CHANTING the HEBREW BIBLE

Student Edition

Publication of this book was made possible
by gifts from

Cantor Perry S. Fine
Cantor Michael A. Shochet
Cantor Rhoda J.H. Silverman
Cantors Rachel Stock Spilker and Jennifer Blum
Temple Emanu-El, Providence, Rhode Island
Temple Isaiah, Lafayette, CA
Hazzan Eliot I. Vogel

CHANTING the HEBREW BIBLE

Student Edition

Joshua R. Jacobson

2005 • 5765

THE JEWISH PUBLICATION SOCIETY

Philadelphia

The Jewish Publication Society
2100 Arch Street, 2nd Floor
Philadelphia, PA 19103
www.jewishpub.org

Design and composition by the author
Manufactured in the United States of America

07 08 09 10 10 9 8 7 6 5 4 3 2

Library of Congress Cataloging-in-Publication Data

Jacobson, Joshua R.
Chanting the Hebrew Bible/Joshua R. Jacobson.—Student ed. p. cm.
Includes bibliographical references (p. 239) and indexes.

ISBN 0-8276-0816-0 (alk. paper)
1. Cantillation—Instruction and study. I. Title
MT860.J32 2005
782.3'6—dc22

2004056903

מוקדש לבני היקר בנימין חיים ולכלתו היקרה שירה תמוז

Contents

Acknowledgments

In *Chanting the Hebrew Bible: Student Edition,* I have tried to present some of the material from my big book, *Chanting the Hebrew Bible: The Complete Guide to the Art of Cantillation,* in a manner that is accessible to the nonspecialist and user-friendly for all.

I would like to express my thanks to the many people who have made it possible for this book to come to press. To Dr. Ellen Frankel at The Jewish Publication Society for your enthusiasm, confidence, and assistance; to Carol Hupping, Emily Law, Michelle Kwitkin-Close, and Christine Sweeney for your careful reading and insightful suggestions; and to Robin Norman and Janet Liss for your production expertise.

Thanks also to my students at Hebrew College and to the many readers who called my attention to the typographical errors in the first edition of the big book.

As always, thanks to Ronda for your patience and support. And thanks to Ben for keeping me in touch with Hebrew as a living language.

Photographs by Joshua Jacobson and Ronda Jacobson. The passages from the Bible shown on pages 93, 109, 143, and 195 are reproductions of the Leningrad Codex (1109), the oldest surviving complete Bible, punctuated with the *te'amim.*

Transliterations, Translations, and Text Sources

Transliterations

I have used two different, but related, systems for transcribing Hebrew words. For a complete transliteration chart, see chapter 4.

- The **technical transliteration** is used for demonstrating exact pronunciation. This is a completely phonetic system, based on modern Israeli pronunciation of biblical Hebrew. I have attempted to render the *sounds* rather than the *symbols* of the Hebrew original. Thus, the symbol [s] suffices for both ס and שׂ. The letters א, ה, and י are transcribed only if they are sounded as consonants.
  - Hyphens are used to indicate syllabic division (unless the words are monosyllabic).
  - The stressed syllable is shown in uppercase type, e.g., yis-ra-'**ÉL**.
- The **nontechnical transliteration** is used when Hebrew words are used as a part of the expository text. This transliteration is based on the technical system, with the following simplifications:
  - I omit diacritical signs and superscript; thus, *tsere* (in the technical system transcribed as [é]), *segol* [e], and *sheva* [^{e}] are all represented by [e].
  - I dispense with hyphenation and the designation of the stressed syllable, e.g., *yisra'el.*
  - I transcribe silent ה as [h], e.g., Torah.
  - I transcribe final silent ֵי as [ey], e.g., *ta'amey.*
  - I generally omit the symbols for *alef* and *ayin* at the beginning and end of words, e.g., *oleh, etnaḥta, revia.*
  - Hyphens are used instead of gemination (doubling the consonant) after the demonstrative prefixes הַ, בַּ, כַּ, and לַ, e.g., *ha-torah.*
  - I follow the accepted transliteration of certain Hebrew words and names that are in common usage, e.g., Esther, mitzvah.

Translations

Translations from the Hebrew are taken from the King James Version or from *Tanakh: A New Translation of the Holy Scriptures* (Philadelphia: The Jewish Publication Society, 1985) or are the author's.

Text Sources

Citations from the Hebrew Bible are based on a transcription of the Leningrad Codex, using Accordance software and MacBible software.

1. Introduction

In recent years, I have seen more and more American Jews learning to become Torah readers. Congregants are no longer satisfied to sit passively in synagogue and leave the liturgy exclusively in the hands of professionals. Uncomfortable with their role as audience, Jews have come forward to become players. M

value of the standard synagogue sing-along. People have rediscovered the magic of chanting—the power of a supple, personal incantation in an exotic language. Chanting evokes the consciousness of using our voices as a link to antiquity, a profound sense of belonging to a historical continuum, a connection to the Divine.

Clearly, we cannot approach the cantillation of sacred texts in a casual manner. Spiritual elevation requires preparation. The *ba'al keri'ah* (master reader) senses the awesome nature of the task and becomes elevated through its performance. To maximize this experience, the *ba'al keri'ah* prepares as thoroughly as possible. The *ba'al keri'ah* wants to discover every possible nuance of the text and perform it in a manner such that every listener can sense its majesty, its drama, its historical/mythological depth, its sweetness.

Most Jews are aware that the Hebrew Bible is chanted in the synagogue using an ancient melody. Those who delve deeper discover that this melody is composed of nearly 50 motifs, or musical building blocks. They learn how to apply these motifs to the sacred text, even to predict their occurrence. They learn that the identity of these motifs lies not only in their pitches, but also in their rhythms. The sensitive reader learns that the cantillation motifs illuminate the sense of the words.

More than 1000 years ago, scholars at the academy of Ben-Asher in Tiberias perfected and canonized a system of chant, the goal of which was no less than the revitalization and preservation of the biblical text. These rabbis were concerned about an alarming decline in Hebrew literacy. They were afraid that the original text of the Holy Scriptures would be lost to all but a handful of the intellectual elite. They designed a method that would revolutionize the way we read Hebrew. They developed symbols for vowels, which had up until then been absent from the written language. They also instituted dots that would help the reader distinguish between different phonemes (sounds) that had been written with the same letter. They created an extensive body of marginalia—notes to assist future editors and curious readers. And, most significantly, they came up with an extremely thorough system of punctuation. Associated with each punctuation mark was a unique musical motif, called a *ta'am*.

In premodern Hebrew, *ta'am* could mean "sense" or "reason." Indeed, the function of the *ta'amey ha-mikra* (the cantillation marks) was to help the reader make sense of a text that had previously been lacking in any punctuation. Even today, when you look at a Torah scroll you can see the challenges that faced a reader. Words without vowels are challenging and ambiguous. The word מדבר could mean "speaking" (מְדַבֵּר) or "wilderness" (מִדְבָּר) or "from pestilence" (מִדֶּבֶר). Certain consonant symbols also presented a challenge: Was המן "the mannah" (הַמָּן), or was it the name "Haman" (הָמָן)? And without punctuation, how was one to know when one sentence ended and the next one began?

The scholars of Tiberias (known as the Masoretes) created a system far more elaborate than the commas, colons, semicolons, periods, and dashes that characterize written English. Their system parsed every possible nuance of the text, leaving no room for misinterpretation. Thus the *ba'al keriy'ah* who understood the Masoretic system, its melodies, and its rhythms, could deliver a totally convincing performance, faithful to the traditional meaning of the text.

This book was written for Jews of our time who have experienced the thrilling satisfaction of reading the Torah, the *haftarah,* or the *megillot*. This book was written for Jews who are eager to go beyond a mere casual acquaintance and deepen their relationship with the sacred text and its traditional rendition. Those who have finished this book and want to learn more are urged to consult my more thorough treatment, *Chanting the Hebrew Bible: The Complete Guide to the Art of Cantillation*, available from The Jewish Publication Society.

2. How to Use This Book

To the Student

When I was a lad, I learned to chant by repeating over and over, "*mahpakh pashta zakef katon....*" It did the trick, but I didn't know what I was missing. Then, about 15 years ago, I came to understand that there was a logical system to the placement of the *te'amim*. I realized that the musical sense of the *te'amim* was a direct reflection of sentence structure. This knowledge not only enhanced my performance of cantillation, it also inspired me to propose a better way to learn—a logical method that reinforces the connection between music and meaning. The response from both teachers and students has been overwhelmingly enthusiastic.

This book presents the basics of this system in a language that is accessible to most readers who have at least a rudimentary understanding of Hebrew. The introductory chapters set forth the basic premises of cantillation and some tips on pronunciation. The next chapters present the six systems of cantillation, according to one Eastern European tradition, with musical notation. The first system, Torah, is presented in the greatest detail. The other five—*Haftarah*, Lamentations, Festival *Megillot*, Esther, and High Holiday—are presented with the assumption that you have learned the basic premises set forth in the Torah chapter. The final section of the book contains reference material: charts, helpful hints, a bibliography, a glossary, and indices. A compact disc recording of the cantillation melodies can be found in the inside back cover.

In this book, you'll start by learning the most common and powerful *te'amim*. You'll learn them in logical sequences, and then see how various segments fit together. You shouldn't try to master too much at once; tackle one segment at a time. If you can't read music, use the CD recording. After you listen, chant the name of the *ta'am* over and over, first without and then with its conjunctives.

Before you chant the sample words or verses, read the words aloud without the melody. Make sure you understand the syllabification of each word. Make sure you are reading each segment with the proper phrasing. Then apply the melodies of the *te'amim* to the words. Make sure conjunctives are connected to disjunctives. Make sure you give appropriately more weight to greater disjunctives than to lesser ones.

Then search for more examples. This is an important exercise! Look in a TANAKH for more examples of the paradigm you have just learned, whether it's a single disjunctive or a longer string of *te'amim*. Perhaps you're working on a specific *aliyah* from the Torah, or a *haftarah*, or a chapter from a *megillah*. Photocopy the page(s) you're studying. As you learn a segment of *te'amim* from the book, find examples of that segment on your photocopied sheets and highlight those words with a marker. As you learn more and more *te'amim*, you'll begin to fill up the sheet. Practice only the words you've highlighted.

Working with a Teacher or a Friend

Prepare a set of flash cards. On one side draw only the symbol of a *ta'am*; on the other side write the name of the *ta'am* along with its symbol. Use the cards to make sure you've learned the names and melodies of the *te'amim*. Try arranging the cards in commonly found sequences and then chant the sequence.

side 1 *side 2*

Dictation is a great exercise. One person (either the student or the teacher) is designated the "dictator," and another is the "transcriber." The dictator reads or chants a single word, a phrase, a clause, or a full sentence. The transcriber must write down exactly what he/she hears from the dictator. The dictator repeats the exercise as many times as necessary. Longer segments may be subdivided into shorter units. If the transcriber isn't getting it right, the dictator repeats the exercise until it is perfectly clear.

In some exercises, the dictator will *speak* the words; in others she/he will *chant* the words. In some exercises, she/he will chant just the *melodies* of the *te'amim* using "la la la" and the transcriber will write the *names* of the *te'amim*. In some exercises, the transcriber will be filling in everything she/he hears onto a blank sheet of paper. In others, the text could be provided, but not the *te'amim*. In others, only the consonantal text could be provided, without the vowel signs. In yet others, the transcriber will have the complete text with vowels and *te'amim*; the dictator will make an error (on purpose) and the listener will catch and correct the error. Try it!

You can also play "Fill in the *Ta'am*." The teacher shows the student a verse in which a *ta'am* is missing from one of the words. The student will figure out what the missing *ta'am* is and then chant the verse.

Preparing these exercises can be easy and fun with a computer program such as Oak Tree Software's Accordance. See http://www.accordancebible.com or http://www.davka.com.

Working Alone

After working with a teacher, you're now ready to start preparing cantillation on your own. Sometimes you'll have many weeks to prepare; sometimes you might find yourself having to sight-read. Here are a few suggestions that may be helpful in your self-study.

- Begin by reading the text without its melody. Start with short segments. As you master each segment, chain them together until you are comfortable reading longer units.
- Master the pronunciation of each word. If no one is available to check you, record your performance and listen to yourself.
- Translate the text. Be sure that you understand the overall meaning of the passage as well as the syntactic function of each word.
- Read the text again, this time concentrating on proper word accents, phrase inflection, and rhythm.
- Chant the text with *te'amim*. Chant one phrase at a time. If necessary, go back a step—chant each sequence of *te'amim* using the names of the *te'amim* as lyrics. Then chant the biblical text with the *te'amim*.

- Some students prefer to follow the procedure we use in this book: Begin with the last word of each segment and work forward.
- Chant each segment (word, phrase, or complete verse) several times until you are completely comfortable with it.
- After a verse has been mastered, go on to the next verse. Or, if you prefer, start with the last verse of your portion and work back to the beginning.
- Don't try to master too much material in one session.
- Always review. After you have learned to chant the second sentence, practice chanting two sentences consecutively.
- Continue to use a recording device to check melody and pronunciation.
- Train your eyes to read at least one word ahead of your voice.

Preparing to Read from a Scroll

In a traditional liturgical setting, the Torah and the Book of Esther are read from scrolls. As the *ba'al keri'ah*, you will have before you only the consonantal text; you must memorize the correct pronunciation and melody for each word. You will need to have a *tikkun kore'im*: a book in which the text of the Bible is displayed in two versions: On one side you see the consonantal text as it appears in the liturgical scroll; opposite it you see the text with all *nekudot* and *te'amim*. The *Tikkun Simanim* (2003) is, in many respects, the best edition.

After you have mastered chanting each verse from the fully punctuated column, try chanting the same verse from the consonantal text in the other column. If you have difficulty, practice one small phrase at a time. Continually add to what you have just learned. Gradually increase the number of sentences that you can chant consecutively without peeking at the right-hand column. As before, continue to use a recording device to check melody and pronunciation. Be extremely proud of what you have accomplished!

3. The Art of Cantillation

Mah Nishtanah!

In the synagogue, we read the Torah in a manner quite different from the way we read most books. We chant the Torah using ancient melodic formulas, in a free rhythm that sounds like the natural inflections of speech. The technical term for this chant is "cantillation," But more often we simply call it "reading" the Torah—in English, in Hebrew (קריאה), and in Yiddish (לייענען).

Why don't we just read the Torah (and the other books of the Bible) in the normal way? Two thousand years ago, Roman orators criticized the Jewish style of reading. In the first century B.C.E., Cicero condemned what he called the "Asiatic" practice of chanting a text. And 100 years later, Quintilian wrote: "The practice of chanting instead of speaking ... is the worst feature of ... oratory." Apparently, some Jews must have switched over to the Roman style of reading. In the third century C.E., Rabbi Yohanan had to remind his fellow Jews that it was a requirement to chant the Torah with the appropriate melody. We read in the Talmud (TB *Megillah* 32a), "Rabbi Yohanan said, 'Those people who read Scripture without a melody ..., of them it is written in the Bible, [I scattered them among the nations,] and I gave them laws that were not good.'"

Why do we chant the Torah? Why did Rabbi Yohanan prohibit the reading of the Torah without a melody? There are many reasons.

- Music makes the words of the Torah more beautiful. Just as we adorn our synagogue with beautiful decorations, we adorn our words with beautiful music.
- Music can create an aura of holiness. When we hear a text being chanted, we know immediately that these are not ordinary words; this sounds like a sacred text. This is not a Roman oration. This is not a folk song or a pop song. This is Jewish cantillation.
- Music can serve as a marker of function, time, and place. For example, on Rosh Hashanah we use a special melody for reading the *Akedah* (the story of Abraham's binding of Isaac), but when that same story is read on Shabbat a month later, we use the regular melody. If we simply read the texts, we would lose a significant means of marking the uniqueness of the occasion. On Rosh Hashanah, we replace the regular *parokhet* (the curtain on the ark) with a white one, the cantor puts on a white *kittel* (robe), and the Torah reader chants a special, evocative melody.
- Which is easier to memorize, a song or a poem? Before the Bible was committed to writing, it existed for many centuries as an oral text—words that were performed and listened to. Those who performed these stories kept thousands of sentences in their memory.
- Music can clarify the meaning of the text.

Let's take a close look at that last statement. How can music clarify meaning? Here's an example in English. How do you pronounce the word "invalid"? You may have pronounced it stressing the first syllable, or you may have stressed the second syllable. Does the syllabic stress affect the meaning of the word? In this case, it does. In one pronunciation, it refers to someone with a debilitating disease or medical disorder; in the other, to something that is without foundation in fact, truth, or law.

How do we clarify syllabic stress (or "accent") in our speech? We may speak the stressed syllable at a higher pitch or at a louder dynamic (volume) level, or we might lengthen its duration. Pitch, dynamics, and duration are the musician's most important tools. Even if we don't sing our words, we "inflect" them; we perform them with expressive variety of pitch, dynamics, and duration. Without those three qualities, we would sound like primitive robots. Cantillation is a form of heightened inflection. It is a way of telling a story using the rhythm and dynamics of expressive speech, but with more stylized pitches.

Is it possible to clarify syllabic stress in a *written* document? Generally it's not necessary; we can figure out the text from the context. For example, "The doctor was able to cure the invalid's problem." "The judge ruled that the witness's testimony was invalid." Of course, when you look up a word in a dictionary, you will see a symbol of some sort indicating the syllabic stress; for example, in'-va-lid or in-val'-id.

But what if you're reading a language that you don't understand very well, like Hebrew? The context won't be much help. About 1100 years ago, Jewish scholars in Tiberias put the finishing touches on a system that would help readers who were no longer fluent enough in Hebrew. These scholars expanded the Hebrew alphabet to include symbols for syllabic accents, as well as vowels, consonant modifiers, and punctuation (more about that later). Figure 1 shows a passage from Exodus 18 (12–14) as it would appear in a Torah scroll. Figure 2 shows the same text with the Tiberian marks.

Does it matter if we accent the wrong syllable? Sure it does. Speaking English with improper

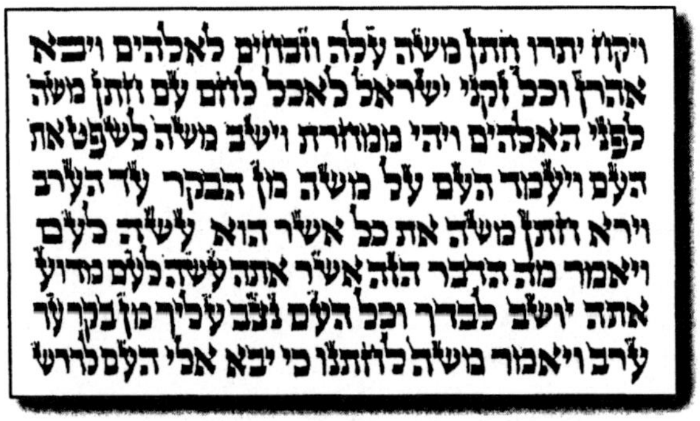
ויקח יתרו חתן משה עלה וזבחים לאלהים ויבא
אהרן וכל זקני ישראל לאכל לחם עם חתן משה
לפני האלהים ויהי ממחרת וישב משה לשפט את
העם ויעמד העם על משה מן הבקר עד הערב
וירא חתן משה את כל אשר הוא עשה לעם
ויאמר מה הדבר הזה אשר אתה עשה לעם מדוע
אתה יושב לבדך וכל העם נצב עליך מן בקר עד
ערב ויאמר משה לחתנו כי יבא אלי העם לדרש

Figure 1: Unpunctuated Hebrew in a Torah scroll

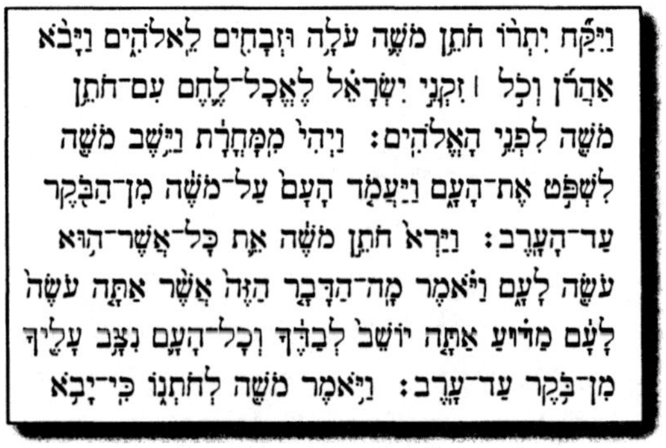
וַיִּקַּח יִתְרוֹ חֹתֵן מֹשֶׁה עֹלָה וּזְבָחִים לֵאלֹהִים וַיָּבֹא
אַהֲרֹן וְכֹל ׀ זִקְנֵי יִשְׂרָאֵל לֶאֱכָל־לֶחֶם עִם־חֹתֵן
מֹשֶׁה לִפְנֵי הָאֱלֹהִים׃ וַיְהִי מִמָּחֳרָת וַיֵּשֶׁב מֹשֶׁה
לִשְׁפֹּט אֶת־הָעָם וַיַּעֲמֹד הָעָם עַל־מֹשֶׁה מִן־הַבֹּקֶר
עַד־הָעָרֶב׃ וַיַּרְא חֹתֵן מֹשֶׁה אֵת כָּל־אֲשֶׁר־הוּא
עֹשֶׂה לָעָם וַיֹּאמֶר מָה־הַדָּבָר הַזֶּה אֲשֶׁר אַתָּה עֹשֶׂה
לָעָם מַדּוּעַ אַתָּה יוֹשֵׁב לְבַדֶּךָ וְכָל־הָעָם נִצָּב עָלֶיךָ
מִן־בֹּקֶר עַד־עָרֶב׃ וַיֹּאמֶר מֹשֶׁה לְחֹתְנוֹ כִּי־יָבֹא

Figure 2: Punctuated Hebrew from a printed Bible

syllabic stress can sound ludicrous and confusing. The same is true in Hebrew. For example, how do we pronounce the word בָּאָה? Do we accent the first syllable or the last syllable? Look at this verse (Genesis 29:6):

וַיֹּאמֶר לָהֶם הֲשָׁלוֹם לוֹ וַיֹּאמְרוּ שָׁלוֹם וְהִנֵּה רָחֵל בִּתּוֹ בָּאָה עִם־הַצֹּאן׃

Jacob is talking to some shepherds and asks them if they know his uncle Laban. They reply that they indeed do know him; Laban is well, and in fact, here comes his daughter Rachel with her sheep. Notice that the word בָּאָה, meaning "comes," has an accent mark on the second syllable.

Three verses later (Genesis 29:9), Jacob is still talking to the shepherds:

עוֹדֶ֖נּוּ מְדַבֵּ֣ר עִמָּ֑ם וְרָחֵ֣ל ׀ בָּ֗אָה עִם־הַצֹּאן֙ אֲשֶׁ֣ר לְאָבִ֔יהָ כִּ֥י רֹעָ֖ה הִֽוא׃

Meanwhile, Rachel the shepherdess had come with her father's sheep. In this case, the word בָּ֗אָה, meaning "had come," has an accent mark on the first syllable. Notice that accent marks are generally placed either above or below the first letter of the accented syllable. (There are a few exceptions, but we'll deal with those later.)

There's another way that cantillation can clarify the meaning of a text. Picture this. I walk into a post office and tell the clerk, "I want twenty three cent stamps." How many stamps am I buying? Twenty or an undefined number? What denomination are these stamps? Are they three-cent stamps or twenty-three-cent stamps? How could I speak that sentence so that the clerk will know exactly what I need? Try it. If you connect certain words, you can clarify the meaning. How could I *write* that sentence so that any reader would know exactly what I mean? I could use hyphens. "I want twenty three-cent stamps." Or "I want twenty-three-cent stamps."

Picture this: I walk into a meeting of a feminist organization and declaim, "Woman without her man is nothing." That would not be a popular statement. But what if I said, "Woman. Without her, man is nothing!"? That would be received a little better. Here I used a period and a comma to create a separation between words. In speech, pauses have the same effect.

In written English, we use periods, semicolons, and commas to indicate a separation between ideas. Punctuation that separates ideas is called "disjunctive." Notice that there is a hierarchy of disjunctives: A period is a stronger separator than a semicolon, which is a stronger separator than a comma, which is a stronger separator than no punctuation at all. We use hyphens to connect words. Punctuation that connects words is called "conjunctive."

Let's see how this works in Hebrew. In the Book of Numbers, we read about the number of Israelites who died in the plague. וַיִּהְיוּ הַמֵּתִים בַּמַּגֵּפָה אַרְבָּעָה וְעֶשְׂרִים אָלֶף

But what is that number? Is it אַרְבָּעָה וְעֶשְׂרִים אָלֶף (four-and-twenty thousand, i.e., 24,000)? Or is it אַרְבָּעָה וְעֶשְׂרִים אָלֶף (four and twenty-thousand, i.e., 20,004)?

To clarify such ambiguous phrases, the Tiberian scholars designated some of their accent marks as disjunctives (separators), and others as conjunctives (joiners). The accent *merekha* (֥) is a conjunctive; it indicates that its word is connected in meaning to the word that follows. The accent *tippeḥa* (֖) is a disjunctive; it usually indicates that its word is less connected in meaning to the word that follows.

So אַרְבָּעָ֥ה וְעֶשְׂרִ֖ים אָֽלֶף indicates 24,000, while אַרְבָּעָ֖ה וְעֶשְׂרִ֥ים אָֽלֶף indicates 20,004.

It is also important for us to understand the hierarchy of the disjunctive accents. The accent *tippeḥa* (֖) is a disjunctive. The accent *tevir* (֛) is also a disjunctive. But *tippeḥa* is a stronger disjunctive than *tevir*. See how important that is for a proper understanding of the following words (Exodus 21:15) וּמַכֵּ֥ה אָבִ֛יו וְאִמּ֖וֹ מ֥וֹת יוּמָֽת.

Usually I hear that verse read with a pause after אָבִ֛יו and no pause after וְאִמּ֖וֹ. The implications of that reading are ungrammatical and absurd.

Reading וּמַכֵּה אָבִיו (pause) וְאִמּוֹ מוֹת יוּמָת
would mean "If a person strikes his father, his mother will be put to death."

Figure 3: Six interpretations of *tevir*, Lithuanian tradition

Figure 4: Seven interpretations of *tevir*, geographical variations

The proper phrasing is מוֹת יוּמָת (pause) וּמַכֵּה אָבִיו וְאִמּוֹ. The proper meaning is, "He who strikes his father or his mother shall be put to death."

These Tiberian accent marks are called *te'amim*, or *ta'amey ha-mikra*. In classical Hebrew, the word *ta'am* means "sense" or "reason." These symbols help us make sense of the reading.

> אלמלא שראיתי טעם המקרא לא הייתי יודע לפרשו.
>
> *Had I not seen the punctuation of the* te'amim,
>
> *I would not have known how to interpret this verse correctly.*
>
> —Rashi (11th century)

We have learned that the *te'amim* indicate (1) which syllable is stressed, and (2) when to connect words and when to separate them. But there is a third function of the *te'amim*, and this brings us back to the beginning of the chapter. The *te'amim* are an elaborate system of musical notation, showing us how to beautify the biblical text with the appropriate chant.

But what kind of notation is this? It's certainly different from the musical notation that we are used to seeing in our culture, in which every symbol represents an absolute pitch with an absolute duration. A *ta'am*, on the other hand, is only the reminder of a musical motif (fragment of a melody); and its musical realization will depend of the liturgical context in which it is found. So the same *ta'am* will have one musical sound when it is read in the Book of Genesis, but a different sound in the Book of Isaiah, a different sound in the Book of Ruth, a different sound in the Book of Lamentations, and a different sound in the Book of Esther. Furthermore, each *ta'am* in the 22nd chapter of Genesis will have one sound when it is read on Shabbat, but a different sound when the same passage is read on Rosh Hashanah. Figure 3 shows six different realizations of the *ta'am tevir* (֛).

And there is another wrinkle. The interpretation of the *te'amim* also varies from community to community. The musical traditions of the Yemenite Jews are different from those of the German Jews. Figure 4 shows seven different geographical traditions for chanting the Torah on a normal Shabbat using the *ta'am tevir*.

Which tradition is the right one? They all are. Each one is probably a variant of the way the Bible was chanted before the beginning of the Diaspora, nearly 2000 years ago. But while the pitches of the *te'amim* differ according to geographical origin and liturgical function, one aspect of the *te'amim* is universal and unchanging: their role as clarifiers and interpreters of the sacred text.

How to Chant

נֹ֥פֶת תִּטֹּ֛פְנָה שִׂפְתוֹתַ֖יִךְ כַּלָּ֑ה
דְּבַ֤שׁ וְחָלָב֙ תַּ֣חַת לְשׁוֹנֵ֔ךְ וְרֵ֥יחַ שַׂלְמֹתַ֖יִךְ כְּרֵ֥יחַ לְבָנֽוֹן׃

Sweetness drips from your lips, O bride.
Honey and milk are under your tongue.
The scent of your robes is like the scent of Lebanon.
—The Song of Songs 4:11

אמר ר׳ לוי אף הקורא מקרא בעינוגו ובניגונו
עליו נאמר דבש וחלב תחת לשונך.

Rabbi Levi said: Surely if one reads Scripture with proper sweetness and melody,
it may be said of him, "honey and milk are under your tongue."
—*Midrash Rabbah*, The Song of Songs 4:24

When chanting the Bible in a liturgical service, keep two principles in mind: beauty and clarity. Your rendition will make the ancient words come alive for your listeners. Those who don't understand Hebrew will appreciate the sweetness of your chant. Those who do understand will recognize every word and every nuance of meaning from your rendition.

Keep in mind the primacy of the text. Your rendition of the melody is an enhancement, not an objective—a means, not an end. Here are a few characteristics of a master cantillator:

- Your pronunciation is clear and accurate in every detail.
- You chant loudly enough so that every member of the congregation can hear you clearly.
- You have a pleasant voice.
- You have memorized the correct melody for every word.
- You have practiced the reading to the point where your performance is confident and smooth.
- Your rhythm is flexible, based on the sense of the words. You chant unstressed syllables faster than stressed syllables. You slow down and pause appropriately on disjunctive words.
- Your tempo is appropriate for the service. (The Torah reading on a weekday morning may be chanted quickly. On Shabbat, the pace is more relaxed. On the High Holidays, the reading is deliberate and dramatic. The Book of Lamentations is always chanted sadly and slowly.)
- You understand the meaning of the text and convey the drama of the story.
- You understand and follow the correct procedures for cantillation, as required by Jewish law and the customs of your congregation.

- You are conscious of the awesome responsibility of the cantillator. You perform with poise, confidence, and joy, thereby enhancing the experience of your listeners. You perform with care and humility, keeping in mind the sanctity of the task at hand and the fact that you are carrying on a tradition that is more than 2000 years old.

In the following pages, you will see a transcription of the *te'amim* into (Western) musical notation. This transcription represents only one of many valid traditions. Your goal is to learn this tradition, master it, internalize it, and then transform it into your own personal oral tradition.

Transcription of the *Te'amim*

The melody for each *ta'am* consists of two parts:

- The *core* is the portion of the *ta'am* that is sung on the accented syllable. In our notational system, we designate the pitches that belong to the core as notes with stems (♪, ♩, and/or 𝅗𝅥). The first stemmed note always represents the beginning of the stressed syllable. The accented syllable is displayed in uppercase type (e.g., NE-fesh). The core is highlighted with a gray screen.

- The *pick-up* is the portion of the *ta'am* that is sung on the unaccented syllable(s) that precede(s) the accented syllable. In our notational system we designate the pitches that belong to the pick-up as notes without stems (•). Pick-up notes are sung quicker than core notes. Pick-up pitches may be altered, at your discretion, to make the reading smoother.

The best way for you to learn the art of cantillation is to sing (and memorize) the name of the *ta'am* to the tune of its motif.

Rhythmic Notation

Durations are approximate. Don't attempt to count out the relative lengths of the rhythms as you would in metered music. Bar lines are inserted at the end of each word. They do not imply the dominance of a time signature.

You generally connect a conjunctive word to the word that follows. But after a disjunctive word, you create an elongation (slowing down) and/or pause. The extent of that elongation and/or pause will depend on the strength of the disjunction. *Siluk* has the greatest stopping power. *Etnaḥta* has only slightly less. Slightly less again for the following *te'amim: segol, shalshelet, zakef, tippeḥa*. Even less stopping power for *tevir, pashta, yetiv, zarka, revia*. The disjunctives with the least stopping power are *pazer, geresh, telishah gedolah*, and *legarmeh*. We'll remind you of these levels as we introduce each *ta'am*.

To help you visualize these relative disjunctions, we have inserted spaces in some of the Hebrew texts. Each space indicates a slight pause. In other examples, we have displayed the strongest disjunctives with the largest type size.

Pitch Notation

Pitches are relative, not fixed or absolute. You should chant in whatever key you find comfortable.

Syllabic Stress

In some diagrams, each syllable is indicated as a box. A colored box represents a stressed syllable.

גַּן כַּלָּה לְשׁוֹנֵךְ שְׂפְתוֹתַיִךְ

Words Accented on the Last Syllable (*Millera*)

Words with Two or More Syllables

The last syllable is stressed and all preceding syllables are unstressed. The stressed syllable is sung on the core of the *ta'am*, and each unstressed syllable is sung on the pick-up note.

תְ בִיר

עָ לָיו

וְאַרְגָּמָן

Note: For purposes of chanting, *sheva-na* is considered a syllable, and *ḥatuf* vowels (*ḥataf-pataḥ, ḥataf-kamats*, and *ḥataf-segol*) are considered syllables.

Words of Only One Syllable

There are no unstressed syllables. Since there are no pick-up notes, the entire word is sung on the core of the *ta'am*. Ignore the pick-up note of the model.

כִּי

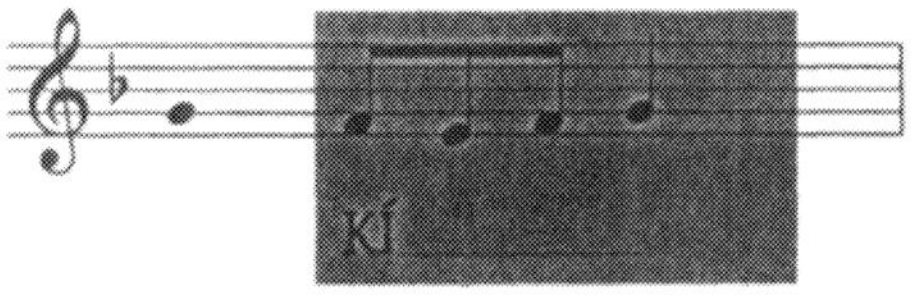

Words Accented on the Next-to-the-Last Syllable (*Mille'el*)

Mille'el words have at least two syllables.

The last syllable is always unstressed and is called a "weak ending."

Two-Syllable Words—The Stressed Syllable Is Followed by One Unstressed Syllable

☐■ דֶּ שֶׁא ☐■ מַ יִם ☐■ שִׁי מוֹ

Both syllables are sung on the core of the *ta'am.*

- If the core of the *ta'am* comprises only one note, both syllables are sung on the same note, but the accented syllable should be sung louder than the unaccented syllable.

☐■ בֶּגֶד

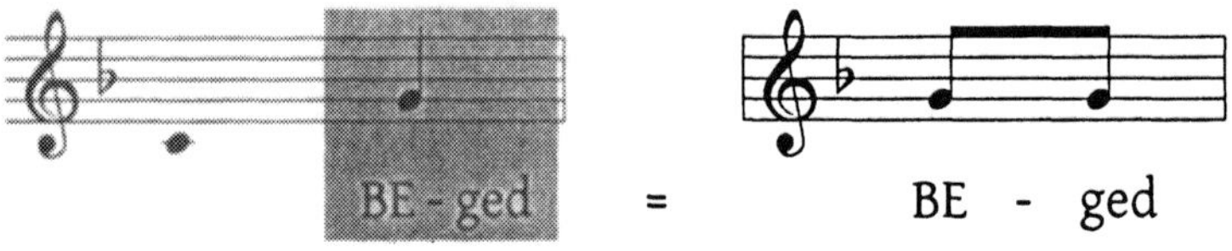

- If the core of the *ta'am* comprises two notes, the accented syllable is sung on the first note and the weak ending is sung on the second note. The *dark gray* indicates the core pitches to be sung on the accented syllable. The *light gray* indicates the final pitch to be sung on the final unaccented syllable.

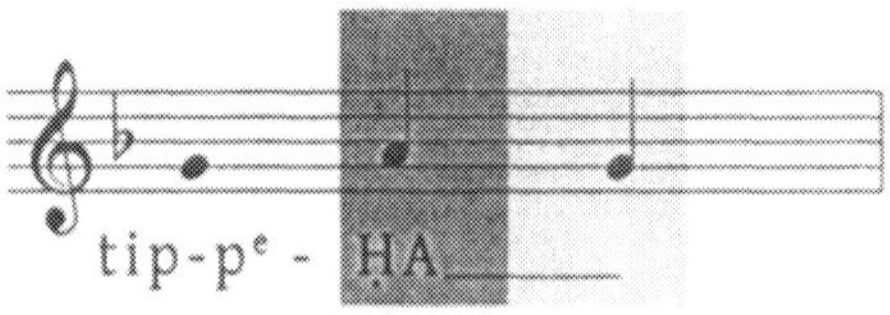

☐■ נֶגַע

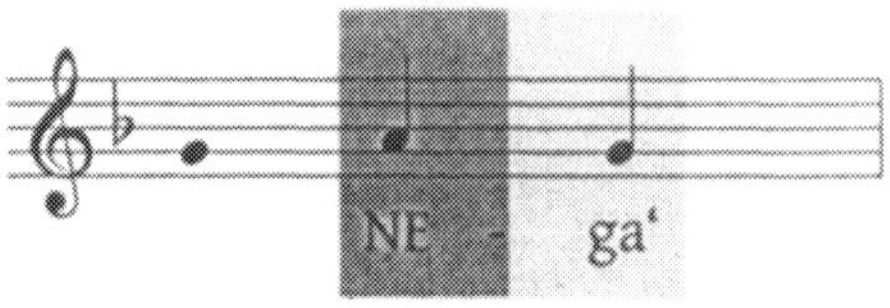

- If the core of the *ta'am* comprises three or more pitches, the accented syllable is sung on all but the last note and the weak ending is sung on the last note.

☐■ אֵלֶּה

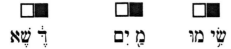

Words with Three or More Syllables

The accented syllable is preceded by one or more unaccented pick-up syllables, and there is one unstressed syllable *following* the stressed syllable.

☐■☐
מִצְרַיִם

☐■☐☐☐
וַיִּפְגְּשֵׁהוּ

The final unaccented syllable (the weak ending) of a disjunctive *mille'el* word is not chanted as quickly as an unaccented pick-up syllable. This syllable ends a phrase, so you should slow down and subtly elongate the final syllable.

Words Accented on the Third Syllable from the End

In a few unusual cases, there are two unstressed syllables following the stressed syllable. The next-to-the-last syllable is always a "quick" vowel (either a *sheva* or a *ḥatuf* vowel).

☐☐■	☐☐■☐	☐☐■☐
צ עֲ רָ ה	הָ אֹ הֱ לָ ה	עִם־יֹ שְׁ בֵ י

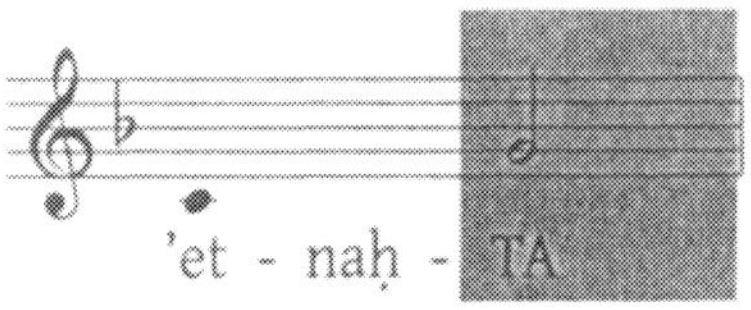

הָאֹהֱלָה

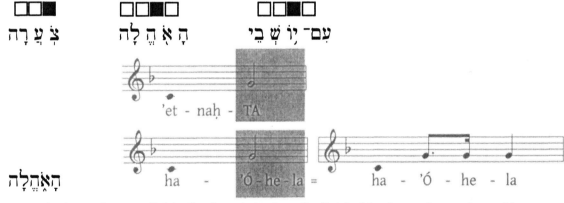

- Both the pick-up syllable (ha-) and the *ḥatuf* syllable (-he-) are chanted quickly.
- The accented syllable (-'Ó-) is chanted louder and somewhat longer.
- The last syllable (-la) is not chanted louder, but is slightly elongated.

Smoothing

The advanced *ba'al keri'ah* may take certain liberties with the *te'amim* to smooth the transitions between words.

Elision

In some combinations of *te'amim*, the allocation of notes to syllables requires adjustment or "elision." Notes that are missing from the beginning of a word are reassigned to the end of the preceding word. This occurs when a conjunctive is followed by a disjunctive that is accented on the first syllable. The pick-up note that is missing from the second word is reassigned to the end of the first word.

- If the first word is accented on the last syllable, that final syllable is chanted on the core of the conjunctive *ta'am and* the pick-up note of the disjunctive.

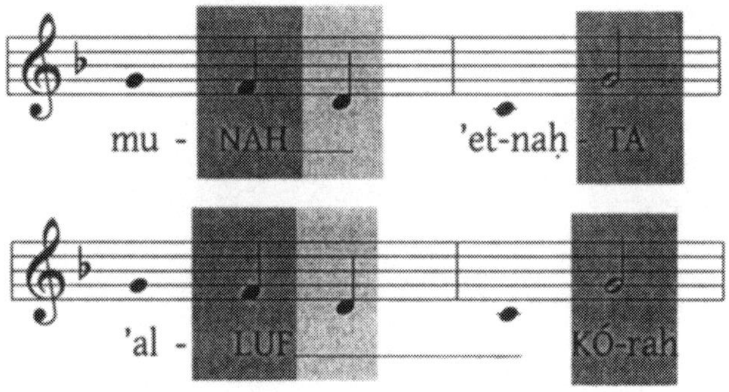

אַלּ֣וּף קֹ֑רַח

- If the first word is accented on the next-to-the-last syllable, that accented syllable is chanted on the core of the *ta'am* and its final syllable is chanted on the pick-up note of the second word.

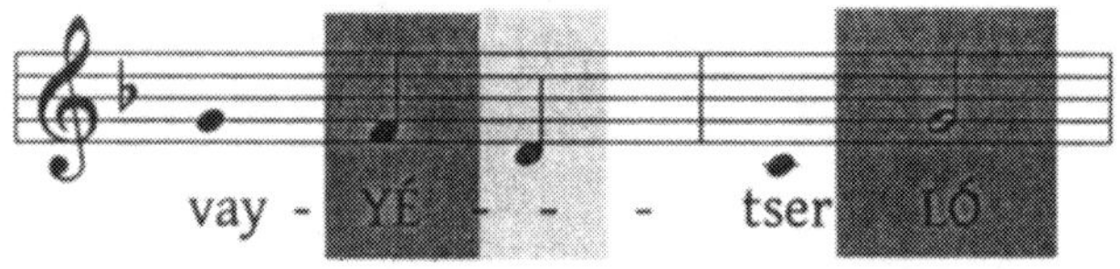

וַיֵּ֖צֶר ל֑וֹ

Disjunctive Elision

Normally, elision takes place between a conjunctive word and the disjunctive word that follows. There are some situations, however, where an experienced *ba'al keri'ah* will create elision between two disjunctive words. For example, in the cantillation of the Torah, even though *tippeḥa* is a disjunctive *ta'am*, it may be elided to the *etnaḥta* word that follows, if that word is accented on the first syllable.

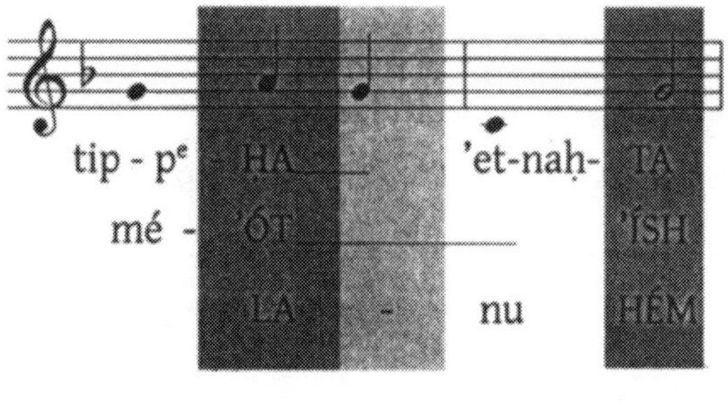

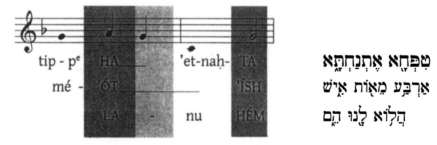

טִפְּחָ֖א אֶתְנַחְתָּ֑א
אַרְבַּ֥ע מֵא֖וֹת אִ֑ישׁ
הֲל֥וֹא לָ֖נוּ הֵֽם

Compensation

Some sequences of *te'amim* are so ubiquitous that when the sequence appears with one of its *te'amim* missing, a *ba'al keri'ah* instinctively compensates for that missing member.

For example, the sequence מֵרְכָ֥א טִפְּחָ֖א מֵרְכָ֥א סִילֽוּק is found in many verses of the Bible. When the מֵרְכָ֥א before the סִילֽוּק is missing, some *ba'aley keri'ah* will insert the notes of the missing conjunctive into the first syllable(s) of the סִילֽוּק word.

For example, in the High Holiday cantillation, מֵרְכָא טִפְּחָא סִילוּק would normally be chanted as:

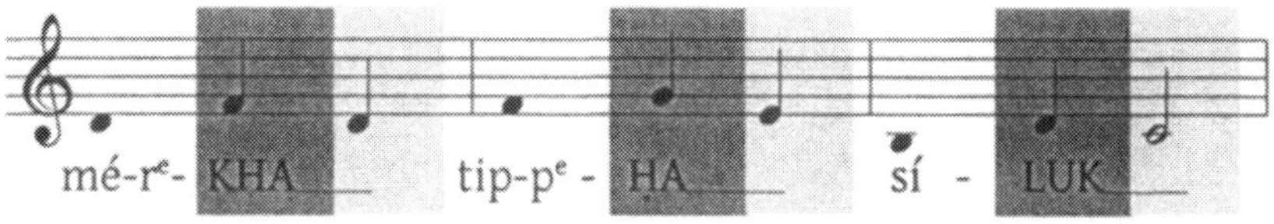

But when reading (Lev 16:8) וְגוֹרָל אֶחָד לַעֲזָאזֵל, instead of chanting:

v^e-gó - RAL ___ 'e - ḤAD ___ la-'a-za-ZÉL ___

you might insert the missing מֵרְכָא and chant instead:

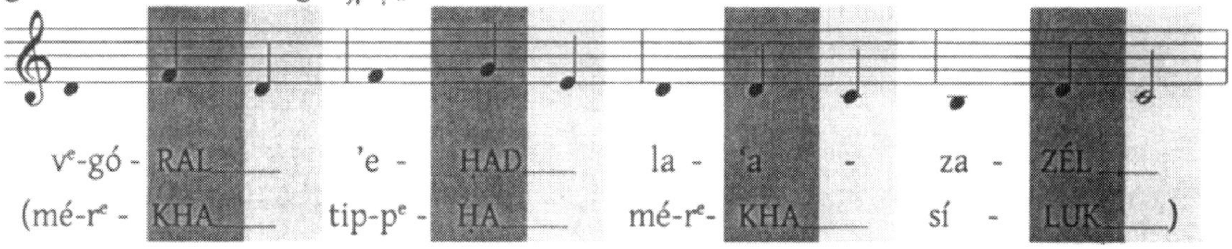

The Style of Biblical Hebrew

Every language has its unique flavor. Some words or expressions are virtually impossible to translate from one language to another. Scholars note that the Hebrew Bible comprises a variety of literary styles. But underlying the entire Bible is a structure that we call parallelism. Most verses of the Hebrew Bible exhibit a binary structure, a division (or dichotomy) into two segments.

- Often the second segment seems to echo or parallel the content of the first.

  הַאֲזִינוּ הַשָּׁמַיִם וַאֲדַבֵּרָה   וְתִשְׁמַע הָאָרֶץ אִמְרֵי־פִי׃

  Give ear, O heavens, let me speak; Let the earth hear the words I utter! (Deut. 32:1)

- Sometimes the second segment will be an intensification of the first, as if to say, "and what's more ..."

  וַיהוָה פָּקַד אֶת־שָׂרָה כַּאֲשֶׁר אָמָר   וַיַּעַשׂ יְהוָה לְשָׂרָה כַּאֲשֶׁר דִּבֵּר׃

  The Lord took note of Sarah as He had promised,
  and [what's more] the Lord did for Sarah as He had spoken. (Gen. 21:1)

  מַרְכְּבֹת פַּרְעֹה וְחֵילוֹ יָרָה בַיָּם   וּמִבְחַר שָׁלִשָׁיו טֻבְּעוּ בְיַם־סוּף׃

  Pharaoh's chariots and his army He has cast into the sea;
  and [what's more] the pick of his officers are drowned in the Sea of Reeds. (Exod. 15:4)

- Sometimes the second segment will contrast with the first.

וַיַּכֵּר יוֹסֵף אֶת־אֶחָיו   וְהֵם לֹא הִכִּרֻהוּ׃

Joseph recognized his brothers, *but they did not recognize him.* (Gen. 42:8)

- Sometimes the second segment will echo only some of the words of the first segment. We call this structure, "elliptical parallelism."

וַיְהִי כָל־הָאָרֶץ שָׂפָה אֶחָת   וּדְבָרִים אֲחָדִים׃

Everyone on earth had the same language, *and [everyone on earth had] the same words.* (Gen. 11:1)

זָבַת חָלָב   וּדְבָשׁ

... flowing with milk *and [flowing with] honey* (Exod. 3:8)

- This binary dichotomy also governs the structure of clauses in the Hebrew Bible. Typically, a clause comprises a verb followed by several words that relate to that verb. Those words could be objects, subjects, or adverbs; we call them "complements" of the verb. The clause is divided into two segments, and the dividing point is usually just before the final complement.

A segment of three words is divided 2+1.

object subject verb

אֶת־פַּרְעֹה   וַיְבָרֶךְ יַעֲקֹב   *Jacob blessed Pharaoh.* (Gen. 47:10)

object subject verb

אֶת־אֶחָיו   יוֹסֵף   וַיַּרְא   *Joseph saw his brothers* (Gen. 42:7)

Sometimes, one of the complements is a phrase comprising two or more words.

subject ind.object verb

מֶלֶךְ מִצְרַיִם   אֲלֵהֶם   וַיֹּאמֶר   *The King of Egypt said to them* (Exod. 5:4)

adverbial phrase subject verb

תַּחַת אַחַד הַשִּׂיחִם   אֶת־הַיֶּלֶד   וַתַּשְׁלֵךְ   *So she left the child under one of the bushes.* (Gen. 21:15)

Generally, the verb is the first word in a clause. So when a noun, pronoun, or adverb is placed *before* the verb, it serves to call attention to that word.

object verb adverb

אֶת־אַבְרָהָם   קָבְרוּ   שָׁמָּה   There *they buried Abraham* (Gen. 49:31)

object verb subject

הִכְבַּדְתִּי אֶת־לִבּוֹ   כִּי־אֲנִי   *For I have hardened his heart* (Exod. 10:1)

- Lists of three items are also usually divided into two segments, in the ratio of 2+1.

  יִשָּׂשכָר זְבוּלֻן וּבִנְיָמִן׃ *Issachar, Zebulun, and Benjamin* (Exod. 1:3)

- If the division is after the first item in the list, it serves to call attention to that item, to set it off from the other two items.

  שֵׁם חָם וָיָפֶת *Shem, Ham and Japheth* (Gen 10:1)

- Based on this binary structure, the Tiberian Masoretes divided each verse into two segments. Each segment, in turn, was further subdivided into two, and so on until the verse had been analyzed down to its smallest possible parts—a segment comprising only one or two words.

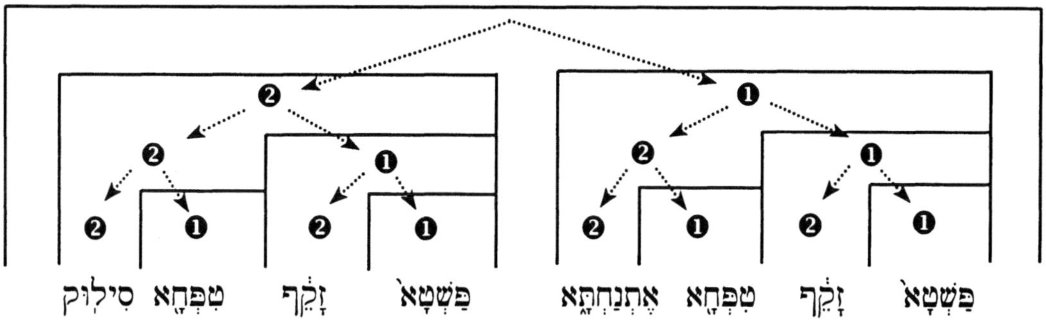

  The last word in each segment is marked with a disjunctive *ta'am*. The strongest disjunctive is the one at the very end of the verse. The weakest disjunctive is one that ends one of the deepest segments.

- In this system, words that seem to be connected in meaning are bound together. The first word of the pair will be marked with a conjunctive accent. "Conjunctive" means that the word is closely connected to the word that follows. Here are some words that typically are bound together:

preposition and noun

בְּתוֹךְ הַמָּיִם *within the-waters*

noun and adjective

הַשָּׁנָה הַהִוא *that year*

noun and apposition (a second noun that serves to identify the first noun)

אֶת־חַוָּה אִשְׁתּוֹ *Eve his-wife*

name and patronym (father's name)

יָאִיר בֶּן־מְנַשֶּׁה *Yair son-of-Menashe*

construct noun and absolute noun

אֱלֹהֵי כֶסֶף *gods-of silver*

coordinate nouns (two objects closely associated with each other, forming an idiomatic unit)

יוֹמָ֣ם וָלַ֔יְלָה *day and-night*

hendiadys (a single concept expressed by two words linked by a conjunction)

חָמָ֣ס וָשֹׁ֑ד *assault and-battery*

words that are paired together for intensification

- infinitive absolute מ֖וֹת תָּמֽוּת *die you shall die (you will surely die)*
- construct שִׁ֥יר הַשִּׁירִ֖ים *the song of songs (the most beautiful song)*
- distributive י֣וֹם י֑וֹם *day day (each day)*
- emphatic צֶ֥דֶק צֶ֖דֶק *justice justice (perfect justice)*

When you read the Hebrew Bible, you will connect pairs of words that begin with a conjunctive accent and you will separate pairs of words that begin with a disjunctive accent. For more information, see *Chanting The Hebrew Bible: The Complete Guide to the Art of Cantillation,* chapter 5.4.*

* In future references to this work, the title will be shortened to *Chanting: The Complete Guide.*

4. Pronunciation

The Importance of Correct Pronunciation

In the art of cantillation, the words are primary; the music is merely a vehicle for an effective and beautiful performance. For centuries, traditional Jews have held the Hebrew text of the Bible to be sacred and unchangeable. While its melodies have evolved, the text has remained constant.

There are certainly many legitimate systems of pronouncing the Hebrew language, and individuals generally follow the practice of their families, teachers, or communities. The pronunciation guide in this book is intended for those who choose to follow the contemporary Israeli Sephardic pronunciation. Nonetheless, there are many principles that are valid for *all* Hebrew pronunciation systems.

Most languages have various "styles" of pronunciation. While colloquial diction is appropriate for a casual conversation among friends, a more elevated style is appropriate for orators, actors, announcers, and classical singers. For example, in colloquial English, "would you" is often pronounced "woojoo," "softness" as "soffniss," "beauty" as "byoodee," "dew" as "doo." The observations in this chapter may not be relevant to the pronunciation of contemporary colloquial Hebrew, but they are appropriate for the "elevated" style required for the cantillation of the Hebrew Bible.

The pronunciation tips below have been selected for four reasons:

- To sharpen your pronunciation skills. For example, the accomplished reader distinguishes between silent ה (as in אִשָּׁה) and *mappik* הּ (as in אִישָׁהּ), and between a normal consonant (as the ל in מִילָה) and one marked with *dagesh ḥazak* (as the לּ in מִלָּה).
- To assist you in reading the Masoretic text. To help distinguish, for example, between signs that look alike but have different pronunciations, such as the two forms of *sheva* (*sheva na* and *sheva naḥ*) or the two forms of *kamats* (*kamats katan* and *kamats gadol*).
- As an aid to the memory. Sometimes you will chant from a scroll containing only the consonantal text; you must memorize the *te'amim* and *nekudot*. Understanding certain patterns of phonology can assist you in predicting the *nekudot*. For example:

  מלפני פרעה The reader who understands the rules of conjunctive words ending with a vowel can predict that the second word will begin with פַ (without a *dagesh*).
- To explain the reasons behind some seemingly strange word forms, such as the the unusual vowel in the first syllable of כֶּלִי (KE-lí, rather than the expected k^e-LÍ).

You will find two different transliteration systems in this book. For prose narrative, we use a nontechnical standardized system. For technical purposes (when dealing with issues of pronunciation and lyrics for chanting), our system is a transcription of the *sounds*, not the *letters*, of Hebrew.

The Hebrew Consonants

Letter	Letter name	Example	Technical transliteration	General transliteration	English equivalent
א א	*alef*	אֵת	ʼ (Omitted when silent)	ʼ (Omitted when silent and at the beginning of words)	Glottal plosive sounded before the first vowel in the second word of "See Edith!"
בּ בּ	*bet*	בֵּין	b	b	b as in big
ב ב	*vet*	בֵין	v	v	v as in vat
גּ גּ	*gimel*	גּוֹיִם	g	g	g as in good
ג ג	*gimel*	גֵר	g	g	g as in good
דּ דּ	*dalet*	דֶּשֶׁא	d	d	d as in dog
ד ד	*dalet*	דוֹר	d	d	d as in dog
ה ה	*he*	הַמַּיִם	h (Omitted when silent)	h	h as in hot
הּ הּ	*he*	אִישָׁהּ	h	h	h as in hot
ו ו	*vav*	וַיִּקְרָא	v	v	v as in vat
ז ז	*zayin*	זֶרַע	z	z	z as in zoo
ח ח	*ḥet*	חַיָּה	ḥ	ḥ	No English equivalent. Similar to German ch as in Bach.
ט ט	*tet*	טֶרֶם	t	t	t as in two
י י	*yod*	יְלִיד	y (Omitted when silent)	y	y as in yes
כּ ךּ כּ ךּ	*kaf*	כִּי	k	k	k as in kit

Letter	Letter name	Example	Technical transliteration	General transliteration	English equivalent
כ ך כ ך	*chaf*	כֹל	kh	kh	ch as in (German) Bach
ל ל	*lamed*	לָהֶם	l	l	l as in let (but use only the tip of the tongue)
מ ם מ ם	*mem*	מְאֹד	m	m	m as in met
נ ן נ ן	*nun*	נֶפֶשׁ	n	n	n as in net
ס ס	*samekh*	סָמַךְ	s	s	s as in set
ע ע	*ayin*	עַד	ʿ	ʿ (Omitted at the beginning and end of words)	No English equivalent. Similar to א.
פּ פּ	*pe*	פְּרוּ	p	p	p as in pet
פ ף פ ף	*fe*	פַּרְעֹה	f	f	f as in fit
צ ץ צ ץ	*tsadi*	צֹאן	ts	tz	ts as in fits
ק ק	*kof*	קַח	k	k	k as in kit
ר ר	*resh*	רֵעִים	r	r	r as in very (flipped, British style)
שׁ שׁ	*shin*	שָׁמַיִם	sh	sh	sh as in show
שׂ שׂ	*sin*	שָׂרֵי	s	s	s as in set
תּ תּ	*tav*	תַּחַת	t	t	t as in two
ת ת	*tav*	תֹהוּ	t	t	t as in two

The Hebrew Vowels

Long Vowels

Hebrew vowel	Vowel name	Example	Technical transliteration	General transliteration	English example
ָ	*kamats gadol*	עָם	a	a	bar
וּ	*shuruk*	שׁוּב	u	u	shoot
וֹ	*ḥolam*	קוֹל	ó	o	coal (but not as a diphthong)
ֹ	*ḥolam*	הַכֹּל	ó	o	coal (but not as a diphthong)
ֵ	*tsere*	נֵר	é	e	gate (but not as a diphthong)
ֵי	*tsere yod*	דִּבְרֵי	é	e	gate (but not as a diphthong)
ִי	*ḥirik gadol*	כִּי	í	i	key

Short Vowels

Hebrew vowel	Vowel name	Example	Technical transliteration	General transliteration	English example
ַ	*pataḥ*	קַל	a	a	bar
ֶ	*segol*	מֶה	e	e	bet
ִ	*ḥirik katan*	דִּבְרֵי	i	i	bit
ֻ	*kubuts*	יֻלַּד	u	u	shoot
ָ	*kamats katan*	כָּל־	o	o	fault (short vowel)

Ultra-short Vowels

Hebrew vowel	Vowel name	Example	Technical transliteration	General transliteration	English example
◌ֲ	*ḥataf-pataḥ*	אֲנִי	a	a	bar (short vowel)
◌ֱ	*ḥataf-segol*	הֶאֱמַנְתִּי	e	e	bet (short vowel)
◌ֳ	*ḥataf-kamats*	חֳדָשִׁים	o	o	fault (short vowel)
◌ְ	*Sheva na*	לְךָ	^{e}	e	Like the short "a" in "above"

Diphthongs

Hebrew vowel	Vowel name	Example	Technical transliteration	General transliteration	English example
◌ַי	*pataḥ yod*	יְלָדַי	ay	ay	rye
◌ָי	*kamats yod*	אֲדֹנָי	ay	ay	rye
◌וֹי	*ḥolam yod*	גּוֹי	oy	oy	soy
◌וּי	*shuruk yod*	גָּלוּי	uy	uy	Like "phooey" shortened to one syllable

א Is Not Always Silent

Alef is silent when it appears with no vowel under (or after) it. Otherwise, it is a consonant. To pronounce the consonant *alef*, you bring the vocal cords together, closing off the passage of air, as if you were lifting a heavy object, then quickly release the air.

What's the difference between "Brenda knows" and "Brendon owes"? In the second example, the word "owes" begins with the *alef* sound.

Compare the pronunciation of the following words:

מַה־לָּךְ	(ma-LLAKH)	*what's with you?*	מַלְאָךְ	(mal-'AKH)	*angel*
בָּא	(BA)	*he came*	בָּאָה	(BA-'a)	*she came*

וַתִּירֶ֫אןָ	(vat-tí-RE-na)	*they saw*	וַתִּרְאֶ֫ינָה	(vat-tir-'E-na)	*they feared*
מוֹרֶ֫ה	(mó-RE)	*shoot*	מָרְאֶ֫ה	(mor-'E)	*are shown*
יָשִׁ֫יר	(ya-SHÍR)	*will sing*	יַשְׁאִ֫יר	(yash-'ÍR)	*will leave*

The Pronunciation of ע

The guttural sound of ע is produced using the swallowing muscles in the back of the throat. Those who have trouble producing this sound may pronounce it like א.

The Difference between "R" and ר

In North America, the letter *r* is pronounced almost like a vowel. In the formal Hebrew required for cantillation, the letter *resh* (ר) is flapped or trilled with the tip of the tongue on the gum ridge. Compare:

English	Hebrew
or	אוֹר
mar	מַר
raid	רֵד
merry	מֶרִי
Abraham	אַבְרָהָם

Beware the Diphthong!

Many Americans pronounce the long vowels *ó* and *é* as diphthongs. For example, the vowel in the word "snow" has two parts: It begins with a long *ó* and ends with a short *u*. The Hebrew *ó* is roughly equivalent to the *first* part of that American diphthong. Similarly, the vowel in the word "tray" has two parts: It begins with a long é and ends with a short *i*. The Hebrew *é* is roughly equivalent to the first part of that American diphthong.

Practice reading these words. Make a distinction between the English and Hebrew words.

English	Hebrew
may	מֵי
bait	בֵּית
ate	אֵת
low	לֹא
ore	אוֹר
coal	קוֹל

What's In a Dot?

Dots in Hebrew can mean different things.

- A dot can mark the difference between שׂ (s) and שׁ (sh).

  שָׁרִים *singers* שָׂרִים *officers*

- A dot can mark the difference between ו (v) and וֹ (o) and וּ (u).

  מִצְוַת *the commandment of* מַצּוֹת *unleavened bread*

  שׁוֹק *leg* שׁוּק *street*

- A dot can mark the difference between ה, which is silent at the end of a word, and הּ, which is "h" at the end of a word. This dot is called *mappik*. You'll use lots of air pronouncing it.

  אִשָּׁה *woman* אִישָׁהּ *her man*

- A dot can mark the difference between ב (v) and בּ (b).

  בַת *daughter* בַּת *daughter*

- A dot can mark the difference between פ (f) and פּ (p).

  פַרְעֹה *Pharaoh* פַּרְעֹה *Pharaoh*

- A dot can mark the difference between כ (kh) and כּ (k).

  כֵן *thus* כֵּן *thus*

  The *dagesh kal* dot changes the pronunciation of בּ, פּ, and כּ, but doesn't change the meaning of the word. The *dagesh kal* dot is also found in the letters גּ, דּ, and תּ, but does not alter their pronunciation.

- A dot can mark the difference between מ (m) and מּ (mm).

  הָמָן *Haman* הַמָּן *the mannah*

  The *dagesh ḥazak* dot changes the pronunciation of almost any letter and can change the meaning of its word. You linger over the sound of a letter containing a *dagesh ḥazak* dot. It's like the difference in the "n" sound between "necessary" and "unnecessary." Any *dagesh* following a vowel is *dagesh ḥazak*. Any *dagesh* following a consonant (or at the beginning of a word) is *dagesh kal*. For more information on the *dagesh* and for exceptions to these rules, see *Chanting: The Complete Guide*, pp. 292-98, 303-8.

- Some dots are even found in a Torah scroll. These dots, placed over the letters, were probably inserted to call attention to the word in some way. These dots do not affect the pronunciation. E.g., וַיִּשָּׁקֵהוּ.

The Hebrew Syllable

A syllable is the building block of a word. Words consist of one or more syllables that are pronounced in an uninterrupted flow. You should be able to break any word into its component syllables.

Every syllable begins with a consonant.

Open Syllables

An "open syllable" consists of a consonant followed by a vowel sound.

Both syllables of the following word are "open."

שָׁנָה (שָׁ נָה) sha-NA

Closed Syllables

A "closed" syllable consists of a consonant followed by a vowel followed by a consonant.

דַּק DAK

מִכְתָּב (מִכְ תָּב) mikh-TAV

- Any syllable that ends with *dagesh ḥazak* is considered a closed syllable. The consonant is doubled: It closes one syllable *and* begins the next syllable.

שִׁבֵּר (שִׁבְ בֵּר) shib-BÉR

- Closed syllables end with either *dagesh ḥazak* or *sheva naḥ*. *Sheva naḥ* is a symbol placed under the last letter of a closed syllable. It is not pronounced; it merely indicates that the syllable preceding it is closed. The symbol consists of two dots arranged vertically under a letter. (But the last letter of a word will usually not have a *sheva naḥ*.)

יִשְׂרָאֵל (יִשְׂ רָ אֵל) yis-ra-'ÉL

- The letters אְ and הְ with *sheva* underneath always close a syllable. The *sheva* is silent.

נֶאְדָּר (נֶאְ דָּר) ne'-DAR

יִהְיוּ (יִהְ יוּ) yih-YU

- Some syllables end with two consonants. "Doubly closed syllables" are found at the end of a few words. A *sheva naḥ* symbol appears under each of the last two letters.

נֵרְדְּ NÉRD

Exceptions

Earlier, we said that every syllable begins with a consonant. There are two exceptions.

- One is found at the beginning of some words: the *shuruk* prefix (וּ), pronounced "u."

וּבֵיתוֹ (וּ בֵי תוֹ) u-vé-TÓ

- The other is found at the end of some words: *pataḥ genuvah*. Most vowels are pronounced *after* the consonant that sits on top of them. But *pataḥ* under final ח, ע, or הּ is pronounced *before* the consonant. So the last syllable of these words will begin with a vowel.

spelled	pronounced
שִׂיחַ	Sí-aḥ
אֱלוֹהַּ	'e-LÓ-ah
פָּרוּעַ	fa-RU-a'

The Conjunctive Soft Form

At the beginning of a word, the letters בּ גּ דּ כּ פּ תּ are normally marked with *dagesh kal.* However, if the preceding word is punctuated with a conjunctive *ta'am* (מֵרְכָא, מוּנַח, דַּרְגָּא, מֵרְכָא־כְפוּלָה, גַּלְגַּל, תְּלִישָׁה־קְטַנָּה, קַדְמָה, מַהְפַּךְ) and ends with a vowel sound, the *dagesh* does *not* appear.

Compare the following three word pairs:

מִלִּפְנֵי פַרְעֹה	The פ is preceded by a word ending in an open syllable and punctuated with *merekha,* which is a conjunctive accent.
לִפְנֵי פַּרְעֹה	The פּ is preceded by a word ending in an open syllable but punctuated with *tippeḥa,* which is a disjunctive accent.
בֵּית פַּרְעֹה	The פּ is preceded by a word punctuated with *merekha,* which is a conjunctive accent, but ending in a closed syllable.

For a list of exceptions, see *Chanting: The Complete Guide,* p. 306.

How Do I Pronounce Those Two Dots (שְׁוָא)?

The symbol for *sheva* is two dots arranged vertically under a consonant. But the problem is there are two kinds of *sheva. Sheva naḥ* (שְׁוָא נָח) is a symbol that signifies the end of a syllable. It has no sound at all. *Sheva na* (שְׁוָא נָע), which has the identical symbol, is a brief, neutral vowel, like the first vowel in the English word "above" (but with a little "eh" flavor). How can you tell when *sheva* is vocal and when it is silent? The easiest way is to use the *Tikkun Simanim,* a book that has a different symbol for *sheva na* (bold typeface). If you want to learn all the rules so that you can predict *sheva na,* see *Chanting: The Complete Guide,* pp. 308-15. In the meantime, here are a few helpful hints.

Sheva is vocal (שְׁוָא נָע) when it is written under the first letter of a syllable. This includes the following cases:

- *Sheva* is vocal under the first letter of a word.

  לְךָ   l^e-KHA   בְּנֵי   b^e-NÉ

  Exception: The *sheva* under the first letter of the word שְׁתַּיִם (as well as derivative forms such as שְׁתֵּים עֶשְׂרֵה and שְׁתֵּי) is a *silent sheva.*

- *Sheva* is vocal under a letter with a *dagesh*.

  בִּתְּךָ bit-t^{e}-KHA מִפְּנֵי mip-p^{e}-NÉ

- *Sheva* is vocal following a long vowel that has no (primary) accent.

  קוֹלְךָ kó-l^{e}-KHA

  But *sheva* following a *normally* accented syllable is silent. These words are normally accented on the next to the last syllable.

  יָכֹלְתִּי ya-KHÓL-tí

- *Sheva* is vocal following a retracted (נָסוֹג אָחוֹר) accent. These words are normally accented on the last syllable, but to make the words flow better, the accent has been shifted back (see p. 33).

  רֹדְפֵי צֶדֶק RÓ-d^{e}-fé הָיְתָה זֹּאת HA-y^{e}-ta

- *Sheva* is vocal under the first of two identical letters.

  הִנְנִי hi-n^{e}-NÍ נָדְדָה na-d^{e}-DA

- When you see two consecutive *shevas*, the second one is vocal and the first one is silent.

  שִׁבְתְּךָ shiv-t^{e}-KHA אִשְׁתְּךָ 'ish-t^{e}-KHA

Two Reminders

- After *vav* conversive (ו׳ הַהִפּוּךְ), *sheva* under *yod* is silent.

וַיְדַבֵּר	(vay-dab-BÉR)	(*not* vay-y^{e}-dab-BÉR)
וַיְהִי	(vay-HÍ)	(*not* vay-y^{e}-HÍ)
וַיְכֻלּוּ	(vay-khul-LU)	(*not* vay-y^{e}-khul-LU)

- After conjunctive *shuruk* (וּ), *sheva* is silent.

וּכְתַבְתָּם	(ukh-tav-TAM)	(*not* u-kh^{e}-tav-TAM)
וּדְבַר	(ud-VAR)	(*not* u-d^{e}-VAR)

Kamats: When Is It "AH" and When Is It "AW"?

The vowel *kamats* (ָ) can be either short (*kamats katan*) or long (*kamats gadol*). Here again, the problem is that the same symbol is used to indicate both sounds. The easiest solution is to use the *Tikkun Simanim*, a book that has different symbols for *kamats katan* and *kamats gadol*. If you want to learn all the rules, see *Chanting: The Complete Guide*, pp. 316-32. But are a few hints that should be helpful for everyone.

Kamats Gadol

The more common *kamats* is long: *Kamats gadol* (קָמַץ גָּדוֹל), pronounced "a" (as in "far").

- *Kamats* is always long in any stressed syllable, whether open or closed. The stressed syllable is marked with a *ta'am* or a *meteg*.

יָם	YAM	(closed stressed syllable)
מִשְׁפָּט	mish-PAT	(closed stressed syllable)
חָֽבְרוּ	ḥa-v^{e}-RU	(open syllable with *meteg*)
חָֽכְמָה	ḥa-kh^{e}-MA	(open syllable with *meteg*)

One exception: The *ta'am metigah* is found only on closed syllables. A *kamats* under a letter marked with *metigah* is short (e.g., בְּאָסְפְּךָ).

- *Kamats* is always long in any open syllable, whether stressed or unstressed. Remember: An open syllable ends with a vowel sound.

שָׁנָה	(שָׁ נָה)	sha-NA
בַּמָּקוֹם	(בַּמ מָ קוֹם)	bam-ma-KÓM
וּבִנְךָ	(וּ בִנְ ךָ)	u-vin-KHA

Kamats Katan

Kamats katan (short *kamats*: קָמַץ קָטָן) is pronounced "aw" (as in "vault"). It is less common than the long *kamats*.

- Any *ḥataf-kamats* (ֳ) is always short.

חֳדָשִׁים	ḥo-da-SHÍM
עֳנִי	'o-NÍ

- *Kamats* is always short in an unstressed, closed syllable.

  Remember: A closed syllable ends with a consonant.

  Remember: A syllable is unstressed if it bears no accent sign.

הָגְלָה	hog-LA
כָּזְבִּי	koz-BÍ
קָרְבָּן	kor-BAN
וַיָּקָם	vay-YA-kom

How do we know if the first *kamats* in the word חָכְמָה is long or short? How do we divide the syllables? Is it:

חָכְ מָה	(closed syllable: *kamats katan*) or
חָ כְ מָה	(open syllable: *kamats gadol*)?

Here we must rely on the *te'amim*. If the *kamats* is marked with a secondary accent, it is considered *kamats gadol*. Compare:

חָֽכְמָה	ḥa-kh^{e}-MA	*she became wise*
חָכְמָה	ḥokh-MA	*wisdom*

Notes:

- *Sheva* that follows *kamats katan* is silent.

חָכְמָה	ḥokh-MA

- *Sheva* that follows *kamats gadol* is vocal.

חָֽכְמָה	ḥa-kh^{e}-MA

- *Kamats* immediately before *dagesh ḥazak* is *kamats katan* (because *dagesh ḥazak* closes its syllable).

עָזִּי	‘oz-ZÍ	*the strength of*
תְּחָגֻּהוּ	t^{e}-ḥog-GU-hu	*you shall celebrate it*
רָנִּי	ron-NÍ	*rejoice*

- *Kamats* is short in certain biblical verb forms.

וַיָּקָם	vay-YA-kom
וַתָּשָׁב	vat-TA-shov
וַיָּמָל	vay-YA-mol
וַיָּגָר	vay-YA-gor
וַתָּמָת	vat-TA-mot

The Pausal Form

Words that are accented with either *etnaḥta* or *siluk* will often experience a transformation of stress and/or vowels. These word forms, called "pausal forms," give a "heavier" feeling to the cadence. Occasionally, words accented with other disjunctives take the pausal form as well.

Change of Stress in the Pausal Form

- The stress advances from the next-to-the-last syllable to the last syllable:

normal	pausal
וַיֹּאמֶר	וַיֹּאמַר
וַיָּמָת	וַיָּמֹת
וַיֵּלֶךְ	וַיֵּלַךְ

- The stress recedes from the last syllable to the next-to-the-last syllable:

normal	pausal
אָנֹכִי	אָנֹכִי

Vowel Changes in Pausal Form

- Accented *pataḥ* may become accented *kamats:*

normal	pausal
מַיִם	מָיִם

- Accented *segol* may become accented *kamats:*

normal	pausal
אֶרֶץ	אָרֶץ

- Accented *tsere* may become accented *pataḥ:*

normal	pausal
יִגָּמֵל	וַיִּגָּמַל

- Unaccented *sheva* may become accented *segol:*

normal	pausal
כְּלִי	כֶּלִי

- Unaccented *sheva* may become accented *tsere:*

normal	pausal
יִתְּנוּ	יִתֵּנוּ

- Others:

normal	pausal
אֲנִי	אָנִי
תְּגַלֶּה	תְּגַלֶּה
לְךָ	לָךְ

Retraction of the Accent נָסוֹג אָחוֹר

The Hebrew Bible was meant to be read (cantillated) aloud. The biblical verses have a smooth but flexible rhythmic flow: Each accented syllable is normally preceded by one or two unaccented syllables. To ensure the appropriate alternation of stressed and unstressed syllables, accents were sometimes moved from one syllable to another.

What happens when a word that is accented on the final syllable is followed by a word that is accented on the first syllable?

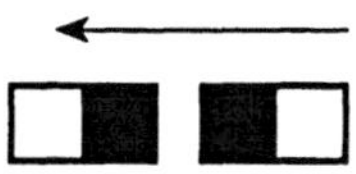

To avoid having two consecutive accents, the accent of the first word is shifted back, or "retracted" (in Hebrew, נָסוֹג אָחוֹר) to the next available syllable.

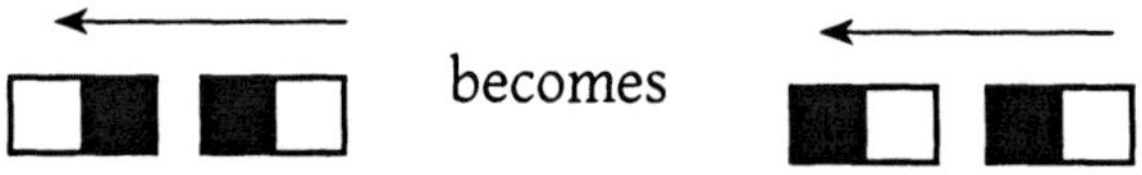

- The word אָבִ֫יא is normally accented on the last syllable. But if the word that follows is accented on the first syllable, a sequence of two consecutive accents has been created (אָבִ֫יא כֶּ֫סֶף). The solution is to move the accent of the word אָבִיא back to the first syllable (אָ֫בִיא כֶּ֫סֶף).

  (Isa. 60:17) תַּ֣חַת הַנְּח֡שֶׁת אָבִ֣יא זָהָ֗ב וְתַ֤חַת הַבַּרְזֶל֙ אָ֣בִיא כֶ֔סֶף

- The word אֱלֹהֵ֫י is normally accented on the last syllable. But if the word that follows is accented on the first syllable, a sequence of two consecutive accents has been created (אֱלֹהֵ֫י כֶּ֫סֶף). The solution is to move the accent of the word אֱלֹהֵי back to the second syllable (אֱלֹ֫הֵי כֶּ֫סֶף).

  (Exod. 20:23) אֱלֹ֤הֵי כֶ֙סֶף֙ וֵאלֹהֵ֣י זָהָ֔ב

- Retraction happens in English, too. The word "thirteen" is normally accented on the last syllable. But the accent is retracted when we say "thirteen bicycles."

Some Words Are Not Pronounced As They Are Written

Some words in the Hebrew Bible have marginal notes attached to them, indicating that they have a special pronunciation. The written form of the word is known by the Aramaic term *ketiv* (כְּתִיב—"what is written"). The corrected pronounciation of the word is known by the Aramaic term *kerey* (קְרֵי—"what is read"). When you encounter these words in a Torah scroll you will see the *ketiv* form. You must memorize the correct pronunciation (*kerey*) and not pronounce the word the way it is written.

Euphemisms

Certain indelicate words were replaced by more polite expressions (the *kerey* is shown here in brackets just after the *ketiv* form; in most books it is shown in the margin):

(Deut. 28:30)

אִשָּׁ֣ה תְאָרֵ֗שׂ וְאִ֤ישׁ אַחֵר֙ יִשְׁגָּלֶ֔נָּה [יִשְׁכָּבֶ֔נָּה]

If you pay the bride-price for a wife, another man shall rape [lie with] her.

Modernizing Archaisms

Sometimes, the early editors of the Bible substituted a more modern expression or spelling:

(2 Kings 4:16)

וַיֹּ֗אמֶר לַמּוֹעֵ֤ד הַזֶּה֙ כָּעֵ֣ת חַיָּ֔ה אַתִּי [אַ֖תְּ] חֹבֶ֣קֶת בֵּ֑ן

Obvious Corrections

Certain spellings seemed to suggest an ancient scribal error:

- (2 Sam. 20:14—metathesis, reversal of letter order)

  וַיִּקְלֻהוּ [וַיִּקָּהֲלוּ] וַיָּבֹאוּ אַף־אַחֲרָיו

- (Ezek. 42:9—an error in the word division)

  וּמִתַּחְתָה לְשָּׁכוֹת [וּמִתַּחַת הַלְּשָׁכוֹת] הָאֵלֶּה

- (Deut. 33:2—omission of a space between words)

  מִימִינוֹ אֵשְׁדָּת [אֵשׁ דָּת] לָמוֹ׃

- (Isa. 49:13—confusion of similar letters [*vav* and *yod*])

  רָנּוּ שָׁמַיִם וְגִילִי אָרֶץ יִפְצְחוּ [וּפִצְחוּ] הָרִים רִנָּה

Kerey ve-la Ketiv

Ten times in the Bible, a word that is not found in the written text must be added when it is read/chanted:

(Judg. 20:13)

וְלֹא אָבוּ [בְּנֵי] בִּנְיָמִן לִשְׁמֹעַ בְּקוֹל אֲחֵיהֶם בְּנֵי־יִשְׂרָאֵל

Ketiv ve-la Kerey

Eight times in the Bible, a word that is written in the text must be ignored when it is read/chanted:

(Ruth 3:12)

וְעַתָּה כִּי אָמְנָם כִּי *אִם גֹאֵל אָנֹכִי וְגַם יֵשׁ גֹּאֵל קָרוֹב מִמֶּנִּי׃

*Do not read the word אִם.

Perpetual *Kerey*

- Certain words are *always* pronounced in a manner at variance with the way they are written. There is no marginal note.

  יְהוָה is always pronounced אֲדֹנָי

  יֱהוִה is always pronounced אֱלֹהִים

  ירושלם is always pronounced יְרוּשָׁלִַם (or, in pausal form, יְרוּשָׁלָיִם)

  יששכר is always pronounced יִשָּׂכָר

- Certain words are *sometimes* pronounced in a manner at variance with the way they are written. There is no marginal note.

  הוא is pronounced הוּא when referring to a male or to an object whose grammatical gender is masculine, but it is pronounced הִיא when referring to a female or to an object whose grammatical gender is feminine.

  נער is pronounced נַעַר when referring to a male, but it is pronounced נַעֲרָה when referring to a female.

Other Exceptions

- The suffix ָיו is not pronounced as written: The *yod* is silent.

  יָמָיו ya-MAV *not* ya-MAYV

- The suffix ֶיךָ is not pronounced as written: The *yod* is silent.

  אֵלֶיךָ 'é-LE-kha *not* 'é-LEY-kha

- The suffix ֶיהָ is not pronounced as written: The *yod* is silent.

  דְרָכֶיהָ d[e]-ra-KHE-ha *not* d[e]-ra-KHEY-ha

5. Torah

The Cycle of Readings

In traditional synagogues, the Torah is read every Shabbat at the end of the morning (*shaḥarit*) service. On Shabbat afternoons and on Monday and Thursday mornings, the first portion of the reading for the following Shabbat is read. The Torah is divided into 54 sections, called "pericopes" in English, or *parashiyot* in Hebrew. Each *parashah* is referred to by the first word (or the first key word) of its text. The first *parashah*, called Bereshit (Gen. 1:1-6:8), is read at the morning service of the first Shabbat after the festival of Simḥat Torah. The following Shabbat, the *parashah* of Noaḥ (Gen. 6:9-11:32) is read, and the reading continues each week in sequence, until—by the next Simḥat Torah—the entire scroll has been read. In nontraditional synagogues, the congregational rabbi may select which verses will be read in a given service. In some Conservative congregations, the Torah is read in a modified triennial cycle.

On festivals, new moons, and fast days, an appropriate *parashah* relating to the theme of the day is read. If one of these festivals coincides with Shabbat, the festival *parashah* takes the place of the reading that would normally have been assigned to that day in the annual cycle. But when the new moon or Hanukkah coincides with Shabbat, the special reading *supplements*, rather than *supplants*, the scheduled reading.

Combined *Parashiyot* פרשיות מחוברות

The Torah is divided into 54 *parashiyot*. On a leap year in the Jewish calendar, there are usually enough weeks to accommodate reading each of the 54 *parashiyot* on a Shabbat. However, the 52 *Shabbatot* of a non-leap-year do not provide sufficient opportunity for reading the 54 *parashiyot*. In fact, the number of available *Shabbatot* may be reduced even further if a major holiday coincides with Shabbat and therefore displaces—defers until the next week—its appropriate *parashah*.

Accordingly, on certain *Shabbatot* the practice is to read two *parashiyot*, joined into one long "combined *parashah*" (פרשה מחוברת). The double *parashah* is divided into seven long *aliyot*. A *ḥumash* will indicate where each reading begins and ends for the combined *parashah* using a designation such as: (שלישי כשהן מחוברין) חמישי. The reader should consult a reliable Jewish calendar (or a rabbi) to determine whether a *parashah* is to be read by itself or combined with another.

The following *parashiyot* may be combined:

ויקהל - פקודי

תזריע - מצורע
אחרי מות - קדשים
בהר - בחקתי
חקת - בלק
מטות - מסעי
נצבים - וילך.

The Division of the *Parashah*

Each liturgical reading of the Torah is divided into three or more segments, called *aliyot* (עליות). The beginning of each *aliyah* for the Shabbat readings is marked in most *ḥumashim*. The division of *aliyot* for other occasions (such as festivals and weekdays) is indicated in some *ḥumashim* and prayer books.

At least three people are called up to the Torah for *aliyot*. On Rosh Ḥodesh, and on the intermediate days of the Pesaḥ and Sukkot festivals, four people are called up. On Rosh Hashanah and the festivals (Pesaḥ, Shavuot, Sukkot) that do not coincide with Shabbat, five people are called. On the morning of Yom Kippur, six people are called. On Shabbat morning (even a Shabbat that coincides with a holiday), seven people are called. At the morning services on festivals, Rosh Hashanah, Yom Kippur, and Shabbat, an extra *oleh*, called the *maftir* (מפטיר), is called to the Torah after the reading has been completed. A *maftir* is also called at the *Minḥah* (afternoon) service of fast days, including Tish'ah Be'Av and Yom Kippur.

When the *maftir* is called, the reader generally repeats the last few verses (three or more) of the *parashah*. On fast days (other than Yom Kippur), the *maftir* is the person called up for the third *aliyah*—no verses are repeated. On other occasions, a second scroll is brought to the table, from which an additional section, appropriate for the occasion, is read. These occasions are the Three Festivals (Pesaḥ, Shavuot, Sukkot), Rosh Hashanah, Yom Kippur, the Shabbat of Ḥanukkah, the Shabbat that coincides with Rosh Ḥodesh, and four special *Shabbatot* that occur in late winter: Shekalim, Zakhor, Parah, and Ha-ḥodesh. If the Shabbat of Ḥanukkah coincides with Rosh Ḥodesh, three scrolls are used. Three scrolls are also used if Rosh Ḥodesh Adar occurs on Shabbat: The first scroll is for the weekly *parashah*, the second scroll is for the Rosh Ḥodesh reading, and the third scroll is for the *maftir* of Shekalim. Likewise, if Rosh Ḥodesh Nisan occurs on Shabbat: The first scroll is for the weekly *parashah*, the second scroll is for the Rosh Ḥodesh reading, and the third scroll is for the *maftir* of Shabbat Ha-ḥodesh.

Simḥat Torah Procedures

On the morning of Simḥat Torah, the reading begins with the last chapters of the Torah (Deut.

33 and 34). The first five *aliyot* may be repeated as many times as necessary to enable every worshiper to be called up to the Torah. The sixth *aliyah*, called *Ḥatan Torah* (חתן תורה—the bridegroom of the Torah)—in which the final 16 verses of Deuteronomy are read—is given, if possible, to an eminent Jewish scholar. Since he is considered to be the "bridegroom," a large *tallit* is extended like a bridal canopy over the *oleh*. After the scroll is put away, a second scroll is opened and the seventh *oleh*, the *Ḥatan Bereshit* (חתן בראשית—the bridegroom of Genesis), is called. This *aliyah*, in which the first 34 verses of the Torah are read, may also be given to an eminent scholar, and the *tallit* canopy is held up again. After the second scroll is put away, the third scroll is opened and the *maftir* is called up for the final reading (Num. 29:35-30:1).

Procedures of Torah Reading

The liturgical chanting of the Torah is held only in the presence of a minyan (מנין): a quorum of ten adult Jews. The Torah is read from a special table called a *shulhan* (שולחן). The scroll is placed in the middle of the *shulhan*, and the *ba'al keri'ah* (בעל קריאה—the reader) stands immediately in front of it. To honor the Torah, the *ba'al keri'ah* wears a *tallit*.

The person who is called up to the Torah (the *oleh*) stands just to the right of the reader. On the sides of the table stand two functionaries called *gabba'im* (גבאים). The first *gabbai* stands at the side of the table to the right of the reader. After chanting an invocation, the *gabbai* will call each *oleh* to the Torah. After each *aliyah*, the first *gabbai* may chant a special blessing for the *oleh*. Special blessings may also be added for those who are dangerously ill, those who have survived a life-threatening situation, or those who are celebrating a joyous milestone. The second *gabbai*, standing at the side of the table to the left of the reader, will ensure that the Torah is covered with a cloth when there is a long pause between *aliyot*, such as when the *ba'al keri'ah* is chanting the *Kaddish* or when the *gabbai* is reciting a blessing. At other times, the Torah may remain on the *shulhan* uncovered, but rolled up. Both *gabba'im* follow the reading from their *ḥumashim*. If the reader makes a serious error, the *gabbai* interrupts the reader, and tactfully explains the proper pronunciation. The reader then repeats the phrase with the correction. Where necessary, the *gabbai* may act as prompter, assisting the reader either by chanting softly just ahead of the reader, or by the use of hand signals that remind the reader of the *te'amim*.

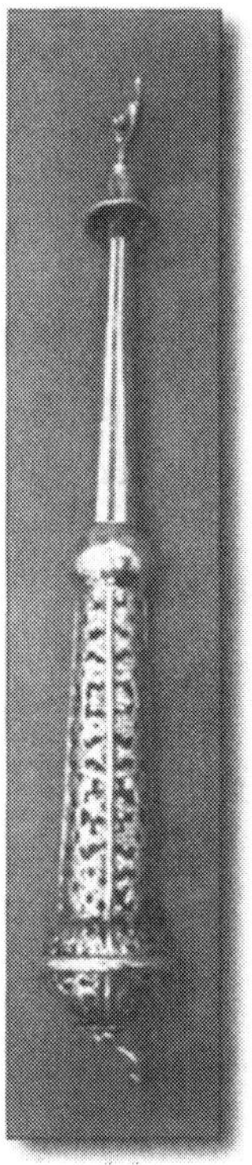

When the *oleh* is called up, the *ba'al keri'ah* opens the scroll and points to the word with which the reading begins. The *oleh* will then touch the Torah with a *tallit* (or some other cloth), kiss the *tallit* (or cloth), and chant the appropriate blessing while holding both of the scroll's wooden handles. The *oleh* does not look at the scroll while chanting the blessing. After the *oleh* has completed the blessing, the *ba'al keri'ah* and the congregation respond, "amen." The *ba'al keri'ah* should respond "amen" immediately following the *oleh*'s blessing, before looking in the scroll. The *ba'al keri'ah* now grasps the left handle with the left hand, leaving the *oleh* to hold the right handle, and begins the cantillation. The *ba'al keri'ah* must read each and every word from the scroll; not one word may be read from memory. It is customary to point to each word, as it is being read, with a special pointer, called a *yad* (יד). Care should taken, however, that the pointer does not actually touch the scroll, lest the letters become scraped off.

The *ba'al keri'ah* chants loudly and clearly enough so that each congregant can hear and understand every word. Simultaneously, the *oleh* is following the reading and, if possible, softly chanting or reading along with the *ba'al keri'ah*. The *ba'al keri'ah* should not interrupt the reading by leaving the room or speaking any words other than the Torah text. (Between *aliyot*, however, some interruption is permitted.)

At the end of the *aliyah*, the *oleh* will again touch the Torah with a *tallit* (or some other cloth), kiss the *tallit* (or cloth), close the scroll, and chant the concluding blessing, while holding both of the handles.

After the last *oleh* (not counting the *maftir*) has concluded the blessing, the reader recites the short *Kaddish* (חצי קדיש). After the reading has been completed, the scroll is re-covered. This act is performed with great ceremony. Two people are called up for this honor. The first (the *magbiah*—מגביה) seizes the Torah by its handles, lifts it with its parchment open for all to see, then sits down. The second (the *gollel*—גולל) rolls and tightens the scroll, ties a sash around the scroll to keep it from unrolling, and covers the Torah with its mantle and other decorative adornments. For further information on the classic laws and customs of Torah reading, see Maimonides, *Mishneh Torah, The Laws of Prayer*, chapters 12 and 13; and the *Shulhan Arukh, Oraḥ Ḥayyim* §135, 137, 139, 141, 142 (as well as the commentaries of the *Mishnah Berurah* and the *Arukh Ha-shulhan*).

Correcting an Error in the Reading

You must read in such a way that every congregant can hear the text and understand it just as if he/she had read it for himself/herself. For this reason, a major error cannot be tolerated and must be corrected immediately. The *gabbai* should quietly indicate what the correct reading is, and then you must repeat the phrase in which the error was made.

What is considered a major error?

- mispronouncing any consonant
- mispronouncing any vowel, if that alters the meaning of the word
- stressing the wrong syllable, if that alters the meaning of the word
- chanting the wrong *ta'am*, if that alters the meaning of the verse

For further information, see *Chanting: The Complete Guide*, chapter 6.2.

A Defect in the Scroll

If, in the course of your reading, you discover a defect in the Torah scroll, finish the verse you are reading and then stop to allow a competent halakhic authority to inspect the scroll.

Tokheḥot

Most of the Torah should be chanted out loud, so that every member of the congregation can hear every word. However, there are several passages that traditionally are chanted softly. These are the passages of "rebuke" (תוכחה) found in Lev. 26:14-41, 43 (*parashat* Beḥukkotay) and Deut. 28:15-68 (*parashat* Ki Tavo). These two passages describe, in horrifically realistic detail, the punishment that God will inflict should the Israelites not uphold the expected high standards of moral behavior. Even though the *ba'al keri'ah* is chanting softly, the congregation must still be able to hear each word.

Chanting the Torah

Siluk

The last word in every verse of the Hebrew Bible is punctuated with a *ta'am* that is called *siluk* (סִילְּוּק). Its symbol is a short vertical line placed under the first letter of the stressed syllable (הַחֹֽשֶׁךְ). If there is a vowel under that letter, the *ta'am* will be placed just to the left of the vowel (הָאָֽרֶץ).

Do not confuse *siluk* with the *sof-pasuk* sign. *Sof-pasuk* (:) is a symbol resembling a colon that is placed at the end of every verse in the Bible. It has nothing to do with chanting.

This is the melody for *siluk* (when it is preceded by *tippeḥa* or *etnaḥta*) **(CD track 1).**

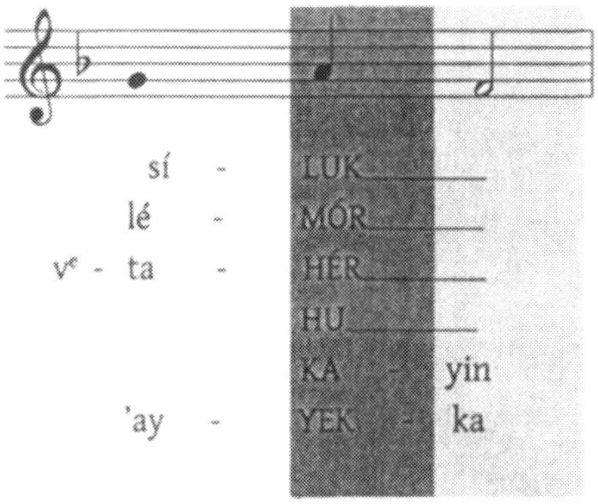

סִילְּוּק
(Lev. 15:1) לֵאמֹֽר
(Lev. 15:13) וְטָהֵֽר
(Lev. 15:2) הֽוּא
(Gen. 4:25) קָֽיִן
(Gen. 3:9) אַיֶּֽכָּה

Two Words in a *Siluk* Segment

Since it is the last word in each verse, *siluk* is the strongest disjunctive. If the preceding word is closely connected in meaning to the *siluk* word, it is usually marked with the conjunctive *ta'am*, *merekha*. The symbol for *merekha* is a small curve extending down and to the left, placed below the first letter of the stressed syllable (לָשֶׁ֖בֶת). Notice that *siluk* has a different melody when it is in the combination *merekha-siluk*.

Merekha siluk מֵרְכָא סִילְּוּק **(CD track 2)**

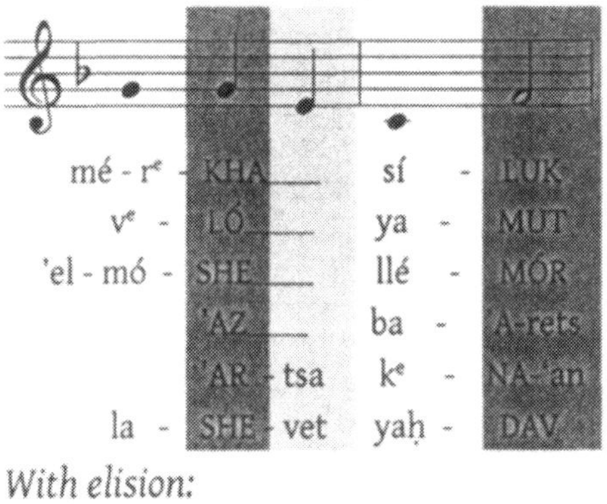

With elision:

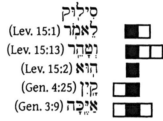

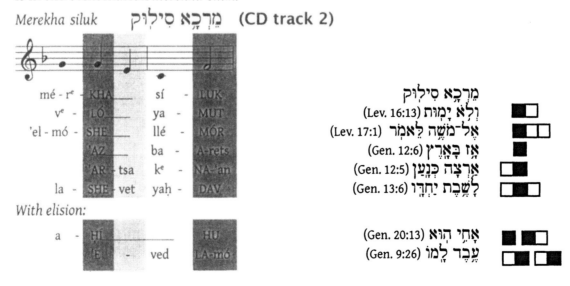

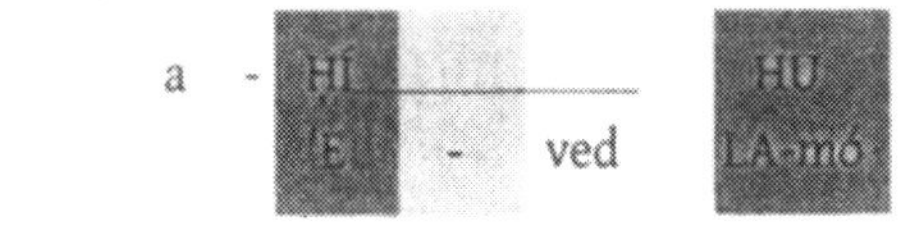

מֵרְכָא סִילְּוּק
(Lev. 16:13) וְלֹ֖א יָמֽוּת
(Lev. 17:1) אֶל־מֹשֶׁ֖ה לֵּאמֹֽר
(Gen. 12:6) אָ֖ז בָּאָֽרֶץ
(Gen. 12:5) אַ֖רְצָה כְּנָֽעַן
(Gen. 13:6) לָשֶׁ֖בֶת יַחְדָּֽו

(Gen. 20:13) אָ֖חִי הֽוּא
(Gen. 9:26) עֶ֖בֶד לָֽמוֹ

Meteg

There is another sign that looks just like *siluk*—the *meteg* (מֶתֶג). The *meteg* is used on some long words to indicate secondary stress. There is no melody associated with *meteg*; it indicates that its syllable is to be chanted slightly louder and/or slower.

Pronounce the word "encyclopedia." The primary accent is on the fourth syllable, and the secondary accent is on the second syllable. Pronounce the Hebrew word אֲחִיסָמָךְ. The primary accent is on the fourth syllable, and the secondary accent is on the second syllable. When we chant the word, we perform the core of the *ta'am* on the final syllable, and we subtly elongate and raise the volume on the second syllable. The *meteg* usually appears two syllables before the primary accent.

Some words will have both a *siluk* and a *meteg* (לְעֵינֵיהֶם). In almost every case, *meteg* appears before *siluk.*

Etnaḥta

Most verses in the Torah are divided into two segments. *Etnaḥta* (אֶתְנַחְתָּא) is the *ta'am* that marks the end of the first segment, and *siluk* marks the end of the second segment. The symbol for *etnaḥta* looks like a wishbone, placed under the first letter of the stressed syllable (אַבְרָהָם).

This is the melody for *etnaḥta.* **(CD track 3)**

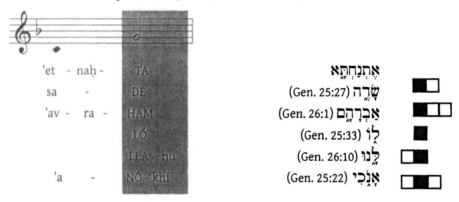

אֶתְנַחְתָּא

(Gen. 25:27) שָׂדֶה

(Gen. 26:1) אַבְרָהָם

(Gen. 25:33) לוֹ

(Gen. 26:10) לָנוּ

(Gen. 25:22) אָנֹכִי

Two Words in an *Etnaḥta* Segment

If the preceding word is closely connected in meaning to the *etnaḥta* word, it is usually marked with the conjunctive *ta'am, munaḥ* (מוּנָח). The symbol for *munaḥ* resembles a backwards letter **L**, placed below the first letter of the stressed syllable (הָלַךְ).

Munah etnahta   מוּנַח אֶתְנַחְתָּא (CD track 4)

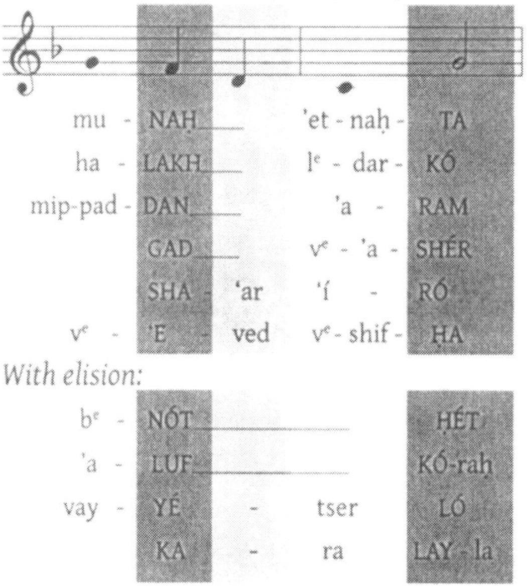

				מוּנַח אֶתְנַחְתָּא	
mu -	NAH	'et - nah -	TA		
ha -	LAKH	lᵉ - dar -	KÓ	הָלַךְ לְדַרְכּוֹ (Gen. 32:2)	
mip-pad -	DAN	'a -	RAM	מִפַּדַּן אֲרָם (Gen. 33:18)	
	GAD	vᵉ - 'a -	SHÉR	גָּד וְאָשֵׁר (Gen. 35:26)	
	SHA	'ar	'í - RÓ	שַׁעַר עִירוֹ (Gen. 34:24)	
vᵉ -	'E	ved vᵉ-shif -	HA	וְעֶבֶד וְשִׁפְחָה (Gen. 32:6)	

With elision:

bᵉ -	NÓT		HÉT	בְּנוֹת חֵת (Gen. 27:46)	
'a -	LUF		KÓ-rah	אַלּוּף קֹרַח (Gen. 36:18)	
vay -	YÉ -	tser	LÓ	וַיֵּצֶר לוֹ (Gen. 32:8)	
	KA -	ra	LAY - la	קָרָא לַיְלָה (Gen. 1:5)	

Tippeha

Usually the *etnahta* segment is subdivided into two parts. The disjunctive *ta'am* that precedes *etnahta* is *tippeha* (טִפְחָא). The symbol for *tippeha* resembles a backwards *merekha*, placed below the first letter of the accented syllable.

Tippeha   טִפְחָא (CD track 5)

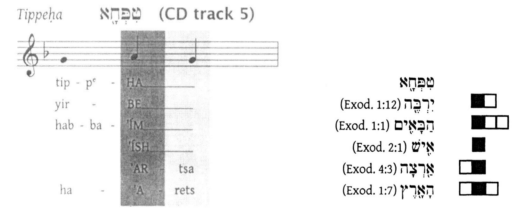

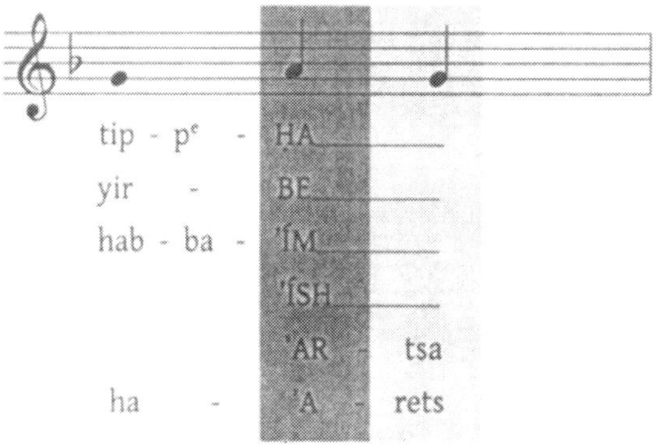

			טִפְחָא	
tip - pᵉ -	HA			
yir -	BE		יִרְבֶּה (Exod. 1:12)	
hab - ba -	'ÍM		הַבָּאִים (Exod. 1:1)	
	'ÍSH		אִישׁ (Exod. 2:1)	
	'AR -	tsa	אַרְצָה (Exod. 4:3)	
ha -	'A -	rets	הָאָרֶץ (Exod. 1:7)	

Two Words in a *Tippeha* Segment

If the preceding word is closely connected in meaning to the *tippeha* word, it is usually marked with the conjunctive *ta'am*, *merekha*. Notice that the melody for *merekha* before *tippeha* is different from the melody of *merekha* before *siluk*. The melody of a conjunctive is dependent on the following *ta'am*.

Merekha tippeḥa **מֵרְכָא טִפְּחָא (CD track 6)**

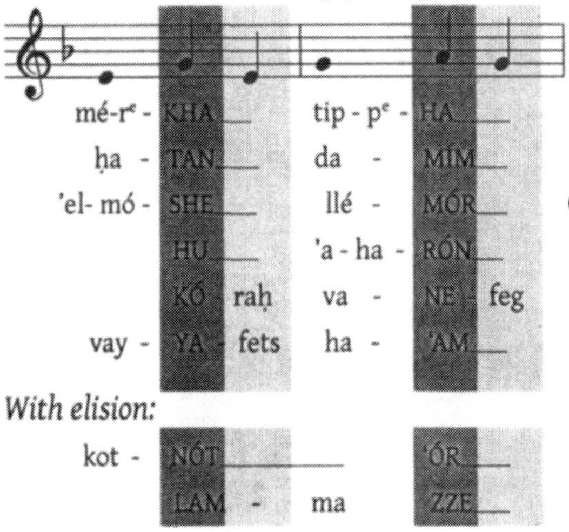

מֵרְכָא טִפְּחָא

חֲתַ֥ן דָּמִ֖ים (Exod. 4:26)

אֶל־מֹשֶׁ֥ה לֵּאמֹֽר (Exod. 6:29)

ה֥וּא אַהֲרֹ֖ן (Exod. 6:26)

קֹ֥רַח וָנֶ֖פֶג (Exod. 6:21)

וַיָּ֥פֶץ הָעָ֖ם (Exod. 5:12)

With elision:

כָּתְנ֥וֹת ע֖וֹר (Gen. 3:21)

לָ֥מָּה זֶּ֖ה (Exod. 5:22)

The *siluk* segment is also subdivided into two parts. The disjunctive *ta'am* that precedes *siluk* is also *tippeḥa.*

Chant the following phrases. Connect each conjunctive (*merekha* or *munaḥ*) to the word that follows. Create a slight elongation or pause after *tippeḥa.* Within each example, an extra white space indicates a slight pause or elongation. The larger the space, the greater the pause or elongation.

מֵרְכָא טִפְּחָא מֵרְכָא סִילוּק

וַיְהִ֥י כִמְצַחֵ֖ק בְּעֵינֵ֥י חֲתָנָֽיו׃ (Gen. 19:14)

עֶ֥בֶד עֲבָדִ֖ים יִֽהְיֶ֥ה לְאֶחָֽיו׃ (Gen. 9:25)

טִפְּחָא מֵרְכָא סִילוּק

אַחַ֖ר תֵּאָסֵ֥ף אֶל־עַמֶּֽיךָ׃ (Num. 31:2)

וַיָּבֹ֖אוּ אַ֥רְצָה כְּנָֽעַן׃ (Gen. 12:5)

מֵרְכָא טִפְּחָא סִילוּק

מְצַוֶּ֥ה אֶתְכֶ֖ם הַיּֽוֹם׃ (Deut. 27:1)

וַיּ֥וֹלֶד בָּנִ֖ים וּבָנֽוֹת׃ (Gen. 11:11)

טִפְּחָא סִילוּק

וְאֶת־הַדֶּ֖לֶת סָגָֽרוּ׃ (Gen. 19:10)

וַיּ֖וֹלֶד אֶת־שָֽׁלַח׃ (Gen. 11:12)

מֵרְכָא טִפְּחָא מוּנַח אֶתְנַחְתָּא

וַיְצַ֥ו פַּרְעֹ֖ה בַּיּ֣וֹם הַה֑וּא (Exod. 5:6)

לִלְבֹּ֧ן הַלְּבֵנִ֖ים כִּתְמ֣וֹל שִׁלְשֹׁ֑ם (Exod. 5:7)

מֵרְכָא טִפְּחָא אֶתְנַחְתָּא

וַיֵּ֥שְׁתְּ מִן־הַיַּ֖יִן וַיִּשְׁכָּ֑ר (Gen. 9:21)

וַיֵּ֥לֶךְ אִתּ֖וֹ ל֑וֹט (*tippeḥa* elision) (Gen. 12:4)

טִפְּחָא מוּנַח אֶתְנַחְתָּא

הַיּ֖וֹם בְּהַ֣ר עֵיבָ֑ל (Deut. 27:4)

וַיֹּ֖אמֶר אָר֣וּר כְּנָ֑עַן (Gen. 9:25)

טִפְּחָא אֶתְנַחְתָּא

אֶ֖לֶף לַמַּטֶּ֑ה (Num. 31:4)

וַיָּ֖קָם וַיֵּלַ֑ךְ (Gen. 25:34)

Now you can chant some complete verses. Remember: The major disjunctives are *siluk* and *etnaḥta*, and the less powerful disjunctive is *tippeḥa.*

בְּרֵאשִׁית בָּרָא אֱלֹהִים אֵת הַשָּׁמַיִם וְאֵת הָאָרֶץ׃ (Gen. 1:1)
וַיְהִי־עֶרֶב וַיְהִי־בֹקֶר יוֹם שְׁלִישִׁי׃ (Gen. 1:13)
וּבְנֵי־דָן חֻשִׁים׃ (Gen. 46:23)
הַאֲזִינוּ הַשָּׁמַיִם וַאֲדַבֵּרָה וְתִשְׁמַע הָאָרֶץ אִמְרֵי־פִי׃ (Deut. 32:1)
תּוֹרָה צִוָּה־לָנוּ מֹשֶׁה מוֹרָשָׁה קְהִלַּת יַעֲקֹב׃ (Deut. 33:4)
וַיְדַבֵּר יְהוָה אֶל־מֹשֶׁה לֵּאמֹר׃ (Num. 28:1)
עֹלַת שַׁבַּת בְּשַׁבַּתּוֹ עַל־עֹלַת הַתָּמִיד וְנִסְכָּהּ׃ (Num. 28:10)
וְעָשׂוּ לִי מִקְדָּשׁ וְשָׁכַנְתִּי בְּתוֹכָם׃ (Exod. 25:8)

Tevir

Sometimes there is a subdivision within the *tippeḥa* segment. *Tevir* (תְּבִיר) is the *ta'am* that marks that subdivision. The symbol for *tevir* looks like a *merekha* with a dot inside, placed under the first letter of the stressed syllable (עָלָיו).

Tevir תְּבִיר (CD track 9)

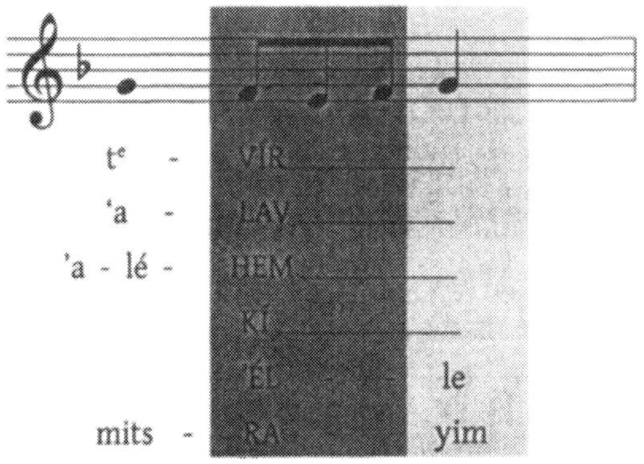

תְּבִיר
עָלָיו (Exod. 25:11)
אֲלֵהֶם (Gen. 50:19)
כִּי (Gen. 50:3)
אֵלֶּה (Exod. 6:19)
מִצְרָיִם (Exod. 1:13)

Two Words in a *Tevir* Segment

If the preceding word is closely connected in meaning to the *tevir* word, it is usually marked with a conjunctive *ta'am*. If there are two or more syllables separating the accents, the conjunctive will be *darga*. The symbol for *darga* resembles a backward letter "z," placed under the first letter of the stressed syllable.

Darga tevir דַּרְגָּא תְּבִיר (CD track 11)

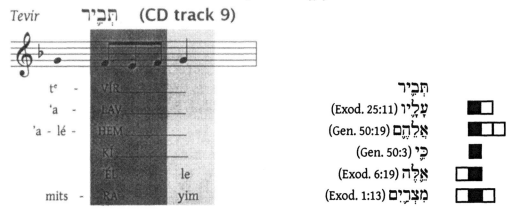

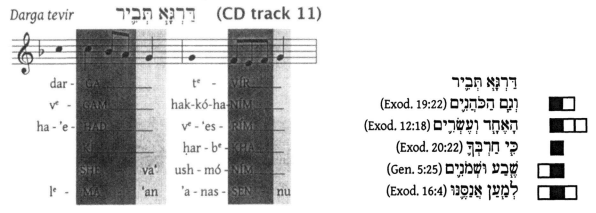

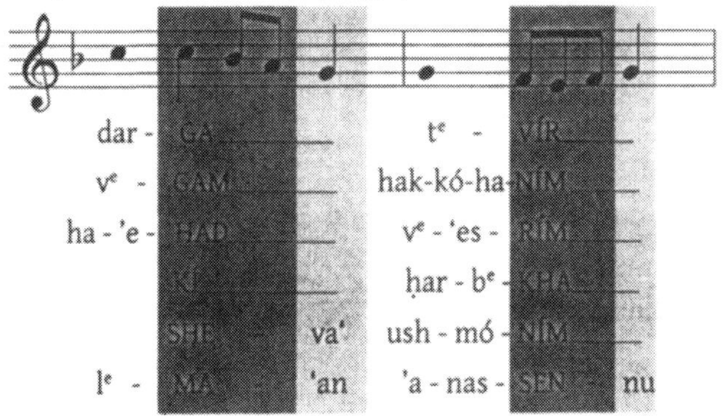

דַּרְגָּא תְּבִיר
וְגַם הַכֹּהֲנִים (Exod. 19:22)
הָאֶחָד וְעֶשְׂרִים (Exod. 12:18)
כִּי חַרְבְּךָ (Exod. 20:22)
שֶׁבַע וּשְׁמֹנִים (Gen. 5:25)
לְמַעַן אֲנַסֶּנּוּ (Exod. 16:4)

If the accents are close to each other, the conjunctive will be *merekha*. This is the third use of *merekha* that we have encountered so far. In each case, it has a different melody.

Merekha tevir מֵרְכָא תְּבִיר **(CD track 10)**

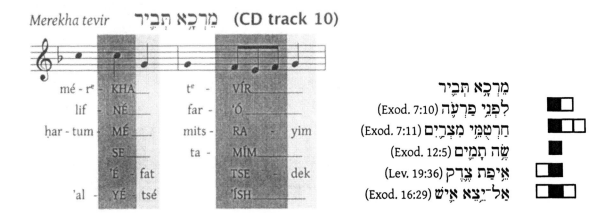

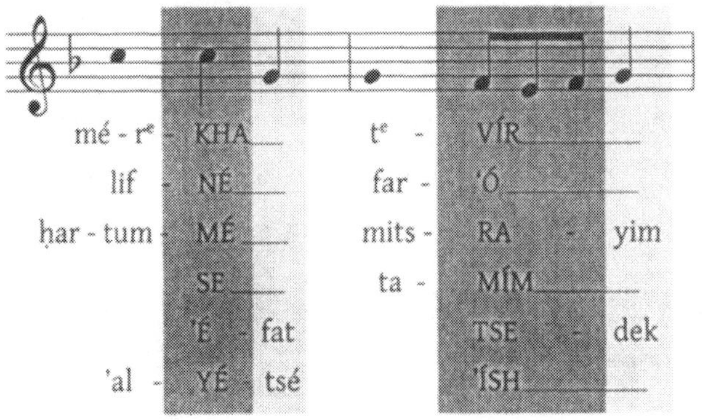
mé - rᵉ - KHA
tᵉ - VÍR
lif - NÉ
far - 'Ó
ḥar - tum - MÉ
mits - RA - yim
SE
ta - MÍM
'É - fat
TSE - dek
'al - YÉ - tsé
'ÍSH

מֵרְכָא תְּבִיר
לִפְנֵי פַרְעֹה (Exod. 7:10)
חַרְטֻמֵּי מִצְרַיִם (Exod. 7:11)
שֶׂה תָמִים (Exod. 12:5)
אֵיפַת צֶדֶק (Lev. 19:36)
אַל־יֵצֵא אִישׁ (Exod. 16:29)

Chant these phrases. Connect each conjunctive word to the word that follows. Create a slight elongation or pause after *tippeḥa*. There is very little elongation or pause after *tevir*. The sense of the words dictates that *tippeḥa* is a stronger disjunctive than *tevir*.

תְּבִיר טִפְּחָא **אֶתְנַחְתָּא**

תְּבִיר טִפְּחָא **סִילוּק**

מֵרְכָא תְּבִיר טִפְּחָא מוּנַח אֶתְנַחְתָּא
אַרְבָּעָה עָשָׂר אֶלֶף וּשְׁבַע מֵאוֹת (Num. 17:14)
אִם־זָרְחָה הַשֶּׁמֶשׁ עָלָיו דָּמִים לוֹ (Exod. 22:2)

דַּרְגָּא תְּבִיר טִפְּחָא מוּנַח אֶתְנַחְתָּא
שֶׁבַע וּשְׁמֹנִים שָׁנָה וּמְאַת שָׁנָה (Gen. 5:25)

דַּרְגָּא תְּבִיר מֵרְכָא טִפְּחָא מֵרְכָא סִילוּק
הֵמָּה הַגִּבֹּרִים אֲשֶׁר מֵעוֹלָם אַנְשֵׁי הַשֵּׁם׃ (Gen. 6:4)
וַיְהִי חֹשֶׁךְ־אֲפֵלָה בְּכָל־אֶרֶץ מִצְרַיִם שְׁלֹשֶׁת יָמִים׃(Exod. 10:22)

תְּבִיר מֵרְכָא טִפְּחָא מֵרְכָא סִילוּק
וּמֵת אוֹ־נִשְׁבַּר אוֹ־נִשְׁבָּה אֵין רֹאֶה׃ (Exod. 22:9)
וַיֹּאמֶר מֹשֶׁה מֹשֶׁה וַיֹּאמֶר הִנֵּנִי׃(Exod. 3:4)

Chant these verses. (In the first four examples, we have inserted spaces to help you remember the relative disjunctions.)

וְלֹא־תוֹתִירוּ מִמֶּנּוּ עַד־בֹּקֶר וְהַנֹּתָר מִמֶּנּוּ עַד־בֹּקֶר בָּאֵשׁ תִּשְׂרֹפוּ׃(Exod. 12:10)
וּמַכֵּה אָבִיו וְאִמּוֹ מוֹת יוּמָת׃ (Exod. 21:15)
וְאִם־שֵׁן עַבְדּוֹ אוֹ־שֵׁן אֲמָתוֹ יַפִּיל לַחָפְשִׁי יְשַׁלְּחֶנּוּ תַּחַת שִׁנּוֹ׃ (Exod. 21:27)
וַיִּקְרָא הָאָדָם שֵׁם אִשְׁתּוֹ חַוָּה כִּי הִוא הָיְתָה אֵם כָּל־חָי׃ (Gen. 3:20)
וַיַּרְא אֱלֹהִים אֶת־הָאָרֶץ וְהִנֵּה נִשְׁחָתָה כִּי־הִשְׁחִית כָּל־בָּשָׂר אֶת־דַּרְכּוֹ עַל־הָאָרֶץ׃ (Gen. 6:12)

וּבַיּ֥וֹם הַחֲמִישִׁ֛י פָּרִ֥ים תִּשְׁעָ֖ה אֵילִ֣ם שְׁנָ֑יִם כְּבָשִׂ֧ים בְּנֵי־שָׁנָ֛ה אַרְבָּעָ֥ה עָשָׂ֖ר תְּמִימִֽם׃ (Num. 29:26)

וַיֵּ֥ט מֹשֶׁ֛ה אֶת־יָד֖וֹ עַל־הַשָּׁמָ֑יִם וַיְהִ֧י חֹֽשֶׁךְ־אֲפֵלָ֛ה בְּכָל־אֶ֥רֶץ מִצְרַ֖יִם שְׁלֹ֥שֶׁת יָמִֽים׃ (Exod. 10:22)

Three Words in a *Tevir* Segment

Sometimes *tevir* is preceded by a series of two or more conjunctives. In these segments, there will be a very slight pause or elongation just before *tevir*.

The second conjunctive before *tevir* (preceding either *merekha* or *darga*) may be *kadmah*. The symbol for *kadmah* resembles an upside-down *merekha*, placed over the first letter of the stressed syllable.

Kadmah darga tevir קַדְמָ֨ה דַרְגָּ֧א תְּבִ֛יר **(CD track 13)**

קַדְמָ֨ה דַרְגָּ֧א תְּבִ֛יר

(Exod. 5:7) לָתֵ֥ת תֶּ֛בֶן לָעָ֖ם

(Lev. 6:5) וּבִעֵ֨ר עָלֶ֧יהָ הַכֹּהֵ֛ן

(Gen. 24:29) וַיָּ֨רָץ לָבָ֧ן אֶל־הָאִ֛ישׁ

Kadmah merekha tevir קַדְמָ֨ה מֵרְכָ֥א תְּבִ֛יר **(CD track 12)**

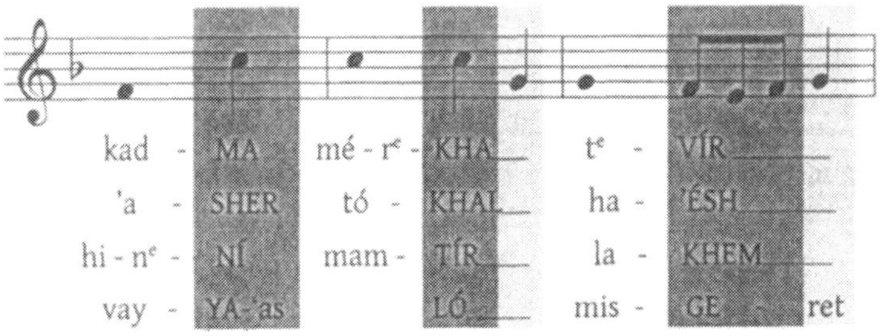

קַדְמָ֨ה מֵרְכָ֥א תְּבִ֛יר

(Lev. 6:3) אֲשֶׁ֨ר תֹּאכַ֥ל הָאֵ֛שׁ

(Exod. 16:4) הִנְנִ֨י מַמְטִ֥יר לָכֶ֛ם

(Exod. 37:12) וַיַּ֨עַשׂ ל֥וֹ מִסְגֶּ֛רֶת

If the second conjunctive before *tevir* (preceding either *merekha* or *darga*) is accented on the first syllable, it will be *munaḥ* instead of *kadmah*. When we refer to this use of the *ta'am*, we will accent its first syllable: *MU-naḥ*.

Munaḥ darga tevir מ֣וּנַח דַרְגָּ֧א תְּבִ֛יר **(CD track 15)**

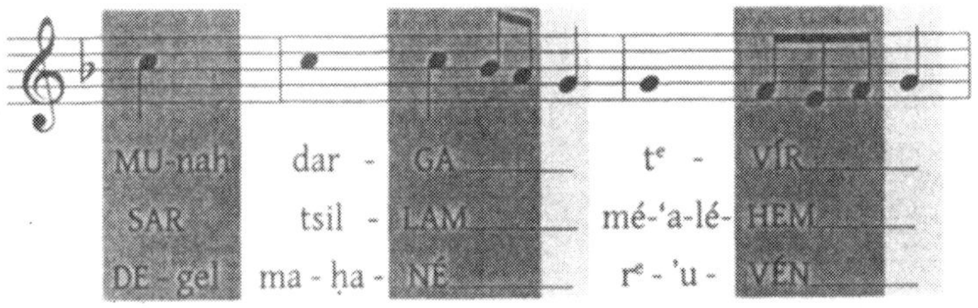

מ֣וּנַח דַרְגָּ֧א תְּבִ֛יר

(Num. 14:9) סָ֣ר צִלָּ֧ם מֵעֲלֵיהֶ֛ם

(Num. 2:10) דֶּ֣גֶל מַחֲנֵ֧ה רְאוּבֵ֛ן

Munaḥ merekha tevir מ֣וּנַח מֵרְכָ֥א תְּבִ֛יר **(CD track 14)**

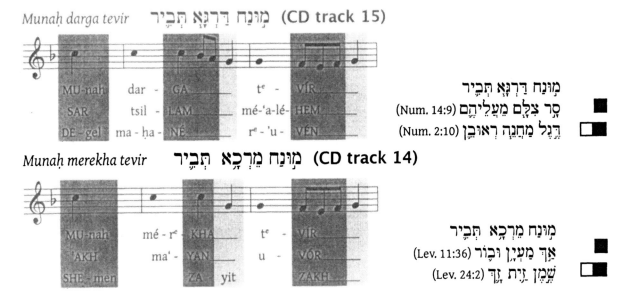

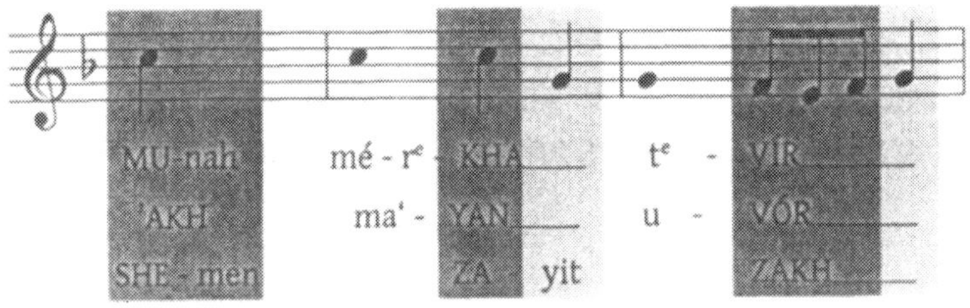

מ֣וּנַח מֵרְכָ֥א תְּבִ֛יר

(Lev. 11:36) אַ֣ךְ מַעְיָ֥ן וּב֛וֹר

(Lev. 24:2) שֶׁ֣מֶן זַ֥יִת זָ֛ךְ

Chant these words to the appropriate *te'amim.*

קַדְמָ֨ה מֵרְכָ֥א תְּבִ֛יר

הָבִ֨יאָה לִּ֥י צַ֛יִד וַעֲשֵׂה־לִ֥י מַטְעַמִּ֖ים וְאֹכֵ֑לָה (Gen. 27:7)

וְהֶ֨בֶל הֵבִ֥יא גַם־ה֛וּא מִבְּכֹר֥וֹת צֹאנ֖וֹ וּמֵֽחֶלְבֵהֶ֑ן (Gen. 4:4)

חֲמ֨וֹר אוֹ־שׁ֥וֹר אוֹ־שֶׂ֛ה וְכָל־בְּהֵמָ֖ה לִשְׁמֹ֑ר (Exod. 22:9)

קַדְמָ֨ה דַּרְגָּ֧א תְּבִ֛יר

אֲשֶׁ֨ר יִקְרָא־ל֧וֹ הָאָדָ֛ם נֶ֥פֶשׁ חַיָּ֖ה ה֥וּא שְׁמֽוֹ׃ (Gen. 2:19)

וְגֹנֵ֨ב אִ֧ישׁ וּמְכָר֛וֹ וְנִמְצָ֥א בְיָד֖וֹ מ֥וֹת יוּמָֽת׃ (Exod. 21:16)

וְעֹרֹ֨ת אֵילִ֧ם מְאָדָּמִ֛ים וְעֹרֹ֥ת תְּחָשִׁ֖ים וַעֲצֵ֥י שִׁטִּֽים׃ (Exod. 35:7)

מוּנַח מֵרְכָ֥א תְּבִ֛יר

עַ֣ד אַרְבָּעָ֥ה עָשָׂ֛ר י֖וֹם לַחֹ֣דֶשׁ הַזֶּ֑ה (Exod. 12:6)

כֶּ֣בֶשׂ אֶחָ֥ד אָשָׁ֛ם לִתְנוּפָ֖ה לְכַפֵּ֣ר עָלָ֑יו (Lev. 14:21)

מוּנַח דַּרְגָּ֧א תְּבִ֛יר

נֶ֣גֶד אַחֵ֧ינוּ הַֽכֶּר־לְךָ֛ מָ֥ה עִמָּדִ֖י וְקַֽח־לָ֑ךְ (Gen. 31:32)

אַ֣יִל תָּמִ֧ים מִן־הַצֹּ֛אן בְּעֶרְכְּךָ֥ לְאָשָׁ֖ם אֶל־הַכֹּהֵ֑ן (Lev. 5:18)

Four Words in a *Tevir* Segment

Sometimes *tevir* is preceded by a series of three conjunctives. The third conjunctive before *tevir* is *telishah ketanah.* The symbol for *telishah ketanah* is a small circle with a tail pointing down to the right (תְּלִישָׁה֠). This *ta'am* is unusual in that it is not necessarily placed on the stressed syllable. *Telishah ketanah* is always placed at the very end of the word. So how can you tell which syllable to stress? Consult an edition of the Bible (such as *Koren* or *Simanim*) that "doubles" the *ta'am* when necessary. In these editions, you will still find *telishah ketanah* placed at the very end of the word. But unless the stress is on the last syllable, you will find a second *telishah ketanah* over the first letter of the stressed syllable (קֹ֠דֶשׁ֠).

Another interesting fact about *telishah ketanah* is that it is always followed by *kadmah* (even if that word is accented on the first syllable).

Telishah kadmah darga tevir תְּלִישָׁה֠ קַדְמָ֨ה דַּרְגָּ֧א תְּבִ֛יר **(CD track 18)**

וְכֹל֩ אֲשֶׁ֨ר יִקְרָא־ל֧וֹ הָאָדָ֛ם נֶ֥פֶשׁ חַיָּ֖ה ה֥וּא שְׁמֽוֹ׃ (Gen. 2:19)

וַיִּבְכּ֨וּ֩ בְנֵ֨י יִשְׂרָאֵ֧ל אֶת־מֹשֶׁ֛ה בְּעַרְבֹ֥ת מוֹאָ֖ב שְׁלֹשִׁ֣ים י֑וֹם (Deut. 34:8)

כֹּל֩ אֲשֶׁ֨ר אָמַ֧ר אֱלֹהִ֛ים אֵלֶ֖יךָ עֲשֵֽׂה׃ (Gen. 31:16)

אֶ֩רֶץ֩ אַרְבַּ֨ע מֵאֹ֧ת שֶֽׁקֶל־כֶּ֛סֶף בֵּינִ֥י וּבֵינְךָ֖ מַה־הִ֑וא (Gen. 23:15)

וַתַּ֩הַר֩ וַתֵּ֨לֶד שָׂרָ֧ה לְאַבְרָהָ֛ם בֵּ֖ן לִזְקֻנָ֑יו (Gen. 21:2)

Telishah kadmah merekha tevir תְּלִישָׁה קַדְמָה מֵרְכָא תְּבִיר (CD track 16)

וְכֹל אֲשֶׁר יִהְיֶה בָעִיר כָּל־שְׁלָלָהּ תָּבֹז לָךְ (Deut. 20:14)

הֵן קָנִיתִי אֶתְכֶם הַיּוֹם וְאֶת־אַדְמַתְכֶם לְפַרְעֹה (Gen. 47:23)

קֹדֶשׁ קָדָשִׁים הוּא לוֹ מֵאִשֵּׁי יְהוָה חָק־עוֹלָם׃ (Lev. 24:9)

וַיָּשָׁב בַּיּוֹם הַהוּא עֵשָׂו לְדַרְכּוֹ שֵׂעִירָה׃ (Gen. 33:16)

Five Words in a *Tevir* Segment

Sometimes *tevir* is preceded by a series of four conjunctives. The fourth conjunctive before *tevir* (preceding *telishah ketanah*) is *munaḥ*.

Munaḥ telishah kadmah darga tevir מוּנַח תְּלִישָׁה קַדְמָה דַּרְגָּא תְּבִיר (CD track 17)

שְׁנֵים עָשָׂר עֲבָדֶיךָ אַחִים ׀ אֲנַחְנוּ בְּנֵי אִישׁ־אֶחָד בְּאֶרֶץ כְּנָעַן (Gen. 42:13)

יִהְיֶה לָכֶם לְזֶרַע הַשָּׂדֶה וּלְאָכְלְכֶם וְלַאֲשֶׁר בְּבָתֵּיכֶם וְלֶאֱכֹל לְטַפְּכֶם׃ (Gen. 47:24)

Munaḥ telishah kadmah merekha tevir מוּנַח תְּלִישָׁה קַדְמָה מֵרְכָא תְּבִיר (CD track 19)

בִּכְלִי עֵץ־יָד אֲשֶׁר־יָמוּת בּוֹ הִכָּהוּ וַיָּמֹת רֹצֵחַ הוּא (Num. 35:18)

בְּאֶבֶן יָד אֲשֶׁר־יָמוּת בָּהּ הִכָּהוּ וַיָּמֹת רֹצֵחַ הוּא (Num. 35:17)

Merekha-Khefulah

Merekha-khefulah (מֵרְכָא־כְפוּלָה) is a *ta'am* that resembles *tevir*. Like *tevir*, it is followed by *tippeḥa* and preceded by *darga*. However, *merekha-khefulah* is actually a conjunctive *ta'am*, a rare substitution for the normal *merekha*. *Merekha-khefulah* is a doubled *merekha*, placed under the first letter of the stressed syllable. It is found only five times in the Torah (Gen. 27:25, Exod. 5:15, Lev. 10:1, Num. 14:3, Num. 32:42).

Darga merekha-khefulah tippeḥa דַּרְגָּא מֵרְכָא־כְפוּלָה טִפְּחָא (CD track 8)

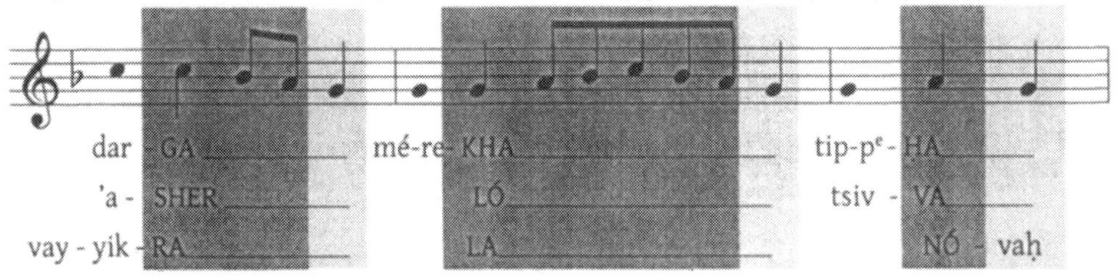
dar - GA mé-re - KHA tip-pᵉ - HA
'a - SHER LÓ tsiv - VA
vay - yik - RA LA NÓ - vaḥ

אֲשֶׁר לֹא צִוָּה אֹתָם׃ (Lev. 10:1)

וַיִּקְרָא לָה נֹבַח בִּשְׁמוֹ׃ (Num. 32:42)

Zakef

Zakef is a strong disjunctive; only *siluk* and *etnaḥta* are stronger. A *zakef* segment will always be followed by a *tippeḥa* segement. *Zakef* is stronger than the ensuing *tippeḥa*. A *zakef* segment may also be followed by one or more other *zakef* segments, but they will eventually be followed by a *tippeḥa* segement. When you see two *zakefs* (or two *zakef* segments) in a row, the first is always stronger.

זָקֵף טִפְּחָא אֶתְנַחְתָּא

זָקֵף זָקֵף טִפְּחָא אֶתְנַחְתָּא

There are two basic forms of *zakef*, each with its own distinct melody: *zakef gadol* and *zakef katon*. There are also two compound *te'amim*, in which two symbols appear on a single word: *munaḥ-zakef* and *metigah-zakef.*

Zakef Gadol

The symbol for *zakef gadol* comprises a vertical line with a pile of two dots on its right, placed over the first letter of the stressed syllable (זָקֵף). A word marked with *zakef gadol* is short, and has no conjunctives immediately before it.

Zakef gadol זָקֵף־גָּדוֹל (CD track 20)

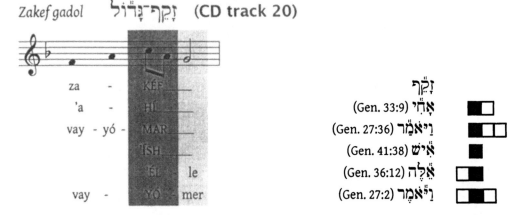

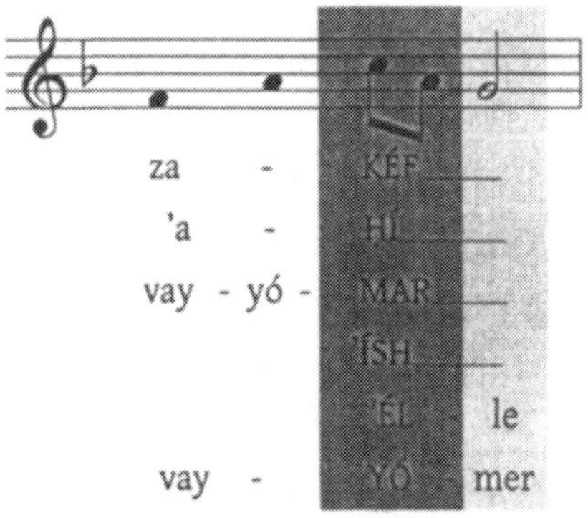
za - KÉF
'a - HÍ
vay - yó - MAR
ÍSH
ÉL le
vay - YÓ mer

זָקֵף

(Gen. 33:9) אָחִי

(Gen. 27:36) וַיֹּאמֶר

(Gen. 41:38) אִישׁ

(Gen. 36:12) אֵלֶּה

(Gen. 27:2) וַיֹּאמֶר

Note: In the case of words that have only a one-syllable pick-up, the F could be omitted.

Zakef is usually followed by *(merekha-) tippeḥa*. Chant these examples. Make a pause or elongation after *zakef*. Make a more subtle pause or elongation after *tippeḥa*. Connect each conjunctive to the word that follows.

מְקֹ֔ום אֲשֶׁ֥ר יֹוסֵ֖ף אָס֥וּר שָֽׁם׃ (Gen. 40:3)
אֹתִ֔י וְאֵ֖ת שַׂ֥ר הָאֹפִֽים׃ (Gen. 41:10)
כִּי־דֶ֥רֶךְ נָשִׁ֖ים לִ֑י וַיְחַפֵּ֕שׂ וְלֹ֥א מָצָ֖א אֶת־הַתְּרָפִֽים׃ (Gen. 31:35)
וַיֹּ֖אמֶר אֲלֵהֶ֑ם לֹ֕א כִּֽי־עֶרְוַ֥ת הָאָ֖רֶץ בָּאתֶ֥ם לִרְאֹֽות׃ (Gen. 42:12)
וּנְתָנָ֖הּ לָ֑נוּ אֶ֕רֶץ אֲשֶׁר־הִ֛וא זָבַ֥ת חָלָ֖ב וּדְבָֽשׁ׃ (Num. 14:8)

Zakef Katon

The symbol for *zakef katon* is a pile of two dots, like a colon, placed over the first letter of the stressed syllable (זָקֵ֔ף).

Zakef katon זָקֵף־קָטֹ֔ון **(CD track 21)**

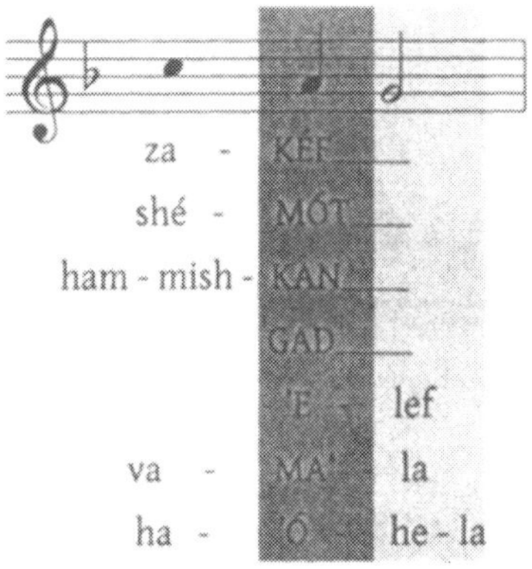

זָקֵ֔ף
שְׁמֹ֔ות (Num. 1:2)
הַמִּשְׁכָּ֔ן (Num. 1:51)
גָּ֔ד (Num. 1:24)
אֶ֔לֶף (Num. 1:25)
וָמַ֔עְלָה (Num. 1:3)
הָאֹ֔הֱלָה (Exod. 33:9)

Two Words in a *Zakef* Segment

A word marked with *zakef katon* is usually preceded by the conjunctive *munaḥ*.

Munaḥ zakef katon מוּנַ֣ח זָקֵף־קָטֹ֔ון **(CD track 22)**

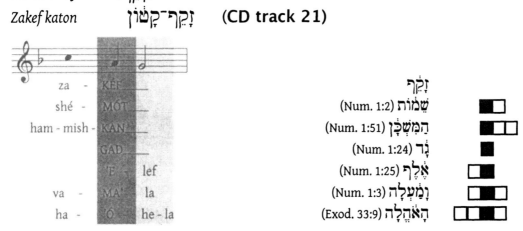

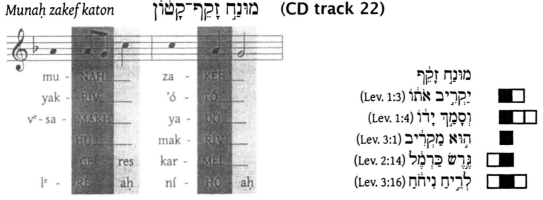

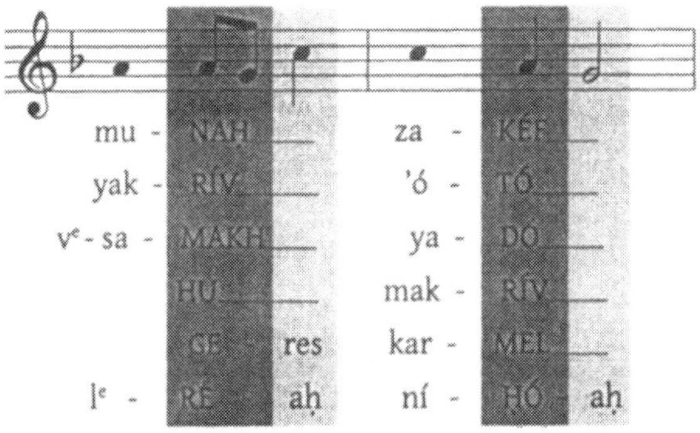

מוּנַ֣ח זָקֵ֔ף
יַקְרִ֣יב אֹתֹ֔ו (Lev. 1:3)
וְסָמַ֣ךְ יָדֹ֔ו (Lev. 1:4)
ה֣וּא מַקְרִ֔יב (Lev. 3:1)
גֶּ֣רֶשׂ כַּרְמֶ֔ל (Lev. 2:14)
לְרֵ֣יחַ נִיחֹ֔חַ (Lev. 3:16)

Sometimes *munah* appears on the same word that is marked with *zakef*. This *munaḥ* takes the place of *meteg* to indicate secondary stress on long words.

וְנָ֣תַתָּ֔ה (Exod. 25:12) וְאֶל־הָ֣אָרֹ֔ן (Exod. 25:21)
בְּעֵ֣ינֵיכֶ֔ם (Num. 33:55) וְלֹא־תִלָּ֣חֲמ֔וּ (Deut. 1:42)
עַל־שֹׂ֣נְאֵ֔ינוּ (Exod. 1:10) וּמִבָּ֣תֶּ֔יךָ (Exod. 8:7)

Metigah–Zakef

Sometimes, *metigah* appears on the same word that is marked with *zakef. Metigah* appears as a secondary *ta'am* on a closed syllable, while *munaḥ* appears as a secondary *ta'am* on an open syllable. *Metigah* looks just like *kadmah*. (For more information on closed syllables, see page 28.)

Metigah-zakef מְתִיגָה־זָקֵף **(CD track 23)**

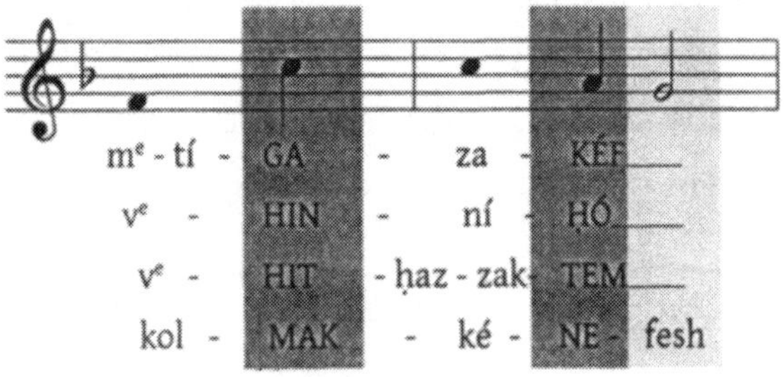

מְתִיגָה־זָקֵף
וְהִנִּיח֔וֹ (Deut. 26:4)
וְהִתְחַזַּקְתֶּ֔ם (Num. 13:20)
כָּל־מַכֵּה־נֶ֔פֶשׁ (Num. 35:30)

Zakef (any form) is usually followed by *(merekha-) tippeḥa*. Chant these examples. Make a pause or elongation after *zakef*. Make a more subtle pause or elongation after *tippeḥa*. Connect each conjunctive to the word that follows.

מוּנַ֣ח זָקֵ֔ף טִפְּחָ֖א
וְאָכְלָ֣ה אֶתְכֶ֔ם אֶ֖רֶץ אֹיְבֵיכֶֽם׃ (Lev. 26:38)
וַיְדַבֵּ֣ר מֹשֶׁ֔ה אֶֽל־אַהֲרֹ֖ן וְאֶל־בָּנָ֑יו (Lev. 21:24)
וְאָמַרְתָּ֣ אֲלֵהֶ֔ם לְנֶ֥פֶשׁ לֹֽא־יִטַּמָּ֖א בְּעַמָּֽיו׃ (Lev. 21:1)
וְכִֽי־יָמ֣וּךְ אָחִ֔יךָ וּמָ֥טָה יָד֖וֹ עִמָּ֑ךְ (Lev. 25:35)

מוּנַ֣ח זָקֵ֔ף תְּבִ֛יר מֵרְכָ֥א טִפְּחָ֖א
וַיֹּ֣אמֶר עֵשָׂ֔ו הִנֵּ֛ה אָנֹכִ֥י הוֹלֵ֖ךְ לָמ֑וּת (Gen. 25:32)
וְאִם־הָמֵ֣ר יְמִירֶ֔נּוּ וְהָֽיָה־ה֥וּא וּתְמוּרָת֛וֹ יִֽהְיֶה־קֹּ֖דֶשׁ לֹ֥א יִגָּאֵֽל׃ (Lev. 27:33)
בְּקֶ֣רֶב הָאָ֔רֶץ אֲשֶׁ֥ר אַתֶּ֛ם בָּאִ֥ים שָׁ֖מָּה לְרִשְׁתָּֽהּ׃ (Deut. 4:5)

זָקֵף־גָּד֕וֹל טִפְּחָ֖א
לַהֲבִיאָ֕ם אֶל־הָאָ֖רֶץ אֲשֶׁר־דִּבֶּ֣ר לָהֶ֑ם (Deut. 9:28)
וַיֹּאמְר֑וּ הַכְזוֹנָ֕ה יַעֲשֶׂ֖ה אֶת־אֲחוֹתֵֽנוּ׃ (Gen. 34:31)
וְאִ֕ישׁ כִּֽי־יֹאכַ֥ל קֹ֖דֶשׁ בִּשְׁגָגָ֑ה (Lev. 22:14)

זָקֵף־גָּד֕וֹל תְּבִ֛יר מֵרְכָ֥א טִפְּחָ֖א
וַיֹּ֕אמֶר אִם־יָב֥וֹא עֵשָׂ֛ו אֶל־הַמַּחֲנֶ֥ה הָאַחַ֖ת וְהִכָּ֑הוּ (Gen. 32:9)
וַיֹּ֕אמֶר כִּֽי־אֵרֵ֧ד אֶל־בְּנִ֛י אָבֵ֖ל שְׁאֹ֑לָה (Gen. 37:35)

מוּנַ֣ח זָקֵ֔ף זָקֵף־גָּד֕וֹל טִפְּחָ֖א
בַּצַּ֣ר לְךָ֔ וּמְצָא֕וּךָ כֹּ֖ל הַדְּבָרִ֣ים הָאֵ֑לֶּה (Deut. 4:30)
וַיֹּ֣אמֶר ל֔וֹ בַּחֲלוֹמִ֕י וְהִנֵּה־גֶ֖פֶן לְפָנָֽי׃ (Gen. 40:9)

זָקֵף־גָּדֹול   מוּנַח זָקֵף   מֵרְכָא טִפְחָא
וַיֹּ֕אמֶר   הִנֵּ֣ה שָׁמַ֔עְתִּי   כִּי יֶשׁ־שֶׁ֖בֶר בְּמִצְרָֽיִם   (Gen. 42:2)

זָקֵף־גָּדֹול   זָקֵף־גָּדֹול טִפְחָא
וַיֹּ֕אמֶר   אָנֹכִ֕י   אֱלֹהֵ֖י אַבְרָהָ֣ם אָבִ֑יךָ   (Gen. 26:24)

מוּנַח זָקֵף   מוּנַח זָקֵף טִפְחָא
וְלָקַחְתָּ֣ סֹ֔לֶת   וְאָפִיתָ֣ אֹתָ֔הּ   שְׁתֵּ֥ים עֶשְׂרֵ֖ה חַלֹּֽות   (Lev. 24:5)

מְתִיגָה־זָקֵף   טִפְחָא
וְאִם־עַד־אֵ֕לֶּה   לֹ֥א תִשְׁמְע֖וּ לִ֑י   (Lev. 26:18)
וַהֲקֵמֹתָ֖ אֶת־הַמִּשְׁכָּ֑ן   כְּמִ֨שְׁפָּט֔וֹ   אֲשֶׁ֥ר הָרְאֵ֖יתָ בָּהָֽר: (Exod. 26:30)

מְתִיגָה־זָקֵף   זָקֵף־גָּדֹול טִפְחָא
וְלָקַ֧ח הַכֹּהֵ֛ן הַטֶּ֖נֶא מִיָּדֶ֑ךָ   וְהִ֨נִּיח֔וֹ   לִפְנֵ֕י מִזְבַּ֖ח יְהוָ֥ה אֱלֹהֶֽיךָ:   (Deut. 26:4)

מְתִיגָה־זָקֵף   מוּנַח זָקֵף טִפְחָא
כָּל־מַכֵּה־נֶ֗פֶשׁ   לְפִ֣י עֵדִ֔ים יִרְצַ֖ח אֶת־הָרֹצֵ֑חַ   (Num. 35:30)

Chant these verses.

וְנָ֣תַתָּ֔ה אֵ֖ת מִזְבַּ֣ח הָעֹלָ֑ה   לִפְנֵ֕י פֶּ֖תַח מִשְׁכַּ֥ן אֹֽהֶל־מוֹעֵֽד: (Exod. 40:6)
וַיֹּ֥אמֶר פַּרְעֹ֖ה אֶל־עֲבָדָ֑יו   הֲנִמְצָ֣א כָזֶ֔ה אִ֕ישׁ אֲשֶׁ֛ר ר֥וּחַ אֱלֹהִ֖ים בּֽוֹ:   (Gen. 41:38)
וַיֹּ֕אמֶר מִ֥י לְךָ֛ כָּל־הַמַּחֲנֶ֥ה הַזֶּ֖ה אֲשֶׁ֣ר פָּגָ֑שְׁתִּי   וַיֹּ֕אמֶר לִמְצֹא־חֵ֖ן בְּעֵינֵ֥י אֲדֹנִֽי: (Gen. 33:8)
צֵ֖א מִן־הַתֵּבָ֑ה   אַתָּ֕ה וְאִשְׁתְּךָ֛ וּבָנֶ֥יךָ וּנְשֵֽׁי־בָנֶ֖יךָ אִתָּֽךְ:   (Gen. 8:16)
וַֽיְהִ֕י מִקֵּ֖ץ אַרְבָּעִ֣ים יֹ֑ום   וַיִּפְתַּ֣ח נֹ֔חַ אֶת־חַלֹּ֥ון הַתֵּבָ֖ה אֲשֶׁ֥ר עָשָֽׂה: (Gen. 8:6)
לִרְצֹנְכֶ֑ם   תָּמִ֣ים זָכָ֔ר בַּבָּקָ֕ר בַּכְּשָׂבִ֖ים וּבָעִזִּֽים: (Lev. 22:19)

Pashta/Yetiv

Sometimes there is a subdivision within the *zakef* segment. *Pashta* (פַּשְׁטָא) is the *ta'am* that marks that subdivision. The symbol for *pashta* looks like *kadmah* but with one important difference: Kadmah (a conjunctive) is placed over the first letter of the stressed syllable, while *pashta* (a disjunctive) is placed on the extreme left end of the word (דָּבָ֙ר). If the stress is not on the last syllable, a second *pashta* may be placed over the first letter of the stressed syllable (פֶּ֙סֶל֙). See also p. 221.

Pashta פַּשְׁטָא֙ (CD track 25)

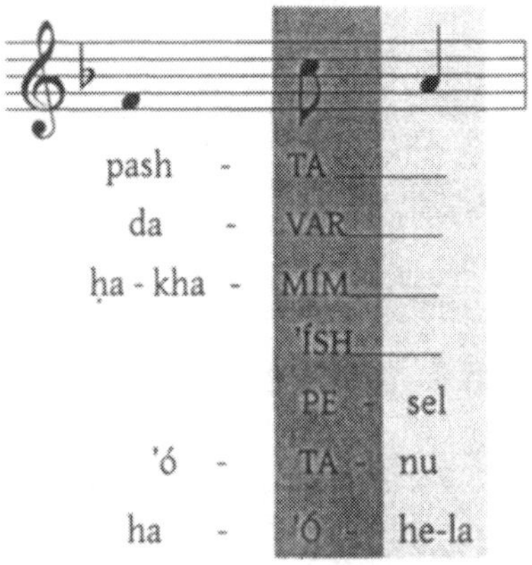

פַּשְׁטָא֙

(Deut. 1:25) דָּבָר֙

(Deut. 1:15) חֲכָמִים֙

(Deut. 1:35) אִישׁ֙

(Deut. 4:25) פֶּסֶל֙

(Deut. 1:22) אֹתָנוּ֙

(Gen. 24:67) הָאֹהֱלָה֙

Two Words in a *Pashta* Segment

If the preceding word is closely connected in meaning to the *pashta* word, it is usually marked with a conjunctive *ta'am.*

If there are two or more syllables separating the accents, the conjunctive will be *mahpakh.* The symbol for *mahpakh* is an arrowhead pointing to the left, placed under the first letter of the stressed syllable (מַהְפַּ֤ךְ).

Mahpakh pashta מַהְפַּ֤ךְ פַּשְׁטָא֙ (CD track 27)

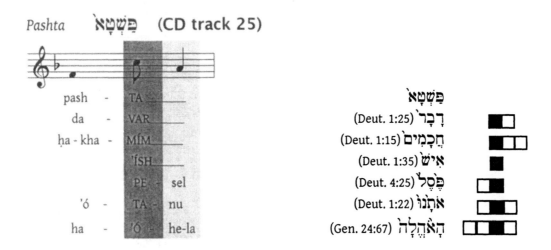

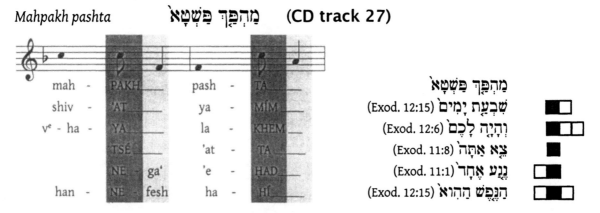

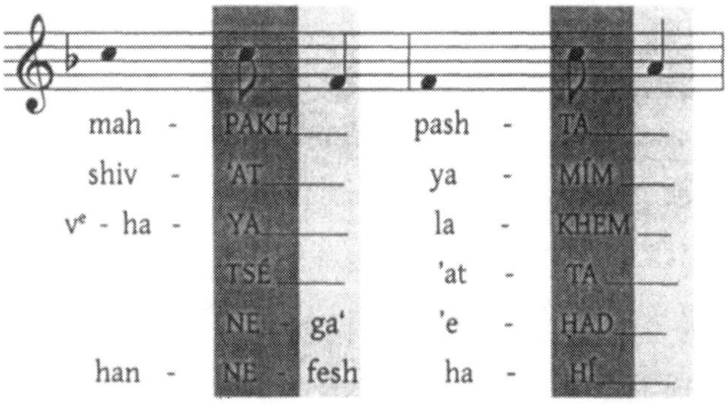

מַהְפַּ֤ךְ פַּשְׁטָא֙

(Exod. 12:15) שִׁבְעַ֤ת יָמִים֙

(Exod. 12:6) וְהָיָ֤ה לָכֶם֙

(Exod. 11:8) צֵ֤א אַתָּה֙

(Exod. 11:1) נֶ֤גַע אֶחָד֙

(Exod. 12:15) הַנֶּ֤פֶשׁ הַהִוא֙

If the accents are close to each other, the conjunctive will be *merekha* instead of *mahpakh.* This is the fourth use of *merekha* that we have encountered so far. In each case, it has a different melody. Remember: A disjunctive *ta'am* can stand by itself and owns a unique melody. But a conjunctive *ta'am* "serves" its ensuing disjunctive; its melodic identity is dependent on that disjunctive.

In the *merekha-pashta* combination, the two accented syllables are contiguous—the *merekha* word is accented on the last syllable, and the *pashta* word has no pick-up. Thus the model is sung on the syllable "TA," dropping the pick-up "pash-."

Merekha pashta מֵרְכָא פַּשְׁטָא֙ (CD track 26)

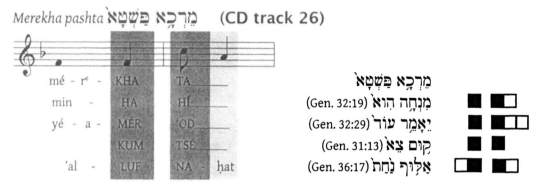

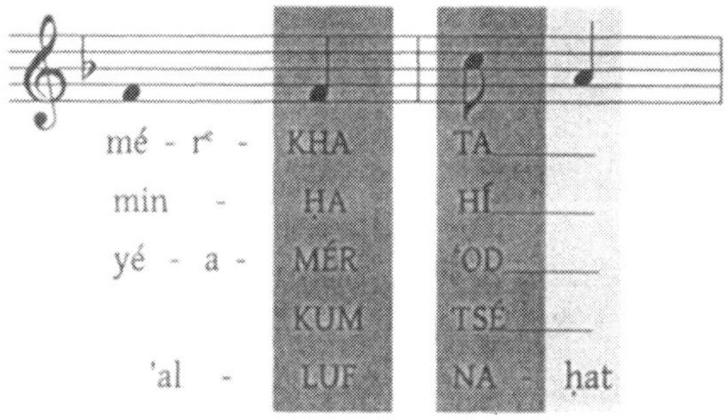
mé - rᵉ - KHA TA
min - HA HÍ
yé - a - MÉR 'OD
KUM TSÉ
'al - LUF NA - ḥat

מֵרְכָא פַּשְׁטָא֙

(Gen. 32:19) מִנְחָ֥ה הִוא֙

(Gen. 32:29) יַֽאָמֵ֥ר עוֹד֙

(Gen. 31:13) ק֥וּם צֵא֙

(Gen. 36:17) אַלּ֥וּף נַ֙חַת֙

Pashta is usually followed by either *zakef katon* or *munaḥ zakef katon*. Chant these examples. Connect each conjunctive word to the word that follows. Make a subtle elongation or pause after *pashta*. Make a stronger elongation or pause after *zakef*.

פַּשְׁטָא֙ זָקֵ֔ף

וַעֲבָדִים֙ וּשְׁפָחֹ֔ת (Gen. 12:16)

וַיֹּ֙אמֶר֙ אֶל־שָׂרַ֣י אִשְׁתּ֔וֹ (Gen. 12:11)

מַהְפַּ֤ךְ פַּשְׁטָא֙ זָקֵ֔ף

וַיַּעֲבֹ֤ר אַבְרָם֙ בָּאָ֔רֶץ (Gen. 12:6)

לָ֤מָה אָמַ֙רְתָּ֙ אֲחֹ֣תִי הִ֔וא (Gen. 12:19)

מֵרְכָא פַּשְׁטָא֙ זָקֵ֔ף

רִאשׁ֥וֹן הוּא֙ לָכֶ֔ם (Exod. 12:2)

וַיַּחֲלֹ֥ם עוֹד֙ חֲל֣וֹם אַחֵ֔ר (Gen. 37:9)

Note: When you see repeating *te'amim*, the first one is a stronger disjunctive than the second one.

פַּ֙שְׁטָא֙ פַּשְׁטָא֙

מַהְפַּ֤ךְ פַּשְׁטָא֙ פַּשְׁטָא֙ מוּנַ֣ח זָקֵ֔ף

יָקֻ֤ם אָבִי֙ וְיֹאכַל֙ מִצֵּ֣יד בְּנ֔וֹ (Gen. 27:31)

מַהְפַּ֤ךְ פַּשְׁטָא֙ מַהְפַּ֤ךְ פַּשְׁטָא֙ זָקֵ֔ף

הַלְעִיטֵ֤נִי נָא֙ מִן־הָאָדֹ֤ם הָאָדֹם֙ הַזֶּ֔ה (Gen. 25:30)

Yetiv

Yetiv (יְ֚תִיב) is used instead of *pashta* if the word is accented on the first syllable and if there are no conjunctive words immediately preceding. The symbol for *yetiv* looks just like *mahpakh*, except that *yetiv* is placed just before the word. Since *yetiv* is found only on words accented on the first syllable, i.e., words with no pick-ups, the model will be sung on the syllable "TÍV," dropping the pick-up "yᵉ-." Remember: A word marked with *yetiv* is never preceded by a conjunctive. See also p. 221.

Yetiv יְתִיב (CD track 24)

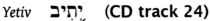

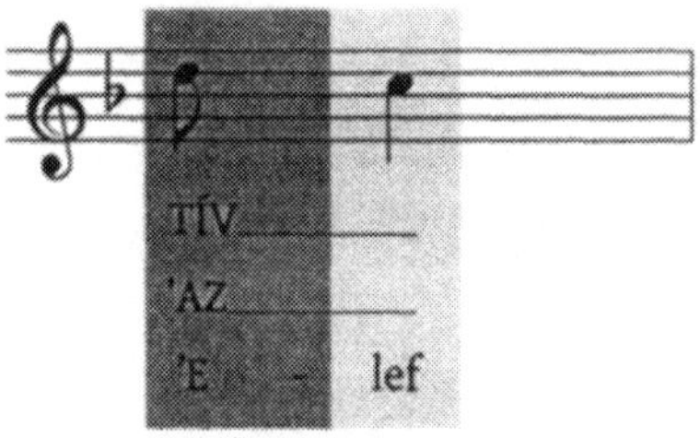

יְתִיב
(Num. 21:17) אָז
(Num. 31:4) אֶלֶף

Yetiv is usually followed by either *zakef katon* or *munaḥ zakef katon*. Chant these examples. Make a subtle elongation or pause after *yetiv*. Make a stronger elongation or pause after *zakef.*

אֵלֶּה הָעֵדֹת וְהַחֻקִּים וְהַמִּשְׁפָּטִים (Deut. 4:45)

קַח אֶת־הַלְוִיִּם מִתּוֹךְ בְּנֵי יִשְׂרָאֵל וְטִהַרְתָּ אֹתָם׃ (Num. 8:6)

רַק עַם־חָכָם וְנָבוֹן הַגּוֹי הַגָּדוֹל הַזֶּה׃ (Deut. 4:6)

There are two places in the Torah where *yetiv* appears immediately before *pashta.* Do not mistake this *yetiv* for a *mahpakh.*

אֶת סִיחֹן מֶלֶךְ הָאֱמֹרִי (Deut. 1:4) אוֹ בְּנִבְלַת בְּהֵמָה טְמֵאָה (Lev. 5:2)

In this clause, *yetiv* is followed by *mahpakh.* יַעַן אֲשֶׁר עָשִׂיתָ אֶת־הַדָּבָר הַזֶּה (Gen. 22:16)

In this clause, *pashta* is followed by *yetiv.* וְלָקַח גַּם מֵעֵץ הַחַיִּים (Gen. 3:22)

Chant these verses.

וַיְבָרְכוּ אֶת־רִבְקָה וַיֹּאמְרוּ לָהּ אֲחֹתֵנוּ אַתְּ הֲיִי לְאַלְפֵי רְבָבָה
וְיִירַשׁ זַרְעֵךְ אֵת שַׁעַר שֹׂנְאָיו׃ (Gen. 24:60)

וַיְהִי רָעָב בָּאָרֶץ מִלְּבַד הָרָעָב הָרִאשׁוֹן אֲשֶׁר הָיָה בִּימֵי אַבְרָהָם וַיֵּלֶךְ
יִצְחָק אֶל־אֲבִימֶלֶךְ מֶלֶךְ־פְּלִשְׁתִּים גְּרָרָה׃ (Gen. 26:1)

וַיֹּאמֶר אֲבִימֶלֶךְ אֶל־יִצְחָק לֵךְ מֵעִמָּנוּ כִּי־עָצַמְתָּ־מִמֶּנּוּ מְאֹד׃ (Gen. 26:16)

וַיֹּאמֶר יִצְחָק אֶל־בְּנוֹ מַה־זֶּה מִהַרְתָּ לִמְצֹא בְּנִי
וַיֹּאמֶר כִּי הִקְרָה יְהוָה אֱלֹהֶיךָ לְפָנָי׃ (Gen. 27:20)

קוּם לֵךְ פַּדֶּנָה אֲרָם בֵּיתָה בְתוּאֵל אֲבִי אִמֶּךָ
וְקַח־לְךָ מִשָּׁם אִשָּׁה מִבְּנוֹת לָבָן אֲחִי אִמֶּךָ׃ (Gen. 28:2)

וַתִּבְלַעְנָה הַשִּׁבֳּלִים הַדַּקּוֹת אֵת שֶׁבַע הַשִּׁבֳּלִים הַבְּרִיאוֹת וְהַמְּלֵאוֹת
וַיִּיקַץ פַּרְעֹה וְהִנֵּה חֲלוֹם׃ (Gen. 41:7)

וְיוֹסֵף בֶּן־שְׁלֹשִׁים שָׁנָה בְּעָמְדוֹ לִפְנֵי פַּרְעֹה מֶלֶךְ־מִצְרָיִם
וַיֵּצֵא יוֹסֵף מִלִּפְנֵי פַרְעֹה וַיַּעֲבֹר בְּכָל־אֶרֶץ מִצְרָיִם׃ (Gen. 41:46)

וַיִּזְכֹּר יוֹסֵף אֵת הַחֲלֹמוֹת אֲשֶׁר חָלַם לָהֶם
וַיֹּאמֶר אֲלֵהֶם מְרַגְּלִים אַתֶּם לִרְאוֹת אֶת־עֶרְוַת הָאָרֶץ בָּאתֶם׃ (Gen. 42:9)

Three Words in a *Pashta* Segment

Sometimes *pashta* is preceded by a series of two or more conjunctives. In these segments, there will be a very slight pause or elongation just before the *pashta.*

The second conjunctive before *pashta* (preceding either *merekha* or *mahpakh*) may be *kadmah.*

Kadmah mahpakh pashta קַדְמָ֨ה מַהְפַּ֤ךְ פַּשְׁטָא֙ **(CD track 29)**

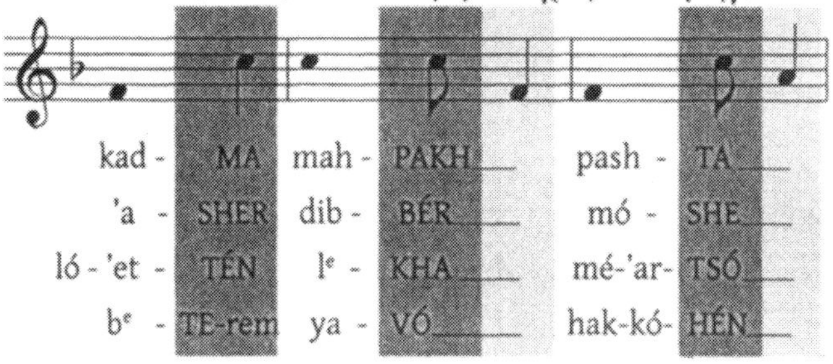

קַדְמָ֨ה מַהְפַּ֤ךְ פַּשְׁטָא֙

אֲשֶׁ֨ר דִּבֶּ֤ר מֹשֶׁה֙ (Deut. 1:1)

לֹֽא־אֶתֵּ֨ן לְךָ֤ מֵֽאַרְצוֹ֙ (Deut. 2:9)

בְּטֶ֨רֶם יָבֹ֤א הַכֹּהֵן֙ (Lev. 14:36)

Chant these phrases.

אֲשֶׁ֨ר שֵׁ֤ם הָֽאַחַת֙ שִׁפְרָ֔ה וְשֵׁ֥ם הַשֵּׁנִ֖ית פּוּעָֽה׃ (Exod. 1:15)

וְיֶ֨תֶר הַגִּלְעָ֤ד וְכָל־הַבָּשָׁן֙ מַמְלֶ֣כֶת ע֔וֹג נָתַ֕תִּי לַחֲצִ֖י שֵׁ֣בֶט הַֽמְנַשֶּׁ֑ה (Deut. 3:13)

Kadmah merekha pashta קַדְמָ֨ה מֵרְכָ֥א פַּשְׁטָא֙ **(CD track 28)**

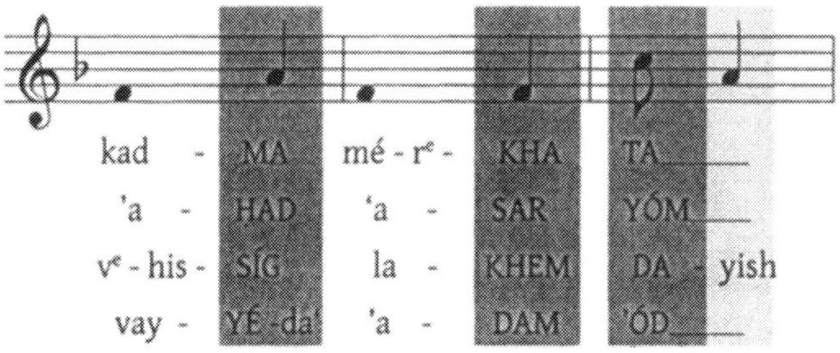

קַדְמָ֨ה מֵרְכָ֥א פַּשְׁטָא֙

אַחַ֨ד עָשָׂ֥ר יוֹם֙ (Deut. 1:2)

וְהִשִּׂ֨יג לָכֶ֥ם דַּ֙יִשׁ֙ (Lev .26:5)

וַיֵּ֨דַע אָדָ֥ם עוֹד֙ (Gen. 4:25)

Chant these phrases.

אַחַ֨ד עָשָׂ֥ר יוֹם֙ מֵֽחֹרֵ֔ב דֶּ֖רֶךְ הַר־שֵׂעִ֑יר עַ֖ד קָדֵ֥שׁ בַּרְנֵֽעַ׃ (Deut. 1:2)

וַיִּזְבַּ֨ח יַעֲקֹ֥ב זֶ֙בַח֙ בָּהָ֔ר וַיִּקְרָ֥א לְאֶחָ֖יו לֶאֱכָל־לָ֑חֶם (Gen. 31:54)

If the second conjunctive before *pashta* (preceding either *merekha* or *mahpakh*) is accented on the first syllable, it will be *munaḥ*, instead of *kadmah*. When we refer to this *ta'am*, we accent its first syllable: *MU-naḥ*.

Munaḥ mahpakh pashta מ֣וּנַח מַהְפַּ֤ךְ פַּשְׁטָא֙ **(CD track 31)**

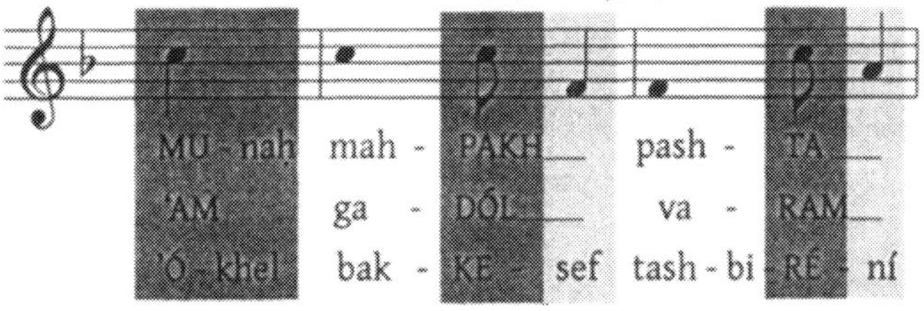

מ֣וּנַח מַהְפַּ֤ךְ פַּשְׁטָא֙

עַ֣ם גָּד֤וֹל וָרָם֙ (Deut. 1:28)

אֹ֣כֶל בַּכֶּ֤סֶף תַּשְׁבִּרֵ֙נִי֙ (Deut. 2:28)

Chant these phrases.

א֣וֹ בֶ֤גֶד אוֹ־עוֹר֙ א֣וֹ שָׂ֔ק כָּל־כְּלִ֕י אֲשֶׁר־יֵעָשֶׂ֥ה מְלָאכָ֖ה בָּהֶ֑ם (Lev. 11:32)

עֵ֣שֶׂב מַזְרִ֤יעַ זֶ֙רַע֙ לְמִינֵ֔הוּ וְעֵ֧ץ עֹֽשֶׂה־פְּרִ֛י אֲשֶׁ֥ר זַרְעוֹ־ב֖וֹ לְמִינֵ֑הוּ (Gen. 1:12)

Munaḥ merekha pashta מ֣וּנַח מֵרְכָ֥א פַּשְׁטָא֙ **(CD track 30)**

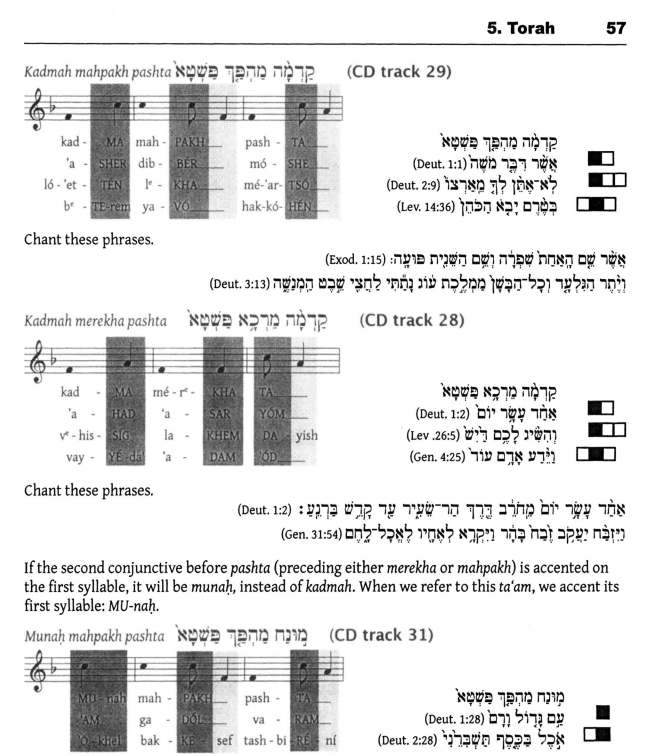

מ֣וּנַח מֵרְכָ֥א פַּשְׁטָא֙

כִּ֣י אָנֹכִ֥י מֵת֙ (Deut. 4:22)

Chant these phrases.

שׁוֹר נַגָּח הוּא מִתְּמוֹל שִׁלְשֹׁם וְלֹא יִשְׁמְרֶנּוּ בְּעָלָיו (Exod 21:36)

זֹאת עֹלַת חֹדֶשׁ בְּחָדְשׁוֹ לְחָדְשֵׁי הַשָּׁנָה׃ (Num. 28:14)

Four Words in a *Pashta* Segment

Sometimes *pashta* is preceded by a series of three conjunctives. The third conjunctive before *pashta* is *telishah ketanah*. Remember: *Telishah ketanah* is always followed by *kadmah*, even if that word is accented on the first syllable.

Telishah kadmah mahpakh pashta תְּלִישָׁה קַדְמָה מַהְפַּךְ פַּשְׁטָא (CD track 34)

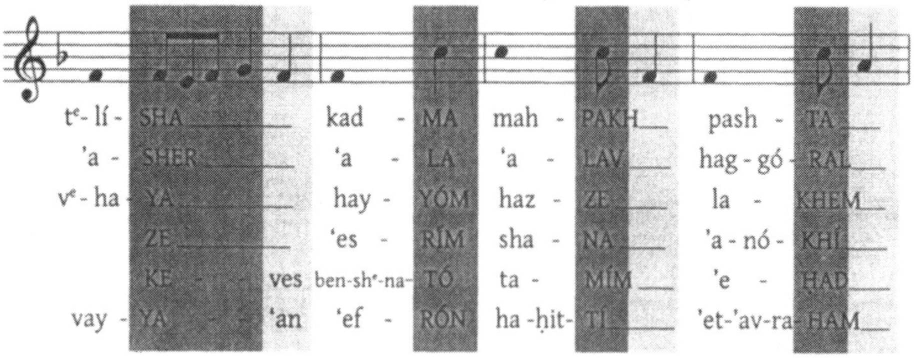

אֲשֶׁר עָלָה עָלָיו הַגּוֹרָל לַעֲזָאזֵל (Lev. 16:10)

וְהָיָה הַיּוֹם הַזֶּה לָכֶם לְזִכָּרוֹן (Exod. 12:14)

זֶה עֶשְׂרִים שָׁנָה אָנֹכִי עִמָּךְ (Gen. 31:38)

כֶּבֶשׂ בֶּן־שְׁנָתוֹ תָמִים אֶחָד לְעֹלָה (Num. 6:14)

וַיַּעַן עֶפְרוֹן הַחִתִּי אֶת־אַבְרָהָם בְּאָזְנֵי בְנֵי־חֵת (Gen. 23:10)

Telishah kadmah merekha pashta תְּלִישָׁה קַדְמָה מֵרְכָא פַּשְׁטָא (CD track 32)

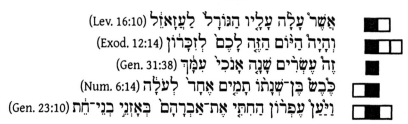

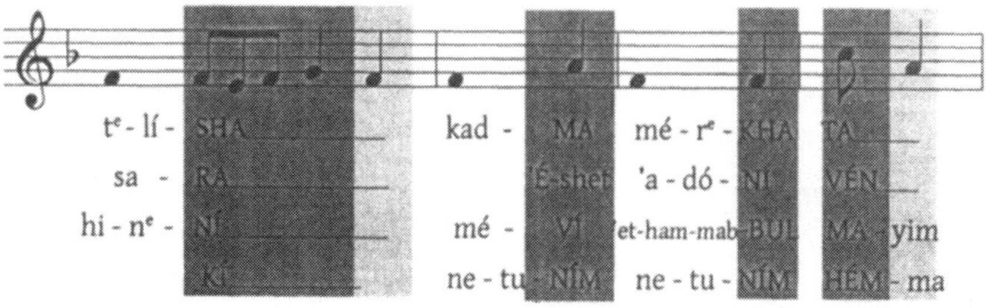

שָׂרָה אֵשֶׁת אֲדֹנִי בֵן לַאדֹנִי (Gen. 24:36)

הִנְנִי מֵבִיא אֶת־הַמַּבּוּל מַיִם עַל־הָאָרֶץ (Gen. 6:17)

כִּי נְתֻנִים נְתֻנִים הֵמָּה לִי (Num. 8:16)

Five Words in a *Pashta* Segment

Sometimes *pashta* is preceded by a series of four conjunctives. The fourth conjunctive before *pashta* (preceding *telishah ketanah*) will be *munaḥ*.

Munaḥ telishah kadmah mahpakh pashta מוּנַח תְּלִישָׁה קַדְמָה מַהְפַּךְ פַּשְׁטָא (CD track 35)

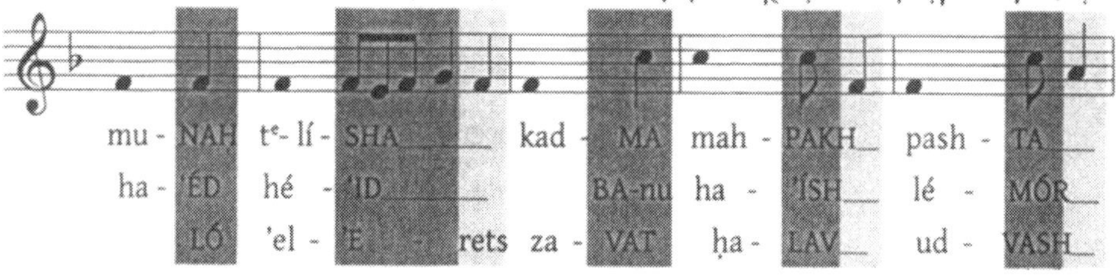

הָעֵד הֵעִד בָּנוּ הָאִישׁ לֵאמֹר לֹא־תִרְאוּ פָנַי (Gen. 43:3)

לֹא אֶל־אֶרֶץ זָבַת חָלָב וּדְבַשׁ הֲבִיאֹתָנוּ (Num. 16:14)

Munaḥ telishah kadmah merekha pashta מוּנַח תְּלִישָׁה קַדְמָה מֵרְכָא פַּשְׁטָא (CD track 33)

אֲשֶׁר אֲנִי מֵבִיא אֶתְכֶם שָׁמָּה לֹא תַעֲשׂוּ (Lev. 18:3)

This is the only occurrence of this combination in the Torah.

Chant these examples. Be sure you know the difference between *kadmah* and *pashta.*

עַד־מָתַי יִהְיֶה זֶה לָנוּ לְמוֹקֵשׁ שַׁלַּח אֶת־הָאֲנָשִׁים (Exod. 10:7)

וַיֹּאמֶר לוֹ אִם־נָא מָצָאתִי חֵן בְּעֵינֶיךָ שִׂים־נָא יָדְךָ תַּחַת יְרֵכִי (Gen. 47:29)

וַיֵּט אַהֲרֹן אֶת־יָדוֹ בְמַטֵּהוּ וַיַּךְ אֶת־עֲפַר הָאָרֶץ וַתְּהִי הַכִּנָּם בָּאָדָם וּבַבְּהֵמָה (Exod. 8:13)

אֲשֶׁר הֵם עֹשִׂים תְּמוֹל שִׁלְשֹׁם תָּשִׂימוּ עֲלֵיהֶם לֹא תִגְרְעוּ מִמֶּנּוּ (Exod. 5:8)

Segol/Shalshelet

Segol is another strong disjunctive, stronger even than *zakef*; only *siluk* and *etnaḥta* are stronger. A *segol* segment will usually be followed by one or more *zakef* segments, and will always be followed eventually by *tippeḥa* and then *etnaḥta.* A *segol* segment may also be followed by one or more other *segol* segments, but they will eventually be followed by a *tippeḥa* segement. *Segol* is always stronger than the others (*zakef* or *tippeḥa*) that follow.

סֶגוֹל טִפְּחָא אֶתְנַחְתָּא

סֶגוֹל זָקֵף טִפְּחָא אֶתְנַחְתָּא

The symbol for *segol* is a cluster of three dots, arranged in the shape of a pyramid (סֶגוֹל). *Segol* is not placed on the first letter of the stressed syllable. It is always found on the very end of the word, over the left edge of the last letter. If the stress is not on the last syllable, a second *segol* may be placed over the first letter of the stressed syllable (בָּאנוּ).

Segol סֶגוֹל֒ **(CD track 37)**

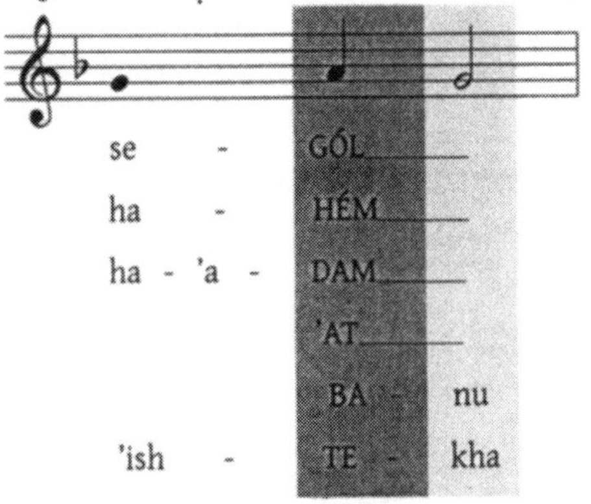
se - GÓL
ha - HÉM
ha - 'a - DAM
'AT
BA - nu
'ish - TE - kha

סֶגוֹל֒
(Gen. 6:4) הָהֵם֒
(Gen. 2:23) הָאָדָם֒
(Gen. 24:47) אֹתָ֒
(Gen. 47:4) בָּאנוּ֒
(Gen. 3:17) אִשְׁתֶּךָ֒

Two Words in a *Segol* Segment

Segol is never the first word in its segment. If the preceding word is closely connected in meaning to the *segol* word, it is usually marked with the conjunctive *munaḥ*.

Munaḥ segol מוּנַח סֶגוֹל֒ **(CD track 38)**

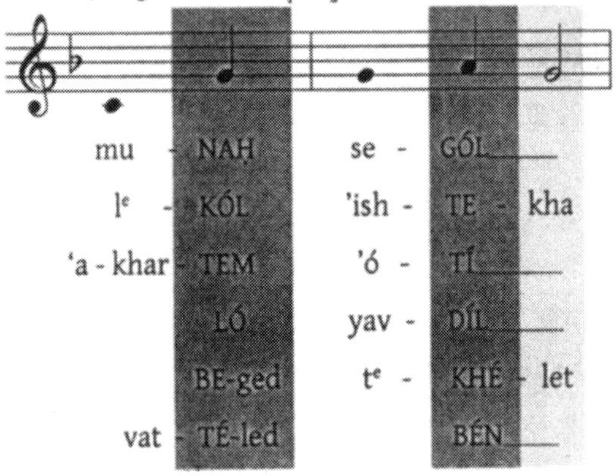
mu - NAH se - GÓL
le - KÓL 'ish - TE - kha
'a - khar - TEM 'ó - TÍ
LÓ yav - DÍL
BE-ged te - KHÉ - let
vat - TÉ-led BÉN

מוּנַח סֶגוֹל֒
(Gen. 3:17) לְקוֹל אִשְׁתֶּךָ֒
(Gen. 34:30) עֲכַרְתֶּם אֹתִי֒
(Lev. 1:17) לֹא יַבְדִּיל֒
(Num. 4:7) בֶּגֶד תְּכֵלֶת֒
(Gen. 29:33) וַתֵּלֶד בֵּן֒

Shalshelet

Shalshelet (שַׁ֓לְשֶׁלֶת ׀) is a rare *ta'am* that is used instead of *segol* on the first word of a verse. *Shalshelet* is found only four times in the Torah. Its symbol has two parts: a pile of three left-pointing arrowheads placed over the first letter of the stressed syllable, and a vertical line placed after the word (וַיֹּ֓אמַר ׀).

Shalshelet שַׁ֓לְשֶׁלֶת ׀ **(CD track 36)**

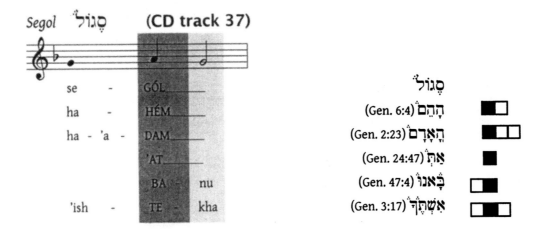

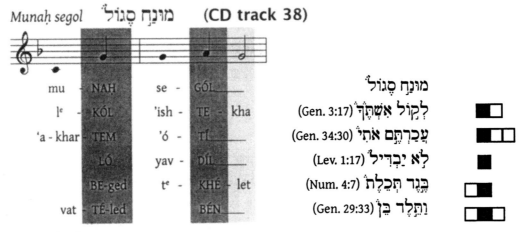

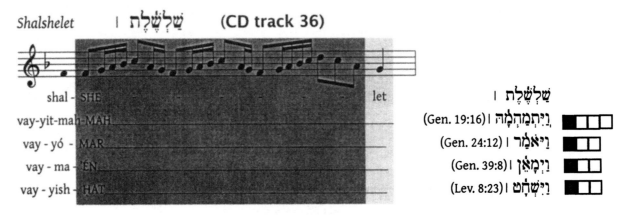

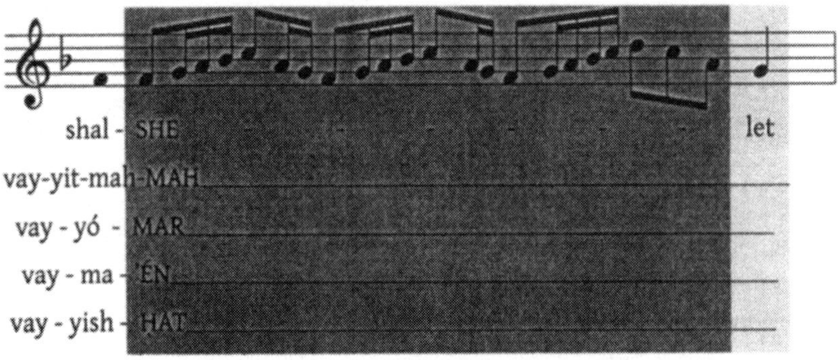
shal - SHE let
vay-yit-mah - MAH
vay - yó - MAR
vay - ma - 'ÉN
vay - yish - HAT

שַׁ֓לְשֶׁלֶת ׀
(Gen. 19:16) וַיִּתְמַהְמָ֓הּ ׀
(Gen. 24:12) וַיֹּ֓אמַר ׀
(Gen. 39:8) וַיְמָ֓אֵן ׀
(Lev. 8:23) וַיִּשְׁחָ֓ט ׀

Pasek

The long vertical line appears in another form in the Torah (and other books of the Tanakh). *Pasek* (| פָּסֵק) is a symbol that the editors of the Masoretic text inserted after certain conjunctive words, if they felt that a slight pause was appropriate. *Pasek* has no melody; it merely indicates a subtle pause (see *Chanting: The Complete Guide*, pp. 105–7).

וַיֹּאמֶר אַבְרָהָם | אַבְרָהָם (Gen. 22:11)

שְׁנֵיהֶם | מְלֵאִים (Num 7:13)

וַיֹּאמֶר | לֹא כִּי צָחָקְתְּ (Gen 18:15)

Chant these verses. *Shalshelet* is the strongest disjunctive until *etnaḥta.*

וַיְמָאֵן | וַיֹּאמֶר אֶל־אֵשֶׁת אֲדֹנָיו הֵן אֲדֹנִי לֹא־יָדַע אִתִּי מַה־בַּבָּיִת

וְכֹל אֲשֶׁר־יֶשׁ־לוֹ נָתַן בְּיָדִי׃ (Gen. 39:8)

וַיִּשְׁחָט | וַיִּקַּח מֹשֶׁה מִדָּמוֹ וַיִּתֵּן עַל־תְּנוּךְ אֹזֶן־אַהֲרֹן הַיְמָנִית

וְעַל־בֹּהֶן יָדוֹ הַיְמָנִית וְעַל־בֹּהֶן רַגְלוֹ הַיְמָנִית׃ (Lev. 8:23)

Zarka

Sometimes there is a subdivision within the *segol* segment. *Zarka* (זַרְקָא) is the *ta'am* that marks that subdivision. The symbol for *zarka* looks like an inverted letter "s" that has fallen down to the left. It is always found on the very end of the word, over the left edge of the last letter (דַּבֵּר). If the stress is not on the last syllable, a second *zarka* may be placed over the first letter of the stressed syllable (טֶּרֶם).

Zarka זַרְקָא (CD track 39)

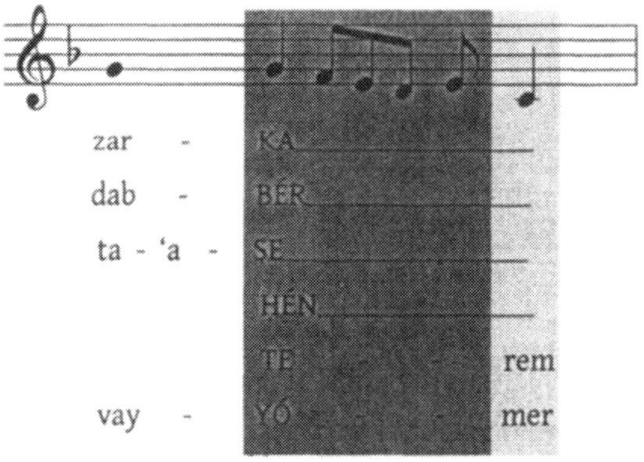

זַרְקָא

(Exod. 14:2) דַּבֵּר

(Exod. 26:5) תַּעֲשֶׂה

(Gen. 19:19) חֵן

(Gen. 19:4) טֶּרֶם

(Gen. 32:10) וַיֹּאמֶר

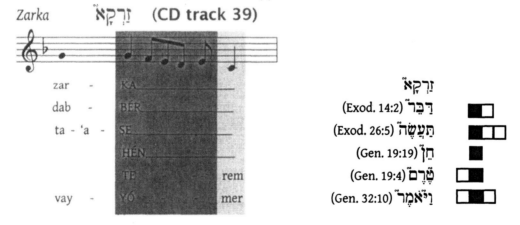

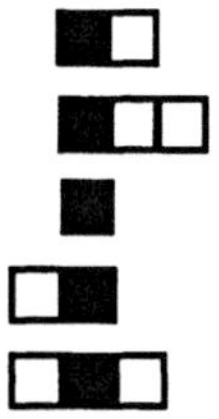

Two Words in a *Zarka* Segment

If there are two words in a *zarka* segment, the first word is usually marked with either of two conjunctives, *munaḥ* or *merekha.* They are chanted to the same melody.

Munaḥ zarka מוּנַח זַרְקָא and *merekha zarka* מֵרְכָא זַרְקָא **(CD track 40)**

מוּנַח זַרְקָא

מֵרְכָא זַרְקָא

הִכָּה כָל־בְּכוֹר (Exod. 12:29)

אֱמֹר לִבְנֵי־יִשְׂרָאֵל (Exod. 6:6)

בְּשַׁלַּח פַּרְעֹה (Exod. 13:17)

כִּי לִי (Num. 3:13)

שֵׁשֶׁת יָמִים (Exod. 31:15)

וְעָשָׂה פֶסַח (Exod. 12:48)

Zarka is always followed (eventually) by *segol.* Chant these phrases.

דַּבֵּר אֶל־בְּנֵי יִשְׂרָאֵל (Exod. 14:2)

וַיֹּאמְרוּ אֶל־מֹשֶׁה (Exod. 14:11)

מִזְבַּח אֲדָמָה תַּעֲשֶׂה־לִּי (Exod. 20:24)

בַּקָּנֶה הָאֶחָד כַּפְתֹּר וָפֶרַח (Exod. 25:33)

Three Words in a *Zarka* Segment

Sometimes *zarka* is preceded by a series of two or more conjunctives. In these segments, there will be a very slight pause or elongation just before the *zarka.* The second conjunctive before *zarka* (preceding either *merekha* or *munaḥ*) is *kadmah.*

Kadmah munaḥ/merekha zarka קַדְמָה מוּנַח\מֵרְכָא זַרְקָא **(CD track 41)**

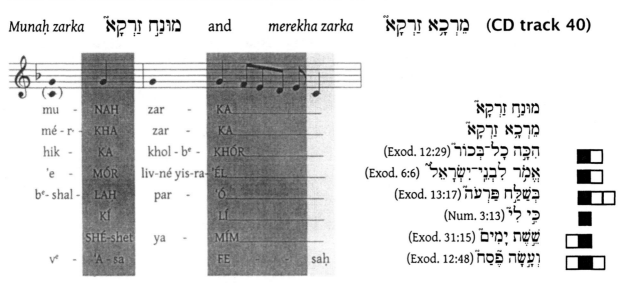

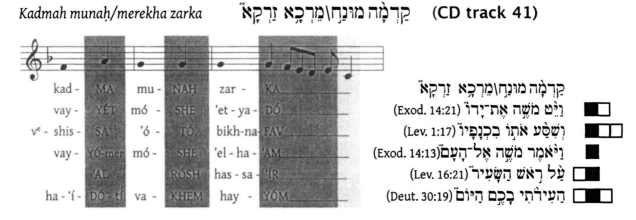

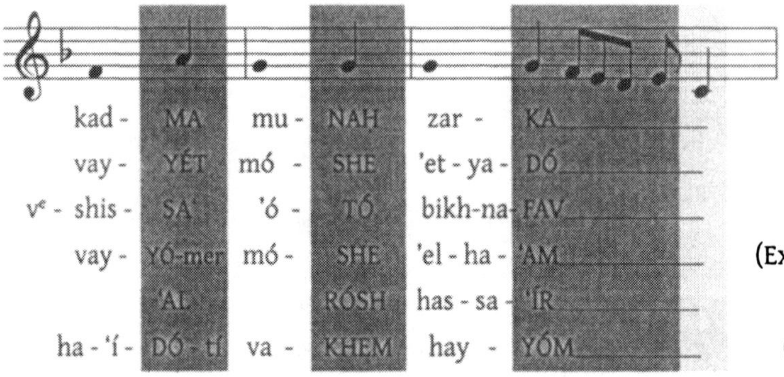

קַדְמָה מוּנַח\מֵרְכָא זַרְקָא

וַיֵּט מֹשֶׁה אֶת־יָדוֹ (Exod. 14:21)

וְשִׁסַּע אֹתוֹ בִכְנָפָיו (Lev. 1:17)

וַיֹּאמֶר מֹשֶׁה אֶל־הָעָם (Exod. 14:13)

עַל רֹאשׁ הַשָּׂעִיר (Lev. 16:21)

הַעִידֹתִי בָכֶם הַיּוֹם (Deut. 30:19)

Four or Five Words in a *Zarka* Segment

Sometimes *zarka* is preceded by three or four conjunctives. The third conjunctive before *zarka* is *telishah ketanah. Telishah ketanah* may be preceded by its conjunctive, *munaḥ.*

(Munah) telishah kadmah merekha zarka (מוּנַח) תְּלִישָׁה קַדְמָה מֵרְכָא זַרְקָא (CD track 42)

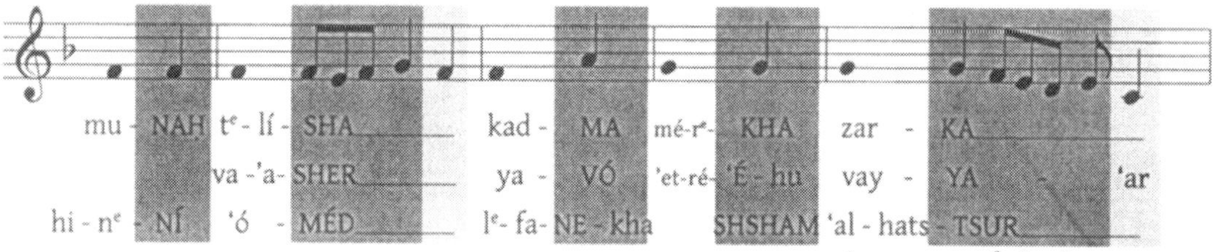

וַאֲשֶׁר יָבֹא אֶת־רֵעֵהוּ בַיַּעַר לַחְטֹב עֵצִים (Deut. 19:5)

הִנְנִי עֹמֵד לְפָנֶיךָ שָּׁם ׀ עַל־הַצּוּר בְּחֹרֵב (Exod. 17:6)

Chant these verses.

וְנִגְּשָׁה יְבִמְתּוֹ אֵלָיו לְעֵינֵי הַזְּקֵנִים וְחָלְצָה נַעֲלוֹ מֵעַל רַגְלוֹ וְיָרְקָה בְּפָנָיו
וְעָנְתָה וְאָמְרָה כָּכָה יֵעָשֶׂה לָאִישׁ אֲשֶׁר לֹא־יִבְנֶה אֶת־בֵּית אָחִיו׃ (Deut. 25:9)

וַיֹּאמְרוּ אֶל־מֹשֶׁה הֲמִבְּלִי אֵין־קְבָרִים בְּמִצְרַיִם לְקַחְתָּנוּ לָמוּת בַּמִּדְבָּר
מַה־זֹּאת עָשִׂיתָ לָּנוּ לְהוֹצִיאָנוּ מִמִּצְרָיִם׃ (Exod. 14:11)

תָּכִין לְךָ הַדֶּרֶךְ וְשִׁלַּשְׁתָּ אֶת־גְּבוּל אַרְצְךָ אֲשֶׁר יַנְחִילְךָ יְהוָה אֱלֹהֶיךָ
וְהָיָה לָנוּס שָׁמָּה כָּל־רֹצֵחַ׃ (Deut. 19:3)

הַעִידֹתִי בָכֶם הַיּוֹם אֶת־הַשָּׁמַיִם וְאֶת־הָאָרֶץ הַחַיִּים וְהַמָּוֶת נָתַתִּי לְפָנֶיךָ
הַבְּרָכָה וְהַקְּלָלָה וּבָחַרְתָּ בַּחַיִּים לְמַעַן תִּחְיֶה אַתָּה וְזַרְעֶךָ׃ (Deut. 30:19)

וְהֵנִיף אוֹתָם הַכֹּהֵן ׀ תְּנוּפָה לִפְנֵי יְהוָה קֹדֶשׁ הוּא לַכֹּהֵן עַל חֲזֵה הַתְּנוּפָה
וְעַל שׁוֹק הַתְּרוּמָה וְאַחַר יִשְׁתֶּה הַנָּזִיר יָיִן׃ (Num. 6:20)

Revia

Revia is medium-level disjunctive, found before *pashta, tevir,* and *zarka* segments. *Revia* is a stronger disjunctive than either *pashta, tevir,* or *zarka* that follow.

רְבִיעַ פַּשְׁטָא זָקֵף
רְבִיעַ זַרְקָא סֶגוֹל
רְבִיעַ תְּבִיר טִפְּחָא

The symbol for *revia* is a single diamond-shaped dot, placed above the first letter of the stressed syllable (רְבִיעַ).

Revia רְבִיעַ (CD track 43)

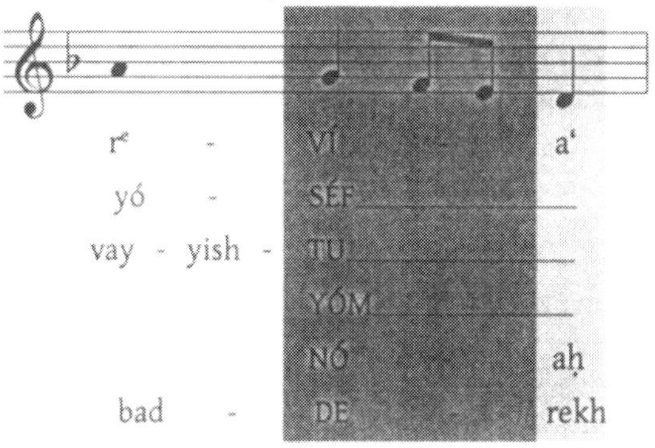

רְבִיעַ
יוֹסֵף (Gen. 48:17)
וַיִּשְׁתּוּ (Gen. 24:54)
יוֹם (Deut. 4:10)
נֹחַ (Gen. 7:13)
בַּדֶּרֶךְ (Deut. 1:33)

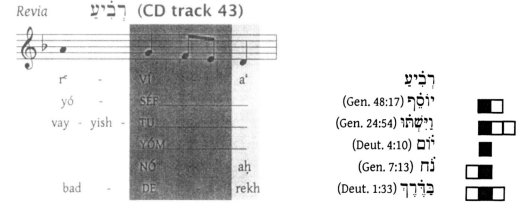

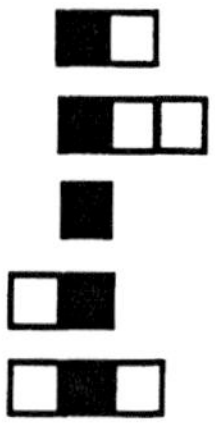

Two Words in a *Revia* Segment

If the preceding word is closely connected in meaning to the *revia* word, it is usually marked with the conjunctive *munaḥ*.

Munaḥ revia מוּנַח רְבִיעַ (CD track 44)

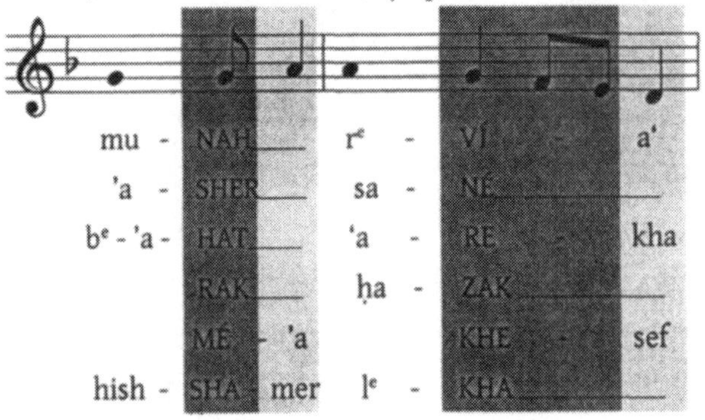

מוּנַח רְבִיעַ
אֲשֶׁר שָׂנֵא (Deut. 12:31)
בְּאַחַת עָרֶיךָ (Deut. 13:13)
רַק חֲזַק (Deut. 12:23)
מֵאָה כֶסֶף (Deut. 22:19)
הִשָּׁמֶר לְךָ (Deut. 12:30)

Three Words in a *Revia* Segment

Sometimes *revia* is preceded by two conjunctives. In these segments there will be a very slight pause or elongation just before the *revia*. The second conjunctive before *revia* (preceding *munaḥ*) is *darga*.

Darga munaḥ revia דַּרְגָּא מוּנַח רְבִיעַ (CD track 45)

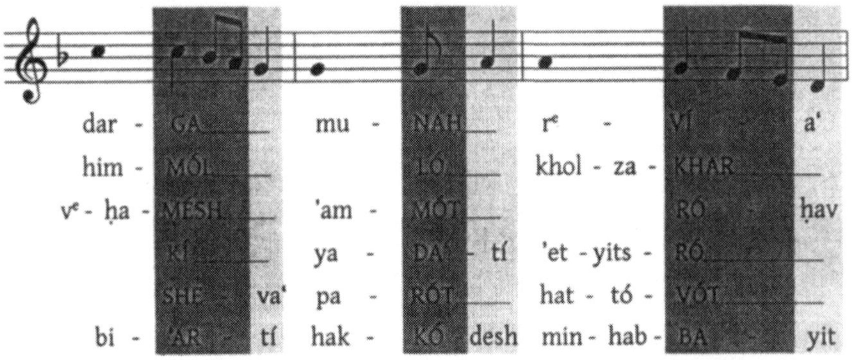

הִמּוֹל לוֹ כָל־זָכָר (Exod. 12:48)
וְחָמֵשׁ אַמּוֹת רֹחַב (Exod. 27:1)
כִּי יָדַעְתִּי אֶת־יִצְרוֹ (Deut. 31:21)
שֶׁבַע פָּרֹת הַטֹּבֹת (Gen. 41:26)
בִּעַרְתִּי הַקֹּדֶשׁ מִן־הַבַּיִת (Deut. 26:13)

Four Words in a *Revia* Segment

Only once in the Torah, *revia* is preceded by three conjunctives. The third conjunctive before *revia* (preceding *darga* and *munaḥ*) is *munaḥ*.

Munaḥ darga munaḥ revia' מוּנַח דַּרְגָּא מוּנַח רְבִיעַ (CD track 46)

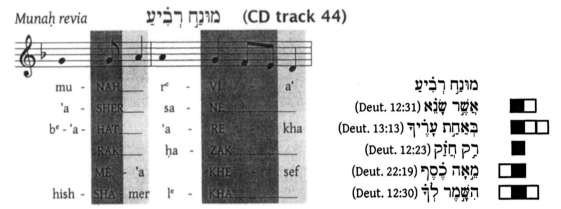

אֲשֶׁר יְשָׁרְתוּ עָלָיו בָּהֶם (Num. 4:14)

Chant these examples. Connect each conjunctive to the word that follows. Create an elongation or pause after *revia*. Create only a slight elongation or pause after *pashta, tevir,* or *zarka*.

רְבִ֗יעַ פַּשְׁטָא֙

וְנִסְלַ֗ח לְכָל־עֲדַת֙ בְּנֵ֣י יִשְׂרָאֵל (Num. 15:26)

מוּנַ֣ח רְבִ֗יעַ פַּשְׁטָא֙

וַיַּ֣עַן בִּלְעָ֗ם וַיֹּאמֶר֙ אֶל־עַבְדֵ֣י בָלָק (Num. 22:18)

רְבִ֗יעַ יְ֚תִיב

וַיָּ֣שֶׂם לִפְנֵיהֶ֗ם אֵ֚ת כָּל־הַדְּבָרִ֣ים הָאֵלֶּה (Exod. 19:7)

רְבִ֗יעַ מַהְפַּ֤ךְ פַּשְׁטָא֙

מָחָ֗ר אָנֹכִ֤י נִצָּב֙ עַל־רֹ֣אשׁ הַגִּבְעָה (Exod. 17:9)

מוּנַ֣ח רְבִ֗יעַ מַהְפַּ֤ךְ פַּשְׁטָא֙

וַיִּקַּ֣ח מִיָּדָ֗ם וַיָּ֤צַר אֹתוֹ֙ בַּחֶרֶט (Exod. 32:4)

דַּרְגָּ֧א מוּנַ֣ח רְבִ֗יעַ מַהְפַּ֤ךְ פַּשְׁטָא֙

דֶּ֧רֶךְ הַמֶּ֣לֶךְ נֵלֵ֗ךְ לֹ֤א נִטֶּה֙ יָמִ֣ין וּשְׂמֹאול (Num. 20:17)

רְבִ֗יעַ מֵרְכָ֥א פַּשְׁטָא֙

עַתָּ֗ה ק֥וּם צֵא֙ מִן־הָאָ֣רֶץ הַזֹּאת (Gen. 31:13)

רְבִ֗יעַ קַדְמָ֨ה מַהְפַּ֤ךְ פַּשְׁטָא֙

אֶת־בְּרִית֗וֹ אֲשֶׁ֨ר צִוָּ֤ה אֶתְכֶם֙ לַעֲשׂוֹת (Deut. 4:13)

מוּנַ֣ח רְבִ֗יעַ קַדְמָ֨ה מַהְפַּ֤ךְ פַּשְׁטָא֙

אֵ֣לֶּה הַדְּבָרִ֗ים אֲשֶׁ֨ר דִּבֶּ֤ר מֹשֶׁה֙ אֶל־כָּל־יִשְׂרָאֵל (Deut. 1:1)

מוּנַ֣ח רְבִ֗יעַ קַדְמָ֨ה מֵרְכָ֥א פַּשְׁטָא֙

שׁ֣וֹר וָשֶׂ֗ה אֲשֶׁ֨ר יִהְיֶ֥ה בוֹ֙ מוּם (Deut. 17:1)

מוּנַ֣ח רְבִ֗יעַ תְּלִישָׁה֩ קַדְמָ֨ה מַהְפַּ֤ךְ פַּשְׁטָא֙

אֶל־פֶּ֣תַח בֵּית־אָבִ֗יהָ וּסְקָל֩וּהָ֩ אַנְשֵׁ֨י עִירָ֤הּ בָּאֲבָנִים֙ וָמֵתָה (Deut. 22:21)

רְבִ֗יעַ תְּבִ֛יר

אָר֗וּר מַטֶּ֛ה מִשְׁפַּ֥ט גֵּר־יָת֛וֹם וְאַלְמָנָה (Deut. 27:19)

מוּנַ֣ח רְבִ֗יעַ תְּבִ֛יר

וַיֹּאכְל֣וּ וַיִּשְׁתּ֗וּ ה֛וּא וְהָאֲנָשִׁ֥ים אֲשֶׁר־עִמּ֖וֹ וַיָּלִינוּ (Gen. 24:54)

דַּרְגָּ֧א מוּנַ֣ח רְבִ֗יעַ תְּבִ֛יר

שְׁתֵּ֧י כְתֵפֹ֣ת חֹבְרֹ֗ת יִֽהְיֶה־לּ֛וֹ אֶל־שְׁנֵ֥י קְצוֹתָ֖יו וְחֻבָּר׃ (Exod. 28:7)

מוּנַ֣ח רְבִ֗יעַ דַּרְגָּ֧א תְּבִ֛יר

וְעָשִׂ֣יתָ פָרֹ֗כֶת תְּכֵ֧לֶת וְאַרְגָּמָ֛ן וְתוֹלַ֥עַת שָׁנִ֖י וְשֵׁ֣שׁ מָשְׁזָר (Exod. 26:31)

רְבִ֗יעַ מֵרְכָ֥א תְּבִ֛יר

אַל־תּ֗וֹסֶף דַּבֵּ֥ר אֵלַ֛י ע֖וֹד בַּדָּבָ֥ר הַזֶּה׃ (Deut. 3:26)

רְבִ֗יעַ קַדְמָ֨ה דַּרְגָּ֧א תְּבִ֛יר

וַיַּ֣רְא פַּרְעֹ֗ה כִּֽי־חָדַ֨ל הַמָּטָ֧ר וְהַבָּרָ֛ד וְהַקֹּלֹ֖ת וַיֹּ֣סֶף לַחֲטֹא (Exod. 9:34)

מוּנַ֣ח רְבִ֗יעַ מוּנַ֣ח זַרְקָא֮ מוּנַ֣ח סֶגּוֹל֒

וַיִּתֹּ֣ם הַכֶּ֔סֶף מֵאֶ֤רֶץ מִצְרַ֙יִם֙ וּמֵאֶ֣רֶץ כְּנַ֔עַן) Gen. 47:15)

רְבִ֗יעַ זַרְקָא֮ מוּנַ֣ח סֶגּוֹל֒

שָׁמַ֕עְתִּי אֶת־תְּלוּנֹּת֙ בְּנֵ֣י יִשְׂרָאֵ֔ל) Exod. 16:12)

רְבִ֗יעַ מוּנַ֣ח זַרְקָא֮ סֶגּוֹל֒

וַיְהִ֗י בְּשַׁלַּ֤ח פַּרְעֹה֙ אֶת־הָעָ֔ם) Exod. 13:17)

דַּרְגָּ֧א מוּנַ֣ח רְבִ֗יעַ מוּנַ֣ח זַרְקָא֮ סֶגּוֹל֒

וְכֵ֣ן תַּעֲשֶׂ֣ה לַחֲמֹר֗וֹ וְכֵ֣ן תַּעֲשֶׂה֙ לְשִׂמְלָת֔וֹ) Deut. 22:3)

מוּנַ֣ח רְבִ֗יעַ זַרְקָא֮ סֶגּוֹל֒

וַיִּקְרָ֣א מֹשֶׁ֗ה אֶל־בְּצַלְאֵ֛ל וְאֶל־אָֽהֳלִיאָ֑ב) Exod. 36:2)

מוּנַ֣ח רְבִ֗יעַ קַדְמָ֥ה מוּנַ֣ח זַרְקָא֮ סֶגּוֹל֒

כָּל־אִ֣ישׁ וְאִשָּׁ֗ה אֲשֶׁ֨ר נָדַ֤ב לִבָּם֙ אֹתָ֔ם) Exod. 35:29)

Chant these verses.

דַּבְּר֗וּ אֶֽל־כָּל־עֲדַ֤ת יִשְׂרָאֵל֙ לֵאמֹ֔ר בֶּעָשֹׂ֖ר לַחֹ֥דֶשׁ הַזֶּ֑ה

וְיִקְח֣וּ לָהֶ֗ם אִ֛ישׁ שֶׂ֥ה לְבֵית־אָבֹ֖ת שֶׂ֥ה לַבָּֽיִת׃) Exod. 12:3)

וַיֹּֽאמֶר־ל֥וֹ פַרְעֹ֖ה לֵ֣ךְ מֵעָלָ֑י

הִשָּׁ֣מֶר לְךָ֗ אַל־תֹּ֙סֶף֙ רְא֣וֹת פָּנַ֔י כִּ֗י בְּי֛וֹם רְאֹתְךָ֥ פָנַ֖י תָּמֽוּת׃) Exod. 10:28)

נַעְבְּרָה־נָּ֣א בְאַרְצֶ֗ךָ לֹ֤א נַעֲבֹר֙ בְּשָׂדֶ֣ה וּבְכֶ֔רֶם וְלֹ֥א נִשְׁתֶּ֖ה מֵ֣י בְאֵ֑ר

דֶּ֧רֶךְ הַמֶּ֣לֶךְ נֵלֵ֗ךְ לֹ֤א נִטֶּה֙ יָמִ֣ין וּשְׂמֹ֔אול עַ֥ד אֲשֶֽׁר־נַעֲבֹ֖ר גְּבֻלֶֽךָ׃) Num. 20:17)

פֶּן־יֹאמְר֗וּ הָאָ֙רֶץ֙ אֲשֶׁ֣ר הוֹצֵאתָ֣נוּ מִשָּׁ֔ם מִבְּלִ֙י יְכֹ֣לֶת יְהֹוָ֔ה

לַהֲבִיאָ֗ם אֶל־הָאָ֙רֶץ֙ אֲשֶׁר־דִּבֶּ֣ר לָהֶ֔ם וּמִשִּׂנְאָת֣וֹ אוֹתָ֔ם הוֹצִיאָ֖ם לַהֲמִתָ֥ם בַּמִּדְבָּֽר׃) Deut. 9:28)

Legarmeh

Sometimes there is a subdivision within the *revia* segment. The *ta'am* that marks that subdivision may be *legarmeh*. The symbol for *legarmeh* looks like a *munaḥ* followed by a *pasek* (לְגַרְמֵ֣הּ ׀).

Legarmeh   לְגַרְמֵ֣הּ ׀   **(CD track 47)**

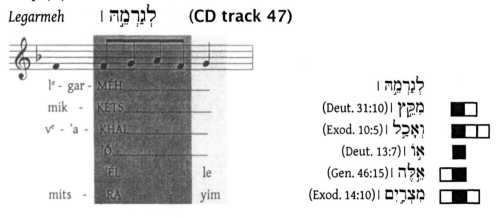

lᵉ - gar - MÉH		le	לְגַרְמֵ֣הּ ׀	
mik - KÉTS			מִקֵּ֣ץ ׀ (Deut. 31:10)	■□
vᵉ - 'a - KHÁL			וְאָכַ֣ל ׀ (Exod. 10:5)	■□□
'Ó			א֣וֹ ׀ (Deut. 13:7)	■
ÉL	le		אֵ֣לֶּה ׀ (Gen. 46:15)	□■□
mits - RÁ - yim			מִצְרַ֣יִם ׀ (Exod. 14:10)	□■□

How can you tell the difference between the conjunctive *munaḥ* followed by *pasek* and the disjunctive *legarmeh*? *Legarmeh* is followed by *munaḥ revia*. There are only three exceptions to that rule, and they are shown below.

Chant these examples.

לְגַרְמֵ֣הּ ׀ מוּנַ֣ח רְבִ֗יעַ

וְגַ֣ם ׀ אֲנִ֣י שָׁמַ֗עְתִּי (Exod. 6:5)

כֹּ֣ל ׀ מַפְרֶ֣סֶת פַּרְסָ֗ה (Lev. 11:3)

כֶּ֣סֶף ׀ שְׁלֹשִׁ֤ים שְׁקָלִים (Exod. 21:32)

Two Words in a *Legarmeh* Segment

If the preceding word is closely connected in meaning to the *legarmeh* word, it is marked with the conjunctive *merekha*. The *merekha-legarmeh* sequence is found only nine times in the Torah.

Merekha legarmeh ׀ מֵרְכָא לְגַרְמֵ֣הּ (CD track 48)

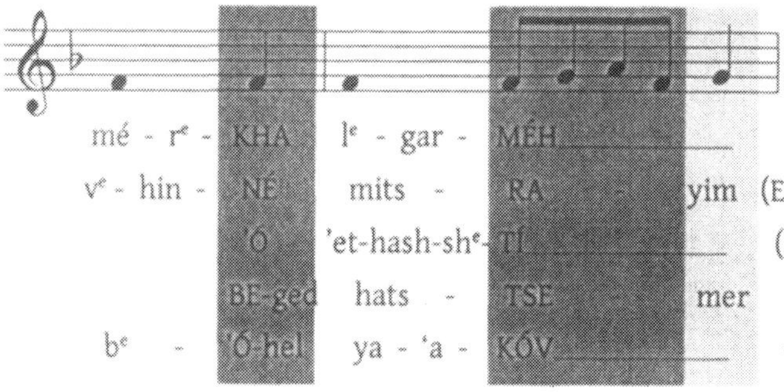

מֵרְכָא לְגַרְמֵ֣הּ ׀

וְהִנֵּ֥ה מִצְרַ֣יִם ׀ נֹסֵ֣עַ אַחֲרֵיהֶ֗ם (Exod. 14:10)

א֥וֹ אֶת־הַשְּׁתִ֣י ׀ א֣וֹ אֶת־הָעֵ֗רֶב (Lev. 13:52)

בֶּ֥גֶד הַצֶּ֣מֶר ׀ א֣וֹ הַפִּשְׁתִּ֗ים (Lev. 13:59)

בְּאֹ֥הֶל יַעֲקֹ֣ב ׀ וּבְאֹ֣הֶל לֵאָ֗ה (Gen. 31:33)

Here are the three instances where *legarmeh* is not followed by *munaḥ revia*.

רָֽאשֵׁיכֶ֣ם אַל־תִּפְרָ֣עוּ ׀ וּבִגְדֵיכֶ֤ם לֹֽא־תִפְרֹ֙מוּ֙ וְלֹ֣א תָמֻ֔תוּ (Lev. 10:6)

אֲשֶׁר־יוּצַ֥ק עַל־רֹאשׁ֣וֹ ׀ שֶׁ֣מֶן הַמִּשְׁחָ֗ה וּמִלֵּ֥א אֶת־יָד֖וֹ (Lev. 21:10)

אֶת־מָחֲלַ֣ת ׀ בַּת־יִשְׁמָעֵ֨אל בֶּן־אַבְרָהָ֜ם (Gen. 28:9)

Geresh

Another *ta'am* that can subdivide the *revia* segment is *geresh*. There are two basic forms of *geresh*, each with its own distinct melody: (single) *geresh*, and double *geresh*, called *gereshayim*.

The symbol for (single) *geresh* looks like the mirror image of *kadmah*. *Geresh* is placed above the first letter of the stressed syllable (גֵּ֜רֶשׁ)

This is how *geresh* is sung when no conjunctive precedes it.

Geresh גֵּ֜רֶשׁ (CD track 49)

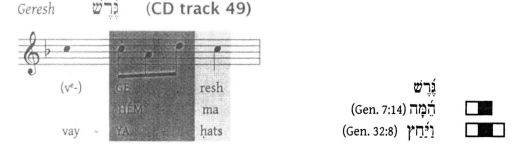

גֵּ֜רֶשׁ

הֵ֜מָּה (Gen. 7:14)

וַיֵּ֜חַץ (Gen. 32:8)

Geresh without a preceding conjunctive is always accented on the next-to-the-last syllable. To construct a model for *geresh* words that have a pick-up (i.e., that comprise more than two syllables), we supply the prefix "v^{e}-."

Two Words in the (Single) *Geresh* Segment

If the preceding word is closely connected in meaning to the *geresh* word, it is usually marked with a conjunctive *ta'am*. Most often the conjunctive of *geresh* is *kadmah.*

Kadmah geresh קַדְמָ֨ה גֵּ֜רֶשׁ **(CD track 51)**

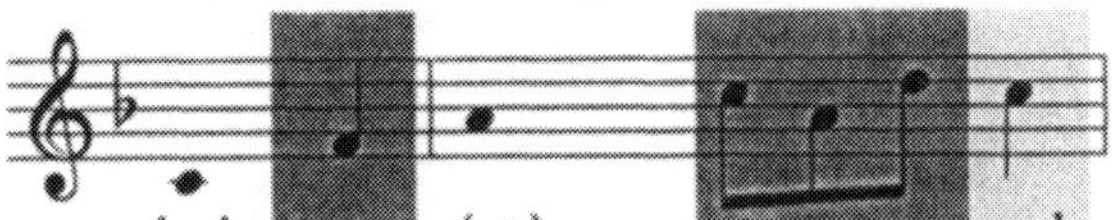

kad - MA (v^{e}-) GE - resh קַדְמָ֨ה גֵּ֜רֶשׁ

v^{e} - SHÓR va - 'A - yil (Lev. 9:4) וְשׁ֨וֹר וָאַ֜יִל

vay - yim - SHAḤ 'et-ham-miz - BÉ - aḥ (Lev. 8:11) וַיִּמְשַׁ֨ח אֶת־הַמִּזְבֵּ֜חַ

ba - NE-kha uv - nó - TE - kha (Deut. 28:32) בָּנֶ֨יךָ וּבְנֹתֶ֜יךָ

Elision will take place if the *geresh* word is accented on the first syllable.

hay - YÓM LÓ (Deut. 29:12) הַיּ֨וֹם ׀ ל֜וֹ

vay - YÓ - mer LÓ (Gen. 20:9) וַיֹּ֨אמֶר ל֜וֹ

Kadmah-geresh on one word:

v^{e} - na - g^{e} - FU (Exod. 21:22) וְנָ֨גְפ֜וּ

Since, strictly speaking, only words accented on the next-to-the-last syllable can be marked with *geresh*, some books refer to this combination as *kadmah azla* when the second word is accented on the last syllable. In this book, we do not use the term *azla.*

קַדְמָ֨ה גֵּ֜רֶשׁ (קַדְמָ֨ה אַזְלָ֜א)

na - SÍ 'e - ḤAD (Num. 7:11) נָשִׂ֨יא אֶחָ֜ד

If the conjunctive word is accented on the first syllable, it will be marked with *munaḥ* instead of *kadmah.* The *munaḥ-geresh* sequence is found only eight times in the Torah.

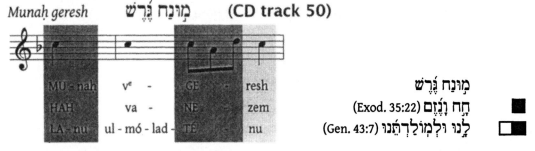

Munaḥ geresh מ֣וּנַח גֵּ֜רֶשׁ **(CD track 50)**

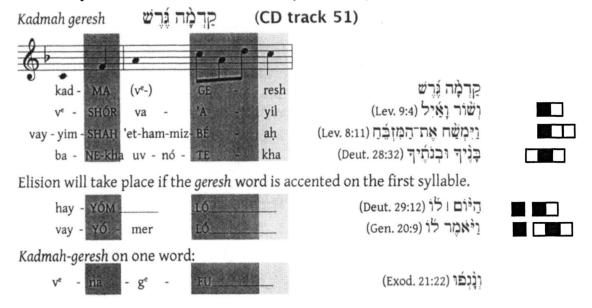

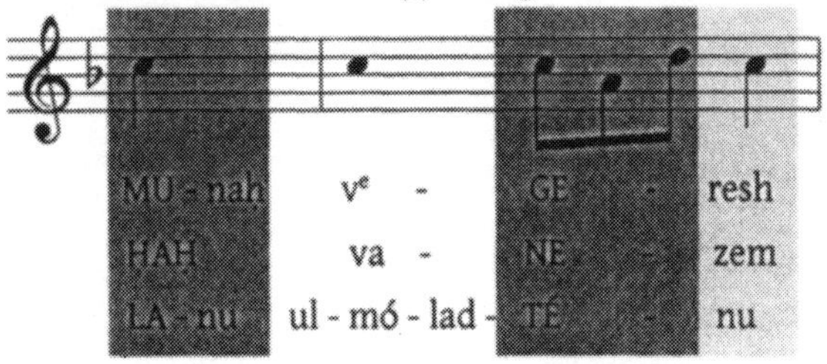

MU - naḥ v^{e} - GE - resh מ֣וּנַח גֵּ֜רֶשׁ

ḤAḤ va - NE - zem (Exod. 35:22) חָ֣ח וָנֶ֜זֶם

LA - nu ul - mó - lad - TÉ - nu (Gen. 43:7) לָ֣נוּ וּלְמוֹלַדְתֵּ֜נוּ

Three Words in the (Single) *Geresh* Segment

Sometimes *geresh* is preceded by two or more conjunctives. The second conjunctive before *geresh* (preceding *kadmah*) is *telishah.* Remember: *Telishah* is always followed by *kadmah.*

Telishah kadmah geresh תְּלִישָׁה קַדְמָה גֶּרֶשׁ (CD track 52)

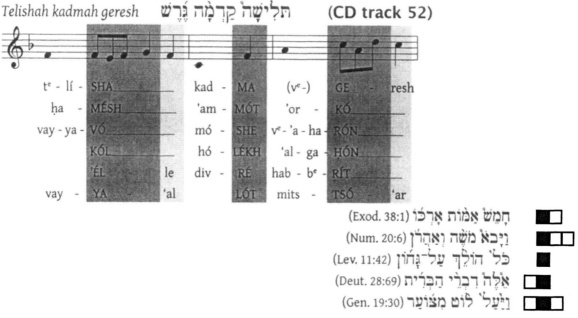

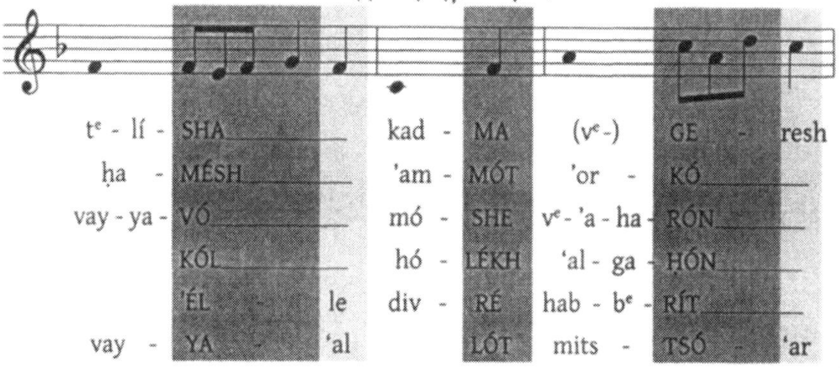
tᵉ - lí - SHA kad - MA (vᵉ-) GE - resh
ḥa - MÉSH 'am - MÓT 'or - KÓ
vay - ya - VÓ mó - SHE vᵉ - 'a - ha - RÓN
KÓL hó - LÉKH 'al - ga - HÓN
'ÉL - le div - RÉ hab - bᵉ - RÍT
vay - YA - 'al LÓT mits - TSÓ - 'ar

חָמֵשׁ אַמּוֹת אָרְכּוֹ (Exod. 38:1)
וַיָּבֹא מֹשֶׁה וְאַהֲרֹן (Num. 20:6)
כֹּל הוֹלֵךְ עַל־גָּחוֹן (Lev. 11:42)
אֵלֶּה דִבְרֵי הַבְּרִית (Deut. 28:69)
וַיַּעַל לוֹט מִצּוֹעַר (Gen. 19:30)

Telishah kadmah-geresh or *Telishah-kadmah geresh*

When chanting *telishah-kadmah-geresh*, you will determine in each case whether the sense of the text demands greater connection between the first and second words or between the second and third words. The rhythm of your chant will reflect the appropriate pairing.

תְּלִישָׁה קַדְמָה גֶּרֶשׁ	תְּלִישָׁה קַדְמָה גֶּרֶשׁ
וְשֵׁם הַשֵּׁנִי מֵידָד (Num. 11:26)	בְּיוֹם הַכֹּתִי כָל־בְּכוֹר (Num. 3:13)
וּבְאַרְבַּע עֶשְׂרֵה שָׁנָה (Gen. 14:5)	בְּיוֹמוֹ תִתֵּן שְׂכָרוֹ (Deut. 24:15)
וְכָל־מַדְוֵי מִצְרַיִם הָרָעִים (Deut. 7:15)	וּבֶעָשׂוֹר לַחֹדֶשׁ הַשְּׁבִיעִי (Num. 29:7)
וְכִי־יָגוּר אִתְּכֶם גֵּר (Num. 15:14)	אוֹ בְדֶרֶךְ רְחֹקָה (Num. 9:10)
וְשִׂימוּ עֲלֵיהֶן קְטֹרֶת (Num. 16:7)	דֶּרֶךְ שְׁלֹשֶׁת יָמִים Exod. 5:3)
וַיַּעַל אַבְרָם מִמִּצְרַיִם (Gen. 13:1)	וַיַּעַל אַהֲרֹן הַכֹּהֵן (Num. 33:38)

Four Words in the (Single) *Geresh* Segment

Sometimes *geresh* is preceded by three conjunctives. The third conjunctive before *geresh* (immediately before *telishah ketanah*) is *munaḥ*.

Munaḥ telishah kadmah geresh   מוּנַ֣ח תְּלִישָׁ֩ה קַדְמָ֨ה גֵּ֜רֵשׁ   **(CD track 53)**

mu-	NAH	tᵉ - lí-	SHA	kad-	MA	(vᵉ-)	GE-	resh
'a-	SHER	ka-	NA	'av-ra-	HAM	'et-has-sa-	DE	
vay - yi-	KAḤ	'av -	RAM	'et-sa-	RAY	'ish -	TÓ	
	KÍ		VA		SUS	par -	TÓ	
'Ó-rekh	he - ḥa-	TSÉR		mé -	A	va - 'am-	MA	
vay - YO-mer	yᵉ - hu-	DA		lᵉ-ta-	MAR	kal - la -	TÓ	

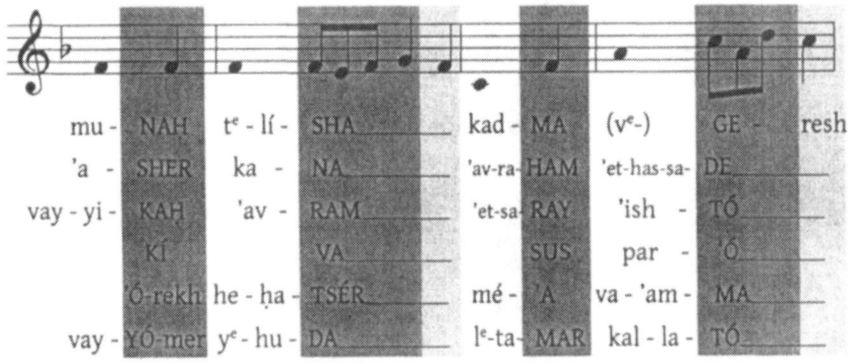

אֲשֶׁר֩ קָנָ֨ה אַבְרָהָ֜ם אֶת־הַשָּׂדֶ֗ה (Gen. 50:13)

וַיִּקַּ֨ח אַבְרָ֜ם אֶת־שָׂרַ֣י אִשְׁתּ֗וֹ (Gen. 12:5)

כִּ֣י בָא֩ ס֨וּס פַּרְעֹ֜ה (Exod 15:19)

אֹ֣רֶךְ הֶחָצֵר֩ מֵאָ֨ה בָֽאַמָּ֜ה (Exod. 27:18)

וַיֹּ֨אמֶר יְהוּדָ֜ה לְתָמָ֣ר כַּלָּת֗וֹ (Gen. 38:11)

Chant these verses.

וַיָּ֨קָם פַּרְעֹ֜ה לַ֗יְלָה ה֤וּא וְכָל־עֲבָדָיו֙ וְכָל־מִצְרַ֔יִם וַתְּהִ֛י צְעָקָ֥ה גְדֹלָ֖ה בְּמִצְרָ֑יִם
כִּֽי־אֵ֣ין בַּ֔יִת אֲשֶׁ֥ר אֵֽין־שָׁ֖ם מֵֽת׃ (Exod. 12:30)

אִם־הִמָּצֵא֩ תִמָּצֵ֨א בְיָד֜וֹ הַגְּנֵבָ֗ה מִשּׁ֧וֹר עַד־חֲמ֛וֹר עַד־שֶׂ֖ה חַיִּ֑ים שְׁנַ֖יִם יְשַׁלֵּֽם׃ (Exod. 22:3)

וַיִּקַּ֣ח אַבְרָ֣ם אֶת־שָׂרַ֣י אִשְׁתּ֗וֹ וְאֶת־ל֣וֹט בֶּן־אָחִ֔יו וְאֶת־כָּל־רְכוּשָׁם֙ אֲשֶׁ֣ר רָכָ֔שׁוּ
וְאֶת־הַנֶּ֖פֶשׁ אֲשֶׁר־עָשׂ֣וּ בְחָרָ֑ן וַיֵּצְא֗וּ לָלֶ֙כֶת֙ אַ֣רְצָה כְּנַ֔עַן וַיָּבֹ֖אוּ אַ֥רְצָה כְּנָֽעַן׃ (Gen. 12:5)

Gereshayim

The double *geresh* is called *gereshayim*. *Gereshayim* is placed above the first letter of the stressed syllable (גֵּרְשַׁ֞יִם) Words that bear this accent are stressed on the last syllable.

Gereshayim   גֵּרְשַׁ֞יִם   **(CD track 54)**

gé - rᵉ - sha -	YIM	
	'el -	PE
vay - yik -	HU
	HÉM

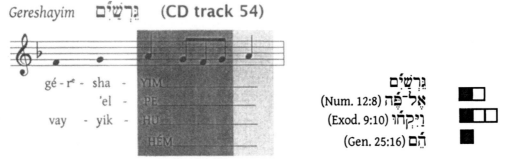

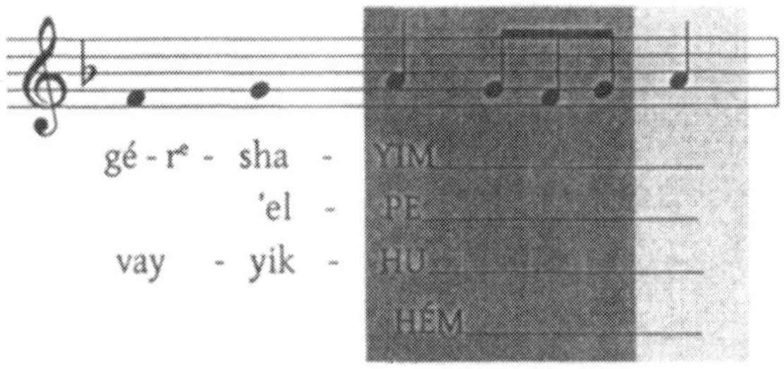

גֵּרְשַׁ֞יִם

אֶל־פֶּ֞ה (Num. 12:8)

וַיִּקְח֞וּ (Exod. 9:10)

הֵ֞ם (Gen. 25:16)

Note: This accent has a double pick-up. If the word has one pick-up syllable, sing that syllable on G. If the word has two pick-up syllables, sing the first pick-up on F and the second on G. If the word has three pick-up syllables, sing the first two pick-ups on F and the third on G.

Two Words in the *Gereshayim* Segment

The conjunctive of *gereshayim* is *munaḥ*. The word bearing the *gereshayim* is always accented on the last syllable, and the word bearing the *munaḥ* is always accented on the first syllable.

Munaḥ gereshayim מ֣וּנַח גֵּרְשַׁ֞יִם **(CD track 55)**

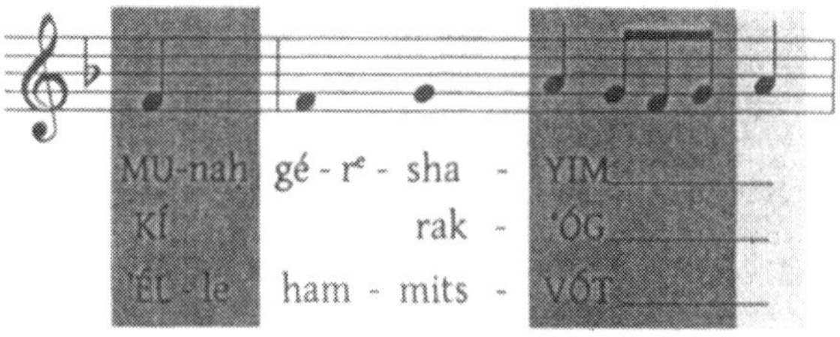

מ֣וּנַח גֵּרְשַׁ֞יִם
כִּ֣י רַק־ע֞וֹג (Deut. 3:11)
אֵ֣לֶּה הַמִּצְוֺ֞ת (Num. 36:13)

Note: *Legarmeh* is found (almost) exclusively before *revia*, but *geresh* (or *gereshayim*) can subdivide any of the following segments: *revia, pashta, tevir,* or *zarka.*

Chant these phrases. Connect each conjunctive to the word that follows. Create an appropriate elongation or pause after *revia, pashta, tevir,* or *zarka.* Create only a slight elongation or pause after *geresh* or *gereshayim.*

קַדְמָ֨ה גֵּ֜רֶשׁ רְבִ֗יעַ	אִם־תַּעֲשֵׂ֨ה עִמָּ֜נוּ רָעָ֗ה (Gen. 26:29)
קַדְמָ֨ה גֵּ֜רֶשׁ מוּנַ֣ח רְבִ֗יעַ	וְצִפִּ֨יתָ אֹת֜וֹ זָהָ֣ב טָה֗וֹר (Exod. 30:3)
גֵּ֜רֶשׁ מוּנַ֣ח רְבִ֗יעַ	וְהַנֶּ֜פֶשׁ אֲשֶׁר־תֹּאכַ֣ל בָּשָׂ֗ר (Lev. 7:20)
מ֣וּנַח גֵּ֜רֶשׁ מוּנַ֣ח רְבִ֗יעַ	אֵ֣ת כְּדָרְלָעֹ֜מֶר מֶ֣לֶךְ עֵילָ֗ם (Gen. 14:9)
קַדְמָ֨ה גֵּ֜רֶשׁ לְגַרְמֵ֣הּ ׀ מוּנַ֣ח רְבִ֗יעַ	וַיִּֽירְשׁ֨וּ אֶת־אַרְצ֜וֹ וְאֶת־אֶ֣רֶץ ׀ ע֣וֹג מֶֽלֶךְ־הַבָּשָׁ֗ן (Deut. 4:47)
קַדְמָ֨ה גֵּ֜רֶשׁ דַּרְגָּ֧א מוּנַ֣ח רְבִ֗יעַ	הָאֲנָשִׁ֨ים הָאֵ֜לֶּה שְֽׁלֵמִ֧ים הֵ֣ם אִתָּ֗נוּ (Gen. 34:21)
גֵּרְשַׁ֞יִם מוּנַ֣ח רְבִ֗יעַ	וְהָי֞וּ הַדְּבָרִ֣ים הָאֵ֗לֶּה (Deut. 6:6)
גֵּרְשַׁ֞יִם רְבִ֗יעַ	אֶת־בַּת־בְּנָ֞הּ וְאֶת־בַּת־בִּתָּ֗הּ (Lev. 18:17)
גֵּרְשַׁ֞יִם דַּרְגָּ֧א מוּנַ֣ח רְבִ֗יעַ	וְהִנֵּ֞ה שֶׁ֧בַע פָּר֣וֹת אֲחֵר֗וֹת (Gen. 41:3)
גֵּרְשַׁ֞יִם לְגַרְמֵ֣הּ ׀ מוּנַ֣ח רְבִ֗יעַ	וַיִּשָּׂ֞א אֶת־רֹ֣אשׁ ׀ שַׂ֣ר הַמַּשְׁקִ֗ים (Gen. 40:20)
מ֣וּנַח גֵּרְשַׁ֞יִם רְבִ֗יעַ	לֵ֣ךְ אֶל־פַּרְעֹ֞ה בַּבֹּ֗קֶר (Exod. 7:15)
מ֣וּנַח גֵּרְשַׁ֞יִם מוּנַ֣ח רְבִ֗יעַ	זֹ֣את בְּרִיתִ֞י אֲשֶׁ֣ר תִּשְׁמְר֗וּ (Gen. 17:10)
תְּ֠לִישָׁה קַדְמָ֨ה גֵּ֜רֶשׁ מוּנַ֣ח רְבִ֗יעַ	וַיַּ֩עַל֩ ל֨וֹט מִצּ֜וֹעַר וַיֵּ֣שֶׁב בָּהָ֗ר (Gen. 19:30)
גֵּ֜רֶשׁ מַהְפַּ֤ךְ פַּשְׁטָא֙	וְעָשִׂ֜יתָ לְאַהֲרֹ֤ן וּלְבָנָיו֙ כָּ֔כָה (Exod. 29:35)
קַדְמָ֨ה גֵּ֜רֶשׁ מֵרְכָ֥א פַּשְׁטָא֙	אֲשֶׁ֨ר אַתֶּ֜ם עֹבְרִ֥ים שָׁ֙מָּה֙ לְרִשְׁתָּ֔הּ (Deut. 11:11)
קַדְמָ֨ה גֵּ֜רֶשׁ מַהְפַּ֤ךְ פַּשְׁטָא֙	וַיִּפְתַּ֨ח יוֹסֵ֜ף אֶֽת־כָּל־אֲשֶׁ֤ר בָּהֶם֙ וַיִּשְׁבֹּ֣ר לְמִצְרַ֔יִם (Gen. 41:56)
קַדְמָ֨ה גֵּ֜רֶשׁ קַדְמָ֨ה מַהְפַּ֤ךְ פַּשְׁטָא֙	וַיֵּצֵ֨א הָאֱמֹרִ֜י הַיֹּשֵׁ֨ב בָּהָ֤ר הַהוּא֙ לִקְרַאתְכֶ֔ם (Deut. 1:44)
קַדְמָ֨ה גֵּ֜רֶשׁ קַדְמָ֨ה מֵרְכָ֥א פַּשְׁטָא֙	מֵאֵ֨ין יְבָמִ֜י לְהָקִ֨ים לְאָחִ֥יו שֵׁם֙ בְּיִשְׂרָאֵ֔ל (Deut. 25:7)
קַדְמָ֨ה גֵּ֜רֶשׁ פַּשְׁטָא֙	וְהִקְטִ֨יר הַכֹּהֵ֜ן אֶת־אַזְכָּרָתָהּ֙ הַמִּזְבֵּ֔חָה (Lev. 2:2)
תְּ֠לִישָׁה קַדְמָ֨ה גֵּ֜רֶשׁ מַהְפַּ֤ךְ פַּשְׁטָא֙	חָמֵ֩שׁ אַמּ֨וֹת אָרְכּ֜וֹ וְחָמֵֽשׁ־אַמּ֤וֹת רָחְבּוֹ֙ רָב֔וּעַ (Exod. 38:1)
גֵּרְשַׁ֞יִם מֵרְכָ֥א פַּשְׁטָא֙	וַיֶּאֱסֹ֞ף שִׁבְעִ֥ים אִישׁ֙ מִזִּקְנֵ֣י הָעָ֔ם (Num. 11:24)
גֵּרְשַׁ֞יִם מַהְפַּ֤ךְ פַּשְׁטָא֙	לֹֽא־יָמִ֞ישׁ עַמּ֤וּד הֶֽעָנָן֙ יוֹמָ֔ם (Exod. 13:22)

גֵּרְשַׁיִם קַדְמָה מַהְפַּךְ פַּשְׁטָא	וְעַל־דְּבַר כָּזְבִּי בַת־נְשִׂיא מִדְיָן אֲחֹתָם (Num. 25:18)
מוּנַח גֵּרְשַׁיִם מַהְפַּךְ פַּשְׁטָא	אֵלֶּה הֵם בְּנֵי יִשְׁמָעֵאל וְאֵלֶּה שְׁמֹתָם (Gen. 25:16)
גֵּרְשַׁיִם תְּבִיר	אַלּוּפֵי אָהֳלִיבָמָה בַּת־עֲנָה אֵשֶׁת עֵשָׂו׃ (Gen. 36:18)
גֵּרְשַׁיִם מֵרְכָא תְּבִיר	תִּקְרָא אֶת־הַתּוֹרָה הַזֹּאת נֶגֶד כָּל־יִשְׂרָאֵל בְּאָזְנֵיהֶם׃ (Deut. 31:11)
גֵּרְשַׁיִם דַּרְגָּא תְּבִיר	הוּא יִתְחַטָּא־בוֹ בַּיּוֹם הַשְּׁלִישִׁי וּבַיּוֹם הַשְּׁבִיעִי יִטְהָר (Num. 19:12)
קַדְמָה גֵּרֵשׁ דַּרְגָּא תְּבִיר	וַיִּקְרָא אַבְרָהָם אֶת־שֶׁם־בְּנוֹ הַנּוֹלַד־לוֹ אֲשֶׁר־יָלְדָה־לּוֹ שָׂרָה יִצְחָק׃ (Gen. 21:3)
קַדְמָה גֵּרֵשׁ מֵרְכָא תְּבִיר	בְּכֶסֶף מָלֵא יִתְּנֶנָּה לִּי בְּתוֹכְכֶם לַאֲחֻזַּת־קָבֶר׃ (Gen. 23:9)
קַדְמָה גֵּרֵשׁ קַדְמָה מֵרְכָא תְּבִיר	וַיַּעֲנוּ בְנֵי־יַעֲקֹב אֶת־שְׁכֶם וְאֶת־חֲמוֹר אָבִיו בְּמִרְמָה וַיְדַבֵּרוּ (Gen. 34:13)
קַדְמָה גֵּרֵשׁ קַדְמָה דַּרְגָּא תְּבִיר	וַיֵּצְאוּ מֹשֶׁה וְאֶלְעָזָר הַכֹּהֵן וְכָל־נְשִׂיאֵי הָעֵדָה לִקְרָאתָם (Num. 31:13)
גֵּרְשַׁיִם קַדְמָה דַּרְגָּא תְּבִיר	לֹא תֹאסִפוּן לָתֵת תֶּבֶן לָעָם לִלְבֹּן הַלְּבֵנִים כִּתְמוֹל שִׁלְשֹׁם (Exod. 5:7)
גֵּרְשַׁיִם קַדְמָה מֵרְכָא תְּבִיר	וַיָּבֹא יִתְרוֹ חֹתֵן מֹשֶׁה וּבָנָיו וְאִשְׁתּוֹ אֶל־מֹשֶׁה (Exod. 18:5)
גֵּרְשַׁיִם מוּנַח דַּרְגָּא תְּבִיר	וַיִּסַּע דֶּגֶל מַחֲנֵה בְנֵי־יְהוּדָה בָּרִאשֹׁנָה לְצִבְאֹתָם (Num. 10:14)
קַדְמָה גֵּרֵשׁ מוּנַח דַּרְגָּא תְּבִיר	וְשָׁחַט אֹתוֹ עַל יֶרֶךְ הַמִּזְבֵּחַ צָפֹנָה לִפְנֵי יְהוָה (Lev. 1:11)
קַדְמָה גֵּרֵשׁ מוּנַח מֵרְכָא תְּבִיר	וְיִקְחוּ אֵלֶיךָ שֶׁמֶן זַיִת זָךְ כָּתִית לַמָּאוֹר (Exod. 27:20)
קַדְמָה גֵּרֵשׁ תְּבִיר	וַיִּכְתֹּב מֹשֶׁה אֶת־מוֹצָאֵיהֶם לְמַסְעֵיהֶם עַל־פִּי יְהוָה (Num. 33:2)
תְּלִישָׁה קַדְמָה גֵּרֵשׁ דַּרְגָּא תְּבִיר	וְכִפֶּר עָלָיו הַכֹּהֵן עַל־חַטָּאתוֹ אֲשֶׁר־חָטָא מֵאַחַת מֵאֵלֶּה וְנִסְלַח לוֹ (Lev. 5:13)
גֵּרֵשׁ דַּרְגָּא תְּבִיר	וַיַּקְהִלוּ מֹשֶׁה וְאַהֲרֹן אֶת־הַקָּהָל אֶל־פְּנֵי הַסָּלַע (Num. 20:10)
גֵּרֵשׁ מֵרְכָא תְּבִיר	הַנֹּגֵעַ בָּאִישׁ הַזֶּה וּבְאִשְׁתּוֹ מוֹת יוּמָת׃ (Gen. 26:11)

קַדְמָה גֵּרֵשׁ מוּנַח זַרְקָא מוּנַח סֶגוֹל	וַיֹּאמֶר אֵלָיו לְעֵינֵי כָל־יִשְׂרָאֵל חֲזַק וֶאֱמָץ (Deut 31:7)
גֵּרֵשׁ מוּנַח זַרְקָא מוּנַח סֶגוֹל	וְאֶל־פֶּתַח אֹהֶל מוֹעֵד לֹא הֱבִיאוֹ (Lev. 17:4)
קַדְמָה גֵּרֵשׁ זַרְקָא מוּנַח סֶגוֹל	וַיְדַבֵּר אֶל־קֹרַח וְאֶל־כָּל־עֲדָתוֹ לֵאמֹר (Num. 16:5)
גֵּרְשַׁיִם מוּנַח זַרְקָא מוּנַח סֶגוֹל	וַיְכַס אֶת־עֵין כָּל־הָאָרֶץ וַתֶּחְשַׁךְ הָאָרֶץ (Exod. 10:15)
גֵּרְשַׁיִם מוּנַח זַרְקָא סֶגוֹל	זֶה־לִּי עֶשְׂרִים שָׁנָה בְּבֵיתֶךָ (Gen. 31:41)
תְּלִישָׁה קַדְמָה גֵּרֵשׁ מוּנַח זַרְקָא סֶגוֹל	וְרָאָה הַכֹּהֵן אֹתוֹ בַּיּוֹם הַשְּׁבִיעִי שֵׁנִית (Lev. 13:6)
גֵּרְשַׁיִם קַדְמָה מֵרְכָא זַרְקָא מוּנַח סֶגוֹל	וְלָקַחְתָּ מִן־הַדָּם אֲשֶׁר עַל־הַמִּזְבֵּחַ וּמִשֶּׁמֶן הַמִּשְׁחָה (Exod. 29:21)

Chant these verses.

הוּא יִתְחַטָּא־בוֹ בַּיּוֹם הַשְּׁלִישִׁי וּבַיּוֹם הַשְּׁבִיעִי יִטְהָר
וְאִם־לֹא יִתְחַטָּא בַּיּוֹם הַשְּׁלִישִׁי וּבַיּוֹם הַשְּׁבִיעִי לֹא יִטְהָר׃ (Num. 19:12)

וַיִּגְוַע כָּל־בָּשָׂר ׀ הָרֹמֵשׂ עַל־הָאָרֶץ בָּעוֹף וּבַבְּהֵמָה וּבַחַיָּה
וּבְכָל־הַשֶּׁרֶץ הַשֹּׁרֵץ עַל־הָאָרֶץ וְכֹל הָאָדָם׃ (Gen. 7:21)

וְזָכַרְתָּ אֶת־כָּל־הַדֶּרֶךְ אֲשֶׁר הֹלִיכֲךָ יְהוָה אֱלֹהֶיךָ זֶה אַרְבָּעִים שָׁנָה בַּמִּדְבָּר
לְמַעַן עַנֹּתְךָ לְנַסֹּתְךָ לָדַעַת אֶת־אֲשֶׁר בִּלְבָבְךָ הֲתִשְׁמֹר מִצְוֺתָיו אִם־לֹא׃ (Deut. 8:2)

שִׁבְעַת יָמִים שְׂאֹר לֹא יִמָּצֵא בְּבָתֵּיכֶם כִּי ׀ כָּל־אֹכֵל מַחְמֶצֶת
וְנִכְרְתָה הַנֶּפֶשׁ הַהִוא מֵעֲדַת יִשְׂרָאֵל בַּגֵּר וּבְאֶזְרַח הָאָרֶץ׃ (Exod. 12:19)

אִם־הִמָּצֵא תִמָּצֵא בְיָדוֹ הַגְּנֵבָה מִשּׁוֹר עַד־חֲמוֹר עַד־שֶׂה חַיִּים שְׁנַיִם יְשַׁלֵּם׃ (Exod. 22:3)

וַיִּקַּח אַבְרָם אֶת־שָׂרַי אִשְׁתּוֹ וְאֶת־לוֹט בֶּן־אָחִיו וְאֶת־כָּל־רְכוּשָׁם אֲשֶׁר רָכָשׁוּ
וְאֶת־הַנֶּפֶשׁ אֲשֶׁר־עָשׂוּ בְחָרָן וַיֵּצְאוּ לָלֶכֶת אַרְצָה כְּנַעַן וַיָּבֹאוּ אַרְצָה כְּנָעַן׃ (Gen. 12:5)

Telishah Gedolah

Telishah gedolah (תְּלִישָׁה֠) is a minor disjunctive that may be used to subdivide any of the following segments: *revia, pashta, tevir,* or *zarka*. Sometimes it subdivides a *geresh* segment. And sometimes it appears in place of *telishah ketanah*. The symbol for *telishah gedolah* is a mirror image of *telishah ketanah* and is placed on the extreme right edge of the word (אֵ֠לֶּה). If the stress is not on the first syllable, a second *telishah gedolah* may be placed over the first letter of the stressed syllable (אֲ֠שֶׁ֠ר).

Telishah תְּלִישָׁה֠ **(CD track 56)**

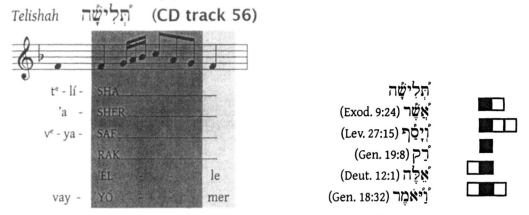

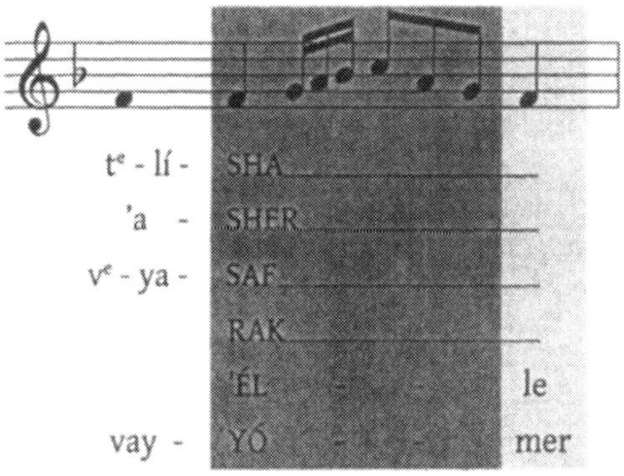

תְּלִישָׁה֠
אֲ֠שֶׁ֠ר (Exod. 9:24)
וְ֠יָסַ֠ף (Lev. 27:15)
רַ֠ק (Gen. 19:8)
אֵ֠לֶּה (Deut. 12:1)
וַ֠יֹּ֠אמֶר (Gen. 18:32)

There are two instances in the Torah where *gereshayim* and *telishah gedolah* appear on the same word. Chant both *te'amim* on the stressed syllable: first the *gereshayim*, then the *telishah*.
(Gen. 5:29) זֶ֠֞ה   (Lev. 10:4) קִ֠רְב֞וּ

Two Words in a *Telishah Gedolah* Segment

The conjunctive of *telishah gedolah* is *munaḥ.*

Munaḥ telishah מוּנַ֣ח תְּלִישָׁ֠ה (CD track 57)

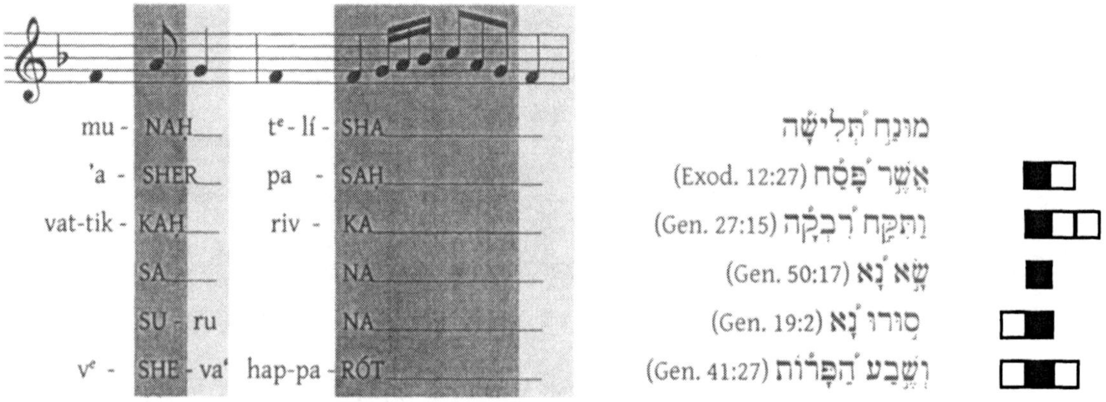

Three or More Words in a *Telishah Gedolah* Segment

The conjunctive *munaḥ* may be repeated before *telishah gedolah.*

(Deut. 29:6) וַיֵּצֵ֣א סִיחֹ֣ן מֶֽלֶךְ־֠חֶשְׁבּוֹן

(Lev. 13:3) וְרָאָ֣ה הַכֹּהֵ֣ן אֶת־הַנֶּ֣גַע בְּעוֹר־֠הַבָּשָׂר

Pazer

Pazer (פָּזֵ֡ר) is another minor disjunctive that may be used to subdivide any of the following segments: *revia, pashta, tevir,* or *zarka.* Sometimes it subdivides a *geresh* segment. Often a *pazer* segment will be followed by a *geresh* segment. The symbol for *pazer* resembles an upside-down **h**, placed above the first letter of the stressed syllable (הָאִ֡ישׁ).

Pazer פָּזֵ֡ר (CD track 58)

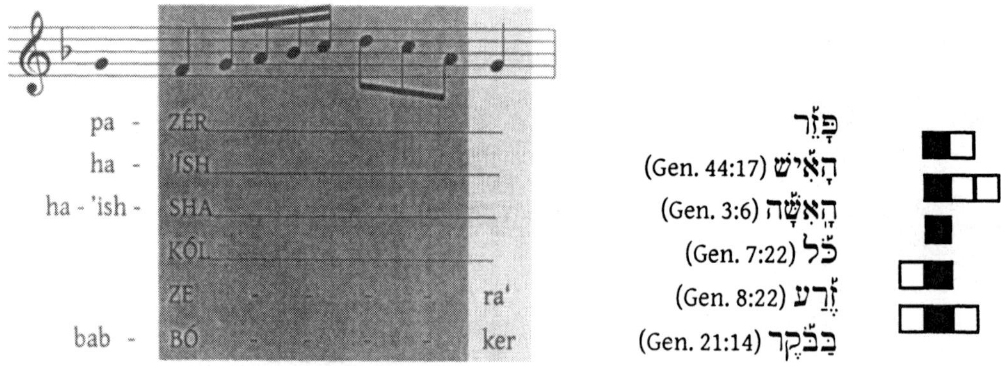

Two Words in a *Pazer* Segment

The conjunctive of *pazer* is *munaḥ.*

Munaḥ pazer מוּנַח פָּזֵר (CD track 59)

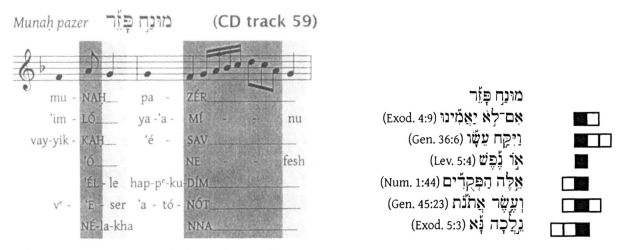

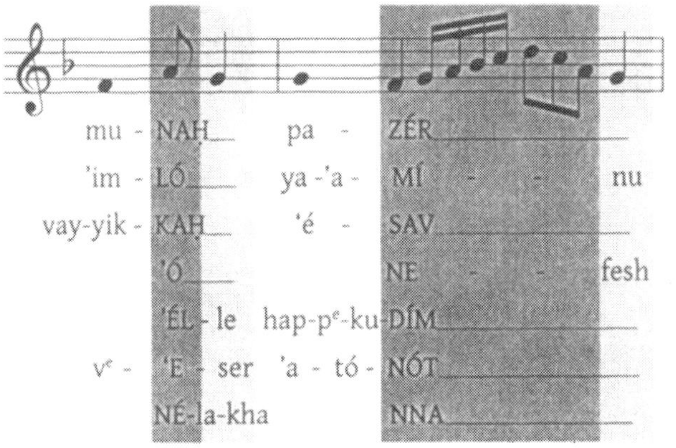

מוּנַח פָּזֵר
אִם־לֹ֣א יַֽאֲמִ֡ינוּ (Exod. 4:9)
וַיִּקַּ֣ח עֵשָׂ֡ו (Gen. 36:6)
א֡וֹ נֶ֣פֶשׁ (Lev. 5:4)
אֵ֣לֶּה הַפְּקֻדִ֡ים (Num. 1:44)
וְעֶ֣שֶׂר אֲתֹנֹ֡ת (Gen. 45:23)
נֵ֣לְכָה נָּ֡א (Exod. 5:3)

Three or More Words in a *Pazer* Segment

The conjunctive *munaḥ* may be repeated before *pazer.*

וַיָּ֣שֶׂם אֹתָ֣הּ יוֹסֵ֡ף (Gen. 47:26)
אִ֣ישׁ אִ֣ישׁ כִּֽי־יִהְיֶֽה־טָמֵ֣א ׀ לָנֶ֡פֶשׁ (Num. 9:10)
וַיָּ֣מָת נָדָ֣ב וַאֲבִיה֣וּא לִפְנֵ֣י יְהוָ֡ה (Num. 3:4)

Chant these verses, which contain *pazer* and/or *telishah-gedolah.*

וּמִצְרַ֡יִם יָלַ֞ד אֶת־לוּדִ֧ים וְאֶת־עֲנָמִ֛ים וְאֶת־לְהָבִ֖ים וְאֶת־נַפְתֻּחִֽים׃ (Gen. 10:13)

וַתִּקַּ֣ח רִ֠בְקָה אֶת־בִּגְדֵ֨י עֵשָׂ֜ו בְּנָ֤הּ הַגָּדֹל֙ הַחֲמֻדֹ֔ת אֲשֶׁ֥ר אִתָּ֖הּ בַּבָּ֑יִת
וַתַּלְבֵּ֥שׁ אֶֽת־יַעֲקֹ֖ב בְּנָ֥הּ הַקָּטָֽן׃ (Gen. 27:15)

וּמִכָּל־הָ֠חַי מִֽכָּל־בָּשָׂ֞ר שְׁנַ֧יִם מִכֹּ֛ל תָּבִ֥יא אֶל־הַתֵּבָ֖ה לְהַחֲיֹ֣ת אִתָּ֑ךְ
זָכָ֥ר וּנְקֵבָ֖ה יִהְיֽוּ׃ (Gen. 6:19)

וַתֵּ֣רֶא הָֽאִשָּׁ֡ה כִּ֣י טוֹב֩ הָעֵ֨ץ לְמַאֲכָ֜ל וְכִ֧י תַֽאֲוָה־ה֣וּא לָעֵינַ֗יִם
וְנֶחְמָ֤ד הָעֵץ֙ לְהַשְׂכִּ֔יל וַתִּקַּ֥ח מִפִּרְי֖וֹ וַתֹּאכַ֑ל וַתִּתֵּ֧ן גַּם־לְאִישָׁ֛הּ עִמָּ֖הּ וַיֹּאכַֽל׃ (Gen. 3:6)

מִכֹּ֣ל ׀ הַבְּהֵמָ֣ה הַטְּהוֹרָ֗ה תִּֽקַּח־לְךָ֛ שִׁבְעָ֥ה שִׁבְעָ֖ה אִ֣ישׁ וְאִשְׁתּ֑וֹ
וּמִן־הַבְּהֵמָ֡ה אֲ֠שֶׁר לֹ֣א טְהֹרָ֥ה הִ֛וא שְׁנַ֖יִם אִ֥ישׁ וְאִשְׁתּֽוֹ׃ (Gen. 7:2)

וְזֶ֨ה הַדָּבָ֜ר אֲשֶׁר־תַּעֲשֶׂ֥ה לָהֶ֛ם לְקַדֵּ֥שׁ אֹתָ֖ם לְכַהֵ֣ן לִ֑י
לְ֠קַח פַּ֣ר אֶחָ֧ד בֶּן־בָּקָ֛ר וְאֵילִ֥ם שְׁנַ֖יִם תְּמִימִֽם׃ (Exod. 29:1)

וַ֠יַּקְרִבוּ בְּנֵ֨י אַהֲרֹ֣ן אֶת־הַדָּם֮ אֵלָיו֒ וַיִּטְבֹּ֤ל אֶצְבָּעוֹ֙ בַּדָּ֔ם וַיִּתֵּ֖ן עַל־קַרְנ֣וֹת הַמִּזְבֵּ֑חַ
וְאֶת־הַדָּ֣ם יָצַ֔ק אֶל־יְס֖וֹד הַמִּזְבֵּֽחַ׃ (Lev. 9:9)

וַיֹּאמְר֡וּ שָׁא֣וֹל שָֽׁאַל־הָ֠אִישׁ לָ֣נוּ וּלְמֽוֹלַדְתֵּ֜נוּ לֵאמֹ֗ר הַע֨וֹד אֲבִיכֶ֥ם חַי֙ הֲיֵ֣שׁ לָכֶ֣ם אָ֔ח
וַנַּ֨גֶּד־ל֔וֹ עַל־פִּ֖י הַדְּבָרִ֣ים הָאֵ֑לֶּה הֲיָד֣וֹעַ נֵדַ֔ע כִּ֣י יֹאמַ֔ר הוֹרִ֖ידוּ אֶת־אֲחִיכֶֽם׃ (Gen. 43:7)

Pazer-Gadol

Pazer-gadol (פָּזֵר־גָּדוֹל) is another minor disjunctive, used once in the Torah in place of the regular *pazer*. The symbol for *pazer gadol* comprises *telishah gedolah* and *telishah ketanah* symbols, linked together, placed above the first letter of the stressed syllable (בָּאַמָּה). Its melody also comprises *telishah gedolah* and *telishah ketanah*.

Pazer gadol is preceded by its unique disjunctive, *galgal*. The symbol for *galgal* resembles an upside-down *etnaḥta*, placed under the first letter of the stressed syllable. *Galgal* is preceded by *munaḥ*. *Pazer gadol* is also known as *karney-farah*, and *galgal* is also known as *yeraḥ-ben-yomo*.

Munaḥ galgal pazer-gadol מוּנַח גַּלְגַּל פָּזֵר־גָּדוֹל **(CD track 60)**

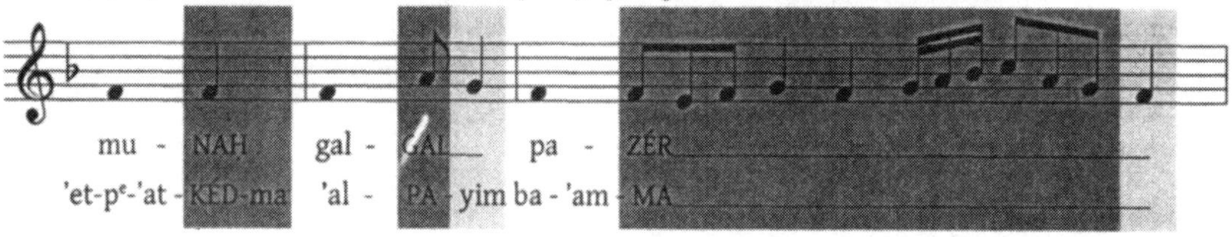

וּמַדֹּתֶם מִחוּץ לָעִיר אֶת־פְּאַת־קֵדְמָה אַלְפַּיִם בָּאַמָּה וְאֶת־פְּאַת־נֶגֶב
אַלְפַּיִם בָּאַמָּה וְאֶת־פְּאַת־יָם ׀ אַלְפַּיִם בָּאַמָּה וְאֵת פְּאַת צָפוֹן אַלְפַּיִם בָּאַמָּה
וְהָעִיר בַּתָּוֶךְ זֶה יִהְיֶה לָהֶם מִגְרְשֵׁי הֶעָרִים׃ (Num. 35:5)

Final Cadence—End of *Aliyah*

In the last verse of each *aliyah*, a special melody is introduced to signal the end of the reading. This melody is applied beginning with the final *tippeḥa* segment. You will chant this cadence slowly.

Siluk סִילוּק **(CD track 61)**

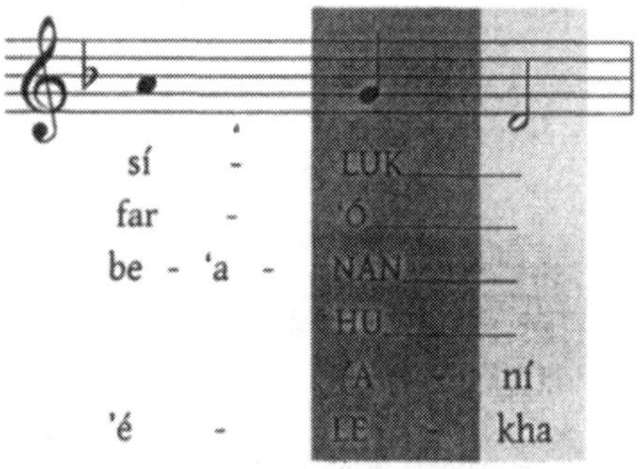

סִילוּק
פַּרְעֹה׃ (Exod. 10:11)
בֶּעָנָן׃ (Exod. 16:10)
הוּא׃ (Exod. 16:36)
אָנִי׃ (Exod. 22:26)
אֵלֶיךָ׃ (Exod. 25:16)

Merekha siluk מֵרְכָא סִילוּק **(CD track 62)**

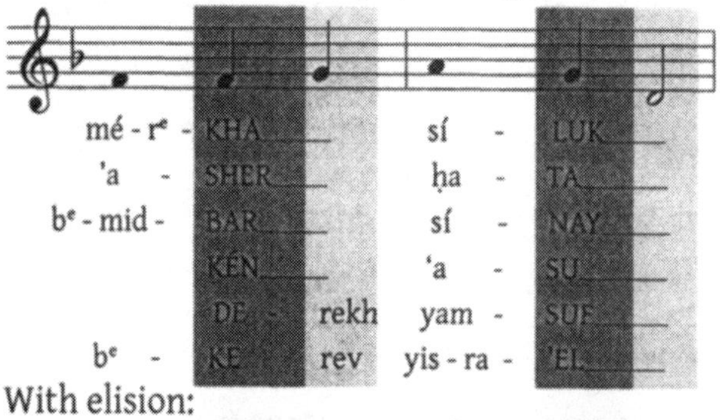

With elision:

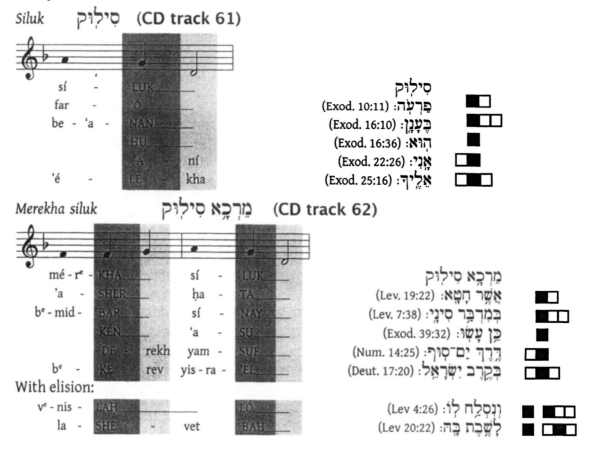

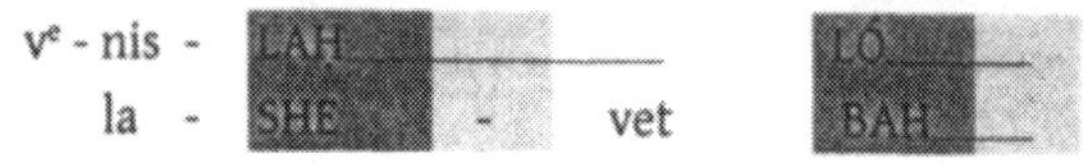

מֵרְכָא סִילוּק
אֲשֶׁר חָטָא׃ (Lev. 19:22)
בְּמִדְבַּר סִינָי׃ (Lev. 7:38)
כֵּן עָשׂוּ׃ (Exod. 39:32)
דֶּרֶךְ יַם־סוּף׃ (Num. 14:25)
בְּקֶרֶב יִשְׂרָאֵל׃ (Deut. 17:20)

וְנִסְלַח לוֹ׃ (Lev 4:26)
לָשֶׁבֶת בָּהּ׃ (Lev 20:22)

Tippeḥa טִפְּחָא (CD track 63)

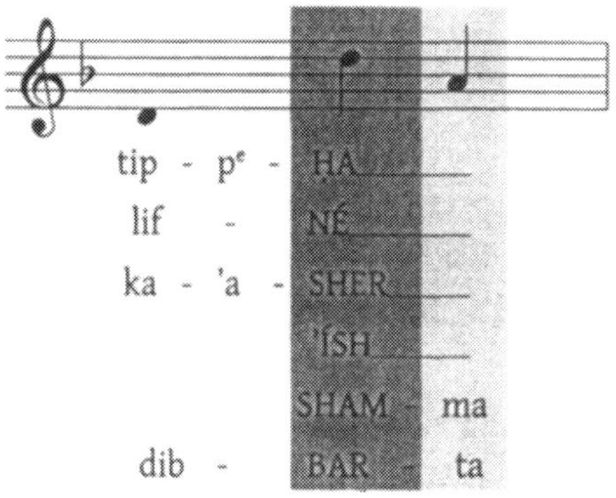

טִפְּחָא
לִפְנֵי (Deut. 24:13)
כַּאֲשֶׁר (Deut. 31:3)
אִישׁ (Lev. 25:13)
שָׁמָּה (Deut. 31:13)
דִּבַּרְתָּ (Deut. 23:24)

Chant these words to the appropriate *te'amim*, using the final cadence.

בְּכֹל אֲשֶׁר תַּעֲשֶׂה: (Deut. 15:18)
וְהַגֵּר אֲשֶׁר בְּקִרְבֶּךָ: (Deut. 26:11)
מִיִּשְׂרָאֵל וְטוֹב לָךְ: (Deut. 19:13)
פֹּה עִמָּנוּ הַיּוֹם: (Deut. 29:14)
רוּחַ יַעֲקֹב אֲבִיהֶם: (Gen. 45:27)
בָּאָרֶץ אַחַר הַמַּבּוּל: (Gen. 10:32)
כָּל־יָמֶיךָ לְעוֹלָם: (Deut. 23:7)

בָּהֶם תְּבוּנָה: (Deut. 32:28)
וּמִשְׁפָּטָיו עִם־יִשְׂרָאֵל: (Deut. 33:21)
אֵת כָּל־אֲשֶׁר תַּעֲשׂוּן: (Deut. 29:8)
תֶּרַח בְּחָרָן: (Gen. 11:32)
אֵלֶיךָ עֲשֵׂה: (Gen. 31:16)
וְאֶת־תַּחַשׁ וְאֶת־מַעֲכָה: (Gen. 22:24)

Merekha tippeḥa מֵרְכָא טִפְּחָא (CD track 64)

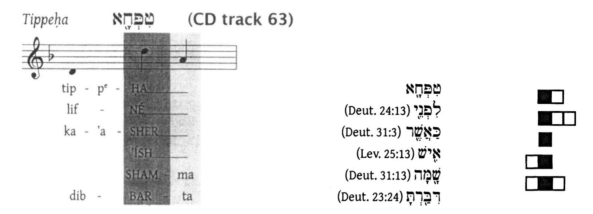

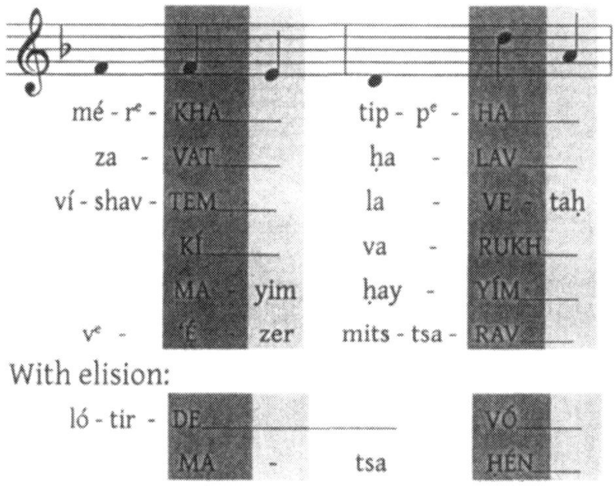

מֵרְכָא טִפְּחָא
זָבַת חָלָב (Deut. 11:9)
וִישַׁבְתֶּם לָבֶטַח (Lev. 26:5)
כִּי בָרוּךְ (Num. 22:12)
מַיִם חַיִּים (Num. 19:17)
וְעֵזֶר מִצָּרָיו (Deut. 33:7)
לֹא־תִרְדֶּה בוֹ (Lev. 25:46)
מָצָא חֵן (Gen. 6:8)

Chant these words to the appropriate *te'amim*, using the final cadence.

נֹתֵן לְךָ נַחֲלָה: (Deut. 24:4)
וּבָרוּךְ אַתָּה בְּצֵאתֶךָ: (Deut. 28:6)
הוּא וּבָנָיו כָּל־הַיָּמִים: (Deut. 18:5)
נֶפֶשׁ חַיָּה הוּא שְׁמוֹ: (Gen. 2:19)
בְּאֶרֶץ פְּלִשְׁתִּים יָמִים רַבִּים: (Gen. 21:34)
כִּי־הִפְרַנִי אֱלֹהִים בְּאֶרֶץ עָנְיִי: (Gen. 41:52)

וְאֵין עִמּוֹ אֵל נֵכָר: (Deut. 32:12)
לְיִצְחָק וּלְיַעֲקֹב לָתֵת לָהֶם: (Deut. 30:20)
רוּחַ אֱלֹהִים בּוֹ: (Gen. 41:38)
וַיַּעַל מִשָּׁם בְּאֵר שָׁבַע: (Gen. 26:23)

Chant these words to the appropriate *te'amim*, using the final cadence. Remember that *tippeḥa* is a stronger disjunctive than *tevir*.

מֵרְכָא טִפְּחָא מֵרְכָא סִילוּק
וְלֹא־תִשְׂא֤וּ עָלָיו֙ חֵ֔טְא בַּהֲרִֽימְכֶ֥ם אֶת־חֶלְבּ֖וֹ מִמֶּ֑נּוּ
וְאֶת־קָדְשֵׁ֧י בְנֵֽי־יִשְׂרָאֵ֛ל לֹ֥א תְחַלְּל֖וּ וְלֹ֥א תָמֽוּתוּ׃ (Num. 18:32)
וְאַתֶּ֧ם תִּהְיוּ־לִ֛י מַמְלֶ֥כֶת כֹּהֲנִ֖ים וְג֣וֹי קָד֑וֹשׁ
אֵ֚לֶּה הַדְּבָרִ֔ים אֲשֶׁ֥ר תְּדַבֵּ֖ר אֶל־בְּנֵ֥י יִשְׂרָאֵֽל׃ (Exod. 19:6)

מֵרְכָא טִפְּחָא סִילוּק
וְאֶת־הַמַּטֶּ֥ה הַזֶּ֖ה תִּקַּ֣ח בְּיָדֶ֑ךָ אֲשֶׁ֥ר תַּעֲשֶׂה־בּ֖וֹ אֶת־הָאֹתֹֽת׃ (Exod. 4:17)
וַיְשַׁלַּ֥ח מֹשֶׁ֖ה אֶת־חֹתְנ֑וֹ וַיֵּ֥לֶךְ ל֖וֹ אֶל־אַרְצֽוֹ׃ (Exod. 18:27)

טִפְּחָא מֵרְכָא סִילוּק
לְהַבְדִּ֕יל בֵּ֥ין הַטָּמֵ֖א וּבֵ֣ין הַטָּהֹ֑ר
וּבֵ֤ין הַֽחַיָּה֙ הַֽנֶּאֱכֶ֔לֶת וּבֵ֣ין הַֽחַיָּ֔ה אֲשֶׁ֖ר לֹ֥א תֵאָכֵֽל׃ (Lev. 11:47)
אֵ֣לֶּה מִשְׁפְּחֹ֧ת בְּנֵי־נֹ֛חַ לְתוֹלְדֹתָ֖ם בְּגוֹיֵהֶ֑ם
וּמֵאֵ֜לֶּה נִפְרְד֧וּ הַגּוֹיִ֛ם בָּאָ֖רֶץ אַחַ֥ר הַמַּבּֽוּל׃ (Gen. 10:32)

טִפְּחָא סִילוּק
וַיִּשְׁמַ֣ע מֹשֶׁ֔ה וַיִּיטַ֖ב בְּעֵינָֽיו׃ (Lev. 10:20)
וְהֶעֱלָ֧ה הַכֹּהֵ֛ן אֶת־הָעֹלָ֥ה וְאֶת־הַמִּנְחָ֖ה הַמִּזְבֵּ֑חָה וְכִפֶּ֥ר עָלָ֛יו הַכֹּהֵ֖ן וְטָהֵֽר׃ (Lev. 14:20)

Ending Each of the Five Books of the Torah

Before you reach the last verse in each book, wait for the congregation to stand. Then chant the final segment to a festive "invitational cadence." This serves as a signal to the congregation to chant חֲזַק חֲזַק וְנִתְחַזֵּק (see below).

Merekha tippeḥa merekha siluk מֵרְכָא טִפְּחָא מֵרְכָא סִילוּק **(CD track 65)**

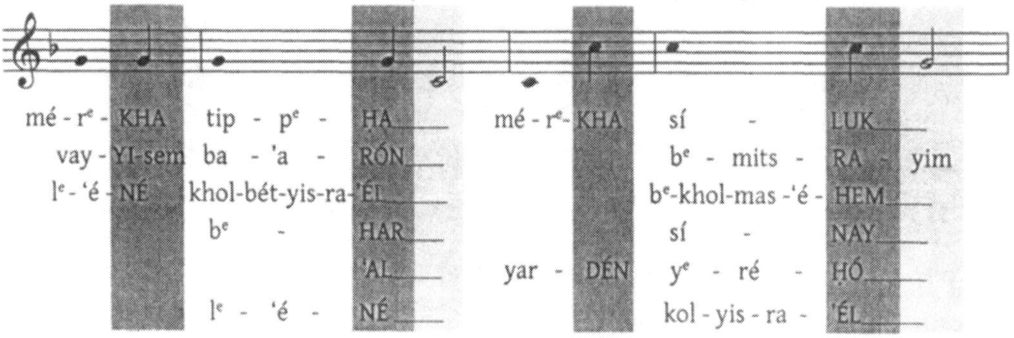

וַיָּ֣מָת יוֹסֵ֔ף בֶּן־מֵאָ֥ה וָעֶ֖שֶׂר שָׁנִ֑ים וַיַּחַנְט֣וּ אֹת֔וֹ וַיִּ֥ישֶׂם בָּאָר֖וֹן בְּמִצְרָֽיִם׃ (Gen. 50:26)
כִּי֩ עֲנַ֨ן יְהוָ֤ה עַֽל־הַמִּשְׁכָּן֙ יוֹמָ֔ם וְאֵ֕שׁ תִּהְיֶ֥ה לַ֖יְלָה בּ֑וֹ
לְעֵינֵ֥י כָל־בֵּֽית־יִשְׂרָאֵ֖ל בְּכָל־מַסְעֵיהֶֽם׃ (Exod. 40:38)
אֵ֣לֶּה הַמִּצְוֹ֗ת אֲשֶׁ֨ר צִוָּ֧ה יְהוָ֛ה אֶת־מֹשֶׁ֖ה אֶל־בְּנֵ֣י יִשְׂרָאֵ֑ל בְּהַ֖ר סִינָֽי׃ (Lev. 27:34)
אֵ֣לֶּה הַמִּצְוֹ֞ת וְהַמִּשְׁפָּטִ֗ים אֲשֶׁ֨ר צִוָּ֧ה יְהוָ֛ה בְּיַד־מֹשֶׁ֖ה אֶל־בְּנֵ֣י יִשְׂרָאֵ֑ל
בְּעַֽרְבֹ֣ת מוֹאָ֔ב עַ֖ל יַרְדֵּ֥ן יְרֵחֽוֹ׃ (Num. 36:13)
וּלְכֹל֙ הַיָּ֣ד הַחֲזָקָ֔ה וּלְכֹ֖ל הַמּוֹרָ֣א הַגָּד֑וֹל אֲשֶׁר֙ עָשָׂ֣ה מֹשֶׁ֔ה לְעֵינֵ֖י כָּל־יִשְׂרָאֵֽל׃ (Deut. 34:12)

In each case, the congregation responds: חֲזַק חֲזַק וְנִתְחַזֵּק

ḥa - ZAK   ḥa - ZAK___   ve - nit - ḥa - ZÉK___

Note: When the same words are chanted again for the *maftir*, you will use the normal motifs for the ending of the *aliyah*.

Cantillation of the Creation on Simḥat Torah

The same "invitational cadence" is used on Simḥat Torah at the end of the account of each of the six days of Creation, just before the words ...וַיְהִי־עֶרֶב וַיְהִי־בֹקֶר.

וַיִּקְרָ֨א אֱלֹהִ֤ים ׀ לָאוֹר֙ י֔וֹם וְלַחֹ֖שֶׁךְ קָ֣רָא לָ֑יְלָה וַֽיְהִי־עֶ֥רֶב וַֽיְהִי־בֹ֖קֶר י֥וֹם אֶחָֽד׃ (Gen. 1:5)

וַיִּקְרָ֧א אֱלֹהִ֛ים לָֽרָקִ֖יעַ שָׁמָ֑יִם וַֽיְהִי־עֶ֥רֶב וַֽיְהִי־בֹ֖קֶר י֥וֹם שֵׁנִֽי׃ (Gen. 1:8)

וַתּוֹצֵ֨א הָאָ֜רֶץ דֶּ֠שֶׁא עֵ֣שֶׂב מַזְרִ֤יעַ זֶ֨רַע֙ לְמִינֵ֔הוּ וְעֵ֧ץ עֹֽשֶׂה־פְּרִ֛י אֲשֶׁ֥ר זַרְעוֹ־ב֖וֹ לְמִינֵ֑הוּ

וַיַּ֥רְא אֱלֹהִ֖ים כִּי־טֽוֹב׃ וַֽיְהִי־עֶ֥רֶב וַֽיְהִי־בֹ֖קֶר י֥וֹם שְׁלִישִֽׁי׃ (Gen. 1:12-13)

וְלִמְשֹׁל֙ בַּיּ֣וֹם וּבַלַּ֔יְלָה וּֽלְהַבְדִּ֔יל בֵּ֥ין הָא֖וֹר וּבֵ֣ין הַחֹ֑שֶׁךְ

וַיַּ֥רְא אֱלֹהִ֖ים כִּי־טֽוֹב׃ וַֽיְהִי־עֶ֥רֶב וַֽיְהִי־בֹ֖קֶר י֥וֹם רְבִיעִֽי׃ (Gen. 1:18-19)

וַיְבָ֧רֶךְ אֹתָ֛ם אֱלֹהִ֖ים לֵאמֹ֑ר פְּר֣וּ וּרְב֗וּ וּמִלְא֤וּ אֶת־הַמַּ֨יִם֙ בַּיַּמִּ֔ים

וְהָע֖וֹף יִ֥רֶב בָּאָֽרֶץ׃ וַֽיְהִי־עֶ֥רֶב וַֽיְהִי־בֹ֖קֶר י֥וֹם חֲמִישִֽׁי׃ (Gen. 1:22-23)

וַיַּ֣רְא אֱלֹהִים֩ אֶת־כׇּל־אֲשֶׁ֣ר עָשָׂ֗ה וְהִנֵּה־ט֖וֹב מְאֹ֑ד

וַֽיְהִי־עֶ֥רֶב וַֽיְהִי־בֹ֖קֶר י֥וֹם הַשִּׁשִּֽׁי׃ (Gen. 1:31)

You chant **(CD track 66)**:

	mé - rᵉ - KHA	tip - pᵉ - HA___	mé - r - KHA	sí - LUK___
	mé - rᵉ - KHA	tip - pᵉ - HA___	mu - NAH	'et - nah - TA___
(1:5)		vᵉ - la - HÓ - shekh	KA - ra	LAY - la
(1:8)		la - ra - KÍ - aʻ		sha - MA - yim
(1:12)	vay - YAR	'e - ló - HÍM___		kí - TÓV___
(1:18)	vay - YAR	'e - ló - HÍM___		kí - TÓV___
(1:22)		vᵉ - ha - ÓF___	Yi - rev	ba - 'A - rets
(1:31)		vᵉ - hin - né - TÓV___		mᵉ - 'ÓD___

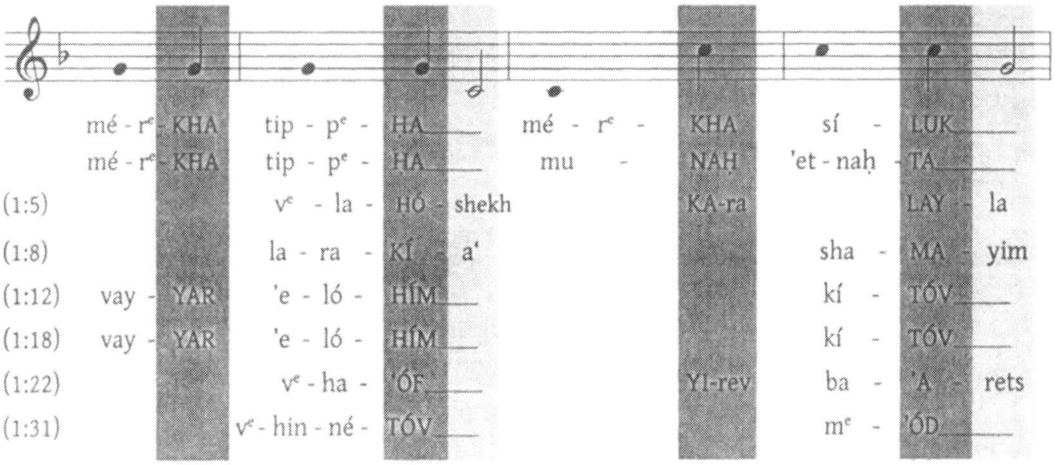

To which the congregation responds, using a High Holiday cantillation motif:

(1:5)	vay-hi - 'E-rev	vay-hi-VÓ - ker	YÓM__	'e - ḤAD______
(1:8)	vay-hi - 'E-rev	vay-hi-VÓ - ker	YÓM__	shé - NÍ______
(1:13)	vay-hi - 'E-rev	vay-hi-VÓ - ker	YÓM__	sh^{e} - lí - SHÍ______
(1:19)	vay-hi - 'E-rev	vay-hi-VÓ - ker	YÓM__	r^{e} - ví - 'Í______
(1:23)	vay-hi - 'E-rev	vay-hi-VÓ - ker	YÓM__	ḥa-mí-SHÍ______
(1:31)	vay-hi - 'E-rev	vay-hi-VÓ - ker	YÓM__	hash-shish-SHÍ______

You then repeat this last phrase (...וַֽיְהִי־עֶ֥רֶב וַֽיְהִי־בֹ֖קֶר).

After you have completed Gen. 1:31, the congregation recites (or chants) Gen. 2:1-3. You then chant Gen. 2:1-3 using the normal *te'amim.*

When these same passages are read on Shabbat, you use the normal *te'amim*, without congregational responses.

Public Fast Days

The invitational cadence is also used three times when chanting the special reading for public fast days (תענית צבור). After you chant the invitational cadence, wait for the congregation to recite the next phrase, using the High Holiday mode. Then you will repeat what the congregation has just recited, using the High Holiday mode. Then continue, using the regular Torah mode. (When these passages are read on any day other than a public fast day, you use the normal *te'amim*, without congregational responses.)

(CD track 67)

Exod. 32:12 לָ֩מָּה֩ יֹאמְר֨וּ מִצְרַ֜יִם לֵאמֹ֗ר בְּרָעָ֤ה הֽוֹצִיאָם֙ לַהֲרֹ֤ג אֹתָם֙ בֶּֽהָרִ֔ים וּ֨לְכַלֹּתָ֔ם מֵעַ֖ל פְּנֵ֣י הָֽאֲדָמָ֑ה
שׁ֚וּב מֵחֲר֣וֹן אַפֶּ֔ךָ וְהִנָּחֵ֥ם עַל־הָרָעָ֖ה לְעַמֶּֽךָ׃

(invitational cadence)

mé - 'AL______ p^{e} - NÉ ha - 'a - da - MA______

(High Holiday)

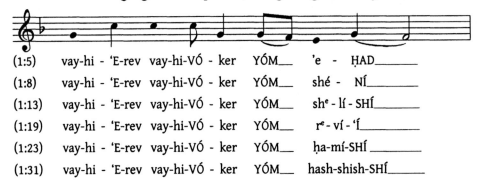

SHUV__ mé–ḥa - RÓN 'ap - PE - kha v^{e}–hin–na - ḤÉM__ 'al–ha–ra - 'A__ l^{e} - 'am - ME - kha

וַיַּעֲבֹ֨ר יְהוָ֥ה ׀ עַל־פָּנָיו֮ וַיִּקְרָא֒ יְהוָ֣ה ׀ יְהוָ֔ה אֵ֥ל רַח֖וּם וְחַנּ֑וּן אֶ֥רֶךְ אַפַּ֖יִם וְרַב־חֶ֥סֶד וֶאֱמֶֽת׃
נֹצֵ֥ר חֶ֨סֶד֙ לָאֲלָפִ֔ים נֹשֵׂ֥א עָוֺ֛ן וָפֶ֖שַׁע וְחַטָּאָ֑ה וְנַקֵּה֙
לֹ֣א יְנַקֶּ֔ה פֹּקֵ֣ד ׀ עֲוֺ֣ן אָב֗וֹת עַל־בָּנִים֙ וְעַל־בְּנֵ֣י בָנִ֔ים עַל־שִׁלֵּשִׁ֖ים וְעַל־רִבֵּעִֽים׃ (Exod. 34:6-7)

וַיֹּ֡אמֶר אִם־נָא֩ מָצָ֨אתִי חֵ֤ן בְּעֵינֶ֙יךָ֙ אֲדֹנָ֔י יֵֽלֶךְ־נָ֥א אֲדֹנָ֖י בְּקִרְבֵּ֑נוּ כִּ֤י עַם־קְשֵׁה־עֹ֙רֶף֙ ה֔וּא
וְסָלַחְתָּ֛ לַעֲוֺנֵ֥נוּ וּלְחַטָּאתֵ֖נוּ וּנְחַלְתָּֽנוּ׃ (Exod. 34:9)

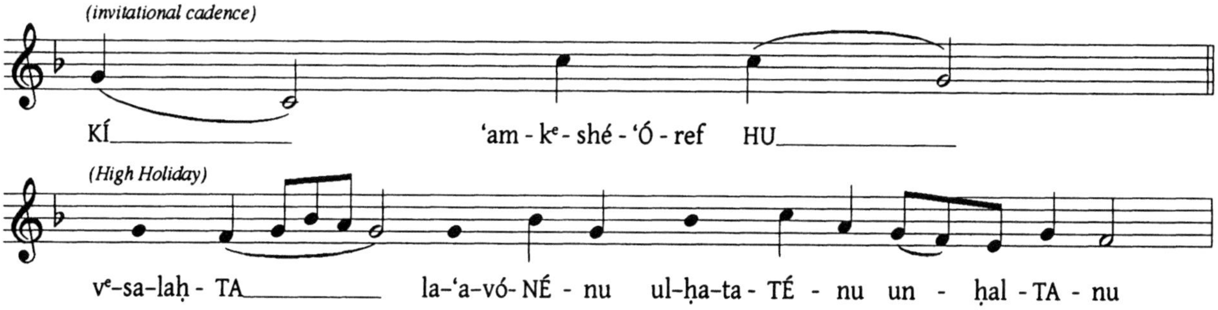

The Song of the Sea (Exodus 14 and 15)

Several portions of the "Song of the Sea" (שירת הים) are chanted to a special melody.
(CD track 68)

The first segment is sung to a free melody—one that does not strictly follow the *te'amim*. If the segment to be sung to this melody comprises only a few words, you will need to abbreviate the melody.

①

The concluding segment is based on the חוק חוק motifs.

②

Most readers use this melody for only the following phrases.

② מִימִינָם וּמִשְּׂמֹאלָם: (.Exod. 14:29)

mí - mí - NAM_____   u-mis-sᵉ-mó - LAM_____

② וַיַּאֲמִ֫ינוּ בַּיהוָ֖ה וּבְמֹשֶׁ֥ה עַבְדּ֑וֹ: (.Exod. 14:31)

vay - ya - 'a - MÍ - nu ba - dó - NAY_____   uv - mó - SHE____ 'av - DÓ_____

① אָשִׁ֤ירָה לַֽיהוָה֙ כִּֽי־גָאֹ֣ה גָּאָ֔ה ② ס֥וּס וְרֹכְב֖וֹ רָמָ֥ה בַיָּֽם: (.Exod. 15:1)

'a - SHÍ - ra la - dó - NAY_____   kí - ga - 'Ó   ga - 'A

SUS ve - ró - khᵉ - VÓ_____   ra - MA____ vay - YAM_____

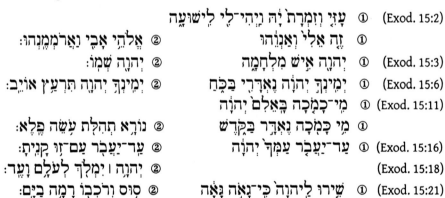

Follow the same pattern for these phrases.

① (Exod. 15:2)	עָזִּ֤י וְזִמְרָת֙ יָ֔הּ וַֽיְהִי־לִ֖י לִֽישׁוּעָ֑ה		
①	זֶ֤ה אֵלִי֙ וְאַנְוֵ֔הוּ	②	אֱלֹהֵ֥י אָבִ֖י וַאֲרֹמְמֶֽנְהוּ:
① (Exod. 15:3)	יְהוָ֖ה אִ֣ישׁ מִלְחָמָ֑ה	②	יְהוָ֖ה שְׁמֽוֹ:
① (Exod. 15:6)	יְמִֽינְךָ֣ יְהוָ֔ה נֶאְדָּרִ֖י בַּכֹּ֑חַ	②	יְמִֽינְךָ֥ יְהוָ֖ה תִּרְעַ֥ץ אוֹיֵֽב:
① (Exod. 15:11)	מִֽי־כָמֹ֤כָה בָּֽאֵלִם֙ יְהוָ֔ה		
①	מִ֥י כָּמֹ֖כָה נֶאְדָּ֣ר בַּקֹּ֑דֶשׁ	②	נוֹרָ֥א תְהִלֹּ֖ת עֹ֥שֵׂה פֶֽלֶא:
① (Exod. 15:16)	עַד־יַעֲבֹ֤ר עַמְּךָ֙ יְהוָ֔ה	②	עַד־יַעֲבֹ֖ר עַם־ז֥וּ קָנִֽיתָ:
(Exod. 15:18)		②	יְהוָ֥ה ׀ יִמְלֹ֖ךְ לְעֹלָ֥ם וָעֶֽד:
① (Exod. 15:21)	שִׁ֤ירוּ לַֽיהוָה֙ כִּֽי־גָאֹ֣ה גָּאָ֔ה	②	ס֥וּס וְרֹכְב֖וֹ רָמָ֥ה בַיָּֽם:

The Journeys and the Chiefs

The festive melody used for the "Song of the Sea" is also used to add a majestic tone to the verses that recount the Israelites' journey in Sinai, as well as the verses that proclaim the names of the tribal chiefs. The custom is to read these verses in pairs.

The Journeys (Num. 33:11–46) (CD track 69)

11. vay - yis - 'U miy - yam - SUF____ vay-ya- ḥa - NU bᵉ-mid-bar - SÍN
13. vay - yis - 'U mid - dof - KA____ vay-ya- ḥa - NU bᵉ - 'a - LUSH

12. vay - yis - 'U mim-mid-bar - SÍN____ vay-ya-ḥa - NU__ bᵉ - dof - KA__
14. vay - yis - 'U mé - 'a - LUSH__ vay-ya-ḥa - NU__ bir - fí - DIM__

11 וַיִּסְעוּ מִיַּם־סוּף וַיַּחֲנוּ בְּמִדְבַּר־סִין׃ 12 וַיִּסְעוּ מִמִּדְבַּר־סִין וַיַּחֲנוּ בְּדָפְקָה׃
13 וַיִּסְעוּ מִדָּפְקָה וַיַּחֲנוּ בְּאָלוּשׁ׃ 14 וַיִּסְעוּ מֵאָלוּשׁ וַיַּחֲנוּ בִּרְפִידִם

(In non-leap-years, when *mas'ey* is read as part of a combined *parashah*, you could begin the pairing with verses 10 and 11, instead of 11 and 12.)

The remainder of verse 14 is cantillated using the normal *te'amim.*

Verses 15-36 are chanted in pairs using the festive melody, as above.

Verses 37-40 are cantillated using the normal *te'amim.*

Verses 41-46 are chanted in pairs using the festive melody.

The Chiefs (Num. 10:15–27) (CD track 70)

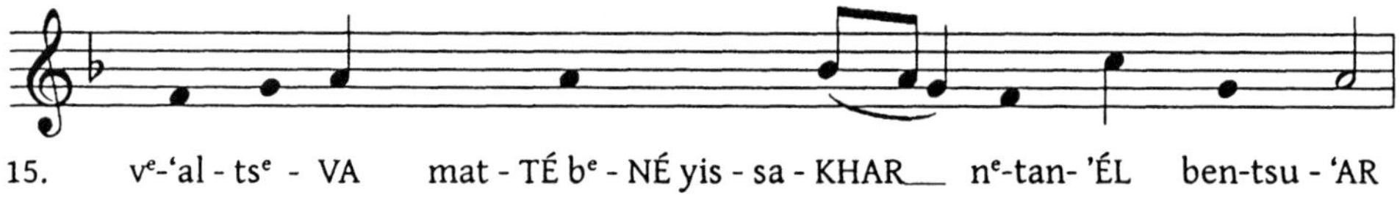
15. vᵉ-'al - tsᵉ - VA mat - TÉ bᵉ - NÉ yis - sa - KHAR__ nᵉ-tan- 'ÉL ben-tsu - 'AR

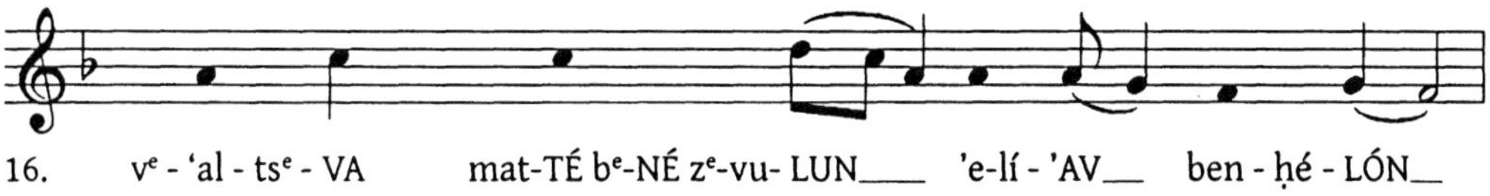
16. vᵉ - 'al - tsᵉ - VA mat-TÉ bᵉ-NÉ zᵉ-vu- LUN____ 'e-lí - 'AV__ ben - ḥé - LÓN__

15 וְעַל־צְבָא מַטֵּה בְּנֵי יִשָּׂשכָר נְתַנְאֵל בֶּן־צוּעָר׃
16 וְעַל־צְבָא מַטֵּה בְּנֵי זְבוּלֻן אֱלִיאָב בֶּן־חֵלוֹן׃

Verses 17-18 are cantillated using the normal *te'amim.*

Verses 19-20 are chanted as a pair using the festive melody, as above.

Verses 21-22 are cantillated using the normal *te'amim.*

Verses 23-24 are chanted as a pair using the festive melody.

Verse 25 is cantillated using the normal *te'amim.*

Verses 26-27 are chanted as a pair using the festive melody.

Some readers will chant the second half (the words after the *etnaḥta*) of verses 10:14, 18, 22, and 25 to the melody of phrase two. In any case, the first half (the words up to the *etnaḥta*) of each of those verses is cantillated using the normal *te'amim*.

Shabbat Ḥazon שבת חזון (CD track 71)

The *parashah* of Devarim is invariably read on the Shabbat before Tish'ah Be'Av, a day of mourning and fasting in commemoration of the destruction of the Sanctuary in Jerusalem. That Shabbat is known as Shabbat Ḥazon (The Shabbat of the Vision), after the first words of its *haftarah* (The Vision of Isaiah). Portions of that *haftarah* are cantillated using the mode of Lamentations (איכה) (see p. 139). One verse of the Torah reading that day (Deut. 1:12) is cantillated using the mode of Lamentations, as well. This verse should be chanted slowly and mournfully.

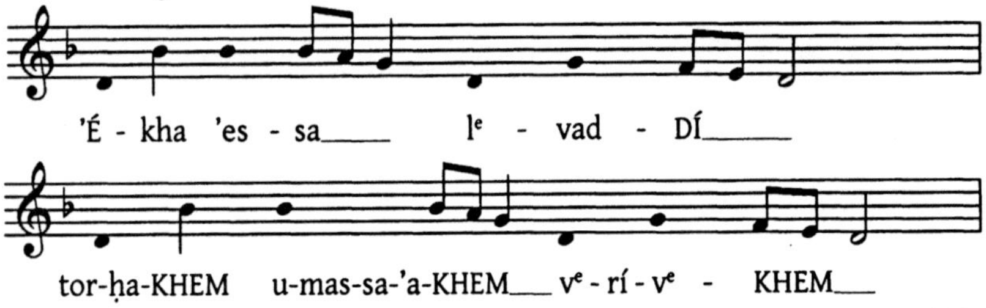

אֵיכָה אֶשָּׂא לְבַדִּי טָרְחֲכֶם וּמַשַּׂאֲכֶם וְרִיבְכֶם׃

Akdamut Millin אקדמות מלין

On the first day of Shavuot, a special hymn (פיוט) is chanted before the Torah reading. After the first *oleh* has been called up, but before the *oleh* chants the blessing, the *ba'al keri'ah* (or the *ḥazzan*) chants this mystical hymn, symbolically asking God's permission to read the Decalogue (the Ten Commandments). It is sung responsively, the leader chanting the odd-numbered verses, and the congregation responding with the even-numbered verses. Each verse is sung to the following melody:

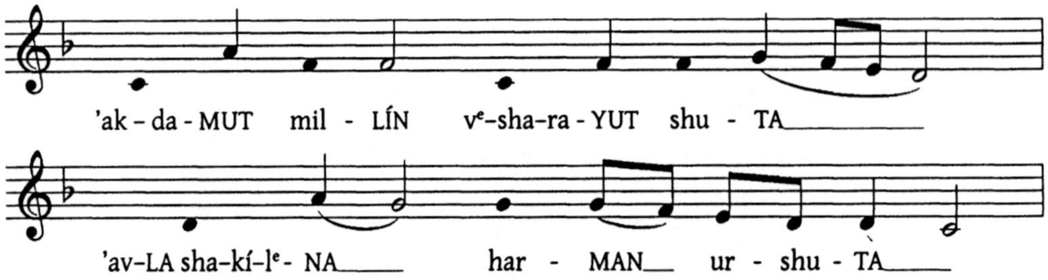

אַקְדָּמוּת מִלִּין וְשָׁרָיוּת שׁוּתָא, אַוְלָא שָׁקִילְנָא הַרְמָן וּרְשׁוּתָא.

The full text of this hymn can be found in a traditional prayer book for Shavuot. After the hymn is concluded, the *oleh* chants the blessing and the *ba'al keri'ah* begins the Festival reading (Exod. 19:1).

High and Low Accents

The Decalogue

There are two traditions for chanting the Decalogue. The Decalogue appears twice in the Bible: one version in Exodus 20 and another version in Deuteronomy 5. When chanting these passages as part of the synagogue liturgy on the festival of Shavuot and on Shabbat for the *parashiyot* of Yitro and Va'etḥanan, the *ba'al keri'ah* utilizes a tradition known as טַעֲמֵי הָעֶלְיוֹן (high cantillation). The *ta'amey ha-'elyon* arrange the Decalogue into ten verses—one verse for each commandment. The aim of this structure is to create a certain theatrical realism: The *ba'al keri'ah* reenacts the Divine revelation at Sinai.

On the other hand, the *ta'amey ha-taḥton* טַעֲמֵי הַתַּחְתּוֹן (low cantillation) represent the normal reading, leaving the text of the Decalogue in twelve verses of more or less average length: not too short, not too long.

In some editions of the Bible, the two sets of *te'amim* are superimposed one over the other, leaving the reader confused as to which is which. For clarification, we have printed the appropriate liturgical cantillation for both versions of the Decalogue.

Exodus 20—*ta'amey ha-'elyon*

אָנֹכִי יְהֹוָה אֱלֹהֶיךָ אֲשֶׁר הוֹצֵאתִיךָ מֵאֶרֶץ מִצְרַיִם מִבֵּית עֲבָדִים׃

לֹא יִהְיֶה־לְךָ אֱלֹהִים אֲחֵרִים עַל־פָּנַי לֹא תַעֲשֶׂה־לְךָ פֶסֶל ׀ וְכָל־תְּמוּנָה
אֲשֶׁר בַּשָּׁמַיִם ׀ מִמַּעַל וַאֲשֶׁר בָּאָרֶץ מִתַּחַת וַאֲשֶׁר בַּמַּיִם ׀ מִתַּחַת לָאָרֶץ
לֹא־תִשְׁתַּחֲוֶה לָהֶם וְלֹא תָעָבְדֵם כִּי אָנֹכִי יְהֹוָה אֱלֹהֶיךָ אֵל קַנָּא
פֹּקֵד עֲוֹן אָבֹת עַל־בָּנִים עַל־שִׁלֵּשִׁים וְעַל־רִבֵּעִים לְשֹׂנְאָי
וְעֹשֶׂה חֶסֶד לַאֲלָפִים לְאֹהֲבַי וּלְשֹׁמְרֵי מִצְוֺתָי׃

לֹא תִשָּׂא אֶת־שֵׁם־יְהֹוָה אֱלֹהֶיךָ לַשָּׁוְא
כִּי לֹא יְנַקֶּה יְהֹוָה אֵת אֲשֶׁר־יִשָּׂא אֶת־שְׁמוֹ לַשָּׁוְא׃

זָכוֹר אֶת־יוֹם הַשַּׁבָּת לְקַדְּשׁוֹ שֵׁשֶׁת יָמִים תַּעֲבֹד וְעָשִׂיתָ כָל־מְלַאכְתֶּךָ
וְיוֹם הַשְּׁבִיעִי שַׁבָּת ׀ לַיהֹוָה אֱלֹהֶיךָ לֹא תַעֲשֶׂה כָל־מְלָאכָה
אַתָּה וּבִנְךָ וּבִתֶּךָ עַבְדְּךָ וַאֲמָתְךָ וּבְהֶמְתֶּךָ וְגֵרְךָ אֲשֶׁר בִּשְׁעָרֶיךָ
כִּי שֵׁשֶׁת־יָמִים עָשָׂה יְהֹוָה אֶת־הַשָּׁמַיִם וְאֶת־הָאָרֶץ אֶת־הַיָּם וְאֶת־כָּל־אֲשֶׁר־בָּם
וַיָּנַח בַּיּוֹם הַשְּׁבִיעִי עַל־כֵּן בֵּרַךְ יְהֹוָה אֶת־יוֹם הַשַּׁבָּת וַיְקַדְּשֵׁהוּ׃

כַּבֵּד אֶת־אָבִיךָ וְאֶת־אִמֶּךָ
לְמַעַן יַאֲרִכוּן יָמֶיךָ עַל הָאֲדָמָה אֲשֶׁר־יְהֹוָה אֱלֹהֶיךָ נֹתֵן לָךְ׃

לֹא תִרְצָח׃

לֹא תִנְאָף׃

לֹא תִגְנֹב׃

לֹא־תַעֲנֶה בְרֵעֲךָ עֵד שָׁקֶר׃

לֹא תַחְמֹד בֵּית רֵעֶךָ
לֹא־תַחְמֹד אֵשֶׁת רֵעֶךָ וְעַבְדּוֹ וַאֲמָתוֹ וְשׁוֹרוֹ וַחֲמֹרוֹ וְכֹל אֲשֶׁר לְרֵעֶךָ׃

Deuteronomy 5—*ta'amey ha-'elyon*

אָנֹכִי֙ יְהוָ֣ה אֱלֹהֶ֔יךָ אֲשֶׁ֧ר הוֹצֵאתִ֛יךָ מֵאֶ֥רֶץ מִצְרַ֖יִם מִבֵּ֥ית עֲבָדִֽים׃

לֹ֣א יִהְיֶ֥ה־לְךָ֛ אֱלֹהִ֥ים אֲחֵרִ֖ים עַל־פָּנָֽי

לֹֽא־תַעֲשֶׂ֨ה־לְךָ֥ פֶ֣סֶל ׀ כָּל־תְּמוּנָ֡ה

אֲשֶׁ֣ר בַּשָּׁמַ֣יִם ׀ מִמַּ֡עַל וַֽאֲשֶׁ֣ר בָּאָ֣רֶץ מִתַּ֗חַת וַאֲשֶׁ֣ר בַּמַּ֣יִם ׀ מִתַּ֣חַת לָאָֽרֶץ

לֹֽא־תִשְׁתַּחֲוֶ֥ה לָהֶ֖ם וְלֹ֣א תָעָבְדֵ֑ם כִּ֣י אָנֹכִ֞י

יְהוָ֣ה אֱלֹהֶ֗יךָ אֵ֣ל קַנָּ֡א פֹּ֠קֵד עֲוֺ֨ן אָבֹ֧ת עַל־בָּנִ֛ים וְעַל־שִׁלֵּשִׁ֥ים וְעַל־רִבֵּעִ֖ים לְשֹׂנְאָֽי

וְעֹ֥שֶׂה חֶ֖סֶד לַֽאֲלָפִ֑ים לְאֹהֲבַ֖י וּלְשֹׁמְרֵ֥י מִצְוֺתָֽי

לֹ֥א תִשָּׂ֛א אֶת־שֵֽׁם־יְהוָ֥ה אֱלֹהֶ֖יךָ לַשָּׁ֑וְא

כִּ֣י לֹ֤א יְנַקֶּה֙ יְהוָ֔ה אֵ֛ת אֲשֶׁר־יִשָּׂ֥א אֶת־שְׁמ֖וֹ לַשָּֽׁוְא׃

שָׁמ֣וֹר אֶת־י֤וֹם   הַשַּׁבָּת֙ לְקַדְּשׁ֔וֹ כַּאֲשֶׁ֥ר צִוְּךָ֖ ׀ יְהוָ֥ה אֱלֹהֶֽיךָ

שֵׁ֤שֶׁת יָמִים֙ תַּֽעֲבֹ֔ד וְעָשִׂ֖יתָ כָּל־מְלַאכְתֶּֽךָ

וְי֙וֹם֙ הַשְּׁבִיעִ֔י שַׁבָּ֖ת ׀ לַיהוָ֣ה אֱלֹהֶ֑יךָ לֹ֣א תַעֲשֶׂ֣ה כָל־מְלָאכָ֡ה

אַתָּ֣ה וּבִנְךָֽ־וּבִתֶּ֣ךָ וְעַבְדְּךָֽ־וַ֠אֲמָתֶךָ וְשׁוֹרְךָ֨ וַחֲמֹֽרְךָ֜ וְכָל־בְּהֶמְתֶּ֗ךָ

וְגֵֽרְךָ֙ אֲשֶׁ֣ר בִּשְׁעָרֶ֔יךָ לְמַ֗עַן יָנ֛וּחַ עַבְדְּךָ֥ וַאֲמָתְךָ֖ כָּמֽוֹךָ

וְזָכַרְתָּ֞ כִּ֣י־עֶ֣בֶד הָיִ֣יתָ ׀ בְּאֶ֣רֶץ מִצְרַ֗יִם וַיֹּצִ֨אֲךָ֜ יְהוָ֤ה אֱלֹהֶ֙יךָ֙ מִשָּׁ֔ם

בְּיָ֤ד חֲזָקָה֙ וּבִזְרֹ֣עַ נְטוּיָ֔ה עַל־כֵּ֗ן צִוְּךָ֙ יְהוָ֣ה אֱלֹהֶ֔יךָ לַעֲשׂ֖וֹת אֶת־י֥וֹם הַשַּׁבָּֽת׃

כַּבֵּ֤ד אֶת־אָבִ֙יךָ֙ וְאֶת־אִמֶּ֔ךָ כַּאֲשֶׁ֥ר צִוְּךָ֖ יְהוָ֣ה אֱלֹהֶ֑יךָ

לְמַ֣עַן ׀ יַאֲרִ֣יכֻן יָמֶ֗יךָ וּלְמַ֙עַן֙ יִ֣יטַב לָ֔ךְ עַ֚ל הָֽאֲדָמָ֔ה אֲשֶׁר־יְהוָ֥ה אֱלֹהֶ֖יךָ נֹתֵ֥ן לָֽךְ׃

לֹ֥א תִּרְצָֽח׃

וְלֹ֖א תִּנְאָֽף׃

וְלֹ֖א תִּגְנֹֽב׃

וְלֹֽא־תַעֲנֶ֥ה בְרֵֽעֲךָ֖ עֵ֥ד שָֽׁוְא׃

וְלֹ֥א תַחְמֹ֖ד אֵ֣שֶׁת רֵעֶ֑ךָ וְלֹ֣א תִתְאַוֶּ֗ה בֵּ֣ית רֵעֶ֔ךָ

שָׂדֵ֜הוּ וְעַבְדּ֤וֹ וַאֲמָתוֹ֙ שׁוֹר֣וֹ וַחֲמֹר֔וֹ וְכֹ֖ל אֲשֶׁ֥ר לְרֵעֶֽךָ׃

The Saga of Reuben

There is one other passage in which you will find two sets of *te'amim* superimposed one over the other: "the saga of Reuben" (מַעֲשֵׂה רְאוּבֵן) in Genesis 35:22. Here is the appropriate liturgical cantillation for this passage.

וַיְהִי בִּשְׁכֹּן יִשְׂרָאֵל֙ בָּאָרֶץ הַהִוא וַיֵּלֶךְ רְאוּבֵן וַיִּשְׁכַּב֙ אֶת־בִּלְהָה֙ פִּילֶגֶשׁ אָבִיו וַיִּשְׁמַע יִשְׂרָאֵל

וַיִּהְיוּ בְנֵי־יַעֲקֹב שְׁנֵים עָשָׂר׃

Chanting the Torah Blessings ברכות התורה

The person who is called up to the Torah is referred to as the *oleh* (עולה). The *oleh* is summoned by Hebrew name to approach the table (שולחן) where the Torah scroll is resting. The *gabbai* removes the cloth that has been covering the scroll, and you point to the first word of the section you are about to read. The *oleh* touches that word lightly with a *tallit* (or some other fabric), kisses the *tallit*, then, holding the two decorative wooden handles (עצי חיים) that protrude from the scroll dowels, chants the following blessing. Although the scroll may be open, the *oleh* should not look at it while reciting the blessings. The blessings are chanted using the melodic motifs (נוסח) that are heard in many Jewish liturgical services, including the weekday *shaḥarit*.

the oleh:

ba - r^e - KHU 'et 'a - dó - NAY ha - m^e - vó - RAKH

congregation, then the oleh:

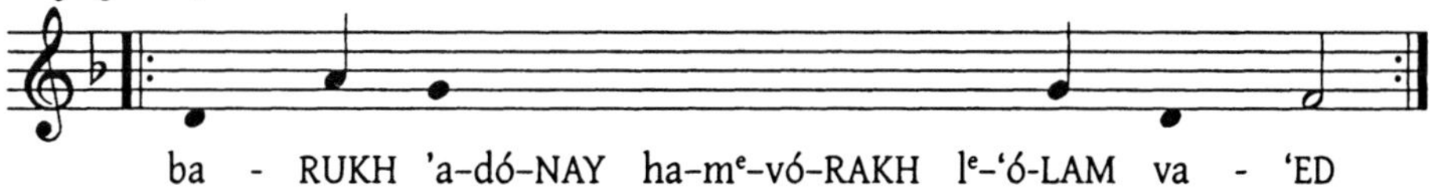
ba - RUKH 'a-dó-NAY ha-m^e-vó-RAKH l^e-'ó-LAM va - 'ED

the oleh:

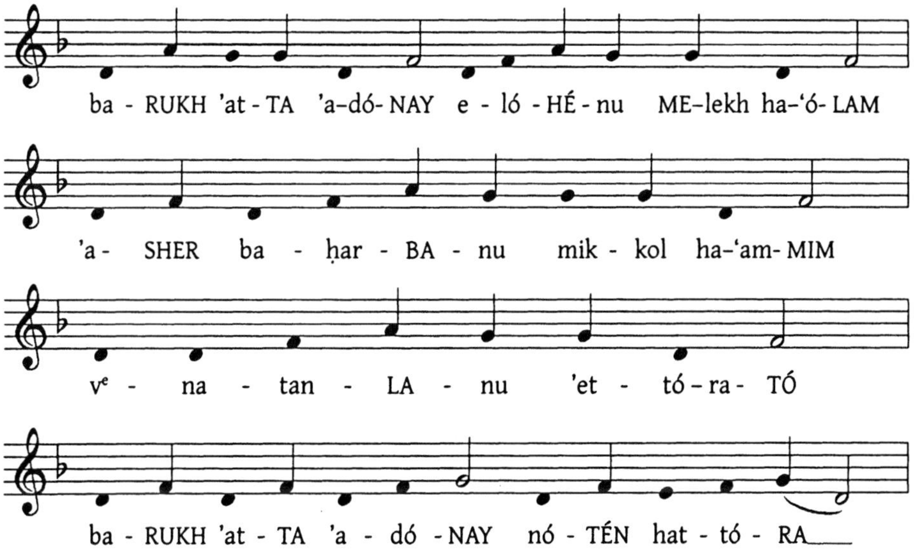
ba - RUKH 'at - TA 'a-dó- NAY e - ló - HÉ - nu ME-lekh ha-'ó- LAM
'a- SHER ba - ḥar - BA - nu mik - kol ha-'am- MIM
v^e - na - tan - LA - nu 'et - tó - ra - TÓ
ba - RUKH 'at - TA 'a - dó - NAY nó - TÉN hat - tó - RA

The congregation (including you, the reader) responds "amen" (אמן) to the blessing that the *oleh* has just chanted. You must respond "amen" *before* looking into the scroll. One normally responds "amen" only to a blessing that someone else has made; if you are the *oleh*, you should not respond "amen" to your own blessing. Chant the "amen" response using the motif of *tevir* or a modified *siluk.*

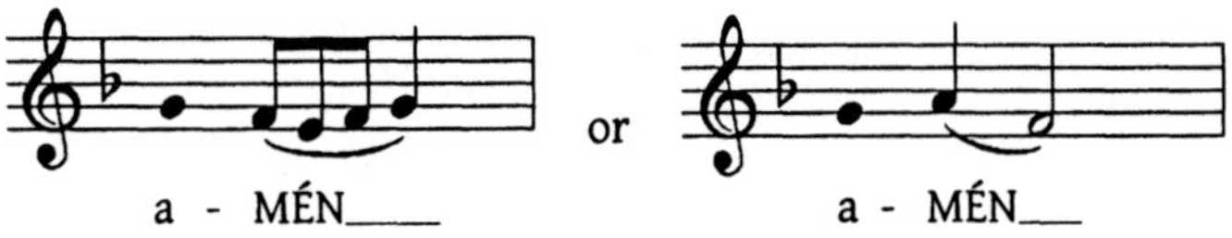
or
a - MÉN
a - MÉN

Take the left handle in your left hand; the *oleh* holds the right handle. Begin to chant the designated section. You will use a pointer (יד) to follow the text, but be careful that the pointer never actually touches the scroll. When you have finished, the *oleh* may gently touch the final word with a *tallit* and then kiss the *tallit*. The *oleh* takes hold of both handles, rolls the scroll shut and chants the next blessing.

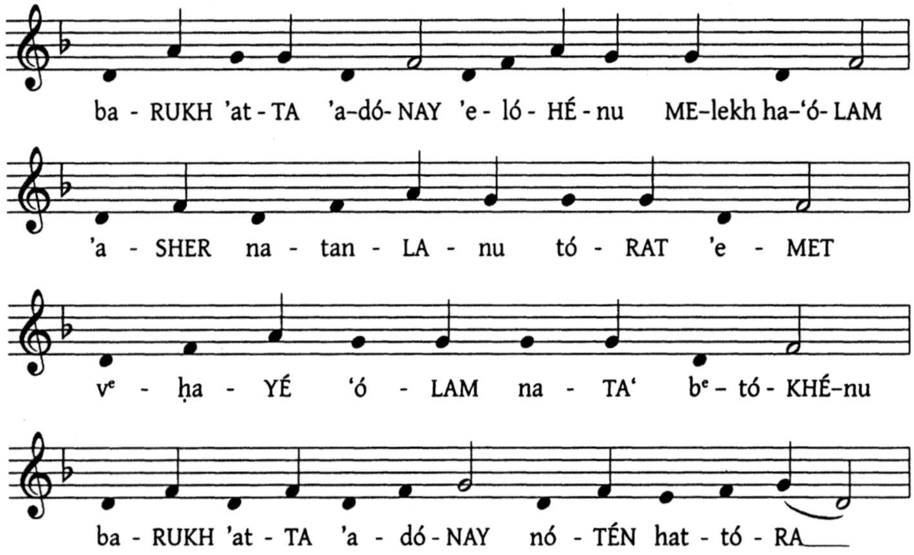
ba - RUKH 'at - TA 'a-dó- NAY 'e - ló - HÉ - nu ME-lekh ha-'ó- LAM
'a - SHER na - tan - LA - nu tó - RAT 'e - MET
vᵉ - ḥa - YÉ 'ó - LAM na - TA' bᵉ - tó - KHÉ-nu
ba - RUKH 'at - TA 'a - dó - NAY nó - TÉN hat - tó - RA

The *Kaddish* חצי קדיש

A "short *Kaddish*" is chanted in the morning service after the Torah reading. Generally, the *ba'al keri'ah* will chant the *Kaddish.* When there is a *maftir*, the *Kaddish* is chanted immediately before calling up the *maftir.* (Tish'ah Be'Av is an exception. Because the *maftir* is the third *oleh*, not an extra, you chant the *Kaddish* after the *maftir* has completed the second Torah blessing.)

When the *Kaddish* is chanted, the Torah scroll should be lying on the table and covered with a cloth. If the *maftir*'s portion is read from a second Torah, both scrolls should be lying on the table. (If three Torah scrolls are used for the reading, you chant the *Kaddish* after the reading from the second Torah. All three scrolls are placed on the table before you chant the *Kaddish.*) After you chant the *Kaddish*, if more than one scroll is lying on the table, remove the first scroll(s) before opening up the next scroll.

The *Kaddish* after Torah Reading on Shabbat

*On Shabbat Shuvah, substitute: l^{e}-'ÉL-la l^{e}-'ÉL-la mik-KOL bir-kha-TA...

The *Kaddish* after Torah Reading on Weekdays

*Between Rosh Hashanah and Yom Kippur, substitute: l^{e}-'ÉL-la l^{e}-'ÉL-la mik-KOL bir-kha-TA...

The *Kaddish* after Torah Reading on Festivals

6. Lamentations

Introduction

The Book of Lamentations, traditionally ascribed to the prophet Jeremiah, describes the siege and devastation of Jerusalem by the Babylonian army in 586 B.C.E. It comprises five chapters, each of which is a self-contained elegiac poem. The first two and last two poems each comprise 22 verses, and all but the last are arranged in an alphabetic acrostic. The third poem, in which the author ponders on the meaning of suffering, is arranged as a triple acrostic in 66 short verses.

Lamentations is customarily chanted in the synagogue on the evening of Tish'ah Be'Av, the ninth day of the Jewish month of Av. The evening (ערבית) service for fast days is recited, up to and including the *Amidah* and the *Kaddish Shalem* that follows. Then the reader, seated like a mourner on the floor or on a low bench, chants Lamentations slowly, in a mournful tone.

Lamentations Motifs in Other Readings

Several melancholy verses in the books of Deuteronomy, Jeremiah, Isaiah, and Esther are chanted according to the musical motifs of Lamentations.

- The *haftarah* of the Shabbat before Tish'ah Be'Av (Shabbat Devarim, also known as Shabbat Ḥazon) is chanted in the following modes:

Isaiah 1:1	*Haftarah* mode
1:2-15	Lamentations mode
1:16-19	*Haftarah* mode
1:20-23	Lamentations mode
1:24-27	*Haftarah* mode

- The *haftarah* for the morning service on Tish'ah Be'Av begins in the Lamentations mode (Jer. 8:13-9:21) and ends in the *Haftarah* mode (9:22-23).
- On the Shabbat before Tish'ah Be'Av, one verse of the Torah portion is chanted in the Lamentations mode (Deut. 1:12—אֵיכָה אֶשָּׂא לְבַדִּי טָרְחֲכֶם וּמַשַּׂאֲכֶם וְרִיבְכֶם). The first word of this verse provides an obvious connection to the opening word of the book of Lamentations.
- In the Book of Esther, several phrases referring to sad events are chanted in the Lamentations mode. See p. 185 for details.

The Melodies of the Cantillation Motifs

Hear the melodies of the Lamentations cantillation on CD tracks 85–87.

The *Siluk* and *Etnaḥta* Segments

The last word in every verse is marked with *siluk*. If the preceding word is closely connected in meaning to the *siluk* word, it is usually marked with the conjunctive *ta'am, merekha* (מֵרְכָ֥א סִילֽוּק).

Most verses are divided into two segments. *Etnaḥta* is the *ta'am* that marks the end of the first segment, and *siluk* marks the end of the second segment. If the *etnaḥta* word and the word before it are closely connected in meaning, they are usually marked *munaḥ etnaḥta* (מוּנַ֣ח אֶתְנַחְתָּ֑א).

The *Tippeḥa* Segment

A *siluk* segment that contains three or more words is subdivided into two parts. The disjunctive *ta'am* that divides the *siluk* segment is *tippeḥa*. If there are two words in the *tippeḥa* segment, the first one is usually marked with the conjunctive *ta'am, merekha* (מֵרְכָ֥א טִפְּחָ֖א מֵרְכָ֥א סִילֽוּק).

An *etnaḥta* segment that contains three or more words is also subdivided into two parts. The disjunctive *ta'am* that divides the *etnaḥta* segment is also *tippeḥa* (מֵרְכָ֥א טִפְּחָ֖א מוּנַ֣ח אֶתְנַחְתָּ֑א).

In the Lamentations mode, *siluk* and *etnaḥta* are chanted to the same melody.

Merekha tippeḥa merekha siluk, Merekha tippeḥa munaḥ etnaḥta

מֵרְכָ֥א טִפְּחָ֖א מֵרְכָ֥א סִילֽוּק   מֵרְכָ֥א טִפְּחָ֖א מוּנַ֣ח אֶתְנַחְתָּ֑א

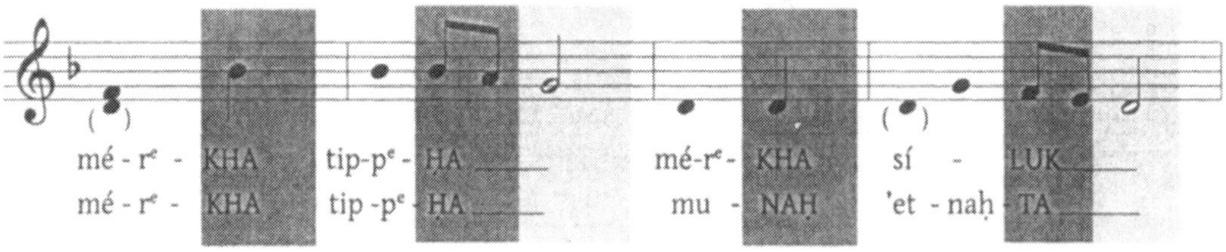

Chant the following phrases.

Unless otherwise indicated, all citations refer to the Book of Lamentations.

מֵרְכָ֥א טִפְּחָ֖א   מֵרְכָ֥א סִילֽוּק
כָּל־רֹדְפֶ֥יהָ הִשִּׂיג֖וּהָ   בֵּ֥ין הַמְּצָרִֽים (1:3)
וַיֵּלְכ֥וּ בְלֹא־כֹ֖חַ   לִפְנֵ֥י רוֹדֵֽף (1:6)
בְּתוּלֹתַ֥י וּבַחוּרַ֖י   הָלְכ֥וּ בַשֶּֽׁבִי (1:18)

מֵרְכָ֥א טִפְּחָ֖א   סִילֽוּק
הָ֥יוּ לָ֖הּ   לְאֹיְבִֽים (1:2)
הָלְכ֥וּ שְׁבִ֖י   לִפְנֵי־צָֽר (1:5)
כִּ֥י הָיִ֖יתִי   זוֹלֵלָֽה (1:11)

מֵרְכָ֥א טִפְּחָ֖א   מוּנַ֣ח אֶתְנַחְתָּ֑א
כֹּהֲנַ֥י וּזְקֵנַ֖י   בָּעִ֣יר גָּוָ֑עוּ (1:19)
פֶּ֥צַע וְחַבּוּרָ֖ה   וּמַכָּ֣ה טְרִיָּ֑ה (Isa. 1:6)
with *merekha-siluk* elision: (1:7) אֲשֶׁ֥ר הָי֖וּ   מִ֣ימֵי קֶ֑דֶם

מֵרְכָ֥א טִפְּחָ֖א   אֶתְנַחְתָּ֑א
אֵ֥ין מְנַחֵ֖ם   לָ֑הּ (1:9)
לֹ֥א מָצְאָ֖ה   מָנ֑וֹחַ (1:3)
אִבַּ֥ד וְשִׁבַּ֖ר   בְּרִיחֶ֑יהָ (2:9)

טִפְחָ֖א מֵרְכָ֥א סִילְוּק
שָׂחֲק֖וּ עַ֥ל מִשְׁבַּתֶּֽהָ (1:7)
מַעֲשֵׂ֖ה יְדֵ֥י יוֹצֵֽר (4:2)
פֹּרֵ֖שׂ אֵ֥ין לָהֶֽם (4:4)

טִפְחָ֖א סִילְוּק
הָיְתָ֖ה לָמַֽס (1:1)
כָּל־הַיּ֖וֹם דָּוָֽה (1:13)
וְיָשִׁ֖יבוּ אֶת־נַפְשָֽׁם (1:19)

טִפְחָ֖א מוּנַ֥ח אֶתְנַחְתָּ֑א
אַיֵּ֖ה דָּגָ֣ן וָיָ֑יִן (2:12)
עַל־כֵּ֖ן לְנִידָ֣ה הָיָ֑תָה (1:8)
לְמִ֖י עוֹלַ֣לְתָּ כֹּ֑ה with *munaḥ-etnaḥta* elision: (2:20)

טִפְחָ֖א אֶתְנַחְתָּ֑א
הָיְתָ֖ה כְּאַלְמָנָ֑ה (1:1)
תִּפְאֶ֖רֶת יִשְׂרָאֵ֑ל (2:1)
כֹּ֖ל מַחֲמַדֵּי־עָ֑יִן (2:4)

Chant these verses.

מַבְלִ֥יגִיתִ֖י עֲלֵ֣י יָג֑וֹן עָלַ֖י לִבִּ֥י דַוָּֽי׃ (Jer. 8:18)
עָבַ֥ר קָצִ֖יר כָּ֣לָה קָ֑יִץ וַאֲנַ֖חְנוּ ל֥וֹא נוֹשָֽׁעְנוּ׃ (Jer. 8:20)
וְנוֹתְרָ֥ה בַת־צִיּ֖וֹן כְּסֻכָּ֣ה בְכָ֑רֶם כִּמְלוּנָ֥ה בְמִקְשָׁ֖ה כְּעִ֥יר נְצוּרָֽה׃ (Isa. 1:8)
כַּסְפֵּ֖ךְ הָיָ֣ה לְסִיגִ֑ים סָבְאֵ֖ךְ מָה֥וּל בַּמָּֽיִם׃ (Isa. 1:22)

The *Tevir* Segment

Sometimes there is a subdivision within the *tippeḥa* segment. *Tevir* is the *ta'am* that marks that subdivision .

One or Two Words in a *Tevir* Segment

If the preceding word is closely connected in meaning to the *tevir* word, it is usually marked with a conjunctive *ta'am*. Most often that conjunctive is *darga*.

Darga tevir דַּרְגָּ֧א תְּבִ֛יר

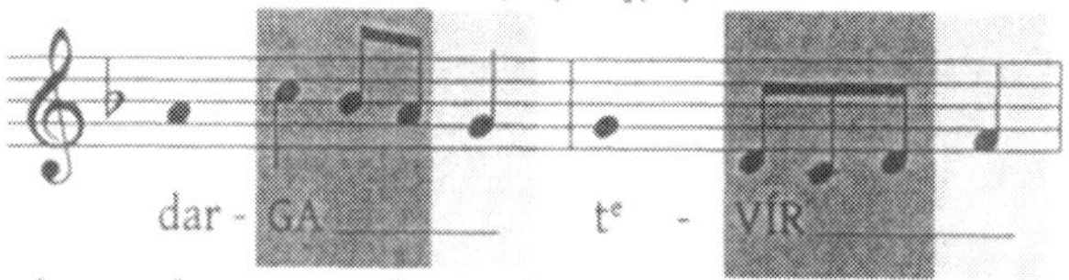

Chant these words to the melody of *darga tevir.*

הָרַ֧ס בְּעֶבְרָת֛וֹ (2:2) אֶל־רָעָ֧ה ׀ יָצָ֛אוּ (Jer. 9:2) קְטֹ֧רֶת תּוֹעֵבָ֛ה (Isa. 1:13)

If the accents are close to each other, the conjunctive will be *merekha* instead of *darga*.

Merekha tevir מֵרְכָ֥א תְּבִ֛יר

Chant these words to the melody of *merekha tevir.*

קָרָ֥א עָלַ֛י (1:15) כִּֽי־רָחַ֥ק מִמֶּ֛נִּי (1:16) חֵ֥ץ שָׁח֛וּט (Jer. 9:7)

Chant these words to the melody of *tevir.*

מִמָּר֛וֹם (1:13) הַאֲזִ֛ינוּ (Isa. 1:10)

Chant these phrases. Connect the conjunctive word to the word that follows. Create a slight elongation or pause after *tippeḥa*. There is very little elongation after *tevir*. The sense of the words dictates that *tippeḥa* is a stronger disjunctive than *tevir*.

דַּרְגָּ֧א תְּבִ֛יר טִפְּחָ֖א

נָתְנ֧וּ מַחֲמַדֵּיהֶ֛ם בְּאֹ֖כֶל לְהָשִׁ֣יב נָ֑פֶשׁ (1:11)

הָיְתָ֧ה יְרוּשָׁלַ֛͏ִם לְנִדָּ֖ה בֵּינֵיהֶֽם (1:17)

וְנָתַתִּ֧י אֶת־יְרוּשָׁלַ֛͏ִם לְגַלִּ֖ים מְע֣וֹן תַּנִּ֑ים (Jer. 9:10)

תְּבִ֛יר מֵרְכָ֥א טִפְּחָ֖א

מִמָּר֛וֹם שָֽׁלַח־אֵ֥שׁ בְּעַצְמֹתַ֖י וַיִּרְדֶּ֑נָּה (1:13)

אִם־יֵהָרֵ֛ג בְּמִקְדַּ֥שׁ אֲדֹנָ֖י כֹּהֵ֥ן וְנָבִֽיא (2:20)

נִֽאֲצ֛וּ אֶת־קְד֥וֹשׁ יִשְׂרָאֵ֖ל נָזֹ֥רוּ אָחֽוֹר (Isa. 1:4)

מֵרְכָ֥א תְּבִ֛יר מֵרְכָ֥א טִפְּחָ֖א

וְלֹ֥א הָיָ֛ה בְּי֥וֹם אַף־יְהוָ֖ה פָּלִ֣יט וְשָׂרִ֑יד (2:22)

קָרַ֥ב קִצֵּ֛ינוּ מָלְא֥וּ יָמֵ֖ינוּ כִּי־בָ֥א קִצֵּֽינוּ (4:18)

יִשְׂתָּֽרְג֥וּ עָל֛וּ עַל־צַוָּארִ֖י הִכְשִׁ֣יל כֹּחִ֑י (1:14)

מֵרְכָ֥א תְּבִ֛יר טִפְּחָ֖א

כִּֽי־רָחַ֥ק מִמֶּ֛נִּי מְנַחֵ֖ם מֵשִׁ֣יב נַפְשִׁ֑י (1:16)

כַּאֲשֶׁ֥ר עוֹלַ֛לְתָּ לִ֖י עַ֣ל כָּל־פְּשָׁעָ֑י (1:22)

הֵשִׁ֥יב אָח֛וֹר יְמִינ֖וֹ מִפְּנֵ֣י אוֹיֵ֑ב (2:3)

דַּרְגָּ֧א תְּבִ֛יר מֵרְכָ֥א טִפְּחָ֖א

הָרַ֧ס בְּעֶבְרָת֛וֹ מִבְצְרֵ֥י בַת־יְהוּדָ֖ה הִגִּ֣יעַ לָאָ֑רֶץ (2:2)

וְאֶת־עָרֵ֧י יְהוּדָ֛ה אֶתֵּ֥ן שְׁמָמָ֖ה מִבְּלִ֥י יוֹשֵֽׁב (Jer. 9:10)

הִנְנִ֧י מַאֲכִילָ֛ם אֶת־הָעָ֥ם הַזֶּ֖ה לַעֲנָ֑ה (Jer. 9:14)

תְּבִ֛יר טִפְּחָ֖א

הִכְעִס֛וּנִי בִּפְסִלֵיהֶ֖ם בְּהַבְלֵ֥י נֵכָֽר (Jer. 8:19)

Three Words in a *Tevir* Segment

Sometimes *tevir* is preceded by two or more conjunctives. In these segments, there will be a very slight elongation just before *tevir*. The second conjunctive before *tevir* (preceding either *merekha* or *darga*) may be *kadmah*.

Kadmah darga tevir קַדְמָ֨ה דַּרְגָּ֧א תְּבִ֛יר

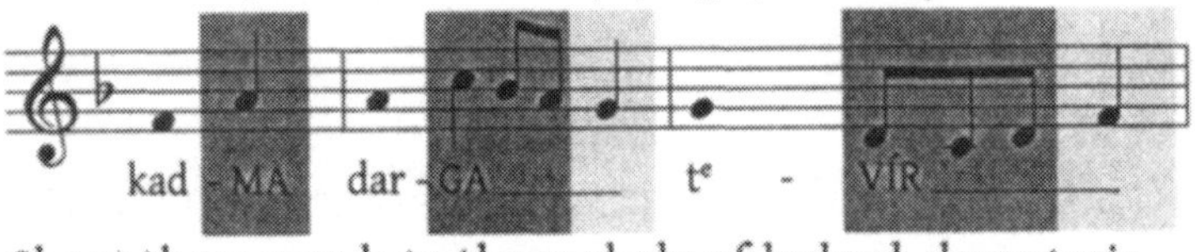
kad - MA dar - GA
tᵉ - VÍR

Chant these words to the melody of *kadmah darga tevir*.

וְדַ֨ם פָּרִ֧ים וּכְבָשִׂ֛ים (Isa. 1:11)   וַאֲשֶׁ֨ר דִּבֶּ֧ר פִּי־יְהוָ֛ה (Jer. 9:11)

Kadmah merekha tevir קַדְמָ֨ה מֵרְכָ֥א תְּבִ֛יר

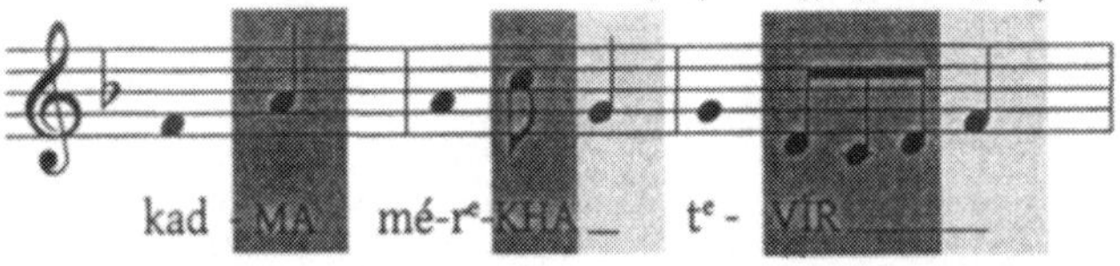
kad - MA mé-rᵉ- KHA
tᵉ - VÍR

Chant these words to the melody of *kadmah merekha tevir*.   דָּבַ֨ק לְשׁ֥וֹן יוֹנֵ֛ק (4:4)

If the second conjunctive before *tevir* (preceding *merekha*) is accented on the first syllable, it will be *munaḥ* instead of *kadmah*. When we refer to this *ta'am*, we accent its first syllable: *MU-naḥ*.

Munaḥ merekha tevir מֻ֣ונַח מֵ֥רְכָ֥א תְּבִ֛יר

Chant these words to the melody of *munaḥ merekha tevir.*

(Isa. 1:5) עַ֣ל מֶ֥ה תֻכּ֛וּ   (Jer. 9:18) כִּ֣י ק֥וֹל נְהִ֛י   (2:16) אַ֣ךְ זֶ֥ה הַיּ֛וֹם

Four Words in a *Tevir* Segment

Sometimes *tevir* is preceded by three conjunctives. The third conjunctive before *tevir* (just before *kadmah*) is *telishah ketanah.*

Telishah kadmah darga tevir תְּלִישָׁ֠ה קַדְמָ֨ה דַּרְגָּ֧א תְּבִ֛יר

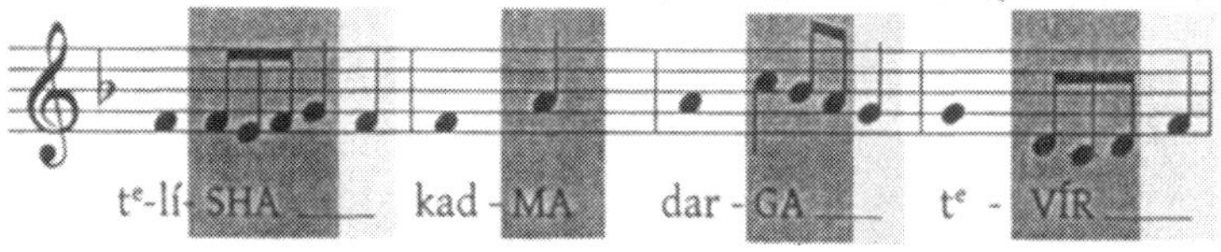

Chant these words to the melody of *telishah kadmah darga tevir.* (Jer. 9:2) כִּ֣י מֵרָעָ֨ה אֶל־רָעָ֧ה ׀ יָצָ֛אוּ

Chant these words to the appropriate *te'amim*. Connect the conjunctive word to the word that follows. Create a slight elongation or pause after *tippeḥa*. There is very little elongation after *tevir.*

קַדְמָ֨ה דַּרְגָּ֧א תְּבִ֛יר טִפְחָ֖א

וַאֲשֶׁ֨ר דִּבֶּ֧ר פִּֽי־יְהוָ֛ה אֵלָ֖יו וְיַגִּדָ֑הּ (Jer. 9:11)

וְדַ֨ם פָּרִ֧ים וּכְבָשִׂ֛ים וְעַתּוּדִ֖ים לֹ֥א חָפָֽצְתִּי׃ (Isa. 1:11)

קַדְמָ֨ה מֵ֥רְכָ֥א תְּבִ֛יר טִפְחָ֖א

דָּבַ֨ק לְשׁ֥וֹן יוֹנֵ֛ק אֶל־חִכּ֖וֹ בַּצָּמָ֑א (4:4)

מֻ֣ונַח מֵ֥רְכָ֥א תְּבִ֛יר (מֵ֥רְכָ֥א) טִפְחָ֖א

אַ֣ךְ זֶ֥ה הַיּ֛וֹם שֶׁקִּוִּינֻ֖הוּ מָצָ֥אנוּ רָאִֽינוּ׃ (2:16)

עַ֣ל מֶ֥ה תֻכּ֛וּ ע֖וֹד תּוֹסִ֣יפוּ סָרָ֑ה (Isa 1:5)

כִּ֣י ק֥וֹל נְהִ֛י נִשְׁמַ֥ע מִצִּיּ֖וֹן אֵ֣יךְ שֻׁדָּ֑דְנוּ (Jer 9:18)

The *Zakef* Segment

Zakef is a strong disjunctive; only *siluk* and *etnaḥta* are stronger. A *zakef* segment will always be followed by a *tippeḥa* segement. *Zakef* is stronger than the ensuing *tippeḥa*. A *zakef* segment may also be followed by one or more other *zakef* segments, but they will eventually be followed by a *tippeḥa* segement. When you see two *zakefs* (or two *zakef* segments) in a row, the first is always stronger.

There are two basic forms of *zakef*, each with its own distinct melody: *zakef gadol* (which occurs only three times), and *zakef katon.*

Zakef Gadol

Zakef gadol זָקֵף־גָּד֕וֹל

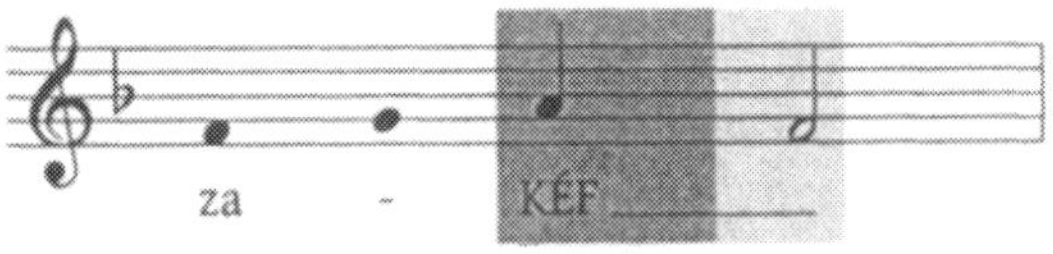

Chant these words to the melody of *zakef gadol.*

קָדַ֕רְתִּי (Jer. 8:21) וּתְמַהֵ֕רְנָה (Jer. 9:17) גַּם־נְבִיאֶ֕יהָ (2:9)

Zakef gadol is usually followed by (*merekha-*) *tippeḥa.* Chant these phrases. Make a pause or elongation after *zakef gadol.* Make a more subtle elongation after *tippeḥa.*

קָדַ֕רְתִּי שַׁמָּ֖ה הֶחֱזִקָתְנִי׃ (Jer. 8:21) וּתְמַהֵ֕רְנָה וְתִשֶּׂ֥נָה עָלֵ֖ינוּ נֶ֑הִי (Jer. 9:17)

גַּם־נְבִיאֶ֕יהָ לֹא־מָצְא֥וּ חָז֖וֹן מֵיְהוָֽה׃ (2:9)

Zakef Katon

Zakef katon זָקֵף־קָטֹ֔ן

This is the melody of *zakef katon* when it is *not* preceded by *munaḥ.*

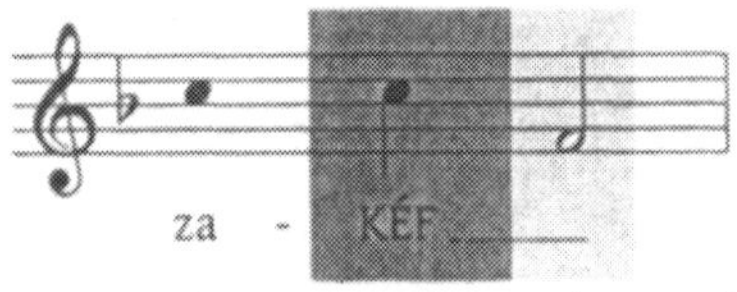

Chant these words to the melody of *zakef katon.*

לִבֵּ֔ךְ (2:19) בַּת־צִיּ֔וֹן (4:22) לָ֔ךְ (2:18) לָ֔מוֹ (4:10) צִפִּ֔ינוּ (4:17)

Two Words in a *Zakef* Segment

A word marked with *zakef katon* is usually preceded by the conjunctive *munaḥ.* Note the change in the melody of *zakef* when preceded by *munaḥ.*

Munaḥ zakef katon מוּנַ֣ח זָקֵף־קָטֹ֔ן

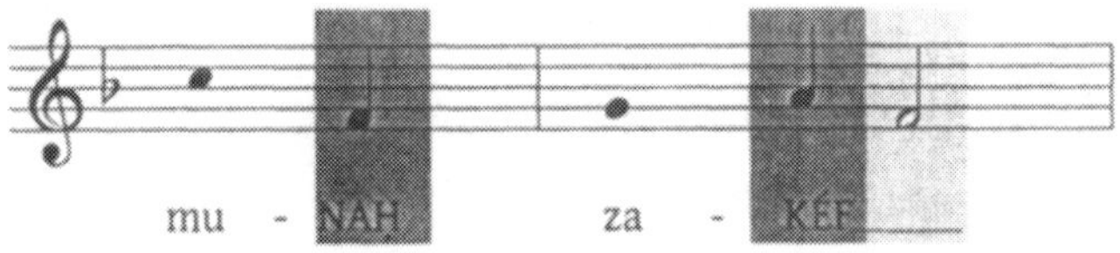

With elision:

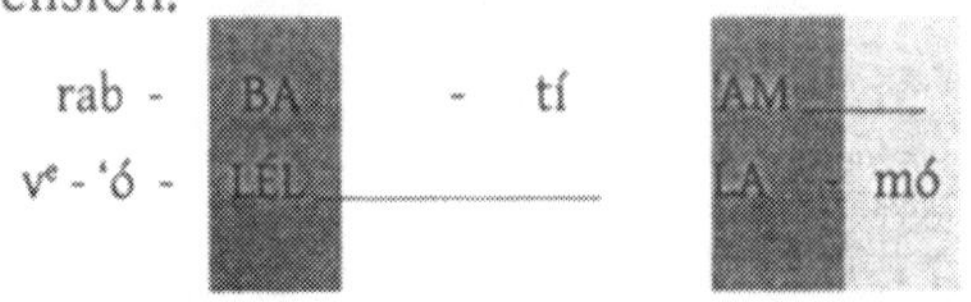

רַבָּ֣תִי עָ֔ם (1:1)
וְעוֹלֵ֣ל לָ֔מוֹ (1:22)

Chant these words to the melody of *munaḥ zakef.*

בָּאֵ֣י מוֹעֵ֔ד (1:4) וּמֵרֹ֣ב עֲבֹדָ֔ה (1:3) עַ֣ל לֶחֱיָ֔הּ (1:2) בָּ֣אוּ מִקְדָּשָׁ֔הּ (1:10) רָא֣וּהָ צָרִ֔ים (1:7)

Sometimes, on long words, *munaḥ* will appear on the same word that is marked with *zakef.*

לְמַ֣עֲדַנִּ֔ים (4:5) רַחֲמָ֣נִיּ֔וֹת (4:10) יְר֣וּשָׁלַ֔ם (1:8) כָּל־א֣וֹיְבַ֔יִךְ (2:16)

Zakef is usually followed by (*merekha-*) *tippeḥa.* Chant these phrases. Make a pause or elongation after *zakef*. Make a more subtle elongation after *tippeḥa*.

מונַח זָקֵף טִפְּחָא
אֲשֶׁר אָמַרְנוּ בְּצִלּוֹ נִחְיֶה בַגּוֹיִם (4:20)
וַיַּצֶּת־אֵשׁ בְּצִיּוֹן וַתֹּאכַל יְסוֹדֹתֶיהָ (4:11)
נָטָה קָו לֹא־הֵשִׁיב יָדוֹ מִבַּלֵּעַ (2:8)

מונַח זָקֵף תְּבִיר מֵרְכָא טִפְּחָא
חֶרֶב תְּאֻכְּלוּ כִּי פִּי יְהוָה דִּבֵּר׃ (Isa 1:20)

The *Pashta/Yetiv* Segment

Sometimes there is a subdivision within a *zakef* segment. *Pashta* is the *ta'am* that marks that subdivision.

One or Two Words in a *Pashta* Segment

If the preceding word is closely connected in meaning to the *pashta* word, it is usually marked with a conjunctive *ta'am*. Most often that conjunctive is *mahpakh*.

Mahpakh pashta מַהְפַּךְ פַּשְׁטָא

Chant these words to the melody of *pashta*. בִּלַּע (2:5) בְּאֹהֶל (2:4)

Chant these words to the melody of *mahpakh pashta*.

יְמֵי עָנְיָהּ (1:7) וַיִּבְעַר בְּיַעֲקֹב (2:3) חֵטְא חָטְאָה (1:8) רוּחַ אַפֵּינוּ (4:20) הוֹרִידוּ לָאָרֶץ (2:10)

With elision: כִּי־עָלָה מָוֶת (Jer. 9:20) חֲזוּ לָךְ (2:14) סוּרוּ סוּרוּ (4:15)

If the accents are close to each other, the conjunctive will be *merekha* instead of *mahpakh*. There are only two examples of *merekha pashta*. In the *merekha-pashta* combination, the two accented syllables are contiguous—the *merekha* word is accented on the last syllable, and the *pashta* word has no pick-up. Thus the model for *pashta* must be sung on the syllable "TA," dropping the pick-up "pash-."

Merekha pashta מֵרְכָא פַּשְׁטָא

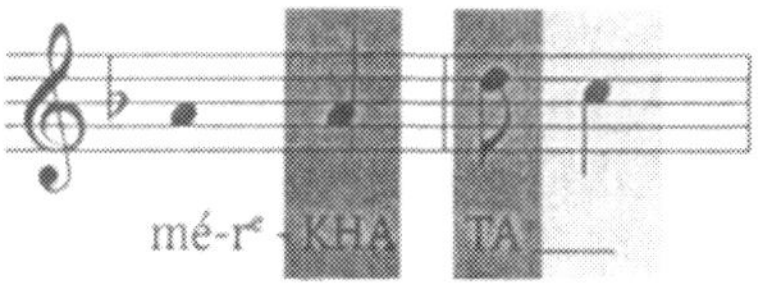

Chant these words to the melody of *merekha pashta*. יָדַע שׁוֹר (Isa. 1:3) כִּי־בִקְשׁוּ אֹכֶל (1:19)

Pashta is usually followed by either *zakef katon* or *munaḥ zakef katon*. Chant these examples. Make a subtle elongation or pause after *pashta*. Make a stronger pause or elongation after *zakef*.

פַּשְׁטָא֙ זָקֵ֔ף

וּרְא֙וּ מַכְאֹבִ֔י בְּתוּלֹתַ֥י וּבַחוּרַ֖י הָלְכ֥וּ בַשֶּֽׁבִי (1:18)

בְּאֹ֙הֶל֙ בַּת־צִיּ֔וֹן שָׁפַ֥ךְ כָּאֵ֖שׁ חֲמָתֽוֹ (2:4)

בִּלַּ֙ע֙ כָּל־אַרְמְנוֹתֶ֔יהָ שִׁחֵ֖ת מִבְצָרָ֑יו (2:5)

מַהְפַּ֤ךְ פַּשְׁטָא֙ זָקֵ֔ף

הָי֤וּ בָנַי֙ שֽׁוֹמֵמִ֔ים כִּ֥י גָבַ֖ר אוֹיֵֽב (1:16)

הִשְׁלִ֤יךְ מִשָּׁמַ֙יִם֙ אֶ֔רֶץ תִּפְאֶ֖רֶת יִשְׂרָאֵ֑ל (2:1)

נִצָּ֤ב יְמִינוֹ֙ כְּצָ֔ר וַֽיַּהֲרֹ֔ג כֹּ֖ל מַחֲמַדֵּי־עָ֑יִן (2:4)

מַהְפַּ֤ךְ פַּשְׁטָא֙ מוּנַ֣ח זָקֵ֔ף

כִּ֤י יָבֹא֙ צַ֣ר וְאוֹיֵ֔ב בְּשַׁעֲרֵ֖י יְרוּשָׁלִָֽם (4:12)

פְּנֵ֤י כֹהֲנִים֙ לֹ֣א נָשָׂ֔אוּ וּזְקֵנִ֖ים לֹ֥א חָנָֽנוּ (4:16)

כִּ֤י כֻלָּם֙ מְנָ֣אֲפִ֔ים עֲצֶ֖רֶת בֹּגְדִֽים (Jer. 9:1)

פַּשְׁטָא֙ זָקֵ֔ף פַּשְׁטָא֙ מוּנַ֣ח זָקֵ֔ף

וַהֲפִיצוֹתִים֙ בַּגּוֹיִ֔ם אֲשֶׁר֙ לֹ֣א יָדְע֔וּ הֵ֖מָּה וַאֲבוֹתָ֑ם (Jer. 9:15)

פַּשְׁטָא֙ פַּשְׁטָא֙ מוּנַ֣ח זָקֵ֔ף

לְנֶגְדְּכֶם֙ זָרִים֙ אֹכְלִ֣ים אֹתָ֔הּ וּשְׁמָמָ֖ה כְּמַהְפֵּכַ֥ת זָרִֽים (Isa. 1:7)

Chant these verses.

חֵ֤טְא חָֽטְאָה֙ יְר֣וּשָׁלַ֔͏ִם עַל־כֵּ֖ן לְנִידָ֣ה הָיָ֑תָה
כָּל־מְכַבְּדֶ֤יהָ הִזִּיל֙וּהָ֙ כִּֽי־רָא֣וּ עֶרְוָתָ֔הּ גַּם־הִ֥יא נֶאֶנְחָ֖ה וַתָּ֥שָׁב אָחֽוֹר׃ (1:8)

יָדַ֥ע שׁוֹר֙ קֹנֵ֔הוּ וַחֲמ֖וֹר אֵב֣וּס בְּעָלָ֑יו
יִשְׂרָאֵל֙ לֹ֣א יָדַ֔ע עַמִּ֖י לֹ֥א הִתְבּוֹנָֽן׃ (Isa. 1:3)

יָדוֹ֙ פָּ֣רַשׂ צָ֔ר עַ֖ל כָּל־מַחֲמַדֶּ֑יהָ
כִּֽי־רָאֲתָ֤ה גוֹיִם֙ בָּ֣אוּ מִקְדָּשָׁ֔הּ אֲשֶׁ֣ר צִוִּ֔יתָה לֹא־יָבֹ֥אוּ בַקָּהָ֖ל לָֽךְ׃ (1:10)

Yetiv

Yetiv is used instead of *pashta* if the word is accented on the first syllable and has no conjunctive words immediately preceding. *Yetiv* is found only on words accented on the first syllable, i.e., words with no pick-up. Thus the model must be sung on the syllable "TÍV," dropping the pick-up "y^{e}-."

Yetiv יְ֚תִיב

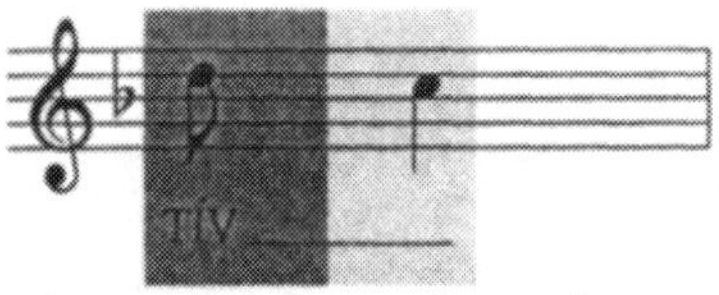

Chant these words to the melody of *yetiv*. הִ֚יא (1:3) כִּ֚י (5:22) כֹּ֚ל (1:7)

Yetiv is usually followed by either *zakef katon* or *munaḥ zakef katon*. Chant:

כֹּ֚ל מַחֲמֻדֶּ֔יהָ אֲשֶׁ֥ר הָי֖וּ מִ֣ימֵי קֶ֑דֶם (1:7)

כִּי אִם־מָאֹס מְאַסְתָּנוּ קָצַפְתָּ עָלֵינוּ עַד־מְאֹד: (5:22)

הִיא יָשְׁבָה בַגּוֹיִם לֹא מָצְאָה מָנוֹחַ (1:3)

כָּל קֶרֶן יִשְׂרָאֵל הֵשִׁיב אָחוֹר יְמִינוֹ מִפְּנֵי אוֹיֵב (2:3)

Three Words in a *Pashta* Segment

Sometimes *pashta* is preceded by two or more conjunctives. In these segments, there is a very slight elongation just before *pashta*.

The second conjunctive before *pashta* (preceding *mahpakh*) may be *kadmah*.

Kadmah mahpakh pashta   קַדְמָ֨ה מַהְפַּ֤ךְ פַּשְׁטָא֙

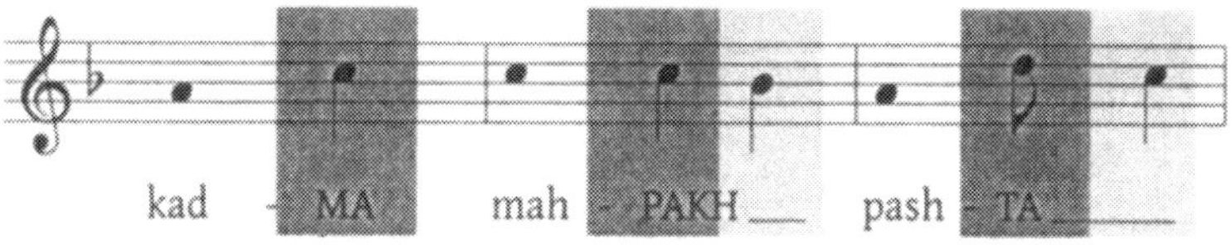

Chant these words to the melody of *kadmah mahpakh pashta*.

הָיוּ צָרֶ֙יהָ לְרֹאשׁ (1:5)   גָּלְתָ֤ה יְהוּדָ֤ה מֵעֹ֙נִי (1:3)   הוֹרִ֤ידִי כַנַּ֙חַל דִּמְעָה֙ (2:18)

If the second conjunctive before *pashta* (preceding *mahpakh*) is accented on the first syllable, it will be *munaḥ* instead of *kadmah*. This *munaḥ* is accented on its first syllable—*MU-nah*. This phrase is found only once in the Lamentations literature. It is also unusual in that *munaḥ* and *mahpakh* occur on the same word (שֶׁהֵ֤ם).

Munaḥ mahpakh pashta   מוּנַח מַהְפַּ֤ךְ פַּשְׁטָא֙

Chant these words to the melody of *munah mahpakh pashta*.   שֶׁהֵ֤ם יָז֙וּבוּ֙ (4:9)

Four Words in a *Pashta* Segment

On two occasions, *pashta* is preceded by three conjunctives. The third conjunctive before *pashta* (immediately preceding *kadmah*) is *telishah ketanah*.

Telishah kadmah mahpakh pashta   תְּלִישָׁה֙ קַדְמָ֨ה מַהְפַּ֤ךְ פַּשְׁטָא֙

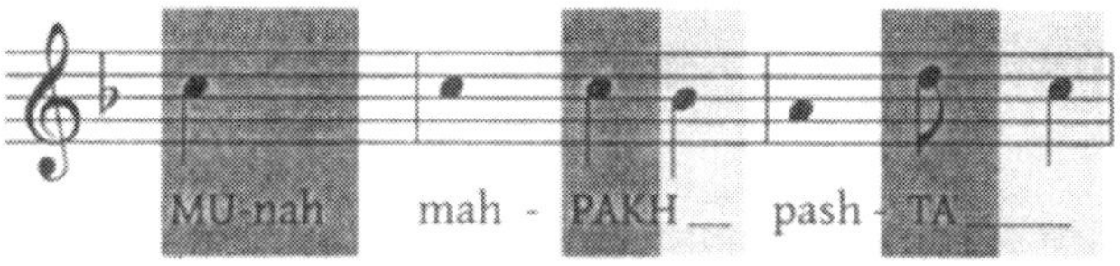

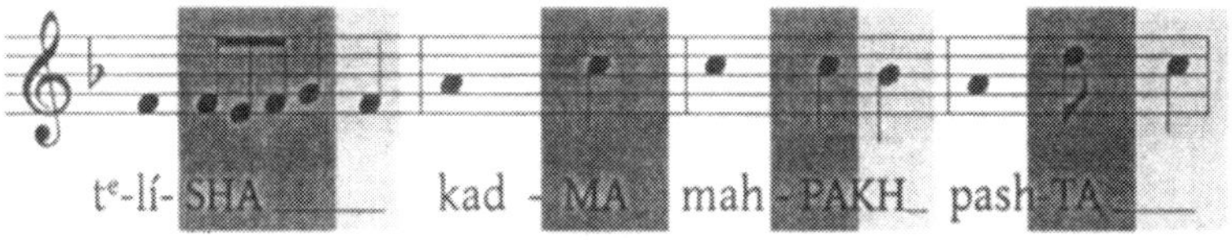

Chant these words to the melody of *telishah kadmah mahpakh pashta*.

אֵיכָ֙ה יָעִ֙יב בְּאַפּ֣וֹ ׀ אֲדֹנָי֙ (2:1)   תִּקְרָ֙א כְי֤וֹם מוֹעֵד֙ מְגוּרַי֙ (2:22)

Chant these verses.

הָי֨וּ צָרֶ֤יהָ לְרֹאשׁ֙ אֹיְבֶ֣יהָ שָׁל֔וּ כִּֽי־יְהוָ֥ה הוֹגָ֖הּ עַ֣ל רֹב־פְּשָׁעֶ֑יהָ עוֹלָלֶ֛יהָ הָלְכ֥וּ שְׁבִ֖י לִפְנֵי־צָֽר׃ (1:5)

גָּלְתָ֨ה יְהוּדָ֤ה מֵעֹ֙נִי֙ וּמֵרֹ֣ב עֲבֹדָ֔ה הִ֚יא יָשְׁבָ֣ה בַגּוֹיִ֔ם לֹ֥א מָצְאָ֖ה מָנ֑וֹחַ

כָּל־רֹדְפֶ֥יהָ הִשִּׂיג֖וּהָ בֵּ֥ין הַמְּצָרִֽים׃ (1:3)

טוֹבִ֤ים הָיוּ֙ חַֽלְלֵי־חֶ֔רֶב מֵחַלְלֵ֖י רָעָ֑ב שֶׁ֣הֵ֞ם יָז֣וּבוּ מְדֻקָּרִ֔ים מִתְּנוּבֹ֖ת שָׂדָֽי׃ (4:9)

אֵיכָה֩ יָעִ֨יב בְּאַפּ֤וֹ ׀ אֲדֹנָי֙ אֶת־בַּת־צִיּ֔וֹן הִשְׁלִ֤יךְ מִשָּׁמַ֙יִם֙ אֶ֔רֶץ תִּפְאֶ֖רֶת יִשְׂרָאֵ֑ל

וְלֹא־זָכַ֥ר הֲדֹם־רַגְלָ֖יו בְּי֥וֹם אַפּֽוֹ׃ (2:1)

The *Segol* Segment

Segol is the strongest disjunctive before *etnaḥta. Zarka* marks the subdivision within the *segol* segment. There is only one occurrence of a *segol* segment.

Munaḥ zarka munaḥ segol מוּנַ֣ח זַרְקָא֮ מוּנַ֣ח סֶגּוֹל֒

Chant these words to the melody of *munaḥ zarka munaḥ segol* .

לֹ֣וא אֲלֵיכֶם֮ כָּל־עֹ֣בְרֵי דֶרֶךְ֒ (1:12)

The *Revia* Segment

Revia is a medium-level disjunctive, found before *pashta* and *tevir* segments. *Revia* is stronger than any *pashta* or *tevir* that follow, but not as strong as *zakef* or *tippeḥa.*

One or Two Words in a *Revia* Segment

If the preceding word is closely connected in meaning to the *revia* word, it is usually marked with the conjunctive *munaḥ.*

Munaḥ revia מוּנַ֣ח רְבִ֗יעַ

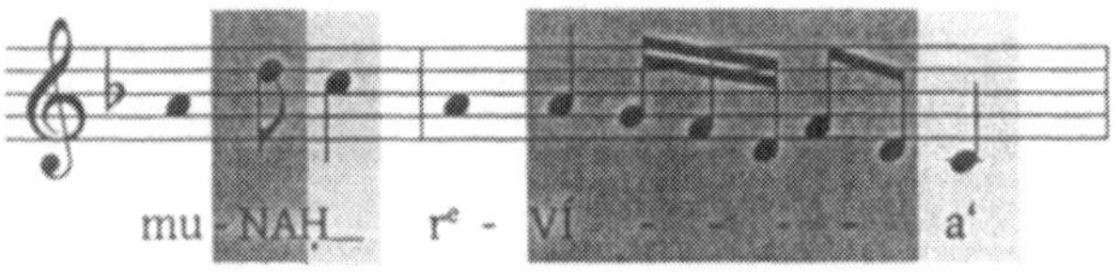

Chant these words to the melody of *revia.* (2:14) נְבִיאַ֗יִךְ (Jer. 8:22) כִּ֗י (Jer. 9:6) לָכֵ֗ן

Chant these words to the melody of *munaḥ revia.*

הָי֣וּ שָׂרֶ֗יהָ (1:6) מָ֣ה אֲדַמֶּה־לָּ֗ךְ (2:13) רֹ֣נִּי בַלַּ֗יְלָה (2:19) רַבָּ֣תִי בַגּוֹיִ֗ם (1:1)

The melody for this מוּנַ֣ח appears to be identical to that for פַּשְׁטָא֙. However, מוּנַ֣ח is chanted much quicker than פַּשְׁטָא֙, since the former is a conjunctive and the latter, a disjunctive.

Three Words in a *Revia* Segment

On four occasions, *revia* is preceded by two conjunctives. The second conjunctive before *revia* (preceding *munaḥ*) is *darga*. In these segments, there will be a very slight elongation just before *revia.*

Darga munaḥ revia דַּרְגָּא מוּנַח רְבִיעַ

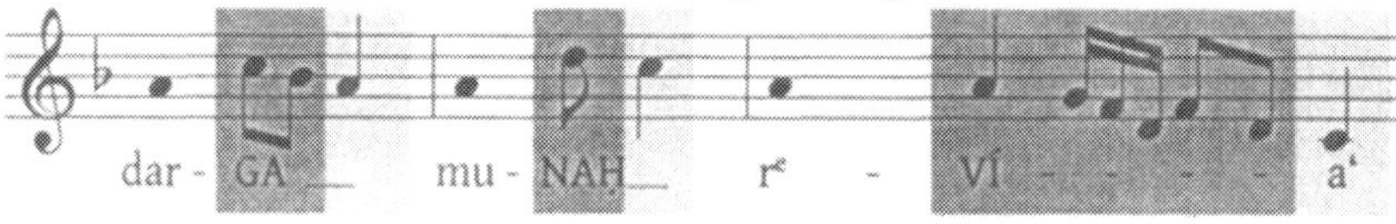

Chant these words to the melody of *darga munaḥ revia.*

בִּנְפֹל עַמָּהּ בְּיַד־צָר (1:7) שְׂאִי אֵלָיו כַּפַּיִךְ (2:19) אֶשָּׂא בְכִי וָנֶהִי (Jer. 9:9) כִּי נֶאֱנָחָה אָנִי (1:21)

Chant these examples. Connect each conjunctive word to the word that follows. Create an elongation or pause after *revia.* Create a very slight elongation after *pashta* or *tevir.*

(מוּנַח) רְבִיעַ פַּשְׁטָא מוּנַח זָקֵף
הָיוּ שָׂרֶיהָ כְּאַיָּלִים לֹא־מָצְאוּ מִרְעֶה (1:6)
הֲזֹאת הָעִיר שֶׁיֹּאמְרוּ כְּלִילַת יֹפִי (2:15)
כִּי מַדּוּעַ לֹא עָלְתָה (Jer. 8:22)

רְבִיעַ פַּשְׁטָא פַּשְׁטָא מוּנַח זָקֵף
אַדְמַתְכֶם לְנֶגְדְּכֶם זָרִים אֹכְלִים אֹתָהּ (Isa. 1:7)

דַּרְגָּא מוּנַח רְבִיעַ מַהְפַּךְ פַּשְׁטָא זָקֵף
בִּנְפֹל עַמָּהּ בְּיַד־צָר וְאֵין עוֹזֵר לָהּ (1:7)
אֶשָּׂא בְכִי וָנֶהִי וְעַל־נְאוֹת מִדְבָּר קִינָה (Jer. 9:9)

(מוּנַח) רְבִיעַ מַהְפַּךְ פַּשְׁטָא (מוּנַח) זָקֵף
זָכְרָה יְרוּשָׁלִַם יְמֵי עָנְיָהּ וּמְרוּדֶיהָ (1:7)
נְבִיאַיִךְ חָזוּ לָךְ שָׁוְא וְתָפֵל (2:14)
בְּפִיו שָׁלוֹם אֶת־רֵעֵהוּ יְדַבֵּר (Jer. 9:7)

דַּרְגָּא מוּנַח רְבִיעַ פַּשְׁטָא זָקֵף
שְׂאִי אֵלָיו כַּפַּיִךְ עַל־נֶפֶשׁ עוֹלָלַיִךְ (2:19)

(מוּנַח) רְבִיעַ יְתִיב (מוּנַח) זָקֵף
גָּדַע בָּחֳרִי־אַף כֹּל קֶרֶן יִשְׂרָאֵל (2:3)
דַּבֵּר כֹּה נְאֻם־יְהוָה (Jer. 9:21)

מוּנַח רְבִיעַ תְּבִיר מֵרְכָא טִפְּחָא
מְלֵאֲתִי מִשְׁפָּט צֶדֶק יָלִין בָּהּ וְעַתָּה מְרַצְּחִים׃ (Isa. 1:21)

Chant these verses.

סָפְקוּ עָלַיִךְ כַּפַּיִם כָּל־עֹבְרֵי דֶרֶךְ שָׁרְקוּ וַיָּנִעוּ רֹאשָׁם עַל־בַּת יְרוּשָׁלִָם
הֲזֹאת הָעִיר שֶׁיֹּאמְרוּ כְּלִילַת יֹפִי מָשׂוֹשׂ לְכָל־הָאָרֶץ׃ (2:15)

מִי־יִתְּנֵנִי בַמִּדְבָּר מְלוֹן אֹרְחִים וְאֶעֶזְבָה אֶת־עַמִּי וְאֵלְכָה מֵאִתָּם
כִּי כֻלָּם מְנָאֲפִים עֲצֶרֶת בֹּגְדִים׃ (Jer. 9:1)

אַרְצְכֶם שְׁמָמָה עָרֵיכֶם שְׂרֻפוֹת אֵשׁ
אַדְמַתְכֶם לְנֶגְדְּכֶם זָרִים אֹכְלִים אֹתָהּ וּשְׁמָמָה כְּמַהְפֵּכַת זָרִים׃ (Isa. 1:7)

The *Legarmeh* Segment

Sometimes there is a subdivision within a *revia* segment. On four occasions, the *ta'am* that marks that subdivision will be *legarmeh.*

Legarmeh לְגַרְמֵה ׀

Chant these words to the melody of *legarmeh.*

אֵיכָה ׀ (1:1)   הוֹי ׀ (Isa. 1:4)   קוּמִי ׀ (2:19)   עַל־אֵלֶּה ׀ (1:16)

The melody for *legarmeh* appears to be identical to that of *telishah ketanah*. However *telishah ketanah* is chanted quicker than *legarmeh*, since the former is a conjunctive and the latter, a minor disjunctive.

Legarmeh is always followed by *munaḥ revia*. Chant these phrases.

אֵיכָה ׀ יָשְׁבָה בָדָד הָעִיר רַבָּתִי עָם (1:1)

קוּמִי ׀ רֹנִּי בַלַּיְלָה לְרֹאשׁ אַשְׁמֻרוֹת (2:19)

הוֹי ׀ גּוֹי חֹטֵא עַם כֶּבֶד עָוֹן (Isa. 1:4)

The *Geresh* Segment

Another *ta'am* that can subdivide a *revia* segment (or a *pashta* segment) is *geresh*. There are two basic forms of *geresh*, each with its own distinct melody: (single) *geresh*, and double *geresh*, called *gereshayim*.

Two Words in a *Geresh* Segment

In Lamentations, *geresh* always appears with its preceding conjunctive, *kadmah*.

Kadmah (ve-)geresh קַדְמָה גֶּרֶשׁ

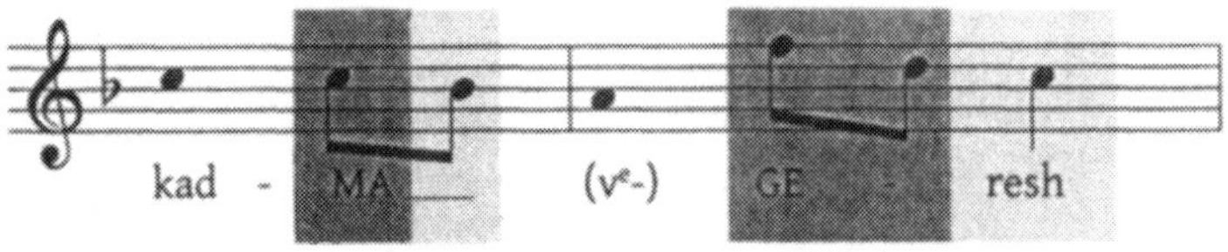

Chant these words to the melody of *kadmah geresh.*

בָּכוֹ תִבְכֶּה (1:2)   פֵּרְשָׂה צִיּוֹן (1:17)   בִּלַּע אֲדֹנָי (2:2)   עֹל פְּשָׁעַי (1:14)

Kadmah geresh is followed by either *revia* or *pashta*:

בָּכוֹ תִבְכֶּה בַּלַּיְלָה (1:2)   בִּלַּע אֲדֹנָי וְלֹא חָמַל (2:2)

עַל־הֶהָרִים אֶשָּׂא בְכִי וָנֶהִי (Jer 9:9)   כָּל־אֹיְבַי שָׁמְעוּ רָעָתִי שָׂשׂוּ (1:21)

Three Words in the *Geresh* Segment

On one occasion *geresh* is preceded by two conjunctives.

Telishah kadmah geresh תְּלִישָׁה קַדְמָה גֶּרֶשׁ

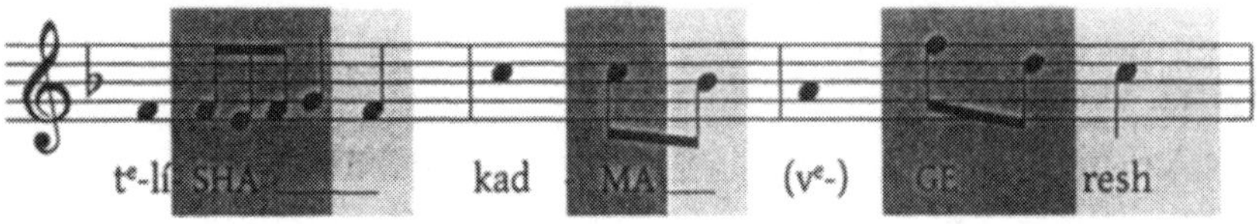

Chant these words to the melody of *telishah kadmah geresh*. נִשְׂקַד֩ עֹ֨ל פְּשָׁעַ֜י (1:14)

Gereshayim

The double *geresh* is called *gereshayim*. The conjunctive of *gereshayim* is *munaḥ*. The word bearing *gereshayim* is always accented on the last syllable, and the word bearing *munaḥ* is always accented on the first syllable. *Gereshayim* appears only five times, once with its conjunctive, *munaḥ*.

Munaḥ gereshayim מֻ֣ונַח גֵּרְשַׁ֞יִם

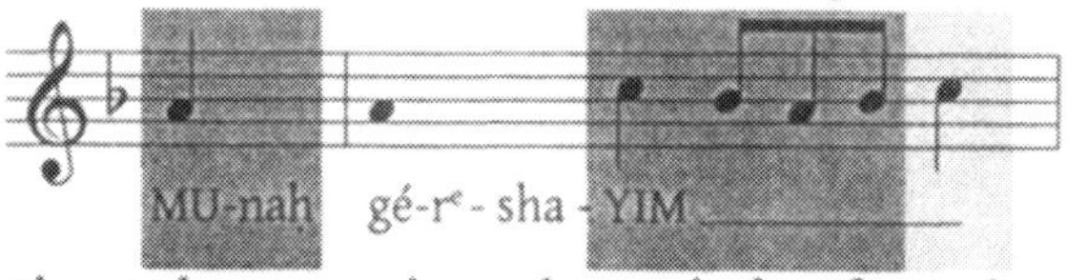

Chant these words to the melody of *gereshayim*. כֹּֽה־אָמַ֞ר (Jer 9:14) מָֽה־אֲעִידֵ֞ךְ (2:13)

Chant these words to the melody of *munaḥ gereshayim*. ס֣וּרוּ טָמֵ֞א (4:15)

Chant these phrases. Connect each conjunctive to the word that follows. Create an appropriate elongation or pause after *revia, pashta,* or *tevir*. Create only a slight elongation after *geresh* or *gereshayim*.

מָֽה־אֲעִידֵ֞ךְ מָ֣ה אֲדַמֶּה־לָּ֗ךְ הַבַּת֙ יְר֣וּשָׁלַ֔͏ִם (2:13)

הִנֵּה־ק֞וֹל שַׁוְעַ֣ת בַּת־עַמִּ֗י מֵאֶ֙רֶץ֙ מַרְחַקִּ֔ים (Jer. 8:19)

ס֣וּרוּ טָמֵ֞א קָ֣רְאוּ לָ֗מוֹ ס֤וּרוּ ס֙וּרוּ֙ אַל־תִּגָּ֔עוּ (4:15)

שָׁמְע֞וּ כִּ֣י נֶאֱנָחָ֣ה אָ֗נִי אֵ֤ין מְנַחֵם֙ לִ֔י (1:21)

לָ֠כֵן כֹּֽה־אָמַ֞ר יְהוָ֤ה צְבָאוֹת֙ אֱלֹהֵ֣י יִשְׂרָאֵ֔ל (Jer. 9:14)

Telishah Gedolah

Telishah gedolah is a minor disjunctive that appears twice as a subdivision of a *pashta* segment. Once, it appears with its conjunctive, *munaḥ*.

Munaḥ telishah (gedolah) מ֣וּנַח תְּ֠לִישָׁה

Chant these words to the melody of *munaḥ telishah gedolah*. חוֹמַ֣ת בַּת־צִ֠יּוֹן (2:18)

Chant these phrases.

חוֹמַ֣ת בַּת־צִ֠יּוֹן הוֹרִ֨ידִי כַנַּ֤חַל דִּמְעָה֙ יוֹמָ֣ם וָלַ֔יְלָה (2:18)

כִּ֠י אֵיכָכָ֤ה אוּכַל֙ וְֽרָאִ֔יתִי בָּרָעָ֖ה אֲשֶׁר־יִמְצָ֣א אֶת־עַמִּ֑י (Esther 8:6)

The Final Cadence

We use a special melody to signal the ending of each chapter of Lamentations. This melody is applied at the final (*merekha-*) *tippeḥa* segment. You'll chant this cadence slowly. This special cadence is not applied to chapter three, which is chanted to a completely different melody (see p. 107).

מֵרְכָא טִפְּחָא מֵרְכָא סִילוּק

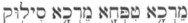

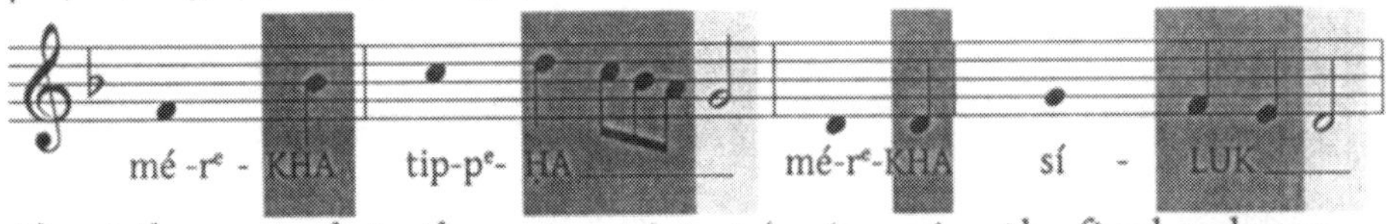
mé -rᵉ - KHA
tip-pᵉ- HA
mé-rᵉ-KHA
sí - LUK

Chant these words to the appropriate *te'amim*, using the final cadence.

כִּֽי־רַבּ֥וֹת אַנְחֹתַ֖י וְלִבִּ֥י דַוָּֽי׃ (1:22)

אֲשֶׁר־טִפַּ֥חְתִּי וְרִבִּ֖יתִי אֹיְבִ֥י כִלָּֽם׃ (2:22)

גִּלָּ֖ה עַל־חַטֹּאתָֽיִךְ׃ (4:22)

חַדֵּ֥שׁ יָמֵ֖ינוּ כְּקֶֽדֶם׃ (5:21)

Chant these verses, using the final cadence.

תָּבֹ֨א כָל־רָעָתָ֤ם לְפָנֶ֙יךָ֙ וְעוֹלֵ֣ל לָ֔מוֹ כַּאֲשֶׁ֧ר עוֹלַ֛לְתָּ לִ֖י עַ֣ל כָּל־פְּשָׁעָ֑י

כִּֽי־רַבּ֥וֹת אַנְחֹתַ֖י וְלִבִּ֥י דַוָּֽי׃ (1:22)

תִּקְרָא֩ כְי֨וֹם מוֹעֵ֤ד מְגוּרַי֙ מִסָּבִ֔יב וְלֹ֥א הָיָ֛ה בְּי֥וֹם אַף־יְהוָ֖ה פָּלִ֣יט וְשָׂרִ֑יד

אֲשֶׁר־טִפַּ֥חְתִּי וְרִבִּ֖יתִי אֹיְבִ֥י כִלָּֽם׃ (2:22)

In a liturgical setting, it is customary to avoid concluding a reading of Scripture with words of discouragement. Therefore, the end of the book of Lamentations is chanted in the following manner.

- The reader chants through verse 20 of chapter 5. (In some traditions, the congregation chants verse 21 aloud.)
- The reader then chants verses 21 and 22, using the normal melody.
- The congregation chants verse 21 using the final cadence.
- The reader chants verse 21 using the final cadence.

Chanting Chapter Three

The third chapter of Lamentations, consisting of 66 short verses, is not cantillated according to the *te'amim*. Instead, it is chanted to a special melody that combines every three verses into one strophe of melody. The half-cadence of each line of the strophe (indicated by the first fermata of each line) is chanted on the first word marked with *zakef* (or, if there is no *zakef*, *tippeḥa*).

Hear the chanting of chapter three on CD track 87.

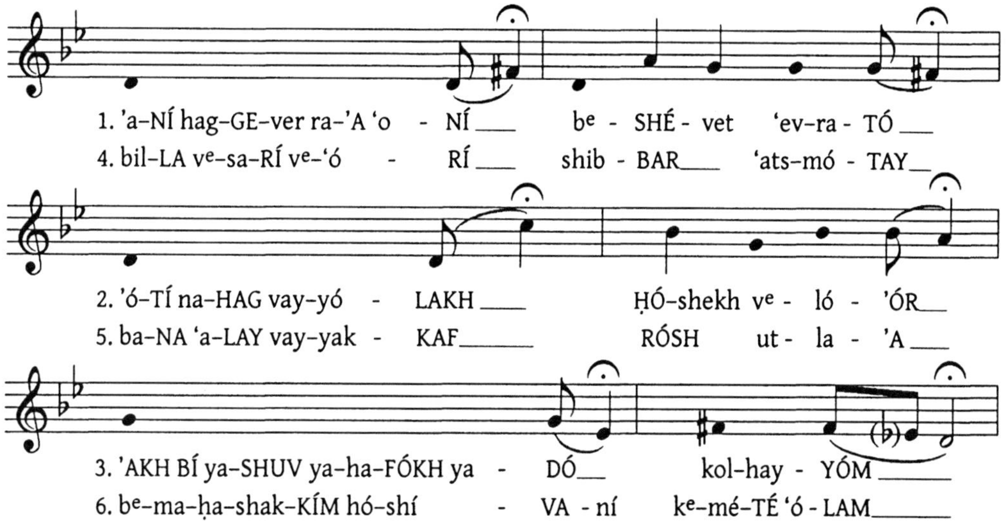
1. 'a–NÍ hag–GE–ver ra–'A 'o - NÍ___ be - SHÉ - vet 'ev–ra - TÓ___
4. bil–LA ve–sa–RÍ ve–'ó - RÍ___ shib - BAR___ 'ats–mó - TAY___
2. 'ó–TÍ na–HAG vay–yó - LAKH___ ḤÓ–shekh ve - ló - 'ÓR___
5. ba–NA 'a–LAY vay–yak - KAF___ RÓSH ut - la - 'A___
3. 'AKH BÍ ya–SHUV ya–ha–FÓKH ya - DÓ___ kol–hay - YÓM___
6. be–ma–ḥa–shak–KÍM hó–shí - VA - ní ke–mé–TÉ 'ó - LAM___
(♭)

אֲנִי הַגֶּבֶר רָאָה עֳנִי בְּשֵׁבֶט עֶבְרָתוֹ׃ (3:1)

אוֹתִי נָהַג וַיֹּלַךְ חֹשֶׁךְ וְלֹא־אוֹר׃ (3:2)

אַךְ בִּי יָשֻׁב יַהֲפֹךְ יָדוֹ כָּל־הַיּוֹם׃ (3:3)

בִּלָּה בְשָׂרִי וְעוֹרִי שִׁבַּר עַצְמוֹתָי׃ (3:4)

בָּנָה עָלַי וַיַּקַּף רֹאשׁ וּתְלָאָה׃ (3:5)

בְּמַחֲשַׁכִּים הוֹשִׁיבַנִי כְּמֵתֵי עוֹלָם׃ (3:6)

7. Haftarah

Contemporary Traditional Practice

In traditional synagogues, a portion from one of the "prophetic books" of the Bible is chanted after reading the Torah on *Shabbatot*, festivals, and fast days. This practice is known as the *haftarah* (הפטרה) (*haf-ta-<u>rah</u>*). The person who chants the *haftarah* is called the *maftir* (מפטיר) (*maf-<u>tir</u>*). On *Shabbatot* and festivals, a *haftarah* is chanted during the morning service (שחרית); on most fast days it is chanted at the afternoon service (מנחה) only. On Yom Kippur and Tish'ah Be'Av, a *haftarah* is chanted after the Torah reading in both the morning and afternoon services.

The content of the *haftarah* is usually linked to the Torah reading of the day. For example, on the Shabbat when *parashat* Beshallaḥ (Exod. 13:17–17:16) is read from the Torah, the fourth and fifth chapters of the book of *Shofetim* (Judges) are read as the *haftarah.* Thus the song of Moses and Miriam celebrating the defeat of the Egyptian army (*Shirat Ha-yam*—Exod. 15) is followed by the song of Deborah celebrating the defeat of the armies of Sisera (*Shirat Devorah*—Judg. 4–5).

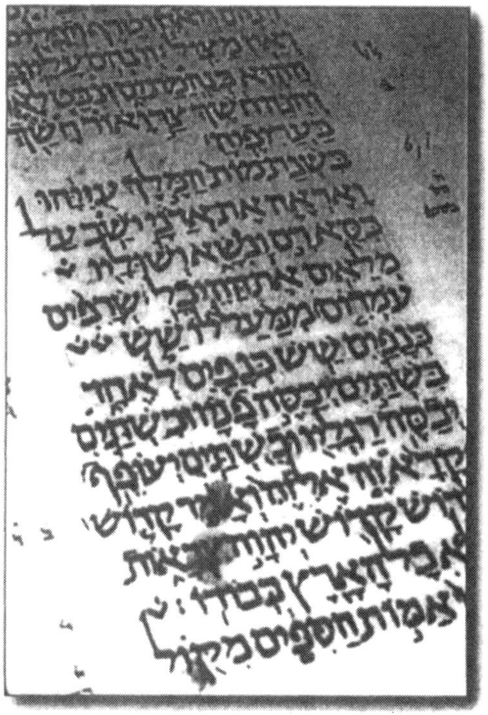

Some *haftarot*, however, are linked to the liturgical calendar rather than to the theme of the Torah portion. On three *Shabbatot* in the middle of the summer, from the Shabbat before the fast of Shiv'ah Asar Betamuz to the Shabbat before the fast of Tish'ah Be'Av, the *haftarot* of punishment (תלתא דפרענותא—שלשה של פרענות) are chanted. The seasonal theme of the destruction of the Sanctuary supersedes the connection with the Torah reading. On the following seven *Shabbatot*, from the Shabbat after the fast of Tish'ah Be'Av until the Shabbat before Rosh Hashanah, the *haftarot* of consolation (שבעה דנחמתא) are chanted. The seasonal theme of consolation after the destruction of the Sanctuary supersedes the connection with the Torah reading.

When Shabbat coincides with Rosh Ḥodesh (celebration of the new moon), and on the Shabbat before a Sunday Rosh Ḥodesh, special *haftarot* are chanted that mention Rosh Ḥodesh celebrations in ancient times. On the Shabbat before Yom Kippur (Shabbat Shuvah), the Shabbat of Hanukkah, and on five "special" *Shabbatot* in late winter (Shekalim, Zakhor, Parah, Ha-ḥodesh, and Ha-gadol), *haftarot* appropriate to the season are read instead of the *haftarah* that is linked to the Torah portion. On festivals and fast days, *haftarot* appropriate to those occasions are chanted.

On a Shabbat when two Torah *parashiyot* are combined, the *haftarah* of the *second parashah* is chanted. For example, in the spring of a non-leap-year, when בהר and בחקתי are both read on the same Shabbat, the *haftarah* of בחקתי is chanted; that year the *haftarah* of בהר is not heard. There is one exception to this rule. When אחרי מות and קדשים are read on the same Shabbat, the *haftarah* of אחרי מות is read (הלא כבני כושיים—Amos 9:7–15). The appropriate *haftarah* for any occasion can be found in most editions of the *Ḥumash*.

The Melodies of the Cantillation Motifs

Hear the melodies of the Haftarah cantillation on CD tracks 74–76.

The *Siluk* Segment and *Tippeḥa* Segment

The last word in every verse is marked with *siluk*. If the preceding word is closely connected in meaning to the *siluk* word, it is usually marked with the conjunctive *ta'am merekha* (מֵרְכָא סִילְוּק).

A *siluk* segment is subdivided by the disjunctive *ta'am tippeḥa*. If there are two words in the *tippeḥa* segment, the first one is usually marked with the conjunctive *ta'am merekha* (מֵרְכָא טִפְּחָא).

Merekha tippeḥa merekha siluk מֵרְכָא טִפְּחָא מֵרְכָא סִילְוּק

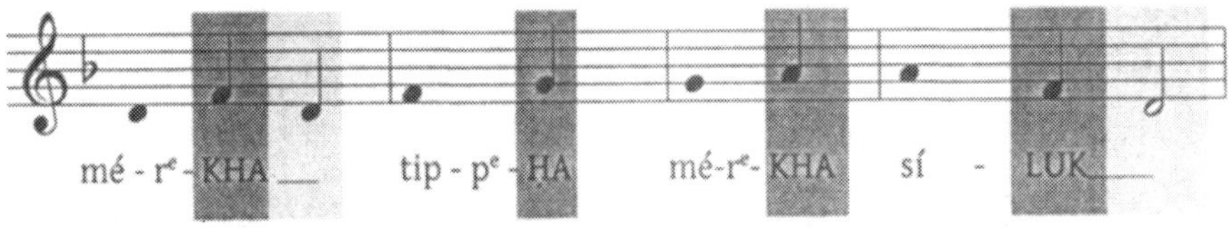

Chant these words to the appropriate *te'amim*. Connect each conjunctive (*merekha*) to the word that follows. Pause slightly after the disjunctive *ta'am, tippeḥa*.

מֵרְכָא טִפְּחָא מֵרְכָא סִילְוּק

לִבְרִית עָם לְאוֹר גּוֹיִם: (Isa. 42:6)

וּלְאֵין אוֹנִים עָצְמָה יַרְבֶּה: (Isa. 40:29)

מִבֵּית כֶּלֶא יֹשְׁבֵי חֹשֶׁךְ: (Isa. 42:7)

זְעֵיר שָׁם זְעֵיר שָׁם: *Merekha tippeḥa* with elision: (Isa. 28:10)

שַׁקַּמְתִּי אֵם בְּיִשְׂרָאֵל: *Merekha tippeḥa* with elision: (Judg. 5:7)

מֵרְכָא טִפְּחָא סִילְוּק

וְנָשָׂא אֶתְכֶם אֵלָיו: (Mal. 2:3)

וַיֶּאְשַׁם בַּבַּעַל וַיָּמֹת: (Hos. 13:1)

וּמוֹשִׁיעַ אַיִן בִּלְתִּי: (Hos. 13:4)

וְנָתָן הַנָּבִיא בָּא: (1 Kings 1:22)

Tippeḥa Elision

Even though *tippeḥa* is a disjunctive *ta'am*, you may elide it to the *siluk* word that follows, if that word is accented on the first syllable.

Merekha tippeḥa siluk מֵרְכָא טִפְּחָא סִילְוּק

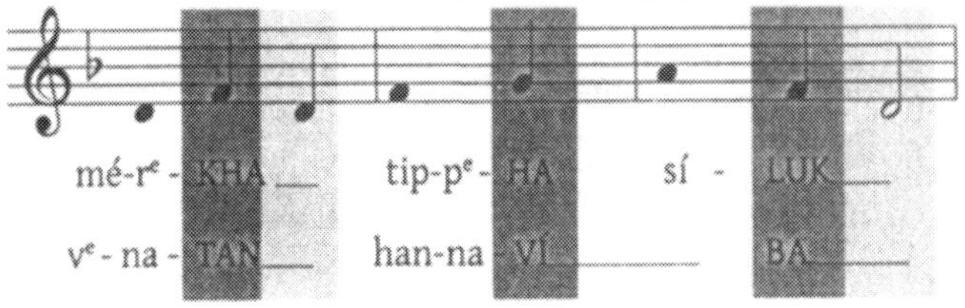

טִפְּחָא מֵרְכָא סִילוּק

יְחִי הַמֶּלֶךְ אֲדֹנִיָּהוּ׃ (1 Kings 1:25)

כִּי אִם־אָסוּךְ שָׁמֶן׃ (2 Kings 4:2)

וַיָּקָם וַיֵּלֶךְ אַחֲרֶיהָ׃ (2 Kings 4:30)

טִפְּחָא סִילוּק

הִיא אִמּוֹ׃ (1 Kings 3:27)

מֻשְׁכָּב עַל־מִטָּתוֹ׃ (2 Kings 4:32)

וַתַּעֲמֹדְנָה לְפָנָיו׃ (1 Kings 3:16)

Merekha-khefulah

Merekha-khefulah is a rare substitution for (single) *merekha*. It occurs in one *haftarah* that is read twice: Shabbat Beha'alotekha and Shabbat Hanukkah. *Merekha-khefulah* is preceded by another conjunctive, *darga*.

Darga merekha-khefulah tippeḥa דַּרְגָא מֵרְכָא־כְפוּלָה טִפְּחָא

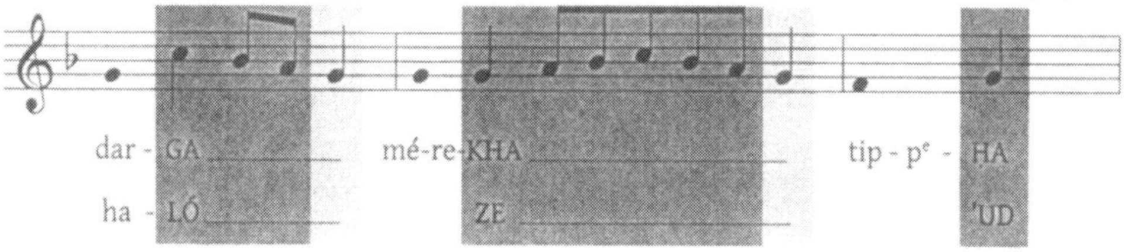

הֲלוֹא זֶה אוּד מֻצָּל מֵאֵשׁ (Zech. 3:2)

The *Etnaḥta* Segment and *Tippeḥa* Segment

Most verses are divided into two segments. *Etnaḥta* is the *ta'am* that marks the end of the first segment, and *siluk* marks the end of the second segment. If the *etnaḥta* word and the word before it are closely connected in meaning, they are usually marked *munaḥ etnaḥta* (מוּנַח אֶתְנַחְתָּא).

An *etnaḥta* segment is also subdivided by the disjunctive *ta'am tippeḥa*. If there are two words in the *tippeḥa* segment, the first one is usually marked with the conjunctive *ta'am merekha* (מֵרְכָא טִפְּחָא).

Merekha tippeḥa munaḥ etnaḥta מֵרְכָא טִפְּחָא מוּנַח אֶתְנַחְתָּא

Chant these words to the appropriate *te'amim*. Connect each conjunctive (*merekha* or *munaḥ*) to the word that follows. Pause slightly after the disjunctive *ta'am*, *tippeḥa*.

מֵרְכָא טִפְּחָא מוּנַח אֶתְנַחְתָּא

אִישׁ לְאָחִיו וְאִישׁ לְרֵעֵהוּ (Jer. 34:17)

לִקְרֹא דְרוֹר אִישׁ לְרֵעֵהוּ (Jer. 34:15)

מִבְּנֵי חֹבָב חֹתֵן מֹשֶׁה (Judg. 4:11)

אִם־לֹ֣א בְרִיתִ֔י יוֹמָ֣ם וָלָ֑יְלָה (Jer. 33:25) *munaḥ etnaḥta* elision:

הוֹצִיאִ֣י אוֹתָ֔ם מֵאֶ֥רֶץ מִצְרָ֑יִם (Jer. 7:22) *munaḥ etnaḥta* elision:)

מֵרְכָ֥א טִפְּחָ֖א אֶתְנַחְתָּ֑א

אֶת־סֻכַּ֥ת דָּוִ֖יד הַנֹּפֶ֑לֶת (Amos 9:11) לֹ֥א יָב֖וֹא לְטָמְאָ֑ה (Ezek. 44:25)

בָּ֥א אֵלֶ֖יךָ לֵאמֹ֑ר (Jer. 32:7)

נָגַ֥ע זֶ֖ה עַל־שְׂפָתֶ֑יךָ (Isa. 6:7) *merekha tippeḥa* elision:

מְדַבֶּ֥רֶת שָׁ֖ם עִם־הַמֶּ֑לֶךְ (1 Kings 1:14) *merekha tippeḥa* elision:

טִפְּחָ֖א מוּנַ֣ח אֶתְנַחְתָּ֑א

בָּאָ֕רֶץ אֲשֶׁ֣ר לֹא־יָדָ֑עְתָּ (Jer. 17:4) עַ֕ד לַעֲל֣וֹת הַמִּנְחָ֑ה (1 Kings 18:29)

וּמְנוּסִ֖י בְּי֣וֹם צָרָ֑ה (Jer. 16:19) הִנֵּ֖ה נָתָ֣ן הַנָּבִ֑יא (1 Kings 1:23)

אַף־יַשִּׂ֖יק וְאָ֣פָה לָ֑חֶם (Isa. 44:15) *munaḥ etnaḥta* elision:

טִפְּחָ֖א אֶתְנַחְתָּ֑א

אֶל־יְהוֹשֻׁ֖עַ בִּן־נ֑וּן (Josh. 2:23) אַחֲרִ֖ישׁ אֶתְאַפָּ֑ק (Isa. 42:14)

עַד־שָׁ֖בוּ הָרֹדְפִ֑ים (Josh. 2:22)

Chant these verses.

וְהָלְכ֥וּ גוֹיִ֖ם לְאוֹרֵ֑ךְ וּמְלָכִ֖ים לְנֹ֥גַהּ זַרְחֵֽךְ׃ (Isa. 60:3)

תָּרֹ֥ם יָדְךָ֖ עַל־צָרֶ֑יךָ וְכָל־אֹיְבֶ֖יךָ יִכָּרֵֽתוּ׃ (Mic. 5:8)

אִ֥ישׁ אֶת־רֵעֵ֖הוּ יַעְזֹ֑רוּ וּלְאָחִ֖יו יֹאמַ֥ר חֲזָֽק׃ (Isa. 41:6)

וַיֹּ֥אמֶר הַמֶּ֖לֶךְ קְח֣וּ לִי־חָ֑רֶב וַיָּבִ֥אוּ הַחֶ֖רֶב לִפְנֵ֥י הַמֶּֽלֶךְ׃ (1 Kings 3:24)

וַיְהִ֥י הַיּ֖וֹם וַיָּ֣בֹא שָׁ֑מָּה וַיָּ֥סַר אֶל־הָעֲלִיָּ֖ה וַיִּשְׁכַּב־שָֽׁמָּה׃ (2 Kings 4:11)

וַיְהִ֖י מִיָּמִ֑ים וַיִּלָּחֲמ֥וּ בְנֵי־עַמּ֖וֹן עִם־יִשְׂרָאֵֽל׃ (Judg. 11:4)

וְהִכְרַתִּ֖י עָרֵ֣י אַרְצֶ֑ךָ וְהָרַסְתִּ֖י כָּל־מִבְצָרֶֽיךָ׃ (Mic. 5:10)

אִם־תֹּאב֖וּ וּשְׁמַעְתֶּ֑ם ט֥וּב הָאָ֖רֶץ תֹּאכֵֽלוּ׃ (Isa. 1:19)

The *Tevir* Segment

Sometimes there is a subdivision within a *tippeḥa* segment. *Tevir* is the *ta'am* that marks that subdivision.

Tevir תְּבִ֛יר

Chant these words to the melody of *tevir.*

יָג֛וּר (Isa. 54:15) יַֽעֲקֹ֛ב (Isa. 42:24) שָׁ֛ם (1 Kings 8:9) לָ֛מָּה (2 Sam. 7:7) עֹשֶׂ֛ךָ (Isa. 44:2)

Two Words in a *Tevir* Segment

If the preceding word is closely connected in meaning to the *tevir* word, it is usually marked with a conjunctive *ta'am.* Most often that conjunctive is *darga.*

Darga tevir דַּרְגָּ֧א תְּבִ֛יר

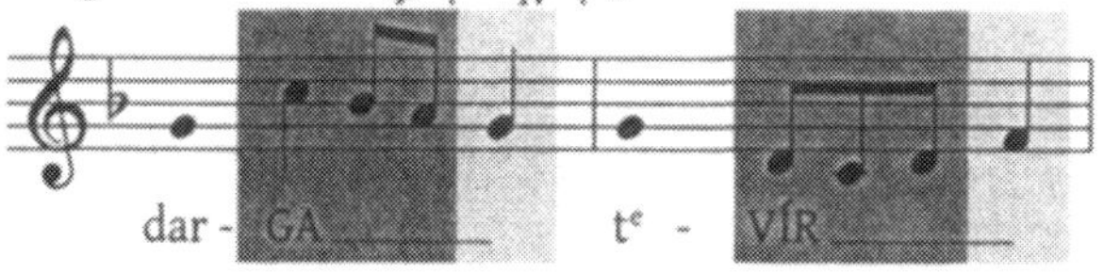

Chant these words to the melody of *darga tevir.*

קָד֧וֹשׁ ׀ קָד֛וֹשׁ (Isa. 6:3) אָנֹכִ֧י אָנֹכִ֛י (Isa. 51:12)

בֵּ֧ין הָֽרָמָ֛ה (Judg. 4:5) יַ֧עַן הֱיוֹתָ֛ם (Ezek. 29:6) וּמֶ֧לֶךְ אֶחָ֛ד (Ezek. 37:22)

If the accents are close to each other, the conjunctive will be *merekha* instead of *darga.*

Merekha tevir מֵרְכָ֥א תְּבִ֛יר

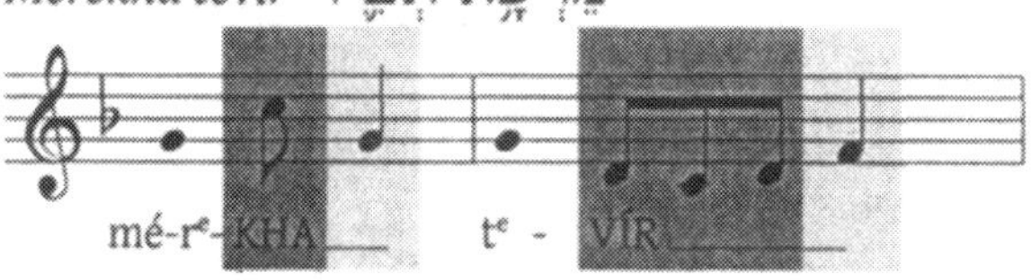

Chant these words to the melody of *merekha tevir.*

רִדְפ֥וּ מַהֵ֛ר (Josh. 2:5) וַאֲשֶׁ֥ר דִּבַּ֛רְתָּ (Jer. 32:24) כִּ֥י לְךָ֛ (Jer. 32:7) הִרְבֵּ֥יתִי לָ֛הּ (Hos. 2:10)

Chant these phrases. Connect each conjunctive to the word that follows. Create a slight elongation or pause after *tippeḥa.* There is very little elongation after *tevir.* The sense of the words dictates that *tippeḥa* is a stronger disjunctive than *tevir.* Remember that the melody for *merekha tippeḥa* before *siluk* is different from the melody of *merekha tippeḥa* before *etnaḥta.* Look at the end of each example before you begin to chant.

תְּבִ֛יר טִפְּחָ֖א

לְהָשִׁ֛יב אֶל־הַיַּבָּשָׁ֖ה וְלֹ֣א יָכֹ֑לוּ (Jon. 1:13)

תְּבִ֛יר מֵרְכָ֥א טִפְּחָ֖א

וְאֶתֶּנְךָ֛ לִבְרִ֥ית עָ֖ם לְא֥וֹר גּוֹיִֽם׃ (Isa. 42:6) הֵ֛ן עֵ֥ד לְאוּמִּ֖ים נְתַתִּ֑יו (Isa. 55:4)

מֵרְכָ֥א תְּבִ֛יר טִפְּחָ֖א

וַיִּשְׂמַ֥ח יוֹנָ֛ה עַל־הַקִּֽיקָי֖וֹן שִׂמְחָ֥ה גְדוֹלָֽה׃ (Jon. 4:6) הִגִּ֥יד לְךָ֛ אָדָ֖ם מַה־טּ֑וֹב (Mic. 6:8)

מֵרְכָ֥א תְּבִ֛יר מֵרְכָ֥א טִפְּחָ֖א

וַתַּ֥ךְ הַשֶּׁ֛מֶשׁ עַל־רֹ֥אשׁ יוֹנָ֖ה וַיִּתְעַלָּ֑ף (Jon. 4:8) עוּרִ֥י עוּרִ֛י לִבְשִׁ֥י עֻזֵּ֖ךְ צִיּ֑וֹן (Isa. 52:1)

דַּרְגָּ֧א תְּבִ֛יר טִפְּחָ֖א

וִירִיע֧וֹת מִשְׁכְּנוֹתַ֛יִךְ יַטּ֖וּ אַל־תַּחְשֹׂ֑כִי (Isa. 54:2) הַסַּ֧עַר הַגָּד֛וֹל הַזֶּ֖ה עֲלֵיכֶֽם׃ (Jon. 1:12)

דַּרְגָּ֧א תְּבִ֛יר מֵרְכָ֥א טִפְּחָ֖א

וְאֵ֧שֶׁת נְעוּרִ֛ים כִּ֥י תִמָּאֵ֖ס אָמַ֥ר אֱלֹהָֽיִךְ׃ (Isa. 54:6) ס֧וּרָה אֲדֹנִ֛י ס֥וּרָה אֵלַ֖י אַל־תִּירָ֑א (Judg. 4:18)

דַּרְגָּ֧א תְּבִ֛יר מֵרְכָ֥א תְּבִ֛יר מֵרְכָ֥א טִפְּחָ֖א

קָחֶ֧נּוּ ׀ וָבֹ֛אָה כִּֽי־שָׁל֥וֹם לְךָ֛ וְאֵ֥ין דָּבָ֖ר חַי־יְהוָֽה׃ (1 Sam. 20:21)

Chant these verses.

וַיְהִ֧י לִשְׁלֹמֹ֛ה שִׁבְעִ֥ים אֶ֖לֶף נֹשֵׂ֣א סַבָּ֑ל וּשְׁמֹנִ֥ים אֶ֛לֶף חֹצֵ֖ב בָּהָֽר׃ (1 Kings 5:29)

כִּֽי־כְאִשָּׁ֧ה עֲזוּבָ֛ה וַעֲצ֥וּבַת ר֖וּחַ קְרָאָ֣ךְ יְהוָ֑ה וְאֵ֧שֶׁת נְעוּרִ֛ים כִּ֥י תִמָּאֵ֖ס אָמַ֥ר אֱלֹהָֽיִךְ׃ (Isa. 54:6)

הֵ֛ן עֵ֥ד לְאוּמִּ֖ים נְתַתִּ֑יו נָגִ֥יד וּמְצַוֵּ֖ה לְאֻמִּֽים׃ (Isa. 55:4)

מֵחֲמַ֛ס אָחִ֥יךָ יַעֲקֹ֖ב תְּכַסְּךָ֣ בוּשָׁ֑ה וְנִכְרַ֖תָּ לְעוֹלָֽם׃ (Obad. 1:10)

וְעָשִׂ֖יתָ כְּחָכְמָתֶ֑ךָ וְלֹֽא־תוֹרֵ֧ד שֵׂיבָת֛וֹ בְּשָׁלֹ֖ם שְׁאֹֽל׃ (1 Kings 2:6)

אַל־תִּירָ֖א מִפְּנֵיהֶ֑ם כִּֽי־אִתְּךָ֛ אֲנִ֥י לְהַצִּלֶ֖ךָ נְאֻם־יְהוָֽה׃ (Jer. 1:8)

Three Words in a *Tevir* Segment

Sometimes *tevir* is preceded by two or more conjunctives. In these segments there will be a very slight elongation just before *tevir*. The second conjunctive before *tevir* (preceding either *darga* or *merekha*) may be *kadmah*.

Kadmah darga tevir קַדְמָ֨ה דַּרְגָּ֧א תְּבִ֛יר

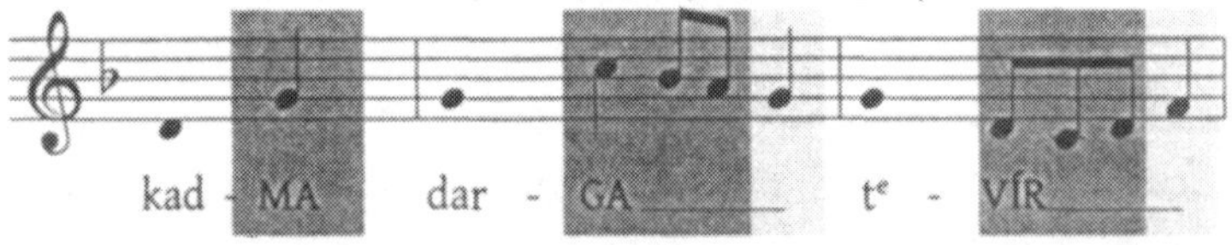
kad - MA dar - GA tᵉ - VÍR

Chant these words to the melody of *kadmah darga tevir.*

לִשְׁפֹּ֨ךְ חֲמָתִ֧י עֲלֵיהֶ֛ם (Ezek. 20:13) מִֽי־נָתַ֨ן לִמְשִׁסָּ֧ה יַעֲקֹ֛ב (Isa. 42:24) וַיַּ֨עַל הַמֶּ֧לֶךְ שְׁלֹמֹ֛ה (1 Kings 5:27)

Kadmah merekha tevir קַדְמָ֨ה מֵרְכָ֥א תְּבִ֛יר

kad - MA mé - rᵉ - KHA tᵉ - VÍR

Chant these words to the melody of *kadmah merekha tevir.*

וְלֹ֨א יֵחָצוּ ע֥וֹד (Ezek. 37:22) לְצַוֺּ֨ת אֹתִ֥י נָגִ֛יד (2 Sam. 6:21) וַיֹּ֨סֶף ע֥וֹד דָּוִ֛ד (2 Sam. 6:1)

Chant these phrases. Connect each conjunctive word to the word that follows. Create a slight elongation or pause after *tippeḥa*. There is very little elongation after *tevir*.

אֲשֶׁ֨ר הִנִּ֥חַ שָׁ֛ם מֹשֶׁ֖ה בְּחֹרֵ֑ב (1 Kings 8:9)

אָנֹכִ֨י אָנֹכִ֥י ה֛וּא מֹחֶ֥ה פְשָׁעֶ֖יךָ לְמַעֲנִ֑י (Isa. 43:25)
וְכֶ֨סֶף הִרְבֵּ֥יתִי לָ֛הּ וְזָהָ֖ב עָשׂ֥וּ לַבָּֽעַל׃ (Hos. 2:10)

הִנֵּ֨ה אֵ֧ל יְשׁוּעָתִ֛י אֶבְטַ֖ח וְלֹ֣א אֶפְחָ֑ד (Isa. 12:2)
וַיְדַבֵּ֨ר יִפְתָּ֧ח אֶת־כָּל־דְּבָרָ֛יו לִפְנֵ֥י יְהוָ֖ה בַּמִּצְפָּֽה׃ (Judg. 11:11)
וּפִתְּח֨וּ שְׁעָרַ֧יִךְ תָּמִ֛יד יוֹמָ֥ם וָלַ֖יְלָה לֹ֣א יִסָּגֵ֑רוּ (Isa. 60:11)
וּבָ֨אתִי לְהַגִּ֧יד לְאַחְאָ֛ב וְלֹ֥א יִמְצָאֲךָ֖ וַהֲרָגָ֑נִי (1 Kings 18:12)

If the second conjunctive before *tevir* (preceding either *darga* or *merekha*) is accented on the first syllable, it will be *munaḥ* instead of *kadmah*. When we refer to this use of the *ta'am*, we accent its first syllable: *MU-naḥ*.

Munaḥ darga tevír מֻ֣ונַח דַּ֧רְגָּ֧א תְּבִ֛יר

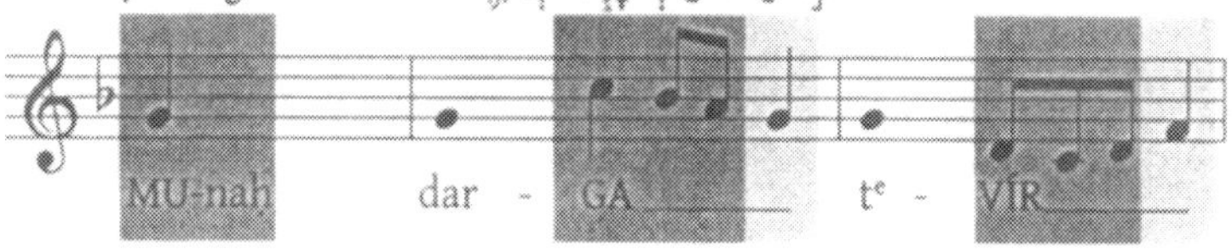

Chant these words to the melody of *munaḥ darga tevir.*

אֵ֣ת אֲשֶׁ֧ר יוֹרִֽישְׁךָ֛ (Judg. 11:24) בָּ֣אוּ הֵ֧נָּה הַלַּ֛יְלָה (Josh. 2:2)

Munaḥ merekha tevir מֻ֣ונַח מֵרְכָ֥א תְּבִ֛יר

Chant these words to the melody of *munaḥ merekha tevir.*

בֵּ֛ית עֹבֵ֥ד אֱדֹ֛ם (2 Sam. 6:11) מַ֛יִם כַּבִּירִ֥ים שֹׁטְפִ֛ים (Isa. 28:2)

Chant these phrases. Connect each conjunctive word to the word that follows. Create a slight elongation or pause after the *tippeḥa*. There is very little elongation after *tevir*.

כִּ֣י לֹ֧א מְצָאתֶ֛ם בְּיָדִ֖י מְא֑וּמָה (1 Sam. 12:5)
כִּ֣י שִׂ֧יחַ וְכִֽי־שִׂ֛יג ל֖וֹ וְכִֽי־דֶ֣רֶךְ ל֑וֹ (1 Kings 18:27)
שָׁ֣ם יִרְעֶ֥ה עֵ֛גֶל וְשָׁ֥ם יִרְבָּ֖ץ וְכִלָּ֥ה סְעִפֶֽיהָ׃ (Isa. 27:10)
כִּ֣י י֧וֹם אֵידָ֛ם בָּ֥א עֲלֵיהֶ֖ם עֵ֥ת פְּקֻדָּתָֽם׃ (Jer. 46:21)

Four or Five Words in the *Tevir* Segment

Sometimes *tevir* is preceded by three or four conjunctives. The third conjunctive before *tevir* is *telishah ketanah*. The fourth conjunctive before *tevir* (preceding *telishah ketanah*) is *munaḥ*.

Munaḥ telishah kadmah darga tevir מ֣וּנַח תְּלִישָׁ֩ה קַדְמָ֨ה דַּ֧רְגָּ֧א תְּבִ֛יר

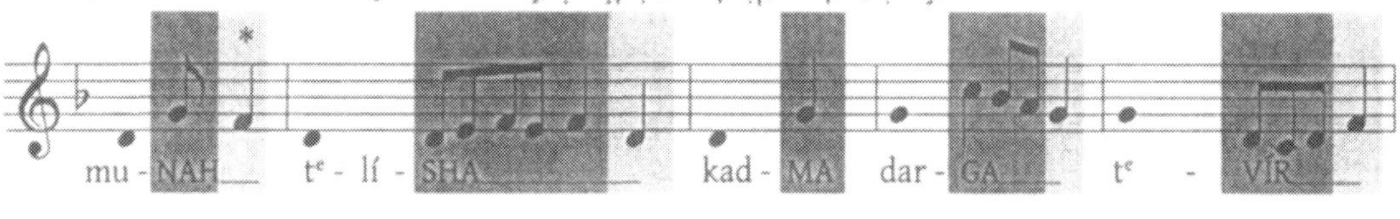

* The final pitch of *munaḥ* is F# in some traditions.

Chant these words to the melody of *telishah kadmah darga tevir.*

וַיְהִי אִישׁ אֶחָד מִצָּרְעָה (Judg. 13:2)

נַחֲלַת עַבְדֵי יְהוָה וְצִדְקָתָם (Isa. 54:17)

אֵת כָּל־אֲשֶׁר צִוִּיתָה לָהֶם (Jer. 32:23)

Chant these words to the melody of *munaḥ telishah kadmah darga tevir.*

כַּאֲשֶׁר יָבִיאוּ בְנֵי יִשְׂרָאֵל אֶת־הַמִּנְחָה (Isa. 66:20)

כֹּל אֲשֶׁר־יֵצֵא מִדַּלְתֵי בֵיתֵךְ ׀ הַחוּצָה (Josh. 2:19)

Munaḥ telishah kadmah merekha tevir (מונח) תְּלִישָׁה קַדְמָה מֵרְכָא תְּבִיר

mu - NAH__
tᵉ-lí - SHA__
kad - MA
mé-rᵉ - KHA__
tᵉ - VÍR__

*F# in some traditions.

Chant these words to the melody of *telishah kadmah merekha tevir.*

וְהִנֵּה אוֹפַן אֶחָד בָּאָרֶץ (Ezek. 1:15)

בְּאַרְבָּעָה עָשָׂר יוֹם לַחֹדֶשׁ (Josh. 5:10)

בְּיוֹם הִצִּיל יְהוָה אֹתוֹ (2 Sam. 22:1)

Chant these words to the melody of *munaḥ telishah kadmah merekha tevir.*

הֲלוֹא כִבְנֵי כֻשִׁיִּים אַתֶּם לִי (Amos 9:7)

Chant these phrases. Connect each conjunctive word to the word that follows. Create a slight elongation or pause after *tippeḥa.* There is very little elongation after *tevir.*

בְּעַד הַחַלּוֹן נִשְׁקְפָה וַתְּיַבֵּב אֵם סִיסְרָא בְּעַד הָאֶשְׁנָב (Judg. 5:28)

עַל אֲשֶׁר פָּרַץ יְהוָה פֶּרֶץ בְּעֻזָּה (2 Sam. 6:8)

וַיְהִי אִישׁ אֶחָד מִצָּרְעָה מִמִּשְׁפַּחַת הַדָּנִי וּשְׁמוֹ מָנוֹחַ וְאִשְׁתּוֹ עֲקָרָה וְלֹא יָלָדָה׃ (Judg. 13:2)

אֵת כָּל־אֲשֶׁר צִוִּיתָה לָהֶם לַעֲשׂוֹת לֹא עָשׂוּ (Jer. 32:23)

הֲלוֹא כִבְנֵי כֻשִׁיִּים אַתֶּם לִי בְּנֵי יִשְׂרָאֵל נְאֻם־יְהוָה (Amos 9:7)

כַּאֲשֶׁר יָבִיאוּ בְנֵי יִשְׂרָאֵל אֶת־הַמִּנְחָה בִּכְלִי טָהוֹר בֵּית יְהוָה׃ (Isa. 66:20)

וְהִנֵּה אוֹפַן אֶחָד בָּאָרֶץ אֵצֶל הַחַיּוֹת לְאַרְבַּעַת פָּנָיו׃ (Ezek. 1:15)

בְּאַרְבָּעָה עָשָׂר יוֹם לַחֹדֶשׁ בָּעֶרֶב בְּעַרְבוֹת יְרִיחוֹ׃ (Josh. 5:10)

בְּיוֹם הִצִּיל יְהוָה אֹתוֹ מִכַּף כָּל־אֹיְבָיו וּמִכַּף שָׁאוּל׃ (2 Sam. 22:1)

The *Zakef* Segment

Zakef is a strong disjunctive; only *siluk* and *etnaḥta* are stronger. A *zakef* segment will always be followed by a *tippeḥa* segement. *Zakef* is stronger than the ensuing *tippeḥa.* A *zakef* segment may also be followed by one or more other *zakef* segments, but they will eventually be followed by a *tippeḥa* segement. When you see two *zakefs* (or two *zakef* segments) in a row, the first is always stronger.

There are two basic forms of *zakef*, each with its own distinct melody: *zakef gadol* and *zakef katon*. There are also two compound *te'amim*, in which two symbols appear on a single word: *munaḥ-zakef* and *metigah-zakef*.

Zakef Gadol

A word marked with *zakef gadol* is short and has no conjunctive immediately before it.

Zakef gadol זָקֵף־גָּד֔וֹל

Chant these words to the melody of *zakef gadol.*

יָשַׁ֔ב (1 Kings 2:12)   וַיָּבֹ֔א (2 Kings 4:33)   הִ֔יא (Ezek. 1:13)   אֶפְרַ֔יִם (Hos. 14:9)

Zakef is usually followed by *(merekha-) tippeḥa*. Chant these phrases. Make a pause or elongation after *zakef*. Make a more subtle pause or elongation after *tippeḥa.*

נָשִׁ֔ים בָּא֖וֹת מְאִ֣ירוֹת אוֹתָ֑הּ (Isa. 27:11)

וְעַתָּ֔ה לְכִ֛י אִיעָצֵ֥ךְ נָ֖א עֵצָ֑ה (1 Kings. 1:12)

וַאֲמַרְתֶּ֕ם בַּמֶּ֖ה בָזִ֥ינוּ אֶת־שְׁמֶֽךָ׃ (Mal. 1:6)

רָב֔וּעַ אֶ֖ל אַרְבַּ֥עַת רְבָעָֽיו׃ (Ezek. 43:16)

One or Two Words in a *Zakef Katon* Segment

A word marked with *zakef katon* is usually preceded by the conjunctive *munaḥ.*

Munaḥ zakef katon מוּנַ֣ח זָקֵף־קָט֔וֹן

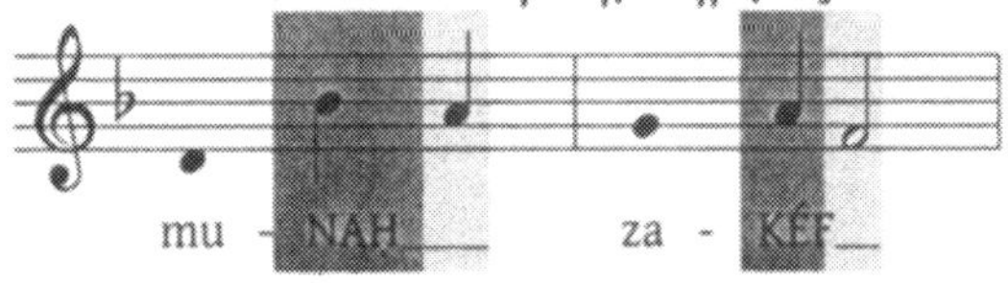

Chant these words to the melody of *zakef.*   שִׁמְשֵׁ֔ךְ (Isa. 60:20)   גּוֹרָל֔וֹת (Jon. 1:17)   מֵיתָרַ֔יִךְ (Isa. 54:2)

Chant these words to the melody of *munaḥ zakef.*

הֵקִ֣ים תַּחְתָּ֔ם (Josh. 5:7)   הַכֹּהֵ֣ן הַגָּד֔וֹל (Zech. 3:1)   ק֣וֹל קוֹרֵ֔א (Isa. 40:3)

וַיֹּ֣אמֶר אֵלַ֔י (Ezek. 37:3)   רֶ֣כֶב בַּרְזֶ֔ל (Judg. 4:13)

הַדֹּבֵ֣ר בִּ֔י (Zech. 1:14)   *With elision:* (Josh. 5:13) וַיֹּ֣אמֶר ל֔וֹ

Sometimes, *munah* will appear on the same word that is marked with *zakef.*

מְשׁ֣וּבָתָ֔ם (Hos. 14:5)   הַכֹּ֣הֲנִ֔ים (Joel 2:17)   לְאֹ֣יְבַ֔יִךְ (Isa. 62:8)   תְּר֣וֹמְמֵ֔נִי (2 Sam. 22:49)

Metigah Zakef

Metigah-zakef מְתִיגָ֣ה־זָקֵ֔ף

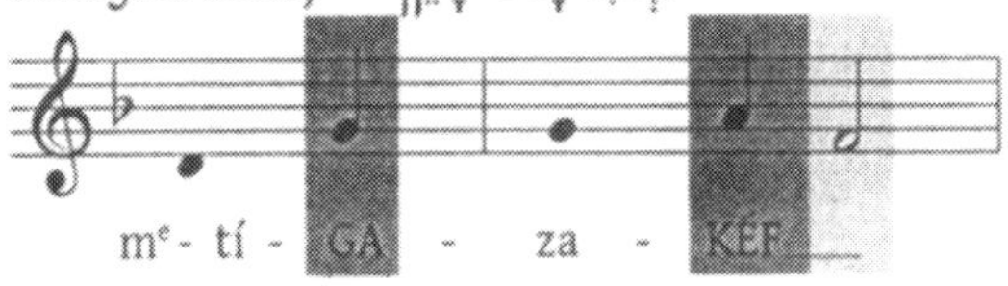

Chant these words to the melody of *metigah zakef.* וְהַנֹּשֶׁה (2 Kings 4:1) בְּמֶלְקַחַיִם (Isa. 6:6)

Zakef is usually followed by *(merekha-) tippeḥa.* Chant these phrases. Make a pause or elongation after *zakef.* Make a more subtle pause or elongation after *tippeḥa.*

מונַח זָקֵף טִפְּחָא

אָנֹכִי הֹלֵךְ בְּדֶרֶךְ כָּל־הָאָרֶץ (1 Kings. 2:2) שִׂים פָּנֶיךָ עַל־פַּרְעֹה מֶלֶךְ מִצְרָיִם (Ezek. 29:2)

וְהוֹדַעְתָּהּ אֵת כָּל־תּוֹעֲבוֹתֶיהָ׃ (Ezek. 22:2)

מונַח זָקֵף מֵרְכָא טִפְּחָא

וְאֹיְבַי תַּתָּה לִּי עֹרֶף (2 Sam. 22:41) כִּי הַיָּם הוֹלֵךְ וְסֹעֵר עֲלֵיהֶם׃ (Jon. 1:13)

וְאַתָּה בֶן־אָדָם הֲתִשְׁפֹּט הֲתִשְׁפֹּט אֶת־עִיר הַדָּמִים (Ezek. 22:2)

מונַח זָקֵף תְּבִיר מֵרְכָא טִפְּחָא

וַתָּקָם חַנָּה אַחֲרֵי אָכְלָה בְשִׁלֹה וְאַחֲרֵי שָׁתֹה (1 Sam. 1:9)

וּבָשָׂר עָלָה וַיִּקְרַם עֲלֵיהֶם עוֹר מִלְמָעְלָה (Ezek. 37:8)

זָקֵף טִפְּחָא

וַיָּשָׁב הַמַּלְאָךְ הַדֹּבֵר בִּי (Zech. 4:1) וַיְעִירֵנִי כְּאִישׁ אֲשֶׁר־יֵעוֹר מִשְּׁנָתוֹ׃ (Zech. 4:1)

זָקֵף מֵרְכָא טִפְּחָא

וָאֹמַר מַקֵּל שָׁקֵד אֲנִי רֹאֶה׃ (Jer. 1:11) וּפְנֵיהֶם וְכַנְפֵיהֶם פְּרֻדוֹת מִלְמָעְלָה (Ezek. 1:11)

זָקֵף תְּבִיר טִפְּחָא

וָאֹמַר יָשִׂימוּ צָנִיף טָהוֹר עַל־רֹאשׁוֹ (Zech. 3:5)

וְאַנְחֵהוּ וַאֲשַׁלֵּם נִחֻמִים לוֹ וְלַאֲבֵלָיו׃ (Isa. 57:18)

מונַח זָקֵף זָקֵף טִפְּחָא

וַיֹּאמֶר אֵלַי בֶּן־אָדָם הֲתִחְיֶינָה הָעֲצָמוֹת הָאֵלֶּה (Ezek. 37:3)

יָבִין מֶלֶךְ־חָצוֹר וּבֵין בֵּית חֶבֶר הַקֵּינִי (Judg. 4:17)

זָקֵף מונַח זָקֵף טִפְּחָא

בֶּן־אָדָם הָעֲצָמוֹת הָאֵלֶּה כָּל־בֵּית יִשְׂרָאֵל הֵמָּה (Ezek. 37:11)

זָקֵף זָקֵף טִפְּחָא

וּשְׁלֹמֹה יָשַׁב עַל־כִּסֵּא דָּוִד אָבִיו (1 Kings 2:12)

מוּנַ֥ח זָקֵ֔ף מוּנַ֥ח זָקֵ֔ף טִפְּחָ֖א
וַתִּשָּׂאֵ֣נִי ר֔וּחַ וָאֶשְׁמַ֣ע אַחֲרַ֔י ק֖וֹל רַ֣עַשׁ גָּד֑וֹל (Ezek. 3:12)

מוּנַ֥ח זָקֵ֔ף מְתִיגָֽה־זָקֵ֔ף טִפְּחָ֖א
פֶּן־אַפְשִׁיטֶ֣נָּה עֲרֻמָּ֔ה וְהִ֨צַּגְתִּ֔יהָ כְּי֖וֹם הִוָּֽלְדָ֑הּ (Hos. 2:5)

The *Pashta/Yetiv* Segment

Sometimes there is a subdivision within a *zakef* segment. *Pashta* is the *ta'am* that marks that subdivision.

Pashta פַּשְׁטָא֙

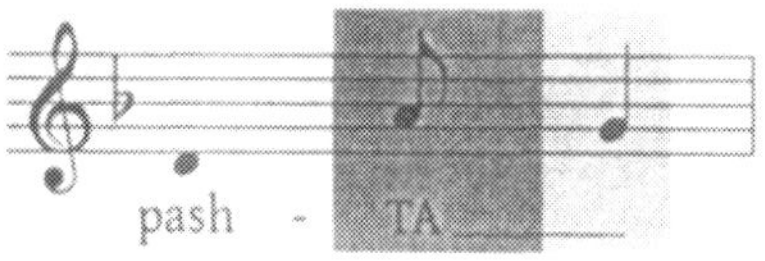

Chant these words to the melody of *pashta.*

שִׁבְעָה֙ (1 Kings 7:17) וַיִּשְׁלַח֙ (1 Kings 7:13) עוֹד֙ (2 Sam. 6:22)

אֲנִי֙ (2 Kings 5:7) מָאתַ֙יִם֙ (1 Kings 7:20)

Two Words in a *Pashta* Segment

If the preceding word is closely connected in meaning to the *pashta* word, it is usually marked with a conjunctive *ta'am.* Most often that conjunctive will be *mahpakh.*

Mahpakh pashta מַהְפַּ֤ךְ פַּשְׁטָא֙

Chant these words to the melody of *mahpakh pashta.*

כְּלֵ֤י גוֹלָה֙ (Jer. 46:19) הוֹצִאִ֤י אוֹתָם֙ (Jer. 34:13) כִּ֤י רַבּוּ֙ (Jer. 46:23) לַבַּ֤יִת סָבִיב֙ (1 Kings 6:6)

If the accents are close to each other, the conjunctive will be *merekha* instead of *mahpakh.* In the *merekha-pashta* combination, the two accented syllables are contiguous—the *merekha* word is accented on the last syllable, and the *pashta* word has no pick-up. Thus the model for *pashta* must be sung on the syllable "TA," dropping the pick-up "pash-."

Merekha pashta מֵרְכָ֥א פַּשְׁטָא֙

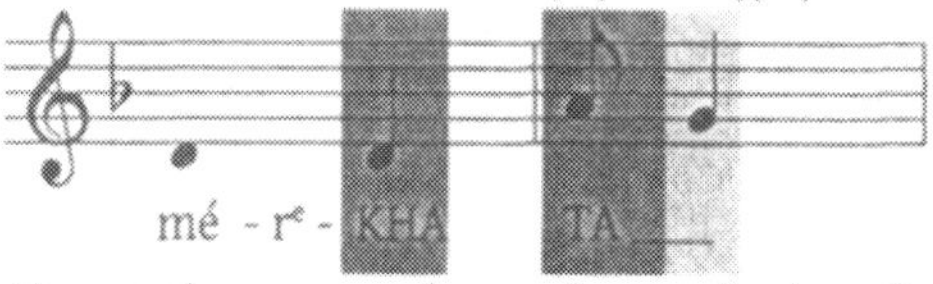

Chant these words to the melody of *merekha pashta.*

שֹׁכֵ֥ן עַד֙ (Isa. 57:15) לֹא־יָב֥וֹא עוֹד֙ (Isa. 60:20) בְּ֥וֹא גוֹג֙ (Ezek. 38:18) כִּי־מֵ֥י נֹחַ֙ (Isa. 54:9)

Pashta is usually followed by either *zakef katon* or *munaḥ zakef katon*. Chant these examples. Connect each conjunctive word to the word that follows. Make only a subtle elongation or pause after *pashta*. Make a stronger elongation or pause after *zakef*.

פַּשְׁטָא זָקֵף

וַיַּפִּלוּ גּוֹרָלוֹת וַיִּפֹּל הַגּוֹרָל עַל־יוֹנָה׃ (Jon. 1:7)

הַאֲרִיכִי מֵיתָרַיִךְ וִיתֵדֹתַיִךְ חַזֵּקִי׃ (Isa. 54:2)

מַהְפַּךְ פַּשְׁטָא זָקֵף

כִּי רַבּוּ מֵאַרְבֶּה וְאֵין לָהֶם מִסְפָּר׃ (Jer. 46:23)

נָתַן חָכְמָה לִשְׁלֹמֹה כַּאֲשֶׁר דִּבֶּר־לוֹ (1 Kings 5:26)

מַהְפַּךְ פַּשְׁטָא מוּנַח זָקֵף

כְּלֵי גוֹלָה עֲשִׂי לָךְ יוֹשֶׁבֶת בַּת־מִצְרָיִם (Jer. 46:19)

וַיִּירְאוּ הָאֲנָשִׁים יִרְאָה גְדוֹלָה וַיֹּאמְרוּ אֵלָיו מַה־זֹּאת עָשִׂיתָ (Jon. 1:10)

מֵרְכָא פַּשְׁטָא זָקֵף

לֹא־יָבוֹא עוֹד שִׁמְשֵׁךְ וִירֵחֵךְ לֹא יֵאָסֵף (Isa. 60:20)

חֲמִשִּׁים אִישׁ בַּמְּעָרָה וָאֲכַלְכְּלֵם לֶחֶם וָמָיִם׃ (1 Kings 18:13)

מֵרְכָא פַּשְׁטָא מוּנַח זָקֵף

שֹׁכֵן עַד וְקָדוֹשׁ שְׁמוֹ מָרוֹם וְקָדוֹשׁ אֶשְׁכּוֹן (Isa. 57:15)

אַתָּה חַסְתָּ עַל־הַקִּיקָיוֹן אֲשֶׁר לֹא־עָמַלְתָּ בּוֹ וְלֹא גִדַּלְתּוֹ (Jon. 4:10)

פַּשְׁטָא פַּשְׁטָא מוּנַח זָקֵף

וַיֹּאמֶר קְרָא אֶל־הַשֻּׁנַמִּית הַזֹּאת וַיִּקְרָאֶהָ וַתָּבוֹא אֵלָיו (2 Kings. 4:36)

לָכֶם הַכֹּהֲנִים בּוֹזֵי שְׁמִי וַאֲמַרְתֶּם בַּמֶּה בָזִינוּ אֶת־שְׁמֶךָ׃ (Mal. 1:6)

מַהְפַּךְ פַּשְׁטָא מַהְפַּךְ פַּשְׁטָא מוּנַח זָקֵף

תִּהְיֶה הַמִּנְחָה אֵיפָה לַפָּר וְאֵיפָה לָאַיִל וְלַכְּבָשִׂים מַתַּת יָדוֹ (Ezek. 46:11)

Chant these verses.

אֲפָפוּנִי מַיִם עַד־נֶפֶשׁ תְּהוֹם יְסֹבְבֵנִי סוּף חָבוּשׁ לְרֹאשִׁי׃ (Jon. 2:6)

שִׁירוּ לַיהוָה שִׁיר חָדָשׁ תְּהִלָּתוֹ מִקְצֵה הָאָרֶץ יוֹרְדֵי הַיָּם וּמְלֹאוֹ אִיִּים וְיֹשְׁבֵיהֶם׃ (Isa. 42:10)

לְקִצְבֵי הָרִים יָרַדְתִּי הָאָרֶץ בְּרִחֶיהָ בַעֲדִי לְעוֹלָם וַתַּעַל מִשַּׁחַת חַיַּי יְהוָה אֱלֹהָי׃ (Jon. 2:7)

הַטּוּ אָזְנְכֶם וּלְכוּ אֵלַי שִׁמְעוּ וּתְחִי נַפְשְׁכֶם וְאֶכְרְתָה לָכֶם בְּרִית עוֹלָם חַסְדֵי דָוִד הַנֶּאֱמָנִים׃ (Isa. 55:3)

Yetiv

Yetiv is used instead of *pashta* if the word is accented on the first syllable and has no conjunctive words immediately preceding. Since *yetiv* is found only on words accented on the first syllable, i.e., words with no pick-ups, the model must be sung on the syllable "TÍV," dropping the pick-up "y^e-."

Yetiv יְתִיב

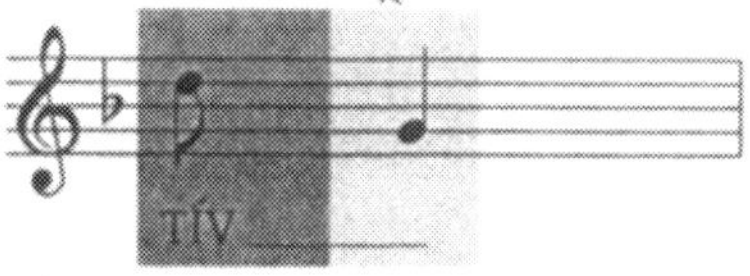

Chant these words to the melody of *yetiv.*

אָז (Judg. 5:13) חֹדֶשׁ (1 Kings 5:28)

Yetiv is usually followed by *zakef katon* or *munaḥ zakef katon.* Chant these examples. Make a subtle elongation or pause after *yetiv.* Make a stronger pause or elongation after *zakef.*

רַק אֶתְכֶם יָדַעְתִּי (Amos 3:2)

אֵלֶּה הַדְּבָרִים (Isa. 42:16)

וַיֹּאמֶר מְשָׁרְתוֹ מָה אֶתֵּן זֶה לִפְנֵי מֵאָה אִישׁ (2 Kings 4:43)

וַאֲנִי אָמַרְתִּי נִגְרַשְׁתִּי מִנֶּגֶד עֵינֶיךָ אַךְ אוֹסִיף לְהַבִּיט אֶל־הֵיכַל קָדְשֶׁךָ׃ (Jon. 2:5)

הֲיִרְצְךָ אוֹ הֲיִשָּׂא פָנֶיךָ אָמַר יְהוָה צְבָאוֹת׃ (Mal. 1:8)

Three Words in a *Pashta* Segment

Sometimes *pashta* is preceded by two or more conjunctives. In these segments, there will be a very slight elongation just before the *pashta.*

The second conjunctive before *pashta* (preceding either *merekha* or *mahpakh*) may be *kadmah.*

Kadmah mahpakh pashta קַדְמָה מַהְפַּךְ פַּשְׁטָא

Chant these words to the melody of *kadmah mahpakh pashta.*

שִׁמְעוּ שָׁמוֹעַ אֵלַי (Isa. 55:2) וָאָשִׂם שָׁם מָקוֹם (1 Kings 8:21) וַיֹּאמֶר שְׁמוּאֵל אֶל־הָעָם (1 Sam. 12:20)

Kadmah merekha pashta קַדְמָה מֵרְכָא פַּשְׁטָא

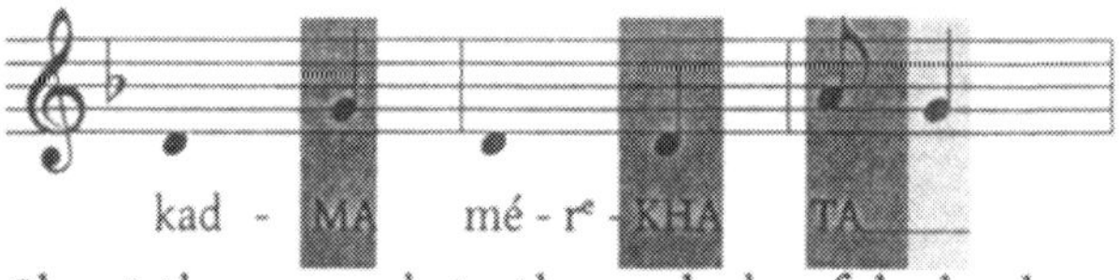

Chant these words to the melody of *kadmah merekha pashta.*

בְּיוֹם בּוֹא גוֹג (Ezek. 38:18) חֲמִשִּׁים חֲמִשִּׁים אִישׁ (1 Kings 18:13) הַגִּישָׁה אֵלַי עוֹד (2 Kings 4:6)

Chant these examples. Connect the *kadmah* word to the word that follows. Make a subtle elongation or pause after *pashta*. Make a stronger pause or elongation after *zakef*.

שִׁמְעוּ שָׁמ֨וֹעַ אֵלַ֙י וְאִכְלוּ־ט֔וֹב וְתִתְעַנַּ֥ג בַּדֶּ֖שֶׁן נַפְשְׁכֶֽם׃ (Isa. 55:2)

וַיֹּ֨אמֶר שְׁמוּאֵ֤ל אֶל־הָעָם֙ אַל־תִּירָ֔אוּ אַתֶּ֣ם עֲשִׂיתֶ֔ם אֵ֥ת כָּל־הָרָעָ֖ה הַזֹּ֑את (1 Sam. 12:20)

אֲשֶׁ֨ר יִהְיֶ֤ה אִתְּךָ֙ בַּבַּ֔יִת דָּמ֣וֹ בְרֹאשֵׁ֔נוּ אִם־יָ֖ד תִּֽהְיֶה־בּֽוֹ׃ (Josh. 2:19)

וְקָרָ֨א זֶ֤ה אֶל־זֶה֙ וְאָמַ֔ר קָד֧וֹשׁ ׀ קָד֛וֹשׁ קָד֖וֹשׁ יְהוָ֣ה צְבָא֑וֹת מְלֹ֥א כָל־הָאָ֖רֶץ כְּבוֹדֽוֹ׃ (Isa. 6:3)

אִם־מְשִׁיבִ֨ים אַתֶּ֤ם אוֹתִי֙ לְהִלָּחֵם֙ בִּבְנֵ֣י עַמּ֔וֹן וְנָתַ֧ן יְהוָ֛ה אוֹתָ֖ם לְפָנָ֑י אָנֹכִ֕י אֶהְיֶ֥ה לָכֶ֖ם לְרֹֽאשׁ׃ (Judg. 11:9)

בָּר֨וּךְ אַתָּ֤ה יי֙ אֱלֹהֵ֙ינוּ֙ מֶ֣לֶךְ הָעוֹלָ֔ם (First blessing before the *haftarah*)

חֲמִשִּׁ֨ים חֲמִשִּׁ֥ים אִישׁ֙ בַּמְּעָרָ֔ה וָאֲכַלְכְּלֵ֖ם לֶ֥חֶם וָמָֽיִם׃ (1 Kings 18:13)

וַתֹּ֨אמֶר אֶל־בְּנָהּ֙ הַגִּ֨ישָׁה אֵלַ֥י עוֹד֙ כֶּ֔לִי וַיֹּ֣אמֶר אֵלֶ֔יהָ אֵ֥ין ע֖וֹד כֶּ֑לִי וַֽיַּעֲמֹ֖ד הַשָּֽׁמֶן׃ (2 Kings 4:6)

בָּֽא־שָׁא֨וּל הַכַּרְמֶ֜לָה וְהִנֵּ֨ה מַצִּ֥יב לוֹ֙ יָ֔ד וַיִּסֹּב֙ וַֽיַּעֲבֹ֔ר וַיֵּ֖רֶד הַגִּלְגָּֽל׃ (1 Sam. 15:12)

מַה־מָּצְא֨וּ אֲבוֹתֵיכֶ֥ם בִּי֙ עָ֔וֶל כִּ֥י רָחֲק֖וּ מֵעָלָ֑י וַיֵּ֥לְכ֛וּ אַחֲרֵ֥י הַהֶ֖בֶל וַיֶּהְבָּֽלוּ׃ (Jer. 2:5)

If the second conjunctive before *pashta* (preceding either *mahpakh* or *merekha*) is accented on the first syllable, it will be *munaḥ* instead of *kadmah*. When we refer to this use of the *ta'am*, we accent its first syllable: *MU-naḥ*.

Munaḥ mahpakh pashta מ֣וּנַח מַהְפַּ֤ךְ פַּשְׁטָא֙

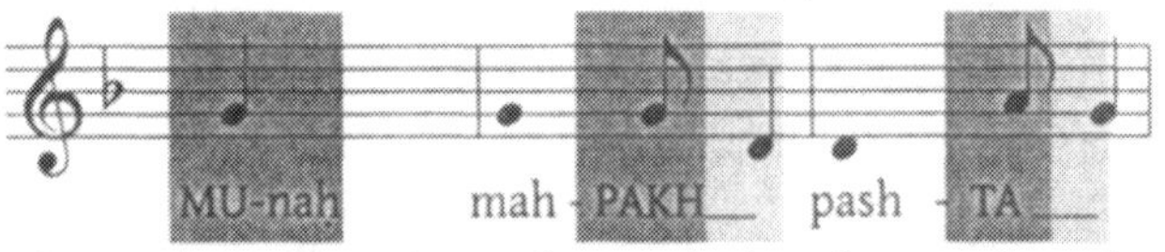
MU-nah
mah - PAKH
pash - TA

Chant these words to the melody of *munaḥ mahpakh pashta*.

כִּ֣י עַ֤יִן בְּעַ֙יִן֙ (Isa. 52:8) סֹ֤לּוּ סֹ֙לּוּ֙ הַֽמְסִלָּ֔ה (Isa. 62:10)

Munaḥ merekha pashta מ֣וּנַח מֵרְכָ֥א פַּשְׁטָא֙

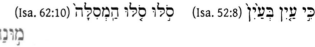

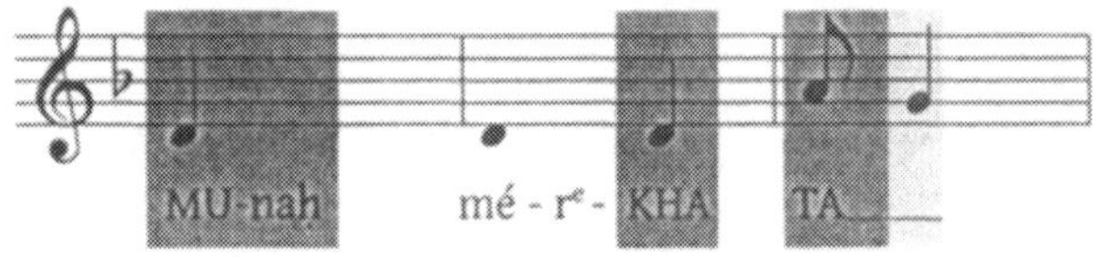
MU-nah
mé - rᵉ - KHA
TA

Chant these words to the melody of *munaḥ merekha pashta*. אֵ֣ין לְשִׁפְחָתְךָ֥ כֹל֙ (2 Kings 4:2)

Chant these examples. Connect the *munaḥ* word to the word that follows. Make a subtle elongation or pause after *pashta*. Make a stronger pause or elongation after *zakef*.

עַ֣ל הַר־גָּבֹ֤הַ עֲלִי־לָךְ֙ מְבַשֶּׂ֣רֶת צִיּ֔וֹן (Isa. 40:9)

וּבְב֖וֹא הַנָּשִׂ֑יא דֶּ֣רֶךְ אוּלָ֤ם הַשַּׁ֙עַר֙ יָב֔וֹא וּבְדַרְכּ֖וֹ יֵצֵֽא׃ (Ezek. 46:8)

ק֥וֹל צֹפַ֛יִךְ נָ֥שְׂאוּ ק֖וֹל יַחְדָּ֣ו יְרַנֵּ֑נוּ כִּ֣י עַ֤יִן בְּעַ֙יִן֙ יִרְא֔וּ בְּשׁ֥וּב יְהוָ֖ה צִיּֽוֹן׃ (Isa. 52:8)

אֵ֣ין לְשִׁפְחָתְךָ֥ כֹל֙ בַּבַּ֔יִת כִּ֖י אִם־אָס֥וּךְ שָֽׁמֶן׃ (2 Kings 4:2)

Four or Five Words in a *Pashta* Segment

Sometimes *pashta* is preceded by three or four conjunctives. The third conjunctive before *pashta* is *telishah ketanah.* The fourth conjunctive before *pashta* (preceding *telishah ketanah*) is *munaḥ.*

Munaḥ telishah kadmah mahpakh pashta מוּנַח תְּלִישָׁה קַדְמָא מַהְפַּךְ פַּשְׁטָא

* F# in some traditions.

Chant these words to the melody of *telishah kadmah mahpakh pashta.*

אֲשֶׁר יַעֲשֶׂה אֹתָם הָאָדָם (Ezek. 20:13) כִּי יֵשׁ שָׂכָר לִפְעֻלָּתֵךְ (Jer. 31:15)

Chant these words to the melody of *munaḥ telishah kadmah mahpakh pashta.*

הָיָה אִישׁ גָּדוֹל לִפְנֵי אֲדֹנָיו (2 Kings. 5:1)

Chant these examples. Connect the *kadmah* word to the word that follows. Make a subtle elongation or pause after *pashta.* Make a stronger pause or elongation after *zakef.*

וְנִבְקַע הַר הַזֵּיתִים מֵחֶצְיוֹ מִזְרָחָה וָיָמָּה גֵּיא גְּדוֹלָה מְאֹד (Zech. 14:4)

וְעָלָה הָאִישׁ הַהוּא מֵעִירוֹ מִיָּמִים ׀ יָמִימָה לְהִשְׁתַּחֲוֹת וְלִזְבֹּחַ לַיהוָה צְבָאוֹת בְּשִׁלֹה (1 Sam. 1:3)

וְגֵר יָתוֹם וְאַלְמָנָה אַל־תֹּנוּ אַל־תַּחְמֹסוּ וְדָם נָקִי אַל־תִּשְׁפְּכוּ בַּמָּקוֹם הַזֶּה׃ (Jer. 22:3)

וְעַל־מֵיטַב הַצֹּאן וְהַבָּקָר וְהַמִּשְׁנִים וְעַל־הַכָּרִים וְעַל־כָּל־הַטּוֹב וְלֹא אָבוּ הַחֲרִימָם (1 Sam. 15:9)

אֶל אֲשֶׁר יִהְיֶה־שָׁמָּה הָרוּחַ לָלֶכֶת יֵלֵכוּ לֹא יִסַּבּוּ בְּלֶכְתָּן׃ (Ezek. 1:12)

Telishah kadmah merekha pashta תְּלִישָׁה קַדְמָא מֵרְכָא פַּשְׁטָא

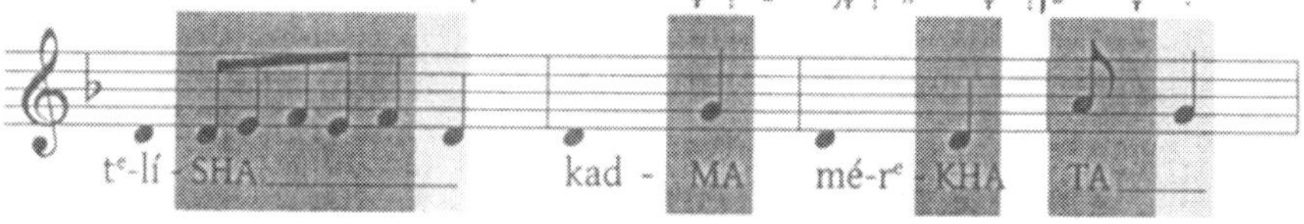

Chant these words to the melody of *telishah kadmah merekha pashta.*

וַיִּפֹּל יְהוֹשֻׁעַ אֶל־פָּנָיו אַרְצָה וַיִּשְׁתָּחוּ (Josh. 5:14)

This is the only example of this combination in the *haftarot.*

The *Segol* Segment

Segol is the strongest disjunctive before *etnaḥta.* A *segol* segment is followed by one or more *zakef* segments, and then by *tippeḥa* and *etnaḥta.*

One or Two Words in a *Segol* Segment

Segol is never the first word in its segment. If the preceding word is closely connected in meaning to the *segol* word, it is usually marked with the conjunctive *munaḥ.*

Munaḥ segol מוּנַ֣ח סֶגוֹל֒

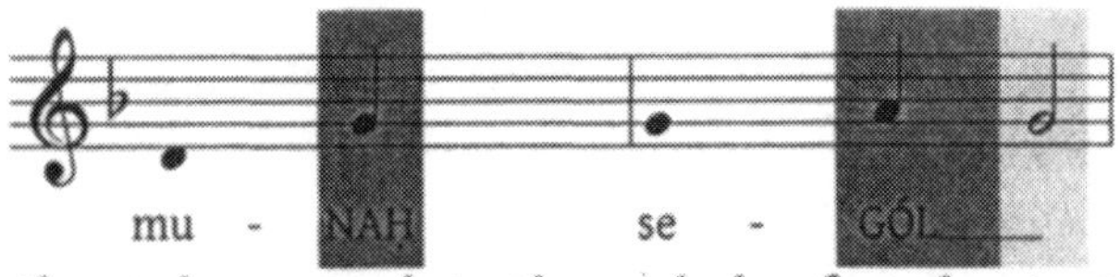

Chant these words to the melody of *segol.* לֵאמֹ֒ר (Isa. 44:19) בָּ֒א (1 Sam. 20:41) לַמִּשְׁפָּ֒ט (Mal. 3:5)

Chant these words to the melody of *munaḥ segol.*

וְאֵ֥ין עוֹנֶ֣ה֒ (Isa. 50:2) בְּשׁוֹפָ֣ר גָּד֒וֹל (Isa. 27:13) בָּ֣א עֲלֵיכֶ֒ם (1 Sam. 12:12) נָ֣טָה קָ֒ו (Isa. 44:13)

The *Zarka* Segment

Sometimes there is a subdivision within the *segol* segment. *Zarka* is the *ta'am* that marks that subdivision.

One or Two Words in a *Zarka* Segment

If there are two words in the *zarka* segment, the first word is usually marked with either of two conjunctives, *munaḥ* or *merekha.* They are chanted to the same melody.

Munaḥ zarka מוּנַ֣ח זַרְקָא֮ and *Merekha zarka* מֵרְכָ֥א זַרְקָא֮

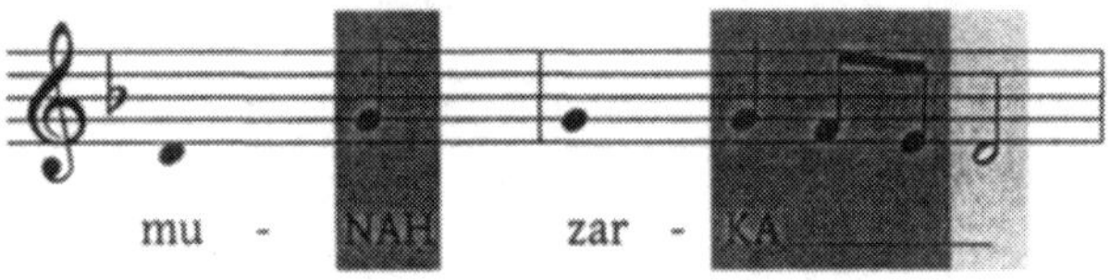

Chant these words to the melody of *zarka.*

עָלַי֮ (Ezek. 37:1) כֹּה־אָמַר֮ (Ezek. 37:12) זֶה֮ (Isa. 58:6) וּבָאוּ֮ (Jer. 31:12)

Chant these words to the melody of *munaḥ zarka.*

חָרַ֣שׁ עֵצִים֮ (Isa. 44:13) הָיְתָ֣ה עָלַי֮ (Ezek. 37:1) בָּ֣אוּ הָעִיר֮ (Jer. 32:24) וַתֹּ֣אמֶר לְאִישָׁהּ֮ (Judg. 13:6)

Zarka is always followed (eventually) by *segol.* Chant these examples.

וּבָאוּ֮ וְרִנְּנ֣וּ בִמְרוֹם־צִיּ֒וֹן (Jer. 31:12) הַנַּ֣עַר֮ בָּ֒א (1 Sam. 20:41)

אֲלֵיכֶם֮ לַמִּשְׁפָּ֒ט (Mal. 3:5)

וְהוּא֮ עַם־בָּז֣וּז וְשָׁסוּי֒ הָפֵ֤חַ בַּֽחוּרִים֙ כֻּלָּ֔ם וּבְבָתֵּ֥י כְלָאִ֖ים הָחְבָּ֑אוּ (Isa. 42:22)

הֲל֣וֹא זֶה֮ צ֣וֹם אֶבְחָרֵ֒הוּ֒ פַּתֵּ֙חַ֙ חַרְצֻבּ֣וֹת רֶ֔שַׁע הַתֵּ֖ר אֲגֻדּ֣וֹת מוֹטָ֑ה (Isa. 58:6)

Three Words in a *Zarka* Segment

Sometimes *zarka* is preceded by two or more conjunctives. In these segments, there will be a very slight elongation just before the *zarka.* The second conjunctive before *zarka* (preceding either *merekha* or *munaḥ*) is usually *kadmah.*

Kadmah munaḥ zarka or Kadmah merekha zarka קַדְמָ֨ה מֵרְכָ֥א זַרְקָא֮ קַדְמָ֨ה מוּנַּ֣ח זַרְקָא֮

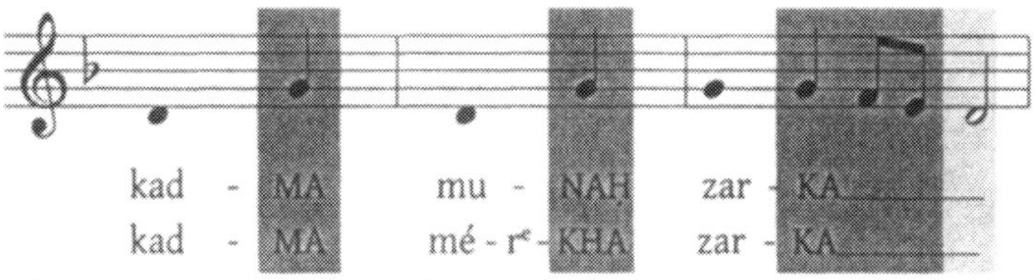
kad - MA mu - NAH zar - KA
kad - MA mé - rᵉ - KHA zar - KA

Chant these words to the melody of *kadmah munaḥ zarka.*

אֲשֶׁ֨ר דִּבֶּ֣ר עָלַי֮ (1 Kings 2:4) אֶת־הַפָּ֨ר אֲשֶׁר־נָתַ֣ן לָהֶם֮ (1 Kings 18:26)

Chant these words to the melody of *kadmah merekha zarka.*

שִׁמְעִ֨י בֶן־גֵּרָ֥א בֶן־הַיְמִינִי֮ מִבַּחֻרִים֒ (1 Kings 2:8) וְלֹ֨א דַ֤עַת וְלֹא־תְבוּנָה֙ לֵאמֹר֮ (Isa. 44:19)

If the second conjunctive before *zarka* is accented on the first syllable, it will be *munaḥ* (MU-naḥ).

Munaḥ munaḥ zarka מֻ֣נַּח מוּנַּ֣ח זַרְקָא֮

MU-nah mu - NAH zar - KA

Chant these words to the melody of *munaḥ munaḥ zarka.*

צֵ֣א וְעָמַדְתָּ֣ בָהָר֮ (1 Kings 19:11) כִּ֣י כֹ֣ה אָמַר֮ (Zech. 2:12)

Four or Five Words in a *Zarka* Segment

Sometimes *zarka* is preceded by three or four conjunctives. The third conjunctive before *zarka* is *telishah ketanah. Telishah ketanah* may be preceded by its conjunctive, *munaḥ.*

Munaḥ telishah kadmah merekha zarka מוּנַּ֣ח תְּלִישָׁ֩ה קַדְמָ֨ה מֵרְכָ֥א זַרְקָא֮

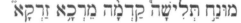

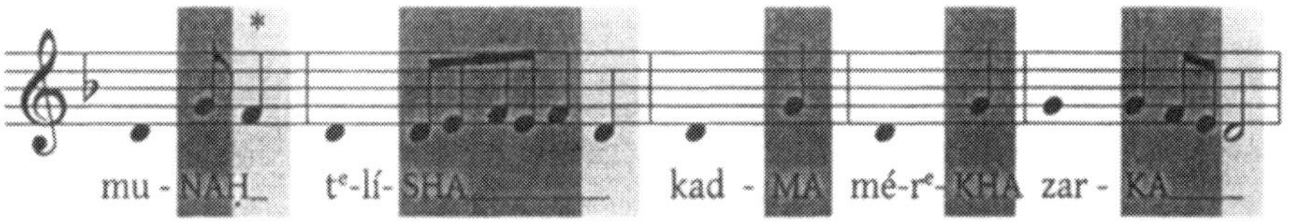
*
mu - NAH tᵉ-lí- SHA kad - MA mé-rᵉ- KHA zar - KA

* F# in some traditions.

Chant these words to the melody of *telishah kadmah merekha zarka.*

וַיָּבֹא֩ דָוִ֨ד וַאֲבִישַׁ֥י ׀ אֶל־הָעָם֮ (1 Sam. 26:7)

Chant these words to the melody of *munaḥ telishah kadmah merekha zarka.*

אֶל־פְּנֵ֣י חֲמִשָּׁ֩ה וְעֶשְׂרִ֨ים אֶ֥לֶף ׀ תְּרוּמָה֮ (Ezek. 48:21)

Chant these examples. Connect each conjunctive to the word that follows. Make only a slight elongation or pause after *zarka.* Make a longer elongation or pause after *segol.*

וַיֹּ֘אמֶר֮ אֵלַי֒ בֶּן־אָדָ֕ם הָעֲצָמ֣וֹת הָאֵ֔לֶּה כָּל־בֵּ֥ית יִשְׂרָאֵ֖ל הֵ֑מָּה (Ezek. 37:11)

וְקִבַּצְתִּים֮ מִיַּרְכְּתֵי־אָרֶץ֒ בָּ֚ם עִוֵּ֣ר וּפִסֵּ֔חַ הָרָ֥ה וְיֹלֶ֖דֶת יַחְדָּ֑ו קָהָ֥ל גָּד֖וֹל יָשׁ֥וּבוּ הֵֽנָּה׃ (Jer. 31:8)

וּדְמ֣וּת פְּנֵיהֶם֮ פְּנֵ֣י אָדָם֒ וּפְנֵ֨י אַרְיֵ֤ה אֶל־הַיָּמִין֙ לְאַרְבַּעְתָּ֔ם

וּפְנֵי־שׁ֥וֹר מֵהַשְּׂמֹ֖אול לְאַרְבַּעְתָּ֑ן וּפְנֵי־נֶ֖שֶׁר לְאַרְבַּעְתָּֽן׃ (Ezek. 1:10)

כִּ֣י כֹ֣ה אָמַר֮ יְהוָ֣ה צְבָאוֹת֒ אַחַ֣ר כָּב֔וֹד שְׁלָחַ֕נִי אֶל־הַגּוֹיִ֖ם הַשֹּׁלְלִ֣ים אֶתְכֶ֑ם (Zech. 2:12)

הֲל֣וֹא זֶה֮ צ֣וֹם אֶבְחָרֵ֒הוּ֒ פַּתֵּ֙חַ֙ חַרְצֻבּ֣וֹת רֶ֔שַׁע הַתֵּ֖ר אֲגֻדּ֣וֹת מוֹטָ֑ה (Isa. 58:6)

וַיַּאֲרִ֙כוּ֙ הַבַּדִּ֔ים וַיֵּרָא֨וּ רָאשֵׁ֤י הַבַּדִּים֙ מִן־הַקֹּ֙דֶשׁ֙ עַל־פְּנֵ֣י הַדְּבִ֔יר וְלֹ֥א יֵרָא֖וּ הַח֑וּצָה (1 Kings 8:8)

אֶל־פְּנֵ֡י חֲמִשָּׁה֩ וְעֶשְׂרִ֨ים אֶ֤לֶף ׀ תְּרוּמָה֙ עַד־גְּב֣וּל קָדִ֔ימָה (Ezek. 48:21)

The *Revia* Segment

Revia is a medium-level disjunctive, found before *pashta, tevir,* and *zarka* segments. *Revia* is stronger than any *pashta, tevir,* or *zarka* that follow, but not as strong as *zakef, tippeḥa,* or *segol.*

One or Two Words in a *Revia* Segment

If the preceding word is closely connected in meaning to the *revia* word, it is usually marked with the conjunctive *munaḥ.*

Munaḥ revia מונַ֣ח רְבִ֗יע

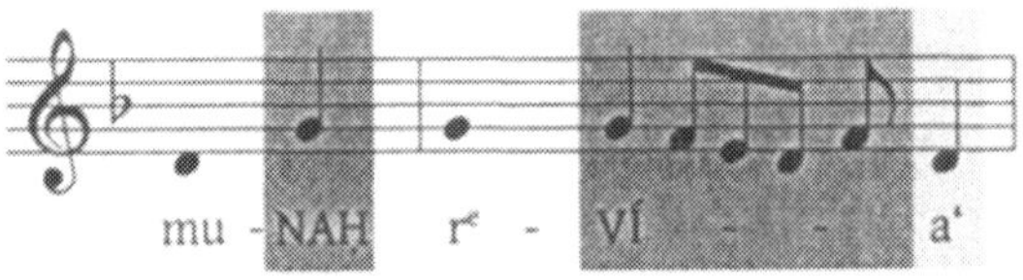

Chant these words to the melody of *revia.*

וַיַּ֗רְא (1 Kings 19:3) לְדָוִ֗ד (1 Sam. 18:25) כִּ֗י (Isa. 41:13) לַ֗יְלָה (2 Kings 7:12) וַיֹּ֗אמֶר (1 Kings 19:11)

Chant these words to the melody of *munaḥ revia.*

בְּנֵ֣י צָד֗וֹק (Ezek. 44:15) וַיִּקְרַ֣ע בְּגָדָ֗יו (2 Kings 5:7) עֵ֣ד מְמַהֵ֗ר (Mal. 3:5)

לָ֣מָּה יָשַׁ֗בְתָּ (Judg. 5:16) וְקֶ֣רֶן יִשְׁעִ֗י (2 Sam. 22:3)

Three Words in a *Revia* Segment

Sometimes *revia* is preceded by two conjunctives. In these segments, there will be a very slight elongation just before the *revia.* The second conjunctive before *revia* (preceding *munaḥ*) is *darga.*

Darga munaḥ revia דַּרְגָּ֧א מונַ֣ח רְבִ֗יע

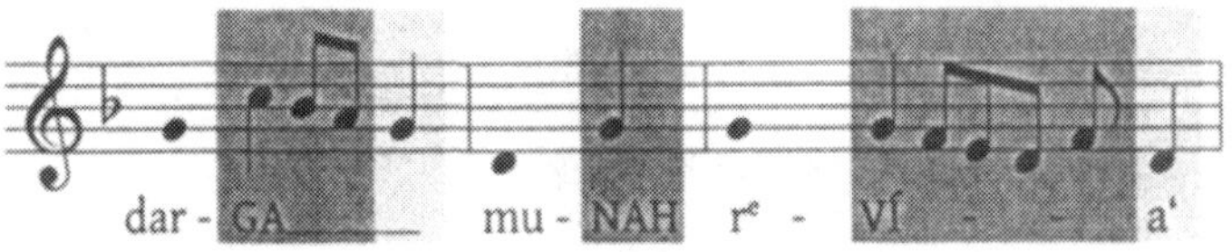

Chant these words to the melody of *darga munaḥ revia.*

אַרְבַּ֧ע עֶשְׂרֵ֣ה אֹ֗רֶךְ (Ezek. 43:17) וַחֲמ֧וֹר מִ֣י לָקַ֗חְתִּי (1 Sam. 12:3) שׂ֧וֹשׂ אָשִׂ֣ישׂ בַּֽיהוָ֗ה (Isa. 61:10)

ר֧וּחַ חָכְמָ֣ה וּבִינָ֗ה (Isa. 11:2) וַיֹּ֧אמֶר ל֣וֹ שָׁא֗וּל (1 Sam. 15:13)

Four Words in a *Revia* Segment

Only once is *revia* preceded by three conjunctives. The third conjunctive before *revia* (preceding *darga* and *munaḥ*) is *munaḥ.*

Munaḥ darga munaḥ revia מוּנַ֣ח דַּרְגָּ֧א מוּנַ֣ח רְבִ֗יעַ

mu - NAH dar - GA mu - NAH rᵉ - VI - - - a'

Chant these words to the melody of *munaḥ darga munaḥ revia.*

וַיִּקַּ֞ח אֶת־צֶ֧מֶד הַבָּקָ֛ר וַיִּזְבָּחֵ֗הוּ (1 Kings 19:21)

Chant these examples. Connect each conjunctive to the word that follows. Make an elongation or pause after *revia.* Make a weaker elongation or pause after *pashta, tevir,* or *zarka.* Make a stronger elongation or pause after *zakef, tippeḥa,* or *segol.*

רְבִ֗יעַ פַּשְׁטָא֙

וַֽיִּמְצְא֗וּ אֶת־אֲבִישַׁג֙ הַשּׁ֣וּנַמִּ֔ית (1 Kings 1:3)

אִ֗ם מֵאֵת֙ אֲדֹנִ֣י הַמֶּ֔לֶךְ נִהְיָ֖ה הַדָּבָ֣ר הַזֶּ֑ה (1 Kings 1:27)

הִנֵּ֣ה שַׂמְתִּ֗יךְ לְמוֹרַג֙ חָר֣וּץ חָדָ֔שׁ בַּ֖עַל פִּיפִיּ֑וֹת (Isa. 41:15)

אֲנִ֤י עָנִ֙יתִי֙ וַאֲשׁוּרֶ֔נּוּ אֲנִי֙ כִּבְר֣וֹשׁ רַעֲנָ֔ן מִמֶּ֖נִּי פֶּרְיְךָ֥ נִמְצָֽא׃ (Hos. 14:9)

רְבִ֗יעַ יְ֚תִיב

עַד־הַגְּבוּל֙ שִׁלְּח֗וּךָ כֹּ֚ל אַנְשֵׁ֣י בְרִיתֶ֔ךָ (Obad. 1:7)

כִּ֣י שָׁל֗וֹם בֵּ֚ין יָבִ֣ין מֶֽלֶךְ־חָצ֔וֹר (Judg. 4:17)

רְבִ֗יעַ מַהְפַּ֤ךְ פַּשְׁטָא֙

לַחְמְךָ֗ יָשִׂ֤ימוּ מָזוֹר֙ תַּחְתֶּ֔יךָ אֵ֥ין תְּבוּנָ֖ה בּֽוֹ׃ (Obad. 1:7)

אֲדֹנִ֣י הַמֶּ֗לֶךְ נִשְׁבַּ֤עְתָּ לַאֲמָֽתְךָ֙ לֵאמֹ֔ר (1 Kings 1:13)

רְבִ֗יעַ מֵרְכָ֥א פַּשְׁטָא֙

וַיֵּ֗לֶךְ בַּבַּ֗יִת אַחַ֥ת הֵ֙נָּה֙ וְאַחַ֣ת הֵ֔נָּה (2 Kings 4:35)

וִֽיהוּדָ֗ה עֹ֥ד רָד֙ עִם־אֵ֔ל וְעִם־קְדוֹשִׁ֖ים נֶאֱמָֽן׃ (Hos. 12:1)

רְבִ֗יעַ קַדְמָ֨ה מַהְפַּ֤ךְ פַּשְׁטָא֙

וְהַיָּמִ֗ים אֲשֶׁ֨ר מָלַ֤ךְ דָּוִד֙ עַל־יִשְׂרָאֵ֔ל (1 Kings 2:11)

וַיְהִ֗י בִּימֵ֨י יְהוֹיָקִ֤ים בֶּן־יֹאשִׁיָּ֙הוּ֙ מֶ֣לֶךְ יְהוּדָ֔ה (Jer. 1:3)

רְבִ֗יעַ קַדְמָ֨ה מֵרְכָ֥א פַּשְׁטָא֙

בְּשֶׁ֣צֶף קֶ֗צֶף הִסְתַּ֨רְתִּי פָנַ֥י רֶ֙גַע֙ מִמֵּ֔ךְ וּבְחֶ֥סֶד עוֹלָ֖ם רִחַמְתִּ֑יךְ (Isa. 54:8)

וַתֹּ֗אמֶר שִׁלְחָ֨ה נָ֥א לִי֙ אֶחָ֣ד מִן־הַנְּעָרִ֔ים (2 Kings 4:22)

רְבִ֗יעַ תְּלִישָׁה֠ קַדְמָ֨ה מַהְפַּ֤ךְ פַּשְׁטָא֙

לְהָדְפָ֔הּ וַיֹּ֩אמֶר֩ אִ֨ישׁ הָאֱלֹהִ֤ים הַרְפֵּה־לָהּ֙ כִּֽי־נַפְשָׁ֣הּ מָֽרָה־לָ֔הּ (2 Kings 4:27)

הַרְאוֹתָ֣ם אֶת־הָאָ֗רֶץ אֲשֶׁ֩ר֩ נִשְׁבַּ֨ע יְהוָ֤ה לַאֲבוֹתָם֙ לָ֣תֶת לָ֔נוּ (Josh. 5:6)

רְבִ֗יעַ תְּבִ֛יר

וְאֶצָּרְךָ֗ וְאֶתֶּנְךָ֛ לִבְרִ֥ית עָ֖ם לְא֥וֹר גּוֹיִֽם׃ (Isa. 42:6)

מִ֗י יֵשֵׁ֛ב עַל־כִּסֵּ֥א אֲדֹנִֽי־הַמֶּ֖לֶךְ אַחֲרָֽיו׃ (1 Kings 1:20)

רְבִ֗יעַ דַּרְגָּ֧א תְּבִ֛יר

דְּבוֹרָ֗ה בֵּ֧ין הָרָמָ֛ה וּבֵ֥ין בֵּֽית־אֵ֖ל בְּהַ֣ר אֶפְרָ֑יִם (Judg. 4:5)

וַתֹּ֣אמֶר אֵלָ֗יו ס֥וּרָֽה אֲדֹנִ֛י ס֥וּרָה אֵלַ֖י אַל־תִּירָ֑א (Judg. 4:18)

רְבִ֗יעַ מֵרְכָ֥א תְּבִ֛יר

אֲשֶׁ֣ר נִשְׁבַּ֗עְתִּי מֵעֲבֹ֥ר מֵי־נֹ֛חַ ע֖וֹד עַל־הָאָ֑רֶץ (Isa. 54:9)

וֶֽאֱמָר־לָ֗הּ הֲשָׁל֥וֹם לָ֛ךְ הֲשָׁל֥וֹם לְאִישֵׁ֖ךְ הֲשָׁל֣וֹם לַיָּ֑לֶד (2 Kings 4:26)

רְבִ֗יעַ קַדְמָ֨ה מֵרְכָ֥א תְּבִ֛יר

וְעַתָּ֗ה שְׁלַ֨ח קְבֹ֥ץ אֵלַ֛י אֶת־כָּל־יִשְׂרָאֵ֖ל אֶל־הַ֣ר הַכַּרְמֶ֑ל (1 Kings 18:19)

רְבִ֗יעַ מוּנַ֣ח זַרְקָא֮ מוּנַ֣ח סֶגוֹל֒

אֶל־הַמֶּ֗לֶךְ כִּֽי־נִכְמְר֣וּ רַחֲמֶיהָ֮ עַל־בְּנָהּ֒ (1 Kings 3:26)

מִמַּטֵּ֣ה נַפְתָּלִ֗י וְאָבִ֣יו אִישׁ־צֹרִי֮ חֹרֵ֣שׁ נְחֹשֶׁת֒ (1 Kings 7:14)

רְבִ֗יעַ זַרְקָא֮ מוּנַ֣ח סֶגוֹל֒

בַּיּ֣וֹם הַה֗וּא יִתָּקַע֮ בְּשׁוֹפָ֣ר גָּדוֹל֒ (Isa. 27:13)

וַיָּבֹ֗אוּ וַֽיִּקְרְאוּ֮ אֶל־שֹׁעֵ֣ר הָעִיר֒ (2 Kings 7:10)

רְבִ֗יעַ קַדְמָ֨ה מוּנַ֣ח זַרְקָא֮ סֶגוֹל֒

אֶת־דְּבָר֗וֹ אֲשֶׁ֨ר דִּבֶּ֣ר עָלַי֮ לֵאמֹר֒ (1 Kings 2:4)

וְלֹֽא־יָשִׁ֣יב אֶל־לִבּ֗וֹ וְלֹ֨א דַ֤עַת וְלֹֽא־תְבוּנָה֙ לֵאמֹ֔ר (Isa. 44:19)

Chant these verses.

אֶפְרַ֕יִם מַה־לִּ֥י ע֖וֹד לָעֲצַבִּ֑ים אֲנִ֧י עָנִ֣יתִי וַאֲשׁוּרֶ֗נּוּ אֲנִי֙ כִּבְר֣וֹשׁ רַעֲנָ֔ן מִמֶּ֖נִּי פֶּרְיְךָ֥ נִמְצָֽא׃ (Hos. 14:9)

הִנֵּ֣ה שַׂמְתִּ֗יךְ לְמוֹרַג֙ חָר֣וּץ חָדָ֔שׁ בַּ֖עַל פִּֽיפִיּ֑וֹת תָּד֤וּשׁ הָרִים֙ וְתָדֹ֔ק וּגְבָע֖וֹת כַּמֹּ֥ץ תָּשִֽׂים׃ (Isa. 41:15)

וַתִּקְרָא֮ אֶל־אִישָׁהּ֒ וַתֹּ֗אמֶר שִׁלְחָ֨ה נָ֥א לִי֙ אֶחָ֣ד מִן־הַנְּעָרִ֔ים וְאַחַ֖ת הָאֲתֹנ֑וֹת

וְאָר֛וּצָה עַד־אִ֥ישׁ הָאֱלֹהִ֖ים וְאָשֽׁוּבָה׃ (2 Kings 4:22)

עַתָּה֮ רֽוּץ־נָ֣א לִקְרָאתָהּ֒ וֶֽאֱמָר־לָ֗הּ הֲשָׁל֥וֹם לָ֛ךְ הֲשָׁל֥וֹם לְאִישֵׁ֖ךְ

הֲשָׁל֣וֹם לַיָּ֑לֶד וַתֹּ֖אמֶר שָׁלֽוֹם׃ (2 Kings 4:26)

וַתִּקֹּ֨ד בַּת־שֶׁ֤בַע אַפַּ֙יִם֙ אֶ֔רֶץ וַתִּשְׁתַּ֖חוּ לַמֶּ֑לֶךְ וַתֹּ֕אמֶר יְחִ֗י אֲדֹנִ֛י הַמֶּ֥לֶךְ דָּוִ֖ד לְעֹלָֽם׃ (1 Kings 1:31)

וִֽידַעְתֶּ֗ם כִּ֣י בְקֶ֤רֶב יִשְׂרָאֵל֙ אָ֔נִי וַאֲנִ֛י יְהוָ֥ה אֱלֹהֵיכֶ֖ם וְאֵ֣ין ע֑וֹד וְלֹא־יֵבֹ֥שׁוּ עַמִּ֖י לְעוֹלָֽם׃ (Joel 2:27)

וַתֹּ֧אמֶר ל֣וֹ אִשְׁתּ֗וֹ ל֣וּ חָפֵ֤ץ יְהוָה֙ לַהֲמִיתֵ֔נוּ לֹא־לָקַ֤ח מִיָּדֵ֙נוּ֙ עֹלָ֣ה וּמִנְחָ֔ה

וְלֹ֥א הֶרְאָ֖נוּ אֶת־כָּל־אֵ֑לֶּה וְכָעֵ֕ת לֹ֥א הִשְׁמִיעָ֖נוּ כָּזֹֽאת׃ (Judg. 13:23)

The *Legarmeh* Segment

Sometimes there is a subdivision within a *revia* segment. The *ta'am* that marks that subdivision may be *legarmeh.*

Legarmeh לְגַרְמֵ֣הּ ׀

Chant these words to the melody of *legarmeh.*

(1 Kings 19:8)׀ בְּכֹ֣חַ (Jer. 46:16)׀ ק֣וּמָה (Zech. 3:9)׀ כִּ֣י (Isa. 27:13)׀ וְהָיָ֣ה (Isa. 28:12)׀ אֲשֶׁ֣ר

Legarmeh is always followed by *munaḥ revia.* לְגַרְמֵ֣הּ ׀ מוּנַ֣ח רְבִ֗יעַ

Chant these examples.

(Jer. 2:24) פֶּ֣רֶה ׀ לִמֻּ֣ד מִדְבָּ֗ר (Zech. 3:9) כִּ֣י ׀ הִנֵּ֣ה הָאֶ֗בֶן (Isa. 28:12) אֲשֶׁ֣ר ׀ אָמַ֣ר אֲלֵיהֶ֗ם

Two Words in the *Legarmeh* Segment

If the preceding word is closely connected in meaning to the *legarmeh* word, it is marked with the conjunctive *merekha.* This sequence occurs only seven times.

Merekha legarmeh מֵרְכָ֥א לְגַרְמֵ֣הּ ׀

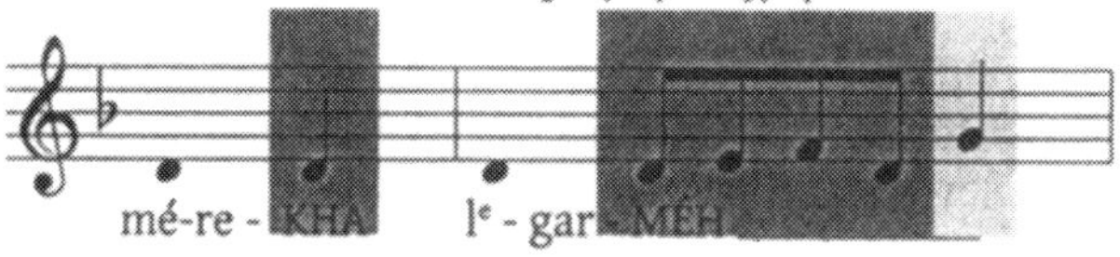

Chant these words to the melody of *merekha legarmeh.*

(1 Sam. 1:11) אִם־רָאֹ֥ה תִרְאֶ֣ה ׀ בָּעֳנִ֣י אֲמָתֶ֗ךָ (1 Sam. 20:21) הִנֵּ֥ה הַחִצִּ֣ים ׀ מִמְּךָ֣ וָהֵ֗נָּה

Chant these examples.

מִ֤י בָכֶם֙ יְרֵ֣א יְהוָ֔ה שֹׁמֵ֖עַ בְּק֣וֹל עַבְדּ֑וֹ

אֲשֶׁ֣ר ׀ הָלַ֣ךְ חֲשֵׁכִ֗ים וְאֵ֥ין נֹ֙גַהּ֙ ל֔וֹ יִבְטַח֙ בְּשֵׁ֣ם יְהוָ֔ה וְיִשָּׁעֵ֖ן בֵּאלֹהָֽיו׃ (Isa. 50:10)

אֲשֶׁ֣ר ׀ אָמַ֣ר אֲלֵיהֶ֗ם זֹ֤את הַמְּנוּחָה֙ הָנִ֣יחוּ לֶֽעָיֵ֔ף וְזֹ֖את הַמַּרְגֵּעָ֑ה וְלֹ֥א אָב֖וּא שְׁמֽוֹעַ׃ (Isa. 28:12)

וַֽיַּעֲמֹד֩ ׀ לִפְנֵ֨י ׀ אֲר֜וֹן בְּרִית־אֲדֹנָ֗י וַיַּ֤עַל עֹלוֹת֙ וַיַּ֣עַשׂ שְׁלָמִ֔ים וַיַּ֥עַשׂ מִשְׁתֶּ֖ה לְכָל־עֲבָדָֽיו׃ (1 Kings 3:15)

הִנֵּ֥ה הַחִצִּ֣ים ׀ מִמְּךָ֣ וָהֵ֗נָּה קָחֶ֛נּוּ ׀ וָבֹ֥אָה כִּֽי־שָׁל֥וֹם לְךָ֛ וְאֵ֥ין דָּבָ֖ר חַי־יְהוָֽה׃ (1 Sam. 20:21)

The *Geresh* Segment

Another *ta'am* that can subdivide a *revia* segment is *geresh*. There are two basic forms of *geresh*, each with its own distinct melody: (single) *geresh*, and double *geresh*, called *gereshayim*.

Geresh without a preceding conjunctive is always accented on the next-to-the-last syllable.

Geresh גֵּ֜רֵשׁ

Note: To construct a model for *geresh* words that have a pick-up (i.e., that comprise three or more syllables), we supply the prefix "vᵉ-."

Chant these words to the melody of *geresh*. (2 Kings 4:35) וַיָּ֜שָׁב (Ezek. 20:16) יַ֜עַן

Two Words in the *Geresh* Segment

If the preceding word is closely connected in meaning to the *geresh* word, it is usually marked with a conjunctive *ta'am*. Most often the conjunctive of *geresh* is *kadmah*.

Kadmah geresh קַדְמָ֨ה גֵּ֜רֵשׁ

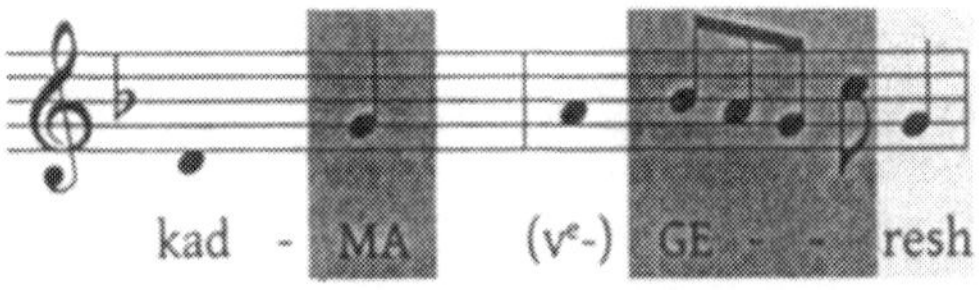

Elision will take place if the *geresh* word is accented on the first syllable.

ma - DU - a' BA - tí (Isa. 50:2) מַדּ֨וּעַ בָּ֜אתִי

vᵉ - ISH BA (2 Kings 4:42) וְאִ֨ישׁ בָּ֜א

Chant these words to the melody of *kadmah geresh*.

(Amos 9:12) לְמַ֨עַן יִֽירְשׁ֜וּ (Jer. 46:28) אֶעֱשֶׂ֨ה כָלָ֜ה (1 Sam. 20:21) אֹמַ֨ר לַנַּ֜עַר

Kadmah-geresh on one word: (1 Sam. 20:25) עַל־מ֨וֹשָׁב֜וֹ (2 Kings 2:9) וְאֵלִיָּ֨הוּ֜

If the conjunctive word is accented on the first syllable, it will be marked with *munaḥ* (MU-naḥ) instead of *kadmah*. The *munaḥ geresh* combination occurs only four times in the *haftarot*.

Munaḥ geresh מֻ֣ונַח גֵּ֜רֵשׁ

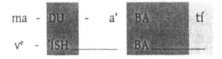

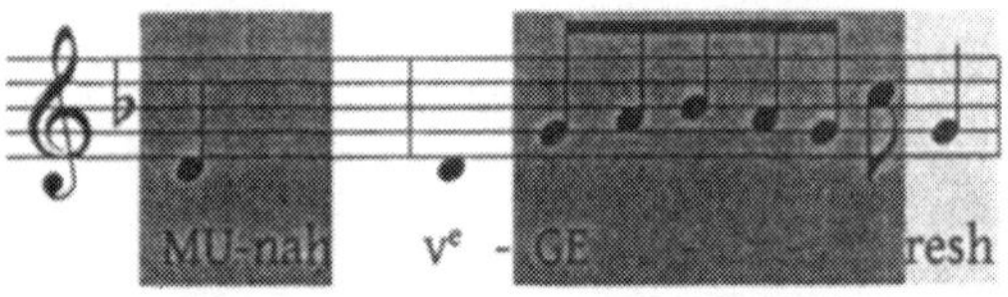

Chant these words to the melody of *munaḥ geresh*. (Isa. 32:14) עֹ֣פֶל וָבַ֜חַן (Mal. 1:11) כִּ֣י מִמִּזְרַח־שֶׁ֜מֶשׁ

Three Words in the *Geresh* Segment

Sometimes *geresh* is preceded by two or more conjunctives. The second conjunctive before *geresh* (preceding *kadmah*) is *telishah*.

Telishah kadmah geresh תְּלִישָׁה קַדְמָה גֵּרֶשׁ

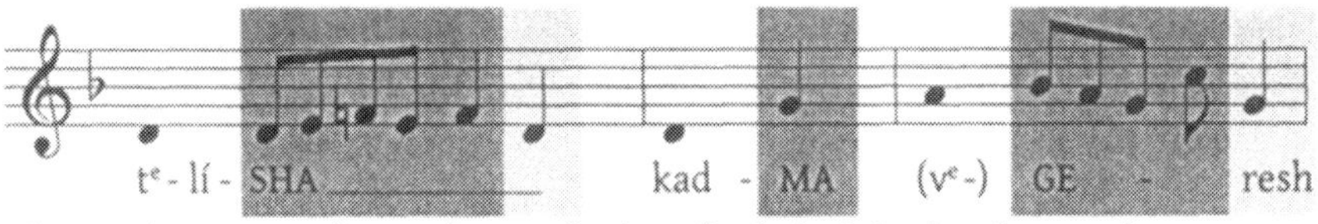

Chant these words to the melody of *telishah kadmah geresh.*

אָשִׂים מַחְשָׁךְ לִפְנֵיהֶם (Isa. 42:16) וַיִּשְׁלַח דָּוִד אֶת־יָדוֹ (1 Sam. 17:49) כִּי הִנָּךְ הָרָה (Judg. 13:5)

סֵפֶר הַמִּקְנָה הַזֶּה (Jer. 32:14) וַתָּקָם בְּתוֹךְ הַלַּיְלָה (1 Kings 3:20)

Telishah kadmah-geresh or *Telishah-kadmah geresh*

When chanting *telishah-kadmah-geresh*, you must determine in each case whether the sense of the text demands greater connection between the first and second words or between the second and third words. The rhythm of your chant will reflect the appropriate pairing.

תְּלִישָׁה קַדְמָה גֵּרֶשׁ	תְּלִישָׁה קַדְמָה גֵּרֶשׁ
וַיִּקְרָא לְכָל־בְּנֵי הַמֶּלֶךְ (1 Kings 1:25)	וַיַּשְׁכֵּם יְהוֹשֻׁעַ בַּבֹּקֶר (Josh. 3:1)
וַיָּבֹא לְאִישׁ הָאֱלֹהִים (2 Kings 4:42)	וַיַּחְמֹל שָׁאוּל וְהָעָם (1 Sam. 15:9)
וַאֲמַרְתֶּם הִנֵּה מַתְּלָאָה (Mal. 1:13)	וְאֶת־נָתָן הַנָּבִיא וּבְנָיָהוּ (1 Kings 1:10)
דֶּרֶךְ אוּלָם הַשַּׁעַר (Ezek. 46:2)	סֵפֶר הַתּוֹרָה הַזֶּה (Josh. 1:8)
וַתֹּאמֶר הָאִשָּׁה הָאַחֶרֶת (1 Kings 3:22)	וַתֹּאמֶר דְּבֹרָה אֶל־בָּרָק (Judg. 4:14)

Four Words in the *Geresh* Segment

Sometimes *geresh* is preceded by three conjunctives. The third conjunctive before *geresh* (just before *telishah*) is *munaḥ*.

Munaḥ telishah kadmah geresh מוּנַח תְּלִישָׁה קַדְמָה גֵּרֶשׁ

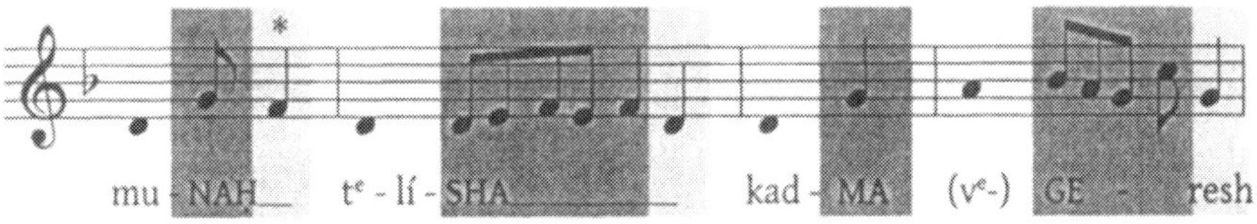

* F# in some traditions.

Chant these words to the melody of *munaḥ telishah kadmah geresh.*

אֲשֶׁר הֵם מִזֶּרַע צָדוֹק (Ezek. 43:19) הִנְנִי קֹרֵא לָכֶם דְּרוֹר (Jer. 34:17)

אֶת סֵפֶר הַמִּקְנָה הַזֶּה (Jer. 32:14) וְגֶשֶׁם שׁוֹטֵף וְאַבְנֵי אֶלְגָּבִישׁ (Ezek. 38:22)

Gereshayim

The double *geresh* is called *gereshayim*. Words that bear this accent are stressed on the last syllable.

Note: This accent has a double pick-up. If the word has one pick-up syllable, sing that syllable on F. If the word has two pick-up syllables, sing the first pick-up on D and the second on F. If the word has three pick-up syllables, sing the first two pick-ups on D and the third on F.

Chant these words to the melody of *gereshayim*. (Hos. 11:8) אֵ֞יךְ (Isa. 54:10) וְחַסְדִּ֞י (1 Kings 1:13) לְכִ֞י

Two Words in the *Gereshayim* Segment

The conjunctive of *gereshayim* is *munaḥ*. The word bearing *gereshayim* is accented on the last syllable, and the word bearing *munaḥ* (MU-naḥ) is accented on the first syllable. The *munaḥ-gereshayim* combination is found only twelve times.

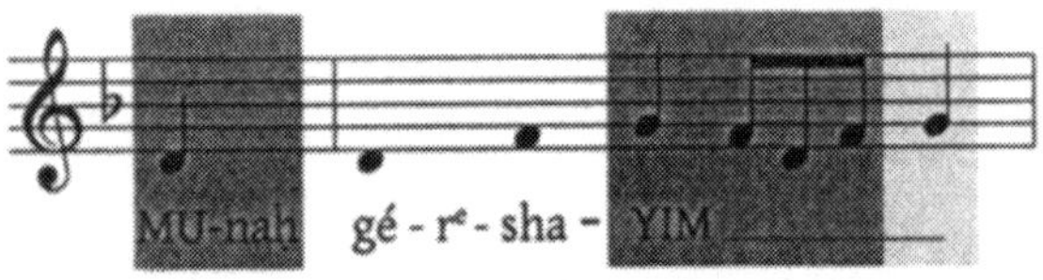

Chant these words to the melody of *munaḥ gereshayim*. (Jer. 2:20) כִּ֤י מֵעוֹלָ֞ם (Isa. 28:13) צַ֤ו לָצָ֞ו

Geresh (or *gereshayim*) can subdivide any of the following segments: *revia, pashta, tevir,* or *zarka*. Chant these phrases. Connect each conjunctive to the word that follows. Make an appropriate elongation or pause after *revia, pashta, tevir,* or *zarka*. Create only a slight elongation or pause after *geresh* or *gereshayim*.

קַדְמָ֨ה גֵּ֜רֶשׁ רְבִ֗יעַ

צָעֲקָ֨ה אֶל־אֱלִישָׁ֜ע לֵאמֹ֗ר (2 Kings 4:1) וַיִּגַּ֤שׁ גֵּיחֲזִי֙ לְהָדְפָ֔הּ (2 Kings 4:27)

קַדְמָ֨ה גֵּ֜רֶשׁ מ֣וּנַח רְבִ֗יעַ

וַיִּקַּ֨ח עֹבַדְיָ֜הוּ מֵ֣אָה נְבִאִ֗ים (1 Kings 18:4) הֲל֨וֹא יָדַ֜עַתְּ אִם־לֹ֣א שָׁמַ֗עַתְּ (Isa. 40:28)

גֵּ֜רֶשׁ מ֣וּנַח רְבִ֗יעַ

וַיָּ֜שָׁב וַיֵּ֣לֶךְ בַּבַּ֗יִת (2 Kings 4:35) וְיִתְּנוּ־לָ֜נוּ שְׁנַ֣יִם פָּרִ֗ים (1 Kings 18:23)

גֵּ֜רֶשׁ דַּרְגָּ֧א מ֣וּנַח רְבִ֗יעַ וַתֹּ֜אמֶר הָלֹ֧ךְ אֵלֵ֣ךְ עִמָּ֗ךְ (Judg. 4:9)

מ֣וּנַח גֵּ֜רֶשׁ רְבִ֗יעַ כִּ֤י מִמִּזְרַח־שֶׁ֜מֶשׁ וְעַד־מְבוֹא֗וֹ (Mal. 1:11)

קַדְמָ֨ה גֵּ֜רֶשׁ לְגַרְמֵ֣הּ ׀ מ֣וּנַח רְבִ֗יעַ וַיָּבֵ֨א שְׁלֹמֹ֜ה אֶת־קָדְשֵׁ֣י ׀ דָּוִ֣ד אָבִ֗יו (1 Kings 7:51)

קַדְמָ֨ה גֵּ֜רֶשׁ דַּרְגָּ֧א מוּנַ֣ח רְבִ֗יעַ
הַיָּצִ֨יעַ הַתַּחְתֹּנָ֜ה חָמֵ֧שׁ בָּאַמָּ֣ה רָחְבָּ֗הּ (1 Kings 6:6)
וְאֶת־נְבִיאֵ֨י הַבַּ֜עַל אַרְבַּ֧ע מֵא֣וֹת וַחֲמִשִּׁ֗ים (1 Kings 18:19)

קַדְמָ֨ה גֵּ֜רֶשׁ מוּנַ֣ח דַּרְגָּ֧א מוּנַ֣ח רְבִ֗יעַ
וַיָּ֨שָׁב מֵאַחֲרָ֜יו וַיִּקַּ֨ח אֶת־צֶ֧מֶד הַבָּקָ֣ר וַיִּזְבָּחֵ֗הוּ (1 Kings 19:21)

גֵּרְשַׁ֞יִם מוּנַ֣ח רְבִ֗יעַ
כָּל־הַגּוֹיִ֞ם נִקְבְּצ֣וּ יַחְדָּ֗ו (Isa. 43:9) אֵ֣יךְ אֶתֶּנְךָ֞ אֶפְרַ֗יִם (Hos. 11:8)

גֵּרְשַׁ֞יִם דַּרְגָּ֧א מוּנַ֣ח רְבִ֗יעַ
וְהָעֲזָרָ֞ה אַרְבַּ֧ע עֶשְׂרֵ֣ה אֹ֗רֶךְ (Ezek. 43:17) וָאֹמַ֞ר לִשְׁפֹּ֧ךְ חֲמָתִ֣י עֲלֵיהֶ֗ם (Ezek. 20:8)

גֵּרְשַׁ֞יִם לְגַרְמֵ֣הּ ׀ מוּנַ֣ח רְבִ֗יעַ וְהָיָ֞ה אֲנִ֣י ׀ אֵלֵ֣ךְ מֵאִתָּ֗ךְ (1 Kings 18:12)

מ֣וּנַח גֵּרְשַׁ֞יִם רְבִ֗יעַ
אֹ֣דֶם פִּטְדָ֞ה וְיָהֲלֹ֗ם (Ezek. 28:13) כִּ֣י עַֽל־כָּל־גִּבְעָ֞ה גְּבֹהָ֗ה (Jer. 2:20)

מ֣וּנַח גֵּרְשַׁ֞יִם מוּנַ֣ח רְבִ֗יעַ
כִּ֣י מֵעוֹלָ֞ם שָׁבַ֣רְתִּי עֻלֵּ֗ךְ (Jer. 2:20) אֵ֣יךְ תֹּאמְרִ֞י לֹ֣א נִטְמֵ֗אתִי (Jer. 2:23)

תְּלִישָׁ֠ה קַדְמָ֨ה גֵּ֜רֶשׁ מוּנַ֣ח רְבִ֗יעַ
וַיֵּ֡לֶךְ וַיִּקַּ֨ח בְּיָד֜וֹ עֶ֣שֶׂר כִּכְּרֵי־כֶ֗סֶף (2 Kings 5:5)
וְאֶצְבְּעֹ֨ת יָדָ֤יו וְאֶצְבְּעֹ֨ת רַגְלָ֜יו שֵׁ֣שׁ וָשֵׁ֗שׁ (2 Sam. 21:20)

תְּלִישָׁ֠ה קַדְמָ֨ה גֵּ֜רֶשׁ רְבִ֗יעַ
אָשִׂים֩ מַחְשָׁ֨ךְ לִפְנֵיהֶ֜ם לָא֗וֹר (Isa. 42:16) וְקָרָ֩אתָ֩ בְאָזְנֵ֨י יְרוּשָׁלַ֜ם לֵאמֹ֗ר (Jer. 2:2)

תְּלִישָׁ֠ה קַדְמָ֨ה גֵּ֜רֶשׁ דַּרְגָּ֧א מוּנַ֣ח רְבִ֗יעַ
וְאִם־לֹ֩א תָשִׂ֨ימוּ עַל־לֵ֜ב לָתֵ֧ת כָּב֣וֹד לִשְׁמִ֗י (Mal 2:2)
וְהָיָ֩ה בֵית־יַעֲקֹ֨ב אֵ֜שׁ וּבֵ֧ית יוֹסֵ֣ף לֶהָבָ֗ה (Obad. 1:18)

תְּלִישָׁ֠ה קַדְמָ֨ה גֵּ֜רֶשׁ לְגַרְמֵ֣הּ ׀ מוּנַ֣ח רְבִ֗יעַ
וְנָתְנ֩וּ אִ֨ישׁ כִּסְא֜וֹ פֶּ֣תַח ׀ שַׁעֲרֵ֣י יְרוּשָׁלַ֗ם (Jer. 1:15)
וּשְׁטָחוּ֩ם לַשֶּׁ֨מֶשׁ וְלַיָּרֵ֜חַ וּלְכֹ֣ל ׀ צְבָ֣א הַשָּׁמַ֗יִם (Jer. 8:2)

תְּלִישָׁ֠ה קַדְמָ֨ה גֵּ֜רֶשׁ לְגַרְמֵ֣הּ ׀ דַּרְגָּ֧א מוּנַ֣ח רְבִ֗יעַ
כִּ֩י אֶעֱשֶׂ֨ה כָלָ֜ה בְּכָל־הַגּוֹיִ֣ם ׀ אֲשֶׁ֧ר הִדַּחְתִּ֣יךָ שָׁ֗מָּה (Jer. 46:28)

מוּנַח תְּלִישָׁה קַדְמָה גֵּרֶשׁ רְבִיעַ

וַתֹּאמֶר הָאִשָּׁה אֲשֶׁר־בְּנָהּ הַחַי אֶל־הַמֶּלֶךְ (1 Kings 3:26)

בְּיַד סִיסְרָא שַׂר־צְבָא חָצוֹר וּבְיַד־פְּלִשְׁתִּים (1 Sam. 12:9)

מוּנַח תְּלִישָׁה קַדְמָה גֵּרֶשׁ מוּנַח רְבִיעַ

מִכֹּל אֲשֶׁר־יֵצֵא מִגֶּפֶן הַיַּיִן לֹא תֹאכַל (Judg. 13:14)

וַיִּשְׁלַח יִשְׂרָאֵל מַלְאָכִים ׀ אֶל־מֶלֶךְ אֱדוֹם ׀ לֵאמֹר אֶעְבְּרָה־נָּא בְאַרְצֶךָ (Judg. 11:17)

מוּנַח תְּלִישָׁה קַדְמָה גֵּרֶשׁ לְגַרְמֵהּ ׀ מוּנַח רְבִיעַ

וְנָתַתִּי אֶת־אֶרֶץ מִצְרַיִם שְׁמָמָה בְּתוֹךְ ׀ אֲרָצוֹת נְשַׁמּוֹת (Ezek. 29:12)

כָּל־הָעָם הַיֹּצֵא מִמִּצְרַיִם הַזְּכָרִים כֹּל ׀ אַנְשֵׁי הַמִּלְחָמָה (Josh. 5:4)

מוּנַח תְּלִישָׁה קַדְמָה גֵּרֶשׁ דַּרְגָּא מוּנַח רְבִיעַ

וַיֹּאמֶר לָהּ אֶלְקָנָה אִישָׁהּ עֲשִׂי הַטּוֹב בְּעֵינַיִךְ (1 Sam. 1:23)

גֵּרֶשׁ מַהְפַּךְ פַּשְׁטָא

וַתֹּאמֶר הָאִשָּׁה הָאַחַת בִּי אֲדֹנִי (1 Kings 3:17) וַתֵּלֶךְ יַד בְּנֵי־יִשְׂרָאֵל הָלוֹךְ וְקָשָׁה (Judg. 4:24)

גֵּרֶשׁ מֵרְכָא פַּשְׁטָא אֶפְרַיִם רֹעֶה רוּחַ וְרֹדֵף קָדִים (Hos. 12:2)

קַדְמָה גֵּרֶשׁ מַהְפַּךְ פַּשְׁטָא

הִנֵּה אָנֹכִי מַרְבִּיץ בַּפּוּךְ אֲבָנַיִךְ (Isa. 54:11) וּבְנָיָהוּ בֶן־יְהוֹיָדָע וְנָתָן הַנָּבִיא וְשִׁמְעִי וְרֵעִי (1 Kings 1:8)

קַדְמָה גֵּרֶשׁ קַדְמָה מַהְפַּךְ פַּשְׁטָא

וְהָיְתָה נִבְלַת הָעָם הַזֶּה לְמַאֲכָל (Jer. 7:33)

אֲשֶׁר לֹא־יַעֲלֶה מֵאֵת מִשְׁפְּחוֹת הָאָרֶץ אֶל־יְרוּשָׁלַם (Zech. 4:17)

קַדְמָה גֵּרֶשׁ מוּנַח תְּלִישָׁה קַדְמָה מַהְפַּךְ פַּשְׁטָא

שַׂר־צְבָא מֶלֶךְ־אֲרָם הָיָה אִישׁ גָּדוֹל לִפְנֵי אֲדֹנָיו וּנְשֻׂא פָנִים (2 Kings 5:1)

תְּלִישָׁה קַדְמָה גֵּרֶשׁ מַהְפַּךְ פַּשְׁטָא

וַיָּשֶׂם פִּיו עַל־פִּיו וְעֵינָיו עַל־עֵינָיו וְכַפָּיו עַל־כַּפָּו (2 Kings 4:34)

הִנֵּה אֲנִי לֹקֵחַ אֶת־עֵץ יוֹסֵף אֲשֶׁר בְּיַד־אֶפְרַיִם (Ezek. 37:19)

תְּלִישָׁה קַדְמָה גֵּרֶשׁ קַדְמָה מַהְפַּךְ פַּשְׁטָא

לִשְׁנֵי מַלְכֵי הָאֱמֹרִי אֲשֶׁר בְּעֵבֶר הַיַּרְדֵּן לְסִיחֹן וּלְעוֹג (Josh. 2:10)

מוּנַח תְּלִישָׁה קַדְמָ֫ה גֵּ֫רֶשׁ קַדְמָ֫ה מַהְפַּ֫ךְ פַּשְׁטָא֑

וַתִּקַּ֨ח רִצְפָּ֤ה בַת־אַיָּ֙ה אֶת־הַשַּׂ֔ק וַתַּטֵּ֤הוּ לָהּ אֶל־הַצּוּר֙ מִתְּחִלַּ֣ת קָצִ֔יר (2 Sam. 21:10)

גֵּרְשַׁ֜יִם מֵרְכָ֖א פַּשְׁטָא֑

וַיַּֽחְבִּיאֵ֥ם חֲמִשִּׁ֖ים אִישׁ֙ בַּמְּעָרָ֔ה (1 Kings 18:40) הַמַּלְאָ֖ךְ הַדֹּבֵ֣ר בִּ֑י וַיֹּ֣אמֶר אֵלַ֔י (Zech. 4:5)

גֵּרְשַׁ֜יִם מַהְפַּ֤ךְ פַּשְׁטָא֑

לָכֵ֞ן הִנֵּֽה־יָמִ֤ים בָּאִים֙ (Jer. 7:32) דַּבֵּ֞ר אֶת־זִקְנֵ֤י יִשְׂרָאֵל֙ וְאָמַרְתָּ֣ אֲלֵהֶ֔ם (Ezek. 20:3)

גֵּרְשַׁ֜יִם קַדְמָ֤ה מַהְפַּ֤ךְ פַּשְׁטָא֑ אַחְאָ֗ב הָלַ֥ךְ בְּדֶ֛רֶךְ אֶחָ֖ד לְבַדּ֑וֹ (1 Kings 18:6)

גֵּרְשַׁ֜יִם מוּנַ֤ח מַהְפַּ֤ךְ פַּשְׁטָא֑ וַיִּקְרָ֞א שֵׁ֣ם הַמָּק֤וֹם הַהוּא֙ גִּלְגָּ֔ל (Josh. 5:9)

מוּנַ֣ח גֵּרְשַׁ֜יִם פַּשְׁטָא֑ לֵ֣ךְ וְהַחֲרַמְתָּ֗ה אֶת־הַֽחַטָּאִים֙ אֶת־עֲמָלֵ֔ק (1 Sam. 18:18)

מוּנַ֣ח גֵּרְשַׁ֜יִם מַהְפַּ֤ךְ פַּשְׁטָא֑

אִ֤ישׁ אֶת־עַבְדּ֙וֹ וְאִ֣ישׁ אֶת־שִׁפְחָת֔וֹ חָפְשִׁ֑ים (Jer. 34:10) צַ֤ו לָצָו֙ צַ֣ו לָצָ֔ו קַ֥ו לָקָ֖ו קַ֥ו לָקָ֑ו (Isa. 28:13)

גֵּרְשַׁ֜יִם מוּנַ֣ח דַּרְגָּ֥א תְּבִ֖יר הֲלֹ֕א אֵ֣ת אֲשֶׁ֣ר יֽוֹרִישְׁךָ֔ (Judg. 11:24)

גֵּרְשַׁ֜יִם מֵרְכָ֖א תְּבִ֑יר

יְלָדָ֑יו מַעֲשֵׂ֣ה יָדַ֔י (Isa. 29:23) וְאַתָּ֗ה עֹשֶׂ֥ה אִתִּ֖י (Judg. 11:27)

גֵּרְשַׁ֜יִם תְּבִ֑יר וְיִשְׁמְר֖וּ אֶת־כָּל־צוּרֹתָ֔יו (Ezek. 43:11)

מוּנַ֣ח גֵּרְשַׁ֜יִם דַּרְגָּ֥א תְּבִ֖יר אִ֤ישׁ אֶת־עַבְדּ֙וֹ וְאִ֣ישׁ אֶת־שִׁפְחָת֔וֹ (Jer. 34:9)

קַדְמָ֤ה גֵּ֣רֶשׁ דַּרְגָּ֥א תְּבִ֑יר

וְקָרַ֣ב אֹתָ֗ם אֶחָ֤ד אֶל־אֶחָד֙ (Ezek. 37:17) וְהָי֤וּ הָֽעֵצִים֙ אֲשֶׁר־תִּכְתֹּ֖ב עֲלֵיהֶ֑ם (Ezek. 37:20)

קַדְמָ֤ה גֵּ֣רֶשׁ מֵרְכָ֖א תְּבִ֑יר

לְעִ֣יר מִבְצָ֗ר וּלְעַמּ֥וּד בַּרְזֶ֖ל (Jer. 1:18) הִנֵּ֣ה אֲנִ֗י מֵבִ֤יא בָכֶ֔ם (Ezek. 37:5)

קַדְמָ֤ה גֵּ֣רֶשׁ קַדְמָ֤ה מֵרְכָ֖א תְּבִ֑יר וְהָאָ֥רֶץ הַֽחֲדָשָׁ֖ה אֲשֶׁ֥ר אֲנִ֣י עֹשֶׂ֔ה (Isa. 66:22)

תְּלִישָׁ֠ה קַדְמָ֤ה גֵּ֣רֶשׁ תְּבִ֑יר וְאֶת־נָתָ֤ן הַנָּבִיא֙ וּבְנָיָ֔הוּ וְאֶת־הַגִּבּוֹרִ֖ים (1 Kings 1:10)

תְּלִישָׁ֠ה קַדְמָ֤ה גֵּ֣רֶשׁ קַדְמָ֤ה מֵרְכָ֖א תְּבִ֑יר

וַיַּ֩עַל֩ אֶת־אֲר֨וֹן הָאֱלֹהִ֜ים מִבֵּ֨ית עֹבֵ֥ד אֱדֹ֛ם (2 Sam. 6:12)

מוּנַח תְּלִישָׁה֩ קַדְמָ֨ה גֶּ֜רֶשׁ דַּרְגָּ֧א תְּבִ֛יר

הִנֵּ֣ה שָׂכַר־עָלֵ֜ינוּ מֶ֣לֶךְ יִשְׂרָאֵ֗ל אֶת־מַלְכֵ֧י הַחִתִּ֛ים (2 Kings 7:6)

גֶּ֜רֶשׁ דַּרְגָּ֧א תְּבִ֛יר לָקַ֣חַת אֶת־שְׁנֵ֧י יְלָדַ֛י (2 Kings 4:1)

גֶּ֜רֶשׁ מֵרְכָ֥א תְּבִ֛יר בָּנַ֜יִךְ עֻלְּפ֥וּ שָׁכְב֛וּ (Isa. 51:20)

קַדְמָ֨ה גֶּ֜רֶשׁ מוּנַ֣ח זַרְקָ֢א מוּנַ֣ח סֶגּוֹל֒

וַיְחַלֵּ֨ק לְכָל־הָעָ֜ם לְכָל־הֲמ֣וֹן יִשְׂרָאֵ֗ל לְמֵאִ֤ישׁ וְעַד־אִשָּׁה֒ (2 Sam. 6:19)
אֶל־הֶחָצֵ֤ר הַחִיצוֹנָה֙ אֶל־הֶחָצֵ֤ר הַחִיצוֹנָה֙ אֶל־הָעָ֒ם (Ezek. 44:19)

קַדְמָ֨ה גֶּ֜רֶשׁ מוּנַ֣ח זַרְקָ֢א סֶגּוֹל֒

אֲשֶׁ֨ר הוֹצֵ֤אתִי אֶת־עַמִּ֤י אֶת־יִשְׂרָאֵל֙ מִמִּצְרַ֔יִם֙ (1 Kings 8:16)
וּבְב֨וֹא עַם־הָאָ֜רֶץ לִפְנֵ֤י יְהוָה֙ בַּמּוֹעֲדִים֒ (Ezek. 46:9)

גֵּרְשַׁ֞יִם מוּנַ֣ח זַרְקָ֢א מוּנַ֣ח סֶגּוֹל֒

כִּֽי־נָחָ֞שׁ מֶ֣לֶךְ בְּנֵֽי־עַמּוֹן֙ בָּ֣א עֲלֵיכֶ֒ם (1 Sam. 12:12)
עַד־מָתַ֞י אַתֶּ֣ם פֹּסְחִים֙ עַל־שְׁתֵּ֣י הַסְּעִפִּים֒ (1 Kings 18:21)

גֵּרְשַׁ֞יִם מוּנַ֣ח זַרְקָ֢א סֶגּוֹל֒

וַיִּגַּ֞שׁ אֵלִיָּ֤הוּ הַנָּבִיא֙ וַיֹּאמַ֒ר (1 Kings 18:36)

תְּלִישָׁה֩ קַדְמָ֨ה גֶּ֜רֶשׁ מוּנַ֣ח זַרְקָ֢א מוּנַ֣ח סֶגּוֹל֒

וְכִֽי־יַעֲשֶׂה֩ הַנָּשִׂ֨יא נְדָבָ֜ה עוֹלָ֣ה אֽוֹ־שְׁלָמִים֙ נְדָבָ֣ה לַֽיהוָה֒ (Ezek. 46:12)
אֶת־חִלְקִיָּ֨הוּ הַכֹּהֵ֜ן הַגָּד֗וֹל וְאֶת־כֹּהֲנֵ֤י הַמִּשְׁנֶה֙ וְאֶת־שֹׁמְרֵ֣י הַסַּ֒ף (2 Kings 23:4)

Telishah Gedolah

Telishah gedolah is another minor disjunctive. The conjunctive of *telishah gedolah* is munaḥ.

One or Two Words in the *Telishah Gedolah* Segment

(Munaḥ) telishah gedolah מוּנַ֣ח תְּלִישָׁה֩

*mu - NAH_____ tᵉ - lí - SHA_____ *Some chant the third pitch of *munaḥ* as F#.

Chant these words to the melody of *telishah gedolah.*

עֵלִ֩י (1 Sam. 4:13) תֵּרָ֩עוּ (Isa. 43:10) בָּ֩א (Jer. 39:1) בְּכֹרַ֩ח (1 Sam. 23:6)

Chant these words to the melody of *munaḥ telishah gedolah.*

הִנֵּ֣ה אֲנָשִׁ֩ים (Josh. 2:2) וְצָד֣וֹק הַכֹּהֵ֩ן (1 Kings 1:8) אֵ֣י זֶ֩ה (Isa. 50:1)
עֶ֣שֶׂר בָּאַמָּ֩ה (1 Kings 7:23) וַיֵּ֣שֶׁב הַמֶּ֩לֶךְ (1 Sam. 20:25)

Three or More Words in the *Telishah Gedolah* Segment

The conjunctive *munaḥ* may be repeated before *telishah gedolah.*

וְגַם אֶת־הָאֹבוֹת וְאֶת־הַיִּדְּעֹנִים (2 Kings 23:24)   וְאִשָּׁה אַחַת מִנְּשֵׁי בְנֵי־הַנְּבִיאִים (2 Kings 4:1)

אֲשֶׁר עָשָׂה לִשְׁנֵי־שָׂרֵי צִבְאוֹת יִשְׂרָאֵל (1 Kings 2:5)

Pazer

Pazer is another minor disjunctive. The conjunctive of *pazer* is *munaḥ.*

One or Two Words in the *Pazer* Segment

Munaḥ pazer מוּנַח פָּזֵר

*Some chant the third pitch of *munaḥ* as F#.

Chant these words to the melody of *pazer.*

הָלֹךְ (Jer. 2:2)   בַּסּוּסִים (Isa. 66:20)   כִּי (Isa. 55:10)   וַיֹּאמֶר (Isa. 6:11)

Chant these words to the melody of *munaḥ pazer.*

אֲשֶׁר יֶשׁ־בָּהּ (Jon. 4:11)   וַיִּמְכֹּר אֹתָם (1 Sam. 12:9)   כִּי אִם־לְאָב (Ezek. 44:25)   וַיֹּאמֶר אֵלַי (Jer. 32:8)

Three or More Words in the *Pazer* Segment

The conjunctive *munaḥ* may be repeated before *pazer.*

וַיַּעַשׂ שְׁלֹמֹה בָעֵת־הַהִיא | אֶת־הֶחָג (1 Kings 8:65)   אָז יַקְהֵל שְׁלֹמֹה אֶת־זִקְנֵי יִשְׂרָאֵל (1 Kings 8:1)

וַיְהִי בִשְׁמוֹנִים שָׁנָה וְאַרְבַּע מֵאוֹת שָׁנָה (1 Kings 6:1)

Chant these verses.

וַיֹּאמֶר שַׁלְּחֵנִי נָא כִּי זֶבַח מִשְׁפָּחָה לָנוּ בָּעִיר וְהוּא צִוָּה־לִי אָחִי
וְעַתָּה אִם־מָצָאתִי חֵן בְּעֵינֶיךָ אִמָּלְטָה נָּא וְאֶרְאֶה אֶת־אֶחָי
עַל־כֵּן לֹא־בָא אֶל־שֻׁלְחַן הַמֶּלֶךְ׃ (1 Sam. 20:29)

מִקֵּץ שֶׁבַע שָׁנִים תְּשַׁלְּחוּ אִישׁ אֶת־אָחִיו הָעִבְרִי אֲשֶׁר־יִמָּכֵר לְךָ
וַעֲבָדְךָ שֵׁשׁ שָׁנִים וְשִׁלַּחְתּוֹ חָפְשִׁי מֵעִמָּךְ וְלֹא־שָׁמְעוּ אֲבוֹתֵיכֶם אֵלַי
וְלֹא הִטּוּ אֶת־אָזְנָם׃ (Jer. 34:14)

וַיְהִי בִּימֵי אָחָז בֶּן־יוֹתָם בֶּן־עֻזִּיָּהוּ מֶלֶךְ יְהוּדָה עָלָה רְצִין מֶלֶךְ־אֲרָם
וּפֶקַח בֶּן־רְמַלְיָהוּ מֶלֶךְ־יִשְׂרָאֵל יְרוּשָׁלִַם לַמִּלְחָמָה עָלֶיהָ
וְלֹא יָכֹל לְהִלָּחֵם עָלֶיהָ׃ (Isa. 7:1)

וַיִּזְבַּח שׁוֹר וּמְרִיא־וְצֹאן לָרֹב וַיִּקְרָא לְכָל־בְּנֵי הַמֶּלֶךְ
וּלְאֶבְיָתָר הַכֹּהֵן וּלְיֹאָב שַׂר הַצָּבָא וְלִשְׁלֹמֹה עַבְדְּךָ לֹא קָרָא׃ (1 Kings 1:19)

וְגַ֣ם אֶת־הָאֹב֣וֹת וְאֶת־הַיִּדְּעֹנִ֡ים וְאֶת־הַתְּרָפִ֣ים וְאֶת־הַגִּלֻּלִ֗ים
וְאֵ֣ת כָּל־הַשִּׁקֻּצִ֗ים אֲשֶׁ֤ר נִרְאוּ֙ בְּאֶ֣רֶץ יְהוּדָ֣ה וּבִירֽוּשָׁלַ֔͏ִם בִּעֵ֖ר יֹֽאשִׁיָּ֑הוּ
לְמַ֗עַן הָקִ֞ים אֶת־דִּבְרֵ֤י הַתּוֹרָה֙ הַכְּתֻבִ֣ים עַל־הַסֵּ֔פֶר אֲשֶׁ֥ר מָצָ֛א חִלְקִיָּ֥הוּ הַכֹּהֵ֖ן בֵּ֥ית יְהוָֽה: (2 Kings 23:24)

בַּשָּׁנָ֣ה הַתְּשִׁעִ֗ית לְצִדְקִיָּ֧הוּ מֶֽלֶךְ־יְהוּדָ֛ה בַּחֹ֥דֶשׁ הָעֲשִׂרִ֖י
בָּ֣א נְבֽוּכַדְרֶאצַּ֣ר מֶֽלֶךְ־בָּבֶ֠ל וְכָל־חֵיל֧וֹ אֶל־יְרֽוּשָׁלַ֛͏ִם וַיָּצֻ֖רוּ עָלֶֽיהָ: (Jer. 39:1)

The Final Cadence

We use a special melody to signal the end of a *haftarah*. This melody is applied beginning with the final *tippeḥa* segment of the last verse. You will chant this cadence slowly.

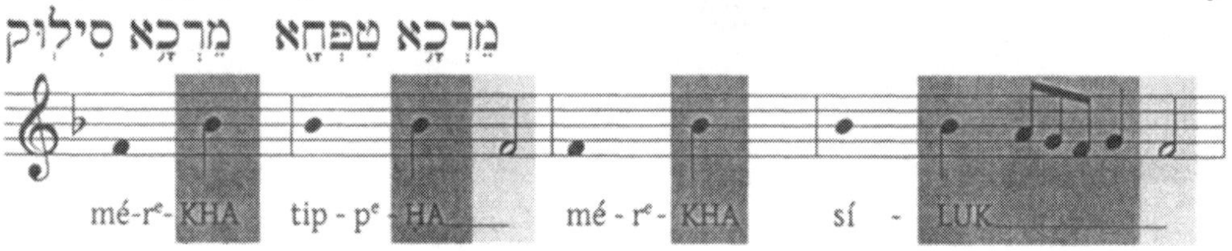

Chant these words to the appropriate *te'amim*, using the final cadence. Remember to pause slightly after *tippeḥa*.

מֶרְכָ֥א טִפְּחָ֖א   מֶרְכָ֥א סִלּֽוּק
כֵּ֣ן יֹאבְד֤וּ כָל־אֽוֹיְבֶ֙יךָ֙ יְהוָ֔ה וְאֹ֣הֲבָ֔יו כְּצֵ֥את הַשֶּׁ֖מֶשׁ בִּגְבֻֽרָת֑וֹ
וַתִּשְׁקֹ֥ט הָאָ֖רֶץ אַרְבָּעִ֥ים שָׁנָֽה: (בשלח) (Judg. 5:31)
וְשָׁ֣כַנְתִּ֔י בְּת֖וֹךְ בְּנֵ֣י יִשְׂרָאֵ֑ל   וְלֹ֥א אֶעֱזֹ֖ב   אֶת־עַמִּ֥י יִשְׂרָאֵֽל: (תרומה) (1 Kings 6:13)

מֶרְכָ֥א טִפְּחָ֖א   סִלּֽוּק
תִּזְרֵם֙ וְר֣וּחַ תִּשָּׂאֵ֔ם וּסְעָרָ֖ה תָּפִ֣יץ אוֹתָ֑ם
וְאַתָּה֙ תָּגִ֣יל בַּֽיהוָ֔ה בִּקְד֥וֹשׁ יִשְׂרָאֵ֖ל   תִּתְהַלָּֽל: (לד-לד) (Isa. 41:16)
וַתִּקֹּ֗ד בַּת־שֶׁ֙בַע֙ אַפַּ֣יִם אֶ֔רֶץ וַתִּשְׁתַּ֖חוּ לַמֶּ֑לֶךְ
וַתֹּ֕אמֶר יְחִ֗י אֲדֹנִ֛י הַמֶּ֥לֶךְ דָּוִ֖ד   לְעֹלָֽם: (חיי שרה) (1 Kings 1:31)
וּשְׁלֹמֹ֔ה יָשַׁ֕ב עַל־כִּסֵּ֖א דָּוִ֣ד אָבִ֑יו   וַתִּכֹּ֥ן מַלְכֻת֖וֹ   מְאֹֽד: (ויחי) (1 Kings 2:12)

טִפְּחָ֖א   מֶרְכָ֥א סִלּֽוּק
אַתֶּ֣ם עֵדַי֩ נְאֻם־יְהוָ֜ה וְעַבְדִּ֣י אֲשֶׁ֣ר בָּחָ֗רְתִּי   לְמַ֤עַן תֵּֽדְעוּ֙
וְתַֽאֲמִ֣ינוּ לִ֗י וְתָבִ֙ינוּ֙ כִּֽי־אֲנִ֣י ה֔וּא לְפָנַי֙ לֹא־נ֣וֹצַר אֵ֔ל וְאַֽחֲרַ֖י   לֹ֥א יִֽהְיֶֽה: (בראשית) (Isa. 43:10)
אַרְיֵ֥ה שָׁאָ֖ג מִ֣י לֹ֣א יִירָ֑א   אֲדֹנָ֤י יְהוִה֙ דִּבֶּ֔ר מִ֖י   לֹ֥א יִנָּבֵֽא: (וישב) (Amos 3:8)

טִפְחָא סִילוּק

וַיְהִי֙ הַמֶּ֣לֶךְ שְׁלֹמֹ֔ה מֶ֖לֶךְ עַל־כָּל־יִשְׂרָאֵֽל׃ (מקץ) (1 Kings 4:1)

וְיָֽדְעוּ֙ הַגּוֹיִ֔ם כִּ֚י אֲנִ֣י יְהוָ֔ה מְקַדֵּ֖שׁ אֶת־יִשְׂרָאֵ֑ל בִּהְי֧וֹת מִקְדָּשִׁ֛י בְּתוֹכָ֖ם לְעוֹלָֽם׃ (ויגש) (Ezek. 37:28)

צִיּ֖וֹן בְּמִשְׁפָּ֣ט תִּפָּדֶ֑ה וְשָׁבֶ֖יהָ בִּצְדָקָֽה׃ (דברים) (Isa. 1:27)

Notes of Sadness

Several melancholy verses in the books of Jeremiah and Isaiah are chanted according to the musical motifs of Lamentations (איכה). The *haftarah* of the Shabbat before Tish'ah Be'Av (Shabbat Devarim, also known as Shabbat Ḥazon) is chanted in the following modes:

Isa. 1:1	*Haftarah* mode
2–15	Lamentations mode
16–19	*Haftarah* mode
20–23	Lamentations mode
24–27	*Haftarah* mode

The *haftarah* for the morning service on Tish'ah Be'Av begins in the Lamentations mode (Jer. 8:13–9:21) and ends in the *Haftarah* mode (9:22–23). The switch away from the Lamentations mode is in keeping with the practice of not ending any reading on a depressing note. The blessings before the *haftarah* for the morning service on Tish'ah Be'Av may be chanted either in the regular mode or in the Lamentations mode. The transcription of the Lamentations *te'amim* is found in chapter 6.

Blessings

The blessings before the *haftarah* are chanted according to *te'amim* that are superimposed on the text.

בָּר֨וּךְ אַתָּ֥ה יְיָ֙ אֱלֹהֵ֙ינוּ֙ מֶ֣לֶךְ הָעוֹלָ֔ם

אֲשֶׁ֤ר בָּחַר֙ בִּנְבִיאִ֣ים טוֹבִ֔ים

וְרָצָ֥ה בְדִבְרֵיהֶ֖ם הַנֶּאֱמָרִ֣ים בֶּאֱמֶ֑ת

בָּר֨וּךְ אַתָּ֥ה יְיָ֙ הַבּוֹחֵ֤ר בַּתּוֹרָה֙ וּבְמֹשֶׁ֣ה עַבְדּ֔וֹ

וּבְיִשְׂרָאֵ֖ל עַמּ֑וֹ וּבִנְבִיאֵ֥י הָאֱמֶ֖ת וָצֶֽדֶק

Note that the *ta'am* on the first word is *kadmah*, not *pashta*!

The blessings after the *haftarah* are chanted to a melody that continues the mode of the *haftarah*'s final cadence. The mood is jubilant, the tempo quick but majestic. No *te'amim* are superimposed on the text; you are expected to be knowledgeable enough to apply the appropriate melodic motifs to the text, with the appropriate phrasing. We have notated the first blessing, as a model for the others. We have also notated the final blessing. The words vary depending on the occasion (Shabbat, holiday, fast day, etc.). The blessings for nontraditional services may have a slightly different wording. In any case, you should consult an appropriate prayer book. For more details, see *Chanting: The Complete Guide*, pp. 721–725, and listen to the supplemental *haftarah* CD.

ba - RUKH 'at - TA 'a-dó - NAI 'e-ló-HÉ-nu ME-lekh ha-'ó-LAM
TSUR KOL ha-'ó-la - MÍM tsad-DÍK b^e-KHOL had-dó - RÓT
ha-'ÉL han-ne-'e - MAN ha-'ó - MÉR v^e-'ó - SE
ha-m^e-da - BÉR um-kay - YÉM shek - KOL d^e-va - RAV 'e-MET va - TSE - dek
ne-'e - MAN 'at-TA HU 'a-dó-NAI 'e-ló - HÉ-nu
v^e-ne-'e-ma - NÍM d^e-vaRE-kha v^e-da-VAR 'e-ḤAD mid-d^e-va - RE - kha
'a-ḤÓR LÓ ya - SHUV ré-KAM KÍ 'ÉL ME-lekh ne-'e - MAN
v^e-ra-ḥa - MAN 'AT - ta ba - RUKH 'at - TA 'a-dó - NAI
ha - 'ÉL han-ne-'e - MAN b^e-KHOL d^e-va - RAV
final blessing:
ba - RUKH 'at - TA 'a-dó - NAI m^e - kad - DÉSH hash-shab - BAT

Yatsiv Pitgam

On the second day of Shavuot, in some congregations a special *piyyut* (hymn) is interpolated into the *haftarah*. The reader chants the first verse of the *haftarah* (Hab. 2:20), then chants the entire *piyyut*, then resumes chanting the *haftarah* from the second verse (Hab. 3:1) to the end (Hab. 3:19).

The first verse of the *piyyut* is sung to the melody of line ❶, the second verse to the melody of line ❷. This alternation continues throughout the *piyyut*.

❶

❷

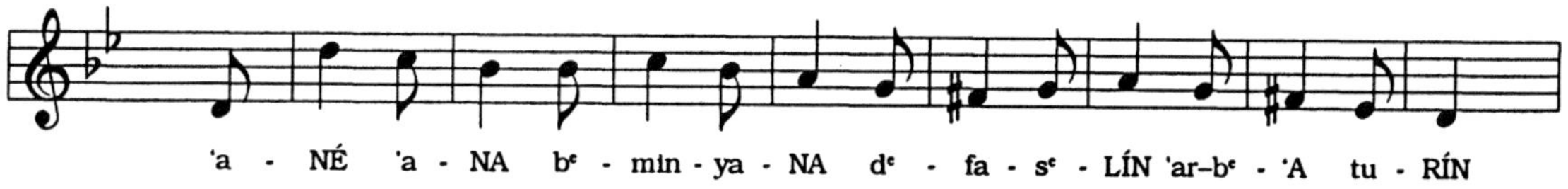

יַצִּיב פִּתְגָם לְאָת וּדְגָם, בְּרִבּוֹ רִבְבָן עִירִין.

אֲנֵה אֲנָא בְּמִנְיָנָא, דְּפָסְלִין אַרְבְּעָה טוּרִין.

8. The Festival Megillot:

Song of Songs, Ruth, and Ecclesiastes

Introduction

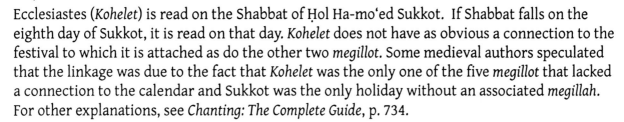

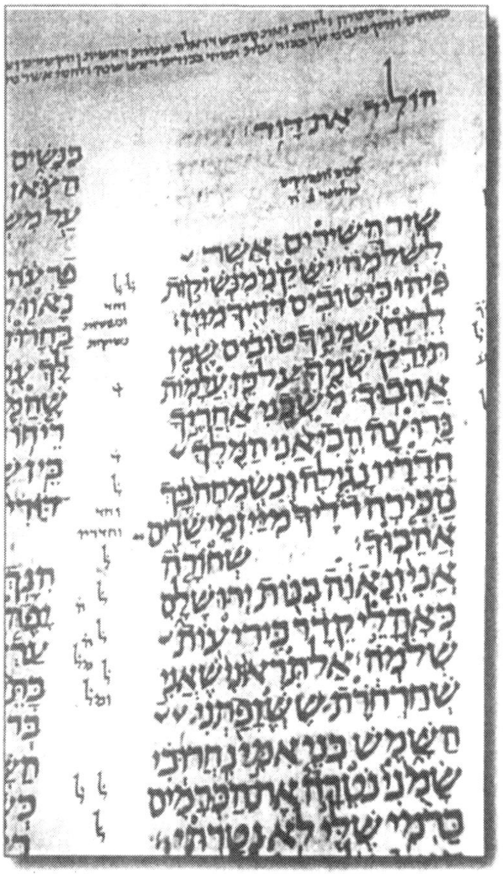

Three books of the Bible are known as the "festival *megillot*," since each is associated with one of the major festivals. The Song of Songs (שיר השירים) is chanted on Pesaḥ, Ruth (רות) on Shavuot, and Ecclesiastes (קהלת) on Sukkot. We use the same melody for chanting the *te'amim* of all three books.

The custom today in most traditional Ashkenazic synagogues is to chant the megillah at the *shaḥarit* service before reading the Torah. In most congregations, these *megillot* are read from a printed book. However, in some communities they are read from a parchment written in the same manner as a Torah scroll. In these communities, the reader chants the appropriate blessings before cantillating the scroll. (See *Chanting: The Complete Guide*, p. 781.)

The Song of Songs (*Shir Ha-shirim*) is read on the Shabbat of Ḥol Ha-mo'ed Pesaḥ. If Shabbat falls on the seventh day of Pesaḥ, it is read on that day. Pesaḥ is known as Ḥag He-aviv, the Festival of Spring. *Shir Ha-shirim* likewise celebrates the end of winter and the coming of springtime.

Ruth is read on the second day of Shavuot. Since the main action in this book takes place during the harvesting season, it is appropriate to be read on Shavuot, the festival of the harvesting of the first fruits.

Ecclesiastes (*Kohelet*) is read on the Shabbat of Ḥol Ha-mo'ed Sukkot. If Shabbat falls on the eighth day of Sukkot, it is read on that day. *Kohelet* does not have as obvious a connection to the festival to which it is attached as do the other two *megillot*. Some medieval authors speculated that the linkage was due to the fact that *Kohelet* was the only one of the five *megillot* that lacked a connection to the calendar and Sukkot was the only holiday without an associated *megillah*. For other explanations, see *Chanting: The Complete Guide*, p. 734.

The Melodies of the Cantillation Motifs

Hear the melodies of the Festival cantillation on CD tracks 81 and 82.

The *Siluk* Segment and *Tippeḥa* Segment

The last word in every verse is marked with *siluk*. If the preceding word is closely connected in meaning to the *siluk* word, it is usually marked with the conjunctive *ta'am merekha.* When *siluk* is not preceded by *merekha,* its melody is slightly different (see below).

A *siluk* segment is usually subdivided by the disjunctive *ta'am tippeḥa,* If there are two words in the *tippeḥa* segment, the first one is usually marked with the conjunctive *ta'am merekha.*

Merekha tippeḥa merekha siluk מֵרְכָא טִפְּחָא מֵרְכָא סִילוּק

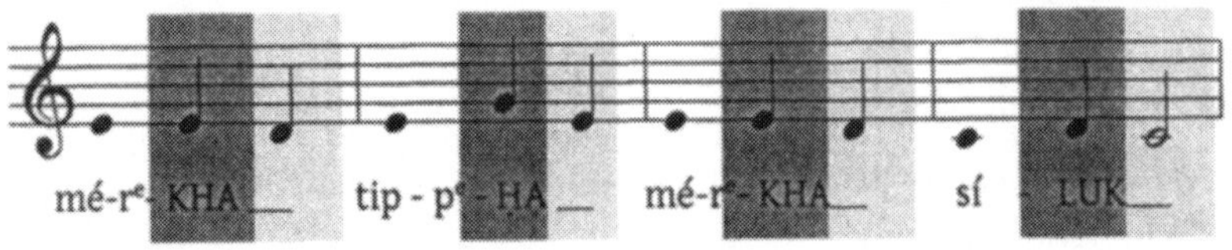
mé-rᵉ-KHA
tip - pᵉ - HA
mé-rᵉ-KHA
sí - LUK

Chant these words to the appropriate *te'amim.* Connect each conjunctive (*merekha*) to the word that follows. Pause slightly after the disjunctive *ta'am tippeḥa,*

מֵרְכָא טִפְּחָא   מֵרְכָא סִילוּק

רָאָה הַרְבֵּה חָכְמָה וָדָעַת: (Eccles. 1:16)   כַּרְמִי שֶׁלִּי לֹא נָטָרְתִּי: (Songs 1:6)

נָצוּר עָלֶיהָ לוּחַ אָרֶז: (Songs 8:9) *merekha siluk* elision:

וְיוֹסִיף דַּעַת יוֹסִיף מַכְאוֹב: (Eccles. 1:18) *merekha tippeḥa* elision:

טִפְּחָא   מֵרְכָא סִילוּק

וְעֵת לַעֲקוֹר נָטוּעַ: (Eccles. 3:2)   וְשַׁכֻּלָה אֵין בָּהֶם: (Songs 6:6)   עַל עֶדְרֵי חֲבֵרֶיךָ: (Songs 1:7)

Here is how we chant *siluk* when it is not preceded by *merekha.*

Tippeḥa siluk טִפְּחָא סִילוּק

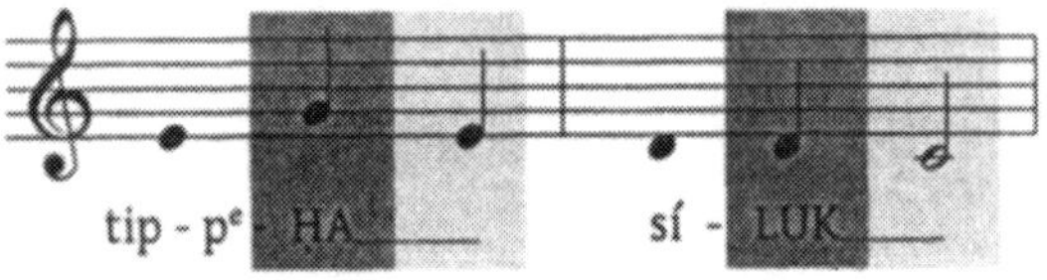
tip - pᵉ - HA
sí - LUK

טִפְּחָא   סִילוּק

וִימִינוֹ תְּחַבְּקֵנִי: (Songs 8:3)   מֶלֶךְ בִּירוּשָׁלִָם: (Eccles. 1:1)   שֹׁכֶבֶת מַרְגְּלֹתָיו: (Ruth 3:8)

מֵרְכָא טִפְּחָא   סִילוּק

וְרֵיחַ אַפֵּךְ כַּתַּפּוּחִים: (Songs 7:9)   כִּי גֹאֵל אָתָּה: (Ruth 3:9)   זוֹרֵחַ הוּא שָׁם: (Eccles. 1:5)

The *Etnaḥta* Segment and *Tippeḥa* Segment

Most verses are divided into two segments. *Etnaḥta* is the *ta'am* that marks the end of the first segment, and *siluk* marks the end of the second segment. If the *etnaḥta* word and the word before it are closely connected in meaning, they are usually marked *munaḥ etnaḥta.* When *etnaḥta* is not preceded by *munaḥ,* its melody is slightly different (see below).

An *etnaḥta* segment is usually subdivided by the disjunctive *ta'am tippeḥa,* If there are two words in the *tippeḥa* segment, the first one is usually marked with the conjunctive *ta'am merekha.*

Merekha tippeḥa munaḥ etnaḥta מֵרְכָא טִפְּחָא מוּנַח אֶתְנַחְתָּא

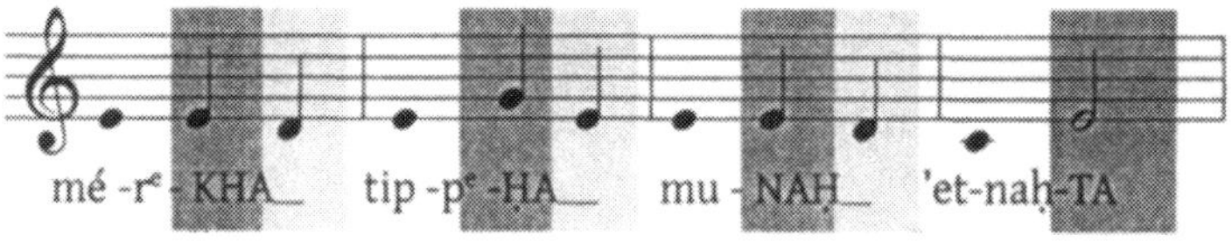
mé -rᵉ -KHA_ tip -pᵉ -HA_ mu -NAH_ 'et-naḥ-TA

Chant these words to the appropriate *te'amim*. Connect each conjunctive (*merekha* or *munaḥ*) to the word that follows. Pause slightly after the disjunctive *ta'am tippeḥa.*

מֵרְכָא טִפְּחָא מוּנַח אֶתְנַחְתָּא

בְּנ֥וֹת צִיּ֖וֹן בַּמֶּ֣לֶךְ שְׁלֹמֹ֑ה (Songs 3:11) עֵ֥ת לָלֶ֖דֶת וְעֵ֣ת לָמ֑וּת (Eccles. 3:2)

וַיָּ֥מָת אֱלִימֶ֖לֶךְ אִ֣ישׁ נָעֳמִ֑י (Ruth 1:3)

טִפְּחָא מוּנַח אֶתְנַחְתָּא

מָשְׁכֵ֖נִי אַחֲרֶ֣יךָ נָּר֑וּצָה (Songs 1:4) לִשְׁכַּ֖ב בִּקְצֵ֣ה הָעֲרֵמָ֑ה (Ruth 3:7) שֶׁ֖מֶן תּוּרַ֣ק שְׁמֶ֑ךָ (Songs 1:3)

Here is how we chant *etnaḥta* when it is not preceded by *munaḥ.*

Tippeḥa etnaḥta טִפְּחָא אֶתְנַחְתָּא

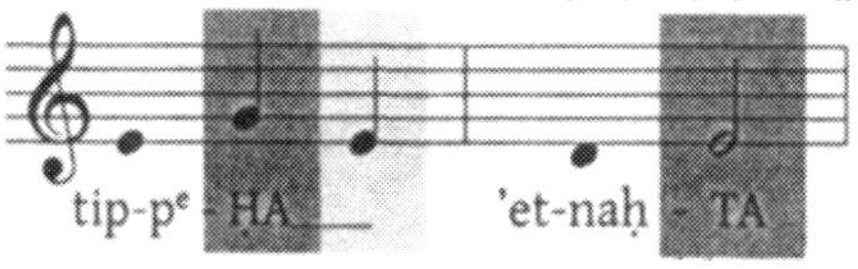
tip-pᵉ -HA_ 'et-naḥ -TA

טִפְּחָא אֶתְנַחְתָּא

וַיֹּ֖אמֶר מִי־אָ֑תְּ (Ruth 3:9) וְכֻלּ֖וֹ מַחֲמַדִּ֑ים (Songs 5:16)

with elision: (Eccles. 10:16) שֶׁמַּלְכֵּ֖ךְ נָ֑עַר

מֵרְכָא טִפְּחָא אֶתְנַחְתָּא

אֵ֥ין זִכְר֖וֹן לָרִאשֹׁנִ֑ים (Eccles. 1:11) וְגִלִּ֥ית מַרְגְּלֹתָ֖יו וְשָׁכָ֑בְתְּ (Ruth 3:4)

with elision: (Eccles. 5:5) כִּ֥י שְׁגָגָ֖ה הִ֑יא

Chant these verses.

וַיָּ֥מָת אֱלִימֶ֖לֶךְ אִ֣ישׁ נָעֳמִ֑י וַתִּשָּׁאֵ֥ר הִ֖יא וּשְׁנֵ֥י בָנֶֽיהָ׃ (Ruth 1:3)

שַׁלַּ֥ח לַחְמְךָ֖ עַל־פְּנֵ֣י הַמָּ֑יִם כִּֽי־בְרֹ֥ב הַיָּמִ֖ים תִּמְצָאֶֽנּוּ׃ (Eccles. 11:1)

The *Tevir* Segment

Sometimes there is a subdivision within a *tippeḥa* segment. *Tevir* is the *ta'am* that marks that subdivision.

One or Two Words in a *Tevir* Segment

If the preceding word is closely connected in meaning to the *tevir* word, it is usually marked with a conjunctive *ta'am.* Most often that conjunctive will be *darga.*

Darga tevir דַּרְגָּ֧א תְּבִ֛יר

Chant these words to the melody of *tevir.* נָתַ֛ן (Eccles. 2:26) נֹ֛פֶת (Songs 4:11) שָׁ֛ם (Songs 7:13)

Chant these words to the melody of *darga tevir.*

אֲשֶׁ֧ר יֶשׁ־לָהֶ֛ם (Eccles. 4:9) עֲשָׂרָ֧ה אֲנָשִׁ֛ים (Ruth 4:2) כִּ֧י עַל־כָּל־אֵ֛לֶּה (Eccles. 11:9)

צְאֶ֧נָה ׀ וּרְאֶ֛ינָה (Songs 3:11)

Merekha tevir מֵרְכָ֥א תְּבִ֛יר

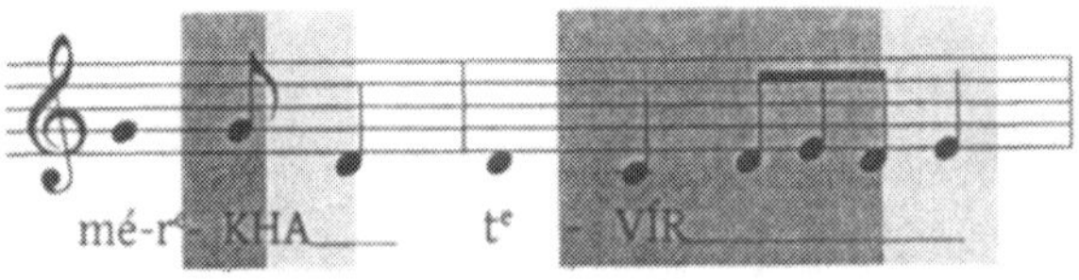

Chant these words to the melody of *merekha tevir.*

כְּיֵ֥ין הַטּ֛וֹב (Songs 7:10) מִמְּלֹ֥א חָפְנַ֛יִם (Eccles. 4:6) יֵ֥שׁ דָּבָ֛ר (Eccles. 1:10) קוּמִ֥י לָ֛ךְ (Songs 2:10)

הָיִ֥יתִי מֶ֛לֶךְ (Eccles. 1:12)

Chant these phrases. Connect the conjunctive word to the word that follows. Create a slight elongation or pause after the *tippeḥa*. There is very little elongation or pause after the *tevir*. The sense of the words dictates that *tippeḥa* is a stronger disjunctive than *tevir*.

דַּרְגָּ֧א תְּבִ֛יר טִפְּחָ֖א

וְלָ֧מָּה חָכַ֛מְתִּי אֲנִ֖י אָ֣ז יוֹתֵ֑ר (Eccles. 2:15) כִּ֧י הַחַיִּ֛ים יוֹדְעִ֖ים שֶׁיָּמֻ֑תוּ (Eccles. 9:5)

וְיָשֹׁ֧ב הֶעָפָ֛ר עַל־הָאָ֖רֶץ כְּשֶׁהָיָ֑ה (Eccles. 12:7)

תְּבִ֛יר מֵרְכָ֥א טִפְּחָ֖א

שָׁ֛ם אֶתֵּ֥ן אֶת־דֹּדַ֖י לָֽךְ׃ (Songs 7:13) אִ֛ישׁ יָבִ֥א בְּפִרְי֖וֹ אֶ֥לֶף כָּֽסֶף׃ (Songs 8:11)

נֹ֛פֶת תִּטֹּ֥פְנָה שִׂפְתוֹתַ֖יִךְ כַּלָּ֑ה (Songs 4:11)

מֵרְכָ֥א תְּבִ֛יר מֵרְכָ֥א טִפְּחָ֖א

יֵ֥שׁ דָּבָ֛ר שֶׁיֹּאמַ֥ר רְאֵה־זֶ֖ה חָדָ֣שׁ ה֑וּא (Eccles. 1:10)

מֵרְכָ֥א תְּבִ֛יר טִפְּחָ֖א

שֶׁיֵּ֥שׁ יִתְר֛וֹן לַֽחָכְמָ֖ה מִן־הַסִּכְל֑וּת (Eccles. 2:13)

דַּרְגָּ֧א תְּבִ֛יר מֵרְכָ֥א טִפְּחָ֖א

אֲשֶׁ֧ר יֶשׁ־לָהֶ֛ם שָׂכָ֥ר ט֖וֹב בַּעֲמָלָֽם׃ (Eccles. 4:9)

Three Words in the *Tevir* Segment

Sometimes *tevir* is preceded by two or more conjunctives. In these segments there will be a very slight pause or elongation just before the *tevir*. The second conjunctive before *tevir* (preceding either *merekha* or *darga*) may be *kadmah*.

Kadmah darga tevir קַדְמָ֨ה דַּרְגָּ֧א תְּבִ֛יר

Chant these words to the melody of *kadmah darga tevir.*

(Ruth 3:13) וְאִם־לֹ֨א יַחְפֹּ֧ץ לְגָֽאֳלֵ֛ךְ (Ruth 2:19) אֲשֶׁ֨ר עָשִׂ֧יתִי עִמּ֛וֹ

Kadmah merekha tevir קַדְמָ֨ה מֵרְכָ֥א תְּבִ֛יר

Chant these words to the melody of *kadmah merekha tevir.* (Ruth 4:13) וַיִּתֵּ֨ן יְהוָ֥ה לָ֛הּ

If the second conjunctive before *tevir* (preceding either *merekha* or *darga*) is accented on the first syllable, it will be *munaḥ* instead of *kadmah*. When we refer to this use of the *ta'am*, we will accent its first syllable: *MU-naḥ*.

Munaḥ darga tevir מֻ֣ונַח דַּרְגָּ֧א תְּבִ֛יר

Chant these words to the melody of *munaḥ darga tevir.*

(Eccles. 9:6) גַּ֣ם אַהֲבָתָ֧ם גַּם־שִׂנְאָתָ֛ם (Ruth 2:15) גַּ֣ם בֵּ֧ין הָעֳמָרִ֛ים

Munaḥ merekha tevir מֻ֣ונַח מֵרְכָ֥א תְּבִ֛יר

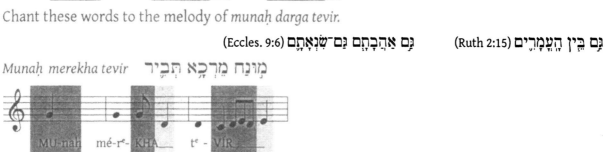

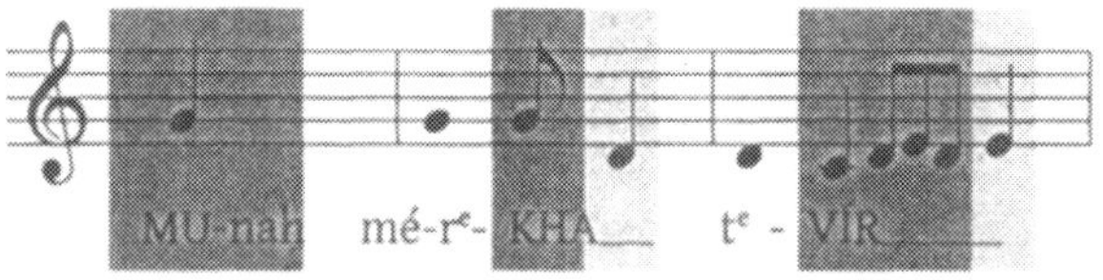

Chant these words to the melody of *munaḥ merekha tevir.* (Ruth 4:14) לֹ֣א הִשְׁבִּ֥ית לָ֛ךְ

Four Words in the *Tevir* Segment

Sometimes *tevir* is preceded by three conjunctives. The third conjunctive before *tevir* (just before *kadmah*) will be *telishah ketanah.*

telishah kadmah darga tevir תְּלִישָׁה קַדְמָה דַרְגָּא תְּבִיר

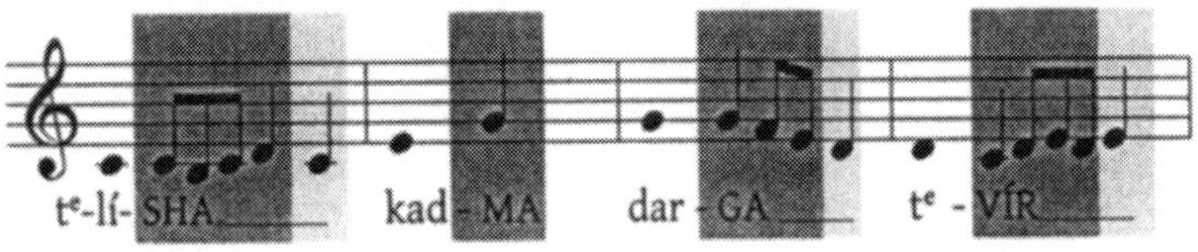

Chant these words to the melody of *telishah kadmah darga tevir.* (Eccles. 2:16) כִּי אֵין זִכְרוֹן לֶחָכָם

Chant these words to the appropriate *te'amim.*

וְאִם־לֹא יַחְפֹּץ לְגָאֳלֵךְ וּגְאַלְתִּיךְ אָנֹכִי חַי־יְהוָה שִׁכְבִי עַד־הַבֹּקֶר׃ (Ruth 3:13)

אֲשֶׁר יַעֲמֹל הָאָדָם לְבַקֵּשׁ וְלֹא יִמְצָא (Eccles. 8:17)

אֲשֶׁר עָשָׂה הָאֱלֹהִים אֶת־הָאָדָם יָשָׁר וְהֵמָּה בִקְשׁוּ חִשְּׁבֹנוֹת רַבִּים׃ (Eccles. 7:29)

גַּם בֵּין הָעֳמָרִים תְּלַקֵּט וְלֹא תַכְלִימוּהָ׃ (Ruth 2:15)

לֹא הִשְׁבִּית לָךְ גֹּאֵל הַיּוֹם וְיִקָּרֵא שְׁמוֹ בְּיִשְׂרָאֵל׃ (Ruth 4:14)

כִּי אֵין זִכְרוֹן לֶחָכָם עִם־הַכְּסִיל לְעוֹלָם (Eccles. 2:16)

The *Zakef* Segment

Zakef is a strong disjunctive; only *siluk* and *etnaḥta* are stronger. A *zakef* segment will always be followed by a *tippeḥa* segement. *Zakef* is stronger than the ensuing *tippeḥa.* A *zakef* segment may also be followed by one or more other *zakef* segments, but they will eventually be followed by a *tippeḥa* segement. When you see two *zakefs* (or two *zakef* segments) in a row, the first is always stronger.

There are two basic forms of *zakef*, each with its own distinct melody: *zakef gadol* and *zakef katon*. There are also two compound *te'amim*, in which two symbols appear on a single word: *munaḥ-zakef* and *metigah-zakef.*

Zakef Gadol

A word marked with *zakef gadol* is short and has no conjunctives immediately before it.

Zakef gadol זָקֵף־גָּדוֹל

Note: This accent has a double pick-up. If the word has one pick-up syllable, sing that syllable on E. If the word has two pick-up syllables, sing the first pick-up on D and the second on E. If the word has three pick-up syllables, sing the first two pick-ups on D and the third on E.

Chant these words to the melody of *zakef gadol.*

עֵינָיו (Songs 5:12) אֲבַקְשָׁה (Songs 3:2) טוֹב (Eccles. 4:6) הַגֶּשֶׁם (Songs 2:11)

Zakef gadol is usually followed by *(merekha-) tippeḥa.* Chant these phrases. Make a pause or elongation after *zakef.* Make a more subtle elongation or pause after *tippeḥa.*

וַיָּבֹא לִשְׁכַּב בִּקְצֵה הָעֲרֵמָה (Ruth 3:7)

וַתָּ֫קָם בְּטֶ֣רֶם יַכִּ֥יר אִ֖ישׁ אֶת־רֵעֵ֑הוּ (Ruth 3:14)

כִּֽי־הִנֵּ֥ה הַסְּתָ֖יו עָבָ֑ר הַגֶּ֕שֶׁם חָלַ֖ף הָלַ֥ךְ לֽוֹ: (Songs 2:11)

בִּקַּ֙שְׁתִּי֙ אֵ֣ת שֶׁאָֽהֲבָ֣ה נַפְשִׁ֔י בִּקַּשְׁתִּ֖יו וְלֹ֥א מְצָאתִֽיו: (Songs 3:1)

קָשָׁ֤ה כִשְׁאוֹל֙ קִנְאָ֔ה רְשָׁפֶ֕יהָ רִשְׁפֵּ֕י אֵ֖שׁ שַׁלְהֶבֶתְיָֽה: (Song 8:6)

Zakef Katon

A word marked with *zakef katon* is usually preceded by the conjunctive *munah*. Sometimes, *munah* will appear on the same word that is marked with zakef. This happens often on long words.

One or Two Words in a *Zakef* Segment

Munah zakef katon   מוּנַ֣ח זָקֵף־קָטֹ֔ן

Chant these words to the melody of *zakef.*

הָאִ֔ישׁ (Ruth 2:20)   וַאֲהָל֔וֹת (Songs 4:14)   יָרַ֖דְתִּי (Songs 6:11)

Chant these words to the melody of *munah zakef.*

אֶל־בֵּ֣ית הַיַּ֔יִן (Songs 2:4)   בַּעֲצֵ֣י הַיַּ֔עַר (Songs 2:3)   בֵּ֣ין הַחוֹחִ֔ים (Songs 2:2)

תַּ֣חַת לְרֹאשִׁ֔י (Songs 2:6)   כְּעֵ֣דֶר הָעִזִּ֔ים (Songs 4:1)   הַשּׁוּלַמִּ֔ית (Songs 7:1)

Metigah-zakef   מְתִיגָה־זָקֵ֔ף

Chant these words to the melody of *metigah-zakef.*

בְּכָל־עֲמָל֔וֹ (Eccles. 1:3)   וְאֶל־מְקוֹמ֔וֹ (Eccles. 1:5)   וַתַּגֶּד־לָ֔הּ (Ruth 3:16)

Zakef is usually followed by (merekha-) tippeha. Chant these phrases. Make a pause or elongation after *zakef*. Make a more subtle elongation or pause after *tippeha*.

מוּנַ֣ח זָקֵ֔ף טִפְּחָ֖א

וַתֵּלַ֣כְנָה שְׁתֵּיהֶ֔ם עַד־בֹּאָ֖נָה בֵּ֣ית לָ֑חֶם (Ruth 1:19)

רְפִידָת֣וֹ זָהָ֔ב מֶרְכָּב֖וֹ אַרְגָּמָ֑ן (Songs 3:10)   ק֣וֹל דּוֹדִ֔י הִנֵּה־זֶ֖ה בָּֽא (Songs 2:8)

מוּנַ֣ח זָקֵ֔ף מֵרְכָ֖א טִפְּחָ֖א

וְאָכַ֣לְתְּ מִן־הַלֶּ֔חֶם וְטָבַ֥לְתְּ פִּתֵּ֖ךְ בַּחֹ֑מֶץ (Ruth 2:14)

אָכְל֣וּ רֵעִ֔ים שְׁת֥וּ וְשִׁכְר֖וּ דּוֹדִֽים: (Songs 5:1)   עַ֣ד שֶׁמְּצָ֔אתִי אֵ֖ת שֶׁאָהֲבָ֥ה נַפְשִֽׁי (Songs 3:4)

מוּנַ֣ח זָקֵ֔ף תְּבִ֨יר מֵרְכָ֥א טִפְחָ֖א

וְגָדַ֣לְתִּי וְהוֹסַ֗פְתִּי מִכֹּ֛ל שֶׁהָיָ֥ה לְפָנַ֖י בִּירוּשָׁלָ֑ם (Eccles. 2:9)

הַכֹּ֣ל נִשְׁכָּ֔ח וְאֵ֛יךְ יָמ֥וּת הֶחָכָ֖ם עִם־הַכְּסִֽיל׃ (Eccles. 2:16)

זָקֵ֕ף־גָּד֖וֹל טִפְחָ֖א

עֵינָ֕יו כְּיוֹנִ֖ים עַל־אֲפִ֣יקֵי מָ֑יִם (Songs 5:12)

ט֕וֹב לִשְׁמֹ֖עַ גַּעֲרַ֣ת חָכָ֑ם מֵאִ֕ישׁ שֹׁמֵ֖עַ שִׁ֥יר כְּסִילִֽים׃ (Eccles. 7:5)

זָקֵ֕ף־גָּד֖וֹל מֵרְכָ֥א טִפְחָ֖א

בִּקַּ֕שְׁתִּי אֵ֥ת שֶׁאָהֲבָ֖ה נַפְשִׁ֑י (Songs 3:1) ט֥וֹב מְלֹ֥א כַ֖ף נָֽחַת (Eccles. 4:6)

אָמַ֕רְתִּי ט֥וֹב מִמֶּ֖נּוּ הַנָּֽפֶל׃ (Eccles. 6:3)

זָקֵ֕ף־גָּד֖וֹל תְּבִ֨יר מֵרְכָ֥א טִפְחָ֖א

וַתָּ֕קָם בְּטֶ֛רֶם יַכִּ֥יר אִ֖ישׁ אֶת־רֵעֵ֑הוּ (Ruth 3:14)

וְדָ֕ע כִּ֣י עַל־כָּל־אֵ֔לֶּה יְבִֽיאֲךָ֥ הָאֱלֹהִ֖ים בַּמִּשְׁפָּֽט׃ (Eccles. 11:9)

מוּנַ֣ח זָקֵ֔ף זָקֵ֕ף־גָּד֖וֹל מֵרְכָ֥א טִפְחָ֖א

וַתֵּלְכִ֗י אֶל־עַ֕ם אֲשֶׁ֥ר לֹא־יָדַ֖עַתְּ תְּמ֥וֹל שִׁלְשֽׁוֹם׃ (Ruth 2:11)

Chant these verses.

לֹ֣א יָדַ֔עְתִּי נַפְשִׁ֣י שָׂמַ֔תְנִי מַרְכְּב֖וֹת עַמִּי־נָדִֽיב׃ (Songs 6:12)

וַתֵּ֕רֶא כִּֽי־מִתְאַמֶּ֥צֶת הִ֖יא לָלֶ֣כֶת אִתָּ֑הּ וַתֶּחְדַּ֖ל לְדַבֵּ֥ר אֵלֶֽיהָ׃ (Ruth 1:18)

אִם־חוֹמָ֣ה הִ֔יא נִבְנֶ֥ה עָלֶ֖יהָ טִ֣ירַת כָּ֑סֶף וְאִם־דֶּ֣לֶת הִ֔יא נָצ֥וּר עָלֶ֖יהָ ל֥וּחַ אָֽרֶז׃ (Songs 8:9)

עֵ֥ת לָלֶ֖דֶת וְעֵ֣ת לָמ֑וּת עֵ֤ת לָטַ֙עַת֙ וְעֵ֖ת לַעֲק֥וֹר נָטֽוּעַ׃ (Eccles. 3:2)

יָדַ֕עְתִּי כִּ֛י אֵ֥ין ט֖וֹב בָּ֑ם כִּ֣י אִם־לִשְׂמ֔וֹחַ וְלַעֲשׂ֥וֹת ט֖וֹב בְּחַיָּֽיו׃ (Eccles. 3:12)

וְשַׁבֵּ֧חַ אֲנִ֛י אֶת־הַמֵּתִ֖ים שֶׁכְּבָ֣ר מֵ֑תוּ מִן־הַ֣חַיִּ֔ים אֲשֶׁ֛ר הֵ֥מָּה חַיִּ֖ים עֲדֶֽנָה׃ (Eccles. 4:2)

The *Pashta/Yetiv* Segment

Sometimes there is a subdivision within a *zakef* segment. *Pashta* is the *ta'am* that marks that subdivision.

This is how *pashta* is sung when no conjunctive precedes it.

Pashta   פַּשְׁטָא֙

pash - TA

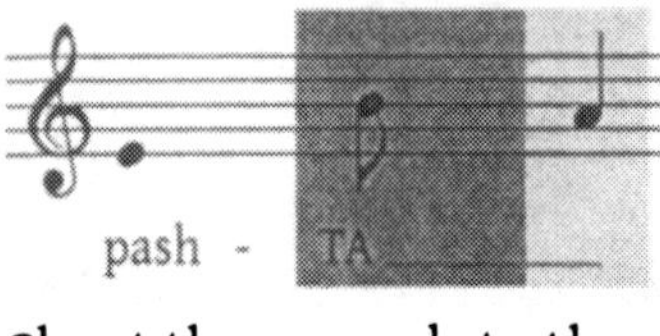

Chant these words to the melody of *pashta*.   וְטוֹב֙ (Eccles. 4:3) לְחָיָו֙ (Songs 5:13) שִׁנַּ֙יִךְ֙ (Songs 6:6)

Pashta is followed by *zakef* or *munaḥ zakef.*

קָנֶה֙ וְקִנָּמ֔וֹן עִ֖ם כׇּל־עֲצֵ֣י לְבוֹנָ֑ה (Songs 4:14)

שְׁלָחַ֙יִךְ֙ פַּרְדֵּ֣ס רִמּוֹנִ֔ים עִ֖ם פְּרִ֣י מְגָדִ֑ים (Songs 4:13)

Two Words in a *Pashta* Segment

If the preceding word is closely connected in meaning to the *pashta* word, it is usually marked with a conjunctive *ta'am*. Most often that conjunctive is *mahpakh.*

Mahpakh pashta מַהְפַּ֤ךְ פַּשְׁטָא֙

with elision:

'A - sa LÓ עָ֤שָׂה לוֹ֙ (Songs 3:9)

Note: Some chant the pick-up to *mahpakh* on G instead of A.

Chant these words to the melody of *mahpakh pashta.*

תּוֹרֵ֤י זָהָב֙ (Songs 1:11) וּמִקְרֶ֤ה אֶחָד֙ (Eccles. 3:19) כִּ֤י תֵֽצְאִי֙ (Ruth 2:22)

אָרִ֤יתִי מוֹרִי֙ (Songs 5:1) ע֤וּרִי צָפוֹן֙ (Songs 4:16)

If the accents are close to each other, the conjunctive will be *merekha* instead of *mahpakh.* In the *merekha-pashta* combination, the two accented syllables are contiguous—the *merekha* word is accented on the last syllable, and the *pashta* word has no pick-up. Thus the model for *pashta* must be sung on the syllable "TA," dropping the pick-up "pash-."

Merekha pashta מֵרְכָ֥א פַּשְׁטָא֙

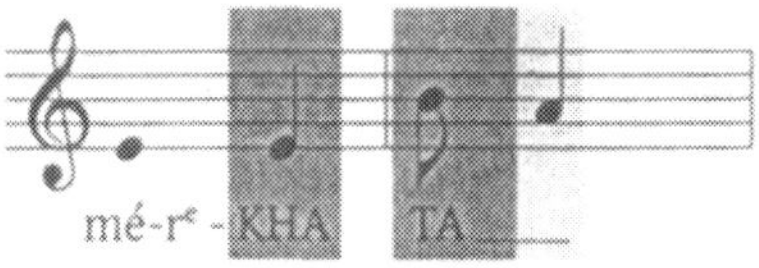

Chant these words to the melody of *merekha pashta.*

דּוֹדִ֥י לִי֙ (Songs 2:16) לֹא־תִשְׂבַּ֥ע עַ֙יִן֙ (Eccles. 1:8) אֵ֥ין טוֹב֙ (Eccles. 3:22) הַכֹּ֥ל הָֽבֶל֙ (Eccles. 2:11)

Pashta is usually followed by *zakef katon* or *munaḥ zakef katon.* Chant these examples. Make a subtle elongation or pause after *pashta.* Make a stronger pause or elongation after *zakef.*

פַּשְׁטָא֙ זָקֵ֔ף

וְטוֹב֙ מִשְּׁנֵיהֶ֔ם (Eccles. 4:3) נָשִׁים֙ מֹֽאֲבִיּ֔וֹת (Ruth 1:4)

מַהְפַּ֤ךְ פַּשְׁטָא֙ זָקֵ֔ף

אֶל־גִּנַּ֤ת אֱגוֹז֙ יָרַ֔דְתִּי (Songs 6:11) אָמַ֤רְתִּי אֲנִי֙ בְּלִבִּ֔י (Eccles. 2:1)

מַהְפַּךְ פַּשְׁטָא֙   מוּנַח זָקֵף

שׁוּבִי שׁוּבִי֙ הַשּׁוּלַמִּית (Songs 7:1)   לְכָה דוֹדִי֙ נֵצֵא הַשָּׂדֶ֜ה (Songs 7:12)

מֵרְכָא פַּשְׁטָא֙   זָקֵף

דּוֹדִי צַח֙ וְאָד֜וֹם (Songs 5:10)   אָח֥וֹת לָ֖נוּ֙ קְטַנָּ֔ה (Songs 8:8)

מֵרְכָא פַּשְׁטָא֙   מוּנַח זָקֵף

אֹהֵב כֶּסֶף֙ לֹא־יִשְׂבַּ֣ע כֶּ֔סֶף (Eccles. 5:9)   אַחַת הִיא֙ יוֹנָתִי תַמָּתִ֔י (Songs 6:9)

פַּשְׁטָא פַּשְׁטָא֙   מוּנַח זָקֵף

כַּדָּגִים֙ שֶׁנֶּאֱחָזִים֙ בִּמְצוֹדָ֣ה רָעָ֔ה (Eccles. 9:12)   וְיָדַ֗עַתְּ֙ אֶת־הַמָּק֣וֹם אֲשֶׁ֣ר יִשְׁכַּב־שָׁ֔ם (Ruth 3:4)

Yetiv

Yetiv is used instead of *pashta* if the word is accented on the first syllable and has no conjunctive words immediately preceding. Since *yetiv* is found only on words accented on the first syllable, i.e., words with no pick-ups, the model is sung on the syllable "TÍV," dropping the pick-up "yᵉ-."

Yetiv   יְתִ֚יב

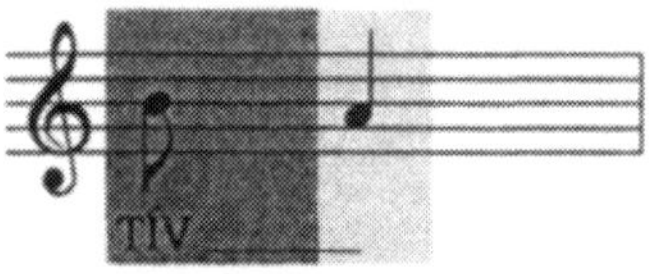

Chant these words to the melody of *yetiv*.   בָּ֚אוּ (Ruth 1:22)   מֹ֚ר (Songs 4:14)

Yetiv is followed by *zakef katon* or *munaḥ zakef katon*. Chant these examples. Make a subtle elongation or pause after *yetiv*. Make a stronger pause or elongation after *zakef*.

אָ֣נָה הָלַ֤ךְ דּוֹדֵ֙ךְ֙ הַיָּפָ֣ה בַּנָּשִׁ֔ים אָ֚נָה פָּנָ֣ה דוֹדֵ֔ךְ וּנְבַקְשֶׁ֖נּוּ עִמָּֽךְ׃ (Songs 6:1)

מֹ֚ר וַאֲהָל֔וֹת עִ֖ם כָּל־רָאשֵׁ֥י בְשָׂמִֽים׃ (Song 4:14)

Chant these segments.

וְאֵ֙לֶּה֙ תּוֹלְד֣וֹת פָּ֔רֶץ פֶּ֖רֶץ הוֹלִ֥יד אֶת־חֶצְרֽוֹן׃ (Ruth 4:18)

עַד־שֶׁ֚הַמֶּ֙לֶךְ֙ בִּמְסִבּ֔וֹ נִרְדִּ֖י נָתַ֥ן רֵיחֽוֹ׃ (Songs 1:12)

נֹ֣פֶת תִּטֹּ֤פְנָה שִׂפְתוֹתַ֙יִךְ֙ כַּלָּ֔ה דְּבַ֤שׁ וְחָלָב֙ תַּ֣חַת לְשׁוֹנֵ֔ךְ וְרֵ֥יחַ שַׂלְמֹתַ֖יִךְ כְּרֵ֥יחַ לְבָנֽוֹן׃ (Songs 4:11)

Three Words in a *Pashta* Segment

Sometimes *pashta* is preceded by two or more conjunctives. In these segments, there will be a very slight pause or elongation just before the *pashta*.

The second conjunctive before *pashta* (preceding either *merekha* or *mahpakh*) may be *kadmah*.

Kadmah mahpakh pashta קַדְמָ֨ה מַהְפַּ֤ךְ פַּשְׁטָא֙

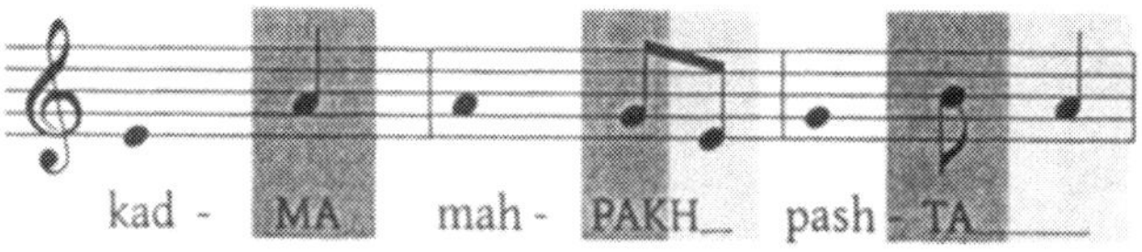
kad - MA mah - PAKH pash - TA

Chant these words to the melody of *kadmah mahpakh pashta.*

צְר֨וֹר הַמֹּ֤ר ׀ דּוֹדִי֙ (Songs 1:13) וַיִּקַּ֨ח בֹּ֤עַז אֶת־רוּת֙ (Ruth 4:13) דִּבַּ֨רְתִּי אֲנִ֤י עִם־לִבִּי֙ (Eccles. 1:16)

Kadmah merekha pashta קַדְמָ֨ה מֵרְכָ֥א פַּשְׁטָא֙

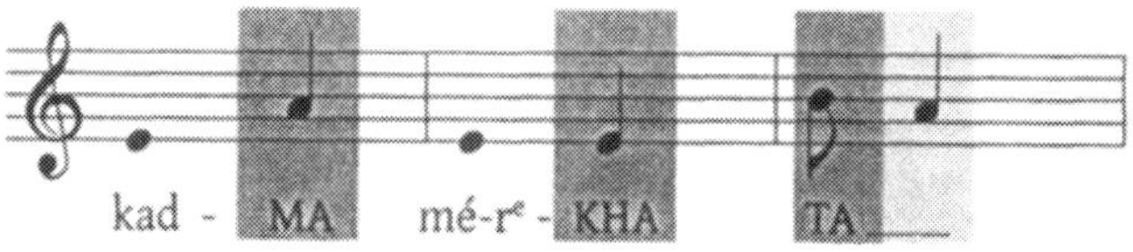
kad - MA mé-r[e] - KHA TA

Chant these words to the melody of *kadmah merekha pashta.*

וְהִנֵּ֨ה הַכֹּ֥ל הֶ֙בֶל֙ (Eccles. 2:11) וְחֵ֨לֶק אֵין־לָהֶ֥ם עוֹד֙ (Eccles. 9:6)

If the second conjunctive before *pashta* (preceding either *merekha* or *mahpakh)* is accented on the first syllable, it will be *munaḥ* instead of *kadmah.* When we refer to this *ta'am,* we will accent its first syllable: *MU-naḥ.*

Munaḥ mahpakh pashta מ֣וּנַח מַהְפַּ֤ךְ פַּשְׁטָא֙

MU-naḥ mah - PAKH pash - TA

Chant these words to the melody of *munaḥ mahpakh pashta.*

כִּ֣י אֵ֤ין זוּלָֽתְךָ֙ (Ruth 4:4) כֶּ֣רֶם הָיָ֤ה לִשְׁלֹמֹה֙ (Songs 8:11)

Munaḥ merekha pashta מ֣וּנַח מֵרְכָ֥א פַּשְׁטָא֙

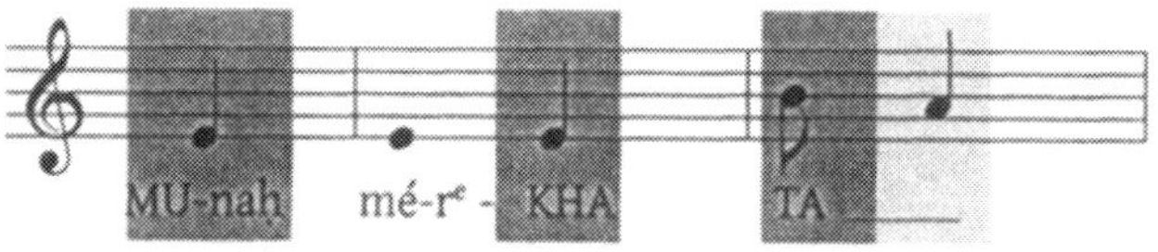
MU-naḥ mé-r[e] - KHA TA

Chant these words to the melody of *munaḥ merekha pashta.* כִּ֣י אֵ֥ין טוֹב֙ (Eccles. 3:22)

Four or Five Words in a *Pashta* Segment

Sometimes *pashta* is preceded by three or four conjunctives. The third conjunctive before *pashta* is *telishah ketanah.* The fourth conjunctive before *pashta* (preceding *telishah ketanah)* is *munaḥ.*

(Munaḥ) telishah kadmah mahpakh pashta מוּנַ֣ח תְלִישָׁה֩ קַדְמָ֨ה מַהְפַּ֤ךְ פַּשְׁטָא֙

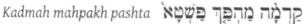

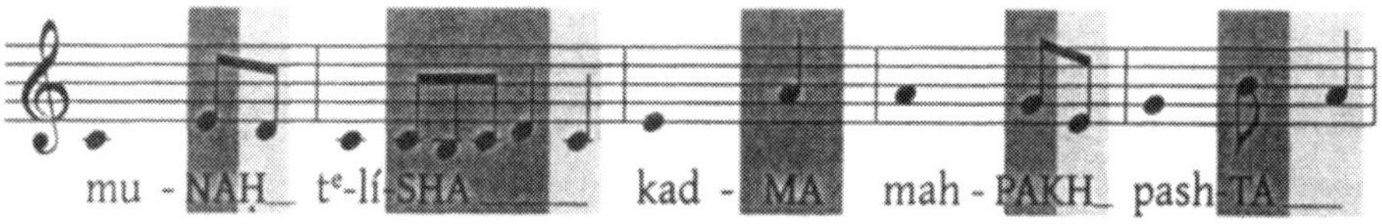
mu - NAḤ t[e]-lí-SHA kad - MA mah - PAKH pash TA

Chant these words to the melody of *telishah kadmah mahpakh pashta.*

מַדּ֫וּעַ מָצָ֨אתִי חֵ֤ן בְּעֵינֶ֙יךָ֙ (Ruth 2:10)   כִּ֠י אֵ֨ין מַעֲשֶׂ֤ה וְחֶשְׁבּוֹן֙ (Eccles. 9:10)

Chant these words to the melody of *munaḥ telishah kadmah mahpakh pashta.*

גַּ֣ם מִקְנֶה֩ בָקָ֨ר וָצֹ֤אן הַרְבֵּה֙ (Eccles. 2:7)

Telishah kadmah merekha pashta תְּלִישָׁה֩ קַדְמָ֨א מֵרְכָ֥א פַּשְׁטָא֙

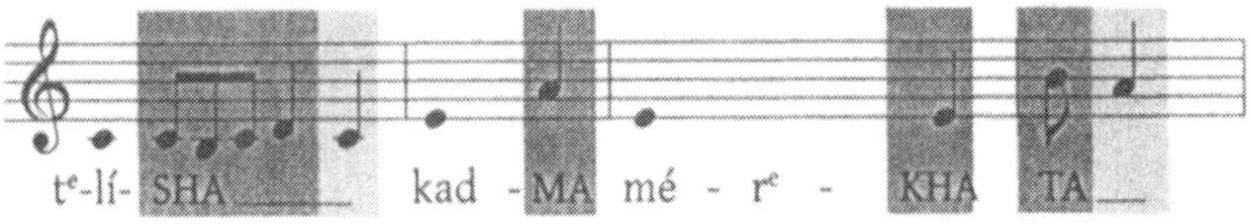

Chant these words to the melody of *telishah kadmah merekha pashta.*

כֹּה֩ יַעֲשֶׂ֨ה יְהוָ֥ה לִי֙ (Ruth 1:17)   וַתִּקְרֶ֩אנָה֩ ל֨וֹ הַשְּׁכֵנ֥וֹת שֵׁם֙ (Ruth 4:17)

Chant these phrases. Connect *telishah* and *kadmah* words to the word that follows. Create only a slight elongation and pause after *pashta.* Create a longer elongation and pause after *zakef.*

קַדְמָ֨א מֵרְכָ֥א פַּשְׁטָא֙

וְחֵ֨לֶק אֵין־לָהֶ֥ם עוֹד֙ לְעוֹלָ֔ם בְּכֹ֥ל אֲשֶׁר־נַעֲשָׂ֖ה תַּ֥חַת הַשָּֽׁמֶשׁ׃ (Eccles. 9:6)

אִם־יִמָּלְא֨וּ הֶעָבִ֥ים גֶּ֙שֶׁם֙ עַל־הָאָ֣רֶץ יָרִ֔יקוּ וְאִם־יִפּ֥וֹל עֵ֛ץ בַּדָּר֖וֹם וְאִ֣ם בַּצָּפ֑וֹן (Eccles. 11:3)

קַדְמָ֨א מַהְפַּ֤ךְ פַּשְׁטָא֙

אֵיפֹה֩ לִקַּ֨טְתְּ הַיּ֜וֹם וְאָ֤נָה עָשִׂ֙ית֙ יְהִ֥י מַכִּירֵ֖ךְ בָּר֑וּךְ (Ruth 2:19)

וְהִנֵּ֨ה הַגֹּאֵ֤ל עֹבֵר֙ אֲשֶׁ֣ר דִּבֶּר־בֹּ֔עַז וַיֹּ֛אמֶר ס֥וּרָה שְׁבָה־פֹּ֖ה פְּלֹנִ֣י אַלְמֹנִ֑י וַיָּ֖סַר וַיֵּשֵֽׁב׃ (Ruth 4:1)

מֻונַח מֵרְכָ֥א פַּשְׁטָא֙

כִּ֣י אֵ֥ין טוֹב֙ מֵאֲשֶׁ֨ר יִשְׂמַ֤ח הָאָדָם֙ בְּמַעֲשָׂ֔יו כִּי־ה֖וּא חֶלְק֑וֹ (Eccles. 3:22)

מֻונַח מַהְפַּ֤ךְ פַּשְׁטָא֙

כִּ֣י לֹ֤א יִשְׁקֹט֙ הָאִ֔ישׁ כִּֽי־אִם־כִּלָּ֥ה הַדָּבָ֖ר הַיּֽוֹם׃ (Ruth 3:18)

כִּ֣י אֵ֤ין זוּלָֽתְךָ֙ לִגְא֔וֹל וְאָנֹכִ֖י אַחֲרֶ֑יךָ וַיֹּ֖אמֶר אָנֹכִ֥י אֶגְאָֽל׃ (Ruth 4:4)

תְּלִישָׁה֩ קַדְמָ֨א מֵרְכָ֥א פַּשְׁטָא֙

כֹּה֩ יַעֲשֶׂ֨ה יְהוָ֥ה לִי֙ וְכֹ֣ה יֹסִ֔יף כִּ֣י הַמָּ֔וֶת יַפְרִ֖יד בֵּינִ֥י וּבֵינֵֽךְ׃ (Ruth 1:17)

וַתִּקְרֶ֩אנָה֩ ל֨וֹ הַשְּׁכֵנ֥וֹת שֵׁם֙ לֵאמֹ֔ר יֻלַּד־בֵּ֖ן לְנָעֳמִ֑י (Ruth 4:17)

תְּלִישָׁה֩ קַדְמָ֨א מַהְפַּ֤ךְ פַּשְׁטָא֙

כִּ֠י אֵ֨ין מַעֲשֶׂ֤ה וְחֶשְׁבּוֹן֙ וְדַ֣עַת וְחָכְמָ֔ה בִּשְׁא֕וֹל אֲשֶׁ֥ר אַתָּ֖ה הֹלֵ֥ךְ שָֽׁמָּה׃ (Eccles. 9:10)

מַדּ֫וּעַ מָצָ֨אתִי חֵ֤ן בְּעֵינֶ֙יךָ֙ לְהַכִּירֵ֔נִי וְאָנֹכִ֖י נָכְרִיָּֽה׃ (Ruth 2:10)

מוּנַ֣ח תְּלִישָׁה֩ קַדְמָ֨ה מַהְפַּ֤ךְ פַּשְׁטָא֙

גַּם מִקְנֶה֩ בָקָ֨ר וָצֹ֤אן הַרְבֵּה֙ הָ֣יָה לִּ֔י מִכֹּ֛ל שֶׁהָי֥וּ לְפָנַ֖י בִּירוּשָׁלִָֽם׃ (Eccles. 2:7)

The *Segol* Segment

Segol is the strongest disjunctive before *etnaḥta*. A *segol* segment is followed by one or more *zakef* segments, and then by *tippeḥa* and *etnaḥta*. The *segol* segment appears only five times in the festival *megillot*.

Zarka is the *ta'am* that marks a subdivision within the *segol* segment.

Both *segol* and *zarka* can be preceded by the conjunctive *munaḥ*. In one verse, *zarka* is preceded by two conjunctives: *kadmah and munaḥ*.

Kadmah munaḥ zarka munaḥ segol קַדְמָ֨א מוּנַ֣ח זַרְקָא֮ מוּנַ֣ח סֶגּוֹל֒

kad - MA mu - NAH zar - KA mu - NAH se - GOL

Chant these words to the appropriate *te'amim*.

בָּ֣אתִי לְגַנִּי֮ אֲחֹתִ֣י כַלָּה֒ (Songs 5:1)

נֶ֣גֶד הַיֹּשְׁבִים֮ וְנֶ֣גֶד זִקְנֵ֣י עַמִּי֒ (Ruth 4:4)

וְרָאִיתִי֮ אֶת־כָּל־מַעֲשֵׂ֣ה הָאֱלֹהִים֒ (Eccles. 8:17)

יֶשׁ־הֶ֘בֶל֮ אֲשֶׁ֣ר נַעֲשָׂ֣ה עַל־הָאָ֒רֶץ֒ (Eccles. 8:14)

וּבֹ֨עַז עָלָ֣ה הַשַּׁעַר֮ וַיֵּ֣שֶׁב שָׁם֒ (Ruth 4:1)

Chant this verse.

בָּ֣אתִי לְגַנִּי֮ אֲחֹתִ֣י כַלָּה֒ אָרִ֤יתִי מוֹרִי֙ עִם־בְּשָׂמִ֔י אָכַ֤לְתִּי יַעְרִי֙ עִם־דִּבְשִׁ֔י שָׁתִ֥יתִי יֵינִ֖י עִם־חֲלָבִ֑י
אִכְל֣וּ רֵעִ֔ים שְׁת֥וּ וְשִׁכְר֖וּ דּוֹדִֽים׃ (Songs 5:1)

The *Revia* Segment

Revia is a medium-level disjunctive, found before *pashta* and *tevir* segments. *Revia* is a stronger disjunctive than the others (*pashta* or *tevir*) that follow.

One or Two Words in a *Revia* Segment

If the preceding word is closely connected in meaning to the *revia* word, it is usually marked with the conjunctive *munaḥ*.

Munaḥ revia מוּנַ֣ח רְבִ֗יעַ

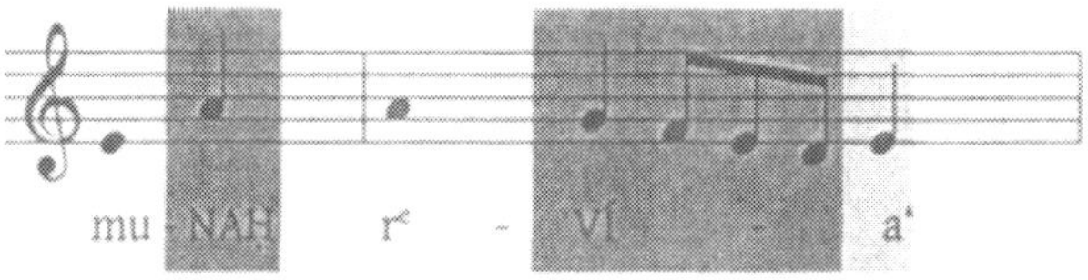
mu - NAH r' - VI - a'

Chant these words to the melody of *revia*.

הִנֵּ֗ה (Songs 3:7) וַתֵּ֗צֵא (Ruth 1:7) וַתֹּ֗אמֶר (Ruth 1:15)

Chant these words to the melody of *munaḥ revia.*

לְעֵ֣ת הָאֹ֗כֶל (Ruth 2:14) וַיִּשְׂא֣וּ לָהֶ֗ם (Ruth 1:4) אַ֣ל בְּנֹתַ֗י (Ruth 1:13)

וַתָּ֣שָׁב נָעֳמִ֗י (Ruth 1:22) מַ֣יִם רַבִּ֗ים (Songs 8:7)

Three Words in a *Revia* Segment

Sometimes *revia* is preceded by two conjunctives. In these segments there will be a very slight pause or elongation just before *revia.* The second conjunctive before *revia* (preceding *munaḥ*) is *darga.*

Darga munaḥ revia דַּרְגָּ֧א מוּנַ֣ח רְבִ֗יעַ

dar - GA
mu - NAH
r^e - VI - a'

Chant these words to the melody of *darga munaḥ revia.*

בְּנֵ֧י אִמִּ֣י נִֽחֲרוּ־בִ֗י (Songs 1:6) כִּ֧י כָל־יָמָ֣יו מַכְאֹבִ֗ים (Eccles. 2:23) וַתֹּ֧אמֶר לָ֣הּ נָעֳמִ֗י (Ruth 2:20)

There should be no pause at all between *darga* and *munaḥ*. There should be a very slight pause between *munaḥ* and *revia.*

Four Words in a *Revia* Segment

Revia may be preceded by three conjunctives. The third conjunctive before *revia* (preceding *darga*) is *munaḥ.*

Munaḥ darga munaḥ revia מוּנַ֣ח דַּרְגָּ֧א מוּנַ֣ח רְבִ֗יעַ

mu - NAH
dar - GA
mu - NAH
r^e - VI - a'

Chant these words to the melody of *munaḥ darga munaḥ revia.* גַּ֣ם בֵּ֧ן וָאָ֣ח אֵֽין־ל֗וֹ (Eccles. 4:8)

Chant these examples. Connect each conjunctive word to the word that follows. Create an elongation or pause after *revia.* Create only a slight elongation or pause after *pashta* or *tevir.*

רְבִ֗יעַ פַּשְׁטָא֙

וַיִּשְׂא֣וּ לָהֶ֗ם נָשִׁים֙ מֹֽאֲבִיּ֔וֹת (Ruth 1:4) ע֗וֹד לִמַּד־דַּ֙עַת֙ אֶת־הָעָ֔ם (Eccles. 12:9)

וַיְהִ֗י בִּימֵי֙ שְׁפֹ֣ט הַשֹּׁפְטִ֔ים (Ruth 1:1)

רְבִ֗יעַ יְתִיב֩

מוֹדַ֣ע לְאִישָׁ֗הּ אִ֚ישׁ גִּבּ֣וֹר חַ֔יִל (Ruth 2:1) וְהִנֵּה־בֹ֗עַז בָּ֚א מִבֵּ֣ית לֶ֔חֶם (Ruth 2:4)

רְבִ֗יעַ מַהְפַּ֤ךְ פַּשְׁטָא֙

וַתָּב֣וֹא וַֽתַּעֲמ֗וֹד מֵאָ֤ז הַבֹּ֙קֶר֙ וְעַד־עַ֔תָּה (Ruth 2:7) וַתַּגֵּ֣ד לַחֲמוֹתָ֗הּ אֵ֤ת אֲשֶׁר־עָשְׂתָה֙ עִמּ֔וֹ (Ruth 2:19)

רְבִ֣יעַ מֵרְכָ֥א פַּשְׁטָ֨א

וְעַתָּ֗ה הֲלֹ֥א בֹ֨עַז֙ מֹֽדַעְתָּ֔נוּ (Ruth 3:2)

וַתֹּ֨אמֶר לָ֤הּ נָעֳמִי֙ קָר֥וֹב לָ֨נוּ֙ הָאִ֔ישׁ (Ruth 2:20)

רְבִ֣יעַ קַדְמָ֨א מַהְפַּ֤ךְ פַּשְׁטָא֙

וַתָּ֨שָׁב נָעֳמִ֜י וְר֨וּת הַמּוֹאֲבִיָּ֤ה כַלָּתָהּ֙ עִמָּ֔הּ (Ruth 1:22)

רְבִ֣יעַ תְּלִישָׁה֩ קַדְמָ֨א מַהְפַּ֤ךְ פַּשְׁטָא֙

וַתֹּ֣אמֶר אֵלָ֗יו מַדּ֨וּעַ֩ מָצָ֨אתִי חֵ֤ן בְּעֵינֶ֨יךָ֙ לְהַכִּירֵ֔נִי (Ruth 2:10)

רְבִ֣יעַ תְּבִ֛יר

אֶנְהָֽגְךָ֗ אֲבִֽיאֲךָ֛ אֶל־בֵּ֥ית אִמִּ֖י תְּלַמְּדֵ֑נִי (Songs 8:2)

שָׁרִ֣ים וְשָׁר֗וֹת וְתַעֲנוּגֹ֛ת בְּנֵ֥י הָאָדָ֖ם שִׁדָּ֥ה וְשִׁדּֽוֹת׃ (Eccles. 2:8)

רְבִ֣יעַ דַּרְגָּ֧א תְּבִ֛יר

וְרָחַ֣צְתְּ ׀ וָסַ֗כְתְּ וְשַׂ֧מְתְּ שִׂמְלֹתַ֛יִךְ עָלַ֖יִךְ וְיָרַ֣דְתְּ הַגֹּ֑רֶן (Ruth 3:3)

עִנְיַ֣ן רָ֗ע נָתַ֧ן אֱלֹהִ֛ים לִבְנֵ֥י הָאָדָ֖ם לַעֲנ֥וֹת בּֽוֹ׃ (Eccles. 1:13)

רְבִ֣יעַ מֵרְכָ֥א תְּבִ֛יר

אֲנִ֣י קֹהֶ֗לֶת הָיִ֥יתִי מֶ֛לֶךְ עַל־יִשְׂרָאֵ֖ל בִּירוּשָׁלָֽםִ׃ (Eccles. 1:12)

אֲשֶׁ֣ר חֹטֶ֗א עֹשֶׂ֥ה רָ֛ע מְאַ֖ת וּמַאֲרִ֣יךְ ל֑וֹ (Eccles. 8:12)

רְבִ֣יעַ קַדְמָ֨א דַּרְגָּ֧א תְּבִ֛יר

עֵ֗ת אֲשֶׁ֨ר שָׁלַ֧ט הָאָדָ֛ם בְּאָדָ֖ם לְרַ֥ע לֽוֹ׃ (Eccl. 8:9)

עַל־דִּבְרַ֗ת שֶׁלֹּ֨א יִמְצָ֧א הָאָדָ֛ם אַחֲרָ֖יו מְאֽוּמָה׃ (Eccles. 7:14)

Chant these verses.

מִ֣י יוֹדֵ֗עַ ר֚וּחַ בְּנֵ֣י הָאָדָ֔ם הָעֹלָ֥ה הִ֖יא לְמָ֑עְלָה

וְר֙וּחַ֙ הַבְּהֵמָ֔ה הַיֹּרֶ֥דֶת הִ֖יא לְמַ֥טָּה לָאָֽרֶץ׃ (Eccles. 3:21)

הַגִּ֣ידָה לִּ֗י שֶׁאָֽהֲבָה֙ נַפְשִׁ֔י אֵיכָ֣ה תִרְעֶ֔ה אֵיכָ֖ה תַּרְבִּ֣יץ בַּֽצָּהֳרָ֑יִם

שַׁלָּמָ֤ה אֶֽהְיֶה֙ כְּעֹ֣טְיָ֔ה עַ֖ל עֶדְרֵ֥י חֲבֵרֶֽיךָ׃ (Songs 1:7)

וַיִּשְׂא֣וּ לָהֶ֗ם נָשִׁים֙ מֹֽאֲבִיּ֔וֹת שֵׁ֤ם הָֽאַחַת֙ עָרְפָּ֔ה וְשֵׁ֥ם הַשֵּׁנִ֖ית ר֑וּת

וַיֵּ֥שְׁבוּ שָׁ֖ם כְּעֶ֥שֶׂר שָׁנִֽים׃ (Ruth 1:4)

וְהִנֵּה־בֹ֗עַז בָּ֚א מִבֵּ֣ית לֶ֔חֶם וַיֹּ֥אמֶר לַקּוֹצְרִ֖ים יְהוָ֣ה עִמָּכֶ֑ם

וַיֹּ֥אמְרוּ ל֖וֹ יְבָרֶכְךָ֥ יְהוָֽה׃ (Ruth 2:4)

The *Legarmeh* Segment

Sometimes there is a subdivision within a *revia* segment. The *ta'am* that marks that subdivision may be *legarmeh*. *Legarmeh* appears eleven times in the festival *megillot*.

Legarmeh לְגַרְמֵ֣ה ׀

Chant these words to the melody of *legarmeh*.

אֲשֶׁ֣ר ׀ (Eccles. 8:14)   וְהִנֵּ֣ה ׀ (Eccles. 4:1)   גַּ֣ם ׀ (Ruth 2:21)   תָּשׁ֣וּרִי ׀ (Songs 4:8)

Two or Three Words in a *Legarmeh* Segment

If the preceding word is closely connected in meaning to the *legarmeh* word, it is usually marked with the conjunctive *merekha*. If there are three words in the *legarmeh* string, the first word is marked with *kadmah*.

(Kadmah) merekha legarmeh קַדְמָ֨ה מֵרְכָ֥א לְגַרְמֵ֣ה ׀

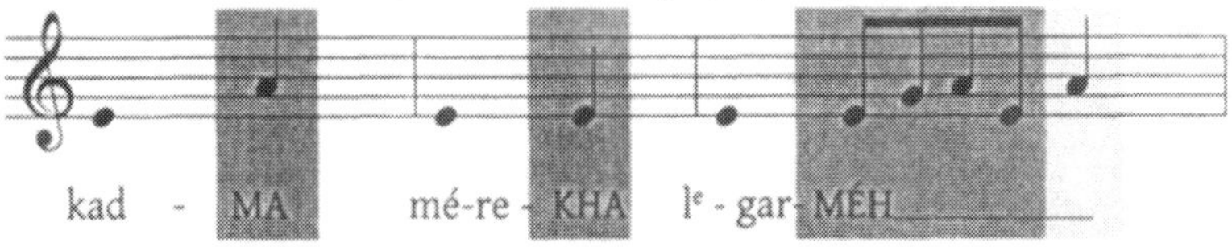

Chant these words to the melody of *merekha legarmeh*. וְשֵׁ֥ם שְׁנֵֽי־בָנָ֣יו ׀ (Ruth 1:2)

Chant these words to the melody of *kadmah merekha legarmeh*. וְֽאֵינֶ֨נּוּ חָסֵ֥ר לְנַפְשׁ֣וֹ ׀ (Eccles. 6:2)

Legarmeh is (nearly) always followed by *munaḥ revia* (or *darga munaḥ revia*).

Chant these words. בְּכָל־עֲמָל֣וֹ ׀ שֶׁיַּעֲמֹ֣ל תַּֽחַת־הַשֶּׁ֔מֶשׁ (Eccles. 5:17)

ק֣וֹל ׀ דּוֹדִ֣י דוֹפֵ֔ק (Songs 5:2)   וְהִנֵּ֣ה ׀ דִּמְעַ֣ת הָעֲשֻׁקִ֔ים (Eccles. 4:1)

Chant this rare appearance of *legarmeh* in a *pashta* segment.

וְשֵׁ֥ם שְׁנֵֽי־בָנָ֣יו ׀ מַחְל֤וֹן וְכִלְיוֹן֙ אֶפְרָתִ֔ים (Ruth 1:2)

The *Geresh* Segment

Another *ta'am* that can subdivide a *revia* segment is *geresh*. There are two basic forms of *geresh*, each with its own distinct melody: (single) *geresh*, and double *geresh*, called *gereshayim*.

Geresh without a preceding conjunctive is always accented on the next-to-the-last syllable. *But geresh* rarely appears by itself. More commonly, *geresh* is preceded by a closely connected word, marked with the conjunctive *ta'am kadmah*.

One or Two Words in a *Geresh* Segment

(Kadmah) geresh קַדְמָ֨ה גֶּ֜רֶשׁ

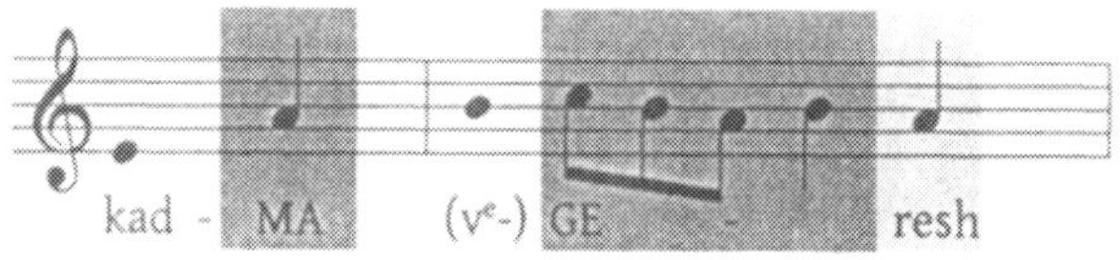

Note: To construct a model for *geresh* words that have a pick-up, we supply the prefix "vᵉ-."

Elision will take place if the *geresh* word is accented on the first syllable.

'é - ZE TÓV (Eccles. 2:3) אֵי־זֶ֣ה ט֗וֹב

vay - YÉ - lekh 'ÍSH (Ruth 1:1) וַיֵּ֨לֶךְ אִ֜ישׁ

Chant these words to the melody of *geresh.*

(Eccles. 9:14) וּבָֽא־אֵלֶ֜יהָ (Ruth 2:9) עֵינַ֜יִךְ (Eccles. 9:11) שַׁ֜בְתִּי

Chant these words to the melody of *kadmah geresh.*

(Songs 8:6) שִׂימֵ֨נִי כַחוֹתָ֜ם (Ruth 4:4) וַאֲנִ֨י אָמַ֜רְתִּי (Ruth 2:11) הֻגֵּ֨ד הֻגַּ֜ד

If the conjunctive word is accented on the first syllable, it will be marked with *munaḥ* instead of *kadmah.* The rare combination of *munaḥ geresh* occurs only once.

munaḥ geresh מ֣וּנַח גֶּ֜רֶשׁ

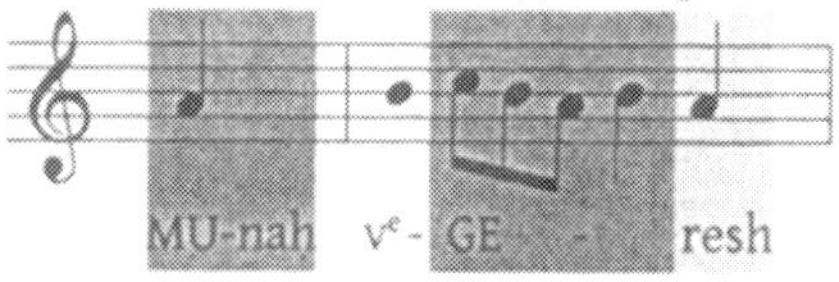

Chant these words to the melody of *munaḥ geresh.* (Eccles. 5:7) כִּ֣י גָבֹ֜הַ

Three Words in a *Geresh* Segment

Sometimes *geresh* is preceded by two conjunctives. The second conjunctive before *geresh* (preceding *kadmah*) is *telishah.*

Telishah kadmah geresh תְּלִישָׁ֠ה קַדְמָ֨ה גֶּ֜רֶשׁ

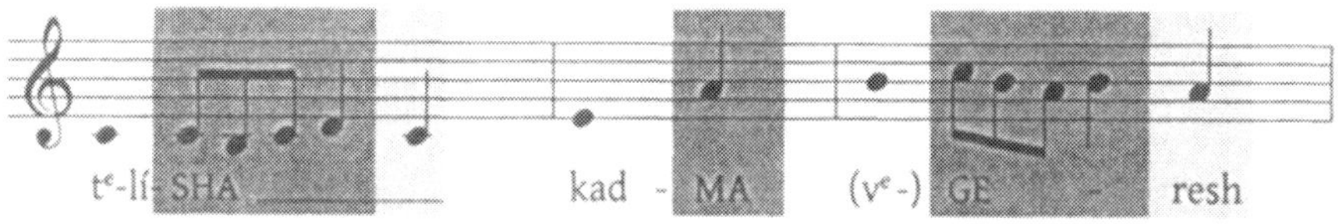

Chant these words to the melody of *telishah kadmah geresh.*

(Eccles. 11:6) כִּ֠י אֵינְךָ֨ יוֹדֵ֜עַ (Eccles. 5:3) כַּאֲשֶׁ֠ר תִּדֹּ֨ר נֶ֜דֶר (Ruth 4:7) וְז֠את לְפָנִ֨ים בְּיִשְׂרָאֵ֜ל

(Eccles. 6:2) עֹ֠שֶׁר וּנְכָסִ֨ים וְכָב֜וֹד (Ruth 2:19) וַתֹּ֠אמֶר לָ֨הּ חֲמוֹתָ֜הּ

When chanting *telishah-kadmah-geresh*, you must determine in each case whether the sense of the text demands greater connection between the first and second words or between the second and third words. The rhythm of your chant will reflect the appropriate pairing.

תְּלִישָׁה קַדְמָ֨ה גֶּ֜רֶשׁ	תְּלִישָׁה קַדְמָ֨ה גֶּ֜רֶשׁ
וַיְצַו֩ בֹּ֨עַז אֶת־נְעָרָ֜יו (Ruth 2:15)	סֹ֒ב דְּמֵה־לְךָ֣ דוֹדִ֜י (Songs 2:17)
וְשֵׁ֤ם אִשְׁתּוֹ֙ נָעֳמִ֔י (Ruth 1:2)	וַתֹּ֗אמֶר ר֤וּת הַמּוֹאֲבִיָּה֙ (Ruth 2:2)
וְשָׁנִים֩ רַבּ֨וֹת יִֽחְיֶ֜ה (Eccles. 6:3)	רָאִ֨יתִי רְשָׁעִ֜ים קְבֻרִ֗ים (Eccles. 8:10)

Four Words in a *Geresh* Segment

Munaḥ telishah kadmah geresh מוּנַ֣ח תְּלִישָׁה קַדְמָ֨ה גֶּ֜רֶשׁ

Sometimes *geresh* is preceded by three conjunctives. The third conjunctive before *geresh* (just before *telishah*) is *munaḥ*. This combinaton is found only five times.

Munaḥ telishah kadmah geresh מוּנַ֣ח תְּלִישָׁה קַדְמָ֨ה גֶּ֜רֶשׁ

Chant these words to the melody of *munaḥ telishah kadmah geresh*.

וְגַם אֶת־ר֣וּת הַמֹּאֲבִיָּה֩ אֵ֨שֶׁת מַחְלוֹן֙ (Ruth 4:10)   יֵ֣שׁ אֶחָד֩ וְאֵ֨ין שֵׁנִ֜י (Eccles. 4:8)

Gereshayim

The double *geresh* is called *gereshayim*. Words that bear this accent are stressed on the last syllable.

Gereshayim גֵּרְשַׁ֞יִם

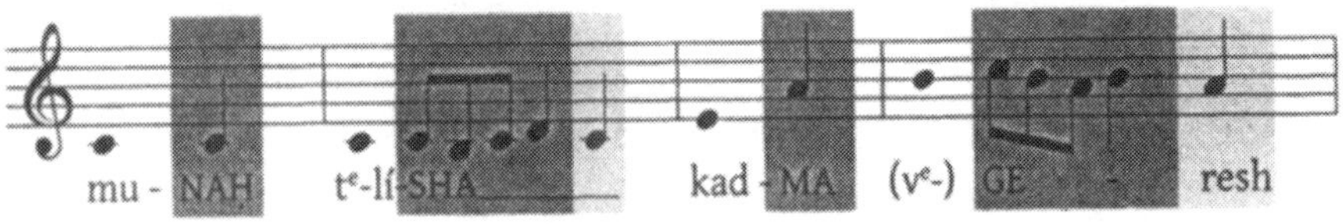

Note: This accent has a double pick-up. If the word has one pick-up syllable, sing that syllable on G. If the word has two pick-up syllables, sing the first pick-up on E and the second on G. If the word has three pick-up syllables, sing the first two pick-ups on E and the third on G.

Chant these words to the melody of *gereshayim*.

אָדָ֞ם (Eccles. 7:28)   וַתִּדְבַּ֞ק (Ruth 2:23)   ט֞וֹב (Eccles. 7:2)

Two Words in a *Gereshayim* Segment

The conjunctive of *gereshayim* is *munaḥ*. This combination is found only twice.

Munaḥ gereshayim מוּנַ֣ח גֵּרְשַׁ֞יִם

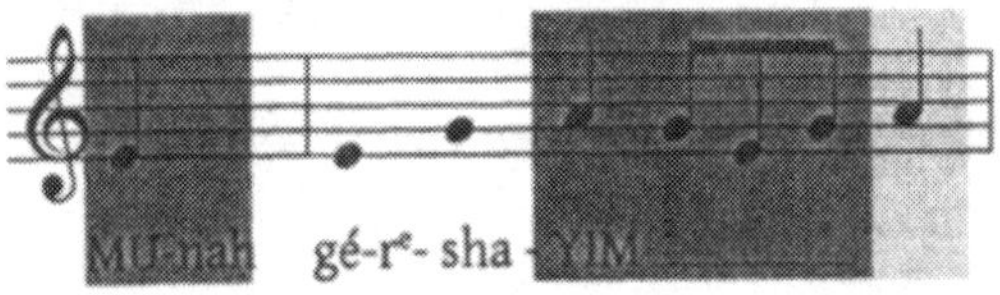

Chant these words to the melody of *munaḥ gereshayim*.

אֵ֣ין אָדָ֞ם (Eccles. 8:8)   כִּ֣י אֶת־כָּל־זֶ֞ה (Eccles. 9:1)

Geresh (or *gereshayim*) can subdivide any of the following segments: *revia, pashta,* or *tevir.*

Chant these phrases. Connect a conjunctive word to the word that follows. Create an elongation or pause after *revia, pashta,* or *tevir.* Create only a slight elongation or pause after *geresh* or *gereshayim.*

קַדְמָ֨ה גֵּ֜רֶשׁ רְבִ֗יעַ

אֶל־אֲשֶׁ֨ר תֵּלְכִ֜י אֵלֵ֗ךְ (Ruth 1:16) הֱבִיאַ֨נִי הַמֶּ֜לֶךְ חֲדָרָ֗יו (Songs 1:4)

קַדְמָ֨ה גֵּ֜רֶשׁ מוּנַ֣ח רְבִ֗יעַ

וְאִם־לֹ֨א יִגְאַ֜ל הַגִּ֣ידָה לִּ֗י (Ruth 4:4) אָק֨וּמָה נָּ֜א וַאֲסוֹבְבָ֣ה בָעִ֗יר (Songs 3:2)

גֵּ֜רֶשׁ מוּנַ֣ח רְבִ֗יעַ

שַׁ֜בְתִּי וְרָאֹ֣ה תַֽחַת־הַשֶּׁ֗מֶשׁ (Eccles. 9:11) עֵינַ֜יִךְ בְּרֵכ֣וֹת בְּחֶשְׁבּ֗וֹן (Songs 7:5)

קַדְמָ֨ה גֵּ֜רֶשׁ לְגַרְמֵ֣ה ׀ מוּנַ֣ח רְבִ֗יעַ

וְלִרְא֨וֹת טוֹבָ֜ה בְּכָל־עֲמָל֣וֹ ׀ שֶׁיַּעֲמֹ֣ל תַּ֣חַת־הַשָּׁ֗מֶשׁ (Eccles. 6:3)

תְּלִישָׁה֩ קַדְמָ֨ה גֵּ֜רֶשׁ לְגַרְמֵ֣ה ׀ מוּנַ֣ח רְבִ֗יעַ

וְשָׁנִ֠ים רַבּ֨וֹת יִֽחְיֶ֜ה וְרַ֣ב ׀ שֶׁיִּהְי֣וּ יְמֵֽי־שָׁנָ֗יו (Eccles. 6:3)

גֵּרְשַׁ֞יִם מוּנַ֣ח רְבִ֗יעַ

הִנֵּ֞ה אֲשֶׁר־רָאִ֣יתִי אָ֗נִי (Eccles. 5:17) יוֹנָתִ֞י בְּחַגְוֵ֣י הַסֶּ֗לַע (Songs 2:14)

גֵּרְשַׁ֞יִם דַּרְגָּ֧א מוּנַ֣ח רְבִ֗יעַ

וְהַמֵּתִ֞ים אֵינָ֧ם יוֹדְעִ֣ים מְא֗וּמָה (Eccles. 9:5) מִבְּלִ֞י אֲשֶׁ֧ר לֹא־יִמְצָ֣א הָאָדָ֗ם (Eccles. 3:11)

קַדְמָ֨ה גֵּ֜רֶשׁ דַּרְגָּ֧א מוּנַ֣ח רְבִ֗יעַ

וַאֲנִ֨י אָמַ֜רְתִּי אֶגְלֶ֧ה אָזְנְךָ֣ לֵאמֹ֗ר (Ruth 4:4) וַיֵּ֨לֶךְ אִ֜ישׁ מִבֵּ֧ית לֶ֣חֶם יְהוּדָ֗ה (Ruth 1:1)

תְּלִישָׁה֩ קַדְמָ֨ה גֵּ֜רֶשׁ רְבִ֗יעַ

וַתֹּ֩אמֶר֩ ר֨וּת הַמּוֹאֲבִיָּ֜ה אֶל־נָעֳמִ֗י (Ruth 2:2) וַיְצַו֩ בֹּ֨עַז אֶת־נְעָרָ֜יו לֵאמֹ֗ר (Ruth 2:15)

תְּלִישָׁה֩ קַדְמָ֨ה גֵּ֜רֶשׁ קַדְמָ֨ה מֵרְכָ֥א לְגַרְמֵ֣ה ׀ רְבִ֗יעַ

עֹ֩שֶׁר֩ וּנְכָסִ֨ים וְכָב֜וֹד וְֽאֵינֶ֨נּוּ חָסֵ֥ר לְנַפְשׁ֣וֹ ׀ מִכֹּ֣ל אֲשֶׁר־יִתְאַוֶּ֗ה (Eccles. 6:2)

תְּלִישָׁה֩ קַדְמָ֨ה גֵּ֜רֶשׁ מוּנַ֣ח רְבִ֗יעַ

כִּי֩ מִקְרֶ֨ה בְנֵי־הָאָדָ֜ם וּמִקְרֶ֣ה הַבְּהֵמָ֗ה (Eccles. 3:19) וַיֹּ֩אמֶר֩ לָ֨ה בֹ֜עַז לְעֵ֣ת הָאֹ֗כֶל (Ruth 2:14)

תְּלִישָׁה֩ קַדְמָ֨ה גֵּ֜רֶשׁ דַּרְגָּ֧א מוּנַ֣ח רְבִ֗יעַ

וַיֹּ֩אמֶר֩ בֹּ֨עַז אֶל־ר֜וּת הֲל֧וֹא שָׁמַ֣עַתְּ בִּתִּ֗י (Ruth 2:8)

וְגַ֣ם אֶת־ר֣וּת הַמֹּאֲבִיָּה֩ אֵ֨שֶׁת מַחְל֜וֹן קָנִ֧יתִי לִ֣י לְאִשָּׁ֗ה (Ruth 4:10)

מוּנַ֣ח תְּלִישָׁ֩ה קַדְמָ֨ה גֵּ֜רֶשׁ מוּנַ֣ח דַּרְגָּ֧א מוּנַ֣ח רְבִ֗יעַ
יֵ֣שׁ אֶחָ֩ד וְאֵ֨ין שֵׁנִ֜י גַּ֣ם בֵּ֧ן וָאָ֣ח אֵֽין־ל֗וֹ (Eccles. 4:8)

גֵּ֜רֶשׁ מַהְפַּ֤ךְ פַּשְׁטָא֙
כִּ֣י גָבֹ֜הַּ מֵעַ֤ל גָּבֹ֙הַּ֙ שֹׁמֵ֔ר (Eccles. 5:7) עֵינַ֜יִךְ בַּשָּׂדֶ֤ה אֲשֶׁר־יִקְצֹרוּן֙ וְהָלַ֣כְתְּ אַחֲרֵיהֶ֔ן (Ruth 2:9)

קַדְמָ֨ה גֵּ֜רֶשׁ מַהְפַּ֤ךְ פַּשְׁטָא֙
הִשְׁבַּ֨עְתִּי אֶתְכֶ֜ם בְּנ֤וֹת יְרוּשָׁלִַ֙ם֙ בִּצְבָא֔וֹת (Songs 2:7, 3:5)
אֵי־זֶ֨ה ט֜וֹב לִבְנֵ֤י הָֽאָדָם֙ אֲשֶׁ֣ר יַעֲשׂ֔וּ תַּ֚חַת הַשָּׁמַ֔יִם (Eccles. 2:3)

תְּלִישָׁ֩ה קַדְמָ֨ה גֵּ֜רֶשׁ קַדְמָ֨ה מַהְפַּ֤ךְ פַּשְׁטָא֙
וַתֹּ֩אמֶר֩ לָ֨הּ חֲמוֹתָ֜הּ אֵיפֹ֨ה לִקַּ֤טְתְּ הַיּוֹם֙ וְאָ֣נָה עָשִׂ֔ית (Ruth 2:19)

תְּלִישָׁ֩ה קַדְמָ֨ה גֵּ֜רֶשׁ מ֣וּנַח מַהְפַּ֤ךְ פַּשְׁטָא֙
כִּ֩י֩ אֵֽינְךָ֨ יוֹדֵ֜עַ אֵ֣י זֶ֤ה יִכְשָׁר֙ הֲזֶ֣ה אוֹ־זֶ֔ה (Eccles. 11:6)

תְּלִישָׁ֩ה קַדְמָ֨ה גֵּ֜רֶשׁ מַהְפַּ֤ךְ פַּשְׁטָא֙
וְזֹ֩את֩ לְפָנִ֨ים בְּיִשְׂרָאֵ֜ל עַל־הַגְּאוּלָּ֤ה וְעַל־הַתְּמוּרָה֙ לְקַיֵּ֣ם כָּל־דָּבָ֔ר (Ruth 4:7)

תְּלִישָׁ֩ה קַדְמָ֨ה גֵּ֜רֶשׁ קַדְמָ֨ה מַהְפַּ֤ךְ פַּשְׁטָא֙
אֲשֶׁ֣ר נָֽתַן־ל֣וֹ הָאֱלֹהִ֩ים֩ עֹ֨שֶׁר וּנְכָסִ֜ים וְהִשְׁלִיט֨וֹ לֶאֱכֹ֤ל מִמֶּ֙נּוּ֙ וְלָשֵׂ֣את אֶת־חֶלְק֔וֹ (Eccles. 5:18)

גֵּרְשַׁ֞יִם מֵרְכָ֥א פַּשְׁטָא֙
וַתִּדְבַּ֞ק בְּנַעֲר֥וֹת בֹּ֙עַז֙ לְלַקֵּ֔ט (Ruth 2:23)

גֵּרְשַׁ֞יִם מַהְפַּ֤ךְ פַּשְׁטָא֙
אָדָ֞ם אֶחָ֤ד מֵאֶ֙לֶף֙ מָצָ֔אתִי (Eccles. 7:28)
כִּ֣י אֶת־כָּל־זֶ֞ה נָתַ֤תִּי אֶל־לִבִּי֙ וְלָב֣וּר אֶת־כָּל־זֶ֔ה (Eccles. 9:1)

תְּלִישָׁ֩ה קַדְמָ֨ה גֵּ֜רֶשׁ מֵרְכָ֥א לְגַרְמֵ֣הּ ׀ מַהְפַּ֤ךְ פַּשְׁטָא֙
וְשֵׁ֩ם֩ אִשְׁתּ֨וֹ נָעֳמִ֜י וְשֵׁ֥ם שְׁנֵֽי־בָנָ֣יו ׀ מַחְל֤וֹן וְכִלְיוֹן֙ אֶפְרָתִ֔ים (Ruth 1:2)

גֵּרְשַׁ֞יִם דַּרְגָּ֧א תְּבִ֛יר
וַיִּקַּ֞ח עֲשָׂרָ֧ה אֲנָשִׁ֛ים מִזִּקְנֵ֥י הָעִ֖יר וַיֹּ֣אמֶר שְׁבוּ־פֹ֑ה (Ruth 4:2)
מָלֵ֞א לֵ֧ב בְּנֵי־הָאָדָ֛ם בָּהֶ֖ם לַעֲשׂ֥וֹת רָֽע׃ (Eccles. 8:11)

קַדְמָ֨ה גֵּ֜רֶשׁ דַּרְגָּ֧א תְּבִ֛יר
וַ֠יֹּאמְרוּ כָּל־הָעָ֧ם אֲשֶׁר־בַּשַּׁ֛עַר וְהַזְּקֵנִ֖ים עֵדִ֑ים (Ruth 4:11)
אַל־תְּבַהֵ֨ל עַל־פִּ֜יךָ וְלִבְּךָ֧ אַל־יְמַהֵ֛ר לְהוֹצִ֥יא דָבָ֖ר לִפְנֵ֣י הָאֱלֹהִ֑ים (Eccles. 5:1)

Telishah Gedolah

Telishah gedolah is another minor disjunctive. The conjunctive of *telishah gedolah* is *munaḥ*.

One or Two Words in a *Telishah Gedolah* Segment

Munaḥ telishah (gedolah) מ֣וּנַח תְ֠לִישָׁה

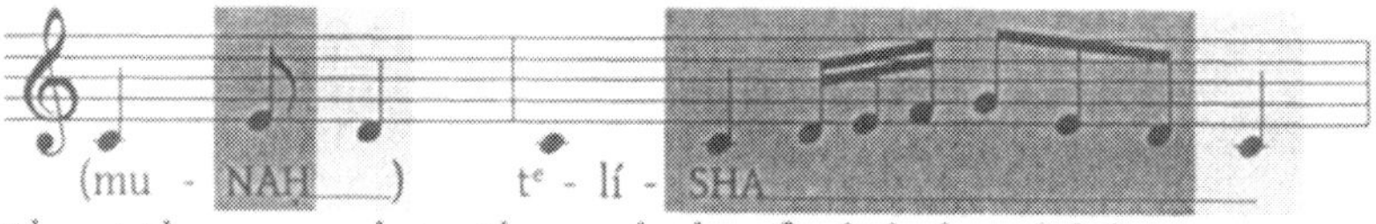

Chant these words to the melody of *telishah gedolah*.

וְגַ֠ם (Eccles. 9:11)   וּ֠מֵאֵת (Ruth 4:5)   כִּ֠י (Ruth 1:16)   וַ֠תֹּאמֶר (Ruth 2:13)

Chant these words to the melody of *munaḥ telishah gedolah*.   אִם־מְעַ֣ט ר֠ שׁ ...

Practice chanting *telishah gedolah* in context.

כִּ֠י אֶל־אֲשֶׁר תֵּלְכִי אֵלֵךְ וּבַאֲשֶׁר תָּלִינִי אָלִין (Ruth 1:16)

וַ֠תֹּאמֶר אֶמְצָא־חֵן בְּעֵינֶיךָ אֲדֹנִי כִּי נִחַמְתָּנִי (Ruth 2:13)

וּ֠מֵאֵת רוּת הַמּוֹאֲבִיָּה אֵשֶׁת־הַמֵּת קָנִיתָה (Ruth 4:5)

הָ֠בִי הַמִּטְפַּחַת אֲשֶׁר־עָלַיִךְ וְאֶחֳזִי־בָהּ וַתֹּאחֶז בָּהּ (Ruth 3:15)

קְ֠נֵה נֶגֶד הַיֹּשְׁבִים וְנֶגֶד זִקְנֵי עַמִּי (Ruth 4:4)

Pazer

Pazer is another minor disjunctive that may be used to subdivide any of the following segments: *revia, pashta, tevir,* or *zarka*. Often a *pazer* segment will be followed by a *geresh* segment.

The conjunctive of *pazer* is *munaḥ*.

One or Two Words in a *Pazer* Segment

(Munaḥ pazer) פָּזֵ֡ר (מ֣וּנַח)

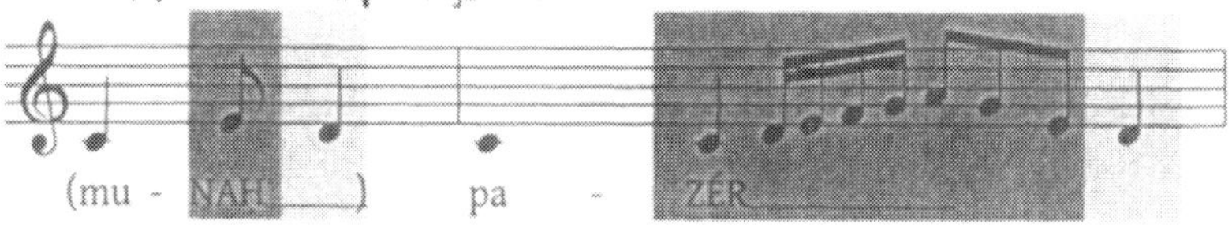

Chant these words to the melody of *pazer*.   מֵאָ֡ה (Eccles. 6:3)   עַל־כֵּ֡ן (Eccles. 8:11)

Chant these words to the melody of *munaḥ pazer*.

וְשֵׁ֣ם הָאִ֣ישׁ אֱלִימֶ֡לֶךְ (Ruth 1:2)   גַּ֣ם כָּל־הָאָדָ֡ם (Eccles. 5:18)

Practice chanting *pazer* in context.

וְשֵׁ֣ם הָאִ֣ישׁ אֱלִימֶ֡לֶךְ וְשֵׁם אִשְׁתּוֹ נָעֳמִי

וְשֵׁ֣ם שְׁנֵֽי־בָנָ֣יו ׀ מַחְלוֹן וְכִלְיוֹן אֶפְרָתִים (Ruth 1:2)

אִם־יוֹלִ֣יד אִ֣ישׁ מֵאָ֡ה וְשָׁנִים רַבּוֹת יִחְיֶה וְרַ֣ב ׀ שֶׁיִּהְי֣וּ יְמֵֽי־שָׁנָיו (Eccles. 6:3)

עַל־כֵּ֡ן מָלֵא לֵב בְּנֵֽי־הָאָדָם בָּהֶם לַעֲשׂוֹת רָע׃ (Eccles. 8:11)

The Final Cadence

We use a special melody to signal the end of each megillah. This melody is applied beginning with the final *tippeḥa* phrase. You will chant this cadence slowly.

Some readers also use this melody for the final cadence of each *parashah* (paragraph in the ancient Jewish division of the text). Other readers use this melody for the final cadence of every chapter according to the Christian division of the text.

Merekha tippeḥa merekha siluk מֵרְכָא טִפְּחָא מֵרְכָא סִילְוּק

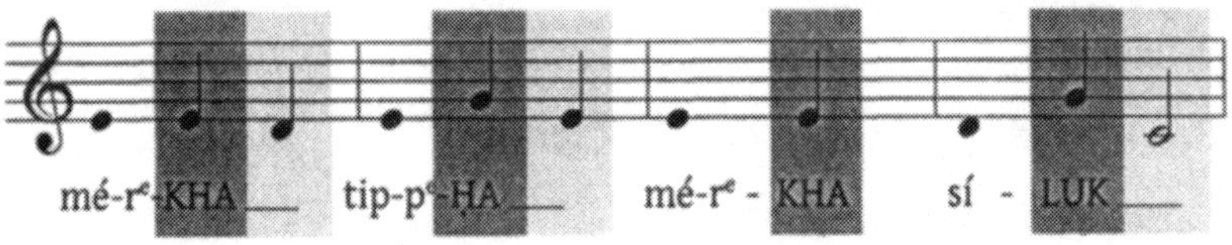

Chant these words to the appropriate *te'amim*, using the final cadence.

וְיִשַׁ֖י הוֹלִ֥יד אֶת־דָּוִֽד׃ (Ruth 4:22)

עַ֖ל הָרֵ֥י בְשָׂמִֽים׃ (Songs 8:14)

כִּי־זֶ֖ה כָּל־הָאָדָֽם׃ (Eccles. 12:13)*

* There is a tradition, when cantillating the Bible in public, not to end a section with a verse that expresses a depressing idea. Thus, when reading the Book of Ecclesiastes (קהלת), after finishing the last verse (12:14) the reader goes back and repeats the penultimate verse (12:13). The final cadence melody should be used only on that repetition of 12:13.

9. Esther

Introduction

Megillat Esther (the Scroll of Esther) is chanted on the Festival of Purim. It is chanted in the synagogue in the presence of a minyan (quorum) in the evening service (ערבית) just before *ve'atah kadosh* and *Aleinu*, and in the morning service (שחרית) after the conclusion of the Torah service. *Megillat Esther* is unique in that it may also be chanted by individuals at home without the presence of a minyan. Every Jew is halakhically required not only to *hear* the megillah, but also to *read* the megillah. In practice, however, the general custom is for the *ba'al keri'ah* to act as agent for the congregation.

Esther is traditionally chanted from a parchment scroll, not from a printed book (as is the general custom for reading the other scrolls: Lamentations, Song of Songs, Ruth, and Ecclesiastes). But unlike the Torah, the scroll of Esther is usually not bound onto wooden dowels, and may be decorated and illustrated. Before reading, the *ba'al keri'ah* unrolls the megillah and then folds it, accordion style, into the shape of a book or a long letter.

Esther is chanted with frivolity, in keeping with the carnival-like spirit of Purim. Some experienced *ba'aley keri'ah* take freedoms with the *te'amim*, altering the melody here and there to dramatize the story, or to create musical "puns." This is the only book in which such deviations from the cantillation are allowed, even encouraged, in keeping with the spirit of the day.

In most communities, it is customary to make raucous noises each time Haman's name is chanted. In view of the importance of the obligation to attend to every word of the megillah, the *ba'al keri'ah* stops reading after mentioning Haman's name and waits until the noisemaking has died down before resuming the chant.

In chapter 9, the 10 sons of Haman are listed among those enemies of the Jews who were slaughtered in the city of Shushan. In the handwritten scroll, these 10 men are given great prominence, each name beginning a new line of text. Before beginning to read these verses, take a deep breath; it is customary to read the 21 words that comprise these 10 names and the following word (עשרת) before taking another breath! For that reason, most *ba'aley keri'ah* will read these words quite fast, even chanting them on a monotone rather than taking the time to articulate the proper *te'amim*.

The *ba'al keri'ah* chants blessings before and after the reading of the megillah (see p. 192). After the chanting of the final blessing, many congregations will chant the *piyyut* (hymn) *Shoshannat Ya'akov* (see *Chanting: The Complete Guide*, p. 840).

The Melodies of the Cantillation Motifs

Hear the melodies of the Esther cantillation on CD tracks 77–80.

The *Siluk* Segment and *Tippeḥa* Segment

The last word in every verse is marked with *siluk.* If the preceding word is closely connected in meaning to the *siluk* word, it is usually marked with the conjunctive *ta'am merekha.* When *siluk* is not preceded by *merekha,* its melody is slightly different (see below).

A *siluk* segment is subdivided by the disjunctive *ta'am tippeḥa.* If there are two words in the *tippeḥa* segment, the first one is usually marked with the conjunctive *ta'am merekha.*

Merekha tippeḥa merekha siluk מֵרְכָ֥א טִפְּחָ֖א מֵרְכָ֥א סִילֽוּק

Chant these words to the appropriate *te'amim.* Connect each conjunctive (*merekha*) to the word that follows. Pause slightly after the disjunctive *ta'am, tippeḥa.*

מֵרְכָ֥א טִפְּחָ֖א מֵרְכָ֥א סִילֽוּק

כִּֽי־הִגִּ֥יד לָהֶ֖ם אֲשֶׁר־ה֥וּא יְהוּדִֽי׃ (3:4)

לֹ֥א יִכְרַ֖ע וְלֹ֥א יִשְׁתַּחֲוֶֽה׃ (3:2)

לַעֲשׂ֥וֹת בּ֖וֹ כַּטּ֥וֹב בְּעֵינֶֽיךָ׃ (3:11)

וַתֹּ֥אמֶר אֶסְתֵּ֖ר לְהָשִׁ֥יב אֶֽל־מָרְדֳּכָֽי׃ (4:15)

טִפְּחָ֖א מֵרְכָ֥א סִילֽוּק

אֲשֶׁ֖ר בְּשׁוּשַׁ֥ן הַבִּירָֽה׃ (1:2)

אֵ֖ת מִצְוַ֥ת הַמֶּֽלֶךְ׃ (3:3)

נֹ֖כַח פֶּ֥תַח הַבָּֽיִת׃ (5:1)

אֶל־הַמִּשְׁתֶּ֖ה אֲשֶׁר־עָשִׂ֥יתִי לֽוֹ׃ (5:4) *merekha-siluk* elision

When *siluk* is not preceded by *merekha,* its melody is slightly different.

Merekha tippeḥa siluk מֵרְכָ֥א טִפְּחָ֖א סִילֽוּק

מֵרְכָ֥א טִפְּחָ֖א סִילֽוּק

וְעֶשְׂרִ֥ים וּמֵאָ֖ה מְדִינָֽה׃ (1:1)

לָדַ֥עַת מַה־זֶּ֖ה וְעַל־מַה־זֶּֽה׃ (4:5)

אֲשֶׁר־כָּתַ֥ב מָרְדֳּכַ֖י אֲלֵיהֶֽם׃ (9:23)

טִפְּחָ֖א סִילֽוּק

וּשְׁלָלָ֖ם לָבֽוֹז׃ (3:13)

וּמַתָּנ֖וֹת לָאֶבְיוֹנִֽים׃ (9:22)

בַּמֶּ֖לֶךְ אֲחַשְׁוֵרֽוֹשׁ׃ (6:2)

Tippeḥa Elision

When *tippeḥa* is followed immediately by *siluk*, and the *siluk* word is accented on the first syllable, the lyrics are elided and melody is slightly altered so that the characteristic B-flat is included.

שְׁמוֹנִ֥ים וּמְאַ֖ת יֽוֹם׃ (1:4)

The *Etnaḥta* Segment and *Tippeḥa* Segment

Most verses are divided into two segments. *Etnaḥta* is the *ta'am* that marks the end of the first segment, and *siluk* marks the end of the second segment. If the *etnaḥta* word and the word before it are closely connected in meaning, they are usually marked *munaḥ etnaḥta.* When *etnaḥta* is not preceded by *munaḥ*, its melody is slightly different (see below).

An *etnaḥta* segment is also subdivided by the disjunctive *ta'am tippeḥa*, If there are two words in the *tippeḥa* segment, the first one is usually marked with the conjunctive *ta'am merekha.*

Merekha tippeḥa munaḥ etnaḥta מֵרְכָ֥א טִפְּחָ֖א מ֣וּנַח אֶתְנַחְתָּ֑א

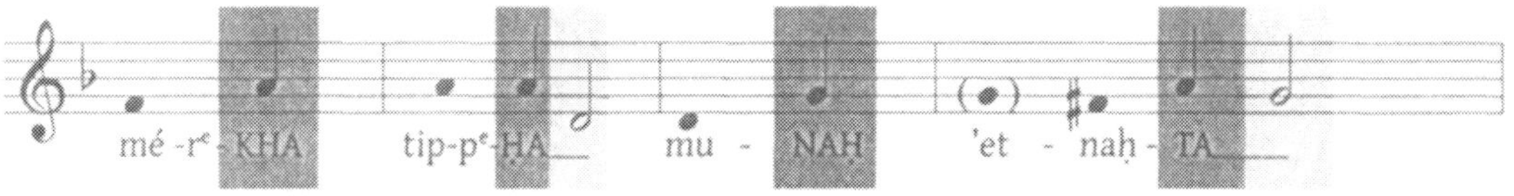

Chant these words to the appropriate *te'amim*. Connect each conjunctive (*merekha* or *munaḥ*) to the word that follows. Pause slightly after the disjunctive *ta'am, tippeḥa*.

מֵרְכָ֥א טִפְּחָ֖א מ֣וּנַח אֶתְנַחְתָּ֑א

וְהַדָּ֥ת נִתְּנָ֖ה בְּשׁוּשַׁ֣ן הַבִּירָ֑ה (3:15) כִּֽי־הִגִּ֥ידוּ ל֖וֹ אֶת־עַ֣ם מָרְדֳּכָ֑י (3:6)

לְהַרְא֥וֹת אֶת־אֶסְתֵּ֖ר וּלְהַגִּ֣יד לָ֑הּ (4:8) *munaḥ etnaḥta* elision

טִפְּחָ֖א מ֣וּנַח אֶתְנַחְתָּ֑א

וַיְהִ֖י בִּימֵ֣י אֲחַשְׁוֵר֑וֹשׁ (1:1) כִּי־כֵ֖ן צִוָּה־ל֣וֹ הַמֶּ֑לֶךְ (3:2)

הַכֶּ֖סֶף נָת֣וּן לָ֑ךְ (3:11) *munaḥ etnaḥta* elision בְּכֹל֙ מְדִינ֣וֹת מַלְכוּתֶ֑ךָ (3:8)

When *etnaḥta* is not preceded by *munaḥ*, its melody is slightly different.

Merekha tippeḥa etnaḥta מֵרְכָ֥א טִפְּחָ֖א אֶתְנַחְתָּ֑א

מֵרְכָ֥א טִפְּחָ֖א אֶתְנַחְתָּ֑א

וְלֹ֥א שָׁמַ֖ע אֲלֵיהֶ֑ם (3:4) וְעַ֥ם וָעָ֖ם כִּלְשׁוֹנ֑וֹ (3:12) וַיֵּצֵ֥א הֲתָ֖ךְ אֶל־מָרְדֳּכָ֑י (4:6)

טִפְּחָ֖א אֶתְנַחְתָּ֑א

לַמֶּ֖לֶךְ אֲחַשְׁוֵר֑וֹשׁ (3:7) יִכָּתֵ֖ב לְאַבְּדָ֑ם (3:9) גָּל֖וּי לְכָל־הָעַמִּ֑ים (3:14)

The *Tevir* Segment

Sometimes there is a subdivision within a *tippeḥa* segment. *Tevir* is the *ta'am* that marks that subdivision.

Tevir תְּבִ֛יר

Chant these words to the melody of *tevir.*

כְּכָ֛ל (4:17) כַּאֲשֶׁ֛ר (2:20) עַ֛ל (1:6) שֶׁ֛בַע (1:1) הַמֶּ֛לֶךְ (4:7)

Two Words in a *Tevir* Segment

If the preceding word is closely connected in meaning to the *tevir* word, it is usually marked with a conjunctive *ta'am.* Most often that conjunctive will be *darga.*

Darga tevir דַּרְגָּ֧א תְּבִ֛יר

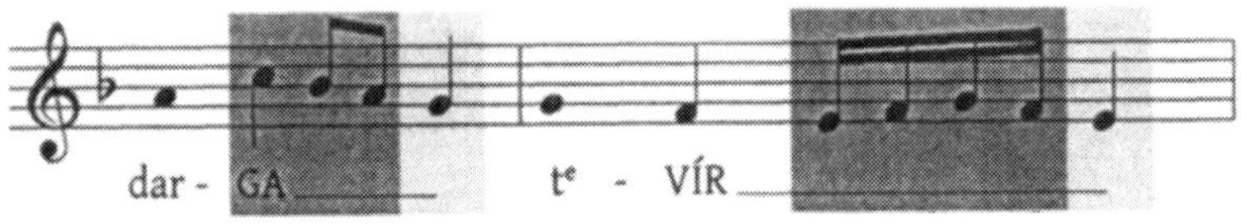

Note: When *tevir* is preceded by *darga (or merekha)*, its pick-up is changed from F to G in order to create a smoother transition. Chant these words to the melody of *darga tevir.*

אֶל־יַ֧ד שַֽׁעַשְׁגַ֛ז (2:14) לְקָחָ֧הּ מָרְדֳּכַ֛י (2:7) כִּ֧י מָרְדֳּכַ֛י (2:10) וַתֹּ֧אמֶר אֶסְתֵּ֛ר (2:22)

If the accents are close to each other, the conjunctive will be *merekha* instead of *darga.*

Merekha tevir מֵרְכָ֥א תְּבִ֛יר

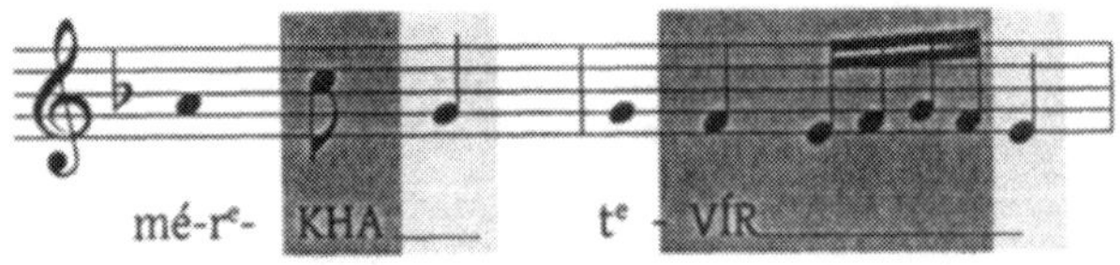

Chant these words to the melody of *merekha tevir.*

וְיֵ֥ין מַלְכ֛וּת (1:7) יְבַקְשׁ֥וּ לַמֶּ֛לֶךְ (2:2) אֵ֥ין לָב֛וֹא (4:2)

Chant these phrases. Connect the conjunctive word to the word that follows. Create a slight elongation and pause after *tippeḥa.* There is very little elongation and pause after *tevir.* The sense of the words dictates that *tippeḥa* is a stronger disjunctive than *tevir.*

מֵרְכָ֥א תְּבִ֛יר טִפְּחָ֖א

וְתָל֥וּ אֹת֛וֹ וְאֶת־בָּנָ֖יו עַל־הָעֵֽץ׃ (9:25) וְיֵ֥ין מַלְכ֛וּת רָ֖ב כְּיַ֥ד הַמֶּֽלֶךְ׃ (1:7)

Note: When *tevir* is followed by *merekha*, the pick-up to *merekha* may be changed from F to E in order to create a smoother transition.

תְּבִיר מֵרְכָא טִפְּחָא

שֶׁבַע וְעֶשְׂרִים וּמֵאָה מְדִינָה׃ (1:1)

וְיִכָּתֵב בְּדָתֵי פָרַס־וּמָדַי וְלֹא יַעֲבוֹר (1:19)

דַּרְגָּא תְּבִיר טִפְּחָא

וַתֹּאמֶר אֶסְתֵּר לַמֶּלֶךְ בְּשֵׁם מָרְדֳּכָי׃ (2:22)

יְקָר וּגְדוּלָּה לְמָרְדֳּכַי עַל־זֶה (6:3)

דַּרְגָּא תְּבִיר מֵרְכָא טִפְּחָא

וַיִּיטַב הַדָּבָר לִפְנֵי הָמָן וַיַּעַשׂ הָעֵץ׃ (5:14)

כִּי מָרְדֳּכַי צִוָּה עָלֶיהָ אֲשֶׁר לֹא־תַגִּיד׃ (2:10)

דַּרְגָּא תְּבִיר תְּבִיר מֵרְכָא טִפְּחָא

לְהַשְׁמִיד אֶת־כָּל־הַיְּהוּדִים אֲשֶׁר בְּכָל־מַלְכוּת אֲחַשְׁוֵרוֹשׁ עַם מָרְדֳּכָי׃ (3:6)

מִיּוֹם ׀ לְיוֹם וּמֵחֹדֶשׁ לְחֹדֶשׁ שְׁנֵים־עָשָׂר הוּא־חֹדֶשׁ אֲדָר׃ (3:7)

מֵרְכָא תְּבִיר מֵרְכָא טִפְּחָא

יְבַקְשׁוּ לַמֶּלֶךְ נְעָרוֹת בְּתוּלוֹת טוֹבוֹת מַרְאֶה׃ (2:2)

נְעָרוֹת רַבּוֹת אֶל־שׁוּשַׁן הַבִּירָה אֶל־יַד הֵגָי (2:8)

Three Words in a *Tevir* Segment

Sometimes *tevir* is preceded by two or more conjunctives. In these segments, there will be a very slight pause or elongation just before *tevir*. The second conjunctive before *tevir* (preceding either *merekha* or *darga*) is *kadmah*.

Kadmah darga tevir קַדְמָה דַּרְגָּא תְּבִיר

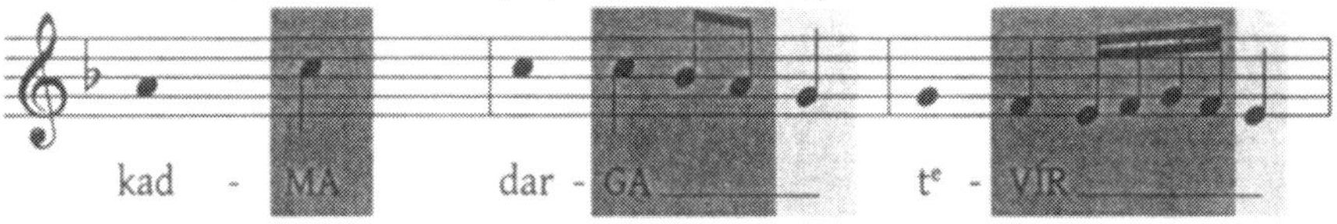

Chant these words to the melody of *kadmah darga tevir*.

אֶסְתֵּר הַמַּלְכָּה עִם־הַמֶּלֶךְ (5:12)

לְהָבִיא אֶת־וַשְׁתִּי הַמַּלְכָּה (1:17)

Kadmah merekha tevir קַדְמָה מֵרְכָא תְּבִיר

Chant these words to the melody of *kadmah merekha tevir*.

מֵאֲשֶׁר יוֹשִׁיט־לוֹ הַמֶּלֶךְ (4:11)

וַיְסַפֵּר לָהֶם הָמָן (5:11)

If the second conjunctive before *tevir* (preceding either *merekha* or *darga*) is accented on the first syllable, it will be *munaḥ* instead of *kadmah*. When we refer to this use of the *ta'am*, we accent its first syllable: *MU-naḥ*.

Munaḥ darga tevir מֻ֣ונַח דַּרְגָּ֧א תְּבִ֛יר

Chant these words to the melody of *munaḥ darga tevir.* בֶּ֣ן יָאִ֧יר בֶּן־שִׁמְעִ֛י (2:5)

Chant these words to the appropriate *te'amim*.

בָּ֣א מִסְפַּ֧ר הַהֲרוּגִ֛ים בְּשׁוּשַׁ֥ן הַבִּירָ֖ה לִפְנֵ֥י הַמֶּֽלֶךְ׃ (9:11)

אֵ֣ת אִגֶּ֧רֶת הַפּוּרִ֛ים הַזֹּ֖את הַשֵּׁנִֽית׃ (9:29)

Munaḥ merekha tevir מֻ֣ונַח מֵרְכָ֥א תְּבִ֛יר

Chant these words to the melody of *munaḥ merekha tevir.* אִ֣ם אֶת־אֲשֶׁ֥ר יֹאמַ֛ר (2:15)

Chant these words to the appropriate *te'amim*.

אִ֣ם אֶת־אֲשֶׁ֥ר יֹאמַ֛ר הֵגַ֥י סְרִיס־הַמֶּ֖לֶךְ שֹׁמֵ֣ר הַנָּשִׁ֑ים (2:15)

כִּ֣י אֵ֥ין לָב֛וֹא אֶל־שַׁ֥עַר הַמֶּ֖לֶךְ בִּלְב֥וּשׁ שָֽׂק׃ (4:2)

כִּ֣י אֵ֥ין הַצָּ֛ר שֹׁוֶ֖ה בְּנֵ֥זֶק הַמֶּֽלֶךְ׃ (7:4)

Four Words in a *Tevir* Segment

Sometimes *tevir* is preceded by three conjunctives. The third conjunctive before *tevir* (just before *kadmah*) will be *telishah ketanah*.

Telishah kadmah darga tevir תְּלִישָׁה֩ קַדְמָ֨ה דַּרְגָּ֧א תְּבִ֛יר

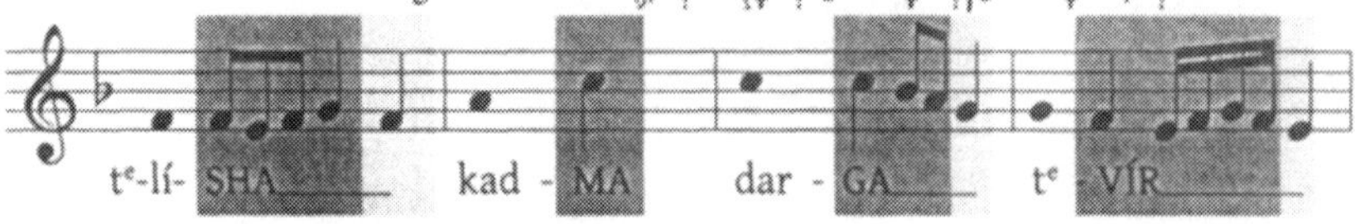

Chant these words to the appropriate *te'amim*.

וַיָּ֩שֶׂם֩ הַמֶּ֨לֶךְ אֲחַשְׁוֵרֹ֥שׁ ׀ מַ֛ס עַל־הָאָ֖רֶץ וְאִיֵּ֥י הַיָּֽם׃ (10:1)

אַ֣ף לֹא־הֵבִ֩יאָה֩ אֶסְתֵּ֨ר הַמַּלְכָּ֧ה עִם־הַמֶּ֛לֶךְ אֶל־הַמִּשְׁתֶּ֥ה אֲשֶׁר־עָשָׂ֖תָה כִּ֣י אִם־אוֹתִ֑י (5:12)

Note: The word אַ֣ף is punctuated with *munaḥ*. Chant it on F—as an extended pick-up to the *telishah*.

The *Zakef* Segment

Zakef is a strong disjunctive; only *siluk* and *etnaḥta* are stronger. A *zakef* segment will always be followed by a *tippeḥa* segement. *Zakef* is stronger than the ensuing *tippeḥa*. A *zakef* segment may also be followed by one or more other *zakef* segments, but they will eventually be followed by a *tippeḥa* segement. When you see two *zakefs* (or two *zakef* segments) in a row, the first is always stronger.

There are two basic forms of *zakef*, each with its own distinct melody: *zakef gadol* and *zakef katon*. There are also two compound *te'amim*, in which two symbols appear on a single word: *munaḥ-zakef* and *metigah-zakef*.

Zakef Gadol

A word marked with *zakef gadol* is short and has no conjunctives immediately before it.

Zakef gadol זָקֵף־גָּד֕וֹל

Chant these words to the melody of *zakef gadol.*

לִפְנֵ֕י (1:13) בַּחֲצַ֕ר (1:5) אִ֕ישׁ (6:7) וַיַּ֕עַשׂ (4:17)

Zakef gadol is usually followed by *(merekha-) tippeḥa*. Chant these phrases. Make a pause or elongation after *zakef*. Make a more subtle elongation or pause after *tippeḥa.*

וְכָל־זֶ֕ה אֵינֶ֥נּוּ שֹׁוֶ֖ה לִ֑י (5:13)   וַיָּב֕וֹא עַ֖ד לִפְנֵ֣י שַֽׁעַר־הַמֶּ֑לֶךְ (4:2)

וְהָעָ֕ם לַעֲשׂ֥וֹת בּ֖וֹ כַּטּ֥וֹב בְּעֵינֶֽיךָ (3:11)   כְּשֹׁ֕ךְ חֲמַ֖ת הַמֶּ֣לֶךְ אֲחַשְׁוֵר֑וֹשׁ (2:1)

One or Two Words in a *Zakef Katon* Segment

A word marked with *zakef katon* is usually preceded by the conjunctive *munaḥ.*

Munaḥ zakef katon מוּנַ֣ח זָקֵף־קָטֹ֔ן

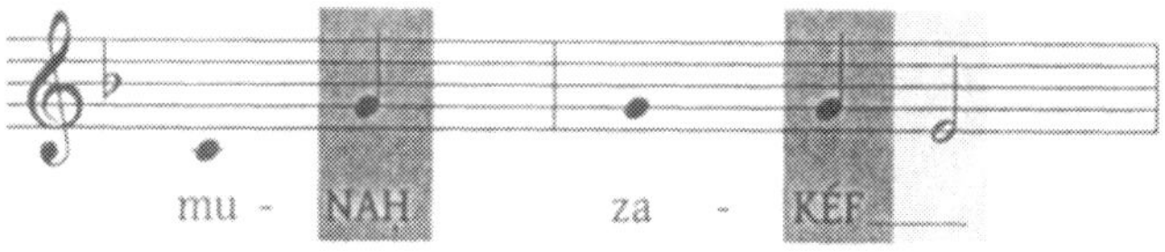

Chant these words to the melody of *zakef.*   אֶל־הַמֶּ֔לֶךְ (2:14) הַמַּלְכ֔וּת (1:9)

Chant these words to the melody of *munaḥ zakef.*

עָשָׂ֥ה מִשְׁתֶּ֔ה (1:3) אֶל־רְח֥וֹב הָעִ֔יר (4:6) בֵּ֣ין הָֽעַמִּ֔ים (3:8) נָ֥תַן ל֔וֹ (4:8) וַיֹּ֣אמֶר הַמֶּ֔לֶךְ (1:13)

Munaḥ Zakef on a Single Word

Sometimes, *munaḥ* will appear on the same word that is marked with *zakef*. This happens often on long words.

הַסָּֽרִיסִ֔ים (1:10) אֶת־שְׁאֵֽלָתִ֔י (5:8) מְשָׁרְתָ֔יו (6:3)

Metigah-zakef katon מְתִיגָ֔ה־זָקֵף־קָטֹ֔ן

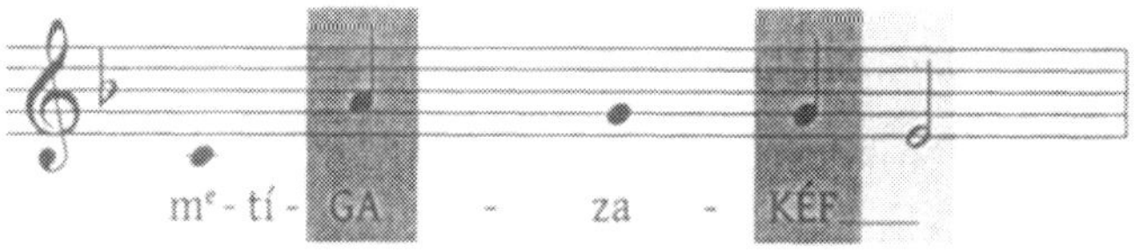

Chant these words to the melody of *metigah zakef.*

וְאֶת־יְקָ֔ר (1:4) וּבַבִּזָּ֔ה (9:15) וּמָרְדֳּכַ֔י (3:2) וְאֶל־הַיְּהוּדִ֔ים (8:9)

Zakef is usually followed by *(merekha-) tippeḥa*. Chant these examples. Make a pause or elongation after *zakef*. Make a more subtle elongation or pause after *tippeḥa*.

מוּנַח זָקֵף טִפְּחָא

בֵּין הָעַמִּים בְּכֹל מְדִינוֹת מַלְכוּתֶךָ (3:8) אִם־עַל־הַמֶּלֶךְ טוֹב יִכָּתֵב לְאַבְּדָם (3:9)

בְּבֵית הַמַּלְכוּת נֹכַח פֶּתַח הַבָּיִת׃ (5:1)

מוּנַח זָקֵף מֵרְכָא טִפְּחָא

אֶל־בֵּית הַמֶּלֶךְ אֶל־יַד הֵגֶי שֹׁמֵר הַנָּשִׁים׃ (2:8) יוֹם וָיוֹם וְלֹא שָׁמַע אֲלֵיהֶם (3:4)

כִּי־אֵין מָרְדֳּכַי כֹּרֵעַ וּמִשְׁתַּחֲוֶה לוֹ (3:5)

מְתִיגָה־זָקֵף מֵרְכָא טִפְּחָא

וּמָרְדֳּכַי לֹא יִכְרַע וְלֹא יִשְׁתַּחֲוֶה׃ (3:2) וּבַבִּזָּה לֹא שָׁלְחוּ אֶת־יָדָם׃ (9:15)

Chant these verses.

וַיַּגִּידוּ לְמָרְדֳּכַי אֵת דִּבְרֵי אֶסְתֵּר׃ (4:12)

וַיֵּצֵא הֲתָךְ אֶל־מָרְדֳּכָי אֶל־רְחוֹב הָעִיר אֲשֶׁר לִפְנֵי שַׁעַר־הַמֶּלֶךְ׃ (4:6)

וַיָּבוֹא הֲתָךְ וַיַּגֵּד לְאֶסְתֵּר אֵת דִּבְרֵי מָרְדֳּכָי׃ (4:9)

וַיַּרְא הָמָן כִּי־אֵין מָרְדֳּכַי כֹּרֵעַ וּמִשְׁתַּחֲוֶה לוֹ וַיִּמָּלֵא הָמָן חֵמָה׃ (3:5)

וַיִּתְאַפַּק הָמָן וַיָּבוֹא אֶל־בֵּיתוֹ וַיִּשְׁלַח וַיָּבֵא אֶת־אֹהֲבָיו וְאֶת־זֶרֶשׁ אִשְׁתּוֹ׃ (5:10)

The *Pashta/Yetiv* Segment

Sometimes there is a subdivision within a *zakef* segment. *Pashta* is the *ta'am* that marks that subdivision.

Pashta פַּשְׁטָא֙

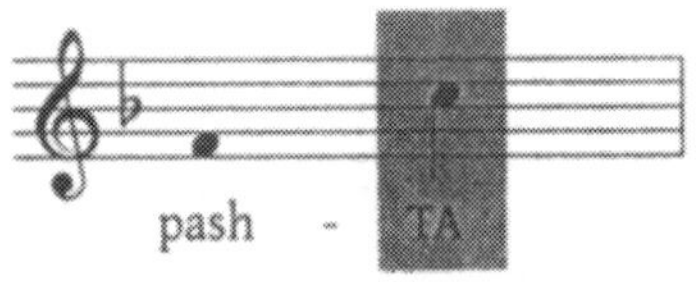

Chant these words to the melody of *pashta*. (1:4) אֶת־עֹ֙שֶׁר֙ (2:13) לָ֙הּ֙ (1:1) הַמֶּ֙לֶךְ֙ (1:10) בַּיּוֹם֙

Two Words in a *Pashta* Segment

If the preceding word is closely connected in meaning to the *pashta* word, it is usually marked with a conjunctive *ta'am*. Most often that conjunctive will be *mahpakh*.

Mahpakh pashta מַהְפַּ֤ךְ פַּשְׁטָא֙

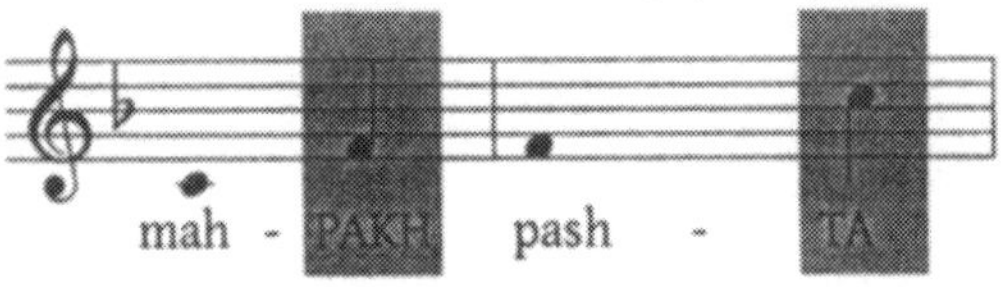

Chant these words to the melody of *mahpakh pashta*.

(2:13) יִנָּ֤תֵֽן לָהּ֙ (2:7) הִ֤יא אֶסְתֵּר֙ (2:15) וַתְּהִ֤י אֶסְתֵּר֙ (1:3) בִּשְׁנַ֤ת שָׁלוֹשׁ֙

If the accents are close to each other, the conjunctive will be *merekha* instead of *mahpakh*. In the *merekha-pashta* combination, the two accented syllables are contiguous—the *merekha* word is accented on the last syllable, and the *pashta* word has no pick-up. Thus the model for *pashta* is sung on the word "TA," dropping the pick-up "pash-."

Merekha pashta מֵרְכָא פַּשְׁטָא֙

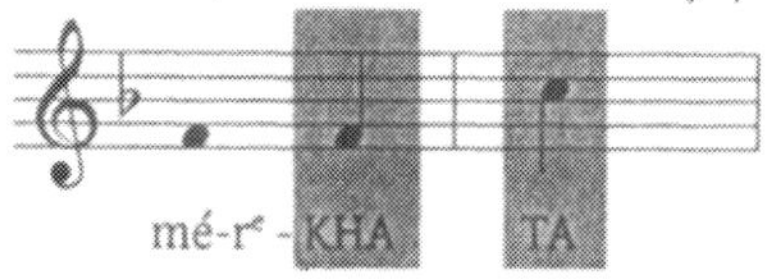

Chant these words to the melody of *merekha pashta*. לֹא־תָבוֹא עוֹד֙ (2:14) וְהִפִּיל פּוּר֙ (9:24)

Yetiv

Yetiv is used instead of *pashta* if the word is accented on the first syllable and has no conjunctive words immediately preceding. Since *yetiv* is found only on words accented on the first syllable, i.e., words with no pick-ups, the model is sung on the word "TÍV," dropping the pick-up "y^e-."

Yetiv יְ֚תִיב

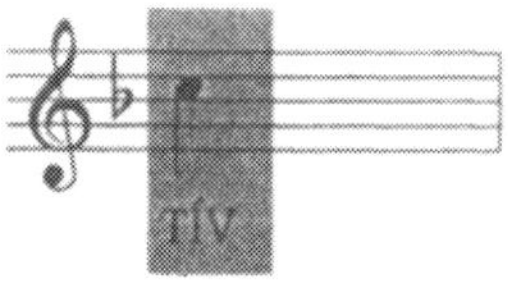

Chant these words to the melody of *yetiv*. עַ֚ל (1:2) כָּ֚כָה (6:9)

Yetiv is usually followed by *zakef katon* or *munaḥ zakef katon*. Chant these examples. Make a more subtle elongation or pause after *yetiv*. Make a stronger pause or elongation after *zakef*.

בֵּ֚ית הַמַּלְכוּת אֲשֶׁר לַמֶּלֶךְ אֲחַשְׁוֵרוֹשׁ׃ (1:9) עַ֚ל כִּסֵּא מַלְכוּתוֹ אֲשֶׁר בְּשׁוּשַׁן הַבִּירָה׃ (1:2)

כָּ֚כָה יֵעָשֶׂה לָאִישׁ אֲשֶׁר הַמֶּלֶךְ חָפֵץ בִּיקָרוֹ׃ (6:9) אִ֚ישׁ צַר וְאוֹיֵב הָמָן הָרָע הַזֶּה (7:6)

Pashta is usually followed by *zakef katon* or *munaḥ zakef katon*. Chant these examples. Make a more subtle elongation or pause after *pashta*. Make a stronger pause or elongation after *zakef*.

פַּשְׁטָא֙ זָקֵף

בַּיּוֹם֙ הַשְּׁבִיעִי כְּטוֹב לֵב־הַמֶּלֶךְ בַּיָּיִן (1:10) כְּדָת֙ מַה־לַּעֲשׂוֹת בַּמַּלְכָּה וַשְׁתִּי (1:15)

מָרְדֳּכַי֙ מִתְהַלֵּךְ לִפְנֵי חֲצַר בֵּית־הַנָּשִׁים (2:11)

פַּשְׁטָא֙ מוּנַח זָקֵף

הַמֶּלֶךְ֙ מֵהֹדּוּ וְעַד־כּוּשׁ שֶׁבַע וְעֶשְׂרִים וּמֵאָה מְדִינָה׃ (1:1)

אֶת־עֹ֙שֶׁר֙ כְּבוֹד מַלְכוּתוֹ וְאֶת־יְקָר תִּפְאֶרֶת גְּדוּלָּתוֹ (1:4)

לָבוֹא֙ בִּדְבַר הַמֶּלֶךְ אֲשֶׁר בְּיַד הַסָּרִיסִים (1:12)

פַּשְׁטָא֙ פַּשְׁטָא֙ מוּנַ֣ח זָקֵ֔ף

לִרְאוֹת֙ הֲיַֽעַמְדוּ֙ דִּבְרֵ֣י מָרְדֳּכַ֔י כִּֽי־הִגִּ֥יד לָהֶ֖ם אֲשֶׁר־ה֥וּא יְהוּדִֽי׃ (3:4)

אֶשְׁקוֹל֙ עַל־יְדֵי֙ עֹשֵׂ֣י הַמְּלָאכָ֔ה לְהָבִ֖יא אֶל־גִּנְזֵ֥י הַמֶּֽלֶךְ׃ (3:9)

מַהְפַּ֤ךְ פַּשְׁטָא֙ זָקֵ֔ף

בִּשְׁנַ֤ת שָׁלוֹשׁ֙ לְמָלְכ֔וֹ עָשָׂ֣ה מִשְׁתֶּ֔ה לְכָל־שָׂרָ֖יו וַעֲבָדָ֑יו (1:3)

לִפְנֵ֤י הַמֶּ֙לֶךְ֙ וְהַשָּׂרִ֔ים לֹ֤א עַל־הַמֶּ֙לֶךְ֙ לְבַדּ֔וֹ עָוְתָ֖ה וַשְׁתִּ֣י הַמַּלְכָּ֑ה (1:16)

הִ֤יא אֶסְתֵּר֙ בַּת־דֹּד֔וֹ כִּ֛י אֵ֥ין לָ֖הּ אָ֣ב וָאֵ֑ם (2:7)

מַהְפַּ֤ךְ פַּשְׁטָא֙ מוּנַ֣ח זָקֵ֔ף

זָכַ֤ר אֶת־וַשְׁתִּי֙ וְאֵ֣ת אֲשֶׁר־עָשָׂ֔תָה וְאֵ֥ת אֲשֶׁר־נִגְזַ֖ר עָלֶֽיהָ׃ (2:1)

אֶל־שׁוּשַׁ֨ן הַבִּירָ֜ה אֶל־בֵּ֣ית הַנָּשִׁ֗ים אֶל־יַ֥ד הֵגֶ֛א סְרִ֥יס הַמֶּ֖לֶךְ שֹׁמֵ֣ר הַנָּשִׁ֑ים (2:3)

וַתִּלָּקַ֤ח אֶסְתֵּר֙ אֶל־בֵּ֣ית הַמֶּ֔לֶךְ אֶל־יַ֥ד הֵגַ֖י שֹׁמֵ֥ר הַנָּשִֽׁים׃ (2:8)

מֵרְכָ֥א פַּשְׁטָא֙ זָקֵ֔ף

לֹא־תָב֥וֹא עוֹד֙ אֶל־הַמֶּ֔לֶךְ כִּ֣י אִם־חָפֵ֥ץ בָּ֛הּ הַמֶּ֖לֶךְ וְנִקְרְאָ֥ה בְשֵֽׁם׃ (2:14)

מֵרְכָ֥א פַּשְׁטָא֙ מוּנַ֣ח זָקֵ֔ף

וְהִפִּ֥יל פּוּר֙ ה֣וּא הַגּוֹרָ֔ל לְהֻמָּ֖ם וּֽלְאַבְּדָֽם׃ (9:24)

Chant these verses.

גַּ֚ם וַשְׁתִּ֣י הַמַּלְכָּ֔ה עָשְׂתָ֖ה מִשְׁתֵּ֣ה נָשִׁ֑ים בֵּ֚ית הַמַּלְכ֔וּת אֲשֶׁ֖ר לַמֶּ֥לֶךְ אֲחַשְׁוֵרֽוֹשׁ׃ (1:9)

וַיֹּ֣אמֶר הַמֶּ֔לֶךְ לַחֲכָמִ֖ים יֹדְעֵ֣י הָֽעִתִּ֑ים כִּי־כֵן֙ דְּבַ֣ר הַמֶּ֔לֶךְ לִפְנֵ֕י כָּל־יֹדְעֵ֖י דָּ֥ת וָדִֽין׃ (1:13)

אַחַר֙ הַדְּבָרִ֣ים הָאֵ֔לֶּה כְּשֹׁ֕ךְ חֲמַ֖ת הַמֶּ֣לֶךְ אֲחַשְׁוֵר֑וֹשׁ

זָכַ֤ר אֶת־וַשְׁתִּי֙ וְאֵ֣ת אֲשֶׁר־עָשָׂ֔תָה וְאֵ֥ת אֲשֶׁר־נִגְזַ֖ר עָלֶֽיהָ׃ (2:1)

וּבְכָל־י֣וֹם וָי֔וֹם מָרְדֳּכַי֙ מִתְהַלֵּ֔ךְ לִפְנֵ֖י חֲצַ֣ר בֵּית־הַנָּשִׁ֑ים

לָדַ֙עַת֙ אֶת־שְׁל֣וֹם אֶסְתֵּ֔ר וּמַה־יֵּעָשֶׂ֖ה בָּֽהּ׃ (2:11)

וַיֹּ֤אמֶר הַמֶּ֙לֶךְ֙ לְהָמָ֔ן הַכֶּ֖סֶף נָת֣וּן לָ֑ךְ וְהָעָ֕ם לַעֲשׂ֥וֹת בּ֖וֹ כַּטּ֥וֹב בְּעֵינֶֽיךָ׃ (3:11)

וַיִּקַּ֤ח הָמָן֙ אֶת־הַלְּב֣וּשׁ וְאֶת־הַסּ֔וּס וַיַּלְבֵּ֖שׁ אֶֽת־מָרְדֳּכָ֑י

וַיַּרְכִּיבֵ֙הוּ֙ בִּרְח֣וֹב הָעִ֔יר וַיִּקְרָ֣א לְפָנָ֔יו כָּ֚כָה יֵעָשֶׂ֣ה לָאִ֔ישׁ אֲשֶׁ֥ר הַמֶּ֖לֶךְ חָפֵ֥ץ בִּיקָרֽוֹ׃ (6:11)

וַתֹּ֣אמֶר־אֶסְתֵּ֔ר אִ֚ישׁ צַ֣ר וְאוֹיֵ֔ב הָמָ֥ן הָרָ֖ע הַזֶּ֑ה וְהָמָ֣ן נִבְעַ֔ת מִלִּפְנֵ֥י הַמֶּ֖לֶךְ וְהַמַּלְכָּֽה׃ (7:6)

Three Words in a *Pashta* Segment

Sometimes *pashta* is preceded by two or more conjunctives. In these segments, there will be a very slight pause or elongation just before *pashta.*

The second conjunctive before *pashta* (preceding either *merekha* or *mahpakh*) may be *kadmah.*

Kadmah mahpakh pashta קַדְמָ֨ה מַהְפַּ֤ךְ פַּשְׁטָא֙

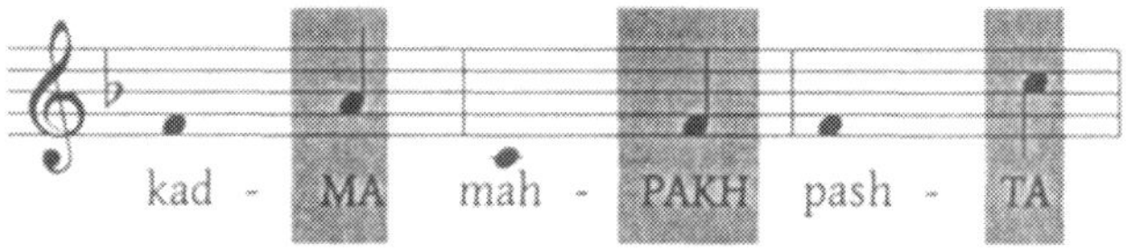
kad - MA mah - PAKH pash - TA

Chant these words to the melody of *kadmah mahpakh pashta.*

יָבֹ֨וא הַמֶּ֤לֶךְ וְהָמָן֙ (5:4)   לַיָּמִ֨ים הָאֵ֤לֶּה פוּרִים֙ (9:26)   וַתַּ֨עַן אֶסְתֵּ֤ר הַמַּלְכָּה֙ (7:3)

Kadmah merekha pashta קַדְמָ֨ה מֵרְכָ֥א פַּשְׁטָא֙

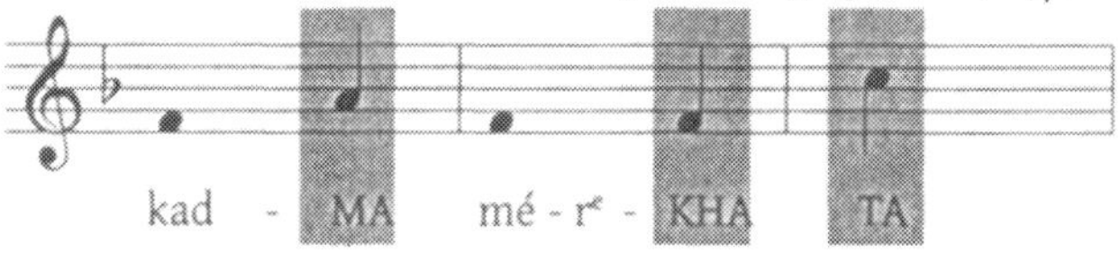
kad - MA mé - rᵉ - KHA TA

Chant these words to the melody of *kadmah merekha pashta.* בִּשְׁלוֹשָׁ֨ה עָשָׂ֥ר יוֹם֙ (9:1)

If the second conjunctive before *pashta* (preceding *mahpakh* or *merekha*) is accented on the first syllable, it will be *munaḥ* instead of *kadmah.* When we refer to this *ta'am*, we accent its first syllable: *MU-naḥ.*

Munaḥ mahpakh pashta מ֣וּנַח מַהְפַּ֤ךְ פַּשְׁטָא֙

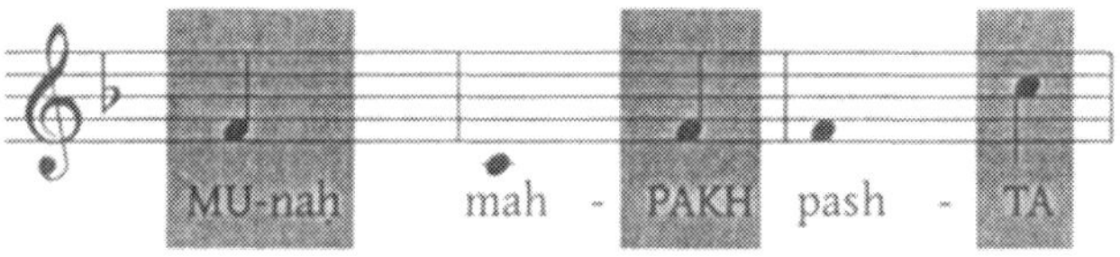
MU-nah mah - PAKH pash - TA

Chant these words to the melody of *munaḥ mahpakh pashta.*

גַּ֣ם בַּיּ֤וֹם הַשֵּׁנִי֙ (7:2)   שֶׁ֣בַע וְעֶשְׂרִ֤ים וּמֵאָה֙ (8:9)

Munaḥ merekha pashta מ֣וּנַח מֵרְכָ֥א פַּשְׁטָא֙

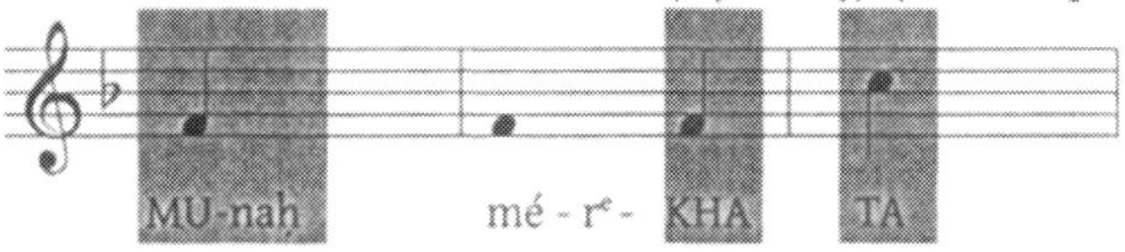
MU-nah mé - rᵉ - KHA TA

Chant these words to the melody of *munaḥ merekha pashta.* מִ֣י ה֥וּא זֶה֙ (7:5)

Four Words in a *Pashta* Segment

Sometimes *pashta* is preceded by three conjunctives. The third conjunctive before *pashta* is *telishah ketanah.*

Telishah kadmah mahpakh pashta תְּלִישָׁה֠ קַדְמָ֨ה מַהְפַּ֤ךְ פַּשְׁטָא֙

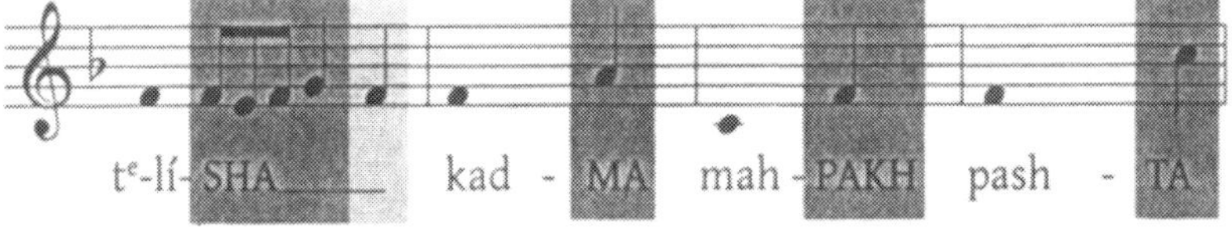
tᵉ-lí- SHA kad - MA mah - PAKH pash - TA

Chant these words to the appropriate *te'amim*.

וְנִשְׁמַע֩ פִּתְגָ֨ם הַמֶּ֤לֶךְ אֲשֶֽׁר־יַעֲשֶׂה֙ בְּכָל־מַלְכוּתֹו֔ (1:20)

וְאֵת֩ כָּל־אֲשֶׁ֨ר גִּדְּל֤וֹ הַמֶּ֙לֶךְ֙ וְאֵ֣ת אֲשֶׁ֣ר נִשְּׂא֔וֹ (5:11)

אֲשֶׁר֩ הַחִלּ֨וֹתָ לִנְפֹּ֤ל לְפָנָיו֙ לֹא־תוּכַ֣ל לֹ֔ו (6:13)

Chant these phrases. Connect the *telishah* and *kadmah* words to the word that follows. Create only a slight elongation and pause after *pashta*. Create a longer elongation and pause after *zakef*.

קַדְמָ֨ה מֵרְכָ֥א פַּשְׁטָא֙

בִּשְׁלוֹשָׁ֨ה עָשָׂ֥ר יוֹם֙ בֹּ֔ו אֲשֶׁ֨ר הִגִּ֧יעַ דְּבַר־הַמֶּ֛לֶךְ וְדָת֖וֹ לְהֵעָשֽׂוֹת (9:1)

קַדְמָ֨ה מַהְפַּ֥ךְ פַּשְׁטָא֙

יָב֨וֹא הַמֶּ֤לֶךְ וְהָמָן֙ הַיֹּ֔ום אֶל־הַמִּשְׁתֶּ֖ה אֲשֶׁר־עָשִׂ֥יתִי לֹֽו׃ (5:4)

אֶל־שֶׁ֨בַע וְעֶשְׂרִ֥ים וּמֵאָה֙ מְדִינָ֔ה מַלְכ֖וּת אֲחַשְׁוֵרֹֽושׁ (9:30)

פַּשְׁטָ֨א קַדְמָ֥ה מַהְפַּ֤ךְ פַּשְׁטָא֙

מְקוֹם֙ אֲשֶׁ֨ר דְּבַר־הַמֶּ֥לֶךְ וְדָתוֹ֙ מַגִּ֔יעַ (4:3)

מ֤וּנַח מֵרְכָ֥א פַּשְׁטָא֙

מִ֣י ה֥וּא זֶה֙ וְאֵֽי־זֶ֣ה ה֔וּא אֲשֶׁר־מְלָא֥וֹ לִבֹּ֖ו לַעֲשֹׂ֥ות כֵּֽן׃ (7:5)

מ֤וּנַח מַהְפַּ֥ךְ פַּשְׁטָא֙

גַּ֣ם בַּיּ֤וֹם הַשֵּׁנִי֙ בְּמִשְׁתֵּ֣ה הַיַּ֔יִן מַה־שְּׁאֵלָתֵ֞ךְ אֶסְתֵּ֤ר הַמַּלְכָּה֙ וְתִנָּ֣תֶן לָ֔ךְ (7:2)

שֶׁ֨בַע וְעֶשְׂרִ֥ים וּמֵאָה֙ מְדִינָ֔ה מְדִינָ֤ה וּמְדִינָה֙ כִּכְתָבָ֔הּ וְעַ֥ם וָעָ֖ם כִּלְשֹׁנֹֽו (8:9)

תְּלִישָׁ֩ה קַדְמָ֨ה מַהְפַּ֥ךְ פַּשְׁטָא֙

אֲשֶׁר֩ הַחִלּ֨וֹתָ לִנְפֹּ֤ל לְפָנָיו֙ לֹא־תוּכַ֣ל לֹ֔ו כִּֽי־נָפ֥וֹל תִּפּ֖וֹל לְפָנָֽיו׃ (6:13)

וְנִשְׁמַע֩ פִּתְגָ֨ם הַמֶּ֤לֶךְ אֲשֶֽׁר־יַעֲשֶׂה֙ בְּכָל־מַלְכוּתֹו֔ כִּ֥י רַבָּ֖ה הִֽיא (1:20)

The *Segol* Segment

Segol is the strongest disjunctive before *etnaḥta*. A *segol* segment is followed by one or more *zakef* segments, and then by *tippeḥa* and *etnaḥta*. The *segol* segment appears 13 times in the Book of Esther.

Zarka is the *ta'am* that marks the subdivision within the *segol* segment.

Both *segol* and *zarka* can be preceded by the conjunctive *munaḥ*. On one occasion, *zarka* is preceded by *kadmah* and *munaḥ*.

Kadmah munaḥ zarka munaḥ segol קַדְמָ֨ה מ֤וּנַח זַרְקָא֮ מ֣וּנַח סֶגּֽוֹל֒

kad - MA   mu - NAH   zar - KA   mu - NAH   se - GÓL

Note: The accent *segol* has a double pick-up. If the word has one pick-up syllable, sing that syllable on F-sharp. If the word has two pick-up syllables, sing the first pick-up on G and the second on F-sharp. If the word has three pick-up syllables, sing the first two pick-ups on G and the third on F-sharp.

Note: The melody of *segol* is identical to that of *etnaḥta.*

Chant these words to the appropriate *te'amim.*

לְקַיֵּ֒ם עֲלֵיהֶ֔ם (9:21)

לְהִקָּהֵל֒ וְלַעֲמֹ֣ד עַל־נַפְשָׁ֔ם (8:11)

בִּשְׁלוֹשָׁ֤ה וְעֶשְׂרִים֙ בּ֔וֹ (8:9)

בִּשְׁלוֹשָׁה עָשָׂ֣ר יוֹם֒ בּ֔וֹ (3:12)

וַיָּבוֹא֒ הָמָ֔ן וַיֹּ֣אמֶר לוֹ֙ הַמֶּ֔לֶךְ מַה־לַּעֲשׂ֕וֹת בָּאִ֕ישׁ אֲשֶׁ֥ר הַמֶּ֖לֶךְ חָפֵ֣ץ בִּיקָר֑וֹ (6:6)

וַיֹּאמֶר֮ הָמָ֒ן אַ֣ף לֹא־הֵבִ֩יאָה֩ אֶסְתֵּ֨ר הַמַּלְכָּ֧ה עִם־הַמֶּ֛לֶךְ אֶל־הַמִּשְׁתֶּ֥ה אֲשֶׁר־עָשָׂ֖תָה כִּ֣י אִם־אוֹתִ֑י (5:12)

The *Revia* Segment

Revia is a medium-level disjunctive, found before *pashta, zarka,* and *tevir* segments. *Revia* is a stronger disjunctive than the others (*pashta, zarka,* or *tevir*) that follow.

One or Two Words in a *Revia* Segment

If the preceding word is closely connected in meaning to the *revia* word, it is usually marked with the conjunctive *munaḥ.*

Munaḥ revia מוּנַ֣ח רְבִ֗יעַ

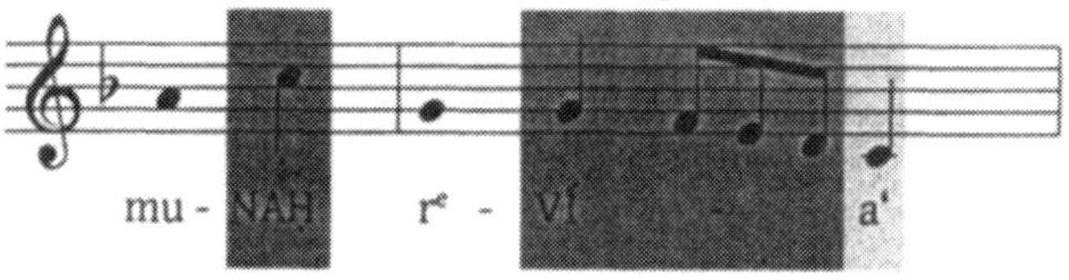

Chant these words to the melody of *revia.* וַיִּכְתֹּ֗ב (8:10) וַשְׁתִּ֗י (1:19)

Chant these words to the melody of *munaḥ revia.*

פָּרַ֣ס וּמָדַ֗י (1:3) הַיָּמִ֣ים הָאֵ֗לֶּה (1:5) אֵ֣ין אֶסְתֵּ֗ר (2:20) וַיֹּ֣אמֶר מְמוּכָ֗ן (1:16)

Three Words in a *Revia* Segment

Sometimes *revia* is preceded by two conjunctives. In these segments, there will be a very slight pause or elongation just before *revia.* The second conjunctive before *revia* (preceding *munaḥ*) is *darga.*

Darga munaḥ revia דַּרְגָּ֧א מוּנַ֣ח רְבִ֗יעַ

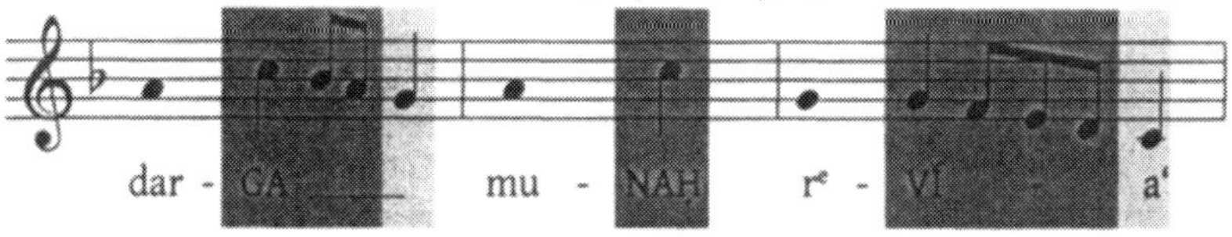

Chant these words to the melody of *darga munaḥ revia.* חֲמֵ֧שׁ מֵא֛וֹת אִ֗ישׁ (9:12)

There should be no pause at all between *darga* and *munaḥ.* There should be a very slight pause between *munaḥ* and *revia.*

Chant these examples. Connect each conjunctive word to the word that follows. Create an elongation and/or pause after *revia*. Create only a slight elongation after *pashta, zarka,* or *tevir*.

דַּרְגָּא) (מוּנַח) רְבִ֗יעַ פַּשְׁטָא֙

כְּתֹ֗ב בְּשֵׁם֙ הַמֶּ֣לֶךְ אֲחַשְׁוֵר֔וֹשׁ (8:10)

אֲשֶׁ֣ר כָּתַ֗ב לְאַבֵּד֙ אֶת־הַיְּהוּדִ֔ים (8:5)

וּא אֲחַשְׁוֵר֗וֹשׁ הַמֹּלֵךְ֙ מֵהֹ֣דּוּ וְעַד־כּ֔וּשׁ (1:1)

חֲמֵ֣שׁ מֵא֗וֹת אִישׁ֙ וְאֵת֙ עֲשֶׂ֣רֶת בְּנֵֽי־הָמָ֔ן (9:12)

רְגָּא מוּנַח רְבִ֗יעַ מַהְפַּ֤ךְ פַּשְׁטָא֙

אִם־מָצָ֨אתִי חֵ֜ן לְפָנָ֗יו וְכָשֵׁ֤ר הַדָּבָר֙ לִפְנֵ֣י הַמֶּ֔לֶךְ (8:5)

וּנַח רְבִ֗יעַ יְ֭תִיב

סַּ֣ד הַמֶּ֗לֶךְ עַ֚ל כָּל־רַ֣ב בֵּית֔וֹ (1:8)

וּנַח רְבִ֗יעַ מ֤וּנַח מַהְפַּ֤ךְ פַּשְׁטָא֙

הֹ֣דּוּ וְעַד־כּ֗וּשׁ שֶׁ֣בַע וְעֶשְׂרִ֤ים וּמֵאָה֙ מְדִינָ֔ה (8:9)

וּנַח רְבִ֗יעַ תְּבִ֛יר

רַ֣ס וּמָדַ֗י הַֽפַּרְתְּמִ֛ים וְשָׂרֵ֥י הַמְּדִינ֖וֹת לְפָנָֽיו׃ (1:3)

זָ֣הָב וָכֶ֗סֶף עַ֚ל רִֽצְפַ֛ת בַּהַט־וָשֵׁ֖שׁ וְדַ֥ר וְסֹחָֽרֶת׃ (1:6)

וּנַח רְבִ֗יעַ דַּרְגָּ֧א תְּבִ֛יר

יְבַקֵּ֣שׁ הָמָ֗ן לְהַשְׁמִ֧יד אֶת־כָּל־הַיְּהוּדִ֛ים אֲשֶׁ֛ר בְּכָל־מַלְכ֥וּת אֲחַשְׁוֵר֖וֹשׁ עַ֥ם מָרְדֳּכָֽי׃ (3:6)

וּנַח רְבִ֗יעַ מ֤וּנַח דַּרְגָּ֧א תְּבִ֛יר

יּ֣וֹם הַה֗וּא בָּ֣א מִסְפַּ֧ר הַהֲרוּגִ֛ים בְּשׁוּשַׁ֥ן הַבִּירָ֖ה לִפְנֵ֥י הַמֶּֽלֶךְ׃ (9:11)

מוּנַח) רְבִ֗יעַ זַרְקָא֮

שֶׁ֣ר בְּכָל־עִ֣יר־וָעִ֗יר לְהִקָּהֵל֮ וְלַעֲמֹ֣ד עַל־נַפְשָׁם֒ (8:11)

יְּהוּדִ֣ים הַפְּרָזִ֗ים הַיֹּשְׁבִים֮ בְּעָרֵ֣י הַפְּרָזוֹת֒ (9:19)

כָּל־אֹהֲבָ֗יו יַֽעֲשׂוּ־עֵץ֮ גָּבֹ֣הַּ חֲמִשִּׁ֣ים אַמָּה֒ (5:14)

וּנַח רְבִ֗יעַ מוּנַח זַרְקָא֮

וּא־חֹ֣דֶשׁ סִיוָ֗ן בִּשְׁלוֹשָׁ֣ה וְעֶשְׂרִים֮ בּוֹ֒ (8:9)

Chant these verses.

וַיְהִ֖י בִּימֵ֣י אֲחַשְׁוֵר֑וֹשׁ ה֣וּא אֲחַשְׁוֵר֗וֹשׁ הַמֹּלֵךְ֙ מֵהֹ֣דּוּ וְעַד־כּ֔וּשׁ

שֶׁ֛בַע וְעֶשְׂרִ֥ים וּמֵאָ֖ה מְדִינָֽה׃ (1:1)

וַיִּ֣בֶז בְּעֵינָ֗יו לִשְׁלֹ֤חַ יָד֙ בְּמָרְדֳּכַ֣י לְבַדּ֔וֹ כִּֽי־הִגִּ֥ידוּ ל֖וֹ אֶת־עַ֣ם מָרְדֳּכָ֑י
וַיְבַקֵּ֣שׁ הָמָ֗ן לְהַשְׁמִ֧יד אֶת־כׇּל־הַיְּהוּדִ֛ים אֲשֶׁ֛ר בְּכׇל־מַלְכ֥וּת אֲחַשְׁוֵר֖וֹשׁ עַ֥ם מָרְדֳּכָֽי׃ (3:6)

וַֽיְהִ֗י כְּאָמְרָ֤ם אֵלָיו֙ י֣וֹם וָי֔וֹם וְלֹ֥א שָׁמַ֖ע אֲלֵיהֶ֑ם
וַיַּגִּ֣ידוּ לְהָמָ֗ן לִרְאוֹת֙ הֲיַֽעַמְדוּ֙ דִּבְרֵ֣י מָרְדֳּכַ֔י כִּֽי־הִגִּ֥יד לָהֶ֖ם אֲשֶׁר־ה֥וּא יְהוּדִֽי׃ (3:4)

The *Legarmeh* Segment

Sometimes there is a subdivision within a *revia* segment. The *ta'am* that marks that subdivision may be *legarmeh.*

Legarmeh ׀ לְגַרְמֵ֣ה

Chant these words to the melody of *legarmeh.*

מִטּ֣וֹת ׀ (1:6) נִקְהֲל֣וֹ ׀ (9:16) חֵ֣יל ׀ (1:3) בָּעֶ֣רֶב ׀ (2:14)

Note: The melody of *legarmeh* is identical to that of *telishah ketanah*. But *legarmeh* is a minor disjunctive, and *telishah ketanah* is a conjunctive.

Legarmeh is always followed by *munaḥ revia.*

בָּעֶ֣רֶב ׀ הִ֣יא בָאָ֗ה (2:14)　　אַחַ֣ר ׀ הַדְּבָרִ֣ים הָאֵ֗לֶּה (3:1)

וּבַבֹּ֣קֶר ׀ אֱמֹ֣ר לַמֶּ֗לֶךְ (5:14)　　נִקְהֲל֣וּ ׀ וְעָמֹ֣ד עַל־נַפְשָׁ֗ם (9:16)

The *Geresh* Segment

Another *ta'am* that can subdivide a *revia* segment is *geresh.* There are two basic forms of *geresh,* each with its own distinct melody: (single) *geresh*, and double *geresh,* called *gereshayim*. *Geresh* without a preceding conjunctive is always accented on the next-to-the-last syllable. *Geresh* appears by itself only twice in the Book of Esther.

One or Two Words in a *Geresh* Segment

More commonly, *geresh* is preceded by a closely connected word, marked with the conjunctive *ta'am kadmah.*

Kadmah geresh קַדְמָ֨א גֵּ֜רֵשׁ

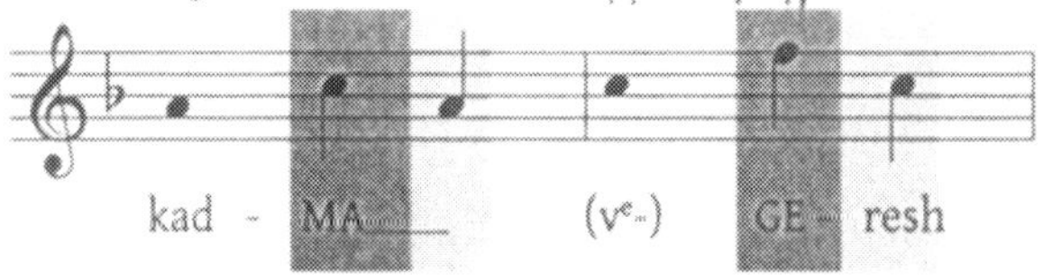

Elision will take place if the *geresh* word is accented on the first syllable.

'a - SAR HÓ desh　　עָשָׂ֨ר חֹ֜דֶשׁ (9:1)

Chant these words to the melody of *geresh*.　　וְהַמֶּ֜לֶךְ (7:7) מַחֲשֶׁ֜בֶת (8:5)

Chant these words to the melody of *kadmah geresh.*

אֲשֶׁ֨ר לֹֽא־תָב֜וֹא (1:19) וְהַיּ֨וֹם הַזֶּ֜ה (1:18) וַיַּ֨עַשׂ הַמֶּ֜לֶךְ (2:18) וַיֹּ֨אמְר֜וּ (3:3)

Three Words in a *Geresh* Segment

Sometimes *geresh* is preceded by two conjunctives. The second conjunctive before *geresh* (preceding *kadmah*) is *telishah.*

Telishah kadmah geresh תְּלִישָׁה קַדְמָה גֵּרֶשׁ

Chant these words to the melody of *telishah kadmah geresh.*

אֲשֶׁר לָקַח־לוֹ לְבַת (2:15) וַתִּקְרָא אֶסְתֵּר לַהֲתָךְ (4:5) תֹּר נַעֲרָה וְנַעֲרָה (2:12) וַיֹּאמֶר הַמֶּלֶךְ לְאֶסְתֵּר (7:2)

Telishah kadmah-geresh or *Telishah-kadmah geresh*

When chanting *telishah-kadmah-geresh*, you will determine in each case whether the sense of the text demands greater connection between the first and second words or between the second and third words. The rhythm of your chant will reflect the appropriate pairing.

תְּלִישָׁה קַדְמָה גֵּרֶשׁ	תְּלִישָׁה קַדְמָה גֵּרֶשׁ
קָצַף בִּגְתָן וָתֶרֶשׁ (2:21)	וַיִּקָּרְאוּ סֹפְרֵי הַמֶּלֶךְ (3:12)
וּבִשְׁנֵים עָשָׂר חֹדֶשׁ (9:1)	בְּיַד הָרָצִים בַּסּוּסִים (8:10)
וַיֹּאמְרוּ לוֹ חֲכָמָיו (6:13)	שָׁב מִגִּנַּת הַבִּיתָן (7:8)

Four Words in a *Geresh* Segment

Sometimes *geresh* is preceded by three conjunctives. The third conjunctive before *geresh* (just before *telishah*) will be *munaḥ.*

Munaḥ telishah kadmah geresh מוּנַח תְּלִישָׁה קַדְמָה גֵּרֶשׁ

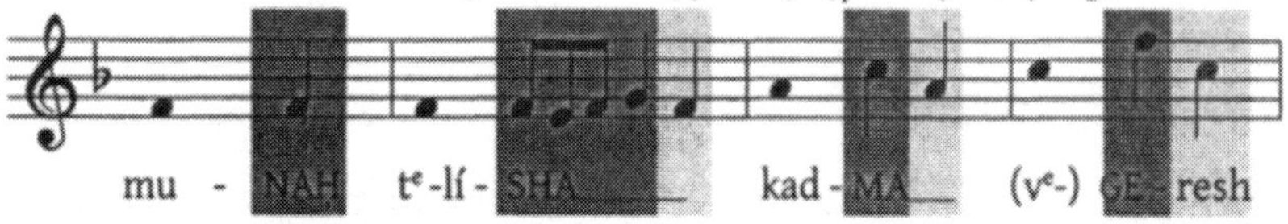

Chant these words to the melody of *munaḥ telishah kadmah geresh.*

הִפִּיל פּוּר הוּא הַגּוֹרָל (3:7) לְכָל־הָעָם הַנִּמְצְאִים בְּשׁוּשַׁן הַבִּירָה (1:5) וַתֹּאמֶר לוֹ זֶרֶשׁ אִשְׁתּוֹ (5:14)

Gereshayim

The double *geresh* is called *gereshayim.* Words that bear this accent are stressed on the last syllable.

Gereshayim גֵּרְשַׁיִם

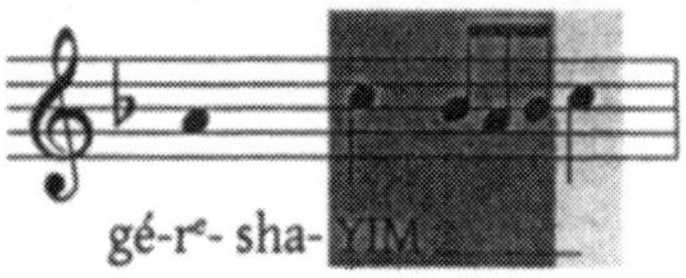

Chant these words to the melody of *gereshayim*. אָמַ֫ר (1:17) הָֽרָצִ֜ים (3:15, 8:14)

Two Words in a *Gereshayim* Segment

The conjunctive of *gereshayim* is *munaḥ*. This combination is found only twice.

Munaḥ gereshayim מ֣וּנַח גֵּרְשַׁ֞יִם

Chant these words to the melody of *munaḥ gereshayim*. הִ֣יא שָׁבָ֞ה (2:14) רֶ֣וַח וְהַצָּלָ֞ה (4:14)

Geresh (or *gereshayim*) can subdivide any of the following segments: *revia, pashta, tevir,* or *zarka*.

Chant these phrases. Connect each conjunctive word to the word that follows. Create an appropriate elongation and pause after *revia, pashta, tevir,* or *zarka*. Create only a slight elongation and pause after *geresh* or *gereshayim*.

קַדְמָ֨א גֵּ֜רֶשׁ רְבִ֗יעַ

אֲשֶׁ֨ר לֹֽא־תָב֜וֹא וַשְׁתִּ֗י לִפְנֵי֙ הַמֶּ֣לֶךְ אֲחַשְׁוֵר֔וֹשׁ (1:19)

וַיְהִ֨י אֹמֵ֜ן אֶת־הֲדַסָּ֗ה הִ֤יא אֶסְתֵּר֙ בַּת־דֹּד֔וֹ (2:7)

מוּנַ֣ח תְּלִישָׁה֩ קַדְמָ֨א גֵּ֜רֶשׁ רְבִ֗יעַ

וַתֹּ֣אמֶר ל֠וֹ זֶ֨רֶשׁ אִשְׁתּ֜וֹ וְכָל־אֹהֲבָ֗יו יַֽעֲשׂוּ־עֵץ֮ גָּבֹ֣הַּ חֲמִשִּׁ֣ים אַמָּה֒ (5:14)

קַדְמָ֨א גֵּ֜רֶשׁ מוּנַ֣ח רְבִ֗יעַ

וַיַּ֨עַשׂ הַמֶּ֜לֶךְ מִשְׁתֶּ֣ה גָד֗וֹל לְכָל־שָׂרָיו֙ וַעֲבָדָ֔יו (2:18)

וַתִּשְׁלַ֨ח בְּגָדִ֜ים לְהַלְבִּ֣ישׁ אֶת־מָרְדֳּכַ֗י וּלְהָסִ֥יר שַׂקּ֛וֹ מֵעָלָ֖יו וְלֹ֥א קִבֵּֽל׃ (4:4)

תְּלִישָׁה֩ קַדְמָ֨א גֵּ֜רֶשׁ מוּנַ֣ח רְבִ֗יעַ

אֲשֶׁר֩ לָֽקַח־ל֨וֹ לְבַ֜ת לָב֣וֹא אֶל־הַמֶּ֗לֶךְ לֹ֤א בִקְשָׁה֙ דָּבָ֔ר (2:15)

וַיְהִי֩ כִרְא֨וֹת הַמֶּ֜לֶךְ אֶת־אֶסְתֵּ֣ר הַמַּלְכָּ֗ה עֹמֶ֙דֶת֙ בֶּֽחָצֵ֔ר (5:2)

תְּלִישָׁה֩ קַדְמָ֨א גֵּ֜רֶשׁ לְגַרְמֵ֣הּ ׀ מוּנַ֣ח רְבִ֗יעַ

אֲשֶׁר֩ נָתַ֨ן הַמֶּ֜לֶךְ לַיְּהוּדִ֣ים ׀ אֲשֶׁ֣ר בְּכָל־עִיר־וָעִ֗יר לְהִקָּהֵל֮ וְלַעֲמֹ֣ד עַל־נַפְשָׁם֒ (8:11)

גֵּרְשַׁ֞יִם מוּנַ֣ח רְבִ֗יעַ

וַתְּמָאֵ֞ן הַמַּלְכָּ֣ה וַשְׁתִּ֗י לָבוֹא֙ בִּדְבַ֣ר הַמֶּ֔לֶךְ (1:12)

וְדָתֵיהֶ֞ם שֹׁנ֣וֹת מִכָּל־עָ֗ם וְאֶת־דָּתֵ֤י הַמֶּ֙לֶךְ֙ אֵינָ֣ם עֹשִׂ֔ים (3:8)

גֵּרְשַׁ֞יִם לְגַרְמֵ֣הּ ׀ מוּנַ֣ח רְבִ֗יעַ

שִׁבְעַ֞ת שָׂרֵ֣י ׀ פָּרַ֣ס וּמָדַ֗י רֹאֵי֙ פְּנֵ֣י הַמֶּ֔לֶךְ (1:14)

וְֽאֶל־הַפַּח֞וֹת אֲשֶׁ֣ר ׀ עַל־מְדִינָ֣ה וּמְדִינָ֗ה וְאֶל־שָׂרֵ֥י עַם֙ וָעָ֔ם (3:12)

קַדְמָ֨א גֵּ֜רֶשׁ מַהְפַּ֤ךְ פַּשְׁטָא֙

בִּזְּתָ֨א חַרְבוֹנָ֜א בִּגְתָ֤א וַאֲבַגְתָא֙ זֵתַ֣ר וְכַרְכַּ֔ס (1:10)

ט֨וֹבַת מַרְאֶ֜ה אֶל־שׁוּשַׁ֤ן הַבִּירָה֙ אֶל־בֵּ֣ית הַנָּשִׁ֔ים (2:3)

תְּלִישָׁה֩ קַדְמָ֨א גֵּ֜רֶשׁ מַהְפַּ֤ךְ פַּשְׁטָא֙

אֵת֩ כָּל־אֲשֶׁ֨ר תֹּאמַ֜ר יִנָּ֤תֵן לָהּ֙ לָב֣וֹא עִמָּ֔הּ (2:13)

קָצַ֩ף בִּגְתָ֨ן וָתֶ֜רֶשׁ שְׁנֵֽי־סָרִיסֵ֤י הַמֶּ֙לֶךְ֙ מִשֹּׁמְרֵ֣י הַסַּ֔ף (2:21)

גֵּרְשַׁ֤יִם מַהְפַּ֤ךְ פַּשְׁטָא֙

הָֽרָצִ֞ים יָצְא֤וּ דְחוּפִים֙ בִּדְבַ֣ר הַמֶּ֔לֶךְ (3:15)

וּבְכֵ֞ן אָב֤וֹא אֶל־הַמֶּ֙לֶךְ֙ אֲשֶׁ֣ר לֹֽא־כַדָּ֔ת (4:16)

מוּנַח גֵּרְשַׁ֤יִם מַהְפַּ֤ךְ פַּשְׁטָא֙

הִ֣יא שָׁבָ֞ה אֶל־בֵּ֤ית הַנָּשִׁים֙ שֵׁנִ֔י (2:14)

גֵּרְשַׁ֞יִם תְּלִישָׁה֩ קַדְמָ֨א מַהְפַּ֤ךְ פַּשְׁטָא֙

מָרְדֳּכַ֞י אֲשֶׁ֩ר הַחִלּ֨וֹתָ לִנְפֹּ֤ל לְפָנָיו֙ לֹא־תוּכַ֣ל ל֔וֹ (6:13)

קַדְמָ֨א גֵּ֜רֶשׁ מֵרְכָ֥א תְּבִ֛יר

וַ֠יֹּאמְרוּ עַבְדֵ֥י הַמֶּ֛לֶךְ אֲשֶׁר־בְּשַׁ֥עַר הַמֶּ֖לֶךְ לְמָרְדֳּכָ֑י (3:3)

תְּלִישָׁה֩ קַדְמָ֨א גֵּ֜רֶשׁ דַּרְגָּ֧א תְּבִ֛יר

גִּדַּ֩ל הַמֶּ֨לֶךְ אֲחַשְׁוֵר֜וֹשׁ אֶת־הָמָ֧ן בֶּן־הַמְּדָ֛תָא הָאֲגָגִ֖י וַֽיְנַשְּׂאֵ֑הוּ (3:1)

מוּנַח תְּלִישָׁה֩ קַדְמָ֨א גֵּ֜רֶשׁ דַּרְגָּ֧א תְּבִ֛יר

לְכָל־הָעָ֣ם הַנִּמְצְאִים֩ בְּשׁוּשַׁ֨ן הַבִּירָ֜ה לְמִגָּ֧דוֹל וְעַד־קָטָ֛ן מִשְׁתֶּ֖ה שִׁבְעַ֣ת יָמִ֑ים (1:5)

גֵּרְשַׁ֞יִם קַדְמָ֨א דַּרְגָּ֧א תְּבִ֛יר

אָמַ֞ר לְהָבִ֨יא אֶת־וַשְׁתִּ֧י הַמַּלְכָּ֛ה לְפָנָ֖יו וְלֹא־בָֽאָה׃ (1:17)

גֵּרְשַׁ֞יִם מֵרְכָ֥א תְּבִ֛יר

וּֽבְהִקָּבֵ֞ץ נְעָר֥וֹת רַבּ֛וֹת אֶל־שׁוּשַׁ֥ן הַבִּירָ֖ה אֶל־יַ֣ד הֵגָ֑י (2:8)

לְמִ֞י יַחְפֹּ֥ץ הַמֶּ֛לֶךְ לַעֲשׂ֥וֹת יְקָ֖ר יוֹתֵ֥ר מִמֶּֽנִּי׃ (6:6)

גֵּרְשַׁ֞יִם דַּרְגָּ֧א תְּבִ֛יר

מַה־נַּעֲשָׂ֞ה יְקָ֧ר וּגְדוּלָּ֛ה לְמָרְדֳּכַ֖י עַל־זֶ֑ה (6:3)

קַדְמָ֨א גֵּ֜רֶשׁ זַרְקָא֮

וְנִשְׁל֨וֹחַ סְפָרִ֜ים בְּיַ֣ד הָרָצִים֮ אֶל־כָּל־מְדִינ֣וֹת הַמֶּלֶךְ֒ (3:13)

Telishah Gedolah

Telishah gedolah is a minor disjunctive. The conjunctive of *telishah gedolah* is *munaḥ*.

One or Two Words in a *Telishah Gedolah* Segment

Munaḥ telishah מוּנַ֣ח תְּלִישָׁ֠ה

Chant these words to the melody of *telishah gedolah.*

לִ֠שְׁקוֹל (4:7) לְ֠הָבִיא (1:11) ֠כִּי (2:15) ֠וַתֹּאמֶר (8:5)

Chant these words to the melody of *munaḥ telishah gedolah.*

וְהַיָּמִ֣ים הָ֠אֵלֶּה (9:28) וְיִקְבְּצ֣וּ את־כָּל־נַעֲרָֽה־בְ֠תוּלָה (2:3) אֶ֣ל אֲחַשְׁוֵרוֹשׁ־פְּנֵי־הַ֠מֶּלֶךְ (3:12)

וַיֹּ֣אמֶר ֠חַרְבוֹנָה (7:9) וְצ֣וּמוּ ֠עָלַי (4:16)

Three or More Words in a *Telishah Gedolah* Segment

The conjunctive *munaḥ* may be repeated before *telishah gedolah.*

וַיִּקָּרְא֣וּ סֹפְרֵֽי־הַמֶּ֣לֶךְ בָּֽעֵת־הַ֠הִיא (8:9) לַהֲרֹ֣ג וּלְאַבֵּ֣ד אֶת־כָּל־הַ֠יְּהוּדִים (3:13)

Practice chanting *telishah gedolah* in context.

לְ֠הָבִיא אֶת־וַשְׁתִּ֧י הַמַּלְכָּ֛ה לִפְנֵ֥י הַמֶּ֖לֶךְ בְּכֶ֣תֶר מַלְכ֑וּת (1:11)

לִ֠שְׁקוֹל עַל־גִּנְזֵ֧י הַמֶּ֛לֶךְ בַּיְּהוּדִ֖ים לְאַבְּדָֽם׃ (4:7)

וַ֠תִּכְתֹּב אֶסְתֵּ֨ר הַמַּלְכָּ֧ה בַת־אֲבִיחַ֛יִל וּמָרְדֳּכַ֥י הַיְּהוּדִ֖י אֶת־כָּל־תֹּ֑קֶף (9:29)

וַיֹּ֣אמֶר ֠חַרְבוֹנָה אֶחָ֨ד מִן־הַסָּרִיסִ֜ים לִפְנֵ֣י הַמֶּ֗לֶךְ (7:9)

וְ֠הַמֶּלֶךְ יוֹשֵׁ֞ב עַל־כִּסֵּ֤א מַלְכוּתוֹ֙ בְּבֵ֣ית הַמַּלְכ֔וּת נֹ֖כַח פֶּ֥תַח הַבָּֽיִת׃ (5:1)

וַ֠יְבַהֵל אֶת־תַּמְרוּקֶ֤יהָ וְאֶת־מָנוֹתֶ֙הָ֙ לָתֵ֣ת לָ֔הּ (2:9)

וַ֠תָּבוֹאנָה נַעֲר֨וֹת אֶסְתֵּ֤ר וְסָרִיסֶ֙יהָ֙ וַיַּגִּ֣ידוּ לָ֔הּ וַתִּתְחַלְחַ֥ל הַמַּלְכָּ֖ה מְאֹ֑ד (4:4)

Pazer

Pazer is another minor disjunctive. Often a *pazer* segment will be followed by a *geresh* segment.

The conjunctive of *pazer* is *munaḥ.*

One or Two Words in a *Pazer* Segment

Munaḥ pazer מוּנַ֣ח פָּזֵ֡ר

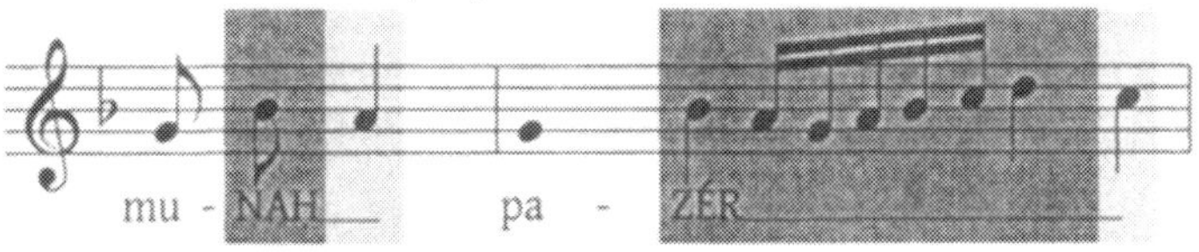

Chant these words to the melody of *pazer.*

אָמַ֡ר (1:10) עַל־כֵּ֡ן (9:26) לְהַשְׁמִ֡יד (3:13) וְהַמֶּ֡לֶךְ (7:8)

Chant these words to the melody of *munaḥ pazer.*

עָשָׂ֥ה הַמֶּ֛לֶךְ (1:5)   בְּשׁוּשַׁ֥ן הַבִּירָ֛ה (9:12)   הַמֶּ֥לֶךְ אֲחַשְׁוֵר֡וֹשׁ (1:17)

Three or More Words in a *Pazer* Segment

The conjunctive *munaḥ* may be repeated before *pazer.*

אִ֣ם מִזֶּ֣רַע הַיְּהוּדִ֡ים (6:13)

וַיִּכָּתֵ֣ב כְּכָל־אֲשֶׁר־צִוָּ֣ה מָרְדֳּכַ֣י אֶל־הַיְּהוּדִ֡ים (8:9)

וּבְהַגִּ֣יעַ תֹּר־אֶסְתֵּ֣ר בַּת־אֲבִיחַ֣יִל דֹּ֣ד מָרְדֳּכַ֡י (2:15)

Practice chanting *pazer* in context:

הַמֶּ֣לֶךְ אֲחַשְׁוֵר֡וֹשׁ אָמַ֞ר לְהָבִ֨יא אֶת־וַשְׁתִּ֧י הַמַּלְכָּ֛ה לְפָנָ֖יו וְלֹא־בָֽאָה׃ (1:17)

וַיִּכָּתֵ֣ב כְּכָל־אֲשֶׁר־צִוָּ֣ה הָמָ֡ן אֶ֣ל אֲחַשְׁדַּרְפְּנֵֽי־הַמֶּ֡לֶךְ (3:12)

כָּל־עַבְדֵ֣י הַמֶּ֡לֶךְ וְעַם־מְדִינ֣וֹת הַמֶּ֡לֶךְ (4:11)

וַיִּשְׁלַ֣ח סְפָרִ֡ים בְּיַ֣ד הָרָצִ֡ים בַּסּוּסִ֡ים (8:10)

עָשָׂ֣ה הַמֶּ֡לֶךְ לְכָל־הָעָ֣ם הַנִּמְצְאִים֩ בְּשׁוּשַׁ֨ן הַבִּירָ֜ה (1:5)

Pazer Gadol

Pazer gadol is another minor disjunctive, found once in place of the regular *pazer*. *Pazer gadol* is preceded by its disjunctive, *galgal*. *Galgal* is preceded by two conjunctives, both *munaḥ.*

Munaḥ galgal pazer-gadol   מוּנַ֣ח גַּלְגַּ֪ל פָּזֵר־גָּד֟וֹל

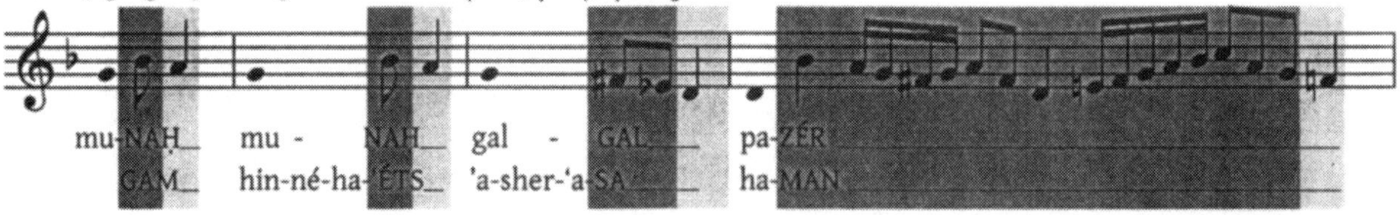
mu-NAH mu - NAH gal - GAL pa-ZER
GAM hin-né-ha-'ÉTS 'a-sher-'a-SA ha-MAN

גַּ֣ם הִנֵּה־הָעֵ֣ץ אֲשֶׁר־עָשָׂ֪ה הָמָ֟ן (7:9)

Here is verse 7:9, complete.

וַיֹּ֣אמֶר חַ֠רְבוֹנָה אֶחָ֨ד מִן־הַסָּרִיסִ֜ים לִפְנֵ֣י הַמֶּ֗לֶךְ

גַּ֣ם הִנֵּה־הָעֵ֣ץ אֲשֶׁר־עָשָׂ֪ה הָמָ֟ן לְמָרְדֳּכַ֞י אֲשֶׁ֧ר דִּבֶּר־ט֣וֹב עַל־הַמֶּ֗לֶךְ

עֹמֵד֙ בְּבֵ֣ית הָמָ֔ן גָּבֹ֖הַּ חֲמִשִּׁ֣ים אַמָּ֑ה וַיֹּ֥אמֶר הַמֶּ֖לֶךְ תְּלֻ֥הוּ עָלָֽיו׃

The Final Cadence

We use a special melody to signal the ending of certain chapters or paragraphs. This melody is applied beginning with the final *tippeḥah* segment. You will slow the tempo for these words.

Some readers use this melody for the final cadence of each *parashah* (paragraph in the ancient Jewish division of the text). Other readers use this melody for the final cadence of every chapter according to the Christian division of the text.

Merekha tippeha merekha siluk מֵרְכָא טִפְּחָא מֵרְכָא סִילוּק

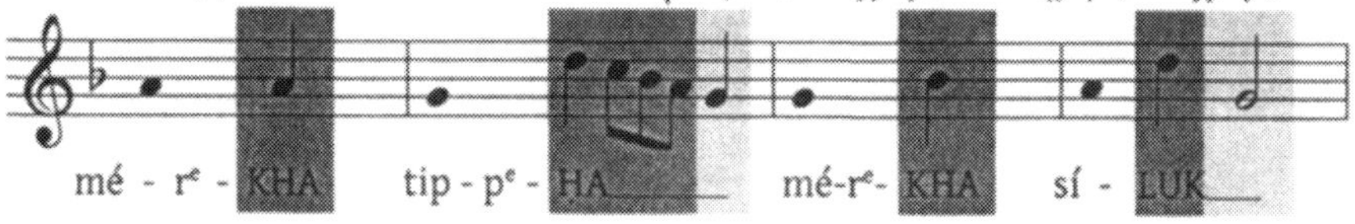

Chant these words to appropriate *te'amim*, using the final cadence.

וַיַּ֥עַשׂ כְּכֹ֛ל אֲשֶׁר־צִוְּתָ֥ה עָלָ֖יו אֶסְתֵּֽר׃ (4:17)

וַיִּיטַ֧ב הַדָּבָ֛ר לִפְנֵ֥י הָמָ֖ן וַיַּ֥עַשׂ הָעֵֽץ׃ (5:14)

אֶל־הַמִּשְׁתֶּ֖ה אֲשֶׁר־עָשְׂתָ֥ה אֶסְתֵּֽר׃ (6:14)

כִּֽי־נָפַ֥ל פַּֽחַד־הַיְּהוּדִ֖ים עֲלֵיהֶֽם׃ (8:17)

וּמַאֲמַ֣ר אֶסְתֵּ֔ר קִיַּ֕ם דִּבְרֵ֥י הַפֻּרִ֖ים הָאֵ֑לֶּה וְנִכְתָּ֖ב בַּסֵּֽפֶר׃ (9:32)

The last verses of chapters 1, 2, 3, 7, and 10 are sung to special melodies (see below).

The Invitational Cadence (CD track 79)

It is customary for the *ba'al keri'ah* to use a special musical cadence (similar to the melody of *geresh*) at the end of four verses (2:4, 8:14, 8:15, and 10:2). This serves as a signal to the congregation to chant the following verse aloud (2:5, 8:15, 8:16, and 10:3). These verses, which represent turning points for the salvation of the Jewish people, are known as "verses of redemption" (פסוקים של גאולה). When the congregation has finished, the *ba'al keri'ah* chants that verse and continues with the cantillation.

Merekha tippeha merekha siluk מֵרְכָא טִפְּחָא מֵרְכָא סִילוּק

Chant these words to appropriate *te'amim*, using the invitational cadence.

בְּעֵינֵ֥י הַמֶּ֖לֶךְ וַיַּ֥עַשׂ כֵּֽן׃ (2:4)

וְהַדָּ֥ת נִתְּנָ֖ה בְּשׁוּשַׁ֥ן הַבִּירָֽה׃ (8:14)

צָהֲלָ֖ה וְשָׂמֵֽחָה׃ (8:15)

לְמַלְכֵ֖י מָדַ֥י וּפָרָֽס׃ (10:2)

Lamentations Verses

Several verses and phrases from the Book of Esther are chanted in the Lamentations mode (see chapter 6 for the musical notation). Common to all these verses is the theme of sadness or mention of the Jews' exile.

וְכֵלִ֥ים מִכֵּלִ֖ים שׁוֹנִ֑ים (1:7)

...beakers of varied design [that had been plundered from the Jerusalem Temple].

אֲשֶׁ֤ר הָגְלָה֙ מִיר֣וּשָׁלַ֔יִם עִם־הַגֹּלָה֙ אֲשֶׁ֣ר הָגְלְתָ֔ה עִ֖ם יְכָנְיָ֣ה מֶֽלֶךְ־יְהוּדָ֑ה
אֲשֶׁ֣ר הֶגְלָ֔ה נְבוּכַדְנֶאצַּ֖ר מֶ֥לֶךְ בָּבֶֽל׃ (2:6)

...that was carried into exile along with King Jeconiah of Judah,
which had been driven into exile by King Nebuchadnezzar of Babylon.

וְהָעִ֥יר שׁוּשַׁ֖ן נָבֽוֹכָה׃ (3:15)

...but the city of Shushan was dumbfounded.

וּמָרְדֳּכַי יָדַע אֶת־כָּל־אֲשֶׁר נַעֲשָׂה וַיִּקְרַע מָרְדֳּכַי אֶת־בְּגָדָיו וַיִּלְבַּשׁ שַׂק וָאֵפֶר
וַיֵּצֵא בְּתוֹךְ הָעִיר וַיִּזְעַק זְעָקָה גְדֹלָה וּמָרָה׃ (4:1)

When Mordecai learned all that had happened, Mordecai tore his clothes and put on sackcloth and ashes. He went through the city, crying out loudly and bitterly

אֵבֶל גָּדוֹל לַיְּהוּדִים וְצוֹם וּבְכִי וּמִסְפֵּד שַׂק וָאֵפֶר יֻצַּע לָרַבִּים׃ (4:3)

...there was great mourning among the Jews, with fasting, weeping, and wailing, and everybody lay in sackcloth and ashes.

וְכַאֲשֶׁר אָבַדְתִּי אָבָדְתִּי׃ (4:16)

...and if I am to perish, I shall perish!

וְעַמִּי בְּבַקָּשָׁתִי׃ (7:3)

...and my people as my request.

כִּי נִמְכַּרְנוּ אֲנִי וְעַמִּי לְהַשְׁמִיד לַהֲרוֹג וּלְאַבֵּד (7:4)

For we have been sold, my people and I, to be destroyed, massacred, and exterminated...

כִּי אֵיכָכָה אוּכַל וְרָאִיתִי בָּרָעָה אֲשֶׁר־יִמְצָא אֶת־עַמִּי
וְאֵיכָכָה אוּכַל וְרָאִיתִי בְּאָבְדַן מוֹלַדְתִּי׃ (8:6)

...For how can I bear to see the disaster which will befall my people! And how can I bear to see the destruction of my kindred!

Exceptional Verses (CD track 80)

Some verses may be sung to special melodies, rather than cantillated according to the *te'amim*. Here are a few suggestions, based on various traditions.

לִהְיוֹת כָּל־אִישׁ שֹׂרֵר בְּבֵיתוֹ וּמְדַבֵּר כִּלְשׁוֹן עַמּוֹ׃ (1:22)

וְהַנַּעֲרָה אֲשֶׁר תִּיטַב בְּעֵינֵי הַמֶּלֶךְ תִּמְלֹךְ תַּחַת וַשְׁתִּי
וַיִּיטַב הַדָּבָר בְּעֵינֵי הַמֶּלֶךְ וַיַּעַשׂ כֵּן׃ (2:4)

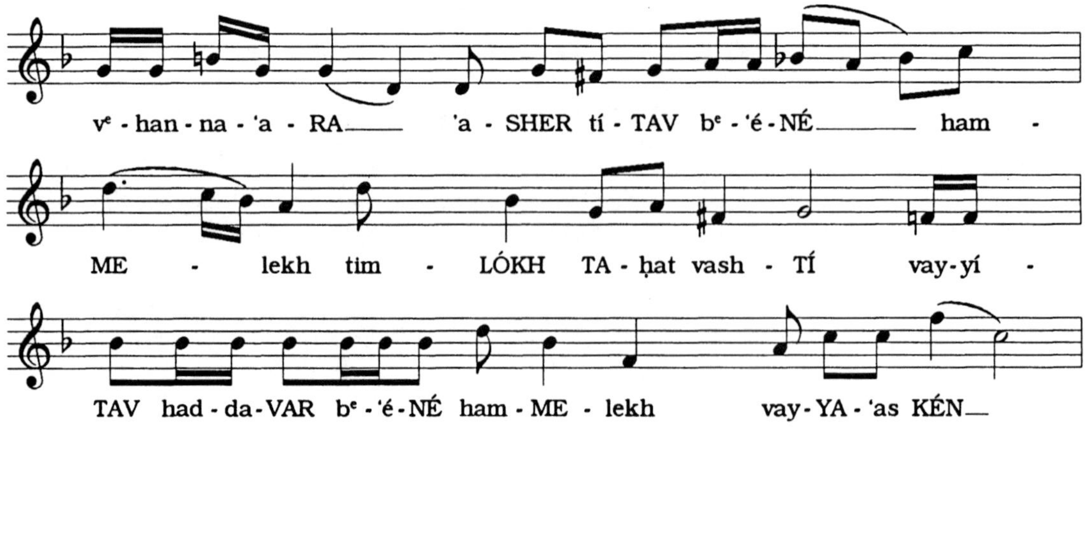

וּבְהַגִּ֣יעַ תֹּר־אֶסְתֵּ֣ר בַּת־אֲבִיחַ֣יִל דֹּ֣ד מָרְדֳּכַ֡י (2:15)

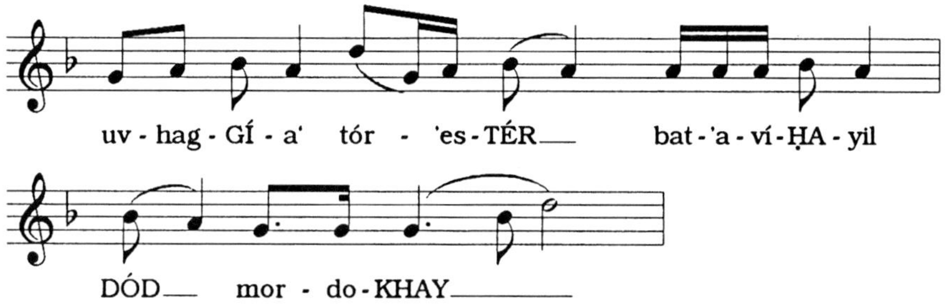
uv - hag - GÍ - a' tór - 'es - TÉR bat - 'a - ví - ḤA - yil
DÓD mor - do - KHAY

וַיֶּאֱהַ֨ב הַמֶּ֤לֶךְ אֶת־אֶסְתֵּר֙ מִכָּל־הַנָּשִׁ֔ים וַתִּשָּׂא־חֵ֥ן וָחֶ֛סֶד
לְפָנָ֖יו מִכָּל־הַבְּתוּלֹ֑ת וַיָּ֤שֶׂם כֶּֽתֶר־מַלְכוּת֙ בְּרֹאשָׁ֔הּ וַיַּמְלִיכֶ֖הָ תַּ֥חַת וַשְׁתִּֽי׃ (2:17)

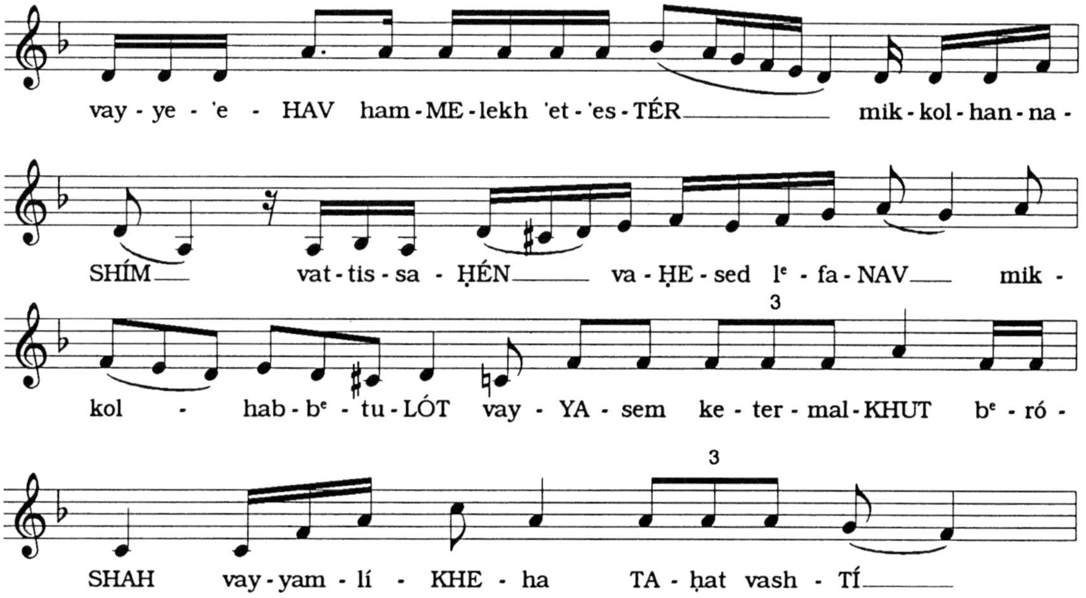
vay - ye - 'e - HAV ham - ME - lekh 'et - 'es - TÉR mik - kol - han - na -
SHÍM vat - tis - sa - ḤÉN va - ḤE - sed lᵉ - fa - NAV mik -
kol - hab - bᵉ - tu - LÓT vay - YA - sem ke - ter - mal - KHUT bᵉ - ró -
SHAH vay - yam - lí - KHE - ha TA - ḥat vash - TÍ

בְּסֵ֥פֶר דִּבְרֵ֥י הַיָּמִ֖ים לִפְנֵ֥י הַמֶּֽלֶךְ׃ (2:23)

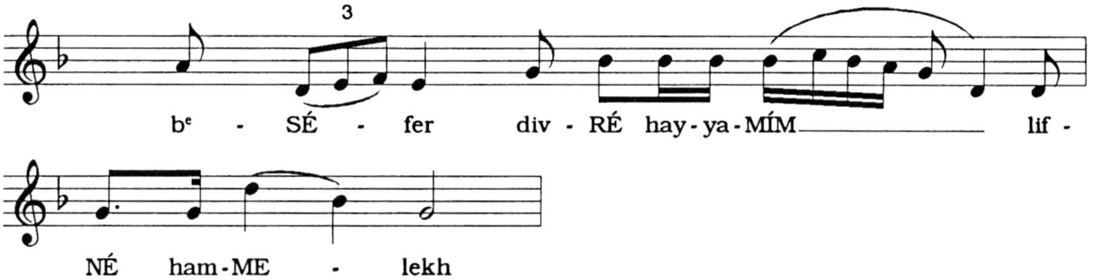
bᵉ - SÉ - fer div - RÉ hay - ya - MÍM lif -
NÉ ham - ME - lekh

יַעֲמ֨וֹד לַיְּהוּדִ֜ים מִמָּק֣וֹם אַחֵ֗ר וְאַ֥תְּ וּבֵית־אָבִ֖יךְ תֹּאבֵ֑דוּ
וּמִ֣י יוֹדֵ֔עַ אִם־לְעֵ֣ת כָּזֹ֔את הִגַּ֖עַתְּ לַמַּלְכֽוּת׃ (4:14)

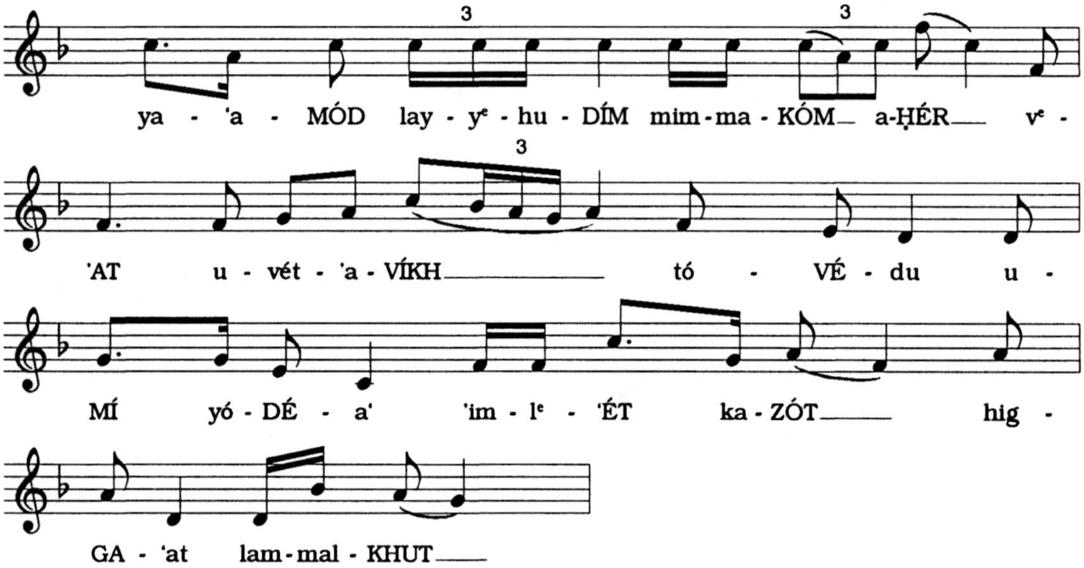

שְׁאֵלָתִ֖י וּבַקָּשָׁתִֽי׃ (5:7)

בַּלַּ֣יְלָה הַה֔וּא נָדְדָ֖ה שְׁנַ֣ת הַמֶּ֑לֶךְ וַיֹּ֗אמֶר לְהָבִ֞יא אֶת־סֵ֤פֶר
הַזִּכְרֹנוֹת֙ דִּבְרֵ֣י הַיָּמִ֔ים וַיִּהְי֥וּ נִקְרָאִ֖ים לִפְנֵ֥י הַמֶּֽלֶךְ׃ (6:1)

קַח אֶת־הַלְּבוּשׁ וְאֶת־הַסּוּס כַּאֲשֶׁר דִּבַּרְתָּ וַעֲשֵׂה־כֵן לְמָרְדֳּכַי הַיְּהוּדִי
הַיּוֹשֵׁב בְּשַׁעַר הַמֶּלֶךְ אַל־תַּפֵּל דָּבָר מִכֹּל אֲשֶׁר דִּבַּרְתָּ׃ (6:10)

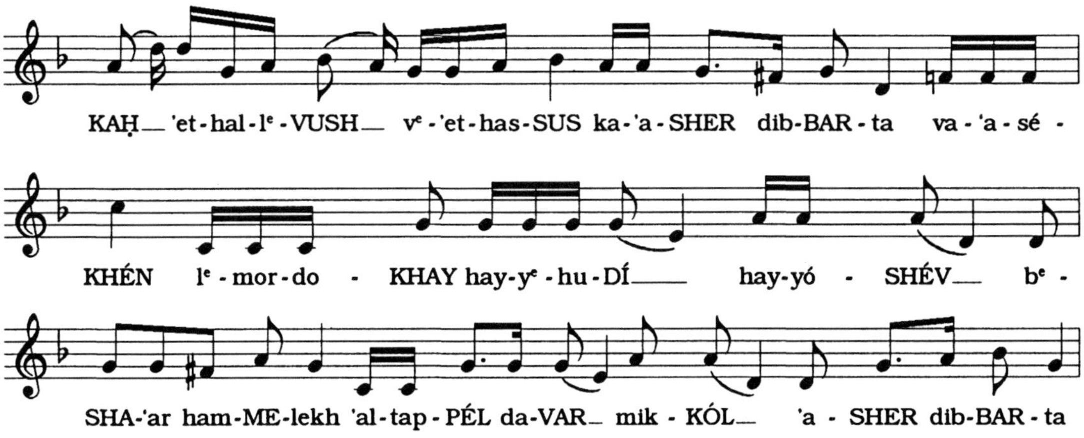
KAḤ — 'et-hal-le-VUSH — ve-'et-has-SUS ka-'a-SHER dib-BAR-ta va-'a-sé-
KHÉN le-mor-do-KHAY hay-ye-hu-DÍ — hay-yó-SHÉV — be-
SHA-'ar ham-ME-lekh 'al-tap-PÉL da-VAR — mik-KÓL — 'a-SHER dib-BAR-ta

תִּנָּתֶן־לִי נַפְשִׁי בִּשְׁאֵלָתִי וְעַמִּי בְּבַקָּשָׁתִי׃ (7:3)

tin-na-ten-LÍ — naf-SHÍ bish-'é-la-TÍ — ve-'am-
MÍ — be-vak-ka-sha-TÍ —

וַיִּתְלוּ אֶת־הָמָן עַל־הָעֵץ אֲשֶׁר־הֵכִין לְמָרְדֳּכָי וַחֲמַת הַמֶּלֶךְ שָׁכָכָה׃ (7:10)

vay-yit-LU 'et-ha-MAN 'al-ha-'ÉTS 'a-sher-hé-
KHÍN le-mor-do-KHAY va-ḥa-MAT ham-ME-lekh sha-KHA-kha

וּמָרְדֳּכַ֞י יָצָ֣א ׀ מִלִּפְנֵ֣י הַמֶּ֗לֶךְ בִּלְב֤וּשׁ מַלְכוּת֙ תְּכֵ֣לֶת וָח֔וּר
וַעֲטֶ֤רֶת זָהָב֙ גְּדוֹלָ֔ה וְתַכְרִ֥יךְ בּ֖וּץ וְאַרְגָּמָ֑ן וְהָעִ֣יר שׁוּשָׁ֔ן צָהֲלָ֖ה וְשָׂמֵֽחָה׃ (8:15)

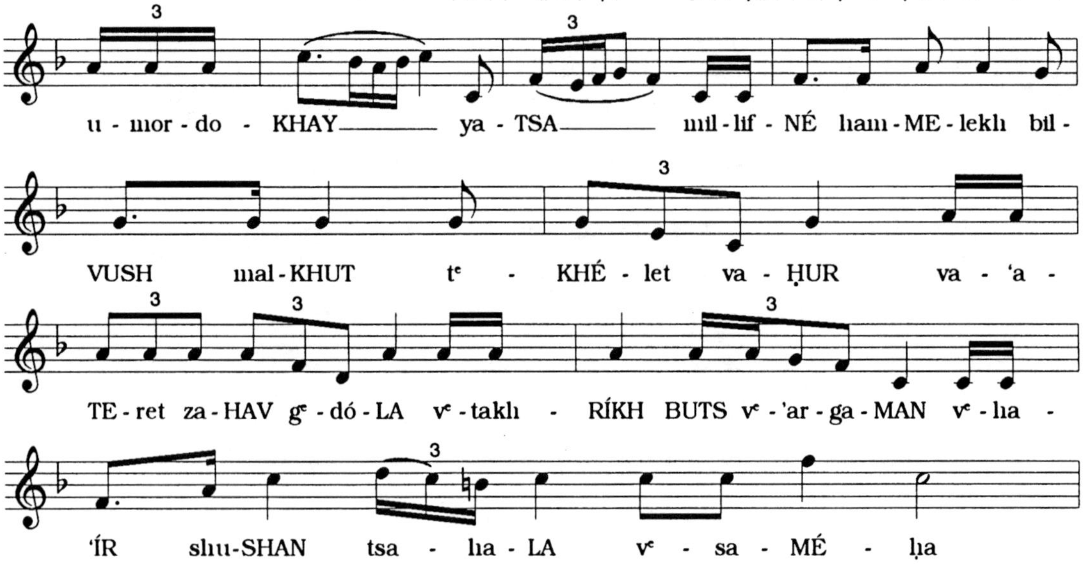

לַיְּהוּדִ֕ים הָֽיְתָ֥ה אוֹרָ֖ה וְשִׂמְחָ֑ה וְשָׂשֹׂ֖ן וִיקָֽר׃ (8:16)

וְכָל־מַעֲשֵׂ֤ה תָקְפּוֹ֙ וּגְב֣וּרָת֔וֹ וּפָרָשַׁת֙ גְּדֻלַּ֣ת מָרְדֳּכַ֔י אֲשֶׁ֥ר גִּדְּל֖וֹ הַמֶּ֑לֶךְ
הֲלוֹא־הֵ֣ם כְּתוּבִ֗ים עַל־סֵ֙פֶר֙ דִּבְרֵ֣י הַיָּמִ֔ים לְמַלְכֵ֖י מָדַ֥י וּפָרָֽס׃ (10:2)

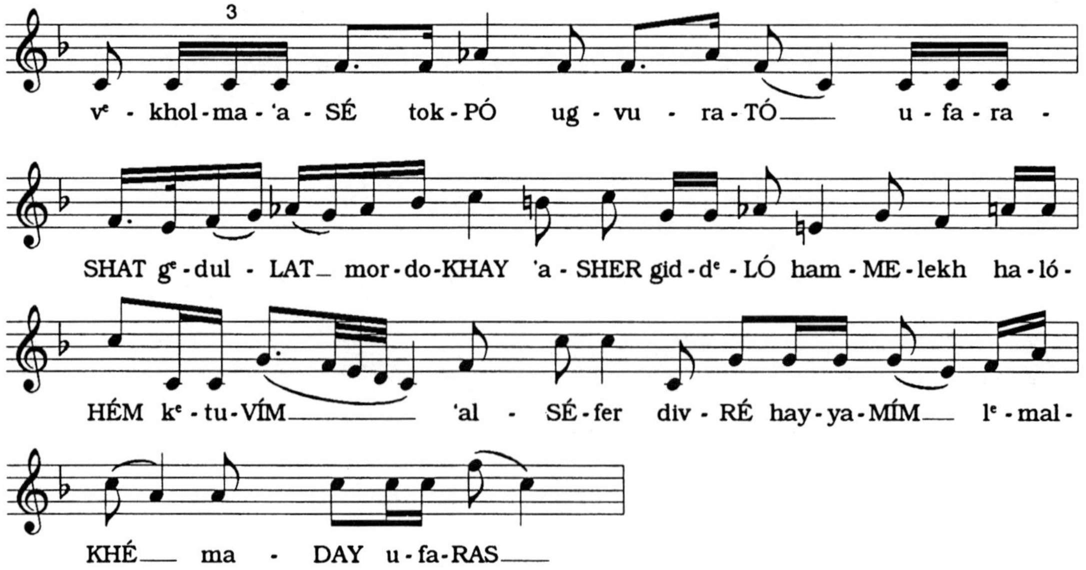

כִּ֣י ׀ מׇרְדֳּכַ֣י הַיְּהוּדִ֗י מִשְׁנֶה֙ לַמֶּ֣לֶךְ אֲחַשְׁוֵר֔וֹשׁ וְגָדוֹל֙ לַיְּהוּדִ֔ים
וְרָצ֖וּי לְרֹ֣ב אֶחָ֑יו דֹּרֵ֥שׁ טוֹב֙ לְעַמּ֔וֹ וְדֹבֵ֥ר שָׁל֖וֹם לְכׇל־זַרְעֽוֹ׃ (10:3)

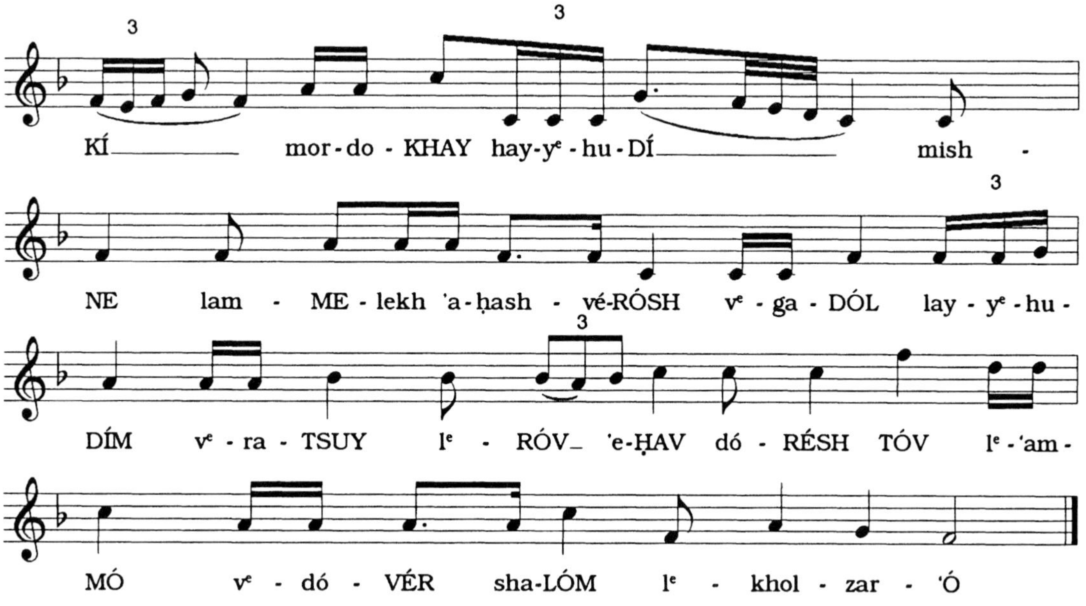

Chanting the Blessings

Before reading the megillah, the *ba'al keri'ah* chants the following three blessings.

Note: Here is an alternate rendition for the first two words of each blessing.

After reading the megillah, the *ba'al keri'ah* chants the following blessing.

ba - RUKH 'at-TA 'a-dó-NAY 'e-ló - HÉ-nu ME-lekh ha-'ó-LAM__ ha-
RAV 'et rí-VÉ-nu v^e-had-DAN 'et dí-NÉ-nu v^e-han-nó-KÉM 'et nik-ma-
TÉ - nu v^e - ham - m^e - sha-LÉM g^e-MUL l^e-khol-ó-y^e-VÉ__ naf-
SHÉ - nu v^e - han-nif-RA' LA - nu mits - tsa - RÉ-nu ba-
RUKH 'at - TA 'a - dó - NAY han - nif -
RA' l^e-'am-MÓ yis - ra - 'ÉL mik-kol-tsa-ré - HEM__ ha-
'ÉL ham-mó - SHÍ - a'

10. High Holiday

At the morning (שחרית) service on the High Holidays (ראש השנה and יום כפור), a special melody is used for chanting the Torah. The High Holidays are unique in this respect; no special melody is used for Torah cantillation on any of the other festivals. The 14th-century German rabbi Jacob Mölin (מהרי"ל) wrote that this special melody was designed to make the worshipers more receptive to the lesson of the Torah reading, to put them in a solemn mood appropriate for these Days of Awe. Accordingly, the reader chants in a slow and dramatically majestic manner.

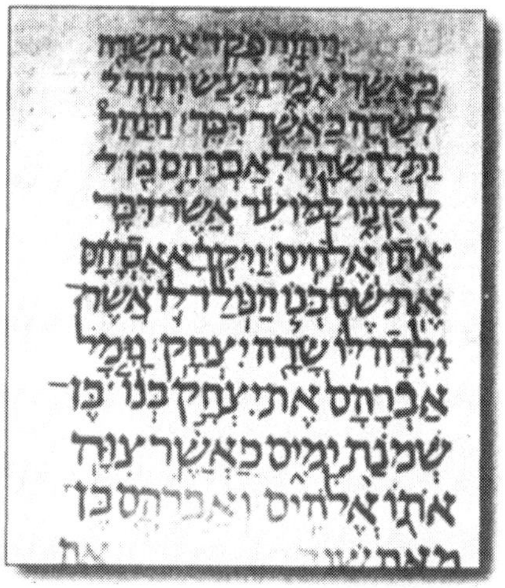

The examples in this chapter are taken from the traditional readings for the morning services of Rosh Hashanah and Yom Kippur.

Rosh Hashanah:
First day: Gen. 21:1–34 and Num. 29:1–6.

Second day: Gen. 22:1–24 and Num. 29:1–6.

Yom Kippur:
Leviticus 16 (complete) and Num. 29:7–11.

On fast days, portions of Exod. 32:12, 34:6–7, and 34:9 are chanted to this melody. On Simḥat Torah, portions of Genesis 1 are chanted to this melody, as well. See pp. 80–81.

The Melodies of the Cantillation Motifs

Hear the melodies of the High Holiday cantillation on CD tracks 83 and 84.

The *Siluk* Segment and *Tippeḥa* Segment

The last word in every verse is marked with *siluk*. If the preceding word is closely connected in meaning to the *siluk* word, it is usually marked with the conjunctive *ta'am merekha*.

A *siluk* segment is usually subdivided by the disjunctive *ta'am tippeḥa*. If there are two words in the *tippeḥa* segment, the first one is usually marked with the conjunctive *ta'am merekha*.

Merekha tippeḥa merekha siluk מֵרְכָא טִפְּחָא מֵרְכָא סִילוּק

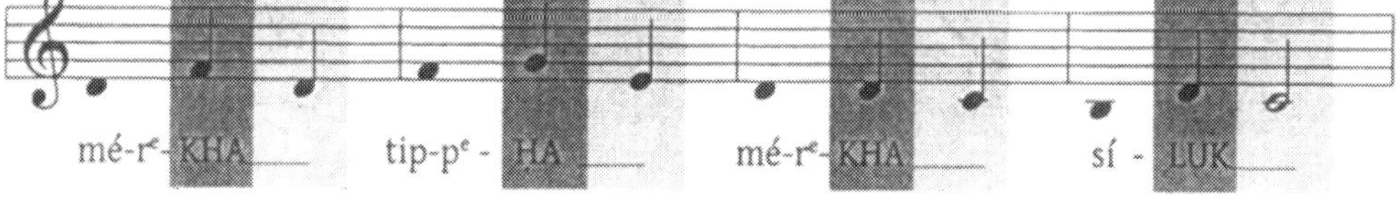
mé-rᵉ-KHA
tip-pᵉ-HA
mé-rᵉ-KHA
sí-LUK

Chant these words to the appropriate *te'amim*. Connect each conjunctive (*merekha*) to the word that follows. Pause slightly after the disjunctive *ta'am, tippeḥa*.

מֵרְכָא טִפְּחָא מֵרְכָא סִילוּק
יוֹם תְּרוּעָה יִהְיֶה לָכֶם׃ (Num. 29:1)
אֲשֶׁר עַל־הָעֵדוּת וְלֹא יָמוּת׃ (Lev. 16:13)
וַיַּעֲלֵהוּ לְעֹלָה תַּחַת בְּנוֹ׃ (Gen. 22:13)

טִפְּחָא מֵרְכָא סִילוּק
כָּל־מְלָאכָה לֹא תַעֲשׂוּ׃ (Num. 29:7)
תַּחַת אַחַד הַשִּׂיחִם׃ (Gen. 21:15)
אֵת יִצְחָק בְּנוֹ׃ (Gen. 21:5)

מֵרְכָא טִפְּחָא סִילוּק (See p. 17)
וְגוֹרָל אֶחָד לַעֲזָאזֵל׃ (Lev. 16:8)
וְאַיִל אֶחָד לְעֹלָה׃ (Lev. 16:5)
וַיַּרְא אֶת־הַמָּקוֹם מֵרָחֹק׃ (Gen. 22:4)

טִפְּחָא סִילוּק
שִׁבְעָה תְּמִימִם׃ (Num. 29:2)
לְכַפֵּר עֲלֵיכֶם׃ (Num. 29:5)
וַיֹּאמֶר הִנֵּנִי׃ (Gen. 22:11)

The *Etnaḥta* Segment and *Tippeḥa* Segment

Most verses are divided into two segments. *Etnaḥta* is the *ta'am* that marks the end of the first segment, and *siluk* marks the end of the second segment. If the *etnaḥta* word and the word before it are closely connected in meaning, they are usually marked *munaḥ etnaḥta.*

An *etnaḥta* segment is usually subdivided by the disjunctive *ta'am tippeḥa*, If there are two words in the *tippeḥa* segment, the first one is usually marked with the conjunctive *ta'am merekha.*

Merekha tippeḥa munaḥ etnaḥta מֵרְכָא טִפְּחָא מוּנַח אֶתְנַחְתָּא

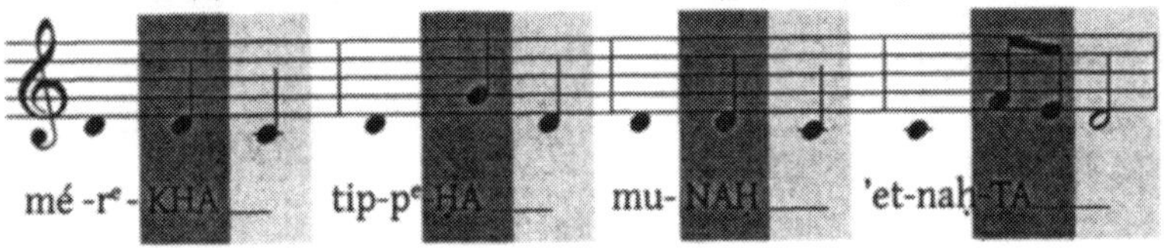
mé -rᵉ- KHA
tip-pᵉ HA
mu- NAH
'et-nah TA

Chant these words to the appropriate *te'amim*. Connect each conjunctive (*merekha* or *munaḥ*) to the word that follows. Pause slightly after the disjunctive *ta'am, tippeḥa.*

מֵרְכָא טִפְּחָא מוּנַח אֶתְנַחְתָּא
פָּקַד אֶת־שָׂרָה כַּאֲשֶׁר אָמָר (Gen. 21:1)
וְגַם אֶת־בֶּן־הָאָמָה לְגוֹי אֲשִׂימֶנּוּ (Gen. 21:13)
וַיֹּאמֶר לָהּ מַה־לָּךְ הָגָר (Gen. 21:17)

מֵרְכָא טִפְּחָא אֶתְנַחְתָּא
הֵינִיקָה בָנִים שָׂרָה (Gen. 21:7)
וַיִּגְדַּל הַיֶּלֶד וַיִּגָּמַל (Gen. 21:8)
נֶאֱחַז בַּסְּבַךְ בְּקַרְנָיו (Gen. 22:13)
יָבֹא אַהֲרֹן אֶל־הַקֹּדֶשׁ (Lev. 16:3)

טִפְּחָא מוּנַח אֶתְנַחְתָּא
סֹלֶת בְּלוּלָה בַשָּׁמֶן (Num. 29:3)
וְאֵת יִצְחָק בְּנוֹ (Gen. 22:3)
שְׁנֵי בְּנֵי אַהֲרֹן (Lev. 16:1)

טִפְּחָא אֶתְנַחְתָּא
וְנִסְכֵּיהֶם כְּמִשְׁפָּטָם (Num. 29:6)
בֶּן־שְׁמֹנַת יָמִים (Gen. 21:4)
אֶל־אֶרֶץ הַמֹּרִיָּה (Gen. 22:2)
מִבֵּית לַפָּרֹכֶת (Lev. 16:2)

Chant these verses.

אֶת־עוּץ בְּכֹרוֹ וְאֶת־בּוּז אָחִיו וְאֶת־קְמוּאֵל אֲבִי אֲרָם׃ (Gen. 22:21)
וּשְׂעִיר־עִזִּים אֶחָד חַטָּאת לְכַפֵּר עֲלֵיכֶם׃ (Num. 29:5)

The *Tevir* Segment

Sometimes there is a subdivision within a *tippeḥa* segment. *Tevir* is the *ta'am* that marks that subdivision.

One or Two Words in a *Tevir* Segment

If the preceding word is closely connected in meaning to the *tevir* word, it is usually marked with a conjunctive *ta'am*. Most often that conjunctive will be *darga*.

Darga tevir דַּרְגָּא תְּבִיר

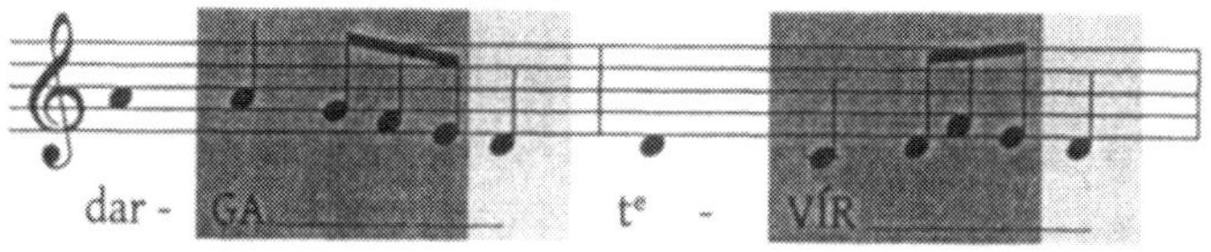

Chant these words to the melody of *darga tevir*.

בְּפַר בֶּן־בָּקָר (Lev. 16:3) וַיִּקְרָא אַבְרָהָם (Gen. 22:14) פַּר בֶּן־בָּקָר (Num. 29:2) וַיֵּרַע הַדָּבָר (Gen. 21:11)

If the accents are close to each other, the conjunctive will be *merekha* instead of *darga*.

Merekha tevir מֵרְכָא תְּבִיר

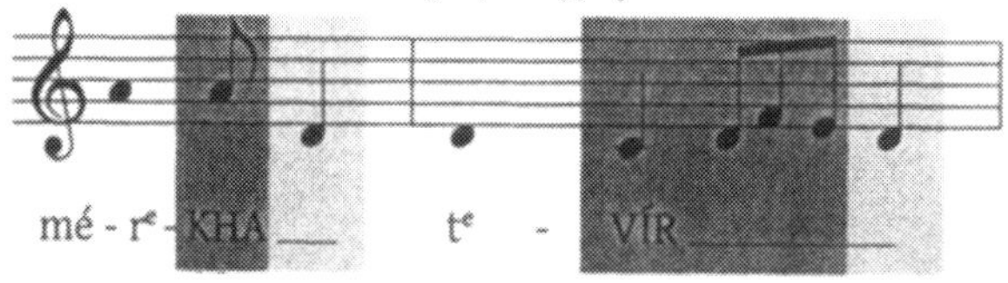

Chant these words to the melody of *merekha tevir*. וְלֹא חָשַׂכְתָּ (Gen. 22:12) וְרָחַץ בַּמַּיִם (Lev. 16:4)

Chant these words to the melody of *tevir*. גָּרֵשׁ (Gen. 21:10) וְשִׁלַּח (Lev. 16:21)

Chant these phrases. Connect the conjunctive word to the word that follows. Create a slight elongation and/or pause after *tippeḥa*. There is very little elongation and/or pause after *tevir*. The sense of the words dictates that *tippeḥa* is a stronger disjunctive than *tevir*.

מֵרְכָא תְּבִיר טִפְּחָא

לְשַׁלַּח אֹתוֹ לַעֲזָאזֵל הַמִּדְבָּרָה: (Lev. 16:10)

וְהִזָּה אֹתוֹ עַל־הַכַּפֹּרֶת וְלִפְנֵי הַכַּפֹּרֶת: (Lev. 16:15)

יִרְאֶה־לּוֹ הַשֶּׂה לְעֹלָה בְּנִי (Gen. 22:8)

מֵרְכָא תְּבִיר מֵרְכָא טִפְּחָא

וְלֹא חָשַׂכְתָּ אֶת־בִּנְךָ אֶת־יְחִידְךָ מִמֶּנִּי: (Gen. 22:12)

כִּי־בַיּוֹם הַזֶּה יְכַפֵּר עֲלֵיכֶם לְטַהֵר אֶתְכֶם (Lev. 16:30)

תְּבִיר מֵרְכָא טִפְּחָא

וְשָׁחַט אֶת־פַּר הַחַטָּאת אֲשֶׁר־לוֹ: (Lev. 16:11)

וְלָבַשׁ אֶת־בִּגְדֵי הַבָּד בִּגְדֵי הַקֹּדֶשׁ: (Lev. 16:32)

גָּרֵשׁ הָאָמָה הַזֹּאת וְאֶת־בְּנָהּ (Gen. 21:10)

קָרָא לַמָּקוֹם הַהוּא בְּאֵר שָׁבַע (Gen. 21:31)

דַּרְגָּא תְּבִיר טִפְּחָא

בְּפַר בֶּן־בָּקָר לְחַטָּאת וְאַיִל לְעֹלָה: (Lev. 16:3)

כְּבָשִׂים בְּנֵי־שָׁנָה שִׁבְעָה תְּמִימִם: (Num. 29:2)

וַיֵּרַע הַדָּבָר מְאֹד בְּעֵינֵי אַבְרָהָם (Gen. 21:11)

דַּרְגָּא תְּבִיר מֵרְכָא טִפְּחָא

אֶת־בֶּן־הָגָר הַמִּצְרִית אֲשֶׁר־יָלְדָה לְאַבְרָהָם מְצַחֵק: (Gen. 21:9)

וְגַם אָנֹכִי לֹא שָׁמַעְתִּי בִּלְתִּי הַיּוֹם: (Gen. 21:26)

Chant these verses.

וַיֵּ֧רַע הַדָּבָ֛ר מְאֹ֖ד בְּעֵינֵ֣י אַבְרָהָ֑ם עַ֖ל אוֹדֹ֥ת בְּנֽוֹ׃ (Gen. 21:11)

וַיִּקְרָ֛א מַלְאַ֥ךְ יְהוָ֖ה אֶל־אַבְרָהָ֑ם שֵׁנִ֖ית מִן־הַשָּׁמָֽיִם׃ (Gen. 22:15)

וַֽיהוָ֛ה פָּקַ֥ד אֶת־שָׂרָ֖ה כַּאֲשֶׁ֣ר אָמָ֑ר וַיַּ֧עַשׂ יְהוָ֛ה לְשָׂרָ֖ה כַּאֲשֶׁ֥ר דִּבֵּֽר׃ (Gen. 21:1)

בְּזֹ֛את יָבֹ֥א אַהֲרֹ֖ן אֶל־הַקֹּ֑דֶשׁ בְּפַ֧ר בֶּן־בָּקָ֛ר לְחַטָּ֖את וְאַ֥יִל לְעֹלָֽה׃ (Lev. 16:3)

Three Words in a *Tevir* Segment

Sometimes *tevir* is preceded by two or more conjunctives. In these segments, there will be a very slight pause or elongation just before the *tevir.* The second conjunctive before *tevir* (preceding either *merekha* or *darga*) is *kadmah.*

Kadmah darga tevir קַדְמָ֨ה דַּרְגָּ֧א תְּבִ֛יר

Chant these words to the melody of *kadmah darga tevir.* וְהִזָּ֨ה עָלָ֧יו מִן־הַדָּ֛ם (Lev. 16:19)

Kadmah merekha tevir קַדְמָ֨ה מֵרְכָ֥א תְּבִ֛יר

Chant these words to the melody of *kadmah merekha tevir.*

אֲשֶׁ֨ר עָלָ֥ה עָלָ֛יו (Lev. 16:9) וְנָשָׂ֨א הַשָּׂעִ֥יר עָלָ֛יו (Lev. 16:22)

Four Words in a *Tevir* Segment

Sometimes *tevir* is preceded by three conjunctives. The third conjunctive before *tevir* (just before *kadmah*) will be *telishah ketanah.*

Telishah kadmah darga tevir תְּלִישָׁ֠ה קַדְמָ֨ה דַּרְגָּ֧א תְּבִ֛יר

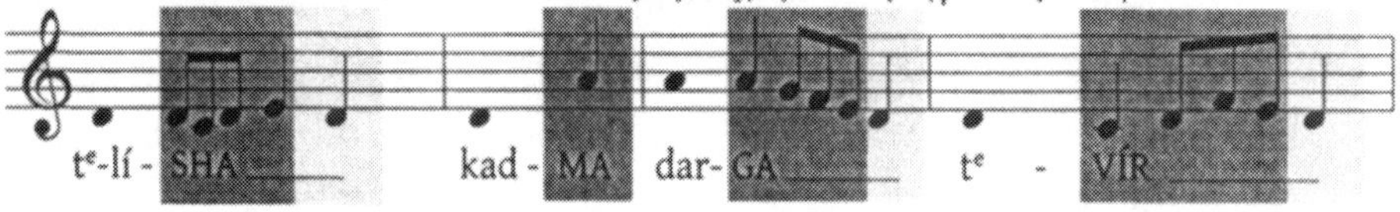

Chant these words to the melody of *telishah kadmah darga tevir.*

וַתַּ֠הַר וַתֵּ֨לֶד שָׂרָ֧ה לְאַבְרָהָ֛ם (Gen. 21:2)

Telishah kadmah merekha tevir תְּלִישָׁ֠ה קַדְמָ֨ה מֵרְכָ֥א תְּבִ֛יר

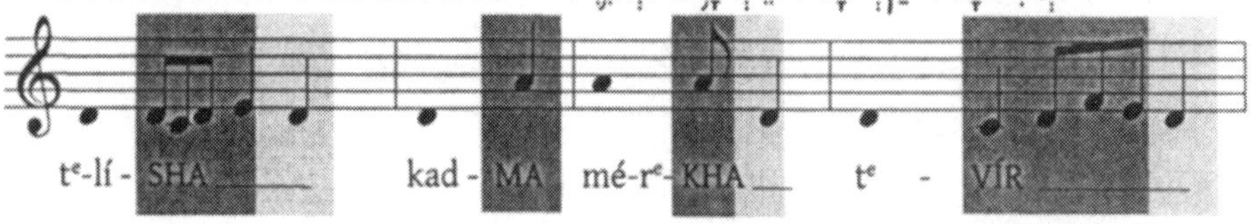

Chant these words to the melody of *telishah kadmah merekha tevir.*

כֹּ֠ל אֲשֶׁ֨ר תֹּאמַ֥ר אֵלֶ֛יךָ (Gen. 21:12)

Chant these words to the appropriate *te'amim*.

וְהִזָּ֨ה עָלָ֧יו מִן־הַדָּ֛ם בְּאֶצְבָּע֖וֹ שֶׁ֣בַע פְּעָמִ֑ים (Lev. 16:19)

וַיִּשָּׂ֨א אַבְרָהָ֧ם אֶת־עֵינָ֛יו וַיַּ֥רְא אֶת־הַמָּק֖וֹם מֵרָחֹֽק׃ (Gen. 22:4)

וְנָשָׂ֨א הַשָּׂעִ֥יר עָלָ֛יו אֶת־כָּל־עֲוֺנֹתָ֖ם אֶל־אֶ֣רֶץ גְּזֵרָ֑ה וְשִׁלַּ֥ח אֶת־הַשָּׂעִ֖יר בַּמִּדְבָּֽר׃ (Lev. 16:22)

אֲשֶׁ֨ר עָלָ֥ה עָלָ֛יו הַגּוֹרָ֖ל לַיהוָ֑ה וְעָשָׂ֖הוּ חַטָּֽאת׃ (Lev. 16:9)

וַתַּ֩הַר֩ וַתֵּ֨לֶד שָׂרָ֧ה לְאַבְרָהָ֛ם בֵּ֖ן לִזְקֻנָ֑יו (Gen. 21:2)

כֹּל֩ אֲשֶׁ֨ר תֹּאמַ֥ר אֵלֶ֛יךָ שָׂרָ֖ה שְׁמַ֣ע בְּקֹלָ֑הּ (Gen. 21:12)

The *Zakef* Segment

Zakef is a strong disjunctive; only *siluk* and *etnaḥta* are stronger. A *zakef* segment will always be followed by a *tippeḥa* segement. *Zakef* is stronger than the ensuing *tippeḥa*. A *zakef* segment may also be followed by one or more other *zakef* segments, but they will eventually be followed by a *tippeḥa* segement. When you see two *zakefs* (or two *zakef* segments) in a row, the first is always stronger.

There are two basic forms of *zakef*, each with its own distinct melody: *zakef gadol* and *zakef katon*. There are also two compound *te'amim*, in which two symbols appear on a single word: *munaḥ-zakef* and *metigah-zakef*.

A word marked with *zakef gadol* is short and has no conjunctives immediately before it.

Zakef Gadol

Zakef gadol זָקֵף־גָּד֕וֹל

Chant these words to the melody of *zakef gadol*.

צְחֹ֕ק (Gen. 21:6) לַמּוֹעֵ֕ד (Gen. 21:2) עֵ֕קֶב (Gen. 22:18) וַיֹּ֕אמֶר (Gen. 21:30)

One or Two Words in a *Zakef Katon* Segment

A word marked with *zakef katon* is usually preceded by the conjunctive *munaḥ*.

Munaḥ zakef katon מוּנַ֣ח זָקֵף־קָטֹ֔ן

With elision:

'im - tish - KÓR ___ LÍ ___ (Gen. 21:23) אִם־תִּשְׁקֹ֣ר לִ֔י

big - dé - KÓ - - desh HÉM ___ (Lev. 16:4) בִּגְדֵי־קֹ֣דֶשׁ הֵ֔ם

Chant these words to the melody of *zakef*.

בַּמִּדְבָּ֔ר (Gen. 21:20) בֶּעָנָ֕ן (Lev. 16:2)

Chant these words to the melody of *munaḥ zakef.*

מִשְׁתֶּ֥ה גָד֖וֹל (Gen. 21:8) אֶת־יִצְחָ֣ק בְּנ֔וֹ (Gen. 21:4) כִּ֣י בְיִצְחָ֔ק (Gen. 21:12) לְרֵ֣יחַ נִיחֹ֔חַ (Num. 29:6)

Sometimes *munaḥ* will appear on the same word that is marked with *zakef.* This happens often on long words.

וְהָֽעֵצִ֔ים (Gen. 22:7) אַל־תִּֽירְאִ֔י (Gen. 21:17)

Metigah-Zakef

Metigah-zakef מְתִיגָה־זָקֵ֔ף

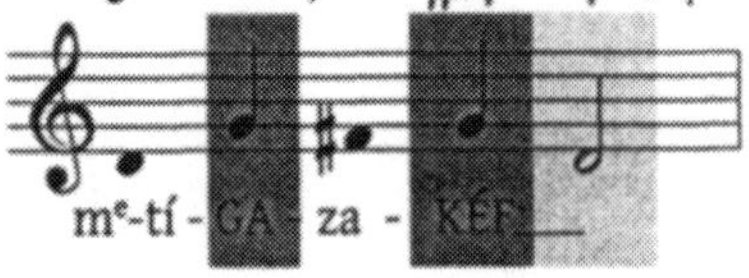

Chant these words to the melody of *metigah zakef.*

וּמִ֨נְחָתָ֔ם (Num. 29:3) וַֽיִּקְרָא־שָׁ֕ם (Gen. 21:33) וְלֶךְ־לְ֔ךָ (Gen. 22:2)

Zakef is usually followed by *(merekha-) tippeḥa.* Chant these examples. Make a pause or elongation after *zakef.* Make a more subtle elongation or pause after *tippeḥa.*

מוּנַ֣ח זָקֵ֔ף טִפְחָ֖א

וַיָּ֣קָם וַיֵּ֔לֶךְ אֶל־הַמָּק֖וֹם אֲשֶׁר־אָֽמַר־ל֥וֹ הָאֱלֹהִֽים׃ (Gen. 22:3) וַאֲנִ֣י וְהַנַּ֔עַר נֵלְכָ֖ה עַד־כֹּ֑ה (Gen. 22:5)

וְיִרַ֣שׁ זַרְעֲךָ֔ אֵ֖ת שַׁ֥עַר אֹיְבָֽיו׃ (Gen. 22:17) וְהִתְבָּרְכ֣וּ בְזַרְעֲךָ֔ כֹּ֖ל גּוֹיֵ֣י הָאָ֑רֶץ (Gen. 22:18)

מוּנַ֣ח זָקֵ֔ף מֵרְכָ֥א טִפְחָ֖א

וְשָׂרְפ֣וּ בָאֵ֔שׁ אֶת־עֹרֹתָ֥ם וְאֶת־בְּשָׂרָ֖ם וְאֶת־פִּרְשָֽׁם׃ (Lev. 16:27)

לֹ֣א יָדַ֔עְתִּי מִ֥י עָשָׂ֖ה אֶת־הַדָּבָ֣ר הַזֶּ֑ה (Gen. 21:26) יְכַבֵּ֣ס בְּגָדָ֔יו וְרָחַ֥ץ אֶת־בְּשָׂר֖וֹ בַּמָּ֑יִם (Lev. 16:26)

זָקֵף־גָּד֕וֹל טִפְחָ֖א

וְכַח֕וֹל אֲשֶׁ֖ר עַל־שְׂפַ֣ת הַיָּ֑ם (Gen. 22:17)

זָקֵף־גָּד֕וֹל מֵרְכָ֥א טִפְחָ֖א

וַיֹּ֕אמֶר בִּ֥י נִשְׁבַּ֖עְתִּי נְאֻם־יְהוָ֑ה (Gen. 22:16) עֵ֕קֶב אֲשֶׁ֥ר שָׁמַ֖עְתָּ בְּקֹלִֽי׃ (Gen. 22:18)

מְתִיגָה־זָקֵ֔ף (מֵרְכָ֥א) טִפְחָ֖א

וּמִ֨נְחָתָ֔ם סֹ֖לֶת בְּלוּלָ֣ה בַשָּׁ֑מֶן (Num. 29:3) וְלֶךְ־לְ֔ךָ אֶל־אֶ֖רֶץ הַמֹּרִיָּ֑ה (Gen. 22:2)

וַֽיִּקְרָא־שָׁ֕ם בְּשֵׁ֥ם יְהוָ֖ה אֵ֥ל עוֹלָֽם׃ (Gen. 21:33)

מוּנַ֣ח זָקֵ֔ף דַּרְגָּ֧א תְּבִ֛יר מֵרְכָ֥א טִפְחָ֖א

אַל־תִּ֣ירְאִ֔י כִּֽי־שָׁמַ֧ע אֱלֹהִ֛ים אֶל־ק֥וֹל הַנַּ֖עַר בַּאֲשֶׁ֥ר הוּא־שָֽׁם׃ (Gen. 21:17)

מוּנַח זָקֵף מֵרְכָא תְּבִיר מֵרְכָא טִפְּחָא

בִּגְדֵי־קֹ֖דֶשׁ הֵ֑ם וְרָחַ֥ץ בַּמַּ֛יִם אֶת־בְּשָׂר֖וֹ וּלְבֵשָֽׁם׃ (Lev. 16:4)

Chant these verses.

וַתַּ֩הַר֩ וַתֵּ֨לֶד שָׂרָ֧ה לְאַבְרָהָ֛ם בֵּ֖ן לִזְקֻנָ֑יו לַמּוֹעֵ֕ד אֲשֶׁר־דִּבֶּ֥ר אֹת֖וֹ אֱלֹהִֽים׃ (Gen. 21:2)

וְאַבְרָהָ֖ם בֶּן־מְאַ֣ת שָׁנָ֑ה בְּהִוָּ֣לֶד ל֔וֹ אֵ֖ת יִצְחָ֥ק בְּנֽוֹ׃ (Gen. 21:5)

וַתֹּ֣אמֶר שָׂרָ֔ה צְחֹ֕ק עָ֥שָׂה לִ֖י אֱלֹהִ֑ים כָּל־הַשֹּׁמֵ֖עַ יִֽצְחַק־לִֽי׃ (Gen. 21:6)

וַיִּכְל֥וּ הַמַּ֖יִם מִן־הַחֵ֑מֶת וַתַּשְׁלֵ֣ךְ אֶת־הַיֶּ֔לֶד תַּ֖חַת אַחַ֥ד הַשִּׂיחִֽם׃ (Gen. 21:15)

וַיִּטַּ֥ע אֶ֖שֶׁל בִּבְאֵ֣ר שָׁ֑בַע וַיִּקְרָא־שָׁ֗ם בְּשֵׁ֛ם יְהוָ֖ה אֵ֥ל עוֹלָֽם׃ (Gen. 21:33)

וְאֶת־כֶּ֣שֶׂד וְאֶת־חֲז֔וֹ וְאֶת־פִּלְדָּ֖שׁ וְאֶת־יִדְלָ֑ף וְאֵ֖ת בְּתוּאֵֽל׃ (Gen. 22:22)

The *Pashta/Yetiv* Segment

Sometimes there is a subdivision within a *zakef* segment. *Pashta* is the *ta'am* that marks that subdivision

Pashta פַּשְׁטָ֙א

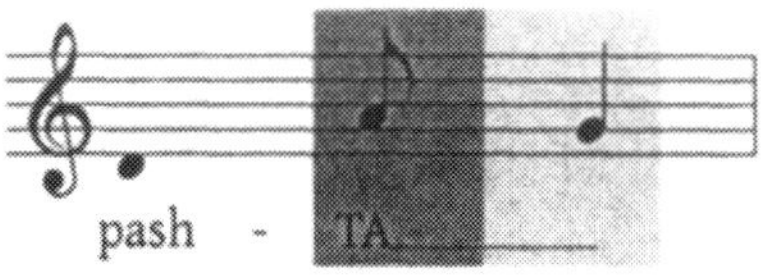

Chant these words to the melody of *pashta.*

יִֽירַשׁ֙ (Gen. 21:10) אַבְרָהָם֙ (Gen. 21:4) שָׁם֙ (Gen. 22:2) וַתֹּ֙אמֶר֙ (Gen. 21:10)

Pashta is followed by *zakef katon* or *munaḥ zakef katon.* Chant these segments.

(Gen. 21:22) וַיְהִי֙ בָּעֵ֣ת הַהִ֔וא (Gen. 21:24) וַיֹּ֙אמֶר֙ אַבְרָהָ֔ם

(Gen. 22:1) אַחַר֙ הַדְּבָרִ֣ים הָאֵ֔לֶּה (Gen. 22:13) וַיַּ֙רְא֙ וְהִנֵּה־אַ֔יִל

Two Words in a *Pashta* Segment

If the preceding word is closely connected in meaning to the *pashta* word, it is usually marked with a conjunctive *ta'am.* Most often that conjunctive will be *mahpakh.*

Mahpakh pashta מַהְפַּ֤ךְ פַּשְׁטָ֙א

With elision:

vᵉ - ha - 'a - LE - - hu SHAM (Gen. 21:23) וְהַעֲלֵ֤הוּ שָׁם֙

Chant these words to the melody of *mahpakh pashta.*

הִנֵּ֤ה הָאֵשׁ֙ (Gen. 22:7) וְהִקְרִ֤יב אַהֲרֹן֙ (Lev. 16:9) מִ֤י מִלֵּל֙ (Gen. 21:7)

וַיַּ֤עַשׂ אַבְרָהָם֙ (Gen. 21:8) שֶׁ֤בַע כְּבָשֹׂת֙ (Gen. 21:29)

Chant these segments. Make a pause or elongation after *zakef* and a lesser pause or elongation after *pashta.*

הִנֵּ֤ה הָאֵשׁ֙ וְהָ֣עֵצִ֔ים וְאַיֵּ֥ה הַשֶּׂ֖ה לְעֹלָֽה׃ (Gen. 22:7)

וַיִּקַּ֤ח אַבְרָהָם֙ צֹ֣אן וּבָקָ֔ר וַיִּתֵּ֖ן לַאֲבִימֶ֑לֶךְ וַיִּכְרְת֥וּ שְׁנֵיהֶ֖ם בְּרִֽית׃ (Gen. 21:27)

וַיֵּ֤לֶךְ אַבְרָהָם֙ וַיִּקַּ֣ח אֶת־הָאַ֔יִל וַיַּעֲלֵ֥הוּ לְעֹלָ֖ה תַּ֥חַת בְּנֽוֹ׃ (Gen. 22:13)

וַיִּשְׁלַ֤ח אַבְרָהָם֙ אֶת־יָד֔וֹ וַיִּקַּ֖ח אֶת־הַֽמַּאֲכֶ֑לֶת לִשְׁחֹ֖ט אֶת־בְּנֽוֹ׃ (Gen. 22:10)

If the accents are close to each other, the conjunctive will be *merekha* instead of *mahpakh.* In the *merekha-pashta* combination, the two accented syllables are contiguous—the *merekha* word is accented on the last syllable, and the *pashta* word has no pick-up. Thus the model for *pashta* must be sung on the syllable "TA," dropping the pick-up "pash-."

Merekha pashta מֵרְכָ֥א פַּשְׁטָא֙

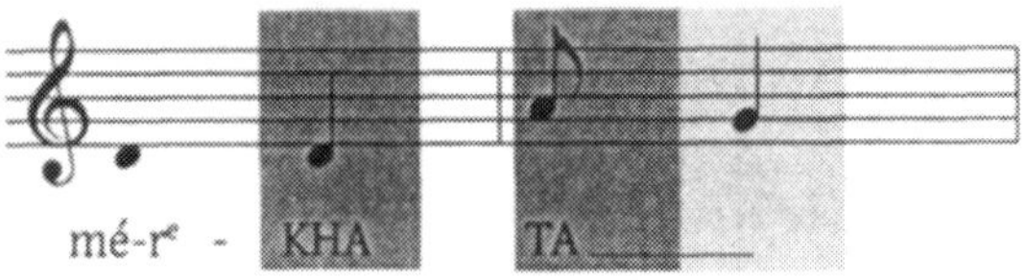

Chant these words to the melody of *merekha pashta.*

וּבְאַבְנֵ֥ט בַּד֙ (Lev. 16:4) שְׁמֹנָ֥ה אֵ֙לֶּה֙ (Gen. 22:23) שְׁבוּ־לָכֶ֥ם פֹּה֙ (Gen. 22:5)

Chant these segments. Make a pause or elongation after *zakef* and a lesser pause or elongation after *pashta.*

וּבְאַבְנֵ֥ט בַּד֙ יַחְגֹּ֔ר וּבְמִצְנֶ֥פֶת בַּ֖ד יִצְנֹ֑ף (Lev. 16:4)

שְׁמֹנָ֥ה אֵ֙לֶּה֙ יָלְדָ֣ה מִלְכָּ֔ה לְנָח֖וֹר אֲחִ֥י אַבְרָהָֽם׃ (Gen. 22:23)

שְׁבוּ־לָכֶ֥ם פֹּה֙ עִֽם־הַחֲמ֔וֹר וַאֲנִ֣י וְהַנַּ֔עַר נֵלְכָ֖ה עַד־כֹּ֑ה (Gen. 22:5)

Yetiv

Yetiv is used instead of *pashta* if the word is accented on the first syllable and has no conjunctive words immediately preceding. Since *yetiv* is found only on words accented on the first syllable, i.e., words with no pick-ups, the model is sung on the syllable "TÍV," dropping the pick-up "yᵉ-."

Yetiv יְ֚תִיב

Chant these words to the melody of *yetiv.* עַ֚ל (Gen. 22:2) ק֚וּמִי (Gen. 21:18)

Yetiv is usually followed by *zakef katon* or *munaḥ zakef katon.* Chant these examples. Make a subtle elongation or pause after *yetiv.* Make a stronger elongation or pause after *zakef.*

עַ֚ל אַחַ֣ד הֶֽהָרִ֔ים אֲשֶׁ֖ר אֹמַ֥ר אֵלֶֽיךָ׃ (Gen. 22:2)

ק֚וּמִי שְׂאִ֣י אֶת־הַנַּ֔עַר וְהַחֲזִ֥יקִי אֶת־יָדֵ֖ךְ בּ֑וֹ כִּֽי־לְג֥וֹי גָּד֖וֹל אֲשִׂימֶֽנּוּ׃ (Gen. 21:18)

כִּ֚י בֶּֽעָנָ֔ן אֵרָאֶ֖ה עַל־הַכַּפֹּֽרֶת׃ (Lev. 16:2)

Note: In this verse, the first word is punctuated with *yetiv*, the second word with *mahpakh*.

יַ֣עַן אֲשֶׁ֤ר עָשִׂ֙יתָ֙ אֶת־הַדָּבָ֣ר הַזֶּ֔ה וְלֹ֥א חָשַׂ֖כְתָּ אֶת־בִּנְךָ֥ אֶת־יְחִידֶֽךָ׃ (Gen. 22:16)

Three Words in a *Pashta* Segment

Sometimes *pashta* is preceded by two or more conjunctives. In these segments, there will be a very slight pause or elongation just before the *pashta*. The second conjunctive before *pashta* (preceding either *merekha* or *mahpakh*) may be *kadmah*.

Kadmah mahpakh pashta קַדְמָ֨א מַהְפַּ֤ךְ פַּשְׁטָא֙

kad - MA mah - PAKH pash - TA

Chant these words to the melody of *kadmah mahpakh pashta*.

אֲשֶׁ֨ר הוּבָ֤א אֶת־דָּמָם֙ (Lev. 16:27) וַיִּ֨בֶן שָׁ֤ם אַבְרָהָם֙ (Gen. 22:9)

Kadmah merekha pashta קַדְמָ֨א מֵרְכָ֥א פַּשְׁטָא֙

kad - MA mé -r^e - KHA TA

Chant these words to the melody of *kadmah merekha pashta*. שַׁבַּ֨ת שַׁבָּת֥וֹן הִיא֙ (Lev. 16:31)

If the second conjunctive before *pashta* (preceding *mahpakh*) is accented on the first syllable, it will be *munaḥ* instead of *kadmah*. When we refer to this *ta'am*, we will accent its first syllable: *MU-naḥ*.

Munaḥ mahpakh pashta מ֣וּנַח מַהְפַּ֤ךְ פַּשְׁטָא֙

MU-nah mah - PAKH pash - TA

Chant these words to the melody of *munaḥ mahpakh pashta*. כִּ֣י לֹ֤א יִירַשׁ֙ (Gen. 21:10)

Four Words in a *Pashta* Segment

Sometimes *pashta* is preceded by three conjunctives. The third conjunctive before *pashta* is *telishah ketanah*.

Telishah kadmah mahpakh pashta תְּלִישָׁה֩ קַדְמָ֨א מַהְפַּ֤ךְ פַּשְׁטָא֙

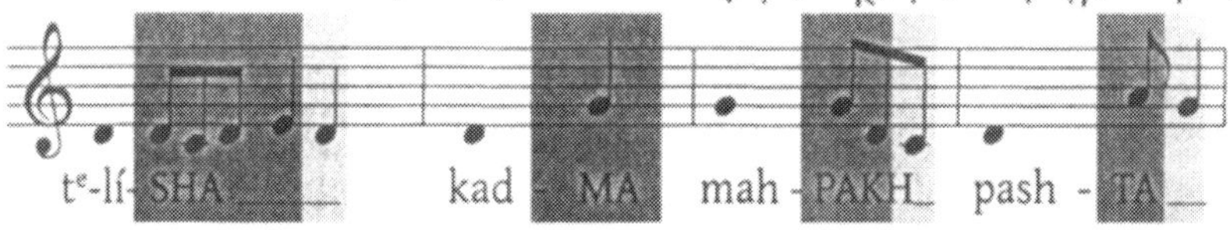
t^e-lí- SHA kad - MA mah - PAKH pash - TA

Chant these words to the melody of *telishah kadmah mahpakh pashta*.

וַיִּקְרָא֩ מַלְאַ֨ךְ אֱלֹהִ֤ים ׀ אֶל־הָגָר֙ (Gen. 21:17)

Chant these examples. Connect the *telishah* and *kadmah* words to the word that follows. Create only a slight elongation and/or pause after *pashta*. Create a longer elongation and/or pause after *zakef.*

קַדְמָ֨ה מֵרְכָ֥א פַּשְׁטָא֙

שַׁבַּ֨ת שַׁבָּת֥וֹן הִיא֙ לָכֶ֔ם וְעִנִּיתֶ֖ם אֶת־נַפְשֹׁתֵיכֶ֑ם חֻקַּ֖ת עוֹלָֽם׃ (Lev. 16:31)

קַדְמָ֨ה מַהְפַּ֤ךְ פַּשְׁטָא֙

אֶת־בִּנְךָ֨ אֶת־יְחִֽידְךָ֤ אֲשֶׁר־אָהַ֙בְתָּ֙ אֶת־יִצְחָ֔ק (Gen. 22:2)

וַיִּ֨בֶן שָׁ֤ם אַבְרָהָם֙ אֶת־הַמִּזְבֵּ֔חַ וַיַּֽעֲרֹ֖ךְ אֶת־הָעֵצִ֑ים (Gen. 22:9)

וְהַרְבָּ֨ה אַרְבֶּ֤ה אֶֽת־זַרְעֲךָ֙ כְּכוֹכְבֵ֣י הַשָּׁמַ֔יִם וְכַח֕וֹל אֲשֶׁ֖ר עַל־שְׂפַ֣ת הַיָּ֑ם (Gen. 22:17)

מ֭וּנַח מַהְפַּ֤ךְ פַּשְׁטָא֙

וַתֹּ֙אמֶר֙ לְאַבְרָהָ֔ם גָּרֵ֛שׁ הָאָמָ֥ה הַזֹּ֖את וְאֶת־בְּנָ֑הּ

כִּ֣י לֹ֤א יִירַשׁ֙ בֶּן־הָאָמָ֣ה הַזֹּ֔את עִם־בְּנִ֖י עִם־יִצְחָֽק׃ (Gen. 21:10)

תְּלִישָׁה֩ קַדְמָ֨ה מַהְפַּ֤ךְ פַּשְׁטָא֙

וַיִּקְרָא֩ מַלְאַ֨ךְ אֱלֹהִ֤ים ׀ אֶל־הָגָר֙ מִן־הַשָּׁמַ֔יִם וַיֹּ֥אמֶר לָ֖הּ מַה־לָּ֣ךְ הָגָ֑ר

אַל־תִּ֣ירְאִ֔י כִּֽי־שָׁמַ֧ע אֱלֹהִ֛ים אֶל־ק֥וֹל הַנַּ֖עַר בַּאֲשֶׁ֥ר הוּא־שָֽׁם׃ (Gen. 21:17)

The *Segol* Segment

Zakef is a strong disjunctive; only *siluk* and *etnaḥta* are stronger. A *zakef* segment will always be followed by a *tippeḥa* segement. *Zakef* is stronger than the ensuing *tippeḥa*. A *zakef* segment may also be followed by one or more other *zakef* segments, but they will eventually be followed by a *tippeḥa* segement. When you see two *zakefs* (or two *zakef* segments) in a row, the first is always stronger.

Zarka is the *ta'am* that marks the subdivision within the *segol* segment.

Both *segol* and *zarka* can be preceded by the conjunctive *munaḥ*.

munaḥ zarka munaḥ segol מוּנַ֣ח זַרְקָא֮ מוּנַ֣ח סֶגּוֹל֒

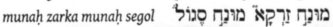

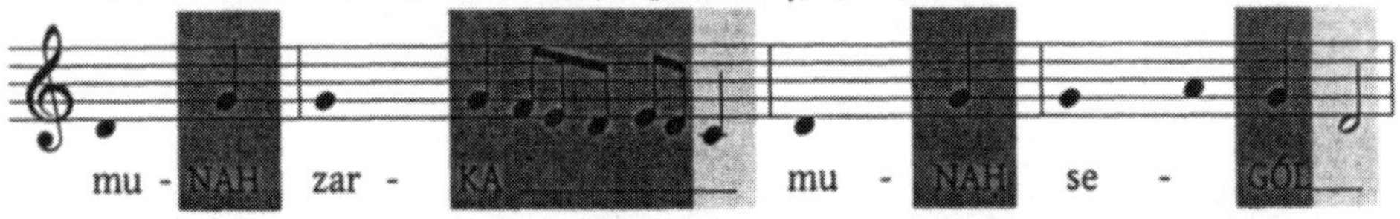
mu -
NAH
zar -
KA
mu -
NAH
se -
GOL

Note: The accent *segol* has a double pick-up. If the word has one pick-up syllable, sing that syllable on A. If the word has two pick-up syllables, sing the first pick-up on G and the second on A. If the word has three pick-up syllables, sing the first two pick-ups on G and the third on A.

Chant these words to the appropriate *te'amim*.

וַיִּשְׁמַ֣ע אֱלֹהִים֮ אֶת־ק֣וֹל הַנַּ֒עַר֒ (Gen. 21:17)

דַּבֵּר֮ אֶל־אַהֲרֹ֣ן אָחִיךָ֒ (Lev. 16:2)

עַל־רֹ֣אשׁ הַשָּׂעִיר֮ הַחַי֒ (Lev. 16:21)

אֶֽל־הַמָּקוֹם֮ אֲשֶׁ֣ר אָֽמַר־ל֣וֹ הָאֱלֹהִים֒ (Gen. 22:9)

וּמִֽכְנְסֵי־בַד֮ יִהְי֣וּ עַל־בְּשָׂרוֹ֒ (Lev. 16:4)

Chant these examples. Connect all conjunctives to the word that follows. Create only a slight elongation and pause after *zarka*. Create a longer elongation and pause after *segol*.

דַּבֵּר֮ אֶל־אַהֲרֹ֣ן אָחִ֒יךָ֒ וְאַל־יָבֹ֤א בְכָל־עֵת֙ אֶל־הַקֹּ֔דֶשׁ מִבֵּ֖ית לַפָּרֹ֑כֶת (Lev. 16:2)

אֶל־הַמָּקוֹם֮ אֲשֶׁ֣ר אָֽמַר־ל֣וֹ הָאֱלֹהִים֒ וַיִּ֨בֶן שָׁ֤ם אַבְרָהָם֙ אֶת־הַמִּזְבֵּ֔חַ וַיַּעֲרֹ֖ךְ אֶת־הָעֵצִ֑ים

וַֽיַּעֲקֹד֙ אֶת־יִצְחָ֣ק בְּנ֔וֹ וַיָּ֤שֶׂם אֹתוֹ֙ עַל־הַמִּזְבֵּ֔חַ מִמַּ֖עַל לָעֵצִֽים׃ (Gen. 22:9)

וַיִּשְׁמַ֣ע אֱלֹהִים֮ אֶת־ק֣וֹל הַנַּ֒עַר֒ וַיִּקְרָא֩ מַלְאַ֨ךְ אֱלֹהִ֤ים ׀ אֶל־הָגָר֙ מִן־הַשָּׁמַ֔יִם

וַיֹּ֥אמֶר לָ֖הּ מַה־לָּ֣ךְ הָגָ֑ר (Gen. 21:17)

The *Revia* Segment

Revia is a medium-level disjunctive, found before *pashta, zarka,* and *tevir* segments. *Revia* is a stronger disjunctive than the others (*pashta, zarka,* or *tevir*) that follow.

One or Two Words in the *Revia* Segment

If the preceding word is closely connected in meaning to the *revia* word, it is usually marked with the conjunctive *munaḥ*.

Munaḥ revia מוּנַ֣ח רְבִ֗יעַ

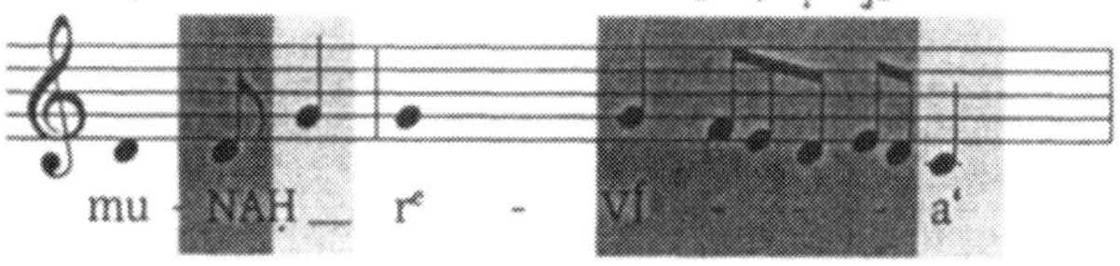

Chant these words to the melody of *revia*.

עָלָ֗יו (Lev. 16:21) וְעַתָּ֗ה (Gen. 21:23) כִּ֗י (Gen. 22:16) הִ֗נֵּה (Gen. 21:29) לַחֹ֗דֶשׁ (Num. 29:1)

Chant these words to the melody of *munaḥ revia*.

בַּיּ֣וֹם הַשְּׁלִישִׁ֗י (Gen. 22:4) וְכִפֶּ֣ר עַל־הַקֹּ֗דֶשׁ (Lev. 16:16) מָ֣ה הֵ֗נָּה (Gen. 21:29) בְּאֹ֣הֶל מוֹעֵ֗ד (Lev.16:17)

Note that the melodies for *revia* and *zarka* are identical in this system.

Chant these examples. Connect each conjunctive word to the word that follows. Create an elongation or pause after *revia*. Create only a slight elongation or pause after *pashta, zarka,* or *tevir*.

רְבִ֗יעַ פַּשְׁטָא֙

בְּאֶחָ֣ד לַחֹ֗דֶשׁ מִֽקְרָא־קֹ֙דֶשׁ֙ יִהְיֶ֣ה לָכֶ֔ם (Num. 29:1)

וַיָּ֣קָם אֲבִימֶ֗לֶךְ וּפִיכֹל֙ שַׂר־צְבָא֔וֹ וַיָּשֻׁ֖בוּ אֶל־אֶ֥רֶץ פְּלִשְׁתִּֽים׃ (Gen. 21:32)

רְבִ֗יעַ מַהְפַּ֤ךְ פַּשְׁטָא֙

וּמִנְחָתָ֗הּ וְעֹלַ֤ת הַתָּמִיד֙ וּמִנְחָתָ֔הּ וְנִסְכֵּיהֶ֖ם כְּמִשְׁפָּטָ֑ם (Num. 29:6)

וַתֹּ֗אמֶר מִ֤י מִלֵּל֙ לְאַבְרָהָ֔ם הֵינִ֥יקָה בָנִ֖ים שָׂרָ֑ה כִּֽי־יָלַ֥דְתִּי בֵ֖ן לִזְקֻנָֽיו׃ (Gen. 21:7)

רְבִ֗יעַ יְ֚תִיב

כִּ֗י יַ֚עַן אֲשֶׁ֤ר עָשִׂ֙יתָ֙ אֶת־הַדָּבָ֣ר הַזֶּ֔ה וְלֹ֥א חָשַׂ֖כְתָּ אֶת־בִּנְךָ֥ אֶת־יְחִידֶֽךָ׃ (Gen. 22:16)

רְבִ֗יעַ קַדְמָ֨ה מַהְפַּ֤ךְ פַּשְׁטָא֙

וְעַתָּ֗ה הִשָּׁ֨בְעָה לִּ֤י בֵֽאלֹהִים֙ הֵ֔נָּה אִם־תִּשְׁקֹ֣ר לִ֔י וּלְנִינִ֖י וּלְנֶכְדִּ֑י (Gen. 21:23)

כִּֽי־בָרֵ֣ךְ אֲבָרֶכְךָ֗ וְהַרְבָּ֨ה אַרְבֶּ֤ה אֶֽת־זַרְעֲךָ֙ כְּכוֹכְבֵ֣י הַשָּׁמַ֔יִם (Gen. 22:17)

רְבִ֗יעַ תְּלִישָׁא֩ קַדְמָ֨ה מַהְפַּ֤ךְ פַּשְׁטָא֙

וְהַשָּׂעִ֗יר אֲשֶׁר֩ עָלָ֨ה עָלָ֤יו הַגּוֹרָל֙ לַעֲזָאזֵ֔ל יָֽעֳמַד־חַ֛י לִפְנֵ֥י יְהוָ֖ה לְכַפֵּ֣ר עָלָ֑יו
לְשַׁלַּ֥ח אֹת֛וֹ לַעֲזָאזֵ֖ל הַמִּדְבָּֽרָה׃ (Lev. 16:10)

רְבִ֗יעַ תְּבִ֛יר

וַיַּצֵּ֣ב אַבְרָהָ֗ם אֶת־שֶׁ֛בַע כִּבְשֹׂ֥ת הַצֹּ֖אן לְבַדְּהֶֽן׃ (Gen. 21:28)

עַל־כֵּ֗ן קָרָ֛א לַמָּק֥וֹם הַה֖וּא בְּאֵ֣ר שָׁ֑בַע כִּ֛י שָׁ֥ם נִשְׁבְּע֖וּ שְׁנֵיהֶֽם׃ (Gen. 21:31)

רְבִ֗יעַ דַּרְגָּ֧א תְּבִ֛יר

וְלִפְנֵ֣י הַכַּפֹּ֗רֶת יַזֶּ֧ה שֶֽׁבַע־פְּעָמִ֛ים מִן־הַדָּ֖ם בְּאֶצְבָּעֽוֹ׃ (Lev. 16:14)

רְבִ֗יעַ קַדְמָ֨ה דַּרְגָּ֧א תְּבִ֛יר

בַּיּ֣וֹם הַשְּׁלִישִׁ֗י וַיִּשָּׂ֨א אַבְרָהָ֧ם אֶת־עֵינָ֛יו וַיַּ֥רְא אֶת־הַמָּק֖וֹם מֵרָחֹֽק׃ (Gen. 22:4)

רְבִ֗יעַ זַרְקָא֮

וַיָּבֹ֗אוּ אֶֽל־הַמָּקוֹם֮ אֲשֶׁ֣ר אָֽמַר־ל֣וֹ הָאֱלֹהִים֒ (Gen. 22:9)

רְבִ֗יעַ מוּנַּ֣ח זַרְקָא֮

אֶת־שְׁתֵּ֣י יָדָ֗ו עַ֣ל רֹ֣אשׁ הַשָּׂעִיר֮ הַחַי֒ (Lev. 16:21)

Chant these verses.

וַיְהִי֙ בָּעֵ֣ת הַהִ֔וא וַיֹּ֣אמֶר אֲבִימֶ֗לֶךְ וּפִיכֹל֙ שַׂר־צְבָא֔וֹ אֶל־אַבְרָהָ֖ם לֵאמֹ֑ר
אֱלֹהִ֣ים עִמְּךָ֔ בְּכֹ֥ל אֲשֶׁר־אַתָּ֖ה עֹשֶֽׂה׃ (Gen. 21:22)

וַיִּכְרְת֥וּ בְרִ֖ית בִּבְאֵ֣ר שָׁ֑בַע וַיָּ֣קָם אֲבִימֶ֗לֶךְ וּפִיכֹל֙ שַׂר־צְבָא֔וֹ
וַיָּשֻׁ֖בוּ אֶל־אֶ֥רֶץ פְּלִשְׁתִּֽים׃ (Gen. 21:32)

וַיְהִ֗י אַחַר֙ הַדְּבָרִ֣ים הָאֵ֔לֶּה וְהָ֣אֱלֹהִ֔ים נִסָּ֖ה אֶת־אַבְרָהָ֑ם וַיֹּ֣אמֶר אֵלָ֔יו אַבְרָהָ֖ם וַיֹּ֥אמֶר הִנֵּֽנִי׃ (Gen. 22:1)

וַיָּבֹ֗אוּ אֶֽל־הַמָּקוֹם֮ אֲשֶׁ֣ר אָֽמַר־ל֣וֹ הָאֱלֹהִים֒
וַיִּ֨בֶן שָׁ֤ם אַבְרָהָם֙ אֶת־הַמִּזְבֵּ֔חַ וַֽיַּעֲרֹ֖ךְ אֶת־הָעֵצִ֑ים
וַֽיַּעֲקֹד֙ אֶת־יִצְחָ֣ק בְּנ֔וֹ וַיָּ֤שֶׂם אֹתוֹ֙ עַל־הַמִּזְבֵּ֔חַ מִמַּ֖עַל לָעֵצִֽים׃ (Gen. 22:9)

The *Legarmeh* Segment

Sometimes there is a subdivision within a *revia* segment. The *ta'am* that marks that subdivision may be *legarmeh*.

Chant these words to the melody of *legarmeh*. (Gen. 22:12) | כִּ֣י (Lev. 16:27) | וְאֵ֣ת

Legarmeh is always followed by *munaḥ revia*. *Legarmeh* appears only four times in the High Holiday readings.

(Lev. 16:13) וְכִסָּ֣ה ׀ עֲנַ֣ן הַקְּטֹ֗רֶת (Gen. 22:12) כִּ֣י ׀ עַתָּ֣ה יָדַ֗עְתִּי

(Lev. 16:27) וְאֵ֣ת ׀ שְׂעִ֣יר הַחַטָּ֗את (Lev. 16:17) לֹא־יִהְיֶ֣ה ׀ בְּאֹ֣הֶל מוֹעֵ֗ד

The *Geresh* Segment

Another *ta'am* that can subdivide a *revia* segment is *geresh*. There are two basic forms of *geresh*, each with its own distinct melody: (single) *geresh*, and double *geresh*, called *gereshayim*.

Geresh without a preceding conjunctive is always accented on the next-to-the-last syllable. *Geresh* appears by itself only twice in the High Holiday readings. More commonly, *geresh* is preceded by a closely connected word, marked with the conjunctive *ta'am kadmah*.

One or Two Words in a *Geresh* Segment

Kadmah geresh קַדְמָ֨א גֵּ֜רֵשׁ

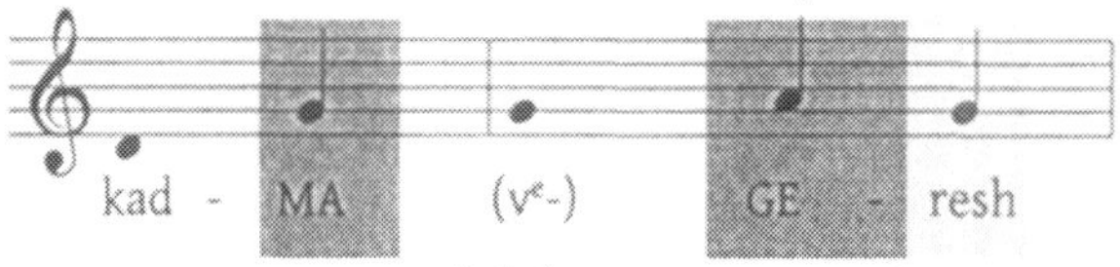

To construct a model for *geresh* words that have a pick-up, we supply the prefix "v^e-".

Chant these words to the melody of *geresh*. (Gen. 21:23) כַּ֜חֶסֶד (Gen. 21:19) וַתֵּ֜לֶךְ

Chant these words to the melody of *kadmah geresh*.

(Gen. 21:16) וַתֵּ֨שֶׁב לָ֜הּ (Lev. 16:27) פַּ֨ר הַחַטָּ֜את (Gen. 22:3) וַיַּשְׁכֵּ֨ם אַבְרָהָ֜ם (Num. 29:6) עֹלַ֨ת הַחֹ֜דֶשׁ

Three Words in a *Geresh* Segment

Sometimes *geresh* is preceded by two conjunctives. The second conjunctive before *geresh* (preceding *kadmah*) is *telishah*. This combination occurs only five times in the High Holiday readings.

Telishah kadmah geresh תְּלִישָׁ֠ה קַדְמָ֨א גֵּ֜רֵשׁ

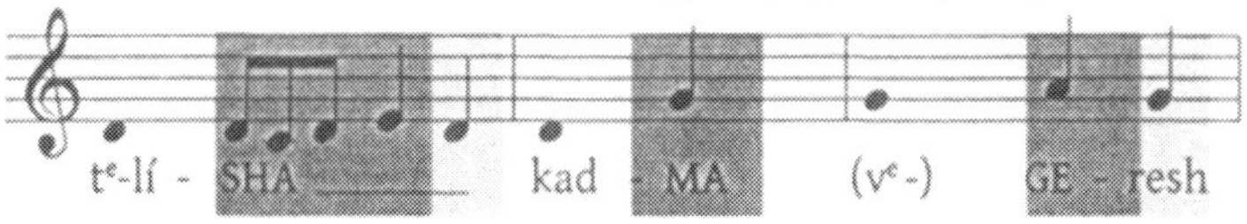

Chant these words to the melody of *telishah kadmah geresh*.

(Gen. 21:16) וַתֵּ֠לֶךְ וַתֵּ֨שֶׁב לָ֜הּ (Lev. 16:27) וְאֵ֠ת פַּ֨ר הַחַטָּ֜את

Gereshayim

The double *geresh* is called *gereshayim*. Words that bear this accent are stressed on the last syllable. *Gereshayim* is found only seven times in the High Holiday readings.

Gereshayim גֵּרְשַׁ֞יִם

Chant these words to the melody of *gereshayim*. וַיִּקַּ֞ח (Gen. 22:3) וְכָל־אָדָ֞ם (Lev. 16:17)

Geresh (or *gereshayim*) can subdivide any of the following segments: *revia, pashta,* or *tevir*.

Chant these phrases. Connect each conjunctive word to the word that follows. Create an elongation or pause after *revia, pashta, tevir,* or *zarka*. Create only a slight elongation or pause after *geresh* or *gereshayim*.

קַדְמָ֨ה גֵּ֜רֶשׁ רְבִ֗יעַ

וַיֹּ֨אמֶר אַבְרָהָ֜ם אֶל־נְעָרָ֗יו (Gen. 22:5)

וַיַּשְׁכֵּ֨ם אַבְרָהָ֜ם בַּבֹּ֗קֶר (Gen. 22:3)

תְּ֠לִישָׁא קַדְמָ֨ה גֵּ֜רֶשׁ רְבִ֗יעַ

מִ֠לְּבַד עֹלַ֨ת הַחֹ֜דֶשׁ וּמִנְחָתָ֗הּ (Num. 29:6)

וַ֠תֵּלֶךְ וַתֵּ֨שֶׁב לָ֜הּ מִנֶּ֗גֶד (Gen. 21:16)

קַדְמָ֨ה גֵּ֜רֶשׁ מוּנַ֣ח רְבִ֗יעַ

וּבַחֹ֨דֶשׁ הַשְּׁבִיעִ֜י בְּאֶחָ֣ד לַחֹ֗דֶשׁ (Num. 29:1)

וַיִּקַּ֨ח אַבְרָהָ֜ם אֶת־עֲצֵ֣י הָעֹלָ֗ה (Gen. 22:6)

תְּ֠לִישָׁא קַדְמָ֨ה גֵּ֜רֶשׁ לְגַרְמֵ֣הּ ׀ מוּנַ֣ח רְבִ֗יעַ

וְאֵ֠ת פַּ֨ר הַֽחַטָּ֜את וְאֵ֣ת ׀ שְׂעִ֣יר הַֽחַטָּ֗את (Lev. 16:27)

גֵּרְשַׁ֞יִם מוּנַ֣ח רְבִ֗יעַ

וְגַם־אַתָּ֞ה לֹא־הִגַּ֣דְתָּ לִּ֗י (Gen. 21:26)

גֵּרְשַׁ֞יִם לְגַרְמֵ֣הּ ׀ מוּנַ֣ח רְבִ֗יעַ

וְכָל־אָדָ֞ם לֹא־יִהְיֶ֣ה ׀ בְּאֹ֣הֶל מוֹעֵ֗ד (Lev. 16:17)

קַדְמָ֨ה גֵּ֜רֶשׁ מַהְפַּ֤ךְ פַּשְׁטָא֙

וַיֹּ֨אמֶר יִצְחָ֜ק אֶל־אַבְרָהָ֤ם אָבִיו֙ וַיֹּ֣אמֶר אָבִ֔י (Gen. 22:7)

אֶל־פְּנֵ֨י הַכַּפֹּ֜רֶת אֲשֶׁ֤ר עַל־הָאָרֹן֙ וְלֹ֣א יָמ֔וּת (Lev. 16:2)

גֵּ֜רֶשׁ מַהְפַּ֤ךְ פַּשְׁטָא֙

וַתֵּ֜לֶךְ וַתְּמַלֵּ֤א אֶת־הַחֵ֙מֶת֙ מַ֔יִם וַתַּ֖שְׁקְ אֶת־הַנָּֽעַר׃ (Gen. 21:19)

כַּחֶ֜סֶד אֲשֶׁר־עָשִׂ֤יתִי עִמְּךָ֙ תַּעֲשֶׂ֣ה עִמָּדִ֔י (Gen. 21:23)

גֵּרְשַׁ֞יִם מַהְפַּ֤ךְ פַּשְׁטָא֙

מִלְּבַ֞ד חַטַּ֤את הַכִּפֻּרִים֙ וְעֹלַ֣ת הַתָּמִ֔יד (Num. 29:11)

וַיִּקַּ֞ח אֶת־שְׁנֵ֤י נְעָרָיו֙ אִתּ֔וֹ (Gen. 22:3)

קַדְמָ֨ה גֵּ֜רֶשׁ דַּרְגָּ֧א תְּבִ֛יר

וַיִּקְרָ֨א אַבְרָהָ֜ם אֶֽת־שֶׁם־בְּנ֧וֹ הַנּֽוֹלַד־ל֛וֹ אֲשֶׁר־יָלְדָה־לּ֥וֹ שָׂרָ֖ה יִצְחָֽק׃ (Gen. 21:3)

וַתֵּ֨רֶא שָׂרָ֜ה אֶֽת־בֶּן־הָגָ֧ר הַמִּצְרִ֛ית אֲשֶׁר־יָלְדָ֥ה לְאַבְרָהָ֖ם מְצַחֵֽק׃ (Gen. 21:9)

גֵּרְשַׁ֞יִם מֵרְכָ֥א תְּבִ֛יר

אֱלֹהִ֞ים יִרְאֶה־לּ֥וֹ הַשֶּׂ֛ה לְעֹלָ֖ה בְּנִ֑י (Gen. 22:8)

Telishah Gedolah

Telishah gedolah is a minor disjunctive that appears only five times in the High Holiday readings. The conjunctive of *telishah gedolah* is *munaḥ.*

One or Two Words in a *Telishah Gedolah* Segment

(Munaḥ) telishah תְּלִישָׁה֠ (מוּנַ֣ח)

Chant this word to the melody of *telishah (gedolah).* (Gen. 22:20) הִנֵּ֠ה

Chant these words to the melody of *munaḥ telishah (gedolah).*

(Lev. 16:29) בַּחֹ֣דֶשׁ הַשְּׁבִיעִ֠י   (Gen. 21:14) וַיִּתֵּ֣ן אֶל־הָ֠גָר

Chant *telishah gedolah* in context.

וַיַּשְׁכֵּ֣ם אַבְרָהָ֣ם ׀ בַּבֹּ֡קֶר

וַיִּֽקַּח־לֶ֩חֶם֩ וְחֵ֨מַת מַ֜יִם וַיִּתֵּ֣ן אֶל־הָ֠גָר שָׂ֧ם עַל־שִׁכְמָ֛הּ וְאֶת־הַיֶּ֖לֶד וַֽיְשַׁלְּחֶ֑הָ
וַתֵּ֣לֶךְ וַתֵּ֔תַע בְּמִדְבַּ֖ר בְּאֵ֥ר שָֽׁבַע׃ (Gen. 21:14)

קַח־נָ֠א אֶת־בִּנְךָ֨ אֶת־יְחִֽידְךָ֤ אֲשֶׁר־אָהַ֙בְתָּ֙ אֶת־יִצְחָ֔ק וְלֶךְ־לְךָ֔ אֶל־אֶ֖רֶץ הַמֹּרִיָּ֑ה
וְהַעֲלֵ֤הוּ שָׁם֙ לְעֹלָ֔ה עַ֚ל אַחַ֣ד הֶֽהָרִ֔ים אֲשֶׁ֖ר אֹמַ֥ר אֵלֶֽיךָ׃ (Gen. 22:2)

וַיְהִ֗י אַחֲרֵי֙ הַדְּבָרִ֣ים הָאֵ֔לֶּה וַיֻּגַּ֥ד לְאַבְרָהָ֖ם לֵאמֹ֑ר
הִנֵּ֠ה יָֽלְדָ֨ה מִלְכָּ֥ה גַם־הִ֛וא בָּנִ֖ים לְנָח֥וֹר אָחִֽיךָ׃ (Gen. 22:20)

וְלָקַ֣ח מְלֹֽא־הַ֠מַּחְתָּה גַּֽחֲלֵי־אֵ֞שׁ מֵעַ֤ל הַמִּזְבֵּ֙חַ֙ מִלִּפְנֵ֣י יְהוָ֔ה וּמְלֹ֣א חָפְנָ֔יו קְטֹ֖רֶת סַמִּ֣ים דַּקָּ֑ה
וְהֵבִ֖יא מִבֵּ֥ית לַפָּרֹֽכֶת׃ (Lev. 16:12)

וְהָיְתָ֥ה לָכֶ֖ם לְחֻקַּ֣ת עוֹלָ֑ם בַּחֹ֣דֶשׁ הַשְּׁבִיעִ֠י בֶּֽעָשׂ֨וֹר לַחֹ֜דֶשׁ תְּעַנּ֣וּ אֶת־נַפְשֹֽׁתֵיכֶ֗ם
וְכָל־מְלָאכָה֙ לֹ֣א תַעֲשׂ֔וּ הָֽאֶזְרָ֔ח וְהַגֵּ֖ר הַגָּ֥ר בְּתוֹכְכֶֽם׃ (Lev. 16:29)

Pazer

Pazer is a minor disjunctive that appears only twice in the High Holiday readings.

The conjunctive of *pazer* is *munaḥ.*

One or Two Words in a *Pazer* Segment

(Munaḥ) pazer פָּזֵ֡ר (מוּנַ֣ח)

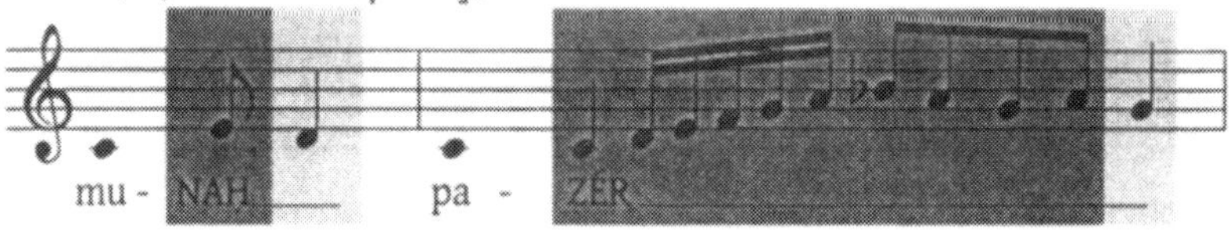

Chant this word to the melody of *pazer.* (Gen. 22:2) וַ֡יֹּאמֶר

Chant these words to the melody of *munaḥ munaḥ pazer.* (Gen. 21:14) וַיַּשְׁכֵּ֣ם אַבְרָהָ֣ם ׀ בַּבֹּ֡קֶר

Practice chanting *pazer* in context.

וַיַּשְׁכֵּ֨ם אַבְרָהָ֜ם ׀ בַּבֹּ֗קֶר וַיִּֽקַּֽח־לֶ֙חֶם֙ וְחֵ֣מַת מַ֔יִם וַיִּתֵּ֣ן אֶל־הָ֠גָר
שָׂ֧ם עַל־שִׁכְמָ֛הּ וְאֶת־הַיֶּ֖לֶד וַֽיְשַׁלְּחֶ֑הָ וַתֵּ֣לֶךְ וַתֵּ֔תַע בְּמִדְבַּ֖ר בְּאֵ֥ר שָֽׁבַע׃ (Gen. 21:14)

וַיֹּ֡אמֶר קַח־נָ֠א אֶת־בִּנְךָ֙ אֶת־יְחִֽידְךָ֤ אֲשֶׁר־אָהַ֙בְתָּ֙ אֶת־יִצְחָ֔ק
וְלֶךְ־לְךָ֔ אֶל־אֶ֖רֶץ הַמֹּרִיָּ֑ה וְהַעֲלֵ֤הוּ שָׁם֙ לְעֹלָ֔ה עַ֚ל אַחַ֣ד הֶֽהָרִ֔ים אֲשֶׁ֖ר אֹמַ֥ר אֵלֶֽיךָ׃ (Gen. 22:2)

The Final Cadence

We use a special melody to signal the end of each *aliyah*. This melody is applied beginning with the final *tippeḥa* segment. You will read this cadence slowly.

(Merekha) tippeḥa (merekha) siluk מֵרְכָ֥א טִפְּחָ֖א מֵרְכָ֥א סִילֽוּק

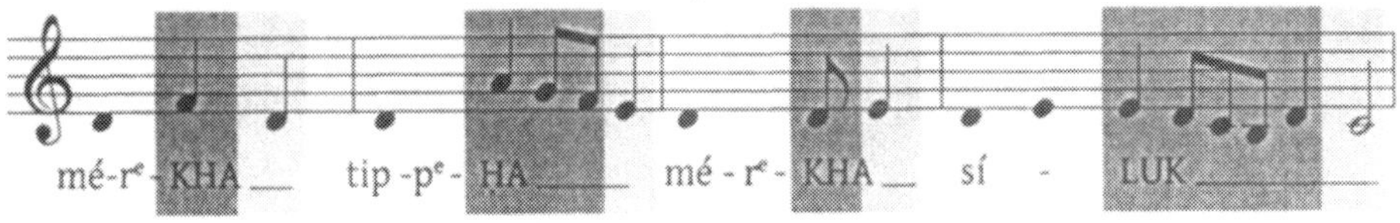

Chant these words to the melody of *(merekha) tippeḥa (merekha) siluk.*

אֶל־ק֥וֹל הַנַּ֖עַר בַּאֲשֶׁ֥ר הוּא־שָֽׁם׃ (Gen. 21:17) וַיֵּ֥שֶׁב אַבְרָהָ֖ם בִּבְאֵ֥ר שָֽׁבַע׃ (Gen. 22:19)

וְכִפֶּ֥ר בַּעֲד֖וֹ וּבְעַ֥ד הָעָֽם׃ (Lev. 16:24) אִשָּׁ֖ה מֵאֶ֥רֶץ מִצְרָֽיִם׃ (Gen. 21:21)

צִוָּ֥ה אֹת֖וֹ אֱלֹהִֽים׃ (Gen. 21:4) יִקָּ֥רֵא לְךָ֖ זָֽרַע׃ (Gen. 21:12) וּמִנְחָתָ֖הּ וְנִסְכֵּיהֶֽם׃ (Num. 29:11)

Chant these segments, using the final cadence.

מֵרְכָ֥א טִפְּחָ֖א מֵרְכָ֥א סִילֽוּק

וַיָּ֧גָר אַבְרָהָ֛ם בְּאֶ֥רֶץ פְּלִשְׁתִּ֖ים יָמִ֥ים רַבִּֽים׃ (Gen. 21:34)
וַיָּ֤שָׁב אַבְרָהָם֙ אֶל־נְעָרָ֔יו וַיָּקֻ֛מוּ וַיֵּלְכ֥וּ יַחְדָּ֖ו אֶל־בְּאֵ֣ר שָׁ֑בַע וַיֵּ֥שֶׁב אַבְרָהָ֖ם בִּבְאֵ֥ר שָֽׁבַע׃ (Gen. 22:19)

טִפְּחָ֖א מֵרְכָ֥א סִילֽוּק

וַיֵּ֖שֶׁב בְּמִדְבַּ֣ר פָּארָ֑ן וַתִּֽקַּֽח־ל֥וֹ אִמּ֛וֹ אִשָּׁ֖ה מֵאֶ֥רֶץ מִצְרָֽיִם׃ (Gen. 21:21)
וְכָל־אָדָ֞ם לֹא־יִהְיֶ֣ה ׀ בְּאֹ֣הֶל מוֹעֵ֗ד בְּבֹא֛וֹ לְכַפֵּ֥ר בַּקֹּ֖דֶשׁ עַד־צֵאת֑וֹ
וְכִפֶּ֤ר בַּעֲדוֹ֙ וּבְעַ֣ד בֵּית֔וֹ וּבְעַ֖ד כָּל־קְהַ֥ל יִשְׂרָאֵֽל׃ (Lev. 16:17)

מֵרְכָ֥א טִפְּחָ֖א סִילֽוּק

וַיֹּ֨אמֶר אֱלֹהִ֜ים אֶל־אַבְרָהָ֗ם אַל־יֵרַ֤ע בְּעֵינֶ֙יךָ֙ עַל־הַנַּ֣עַר וְעַל־אֲמָתֶ֔ךָ
כֹּל֩ אֲשֶׁ֨ר תֹּאמַ֥ר אֵלֶ֛יךָ שָׂרָ֖ה שְׁמַ֣ע בְּקֹלָ֑הּ כִּ֣י בְיִצְחָ֔ק יִקָּ֥רֵא לְךָ֖ זָֽרַע׃ (Gen. 21:12)
וַיֹּ֙אמֶר֙ אַבְרָהָ֔ם אֱלֹהִ֞ים יִרְאֶה־לּ֥וֹ הַשֶּׂ֛ה לְעֹלָ֖ה בְּנִ֑י וַיֵּלְכ֥וּ שְׁנֵיהֶ֖ם יַחְדָּֽו׃ (Gen. 22:8)

טִפְּחָ֖א סִילֽוּק

וּפִֽילַגְשׁ֖וֹ וּשְׁמָ֣הּ רְאוּמָ֑ה וַתֵּ֤לֶד גַּם־הִוא֙ אֶת־טֶ֣בַח וְאֶת־גַּ֔חַם וְאֶת־תַּ֖חַשׁ וְאֶֽת־מַעֲכָֽה׃ (Gen. 22:24)
שְׂעִיר־עִזִּ֥ים אֶחָ֖ד חַטָּ֑את מִלְּבַ֞ד חַטַּ֤את הַכִּפֻּרִים֙ וְעֹלַ֣ת הַתָּמִ֔יד וּמִנְחָתָ֖הּ וְנִסְכֵּיהֶֽם׃ (Num. 29:11)

Chanting the Blessings

The *oleh* chants the blessings using a melody that is based on motifs from the High Holiday cantillation. Before the reading, the *oleh* chants:

oleh:
ba - r^e - KHU 'et 'a - dó - NAY__ ha - m^e - vó - RAKH____
congregation:
ba - RUKH 'a - dó - NAY ha - m^e - vó - RAKH__ l^e - 'ó - lam va - 'ED_____
oleh:
ba - RUKH 'a - dó - NAY ha - m^e - vó - RAKH__ l^e - 'ó - lam va - 'ED_____
ba - RUKH 'at - TA 'a - dó - NAY__ 'e - ló - HÉ - nu me - lekh ha - 'ó - LAM____
'a - SHER BA - ḥar BA - nu mik - kol ha - 'am - MÍM___
v^e - NA - tan LA - nu 'et tó - ra - TÓ____
ba - RUKH 'at - TA 'a - dó - NAY_____ nó - TÉN hat - tó - RA_____

To which the *ba'al keri'ah* responds:

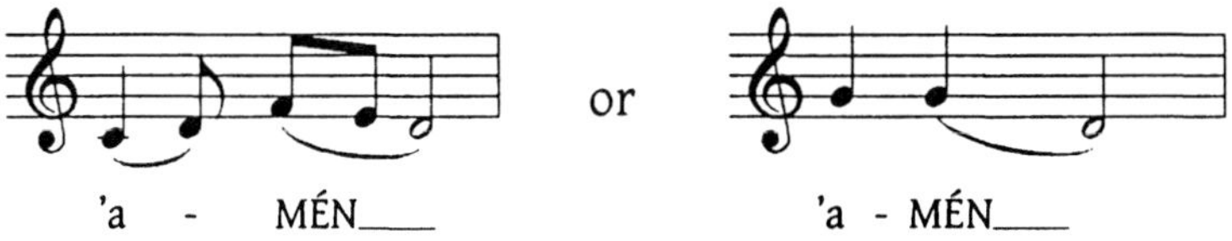
'a - MÉN___
or
'a - MÉN___

and then begins reading from the Torah.

After the reading, the *oleh* chants:

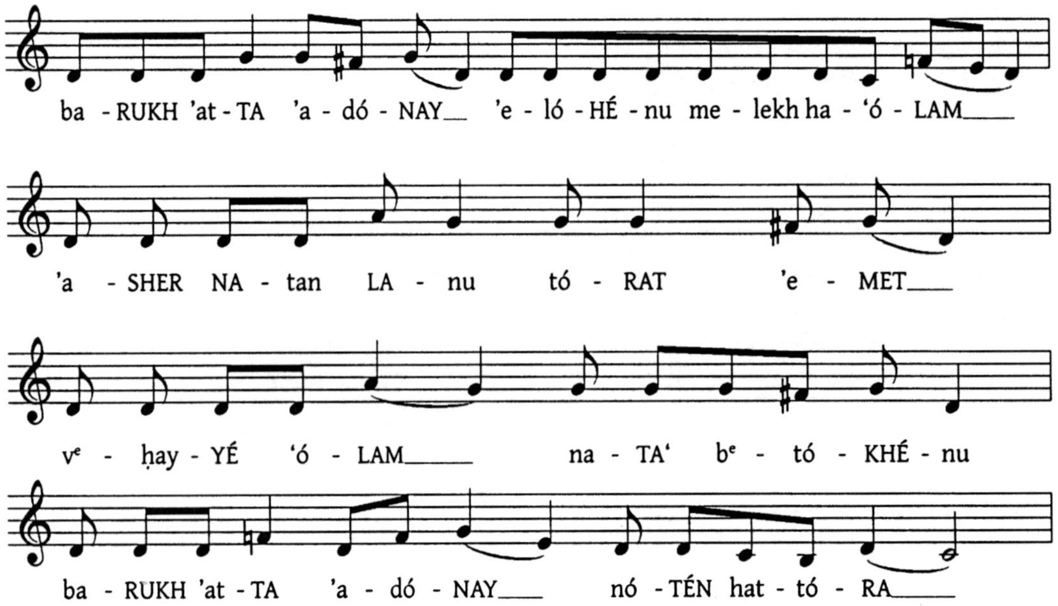
ba - RUKH 'at - TA 'a - dó - NAY__ 'e - ló - HÉ - nu me - lekh ha - ʻó - LAM___
'a - SHER NA - tan LA - nu tó - RAT 'e - MET___
v^{e} - ḥay - YÉ ʻó - LAM___ na - TAʻ b^{e} - tó - KHÉ - nu
ba - RUKH 'at - TA 'a - dó - NAY___ nó - TÉN hat - tó - RA___

Kaddish

Before the *maftir* is called up, the *baʻal keriyah* (or *gabbai*) chants the *ḥatsi kaddish* using a melody that, like the Torah blessings, is based on motifs from the High Holiday cantillation. For a different version, see *Chanting: The Complete Guide*, p. 921.

11. A Guide to the *Te'amim*

Disjunctives

Example	Symbol	Meaning of name	Name
הָאָֽרֶץ	אֽ	separation	סִילֽוּק (סִלֽוּק)
אֽ֑וֹר	א֑	coming to a rest	אֶתְנַחְתָּ֑א
הָאָדָ֒ם	א֒	cluster	סֶגּ֒וֹל
וַיְמָאֵ֓ן ׀	א֓ ׀	chain	שַׁלְשֶׁ֓לֶת ׀
הָאֵ֔לֶּה	א֔	small upright	זָקֵ֔ף (זָקֵף־קָטֹן)
וַתֹּ֕אמֶר	א֕	great upright	זָקֵ֕ף (זָקֵף־גָּדוֹל)
שְׁמ֖וֹ	א֖	handbreath	טִפְחָ֖א
יְהוּדָ֗ה	א֗	resting	רְבִ֗יעַ
אֶחָ֮ד	א֮	scattering	זַרְקָא֮
אֲשֶׁר֙	א֙	extending	פַּשְׁטָא֙
אֵ֚לֶּה	א֚	resting	יְ֚תִיב
הָעִבְרִ֛י	א֛	broken	תְּבִ֛יר
הָאִ֡ישׁ	א֡	scattering	פָּזֵ֡ר
בָּאַמָּ֟ה	א֟	great scattering	פָּזֵר־גָּד֟וֹל
וַיִּפְקֹד֠	א֠	great drawing out	תְּלִישָׁה־גְּדוֹלָה֠
וַתְּחַלֶּ֜ינָה	א֜	expulsion	גֶּ֜רֶשׁ
וַיְהִ֞י	א֞	two expulsions	גֵּרְשַׁ֞יִם
וַיְהִ֣י ׀	א֣ ׀	independent	לְגַרְמֵ֣ה ׀

Conjunctives

Example	Symbol	Meaning of name	Name
יְהִ֣י	א֣	sustained, horizontal	מוּנַ֣ח
וַיֹּ֥אמֶר	א֥	prolonged	מֵרְכָ֥א
בֵּ֤ין	א֤	inverted	מַהְפַּ֤ךְ
וַיִּקְרָ֧א	א֧	step	דַּרְגָּ֧א
הִנֵּה֩	א֩	small drawing out	תְּלִישָׁה־קְטַנָּה֩
וַיֹּ֨אמֶר	א֨	proceeding	קַדְמָ֨ה
תַּעֲשֶׂ֦ה	א֦	double *merekha*	מֵרְכָא־כְּפוּלָ֦ה
הָי֪וּ	א֪	wheel	גַּלְגַּ֪ל

Other Signs

Example	Symbol	Meaning of name	Name
שֹֽׁטְרֵי	אֽ	bridle reins	מֶֽתֶג
לְדֹרֹ֢תֵיכֶם	א֢	inclined	מָאיְלָ֢א
וְהַ֨מְּדָנִים	א֨	bridle reins	מְתִיגָ֨ה־זָקֵף
אֶת־שְׁמוֹ	־א	joiner	מַקֵּף־
יַעֲקֹב ׀ יַעֲקֹב	א ׀	separator	פָּסֵק ׀

Disjunctives with Their Proper Conjunctives

The following chart summarizes the conjunctives that may precede each disjunctive.

Disjunctive	First conjunctive	Second conjunctive	Third conj.	Fourth conj.	Fifth conj.	Sixth conj.
סִילֽוּק	מֵרְכָ֥א					
אֶתְנַחְתָּ֑א	מוּנַ֣ח	מוּנַ֣ח				
זָקֵ֔ף	מוּנַ֣ח	מוּנַ֣ח				
סֶגוֹל֒	מוּנַ֣ח	מוּנַ֣ח				
טִפְחָ֖א	מֵרְכָ֥א					
טִפְחָ֖א	מֵרְכָא־כְפוּלָ֦ה	דַּרְגָּ֧א				
רְבִ֗יעַ	מוּנַ֣ח	דַּרְגָּ֧א	מוּנַ֣ח			
פַּשְׁטָא֙	מֵרְכָ֥א or מַהְפַּ֤ךְ	קַדְמָ֨ה or מ֣וּנַח	תְּלִישָׁה֠	מוּנַ֣ח	מוּנַ֣ח	מוּנַ֣ח
זַרְקָא֮	מֵרְכָ֥א or מוּנַ֣ח	קַדְמָ֨ה or מ֣וּנַח	תְּלִישָׁה֠	מוּנַ֣ח		
תְּבִ֛יר	מֵרְכָ֥א or דַּרְגָּ֧א	קַדְמָ֨ה or מ֣וּנַח	תְּלִישָׁה֠	מוּנַ֣ח		
תְּ֠לִישָׁה	מוּנַ֣ח	מוּנַ֣ח	מוּנַ֣ח	מוּנַ֣ח	מוּנַ֣ח	
פָּזֵ֡ר	מוּנַ֣ח	מוּנַ֣ח	מוּנַ֣ח	מוּנַ֣ח	מוּנַ֣ח	
גֵּ֜רֵשׁ	קַדְמָ֨ה or מ֣וּנַח	תְּלִישָׁה֠	מוּנַ֣ח	מוּנַ֣ח	מוּנַ֣ח	
גֵּרְשַׁ֞ים	מ֣וּנַח					
לְגַרְמֵ֣הּ ׀	מֵרְכָ֥א	קַדְמָ֨ה or מ֣וּנַח				
פָּזֵר־גָּד֟וֹל	גַּלְגַּ֪ל	מוּנַ֣ח	מוּנַ֣ח	מוּנַ֣ח	מוּנַ֣ח	מוּנַ֣ח

The Power of Punctuation

Disjunctives can be classified by relative strength. This chart shows these *te'amim* arranged from strongest to weakest. The strongest are the ones that imply the greatest syntactic separation (the greatest power to separate words).

Category 1: סִילוּק אֶתְנַחְתָּ֑א

Category 2: סֶגוֹל֒ שַׁלְשֶׁ֓לֶת ׀ זָקֵ֔ף זָקֵ֕ף טִפְּחָ֖א

Category 3: רְבִ֗יעַ תְּבִ֛יר יְ֚תִיב פַּשְׁטָ֙א זַרְקָא֮

Category 4: לְגַרְמֵ֣הּ ׀ גֵּרְשַׁ֞יִם גֵּ֜רֶשׁ תְּלִישָׁה־גְּדוֹלָה פָּזֵר־גָּדוֹל פָּזֵ֡ר

Within Category 1, *siluk* (marking the end of the verse) is stronger than *etnaḥta* (marking the main division of the verse).

הַשֶּׁ֙מֶשׁ֙ יָצָ֣א עַל־הָאָ֔רֶץ וְל֖וֹט בָּ֥א צֹֽעֲרָה׃

Category 2 *te'amim* divide the space between the beginning of the verse and *etnaḥta*. Category 2 *te'amim* also divide the space between *etnaḥta* and *siluk*. Within the realm of Category 2, *segol* (or its substitute *shalshelet*) is the strongest. If there is no *segol* (or *shalshelet*), then either form of *zakef* is the strongest. If there are two consecutive *zakefs*, then the first one is stronger than the second. If none of those *te'amim* are present, then *tippeḥa* will be the only Category 2 *ta'am*.

הַשֶּׁ֙מֶשׁ֙ יָצָ֣א עַל־הָאָ֔רֶץ וְל֖וֹט בָּ֥א צֹֽעֲרָה׃

הָיְתָ֣ה עָלַי֮ יַד־יְהוָה֒ וַיּוֹצִאֵ֤נִי בְר֙וּחַ֙ יְהוָ֔ה וַיְנִיחֵ֖נִי בְּת֣וֹךְ הַבִּקְעָ֑ה

וַיֵּרָ֨א אֵלָ֤יו יְהוָה֙ בַּלַּ֣יְלָה הַה֔וּא וַיֹּ֕אמֶר אָנֹכִ֕י אֱלֹהֵ֖י אַבְרָהָ֣ם אָבִ֑יךָ

Category 3 *te'amim* divide the space bounded by any of the Category 2 *te'amim*. Of these, *revia* is the strongest. *Revia* will always be followed by at least one of the other four *te'amim* in that category. *Tevir* is part of a *tippeḥa* segment; either *yetiv* or *pashta* is part of a *zakef* segment; *zarka* is part of a *segol* segment. If any of the Category 3 *te'amim* appear consecutively, the first is the strongest.

וַיִּקְרָ֥א מֹשֶׁ֛ה לְכָל־זִקְנֵ֥י יִשְׂרָאֵ֖ל

וַיַּקְהֵ֣ל מֹשֶׁ֗ה אֶֽת־כָּל־עֲדַ֛ת בְּנֵ֥י יִשְׂרָאֵ֖ל

וַֽיַּחֲנוּ֙ בְּעַרְב֣וֹת מוֹאָ֔ב

וַתֹּ֤אמֶר שָׂרַי֙ אֶל־אַבְרָם֙ חֲמָסִ֣י עָלֶ֔יךָ

וַיֹּ֣אמֶר לְאָבִ֗יו יָקֻ֤ם אָבִי֙ וְיֹאכַל֙ מִצֵּ֣יד בְּנ֔וֹ

Category 4 *te'amim* divide the space bounded by any of the Category 3 *te'amim*. *Legarmeh* is almost always part of a *revia* segment. The others are less predictable.

אֹ֣רֶךְ ׀ הַיְרִיעָ֗ה הָֽאַחַ֑ת

וַיַּֽעֲשׂ֨וּ אֶת־הַפֶּ֜סַח בְּאַרְבָּעָ֨ה עָשָׂ֥ר י֛וֹם לַחֹ֖דֶשׁ

נֵֽלְכָ֞ה אַחֲרֵ֨י אֱלֹהִ֧ים אֲחֵרִ֛ים

Disjunctives That Cannot Be Preceded by Conjunctives

Conjunctives will *never* appear immediately before these disjunctives:

זָקֵף־גָּד֕וֹל, שַׁלְשֶׁ֓לֶת ׀, יְ֚תִיב.

Invariables

Conjunctives

- מַהְפַּ֤ךְ is always followed immediately by פַּשְׁטָ֙א.
- תְּ֠לִישָׁה is always followed immediately by קַדְמָ֨ה.
- גַּלְגַּ֪ל is always followed immediately by פָּזֵר־גָּד֟וֹל.
- מֵרְכָא־כְפוּלָ֦ה is always followed immediately by טִפְחָ֖א.

Disjunctives

- The disjunctive that follows תְּבִ֛יר is טִפְחָ֖א.
- The disjunctive that follows טִפְחָ֖א is סִלּֽוּק or אֶתְנַחְתָּ֑א.
- The disjunctive that follows זַרְקָ֮א is סֶגּוֹל֒.
- The disjunctive that follows לְגַרְמֵ֣הּ ׀ is רְבִ֗יעַ.
- The disjunctive that follows פַּשְׁטָ֙א is זָקֵ֔ף.
- The disjunctive that follows יְ֚תִיב is זָקֵ֔ף.
- זָקֵ֔ף is followed (eventually) by טִפְחָ֖א.
- זָקֵ֕ף is followed (eventually) by טִפְחָ֖א.
- רְבִ֗יעַ is followed (eventually) by פַּשְׁטָ֙א or זַרְקָ֮א or תְּבִ֛יר.
- סֶגּוֹל֒ is followed (eventually) by זָקֵ֔ף except for a few cases, where it is followed by טִפְחָ֖א.

Repeating Te'amim

Te'amim That Do Not Repeat

- סִלּֽוּק will occur once in each verse.
- אֶתְנַחְתָּ֑א will occur no more than once in a verse. *Etnaḥta* does not appear at all in 7 percent of the verses.
- סֶגּוֹל֒ will occur no more than once in a verse, and is never found after אֶתְנַחְתָּ֑א.

- שַׁלְשֶׁ֓לֶת ׀ will occur no more than once in a verse. (*Shalshelet* appears in only 7 verses.)
- פָּזֵ֟ר־גָּד֟וֹל will occur no more than once in each verse. (*Pazer gadol* appears in only 16 verses.)
- טִפְּחָ֖א will occur no more than once in each level-one segment (in other words, no more than once before *etnaḥta* and no more than once before *siluk*).

Te'amim Repeating on Consecutive Words

Some *te'amim* may be found on consecutive words. As a *ta'am* repeats within a segment, its strength diminishes.

- זָקֵ֔ף (*katon* and/or *gadol*) may repeat on consecutive words.
  (Gen. 26:24)... בַּלַּ֣יְלָה הַה֔וּא וַיֹּ֕אמֶר אָנֹכִ֕י אֱלֹהֵ֖י אַבְרָהָ֣ם אָבִ֑יךָ...
- פַּשְׁטָא֙ (and/or יְ֚תִיב) may repeat on consecutive words.
  (Gen. 27:31) ... יָקֻ֣ם אָבִ֗י וְיֹאכַל֙ מִצֵּ֣יד בְּנ֔וֹ ...
  (Exod. 38:30) ... וַיַּ֣עַשׂ בָּ֗הּ אֶת־אַדְנֵי֙ פֶּ֚תַח אֹ֣הֶל מוֹעֵ֔ד
  (Jer. 14:14) ... שֶׁ֚קֶר הַנְּבִאִים֙ נִבְּאִ֣ים בִּשְׁמִ֔י ...
- תְּבִ֛יר may repeat on consecutive words.
  (1 Kings 21:16) וַיָּ֣קָם אַחְאָ֗ב לָרֶ֛דֶת אֶל־כֶּ֛רֶם נָב֖וֹת הַיִּזְרְעֵאלִ֑י לְרִשְׁתּֽוֹ ...
- זַרְקָא֮ may repeat on consecutive words.
  (Isa. 45:14) ... וּסְחַר־כּוּשׁ֮ וּסְבָאִים֮ אַנְשֵׁ֣י מִדָּה֮ ...
- לְגַרְמֵ֣הּ ׀ may repeat on consecutive words.
  (Lev. 10:9) ... יַ֣יִן וְשֵׁכָ֞ר אַל־תֵּ֣שְׁתְּ ׀ אַתָּ֣ה ׀ וּבָנֶ֣יךָ
- פָּזֵ֡ר may repeat on consecutive words.
  (Num. 9:5) ... וַיַּעֲשׂ֡וּ אֶת־הַפֶּ֡סַח בָּרִאשׁ֡וֹן ...
- רְבִ֗יעַ may repeat, but not on consecutive words.
  (Deut. 17:8) ... כִּ֣י יִפָּלֵא֩ מִמְּךָ֨ דָבָ֜ר לַמִּשְׁפָּ֗ט בֵּֽין־דָּ֨ם ׀ לְדָ֜ם בֵּֽין־דִּ֤ין לְדִ֨ין
- גֵּ֜רֶשׁ (and/or גֵּרְשַׁ֞יִם) may repeat, but not on consecutive words.
  (Exod. 19:16) ... וַיְהִ֨י בַיּ֜וֹם הַשְּׁלִישִׁ֗י בִּֽהְיֹ֣ת הַבֹּ֮קֶר֒ וַיְהִי֩ קֹלֹ֨ת וּבְרָקִ֜ים
- תְּלִישָׁא־גְדוֹלָ֠ה may repeat, but not on consecutive words.
  (1 Sam. 17:51) ... וַיָּ֣רָץ דָּוִ֡ד וַיַּעֲמֹ֣ד אֶל־הַפְּלִשְׁתִּי֩ וַיִּקַּ֨ח אֶת־חַרְבּ֜וֹ ...
- Of the conjunctives, only מוּנַ֣ח may repeat on consecutive words.
  (Ezek. 48:21) ... וְהַנּוֹתָ֣ר לַנָּשִׂ֣יא מִזֶּ֣ה ׀ וּמִזֶּ֣ה ׀ לִתְרוּמַֽת־הַקֹּ֡דֶשׁ וְלַאֲחֻזַּ֣ת הָעִ֡יר

The 21 Books and the Three Books

The Hebrew Bible comprises 24 "books." These books are divided into three groups:

- *Torah*—The Five Books of Moses: Genesis, Exodus, Leviticus, Numbers, and Deuteronomy.
- *Nevi'im*—The Prophetic Books: Joshua, Judges, 1 Samuel, 2 Samuel, 1 Kings, 2 Kings, Isaiah, Jeremiah, Ezekiel, and the 12 "Minor" Prophets: Hosea, Joel, Amos, Obadiah, Jonah, Micah, Nahum, Habakkuk, Zephaniah, Haggai, Zechariah, and Malachi.
- *Ketuvim*—The Writings: Psalms, Proverbs, Job, Song of Songs, Ruth, Lamentations, Ecclesiastes, Esther, Daniel, Ezra, Nehemiah, 1 Chronicles, and 2 Chronicles.

If you bothered to count these books, you may have noticed that the total number of books is 39, not 24. The traditional numbering is arrived at by combining 1 and 2 Samuel, 1 and 2 Kings, the 12 minor prophets, Ezra and Nehemiah, and 1 and 2 Chronicles. Twenty-one of these 24 books (ספרי כ"א) are called the "prose books," even though poetic style is not entirely absent. These are punctuated with the *te'amim* that we are studying.

Three of the 24 books are known as "poetic books." These are (most of) Job (איוב), Proverbs (משלי), and Psalms (תהלים), known collectively by their acronym, ספרי אמ"ת. Most of the verses in these books are short and have a clear binary poetic structure. You'll recognize the *te'amim* in these books, but their application is quite different from what we are used to in the other books. The tradition for chanting these *te'amim* has been lost in almost every Jewish community.

A verse from Psalms (6:6)

כִּ֤י אֵ֣ין בַּמָּ֣וֶת זִכְרֶ֑ךָ   בִּ֝שְׁא֗וֹל מִ֣י יֽוֹדֶה־לָּֽךְ׃

For there is no praise of You among the dead;
in Sheol, who can acclaim You?

A verse from Proverbs (1:5)

יִשְׁמַ֣ע חָ֭כָם וְי֣וֹסֶף לֶ֑קַח   וְ֝נָב֗וֹן תַּחְבֻּל֥וֹת יִקְנֶֽה׃

The wise man, hearing them, will gain more wisdom;
The discerning man will learn to be adroit.

A verse from Job (3:10)

כִּ֤י לֹ֣א סָ֭גַר דַּלְתֵ֣י בִטְנִ֑י   וַיַּסְתֵּ֥ר עָ֝מָ֗ל מֵעֵינָֽי׃

Because it did not block my mother's womb,
And hide trouble from my eyes.

12. Troubleshooting

We can fix it before it goes wrong.

Commonly Confused *Te'amim*

Yetiv and *Mahpakh*

- *Yetiv* is placed just before the word. *Mahpakh* is placed under the first letter of the stressed syllable.
- If there is a vowel under the letter, *yetiv* will always be found to the right of a vowel. *Mahpakh* is placed just to the left of the vowel.
- *Yetiv* is a disjunctive indicating a slight separation from the following word. *Mahpakh* is a conjunctive, indicating a connection with the following word.

Yetiv	*Mahpakh*
כִּ֚י	כִּ֤י
א֚וֹ	א֤וֹ
עֵ֚שֶׂב	עֵ֤שֶׂב

- *Mahpakh* is *always* followed by *pashta*.
  (Gen. 4:18) וַיִּוָּלֵ֤ד לַחֲנוֹךְ֙ אֶת־עִירָ֔ד
- *Yetiv* is usually followed by *zakef katon* (or by *munaḥ zakef katon*).
  (Lev. 5:23) א֚וֹ אֶת־הַפִּקָּד֔וֹן
  (Deut. 11:30) דֶּ֚רֶךְ מְב֣וֹא הַשֶּׁ֔מֶשׁ

Kadmah and *Pashta*

- *Pashta* is placed over the left edge of the last letter of the word. *Kadmah* is placed over the center of the first letter of the stressed syllable.
- *Pashta* is a disjunctive indicating a slight separation from the following word. *Kadmah* is a conjunctive, indicating (in most cases) a connection with the following word.
- If the *pashta* word isn't accented on the last syllable, a second *pashta* is placed over the first letter of the stressed syllable. *Kadmah* is never doubled.

pashta	*kadmah*
וְאֵת֙	וְאֵ֨ת
אֲשֶׁר֙	אֲשֶׁ֨ר
זֶ֙רַע֙	זֶ֨רַע

Telishah Ketanah and *Telishah Gedolah*

- *Telishah ketanah* is placed over the left edge of the last letter of the word. *Telishah gedolah* is placed over the right edge of the first letter of the word.
- *Telishah ketanah* is a conjunctive, indicating a connection with the following word. *Telishah gedolah* is a (minor) disjunctive, indicating a slight separation from the following word.

Telishah gedolah	*Telishah ketanah*
אֲ֠שֶׁר	אֲשֶׁר֩
הִ֠נֵּה	הִנֵּה֩
אִ֠תְּךָ	אֶרֶץ֩

Merekha-Tippeḥa and *Tippeḥa/Merekha*

Some readers confuse טִפְּחָ֖א מֵרְכָ֥א with מֵרְכָ֥א טִפְּחָ֖א. You don't think that makes a difference? Read on! A word marked with *merekha* is connected in meaning to the word that follows, while *tippeḥa* indicates a slight separation. Look at this verse (Num. 25:9). How many people died in the plague?

וַיִּהְי֔וּ הַמֵּתִ֖ים בַּמַּגֵּפָ֑ה אַרְבָּעָ֥ה וְעֶשְׂרִ֖ים אָֽלֶף׃

Had the punctuation been אַרְבָּעָ֖ה וְעֶשְׂרִ֥ים אָֽלֶף, we would translate that phrase as "four and twenty thousand (20,004)." But with the punctuation אַרְבָּעָ֥ה וְעֶשְׂרִ֖ים אָֽלֶף, the meaning is "twenty-four thousand (24,000)."

Legarmeh and *Munaḥ-Pasek*

Taken out of context, *legarmeh* and *munaḥ-pasek* look exactly alike.

To differentiate between them, you'll need to scan ahead several words.

- *Legarmeh* is followed by *munaḥ revia*. For example: בְּעֶ֣צֶם ׀ הַיּ֣וֹם הַזֶּ֗ה
- Occasionally a second *legarmeh* or *geresh* or *darga* may intervene between *legarmeh* and *munaḥ revia.*
- In all other circumstances, the *te'amim* in question will be a *munaḥ* followed by a *pasek*. For example: הֲלָהֵ֣ן ׀ תְּשַׂבֵּ֗רְנָה

Meteg and *Siluk*

The symbols for *meteg* and *siluk* look identical.

- *Siluk* marks the last word in a verse. In most books, it is followed by the *sof-pasuk* sign (:).
- *Siluk* is placed under the first letter of the stressed syllable. For example: וַֽיְהִי־עֶ֥רֶב וַֽיְהִי־בֹ֖קֶר י֥וֹם שְׁלִישִֽׁי׃ (Gen. 1:13)
- *Meteg* is a *secondary* accent: It will never appear alone on a word without that word's primary accent. The primary accent is placed on the stressed syllable. *Meteg* indicates a secondary word stress, usually two syllables before the primary stress. For example: לְמִֽינֵהֶֽם.

Errors in Rhythm

Pausing Too Long after *Tevir*

Don't forget that the pause after *tevir* is shorter than the pause after *tippeḥa*. What would this clause mean if you read it (Exod. 31:15) with a long pause after מְלָאכָה ?

Anyone who works on the Sabbath will be put to death.

כָּל־הָעֹשֶׂה מְלָאכָה בְּיוֹם הַשַּׁבָּת מוֹת יוּמָת

Anyone who works on the Sabbath will be put to death.

כָּל־הָעֹשֶׂה מְלָאכָה בְּיוֹם הַשַּׁבָּת מוֹת יוּמָת

Anyone who works on the Sabbath will be put to death.

כָּל־הָעֹשֶׂה מְלָאכָה בְּיוֹם הַשַּׁבָּת מוֹת יוּמָת

Pausing Too Long after *Telishah Ketanah*

In the sequence תְּלִישָׁה קַדְמָה גֵּרֵשׁ, you must determine, based on the meaning of the words, whether to connect *telishah* with *kadmah* or *kadmah* with *geresh*. In the following example, the connection between the first two words is greater than that between the second two. So avoid any pause after the first word.

וּבְאַרְבַּע עֶשְׂרֵה שָׁנָה

Pausing Too Long before "Amen"

After the person who has been called up to the Torah has chanted the blessing, you should respond "amen." Do *not* wait until just before beginning the cantillation, and do *not* look in the Torah scroll when chanting "amen."

Commonly Mispronounced Consonants

Mappik-he

The letter ה at the end of a word is normally silent. However, the letter הּ (with a dot inside) at the end of a word is an aspirated consonant. Be careful—mispronunciation could affect the meaning of the word.

to the land	אַרְצָה	*her land*	אַרְצָהּ
woman	אִשָּׁה	*her husband*	אִישָׁהּ
queen	מַלְכָּה	*her king*	מַלְכָּהּ

Alef

The letter א is silent when it has no vowel sign under (or after) it. But when it is followed by a vowel sign, א is a consonant, a glottal plosive.

Compare and probounce these words:

בָּא	*he came*	בָּאָה (בָּ אָה)	*she came*
מָלַךְ (מָ לַךְ)	*he ruled*	מַלְאַךְ (מַל אַךְ)	*angel (messenger)*
יָשִׁיר (יָ שִׁיר)	*he will sing*	יַשְׁאִיר (יַשְׁ אִיר)	*he will leave*

וֺ and וּ as Consonants

Sometimes *vav* appearing as וֹ or וּ is pronounced as a consonant.

- Remember: every syllable begins with a consonant
- In these examples, וֹ is not a *ḥolam* but the consonant *vav* followed by the *ḥolam* dot.

עָוֺן	'a-VŐN	(Gen. 15:16)	*sin*
עֵדְוֺתָיו	'éd-vó-TAV	(2 Kings 23:3)	*His injunctions*
דְוֺתָה	d^e-vó-TAH	(Lev. 12:2)	*her menstrual infirmity*

- In these examples, וּ is not a *shuruk* but the consonant *vav* with *dagesh ḥazak.*

מְצַוְּךָ	m^e-tsav-v^e-KHA	(Deut. 4:40)	*command you*
יְקַוּוּ	y^e-kav-VU	(Isa. 51:5)	*shall wait*
הִוָּסְדָה	hiv-va-s^e-DA	(Exod. 9:18)	*its founding*
חַוָּה	ḥav-VA	(Gen. 3:20)	*Eve*

Commonly Mispronounced Vowels

Kamats Katan

Kamats katan (ָ in a closed, unaccented syllable) is pronounced "aw" as in "chalk." It is a short vowel and should be chanted quite rapidly. The *hataf-kamats* (ֳ) is pronounced the same way. Read each of the following words.

וַיָּקָם   חֳדָשִׁים   חָכְמָה   עָזִּי

Sheva na

The vowel *sheva* (שְׁוָא) has two pronunciations in Hebrew.

- *sheva na* (שְׁוָא נָע) *Sheva* at the beginning of a syllable is pronounced like the first vowel in the word "above" (or, in the Israeli inflection, like a very short "eh").
- *sheva naḥ* (שְׁוָא נָח) *Sheva* at the end of a syllable is silent.

Practice reading the following words.

silent *sheva*

מֶלֶךְ   הַמַּלְכָּה

sheva as a short vowel

וַיֹּאמְרוּ   בְּנֵי

Sometimes mispronouncing *sheva* could change the meaning of the word.

וַיִּֽירְאוּ is pronounced with a vocal *sheva*. It means "they feared."

וַיִּרְאוּ is pronounced with a silent *sheva*. It means "they saw."

Confusing וְ and וַ

Be careful! The change of a vowel under the prefix ו from *sheva* to *pataḥ* may result in a change in the meaning of the word. Compare the following pairs.

וְתִשְׁכַּב	*and you shall lie*	וַתִּשְׁכַּב	*she lay*
וְיִרְאֶה	*and let him see*	וַיִּרְאֶה	*he saw*

Confusing לְ and לַ; בְּ and בַּ

Be careful! The change of a vowel under the prefixes ל and ב from *sheva* to *pataḥ* (or *kamats* instead of *pataḥ* before certain letters) may result in a change in the meaning of the word. Compare the following pairs.

בְּעִיר	*in a city*	בָּעִיר	*in the city*
לְאִישׁ	*to a man*	לָאִישׁ	*to the man*

Prefixes before the Sacred Name of God

When the prefixes לַ כַּ בַּ וְ are added to the words אֲדֹנָי, אֲדֹנִי and אֱלֹהִים (also when spelled יהוה), the first two syllables become assimilated and the א is silent.

(Gen. 24:3) ba-dó-NAY	בַּיהוָה
(Ps. 73:28) ba-dó-NAY	בַּאדֹנָי
(Gen. 18:30) la-dó-NAY	לַאדֹנָי
(Exod. 8:6) ka-dó-NAY	כַּיהוָה
(Gen. 17:7) lé-ló-HÍM	לֵאלֹהִים
(1 Sam. 14:37) bé-ló-HÍM	בֵּאלֹהִים
(Gen. 3:5) ké-ló-HÍM	כֵּאלֹהִים
(1 Sam. 2:2) ké-ló-HÉ-nu	כֵּאלֹהֵינוּ
(Gen. 46:1) lé-ló-HÉ	לֵאלֹהֵי
(Gen. 13:14) va-dó-NAY	וַיהוָה
(Isa. 49:14) va-dó-NAY	וַאדֹנָי
(Gen. 50:24) vé-ló-HÍM	וֵאלֹהִים
(Ps. 115:3) vé-ló-HÉ-nu	וֵאלֹהֵינוּ

Incorrect Syllabic Stress

In some cases, a change of syllabic stress can result in a change of meaning. Be careful! Sing the core of each *ta'am* on the accented syllable.

Compare the following pairs:

בָּאָה	*she is coming*	בָּאָה	*she came*

וְשָׁ֣בוּ	*they returned*	שָׁ֣בוּ	*they captured*
וּמָֽשַׁחְתָּ֣	*you shall anoint*	מָֽשַׁ֨חְתָּ	*you anointed*

Biblical Hebrew and Contemporary Hebrew

The reader should be careful not to confuse contemporary colloquial pronunciation with the more formal pronunciation required for liturgical reading of classical texts.

מֹשֶׁ֔ה	accent the last syllable
צִפֹּרָ֜ה	accent the last syllable
אַהֲרֹ֔ן	accent the last syllable
דָּוִֽד	accent the last syllable
אַרְבַּ֣ע	accent the last syllable
אֲחֵיהֶ֥ם	accent the last syllable
שְׁמֹנֶ֥ה	accent the last syllable and *sheva na* under the first letter
שְׁלֹמֹֽה	accent the last syllable and *sheva na* under the first letter
צָ֣רְפַּ֔ת	*kamats gadol* and *sheva na* under the second letter
שְׁנֵ֥ים עָשָׂ֖ר	*sheva na* under the first letter
שְׁתֵּ֣י	*sheva naḥ* (silent) under the first letter
צְאֶ֣ינָה	*sheva na* under the first letter
הַסְתָּ֖יו	*sheva na* under the second letter
זְמָ֑ן	*sheva na* under the first letter

Glossary

accents	The graphic symbols used to notate the cantillation motifs.
acrostic	A literary structure in which a name or message can be deciphered by reading just the first letter of each line in sequence. In an alphabetical acrostic, each line begins with a successive letter of the alphabet.
aliyah	(Hebrew; literally, "going up") Calling a congregant to cantillate a portion of the Torah pericope, or (more commonly) to stand by the designated reader and chant a blessing before and after the cantillation.
apposition	A noun that identifies another noun. Generally, one of the pair is a name and the other is a title or relationship, e.g., King David, Uncle Sam.
Arukh Ha-shulḥan	(Hebrew) A commentary on the *Shulḥan Arukh* written by Rabbi Yeḥiel Epstein (1829–1908, Belorussia).
ati-marḥik	(Aramaic) See "conjunctive dagesh."
azla	(Aramaic) (1) Another name for the accent *geresh*, when the word on which it is placed is stressed on the last syllable. (2) Another name for the accent *kadmah*.
azla legarmeh	(Aramaic/Hebrew) A disjunctive accent in the poetic books.
ba'al keri'ah	(Hebrew; plural: *ba'aley keri'ah*) Literally, "the master of the reading." One who is qualified to cantillate.
b.c.e.	Before the common (Christian) era.
cadence	A musical motif that conveys the impression of a (partial or complete) conclusion.
cantillation	The art of chanting Scripture in a liturgical context, according to ancient traditional melodies, unaccompanied, in a free rhythm.
c.e.	The common (Christian) era.
chironomy	A system of hand signals used by a prompter to represent the melodies of the *te'amim*.
circule	A sign, resembling a superscript °, placed over a word in the text of the Hebrew Bible, to indicate the presence of a relevant Masoretic note in the margin.
clause	A group of words that comprises a subject and (usually) a verb (and, optionally, other complements of the verb). An independent clause is one that can stand by itself. A dependent clause is one that functions as a complement of the main verb (either as noun, adjective, or adverb).

closed syllable	A syllable consisting of a consonant followed by a vowel followed by a consonant (or, rarely, two consonants).
codex	A book consisting of multiple pages that are gathered and bound together on the same side.
combined pericope	See "*parashah meḥubberet.*"
complement	As used in this book, a word—whether subject, object, adverb, or indirect object—that gives some information about its verb. (E.g., who is doing the action? To whom is it being done? How or when or where is it being done?)
conjunctive	A word that is connected in meaning to the next word.
conjunctive *dagesh*	A *dagesh* that appears in the first letter of a word that is stressed on the first syllable and that follows a word that is stressed on the penultimate syllable and ends with an open syllable with a *segol* or *kamats* vowel. For example: מִי־אֵ֫לֶּה לָּךְ. The conjunctive *dagesh* may also appear after *kamats-he-makkef, pataḥ-he-makkef,* or *segol-he-makkef.* For example: מַה־לָּךְ.
conjunctive soft form	A word beginning with ב ג ד כ פ ת without a *dagesh*, following a word marked with a conjunctive accent and ending with an open syllable.
consonantal text	The original "proto-Masoretic" text of the Bible as it appears in a liturgical scroll, without vowels, consonant modifiers, cantillation accents, verse numbers, or chapter numbers.
construct	(Hebrew: *semikhut*) A noun that belongs to another noun. For example, בְּנֵי הַמֶּלֶךְ "the sons of the king." The word בְּנֵי (the sons of) is in the construct state.
coordinate nouns	Two objects closely associated with each other, forming an idiomatic unit. For example, "day and night."
core	The portion of the melody that is sung on the stressed syllable.
dagesh ḥazak	A dot that elongates the constriction of a consonant.
dagesh kal	A dot that transforms the letters ב ג ד כ פ ת from their soft (fricative) forms to their hard (plosive) forms.
darga	(Aramaic) A conjunctive accent.
Decalogue	The "Ten Commandments" found in Exodus 20 and, in another version, Deuteronomy 6.
defective spelling	A spelling in which the "matres lectionis" are not used to indicate vowels.
deḥiy	(Aramaic) A disjunctive accent in the poetic books.
deḥik	(Aramaic) See "conjunctive dagesh."
dichotomy	The subdivision of the syntactic unit into two smaller units.

diphthong	A compound vowel, consisting of an initial long vowel sound and a final vanishing vowel sound. For example, in English, the word "low" contains a diphthong. In Hebrew, the word הוֹי contains a diphthong.
directional suffix	See "locative suffix."
disjunctive	A word that is (to some degree) separated in meaning from the word that follows.
distributive repetition	A word that is repeated to indicate constancy. For example, יוֹם יוֹם, "each day."
Ekhah	(Hebrew) The biblical Book of Lamentations.
ekphonetic	A form of notation that indicates inflection patterns and serves as a reminder of musical motifs, but does not indicate absolute pitch.
elision	As used in this book, a reallocation of notes to syllables. For example, if a disjunctive word is monosyllabic (or is stressed on its first syllable), its pick-up note(s) will be sung at the end of the preceding conjunctive.
elliptical parallelism	A form of parallelism in which one or more words are "missing" (or, implied rather than explicitly restated) in the second part of the sentence. For example, נָאווּ לְחָיַיִךְ בַּתֹּרִים צַוָּארֵךְ בַּחֲרוּזִים, *Your cheeks are beautiful with wreaths; your neck [is beautiful] with jewelry* (Songs 1:10).
emphatic repetition	A word that is repeated for intensification. For example, שָׁלוֹם ׀ שָׁלוֹם, *perfect peace.*
enclitic	a word that, by nature of its semantic meaning, tends to be connected with the preceding word with a *makkef.* For example: ־נָא.
etnaḥta	(Aramaic) An accent that is used to mark the first major subdivision in most biblical verses.
euphonic *meteg*	A *meteg* that appears on a short vowel in a closed, unstressed syllable. The euphonic *meteg* may be also found coupled with a *sheva na* or even on a syllable that follows the primary accent. The euphonic *meteg* does not indicate a secondary accent, as does a normal *meteg.* Its function seems to be to caution the reader not to gloss over the unstressed syllable too quickly.
focus marker	A name (or noun or pronoun) placed for emphasis at the beginning of a clause. Generally it has a redundant reference later in the same clause. For example, שָׂרַי אִשְׁתְּךָ לֹא־תִקְרָא אֶת־שְׁמָהּ שָׂרָי — *As for your wife Sarai, her name will no longer be known as Sarai* (Gen. 17:15).
full spelling	A spelling in which the "matres lectionis" are used to indicate vowels.
furtive *pataḥ*	A *pataḥ* vowel appearing under a final ה, ח, or ע. The vowel is pronounced before, rather than after, the consonant under which it appears.

gabbai	(Hebrew) A synagogue functionary who stands next to the Torah reader, ensuring that the latter makes no serious errors in the cantillation and pronunciation. The first *gabbai* also calls the *olim* to the Torah.
galgal	(Hebrew) A rare conjunctive accent serving *pazer gadol.*
ga'ya	(Hebrew) See "*meteg.*"
gemination	The doubling of a consonant. See "*dagesh ḥazak.*"
geresh	(Hebrew) A level-four disjunctive accent.
gereshayim	(Hebrew) A level-four disjunctive accent.
glottal plosive	A consonant created by the constriction and subsequent sudden release of the vocal chords. The sound of א when it is followed by a vowel.
guttural letters	Letters whose sound is produced in the throat: א ה ח ע ר.
haftarah	(Hebrew) A lection from the Prophetic books cantillated in the synagogue.
halakhah	(Hebrew) Jewish law.
ḥaser	(Hebrew) See "defective spelling."
hendiadys	A single concept expressed by two words linked by a conjunction, e.g., וְנִין וָנֶכֶד, *kith and kin* (Isa. 14:22).
hiatus form	A change of syllabic stress from penultimate (מלעל) to ultima (מלרע) in certain words that end with an open syllable and are followed by a word that begins with א, ה, or ע.
Ḥol Ha-mo'ed	(Hebrew) The intermediate days of the holidays of Pesaḥ and Sukkot.
illuy	(Aramaic) (1) A conjunctive accent, also known as *munaḥ.* (2) A conjunctive accent in the poetic books.
immot ha-keri'ah	(Hebrew) See "matres lectionis."
infinitive absolute	A verb in its normal inflection paired with its infinitive form. The meaning of the verb is thus intensified. For example, מוֹת תָּמוּת, *you will surely die* (Gen. 2:17).
intransitive complement	A word or phrase that follows a nontransitive verb and describes its subject. E.g., I am *blue.* Her name is *Sarah.* It was full *of bones.*
Kaddish	(Aramaic) A Jewish doxology (prayer attesting to God's everlasting glory), chanted at the conclusion of a section of the liturgical service. A short form of the *Kaddish* is usually chanted at the conclusion of the Torah cantillation.
kadmah	(Aramaic) A conjunctive accent.
kamats katan	(Hebrew) A vowel pronounced as a short "o." A *kamats* in an unstressed closed syllable is a *kamats katan.* A *ḥataf-kamats* (*kamats* with two dots) is also a *kamats katan.*

karney-farah	(Hebrew) See "*pazer gadol.*"
kerey	(Aramaic) An oral tradition in which certain words in the Bible are pronounced differently from the way they are written (*ketiv*).
ketiv	(Aramaic) The written form of certain words in the Bible that, for various reasons, came to be pronounced differently (*kerey*).
Ketuvim	(Hebrew) The Hagiographa, the third section of the Bible.
Kohelet	(Hebrew) The biblical Book of Ecclesiastes.
Kohen	(Hebrew) (1) A priest. (2) Any Jew who is a (patriarchal) descendant of Aaron the High Priest.
korey	(Hebrew) Reader, or one who cantillates.
lection	The liturgical reading of a text selected from the Bible.
legarmeh	(Hebrew) A level-four disjunctive accent.
leyenen	(Yiddish) See "cantillation."
locative suffix	The suffix *kamats-he* used to indicate direction. For example, הָעִ֫ירָה is the equivalent of אֶל־הָעִ֫יר, *to the city*.
logogenic	Music whose rhythm is derived from the natural rhythms of speech.
Maharil	See "Möllin, Jacob."
maftir	(Hebrew) The person called for the final *aliyah* on festivals, High Holidays, Shabbat, and public fast days. After the Torah is put away, the *maftir* chants the *haftarah*.
mahpakh	(Aramaic) A conjunctive accent serving *pashta*.
mahpakh legarmeh	(Aramaic/Hebrew) A disjunctive accent in the poetic books.
makkef	A symbol resembling a hyphen, used to join two (or more) (usually short) words into a larger word-unit.
male	(Hebrew) See "full spelling."
mappik	(Hebrew) A dot placed inside the letter ה at the end of a word, to change its pronunciation from silent to aspirate. A *mappik* is also found in the letter א four times in the Bible.
Masoretic text	A Bible that incorporates material developed by Tiberian rabbis between the sixth and eighth centuries. This material, developed to preserve the integrity of the text as well as to ensure correct reading, includes graphic symbols to represent the inflection patterns (*te'amim*) and vowels and consonant modifiers (*nekudot*), as well as marginal notes on the form of the words (*masorah*).
matres lectionis	(Latin) Four letters (א ה ו י) that can be used as consonants or vowels.
mayela	(Aramaic) A secondary accent (resembling *tippeḥa*) that is found on the same word as *siluk* or *etnaḥta*.

megillah	(Hebrew) (1) Scroll. (2) Any of the five books of Esther, Lamentations, Ruth, Ecclesiastes, or Song of Songs. (3) The Book of Esther.
melisma	A syllable that is chanted to a long string of pitches.
merekha	(Aramaic) A conjunctive accent.
merekha khefulah	(Aramaic) A rare conjunctive accent.
meteg	(Hebrew) An accent that is used to indicate secondary stress and vowel lengthening.
metigah	(Aramaic) A secondary accent (resembling *kadmah*) that is found on the same word as *zakef.*
mille'el	(Aramaic) A word accented on the penultimate (next-to-last) syllable.
millera	(Aramaic) A word accented on the ultima (last syllable).
minyan	(Hebrew) The quorum for prayer, consisting of 10 adult (male) Jews.
Mishnah	(Hebrew) A code of Jewish law compiled in Palestine, c. 200 C.E.
Mishnah Berurah	(Hebrew) A commentary on the *Shulḥan Arukh* written by Rabbi Yisrael Meir Ha-Cohen Kagan (Radin, Poland; known as "The Chafetz Chayim"), published between 1884 and 1912.
mitzvah	(Hebrew) A sacred commandment, a good deed.
Möllin, Jacob	Ashkenazic rabbi and cantor (c. 1360–1427), known as the "Maharil."
munaḥ	(Hebrew) A conjunctive accent.
nasog aḥor	(Hebrew) See "retraction."
nekudot	Tiberian vocalization symbols used to indicate vowels and gemination, and to distinguish between the double pronunciations of the following letters: ב ג ד ה כ פ ש ת.
nested segment	A segment that is subsumed within a larger segment.
Nevi'im	(Hebrew) The Prophetic books of the Bible
nominal clause	A clause without an expressed verb. For example, מְרַגְּלִים אַתֶּם, meaning, "you [are] spies."
nominal complement	A complement in a nominal (verbless) clause.
oleh	(Hebrew) One who is called to the Torah for an *aliyah*.
oleh veyored	(Hebrew) A disjunctive accent in the poetic books.
open syllable	A syllable consisting of a consonant followed by a vowel.
parallelism	An organizing principle in biblical poetry in which each verse is divided into two sections, the second of which complements the first.

parashah	(Hebrew) (pl. *parashiyot*) (1) A paragraph of text in a biblical scroll. A *parashah setumah* (sealed paragraph) ends with blank space equivalent to the size of nine letters; the next paragraph will begin on the same line. A *parashah petuḥah* (open paragraph) ends with a blank space extending to the end of the column; the next paragraph will begin on a new line. (2) See "pericope."
parashah meḥubberet	A lection comprising two pericopes that have combined to accommodate the Jewish leap-year calendar.
parse	To analyze the syntactic structure of a sentence.
particle	A (usually) short word that is neither noun, verb, adjective, nor adverb. Particles connect to other words (e.g., prepositions, conjunctions, negatives) or are in some way marginal to the sentence structure (e.g., exclamations).
pasek	(Hebrew) A brief pause after a conjunctive word, indicated by a long vertical line following the word.
pashta	(Aramaic) A level-three disjunctive accent.
pataḥ genuvah	(Hebrew) See "furtive *pataḥ*."
pausal form	A change in the pronunciation of a word that comes at the end of a sentence or at the end of a major division of a sentence. Most often this mutation will coincide with *siluk* and/or *etnaḥta*.
patronym	A means of identifying an individual by his/her relationship with his/her father. For example, שְׁכֶם בֶּן־חֲמוֹר, *Shekhem son-of-Ḥamor*.
pazer	(Hebrew) (1) A level-four disjunctive accent. Also known as "*pazer katan*." (2) A disjunctive accent in the poetic books.
pazer gadol	(Hebrew) A rare level-four disjunctive accent. Also known as "*karney-farah*."
pericope	(p^e-RI-k^e-pi) A selection from a book, a lection, or a section of the Bible that is read or chanted as part of a public worship service.
Pesaḥ	(Hebrew) The festival of Passover.
phrase	A group of words used in place of a single word. All the words in a phrase (in biblical Hebrew) are grouped together to function as a noun or an adverb.
pick-up	The portion of the melody that is sung on any syllables that may precede the stressed syllable.
poetic books	Psalms, Proverbs, and (most of the Book of) Job, known in Hebrew by their acronym, ספרי אמת. The cantillation accents for the poetic books are different from those that appear in the rest of the Bible (the "prose" books).
postpositive	An accent that is placed invariably at the very end of the word.
predicate nominative	A noun that follows a copulative verb. For example, "It is *I*."

prepositive	An accent that is placed invariably at the very beginning of the word.
proclitic	A word that, by nature of its semantic meaning, tends to be connected with the following word. A proclitic word is marked with either a conjunctive accent or a *makkef*.
prose books	A designation of all of the Bible other than Psalms, Proverbs, and (most of the book of) Job; known also as "the 21 books."
Purim	(Hebrew) The Jewish holiday celebrating the victory of Mordecai and Esther over the Persian viceroy, Haman.
quotative frame	A clause containing the verb of speaking and, optionally, common nouns, pronouns, or names identifying the speaker and the person being addressed, and adverbs modifying the verb of speaking.
rafeh	The soft (fricative) forms of the letters ב ג ד כ פ ת.
remote conjunctive	A conjunctive word that is followed by another conjunctive word.
retraction	The shifting of syllabic stress from ultima (מִלְּרַע) to penultimate (מִלְּעֵל) (or even antepenultimate). This shift may occur on a conjunctive word when the subsequent word is stressed on its first syllable.
revia	(Aramaic) An initial (or median) level-three disjunctive accent.
revia gadol	(Aramaic/Hebrew) A disjunctive accent in the poetic books.
revia katon	(Aramaic/Hebrew) A disjunctive accent in the poetic books.
revia mugrash	(Aramaic/Hebrew) A disjunctive accent in the poetic books.
ritardando	(Italian) The process of slowing the tempo (the speed).
Rosh Hashanah	(Hebrew) The Jewish New Year holiday.
segment	A group of words ending with a disjunctive. Any words subsumed under a parsing bracket (at any level).
Sephardic	(Hebrew) As used in this book, a contemporary pronunciation of Hebrew, derived from that of Spanish Jews, and adopted as the official pronunciation in the State of Israel.
Septuagint	The ancient Jewish translation of the Bible into Greek. The oldest portion may date from third-century B.C.E. Alexandria.
segol	(Hebrew) An initial level-two disjunctive accent.
sentence	A group of words that (generally) represents a complete thought. A simple sentence consists of a single clause. A compound sentence comprises two or more clauses.
sevirin	(Aramaic) A Masoretic marginal note indicating that the text is correct as written and not in another variant form.
Shabbat	(Hebrew) (pl. *Shabbatot*) The Jewish Sabbath.
shaḥarit	(Hebrew) The morning service.

shalshelet	(Hebrew) A rare initial level-two disjunctive accent.
shalshelet gedolah	(Hebrew) A disjunctive accent in the poetic books.
shalshelet ketanah	(Hebrew) A conjunctive accent in the poetic books.
Shavuot	(Hebrew) The Feats of Weeks, also known as Pentecost.
sheliaḥ tsibbur	(Hebrew) A representative of the congregation who serves as precentor (cantor), leading the chanting of the prayers.
Shemini Atzeret	(Hebrew) See "Sukkot."
sheva	(Hebrew שְׁוָא) A Tiberian pronunciation symbol. *Sheva na* (vocal *sheva*) is an ultra short neutral vowel. *Sheva naḥ* (silent *sheva*) has no sound. *Sheva meraḥef* (intermediate *sheva*) likewise has no sound.
Shir Ha-shirim	(Hebrew) The biblical Song of Songs.
Shulḥan Arukh	(Hebrew) A code of Jewish law written by Joseph Karo in Tiberias and published in 1567.
siddur	(Hebrew) Prayer book (literally, "the order" of prayers).
siluk	(Hebrew) The *ta'am* signifying the end of a biblical verse.
Simḥat Torah	(Hebrew) See "Sukkot."
sofer	(Hebrew) A scribe, an accomplished scholar, skilled in the exact copying of the Bible.
stepping segments	A sequence of segments of descending syntactic disjunction. E.g., a segment ending in *segol* followed by a segment ending in *zakef*, followed by a segment ending in *tippeḥa*.
sublinear accent	An accent that is placed underneath the word.
Sukkot	(Hebrew) The Festival of Booths, also known as Tabernacles. The last days of the festival are known as Shemini Atzeret (the eighth day of the assembly) and Simḥat Torah (rejoicing of the Torah).
superlinear accent	An accent that is placed over the word.
syllabic	A style of chanting in which generally only one note is sung to each syllable.
ta'am	(Hebrew; plural *te'amim* or *ta'amey ha-mikra*) See "accent."
ta'amey ha-'elyon	(Hebrew) A set of accents used for the public liturgical cantillation of three biblical passages (the Decalogue in Exodus 20, the Decalogue in Deuteronomy 5, and the Saga of *Re'uven* in Genesis 35:22), each of which is punctuated with two sets of accents: the *ta'amey ha-taḥton* (low accents), used for private reading, and the *ta'amey ha-'elyon* (high accents), used for public liturgical cantillation.
ta'amey ha-taḥton	(Hebrew) A set of accents used for private reading of three biblical passages. See "*ta'amey ha-'elyon.*"

tag	(Hebrew) A crownlet, a form of decoration consisting of three small strokes rising from the top of certain letters in a liturgical scroll.
Talmud	(Hebrew) A compilation of Jewish law and lore accumulated over a period of seven centuries (c. 200 B.C.E.–c. 500 C.E.) in Palestine (the Jerusalem Talmud) and Babylonia (the Babylonian Talmud). The Talmud comprises the Mishnah, an older compilation, and the Gemara, which elaborates and explicates the Mishnah.
TANAKH	(Hebrew) An acronym for Torah, Nevi'im, Ketuvim; the Hebrew Bible.
Targum	(Aramaic) The ancient Jewish translation of the Bible into Aramaic.
tarḥa	(Aramaic) A conjunctive accent in the poetic books.
te'amim	See "*ta'am*."
telishah gedolah	(Aramaic/Hebrew) A level-four disjunctive accent.
telishah ketanah	(Aramaic/Hebrew) A remote conjunctive accent.
tevir	(Aramaic) A level-three disjunctive accent.
tippeḥa	(Aramaic) The final level-two disjunctive accent.
Tish'ah Be'Av	(Hebrew) The ninth day of the Jewish month of Av, a fast day commemorating many tragic events, including the destruction (twice) of the central sanctuary in Jerusalem.
tokheḥah	(Hebrew) A passage in the Torah that rebukes the Israelites for their sins. The longest of these passages are Lev. 26:14–41, 43; and Deut. 28:15–68. Traditionally, these verses are cantillated softly.
Torah	(Hebrew) Literally, "instruction." More generally, referring to the first five books of the Bible, the Pentateuch.
trop	(Yiddish) See "accent."
tsinnor	(Hebrew) A disjunctive accent, also known as *zarka*.
tsinnorit-merekha	(Hebrew/Aramaic) A conjunctive accent in the poetic books.
tsinnorit-mahpakh	(Hebrew/Aramaic) A conjunctive accent in the poetic books.
unvoiced consonant	A consonant that is articulated without pitch. For example: א הּ ח ט כ כּ ס פ פּ צ ק שׁ שׂ תּ.
upgrading	For reasons relating to the number of words or the length of words in a clause, one word may be accorded a higher syntactic level. For example, while the syntax may determine that a word would be punctuated with a conjunctive accent, for other reasons the word will be punctuated with a disjunctive accent.
vav conversive	(Hebrew: *vav ha-hippukh*) The letter *vav*, used as a prefix to change the tense of a verb from perfect to imperfect, or vice versa.
verb	A word indicating what the subject is doing or what is being done to the subject.

vocative	Directly addressing a person within a speech addressed to that person. For example, the word "LORD" in "LORD, You have been our refuge in every generation."
voiced consonant	A consonant that is articulated with pitch. For example, ב בּ גּ דּ ו ז י ל מ נ ע ר.
yad	(Hebrew) An ornamental pointer used by the *ba'al keri'ah.*
yeraḥ-ben-yomo	(Hebrew) See "*galgal.*"
yetiv	(Aramaic) A level-three disjunctive accent.
Yom Kippur	(Hebrew) The Jewish Day of Atonement.
zakef	(Hebrew) A level-two disjunctive accent. There are four forms of *zakef: zakef gadol, zakef katon, metigah-zakef,* and *munaḥ-zakef.*
zarka	(Aramaic) A level-three disjunctive accent.

Selected Bibliography

Avenary, Hanoch. *The Ashkenazi Tradition of Biblical Chant between 1500 and 1900.* Tel Aviv: Tel Aviv University Press, 1978.

———. "Masoretic Accents." In *Encyclopedia Judaica*, vol. 11, cols. 1098–1111. Jerusalem: Keter, 1972.

Bayer, Batya. "Cantillation." *Encyclopedia Judaica*, vol. 5, cols. 128–129. Jerusalem: Keter, 1972.

Beck, Astrid. *The Leningrad Codex: A Facsimile Edition.* Grand Rapids, Michigan: Eerdmans, 1997.

Ben-Asher, Aharon. *Sefer dikdukey ha-te'amim lerav aharon ben mosheh ben-asher.* Edited by Aharon Dotan. Jerusalem: Ha-Akademiyah Lelashon Ha-ivrit, 1967.

Berlin, Adele. *The Dynamics of Biblical Parallelism.* Bloomington: Indiana University Press, 1985.

Binder, Abraham W. *Biblical Chant.* New York: Sacred Music Press, 1959.

Brettler, Marc Zvi. *Biblical Hebrew for Students of Modern Israeli Hebrew.* New Haven: Yale University Press, 2002.

———. "How the Books of the Hebrew Bible Were Chosen." In *Approaches to the Bible*, vol. 1, edited by Harvey Minkoff. Washington, DC: Biblical Archaeology Society, 1994, pp. 108–113.

Breuer, Mordecai. "Dividing the Decalogue into Verses and Commandments." In *The Ten Commandments in History and Tradition*, edited by Ben-Zion Segal and Gershon Levi. Jerusalem: Magnes Press, 1990 (first appeared in *Biblical Review*, August 1990.)

———. *Ta'amey ha-mikra.* Jerusalem: Ḥorev, 1982.

Dotan, Aharon. "Masorah." In *Encyclopedia Judaica*, vol. 16, cols. 1401–1482. Jerusalem: Keter, 1972.

Elbogen, Ismar. *Jewish Liturgy: A Comprehensive History.* Translated by Raymond Scheindlin. Philadelphia: The Jewish Publication Society, 1993. Original German edition published in 1913.

Freedman, David Noel, editor-in-chief. *The Anchor Bible Dictionary.* New York: Doubleday, 1992.

Gerson-Kiwi, Edith. "Cheironomy." In *The New Grove Dictionary of Music and*

Musicians, vol. 4, edited by Stanley Sadie. London: Macmillan, 1980.

Gesenius, W. *Hebrew Grammar.* Edited and enlarged by E. Kautzch; translated and revised by A. E. Cowley. Oxford: Clarendon Press, 1910.

Hoffman, Lawrence, ed. *My People's Prayer Book: Traditional Prayers, Modern Commentaries.* Volume 4, *Seder K'riat Hatorah (The Torah Service).* Woodstock, Vermont: Jewish Lights Publishing, 2000.

Idelsohn, Abraham Z. *Jewish Music in Its Historical Development.* New York: Holt, Rinehart and Winston, 1929; reprint, New York: Dover, 1992.

———. *Thesaurus of Oriental Hebrew Melodies.* Volume 2, *Songs of the Babylonian Jews.* Berlin: Benjamin Harz, 1923.

Jacobson, Joshua. *Chanting the Hebrew Bible: The Complete Guide to the Art of Cantillation.* Philadelphia: The Jewish Publication Society, 2002.

———. "The Cantillation of the Decalogue." *The Journal of Synagogue Music* 29 (May 1995).

———. "Ta'amey hamikra: A Closer Look." *The Journal of Synagogue Music* (fall 1992).

Janis, Norman. "A Grammar of the Biblical Accents." Ph.D. dissertation, Harvard University, 1987.

Joüon, Paul. *A Grammar of Biblical Hebrew.* Translated and revised by T. Muraoka. Rome: Editrice Pontifico Instituto Biblico, 1993.

Kelley, Page H., Daniel S. Mynatt, and Timothey G. Crawford. *The Masorah of Biblia Hebraica Stuttgartensia: Introduction and Annotated Glossary.* Grand Rapids, Michigan: William B. Eerdmans Publishing Company, 1998.

Klein, Asher, ed. *Tikkun kore'im vesoferim.* Jerusalem: Yerid Ha-sefarim, 1995. Includes excerpts from Norzi's *Minḥat shay* and Heidenheim's *Mishpetey ha-te'amim.*

Kogot, Simcha. *Ha-mikra beyn te'amim lefarshanut.* Jerusalem: Magnes Press, 1994.

Kugel, James. *The Idea of Biblical Poetry: Parallelism and Its History.* New Haven: Yale University Press, 1981; reprint, Baltimore: Johns Hopkins University Press, 1998.

Ne'eman, Yehoshua L. *Tseliley ha-mikra. Volume 1—The Accents and Their Structure, Torah, Haftarah.* Jerusalem: Israel Institute for Sacred Music, 1955.

———. *Tseliley ha-mikra. Volume 2—Shir ha-shirim, Ruth, Kohelet, Ekhah, Esther, High Holidays.* Jerusalem: Israel Institute for Sacred Music, 1971.

Penkower, Jordan. "Minhag Vemassorah: 'Zekher Amalek' Beḥamesh o beshesh nekudot." In *Iyyuney Mikra Ufarshanut*, vol. 4. Ramat Gan, Israel: Bar-Ilan University Press, 1997.

Perlman, Michael. *Dappim lelimud ta'amey ha-mikra*. Jerusalem: Ha-makhon Ha-Yisra'eli Lemusikah Datit, 1962.

———. *Sefer bemidbar*. Tel Aviv: Zimrat, 1981.

———. *Sefer bereshit*. Tel Aviv: Zimrat, 1979.

———. *Sefer devarim*. Tel Aviv: Zimrat, 1981.

———. *Sefer ha-haftarot*. Tel Aviv: Zimrat, 1987.

———. *Sefer shemot*. Tel Aviv: Zimrat, 1981.

———. *Sefer tehillim*. Tel Aviv: Zimrat, 1982.

———. *Sefer vayyikra*. Tel Aviv: Zimrat, 1980.

———. *Sefer yehoshua*. Tel Aviv: Zimrat, 1984.

Price, James D. *Concordance of the Hebrew Accents in the Hebrew Bible*. Lewiston, New York: Edwin Mellen Press, 1996.

———. *The Syntax of Masoretic Accents in the Hebrew Bible*. Lewiston, New York: Edwin Mellen Press, 1990.

Ri'aḥi, Shemu'el Me'ir. *Tikkun kore'im ḥadash: Simanim*. Jerusalem: Feldheim, 2003. (Includes a selection of Norzi's *Minḥat Shay*.)

Rosowsky, Solomon. *The Cantillation of the Bible*. New York: The Reconstructionist Press, 1957.

Sherman-Gold, Rivka. *The Ohs and Ahs of Torah Reading: A Guide to the Kamatz Katan in the Torah, the Haftarot and the Megillot*. Mountain View, California: Yodan Publishing, 1999.

Steiner Yitzhak and Yitzhak Goldstein. *Diney sefer Torah she-nimtsa bo ta'ut (Laws Regarding a Torah Scroll in Which an Error Is Found)*. Jerusalem: Ot, 1984.

Wickes, William. *Two Treatises on the Accentuation of the Old Testament*. 1881–1887; reprint, New York: Ktav, 1970.

Zeitlin, Shneur Zalman, and Haim Bar-Dayan. *Miqraey qodesh: The Megillah of Esther and Its Cantillation*. Jerusalem: Kiryat Sefer, 1974.

The Biblical Text: Recommended Primary Sources

Biblia Hebraica Stuttgartensia. Stuttgart: Deutsche Bibelgesellschaft, 1967–1977. (A new edition of this Bible, *Biblia Hebraica Quinta*, is currently being prepared for publication.)

Breuer, Mordecai, ed. *Keter Yerushalayim.* Jerusalem: Ben-Zvi, 2000.

Dotan, Aharon, ed. *Biblia Hebraica Leningradensia.* Peabody, Massachusetts: Hendrickson Publishers, 2001.

Hebrew-English Tanakh. Philadelphia: The Jewish Publication Society, 1999.

Torah nevi'im ketuvim, Jerusalem: Koren, 1986.

Torah, nevi'im, ketuvim, mahadurat ha-universitah ha-ivrit biyrushalayim. Jerusalem: Magnes Press, 1993–.

Index

Y

Z

CD Index

The compact disc that is included with the book contains detailed instructions on chanting the Torah, and summaries of the other five systems. In most cases, the key is lower than the notation in the book. Additional compact disc recordings of nearly all the music notated in the book are available from the author at <conductor@zamir.org>.

1. Torah	*siluk*	0:16
2. Torah	*merekha siluk*	0:21
3. Torah	*etnaḥta*	0:15
4. Torah	*munaḥ etnaḥta*	0:22
5. Torah	*tippeḥa*	0:16
6. Torah	*merekha tippeḥa*	0:24
7. Torah	*tippeḥa elision*	0:15
8. Torah	*merekha khefulah*	0:18
9. Torah	*tevir*	0:18
10. Torah	*merekha tevir*	0:24
11. Torah	*darga tevir*	0:30
12. Torah	*kadmah merekha tevir*	0:14
13. Torah	*kadmah darga tevir*	0:23
14. Torah	*munaḥ merekha tevir*	0:16
15. Torah	*munaḥ darga tevir*	0:18
16. Torah	*telishah kadmah merekha tevir*	0:16
17. Torah	*munaḥ telishah kadmah merekha tevir*	0:20
18. Torah	*telishah kadmah darga tevir*	0:18
19. Torah	*munaḥ telishah kadmah darga tevir*	0:20
20. Torah	*zakef gadol*	0:20
21. Torah	*zakef katon*	0:19
22. Torah	*munaḥ zakef katon*	0:24
23. Torah	*metigah zakef katon*	0:16
24. Torah	*yetiv*	0:10
25. Torah	*pashta*	0:21
26. Torah	*merekha pashta*	0:19
27. Torah	*mahpakh pashta*	0:24

28. Torah	*kadmah merekha pashta*	0:21
29. Torah	*kadmah mahpakh pashta*	0:23
30. Torah	*munaḥ merekha pashta*	0:12
31. Torah	*munaḥ mahpakh pashta*	0:18
32. Torah	*telishah kadmah merekha pashta*	0:31
33. Torah	*munaḥ telishah kadmah merekha pashta*	0:19
34. Torah	*telishah kadmah mahpakh pashta*	0:44
35. Torah	*munaḥ telishah kadmah mahpakh pashta*	0:25
36. Torah	*shalshelet*	0:29
37. Torah	*segol*	0:16
38. Torah	*munaḥ segol*	0:22
39. Torah	*zarka*	0:22
40. Torah	*munaḥ zarka*	0:28
41. Torah	*kadmah munaḥ zarka*	0:19
42. Torah	*munah telishah kadmah merekha zarka*	0:34
43. Torah	*revia*	0:21
44. Torah	*munaḥ revia*	0:26
45. Torah	*darga munaḥ revia*	0:39
46. Torah	*munaḥ darga munaḥ revia*	0:17
47. Torah	*legarmeh*	0:20
48. Torah	*merekha legarmeh*	0:12
49. Torah	*geresh*	0:13
50. Torah	*munaḥ geresh*	0:16
51. Torah	*kadmah geresh*	0:22
52. Torah	*telishah kadmah geresh*	0:39
53. Torah	*munaḥ telishah kadmah geresh*	0:48
54. Torah	*gereshayim*	0:17
55. Torah	*munaḥ gereshayim*	0:17
56. Torah	*telishah gedolah*	0:27
57. Torah	*munaḥ telishah gedolah*	0:38
58. Torah	*pazer*	0:30
59. Torah	*munaḥ pazer*	0:45
60. Torah	*munaḥ galgal pazer-gadol*	0:23
61. Torah	*siluk* (final)	0:22

62. Torah	*merekha siluk* (final)	0:28
63. Torah	*tippeḥa* (final)	0:21
64. Torah	*merekha tippeḥa* (final)	0:28
65. Torah	ending a book of the Torah	0:50
66. Torah	the Creation on Simḥat Torah	0:51
67. Torah	public fast days	1:20
68. Torah	Song of the Sea	0:47
69. Torah	journeys	0:20
70. Torah	chiefs	0:21
71. Torah	Shabbat Ḥazon	0:17
72. Torah	summary	3:07
73. Torah	sample reading (Torah)	3:31
74. *Haftarah*	summary	3:01
75. *Haftarah*	*haftarah* sample	5:46
76. *Haftarah*	Shabbat Ḥazon	0:42
77. Esther	summary	2:57
78. Esther	Esther sample	2:09
79. Esther	invitational cadence	0:20
80. Esther	exceptions	6:03
81. Festival	summary	2:35
82. Festival	*Shir Ha-shirim* sample	3:36
83. High Holiday	summary	2:08
84. High Holiday	sample	1:18
85. Lamentations	summary	1:54
86. Lamentations	sample reading	2:28
87. Lamentations	chapter 3	0:34

CPSIA information can be obtained at www.ICGtesting.com
Printed in the USA
BVOW031635130912

300356BV00004B/1/P